Global Journalism

Topical Issues and Media Systems

FOURTH EDITION

Editors

Arnold S. de Beer

Stellenbosch University, South Africa

John C. Merrill

University of Missouri, U.S.A.

PEARSON

Boston   New York   San Francisco
Mexico City   Montreal   Toronto   London   Madrid   Munich   Paris
Hong Kong   Singapore   Tokyo   Cape Town   Sydney

Editor: *Molly Taylor*
Editorial Assistant: *Michael Kish*
Production Editor: *Deborah Brown*
Cover Coordinator: *Kristina Mose-Libon*
Editorial Production Service: *P. M. Gordon Associates, Denise Bracken*
Electronic Composition: *Galley Graphics*
Composition Buyer: *Linda Cox*
Manufacturing Buyer: *JoAnne Sweeney*
Marketing Manager: *Mandee Eckersley*

Library of Congress Cataloging-in-Publication data not available at press time.

ISBN 0-8013-3027-0

Printed in the United States of America

10 9 8 7 6 5 4 3 2 1   07 06 05 04 03

Contents

PART II • *The World's Regions*   179

16   *Sub-Saharan Africa (East, West, and South)* • Minabere Ibelema, Mitchell Land, Lyombe Eko, and Elanie Steyn   **299**

Introduction

The world of the twenty-first century is changing at a rapid pace, and so is journalism. This is even more the case with international journalism. Not only did September 11, 2001, change the way we look at international affairs, it also influenced how we perceive the media that bring us news and opinions about peoples and countries far and wide. As with the previous editions of *Global Journalism*, we are trying to provide a survey of the issues facing world journalism and to describe the broad dimensions and trends that characterize international media systems, news, and related issues.

With the vast changes in media and other institutions, we realized we could not just update the third edition. So, for the most part, this is a new book. We also wanted more than simply a revision, because that would have defeated the object of looking at the global stage of journalism from the perspective of the present. Hence, new chapters have been added, and other chapters have been totally revised to address issues pertinent to the mass media world of today and tomorrow.

Since the first edition of *Global Journalism* was published in 1983, the book has been recognized as a course-friendly survey text for international media concerns and comparative journalism systems. University courses in global journalism and media systems (usually comparative, but not always) are now recognized to be as important for journalism and communication majors as, for example, courses in world history would be for students majoring in history. We tried to keep this in mind as we prepared this edition.

The book consists of two interlinked parts. Part I, Global Perspective on Media Issues, provides an overview of the main issues that confront journalists, media organizations, audiences, and other role players in the media world, such as governments and large corporations. Part II takes a closer look at these and other issues affecting the media and journalism in regions all over the globe. For practical reasons, and to a lesser extent for geo-political and language reasons, the world was divided into eight regions, each receiving an emphasis particular to that region in terms of media and journalism issues.

The astute reader will find obvious gaps existing in the theoretical or philosophical perspectives of the book. Although we have tried to increase the number of international contributors to this book, it is still obvious that it has a Western ethnocentric bias, in the same way that Denis McQuail has described a similar situation found in many other media theory publications. We regret this, of course, and have tried to keep such a bias to a minimum. When such a bias shows through, it is not that any cultural arrogance or superiority is intended but only indicates that we, like all people, are to some degree culture-bound. In our opinion, no book is completely free from some bias rooted in culture, race, nationality, or religion. We only hope that if such bias is detected it can be forgiven, even over-looked.

The undertaking of a book such as this is not a simple task. As we noted earlier, the world's media systems are many and complex, and because they are constantly changing, it is impossible to keep up-to-date with all the various media in all parts of the globe. What we have tried to do in this one volume, even if hampered by the lack of a truly international cast of authors, is to provide the reader with a survey or overview of the world's journalism that should at least serve to shake off the Western (mainly American) perspectives that fill Western literature on journalism and mass communication.

Some of the tremendous changes that have taken place in the world's journalism since the 1990s are developments in the field of technology. The information age really got under way with the advent of the Internet in the 1990s, which has changed the way people communicate forever.

Political events, such as the Soviet Union's demise, added a new dimension to the journalism of the final decade of the twentieth century. Countries like Georgia, Belarus, and Poland shook off their communist press trappings and have edged toward a new but uncertain kind of journalism.

At the same time or even before it—starting in many countries in the 1960s—crime and social disorder began to rise, and out-of-wedlock births soared. Confidence in institutions, especially government bureaucracies and even the national state, began a long decline. The Israeli-Palestinian turmoil boiled over; minor wars broke out in the Balkans. We saw genocide and starvation on a large scale in Africa, atrocities in the Balkans, unrest in Southeast Asia and Latin America, and military threats and dangers everywhere in the Middle East, especially Iraq. At the dawn of the twenty-first century, Pakistan and India were on the verge of a full-scale war over the disputed region of Kashmir.

The 1990s also saw the rise of personalities in the news. Princess Diana became an international news figure, and her death, like that of Mother Theresa's, made headlines around the world. Nelson Mandela's release from prison marked the end of apartheid in South Africa, and he became an internationally acclaimed ambassador of peace. In sports, there were people with an almost god-like following, such as soccer star David Beckham. And then, of course, there was Monica Lewinsky, "that woman," who almost single-handedly brought down the mightiest man in the world, Bill Clinton, then President of the United States of America.

Then came September 11, 2001, and the brutal and savage attack on the World Trade Center in New York, which turned the attention of the global press to the continuing threat of Islamic extremist groups, such as Al-Qaeda, and their leaders, such as Osama bin Laden. Foreign news since September 11 has increased modestly worldwide, but a large part of this news has focused on the war against terrorism, the Palestinian-Israeli conflict, and the war in Iraq in 2003.

Although foreign bureaus of major news media have not significantly increased in the new century, more reporters are going abroad for short-term assignments. But, research shows that foreign news is still far down the news scale, with local and domestic news on the top.

The new information age might well be called the "age of crisis," or, as Francis Fukuyama has called it in a book by the same name, "the great disruption." For world journalism it could also be considered "war-to-war" coverage, filled with charges and countercharges and TV screens filled with "talking heads" of military and political personalities. Journalism, of course, has always been drawn to sensation, violence, wars, controversies, and crime, but since about 1990 carnage and international viciousness have become commonplace—and now in vivid color. Global communication has largely become a giant miasma of violence, sporting activities, and political and military propaganda.

Along with technological advances in the communications world, journalism is now faced with new challenges: all kinds of social unrest, prolonged criminal court cases, economic uncertainties, regional wars, and international terrorism. New media are springing up; others are dying. Larger and larger media conglomerates are spreading their identical messages across the globe. Internet users are increasingly becoming a part of journalism (however unreliable) as they dump their observations and gossip into the global informational pool. This is what this book is all about.

In Part I, Global Perspective on Media Issues, John C. Merrill in Chapters 1 and 2 gives an overview of global press philosophies and international media systems, addressing the issues raised in this Introduction in more depth.

Global journalism is about global news and the way it flows within countries and intercontinentally. In chapter 3, Global and National News Agencies, Terhi Rantanan and Oliver Boyd-Barrett show how over the past 150 years, nearly every nation-state has developed a national news agency for the purpose of gathering news from around and about the nation and distributing such news to media and nonmedia clients, both domestic and international. Alongside these national agencies are the major international news agencies. Today the principal international agencies are Agence France-Presse; Associated Press and its television arm, Associated Press Television; and Reuters and its television arm, Reuters Television International. National agencies of the developing world, most of them owned or significantly controlled by their respective governments, have experienced acute difficulties resulting from the combination of local and international pressure to become economically self-sustaining (in highly challenging market conditions) and reduced government subvention. The chapter further describes how the Internet will have a marked effect on news flow.

News, however, does not flow unrestricted from point A to point B. Using Afghanistan as a case study, Paul Parsons in Chapter 4, Barriers to Media Development, explores the many barriers that exist to media development. Until the Taliban lost power in 2001, Afghanistan spent five years as the most media-restrictive country in the world, with no music on the radio, no television, no newspapers, and certainly no Internet. Now, a newly free Afghanistan faces overwhelming obstacles in seeking to restart its media system. Outlining six types of barriers, Parsons explains why the media are economically strong and politically independent in some nations but struggling and submissive in others.

Closely related to the subject of barriers is the age-old issue of press or media freedom. In Chapter 5, Freedom of the Press Around the World, Robert L. Stevenson argues that the "end of history" has reached global press freedom with a near-universal acceptance of the Western definition in theory if not always in practice. Overall, according to Freedom House, the level of freedom peaked in about the mid-1990s and has dropped somewhat since then, but even the violence surrounding September 11, 2001, has not led to a serious restriction on press freedom in the West or in other countries threatened by terrorism. Most of the formerly communist countries of Europe enjoy at least partial freedom of the press, and some countries in Africa are more open than in the past. Even in closed societies, such as most Arab countries and China, efforts to maintain a monopoly on information are challenged more and more and are probably less and less successful. The Internet has affected everything, including press freedom, usually for the better, but not always. Traditionally, press freedom was a national issue, but with the Internet, challenges to government authority can come from anywhere.

Press freedom and ethics go hand in hand. Dean Kruckeberg and Katerina Tsetsura stress in Chapter 6, International Journalism Ethics, the ethical problems and opportunities of recent technological progress in the field of journalism. The authors analyze the new ways of receiving and distributing information and elaborate on potential outcomes of the state of technology applicable to journalism. New questions are raised in relation to ethics of journalists and other communicators in the twenty-first century. The main questions posed in the chapter are: What does the future of journalism look like, and what does it mean to be ethical in the twenty-first century?

The convergence of media, media-related fields, and media technologies is perhaps no more evident than in the way that globalization, the Internet, and exploding world markets have greatly expanded the integrated use of advertising and public relations techniques in global journalism. As Doug Newsom argues in Chapter 7, Global Advertising and Public Relations, the greatest increase in advertising and public relations activity throughout the world occurred in the financial sector, owing to the greater interlocking global economy. A second area of emphasis is issues management and crisis communication. Satellite broadcasting and the Internet create global awareness in times of crisis and are a major factor in the way crises are handled. The Internet is both an information source and a communication tool, and as such is the principal engine for change in advertising and public relations management.

Throughout history, media controversies have ranged from governments trying to close down newspapers to citizens groups protesting the way the media represent certain issues, such as abortion and womens rights. In Chapter 8, Continuing Media Controversies, Paul Grosswiler gives an overview of the intensifying problem of neoliberal media globalization and offers descriptions of the ITU- and the UN-sponsored World Summit on the Information Society, which got underway in 2002. He also considers efforts by France to thwart the influence of U.S. media imperialism. The important rise of coalition advocacy groups such as Voices 21 points to the increasing presence of scholarly and activist organizations in seeking changes to the global media system. The chapter also explores the significance of an emerging protest movement against neoliberal globalization, as well as the growing public dissatisfaction with global corporate media. All of this is situated within the problems and promise presented by the Internet in making global media controversies more visible and urgent, as well as offering an effective means of communication among advocacy groups, which suggest the Internet's democratic potential.

As part of the editors' ongoing efforts to increase the scope of *Global Journalism*, four new chapters have been added to Part I, Global Perspective on Media Issues. Four main issues are addressed in these chapters: How are aspiring journalists taught (or not taught) to become journalists? What are the profiles of journalists, those people bringing the news from around the globe to our doorsteps and into our houses? How do they do their reporting from foreign places? If journalism, also global journalism, is all about news, then what is news?

In Chapter 9, Global Journalism Education, Mark Deuze shows that although education for journalists has many different faces, programs, schools, and courses in journalism across the globe experience many similar developments: the increasing recognition and awareness of (cultural) diversity in society; the merging of entertainment and media industries, genres, and formats; the convergence of digital media technologies (multimedia); and the internationalization of media, journalism, and news (flow).

On the issue of who are the people that bring us the news, David H. Weaver in Chapter 10, Journalists: International Profiles, offers one of the first attempts to systematically compare the characteristics, attitudes, and values of journalists across more than two or three countries at a time. The major assumption behind this work is that individual journalists' backgrounds, education, attitudes, and values have an important impact on news reporting around the world, and that this reporting matters in terms of world public opinion and government policies.

Eric Louw in Chapter 11, Journalists Reporting from Foreign Places, examines why the reporting of foreign places often leads to distortions. He argues that foreign news tends to generate "double misreadings" of foreign situations, chiefly because media audiences have no first-hand knowledge of the places being reported on and no way of checking the validity of this news. Second, when journalists travel to foreign situations, they carry with them their own cultural and newsroom prejudices about these places and people. So foreign news is read through two layers of potential prejudice and misreading, one at the level of the audience and one at the level of journalists.

The issue raised by Louw—namely, how "real" is "news reality"—is taken up by Arnold de Beer in Chapter 12, News—the Fleeting, Elusive and Essential Feature of Global Journalism, where de Beer discusses what is considered to be news and what is not. Moreover, he considers whether it is possible to define this elusive concept in order to understand it better.

Section II, on the world's regions and their media systems, begins with Lianne Fridriksson's discussion in Chapter 13 of the media system in Western Europe. The author examines a number of media trends, both positive and negative, and offers a current country-by-country description of mass media and the challenges facing those print and broadcast outlets. Attention is also given to the challenges the European media landscape faces in the twenty-first century, not the least of which is the controversial notion of a European identity.

In Chapter 14, Allen Palmer and Peter Gross, Katerina Tsetsura and Dean Kruckeberg, and Catherine Cassara take up Eastern Europe, Russia, and Asia. The authors show there is still widespread evidence of the continued struggles over the mass media's role in transitional democracies. Although most of the former Soviet bloc and socialist countries, particularly in Southeastern and Central Europe, are now considered relatively free and open, the economic and political mechanisms of free media are problematic.

The problems in media transition from rigid Marxist-Leninist ideologies toward open, independent media in the late 1990s to early 2000s have been widespread. Yet even those who despair at the slow rate of adaptation and change acknowledge there is systemic movement, however painful and slow, toward a free and responsible media system.

Orayb A. Najjar in Chapter 15 discusses the growing global importance of the Middle East and North Africa and changes in the region's media system. A historical note summarizes the issues currently driving the policies of several nations in this region. The chapter expands information on media issues presented in the previous edition and also provides web site information that gives readers access to the media of each country. An extensive bibliography is included to help readers identify sources on this region.

Who could have guessed just a decade ago that African countries would be letting their voices be heard on the need for freedom of the press? In Chapter 16, Sub-Saharan Africa, Minabere Ibelema, Mitchell Land, Lyombe Eko, and Elanie Steyn show that one of the present-day realities of sub-Saharan Africa is the way media systems are being transformed and are still changing. In the 1980s, most African press systems were groping under authoritarian rule, military and civilian. The 1990s saw the development of a democratic culture that has transformed the press systems profoundly. In a 2002 survey, the formerly Marxist West African country of Benin tied with Britain in a ranking of countries on press freedom. That places Benin ahead of Austria, Spain, and Italy. In all, 19 sub-Saharan African countries placed in the top half of the 139-country survey, with most others following closely behind.

In Chapter 17, Asia and the Pacific, Jiafei Yin and Gregg Payne introduce readers to the major media changes that have taken place in Asia, changes that are reshaping the journalism scene across the continent. This chapter blends the East and the West by bringing Confucian thought into the discussions of government–media relations, freedom of the press, and Western press theories. The chapter calls for a reassessment of the media freedom ratings by Freedom House and holds out the hope that with advanced communication technologies in some parts of Asia, political and economic liberalizations across the continent, and regional media cooperation, Asia may be able to play a significant role in addressing the unbalanced flow of information between the North and the South.

This edition of *Global Journalism* also features another new addition in Chapter 18, Australasia, by Stephen Quinn. Australia's press has traditionally been regarded as free. New Zealand similarly enjoys a high level of freedom of expression.

In Chapter 19, Latin America, Donn Tilson and Rick Rockwell look at the wide variety of forces shaping the media landscape of the region. Although a wave of democratization rolled across the region in the 1990s, economic downturns impeded some of the progress the opportunity of democracy presented for media systems often accustomed to the authoritarian nature of regimes that had ruled much of the area. The authors detail this evolution while examining how globalization, privatization, and media concentration are also reshaping these media systems.

William Briggs in Chapter 20, North America, examines the evolution of media systems in Canada and the United States. Though sharing common British colonial beginnings, the two countries have developed in different ways. The chapter takes a close look at how Canada's close relationship with Britain has shaped its present media systems and fostered its determination to maintain its unique national identity and culture in the shadow of the American colossus to the south, while also facing the cross-cultural challenge of its French-speaking population. Meanwhile, the United States developed a free and mostly responsible press constitutionally protected from government interference. This press freedom, combined with America's unfettered capitalism, has made the United States the dominant media player in a rapidly globalizing world. Today both nations wrestle with the effects of new technologies and of media convergence as the two giant trading partners move together into the twenty-first century.

We hope that this new edition of *Global Journalism* will meet the expectations of readers in general who are interested in the way global journalism works, and especially the faculty who teach courses that introduce students to the mushrooming journalism systems of the world. This volume brings together in one place a handy picture of the global press. We have tried to accomplish a two-pronged objective that should meet the needs of many course syllabi: to present some continuing issues and problems in journalism around the world, and to provide an overview of journalism in the main geographical regions.

Therefore, we hope the book will help in the understanding of some of the major philosophical issues of global journalism, as well as in providing basic information about actual journalism as it is being practiced globally.

We thank the contributors to this book for their input to the Introduction, and for their enthusiasm, time, and expertise to help put this book together. Without their goodwill, endurance, and patience, this book would not have come about.

Arnold S. de Beer
John C. Merrill

Acknowledgments

I am indebted to Nicolette de Beer, who allowed me to turn our home upside-down—changing South Africa night time via e-mail into American day time; keeping the book on track when I was overseas; realizing that while she could not teach an old news dog like myself new tricks, she could master new PC programs to deal with the different obstacles of receiving, retrieving, and sending copy in different formats. To John C. Merrill, a true scholar in every sense of the word, my sincere gratitude for affording me the privilege and honor to work on his *Global Journalism.*

Arnold S. de Beer

Part I

Global Perspectives on Media Issues

Global Press Philosophies

John C. Merrill

Any philosophical discussion of global media always revolves around the topics of responsibility and freedom. In the twentieth century, great emphasis was given to press freedom, whereas responsibility of the press received little or no attention. In some societies, mainly those emanating from the European Enlightenment of the eighteenth and nineteenth centuries, a free and independent press is not only of great importance but essential to proper journalism and a progressive and vital society. Developed Western countries of Europe and North America try to spread this libertarian gospel of press freedom with missionary zeal to the rest of the world.

As a press philosophy, this Enlightenment-inspired system during the twentieth century was the idealistic model (from the Euro-American perspective) for global journalism, although the greater part of the world failed miserably to achieve it. At the end of the previous century many scholars were proposing ever more complex concepts (theories) of the press, but it seems to me that the basic model is a simple spectrum, with authoritarianism at one end and libertarianism at the other. All press systems fall somewhere along this continuum. Just how this model would apply to press responsibility is problematic, however, and it seems possible that there could be responsible authoritarian systems and responsible libertarian systems. Of course, both types of systems could also be irresponsible.

We could also conceive of press systems (and governments) as falling on a circle (Fig. 1.1), with systems toward the top of the circle permitting more freedom and systems toward the bottom being more restricted and controlled. The model in Figure 1.1 also shows that individualistic systems gravitate toward the top of the circle and more collectivistic systems are at the bottom. The new emphasis, even in the West, on communitarianism is expressed in systems found on the left and right sides of the circle, in both cases with an emphasis on feedback and popular cooperation. Again, responsibility is not built into this model. It might appear to some that a free and communitarian press would be more responsible than a controlled and statist press. That would certainly be the major Western position, but

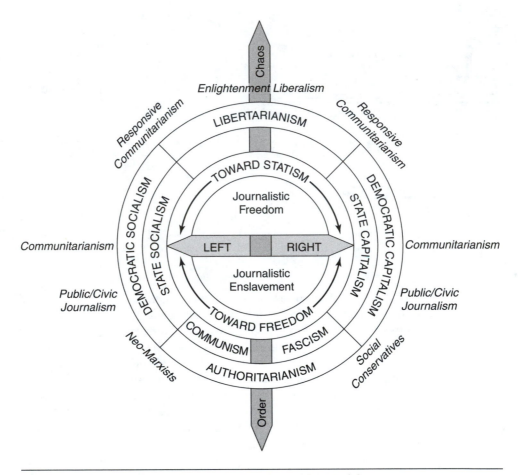

FIGURE 1.1 *Freedom and Authoritarianism: A Circular Model.*

of course, such a position would depend on the definition of responsibility held by the various societies.

The "Responsible Media" Model

Well-entrenched in political-press theory in the developed Western countries is the popular "four theories" concept (Siebert, Peterson, and Schramm 1963), which postulates authoritarian, libertarian, communist, and social responsibility systems. Although this model has been criticized widely for its Western bias (and for other reasons), it is still around and has been very influential. It did much to popularize the so-called "social responsibility" theory, suggested in 1947 by the Hutchins

Commission, that led to support for the late twentieth century idea of "public" (or "civic") journalism.

The Hutchins Commission was seen by many critical observers of modern journalism (many of them anti-Enlightenment neoliberals) as placing a welcome emphasis on "people" and negating the power and importance of the media owners and operators. The basic objective was a shift in emphasis from press freedom to press responsibility. Other theories arose to contest the four theories model, but without much success. For example, the British theorist Denis McQuail proposed the "development" theory and the "democratic participant" theory (1983), and Merrill and Lowenstein (1971) had argued earlier that there were really only two fundamental kinds of theory of press–state relations, authoritarianism and libertarianism, and that all media systems would fall somewhere along that bipolar spectrum.

Ralph Lowenstein (Merrill 1974/1990) presented a "progressive typology," according to which press systems evolved from authoritarian to libertarian, to social libertarian or social centralist (where we are now), and then to a big futuristic question mark. William Hachten (1981) added "revolutionary," "developmental," and "Western" models to the mix. Another U.S. scholar, J. Henry Altschull (1984), insisted that there were three basic media systems, market, communist (Marxist), and developing. And Robert Picard (1985) proposed a "social democratic" model as opposed to social responsibility and free-market systems, one that legitimized public intervention. Other models or classifications of global press systems have been suggested, with many of the newer models attempting to deal with audience participation and democratization in the media.

Habermas and Public Opinion

The German sociologist and communication theorist Juergen Habermas (1989) added much to the concept of a democratic press (at least in terminology) with his discussion of the emergence of a reason-based and discussion-stimulated consensus in what he termed "the public sphere." He saw this public sphere as a public space, existing between the economy and the government, where public opinion develops. It is from this public opinion that the people can supervise government. Habermas saw this occurring from the late seventeenth century through much of the nineteenth century.

The press of that period, according to Habermas, played an important role in public-spirited discussion (in coffeehouses, for example) among "civic-minded elites" (Underwood 2002, p. 10). Men such as Addison, Swift, and Defoe belonged to a healthy civic culture in which people of letters and intellectuals conversed and debated with the political elite and helped form public opinion. But this public sphere, which reached its peak in the eighteenth century, has all but disappeared, mainly because of growing commercialism and a loss of personal journalism. Since then government has expanded and now dominates the public sphere, and the media have ceased being an agent of people empowerment, have lost much of their rationality, and have defined the public debate and sidelined the public.

We must, according to the conservative-sounding Habermas, who—strangely—came out of the leftist student days of the 1960s, get back to this public sphere of bygone times (with the popularity of the salons, coffeehouses, and other public places). Rational discussions must be held, with no restrictions, in which the people decide how they want to see society develop. And, Habermas contends, this would significantly influence government policy. How would the media influence this process? By opening up an area for public debate and by encouraging rational and free discussion, thereby forming a true public sphere with the power of consolidated opinion.

Although Habermas does not deal with it directly, the idea of democratizing the press itself, of establishing a participating and conversing media audience and of providing more accountability mechanisms, is the core of social responsibility, and it is the main philosophical underpinning of the nascent public journalism (or "civic" journalism) of today. Although freedom, used responsibly, is still touted by these audience-centered journalists, it is receding into the shadows. Libertarians have viewed these responsibility-related theories with some concern, seeing them as endangering press freedom and autonomy and as giving journalism a subtle push into a new dimension of authoritarianism.

Certain scholars, among them Doug Underwood (2002), think that Habermas has a narrow view of what the eighteenth century "public sphere" debates were all about and paints an idealized picture of England and France. Habermas "rather blithely dismissed the role of religion," writes Underwood (2002, p. 53), and characterized it as largely unimportant in public debate. But, says Underwood, religion was time and again at the center of controversy in the coffeehouses and played an important part in "the intrigue and scheming" by the conversing insiders. So it might well be that these elite "public spheres" were hardly the breeding places for democracy.

We can probably conclude that Habermas, like so many scholars in critical theory and cultural studies (and public journalism), sees public conversation as essential to democracy. And he, and they, would like to have the media become more aware of public concerns and themselves join the public sphere.

It is difficult for many of us to understand the various intellectual groups that are deprecating the ideas of the Enlightenment. How could such freedom stalwarts as Locke, Voltaire, and Jefferson be wrong? Should not every press system reflect the libertarian ideals of such rational spokesmen? Will not a free press see to it that the truth comes out? Will not a free press ensure that the government is efficient and moral? Will not a free press enhance democracy, seeing to it that citizens have an ever greater impact on their country's actions?

Hard as it is for Americans to realize, there are places on the globe where such questions will be answered in the negative. There are societies where tradition and culture militate against Enlightenment optimism and where stability, religion, and social order take precedence over a free press. There are those who see press freedom as the arrogant possession of one small segment of society, who see press freedom as undermining national development, who see press freedom as harming social unity and community, who see press freedom as destroying religious integrity, and who see press freedom as endangering civil morality.

At the very least, we can say that throughout the world, there are those who are for press freedom and there are those who are against it. And there are those who are in favor of some press freedom but believe there should be controls. There are those who could not care less about the whole subject, having more mundane and practical concerns, such as getting enough to eat or avoiding being bombed.

But in the broad field of journalism and mass communication, freedom of the press and of expression is a continuing hot topic. It is one that is filled with definitional problems (discussed below) and more practical considerations. Context is all-important, and it might be said that if you want to know about press freedom in a country, you must look at the political and economic philosophy and current conditions in that country.

Semantics: Some Antics

Millions of words are poured out each year about such philosophical concepts as press responsibility, the right to know, globalization, democratization, right of access, moral duties, and freedom of the press. For example, all over the world, even in dictatorships and extreme oligarchies, the topic of press freedom receives inexplicable attention. Everyone, at least in rhetoric, seems to be in favor of press freedom.

For one thing, it sounds good. Talk about freedom and democracy tends to put one on the bright side of a darkening world. In journalism, "press freedom" is arguably at the very top of the virtue expressions.

But it is all simply a matter of semantics. Or is it? Voices around the world are talking. Listen:

> We have a free press. We would like to have a free press. Our press is free, but responsible. Our press is not free, but responsible. Our press is not responsible, but it is free. We have some freedom. Our press freedom appears to be temporary and tentative. Our people want security and social stability more than press freedom. Press freedom belongs to those who own the press. Press freedom is in the hands of whoever has the power in the country. Press freedom is empty rhetoric, purely subjective, with no real meaning. Real press freedom is freedom from making decisions. Our press is free vis-à-vis the government.

And again:

> Our press freedom does not extend to the journalists employed by the media. Our press is free to support the policies of the state. We have a free press: one that is free to ignore the will of the people. Our press is not free of social pressures and tradition. Our press is free, but we have codes of ethics. Our press is free except for various laws that limit press actions. Our press is free but largely limited by advertisers. Press

freedom actually belongs to the people, not the press. Freedom of the press belongs to the press, not the people. Our press is a democratic press. Our press cannot be free and democratic. Our press is free from vulgar and immoral material. Our press is free from profit-hungry entrepreneurs. Our press is not free of advertisers' pressures. Our press is free from global media oligarchies and greedy plutocrats.

On and on we could go. But in the United States we say that press freedom is guaranteed in the First Amendment to our constitution. So American journalists surely must know what press freedom is. Not quite. A quick look at the First Amendment reveals that Congress will make no laws to abridge freedom. Not a clue as to what freedom is. Not a clue as to what a responsible press is.

But somehow, possibly due to the power and impact of American journalistic philosophy in the world, a fairly well-defined concept of press freedom has enthroned itself globally. And this in spite of the semantic fog indicated by the hypothetical statements in the above two paragraphs. This Americanized core definition is basically that *press freedom is freedom from government interference*. Note that Americans seldom talk about interference by corporate powers, advertisers, civil pressure groups, publishers, editors, and so on. The concern is with government, and with the press being autonomous, or independent of government.

Of course, the U.S. Constitution does not really say that. It says only that Congress shall not dictate to the press through laws. It says nothing about government—about the executive and judicial branches of government. Constitutionally, the President and the courts can have a merry old time abridging the press's freedom. They, especially the President, however, do have to take public opinion into consideration.

So, when people around the world talk of press freedom in the "American sense," they seem to be talking about freedom from government, but really they are talking about freedom from press laws. No laws, and the press is free? Not by a long shot. As we look at the press globally, we see very quickly that there are many ways to throttle a press system other than legally. Every military regime knows that. Every theocratic regime knows that. Every dictatorial ruler or king knows that. State ownership of the media, threats, imprisonment or exile of journalists, murder, destruction of press property, control of newsprint, and licensing of journalists are all ways to control the press. Even in so-called democratic nations, where the state itself is slow to dictate to the press, there are the terrorist groups, the drug lords and their hit men, religious authorities, the various organized crime syndicates, global cartels, and consumer groups of all kinds exercising their power on the press.

Perhaps press freedom and press responsibility are mainly semantic problems. Certainly the terms have plenty of meanings and depend largely on the cultural-political context for their meanings. But at the core of all the various meanings is the concept of journalists being able to make their own decisions and take their own actions, and taking the consequences (accepting their responsibility). But this core is small, extremely small, and anywhere on the globe this subject is discussed, it must be recognized that in reality there is no freedom or responsibility of the press per se. The global press is always limited by the powerful persons or groups in the society that have reason to see the press go in certain directions. And if the global press has a responsibility, it seems to be to whatever or whomever it feels (or is made to feel) it owes its allegiance and loyalty at the time.

The term *press responsibility* is especially nebulous. Just what do people in various cultures mean by such a term? It is hard to tell, for even in the United States there are various meanings for it. They are implied by the following questions: To whom or what is the press responsible? How is this responsibility operationalized? Who determines what is responsible journalism? Is not responsibility in the eye of the beholder? What is the standard for press responsibility? Can a press system be responsible to some and irresponsible to others at the same time? Is responsibility the same as ethics? On the surface, there is no reason to believe that there is a universal meaning for the term *press responsibility*. It could be that there is, but, if so, communication scholars should still have to find it.

The Philosophy of Authority and Order

There is one media philosophy, itself plagued with semantic problems, that will not go away: *authoritarianism*. The natural tendency for global press systems, as is also true for governments, is toward authority and order. This, of course, always and everywhere curtails liberties of all kinds, especially freedom of expression. Most typologies of government–press relations around the world include "authoritarianism" or some synonym for it. In the well-known four theories model of Siebert, Peterson, and Schramm (1963), the authoritarian press is presented as the oldest of the four and is described as widespread in the noncapitalist Third World nations. Then there was the libertarian press, a creature of the European Enlightenment, followed by the Marxist-Soviet press (which I would consider a genre of the authoritarian press). Finally, there was what the authors called the "social responsible" press, which was presented as evolving from the libertarian or free-press theory.

The four theories model was a kind of progressive, hopeful Westernized model, insinuating that authoritarianism had been losing ground since the Middle Ages (notable exceptions are Napoleon, Hitler, Mussolini, Franco, and assorted military dictatorships in Asia, Africa, and Latin America). The reader of *Four Theories of the Press* would get the idea that the world press was about to come of age and enter an elevated stage called "social responsibility." Vague as this fourth theory is, the authors considered it superior to authoritarianism (and Marxism) and even libertarianism (from which it evolved). Presumably, for the authors, the United States was an example of a press system that at least showed signs of developing an embryonic social responsibility press system. At least, if the United States did not, the Hutchins Commission warned in 1947, the government might have to step in to remedy the situation.

It is true that in the sixties the United States and some other countries were beginning to stress codes of press ethics, ombudspersons, media criticism, capitalistic excesses, and increasing corporatism of the media. A journalistic "conscience"

did seem to be developing—at least in speeches, classrooms, and journalism literature. But wait!

Authoritarianism was still alive and well. And on into the final decades of the
twentieth century, instances of censorship, press harassment, press laws, and the
whole gamut of controlling mechanisms were being placed on journalism throughout the world.

New dictatorships arose in Africa and the Middle East, and Communist
regimes continued to direct their press systems. And in Balkans and scattered parts
of Asia (such as Indonesia and Cambodia), the mass media have been constantly
entrenched in deep authoritarianism.

The situation today is little different. On a scale of 1 to 10 (with 10 being
complete press control), the most likely figure for today's global press would be
about 8. Such organizations as the International Press Institute, Freedom House, the
World Press Freedom Committee, the Inter-American Press Association, the Reporters Committee for Freedom of the Press, the Society of Professional Journalists, and
the American Society of Newspaper Editors regularly publish materials pointing to
the sad (from their perspectives) state of press freedom throughout the world.

It will be noted that most of the organizations and groups just listed as being
concerned with press freedom are American and therefore would be expected to use
Western cultural perspectives in their evaluation of press freedom. The basic premise: Press freedom (editorial self-determinism) is good; government interference in
press freedom is bad.

But it should also be noted that countries with little or no press self-determinism have plenty of justifications for their control of the media. Here are a few of
these justifications (Bullen 2002, pp. 209–211): The press needs to be responsible;
privacy needs to be protected; the press should be truthful; the press needs ethics
codes with teeth; the press needs to be licensed; national security needs protecting;
"hate" speech must be eliminated; there must be a "right of reply"; and public
officials must be respected.

We can see that Enlightenment-style freedom does not really have a place in
authority-based philosophy. Eighteenth and nineteenth century libertarian thinkers
like Turgot and Herbert Spencer and their many ideological colleagues in France
and England unwaveringly saw freedom as freedom from any kind of outside
oppression, political and religious, and freedom to expand individual capacities,
with little or no restriction or guidance. Perhaps the supreme example of a British
radical libertarian was William Godwin, who enthroned individuality and urged
liberation from all restraints.

On the other hand, for the authoritarian, freedom is inseparable from some
group, tribe, community, or state, and warrants some form of discipline or coercion.
As Hegel says (Nisbet 1980, p. 238), true freedom, or "a higher freedom," occurs
when the person dedicates and sublimates himself to the absolute state as an organic
part. Plato, of course, was the grandfather of such an idea, and it has been advocated
by a series of eminent thinkers, among them Marx, Saint-Simon, Comte, Rousseau,
Fichte, and Hegel. Although these men differed in their attachment to social order,
discipline, and authority, they are all examples of anti-Enlightenment thought.

Authoritarianism is seductive, having a beguiling quality, a disciplined aura, a lure for orderly minds that want structure, a sense of security, and institutional stability. It is a potent sociopolitical magnet that pulls unceasingly at nations and people, including journalism. It implies authority, and mass-man wants leadership. In many countries even journalists, among society's intellectuals, feel comfortable having someone make editorial decisions for them. They, too, have a desire to "escape from freedom" (Fromm 1965; Revel 1977).

In Asia, for instance, the family and other communities of cooperation are very important, and respect for an authoritative leader is ingrained in their cultures. An example is Singapore, where in the early 1990s the former prime minister, Lee Kwan Yew, in explaining Singapore's brand of paternalistic authoritarianism (in Fukuyama 1999, p. 130), argued that an Asian culture that stressed "obedience to authority, hard work, family, savings, and education was critical to the rapid and unprecedented postwar economic growth in Asia." He stressed that these values justified the absence of Western-style democracy in places such as Singapore, Malaysia, and Indonesia. But, he added, they also have led to "lower rates of crime, drug use, poverty, and family breakdown." It seems that a chaotic society is anathema in the cultures of the Far East.

It seems to be a rather common belief, following Thomas Hobbes, that humankind's natural condition is "war of all against all," and it was against such anarchy that a powerful state (Leviathan) was needed to impose order. People everywhere, believes Francis Fukuyama tend "to become Hobbesians when faced with the prospect of disorder" (1999, p. 145).

"Order" is the imperative of those who believe that political institutions exist to serve society. Not freedom but order is the main reason for institutions. Therefore authorities (and others) in authoritarian press systems fall back on this imperative in justifying their media control. Order, they say, is related to responsibility, responsibility to virtue, and virtue to the safe and stable society. Of course, it is possible for the free person to seek the good; but if it is not sought voluntarily, then what? Then there must be political enforcement of the good. For a good, moral, and stable society, the good must be enforced by intellectual and moral leaders—by a creative and just oligarchy. Here is the problem. And here is the dilemma for societies.

On the one hand, individuals on their own don't seem to be able to live peaceably and justly with one another, and on the other hand there doesn't seem to be an elite group of "philosopher kings" to lead modern societies. Misused freedom therefore clashes with poor authoritative leadership. This situation is seen in the global press as well as in national states. At present, according to most observers, some form of authoritarianism appears to be winning.

And most of these forms of authoritarianism (in spite of meritocrats like Singapore's Lee Kwan Yew) have control centers that are morally unfit to control. Good people, yes, are often part of the ruling oligarchies of both state and press, but power does seem to corrupt, and individual or private ethics is, as Machiavelli reminds us, generally replaced by the "public" ethics of expediency. So what we had in the twentieth century were the dominant ideologies of fascism, communism, and Stalinism, and the rise of various brands of socialism, positivism, welfarism, and

Libertarians	Communitarians
Individualists, Egocentrists, Enlightenment Liberals	Groupists, Egalitarians, Altruists, Normativists
TRAITS	**TRAITS**
Pluralism	Bonding/conformity
Individualism	Community
Maximum freedom	Restrained freedom
Self-enhancement	Civic transformation
Personal ethical codes	Normative ethical codes
Personal influence	Selflessness
Diversity	Boning/conformity
Competition	Cooperation
Diverse world views	Like-minded world views
Ethical disagreements	Moral consensus
Relativism	Absolutism
Very limited authority	Substantial authority
Anti-professionalization	Media professionalism
Exemplars:	**Exemplars:**
United States, Britain, France Japan, Australia, Canada Germany, Costa Rica, Italy Spain, India	*Iran, Iraq, Saudi Arabia, Syria Pakistan, Libya, Sudan Vietnam, Kuwait, China, Cuba North Korea*

FIGURE 1.2 *Two Global Media Camps: Freedom and Authority.* (The old antinomies survive in the new century!)

pragmatism, all insistent on bringing about some kind of utopia. Factional and ideological authorities increasingly have demanded order, stability, and some type of collectivism or community-oriented societies (Fig. 1.2).

Back to the Community

Bureaucratic authorities go beyond government and civil servants. A vast authoritarian network spreads through any state and is composed of many groups with various functional goals and their own parochial interests. Increasingly, it seems that these groups have a basic unity of ideology or underlying interest. Listen to Frank S. Meyer (1996, p. 104) commenting on this situation:

> [Such a unity] includes, in addition to the bureaucracy of the government, the opinion molders of the mass communications industry and the decisive sections of the

academic personnel of the major universities, where for the past fifty years the ideology of this entire composite elite has been formed.

Most intellectuals in recent years have put great faith in the authority of the state. Even such conservative notables as Russell Kirk, a disciple of the nineteenth century stalwart Edmund Burke (who saw the state as divine), saw the individual as inadequate to take care of human needs. Kirk wrote (Meyer, 1996, p. 125) that government is "a device of Divine wisdom to supply human wants" and that the government "may justly perform all those labors which surpass the reach of individual abilities." Historian Walter Berns (1957, p. 256) has proposed that "government should seek to promote the virtue of citizens." He has also called for the return to the classical concept of the Greek *polis* (a community seen as the norm of human existence).

Many of today's communitarians (such as Robert Nisbet, Leo Strauss, Alasdaire MacIntyre, Amitai Etzioni, and Juergen Habermas) stress the importance of the community. In journalism, some of the communitarian proponents are educationists Kaarle Nordenstreng and Robert Picard (Finland); Yassen Zassoursky (Russia); James Carey, R.C. Harwood, Theodore Glasser, Edmund Lambeth, Lee Wilkins, Jay Rosen, and Cliff Christians (United States). With communitarianism comes the idea of universal morality. And this belief in commonalities in global ethical systems seems to be derived from religion; according to Fukuyama (1999, p. 237), it is "religion alone that first suggested that the final community within which its moral rules should apply—the ultimate radius of trust—should be mankind itself." But, unfortunately, as Fukuyama suggests, in the West at least, the concept of moral authority has been taken away from religion and given to the state, with its elaborate bureaucracy, formal law, elections, and the like. Therefore, modern democracies tend to be political rather than religious in character. As the religious base is disappearing, or at least being shattered into a pluralistic hodgepodge, fewer and fewer common cultural signposts can be taken for granted. Add to this the great diversity of secularized cultural priorities worldwide, and the future does not look good for a universal media ethics—or any other kind.

In spite of the barriers facing a global community, such an ideal remains high on the wish list of communitarians and public journalists, and it is easy to see that individualism in journalism (and in politics) is receding. In addition to the intellectuals who are crying out for more order and stability, there are the kings (Saudi Arabia), the theocrats (Iran), the military dictators (Cambodia, Iraq, Libya), the marauding gangster-tribesmen (Philippines), and the ideological communists (Vietnam, China, North Korea, Cuba) who are inflicting their versions of authoritarianism on the press systems of their nations.

In the 1960s through the 1980s, the Third World, the Soviet Union, and UNESCO were pushing the New World Information and Communication Order (UNESCO), which was expected to usher in a new order of more balanced global communication and an end to Western domination. In 1991, with the fall of the Soviet Union and increasing criticism of the United Nations, NWICO, which had dominated media discussions for so long, disappeared from view. Along with it went certain support organizations (such as the International Organization of Journalists [IOJ], a Marxist global group). However, the emphasis of NWICO—on the role of media in national development, on citizen participation, on meeting the interests of nations, on more balanced communication—has remained, even if largely underground. In 2002, its spirit was awakened, largely by non-governmental organizations (NGOs) in Geneva that were again touting the old "right to communicate" slogans and calling for new regional conferences to revitalize the issues.

The NGO grouping was organized as the Campaign on Communication Rights in the Information Society (CRIS), and the first meeting was held in early 2002 in Mali. American delegates to the meeting (*WPFC Newsletter*, August 7, 2002, p. 2), as they had been in the past, were against the thrust of the meeting, seeing it as a threat to press freedom, American style. They saw among the leading CRIS supporters persons who had been leaders in the earlier NWICO debates—people like Mustapha Masmoudi, former Tunisian and UNESCO official; Antonio Pasquali, former UNESCO communication official, of Venezuela; Cees Hamelink, Dutch information theorist; Wolfgang Kleinwaechter, formerly of Karl Marx University, Leipzig; Antonio Pasquali, a UNESCO communication official; and Kaarle Nordenstreng, former president of the defunct IOJ.

So we can see that the idea of bringing people of a community into the communication process is growing in various venues, such as CRIS. The idea of a right to communicate, defining press freedom as the collective rights of states and social and ethnic groups, thought to be dead at the end of the cold war, is still very much alive. Communitarians of all kinds have kept many of the old ideas of the much discussed NWICO on the media debate agendas of the world. These ideas, contrary to the rigid protestations of libertarian opponents, are not "authoritarian"; in fact, they may well be more liberating and democratic than so-called Western libertarianism. It is true that the emphasis is on the group—the community—and not on the individual journalist or citizen. The question is as old as philosophy, and there is no reason that we can know the "right" answer. I may have my answer, you may have yours. Iran may have its, and Switzerland, its. My position is that *all* states and media systems are *authoritarian*; it just depends on who is the authority—the political power or public sanction.

The Importance of Context

Let us look at authoritarianism in its more usual connotation. Probably, as a philosophy, it goes back at least to Plato, the first great champion of law and order and advocate of submission to an oligarchy of "the best." Plato recognized one standard: the interest of the state (Popper 1930). Everything that threatens the state is bad, believed Plato, and everything that does not further the interest of the state is wicked and unjust.

Today's press controllers, using state interests as a justification, find this Platonic idea appealing. And, in spite of a Western ethnocentrism that enthrones freedom, many of the press controllers may be right. In certain societies, with traditions of tribalism and respect for authority, the press cannot be left to itself; it needs to contribute to the national objectives. It needs to be a stabilizing, not a discordant, factor. Who says, a Nigerian journalist once said to me, that the press must be "an adversary" to government? "Why not a partner with government?" he asked. "After all, many people feel closer to the government than they do to the press," he said.

Throughout the world are many journalists who consider press freedom in a relative manner, generally seeing the cultural contest as probably the most important consideration. For instance, a Pakistani journalist (Isa 2001, p. 136), writing about the press situation in his country, stresses the deep respect for privacy and the media's tendency to invade it. He states emphatically, "the right to or freedom of information must take cognizance of the ingrained value systems in different societies."

Beyond this problem, could it be that press freedom is good for some countries and harmful to others? Is it not reasonable to take many factors into consideration before announcing a verdict on a country's press freedom? Such factors as these, perhaps, should be taken into account: the stage of national development generally, the degree of unrest and instability in the country, the state of journalism education, the firmness of religious tradition, the enlightenment of the ruler or ruling class, basic cultural tendencies of the citizens toward individualism or toward communitarianism.

If a young journalist in, say, Vietnam, has grown up in that culture, such as person is already predisposed to accept, and perhaps even to appreciate, an authoritarian press system. One intercultural scholar (Novinger 2001, p. 17) has written:

> When a person is born into a society, a system already exists into which the person must be assimilated if the society is to sustain itself. If the person's behavior does not become predictable to the degree expected, then he or she must be accorded special treatment, which can range from deification to incarceration. Ultimately the goal is to make the person's behavior predictable enough that society can go about the rest of its business.

This cultural expediency (or even determinism) perhaps should indicate that it is counterproductive or even dangerous for the West to try to impose on all countries a libertarian journalism. Certain countries, due to international power circumstances, may for a time be drawn to a free press, but this might be contrary to the natural national or regional realities.

The Media as Controllers

While less powerful than the state, the mass media communities (bureaucracies, establishments) are important instrumentalities for homogenization of societies. Techniques employed by the press systems of all nations are directed toward the "engineering of consent," the key word here being *engineering*. As the political scientist Frank Meyer has pointed out, the idea of engineering implies persuasive techniques directed toward the mass public, "not the rational and rhetorical persuasion of a critical and highly individualized public" (Meyer 1996, p. 108).

Is this situation good or bad in regard to the development of authoritarianism or despotism in a country? Meyer, for one, believes that it is, for it has substituted "the mass" (the undifferentiated and inarticulate "people") for what he calls "an independent and differentiated middle class."

Critics such as Meyer believe that modern mass media perform the function of creating agreement, which "is indispensable to the well-being of the collectivist state and the composite elite which operates through it" (p. 109). These are strong words and, it should be noted, coming from a modern American conservative thinker. But there are as many, and probably more, left-wing liberal intellectuals saying virtually the same thing, and adding increasing monopolization and lack of democracy to the litany of media criticism. One only has to read writers like Norman Mailer, Gore Vidal, Edward Said, Noam Chomsky, Edward Herman, and Robert McChesney to find similar notions being expressed.

We do know that in every country the press system is potent. Either it is potent as a spokesperson for the ruling elite or, as in some Western countries, it is an important instrument for a certain ideology, pressure group, economic class, race, religion, or some form of "political correctness" that invades the society at the time. Somebody or some group with special powers and influence uses the media for its own purposes everywhere in the world. If the *owners* and *directors* of the press system are using the media for their own purposes then the system is said to be free. If, on the other hand, the *government* or some *non-press entity* is using the press for its own ends, then the system is said to be unfree, or controlled.

The Philosophy of Freedom

So far we have emphasized the pull of authoritarianism. But what about freedom? Just listen for a few minutes to news on television, open almost any magazine or newspaper, turn on your radio to talk show programs. In a country such as the United States, you'll get a surfeit of opinion and information about freedom of expression and the press. So much, in fact, has been published about freedom that the subject has lost most of its earlier impact. By and large, people appear to feel that they have enough freedom, and in fact, that the media have too much freedom. But we always come back to the same questions: What is too little freedom? What is too much freedom? What is the right amount of freedom? What kind of freedom, in what situations, are we talking about?

I won't attempt to answer such questions here, but I will give a few of the assumptions about the benefit of press freedom, largely stemming from the European Enlightenment of the eighteenth and early nineteenth centuries. These centuries had freedom advocates aplenty who placed major stress on the individual person. Arguably the main initiator of individual freedom in the eighteenth century was the Frenchman, Turgot. He was followed by such stalwarts of liberty as Adam

Smith, John Locke, David Hume, the Founding Fathers of the United States, Condocet, William Godwin, Thomas Malthus, Immanuel Kant, Heinrich Heine, John Stuart Mill, and Herbert Spencer. Their ideas filtered naturally into the press philosophy of the time.

Today, when we try to consider press freedom internationally and interculturally, we run into problems. Most of these problems stem from the Western (Euro-American) libertarian assumptions promulgated by influential men such as those listed above. Five such assumptions follow:

- Freedom is good for a media system and a people.
- Freedom is necessary for national or cultural development.
- Freedom is needed for maximum news coverage.
- Freedom is needed for the discovery of truth.
- Freedom is necessary for information pluralism and diversity.

These assumptions of Western journalists are listed in a recent book on global media ethical systems (Atkins 2002, p. 19). Most Americans would probably agree that they are basic assumptions and, by and large, are valid. In reality, however, these assumptions are not embraced by most countries in Africa, the Middle East, and most of Asia and Latin America. Thus, these assumptions represent a Western philosophical perspective.

Lest the reader think that I have turned my back on the libertarianism that I have repeatedly championed in such books as *The Imperative of Freedom* (1974, 1990) and *Existential Journalism* (1977, 1995), let me hasten to say that I have not. I still believe that press freedom will generally lead to the best journalism, especially in countries in the same developmental stage as the United States. I also have my own ideas as to what a responsible press should be. But I cannot force my definition on others around the world. I have no desire to be an ideological missionary for Western journalism. My maxim has always been *preach at home, learn abroad.*

Bibliography

Altschull, J. Henry. *Agents of Power: The Role of News Media in Human Affairs.* New York: Longman, 1984.

Atkins, Joseph. *The Mission: Journalism Ethics and the World.* Ames: Iowa State University Press, 2002.

Berns, Walter. *Freedom, Virtue, and the First Amendment.* Baton Rouge: Louisiana State University Press, 1957.

Bullen, Dana. *Voices of Freedom,* 209–211. Reston, Va.: World Press Freedom Committee, 2002.

Daragahi, Borzou. "Afghanistan: A Nascent Free Press Seizes the Moment, 'Carefully.'" *Columbia Journalism Review* (July/August 2002): 21.

Fromm, Erich. *Escape from Freedom.* New York: Avon Books, 1965.

Fukuyama, Francis. *The Great Disruption.* New York: Simon and Schuster (Touchstone Books), 1999.

Habermas, Juergen. *The Structural Transformation of the Public Sphere.* Cambridge: Polity Press, 1989.

Hachten, William. *The World News Prism.* Ames: Iowa State University Press, 1981.

Hutchins Commission (Commission on Freedom of the Press). *A Free and Responsible Press.* Chicago: University of Chicago Press, 1947.

Isa, Gazi Faez. "Right to Information in Pakistan: Pressing Need for Action." In *Freedom of Information: An Asian Survey,* 136. Singapore: AMIC, 2001.

McQuail, Dennis. *Mass Communication Theory.* London: Sage, 1983.

Merrill, John C. *Existential Journalism.* New York: Hastings House, 1977/Ames: Iowa State University Press, 1995.

Merrill, John C., and Ralph Lowenstein. *Media, Messages, and Men.* New York: Longman, 1971.

———. *The Imperative of Freedom: A Philosophy of Journalistic Autonomy.* New York: Hastings House, 1974.

Meyer, Frank S. *In Defense of Freedom and Related Essays.* Indianapolis, Ind.: Liberty Fund, 1996.

Nisbet, Robert. *History of the Idea of Progress.* New York: Basic Books, 1980.

Novinger, Tracy. *Intercultural Communication,* 17. Austin: University of Texas Press, 2001.

Picard, Robert. *The Press and the Decline of Democracy.* Westport, Conn.: Greenwood Press, 1985.

Popper, Karl. *The Open Society and Its Enemies.* Princeton, N.J.: University Press, 1930.

Revel, Jean-François. *The Totalitarian Temptation.* New York: Penguin Books, 1977.

Siebert, Frederick, Theodore Peterson, and Wilbur Schramm. *Four Theories of the Press.* Urbana: University of Illinois Press, 1963.

Underwood, Doug. *From Yahweh to Yahoo: The Religious Roots of the Secular Press.* Urbana: University of Illinois Press, 2002.

WPFC Newsletter ("Old Game, New Playing Field"), August 7, 2002.

2

International Media Systems: An Overview

John C. Merrill

The world is so full of a number of media systems, we should all be as happy as kings, to revamp Robert Louis Stevenson's optimistic words. But are we? And, for that matter, does a press system contribute substantially to the happiness of people? If so, what kind of press system makes the greatest contribution? This book attempts to make some generalizations about these questions and to provide a survey of the issues and the dimensions of press development throughout the world. Of course, this is a huge undertaking, and the authors of the following chapters are cognizant of the necessary limitations of their contributions.

In spite of the necessary limitations of such a global survey, the reader should find at least an informed, helpful overview of journalism around the world. One thing is evident: states throughout the world are getting and exercising ever greater power over the media, and politicization is becoming a fact of life. As R. M. Hartwell pointed out as far back as 1979 (in Templeton 1979, pp. 14–15):

> Politicization can now be seen in the relationship between all people in the society: between parents and children, between teachers and pupils, between professors and students, between employers and employees, between producers and consumers, between races, between sportsmen, indeed between men and women.

And politicization continues, perhaps at a faster pace than ever. Where once private initiative dominated, especially in areas like personal and private enterprise (such as newspaper publishing), these are now tied to big business or to politics, and private solutions no longer suffice. And, as Hartwell noted, wherever public inquiry and solutions dominate, there is almost invariably "remedial legislation and the establishment of a bureaucracy of enforcement and control" (Templeton 1979, p. 14).

The world's media scene is affected not only by increased politicization but also by globalization—the spread of common values and technologies. Globalization is generally seen by the less-developed countries as largely one-way: from the developed West to the rest of the world. It is often seen as media imperialism, tied largely to Western (or European) values. Globalization has not reduced the seemingly natural tendency for individual nations and press systems (and journalists) to look inward, form egocentric objectives, discard normal ethics if necessary, and do all they can to be successful.

The Machiavellian Pull

In spite of varying moral and religious values found around the world, there is one dominant perspective that affects every press system's ethics: *Machiavellianism*. A basic desire seems to exist everywhere in the media to *succeed in achieving a specified and overriding purpose.* This might be national progress or supremacy; it might be achieving political party objectives; it might be cooperating with or contending with government; it might be making profits for the institution or the individual person or family; it might be propagating certain perspectives or values. But whatever the purpose, the desire everywhere is to *succeed,* and to succeed using whatever means will work.

This Machiavellian emphasis in journalism (described at length in Merrill's *The Princely Press,* 1998) permeates the world and proves a real danger to nonpragmatic or moralistic (principled) media ethics. Such an amoral emphasis is, of course, related to the increase of politicization and with it, state power. Felix Morley (in Templeton, 1979, p. 78) tells us that Machiavelli's name reminds us that a state develops its supremacy with total disregard for morality. Morley believes that "a Machiavellian policy is simply one in which intellectual ability is wholly divorced from moral considerations" and notes that as the state gains power, the inclination to follow the teachings of Machiavelli has increased. We can see this at work today as terrorism is fought by an increasingly insecure Western world. In order to be successful in this war, the Western liberal nations are increasingly compromising previous libertarian values and using means (tactics) formerly disdained.

Modern journalists, like Machiavelli himself in Renaissance Florence, prefer to use normal, respected, and traditional "private" ethics if it can achieve their purpose, but they have little or no reluctance to use more "practical" (public or institutional) ethics to ensure their desired ends. Terrorists and their journalistic, as well as media academic, apologists, for example, would not normally justify the suicide bombings and other acts that kill civilians, but when they find that attacking soldiers only or diplomatic endeavors will not bring them political and social success, they retreat from humanistic ethics. And Western liberal democracies bend their normal ethics as they try to reduce terrorist activities around the world, thereby damaging their loyalty to civil rights and legal guarantees. World crises serve as a catalyst for nations to become more Machiavellian and thereby increase their power.

Machiavellian instrumentalism bestows on the media various objectives, duties, or ends with a kind of positivist disregard for conventional ethics. The business of the press is to achieve certain ends, such as national security and stability, social development, making money for owners and corporations, and consolidating the power of ruling elites. As will be shown in the global survey that follows, the world's journalism is, in one way or another, an instrument of power, of control by the various elites that guide societies. Subsumed in this concern with ends (in themselves probably good) is an uneven pattern of truly ethical concern dealing with such issues as freedom, values, accuracy, significance, respect, and the like. Of course, there is hope for an ethical enlightenment.

In the midst of this instrumental, pragmatic Machiavellian journalism in the world there are, indeed, slivers of moral concern. A new demand (at least in rhetoric) for media ethics, although largely among journalism academics, is manifesting itself. Although this concern is as yet culture-bound, it is trying to break with Machiavellianism, of whatever source, and in some places even proposing a global code of journalism ethics. Yet it cannot avoid the instrumental conformity of achieving predetermined ends—an all-embracing ethical code being one of them. State laws regarding the media are increasing, evidencing a need for more media control. Could it be that a statist or socially sanctioned ethical code will be a further step?

At least five centuries before Machiavelli, a political adviser in India named Kautilya proposed harsh, sometimes ruthless, techniques to get things done. But he mixed pragmatism with compassion for the poor, for women, and for slaves. He was a very early example of moral concern—at least in some areas. His major work, *Arthashastra,* is unique in Indian literature for its open advocacy of *realpolitik* and its clear arguments. Although he is seen as a forerunner of Machiavelli, his ultimate purpose, unlike Machiavelli's, was to serve public welfare, not to protect the sovereign. And Kautilya, unlike Machiavelli, did not justify the principle of any means (to achieve ends) against anybody. He clearly forbade (Chunder 1970, p. 184) the application of devious methods against "the good and virtuous people," and advised the king to use duplicity in his military efforts only when peaceful methods failed.

Thus, Machiavellianism, like so many other European philosophies, originated in the East. It has remained a powerful force in the world and lends potency today to the idea of state power and authoritarianism, however much the rationale of public service may be attached to it. Increased consideration of the benefits to society obviously decreases the emphasis on individualism and plays into the hands of those advocating big government. The noted American sociologist Robert Nisbet has warned persistently against this increasing state power. In his *Twilight of Authority* (1975), he points out the incessant loss of individual liberties to state power and, in his Preface (xi), he notes "something like a vacuum obtains in the moral order for large numbers of people."

What he says can easily be applied to the global press. Listen to these incisive words as he proceeds (xi):

> Human loyalties, uprooted from accustomed soil, can be seen tumbling across the landscape with no scheme of larger purpose to fix them. Individualism reveals itself less as achievement and enterprise than as egoism and mere performance. Retreat

from the major to the minor, from the noble to the trivial, the communal to the personal, and from the objective to the subjective is commonplace. There is a widely expressed sense of degradation of values and of corruption of culture. The sense of estrangement from community is strong.

The communitarians of today, of whom Nisbet is an outstanding example, are trying to reestablish community and values, to put society above egoistic individualism, and to stress social obligation rather than an obsession with personal freedom. Although it has not permeated the far reaches of the globe (and how could it, in unfree societies?), communitarianism's media offspring, public or civic journalism, has reared its head, especially in the United States (Merrill et al. 2001). It is attempting to democratize journalism by involving the public in the daily editorial decision making of the media.

All this suggests two main traditions of citizenship, at least in the West, emanating from Plato and Aristotle. Plato stressed the unitary state—the power center of the society—and believed that loyalties other than to this state were counterproductive.

A Platonic Future?

According to Nisbet (1975, p. 262), the Platonic tradition has come down through Hobbes and Rousseau to today's social and political scene—and, logically, to today's journalistic scene. Nisbet notes that today the state (in some countries I would add Big Business) is a form of Hobbes's Leviathan and has "become the overriding form of oppression and exploitation." It is also quite possible that the press too, as a part of Big Business in its giant corporate and internationalized power, has become a kind of mental and emotional form of Leviathan that oppresses and exploits. It certainly has "the last word" in any critical debate or situation and sets the agenda for global dialogue.

Thomas Hobbes, a key figure in modern political thought, believed that a strong authority was necessary to avoid anarchy and to maintain social order. People tend to become Hobbesians when they face danger and the prospect of social disorder. According to Francis Fukuyama (1999, p. 145), if they are "progressives, suspicious of 'untrammeled markets,'" they want order imposed by the state for regulation, and if they are traditional conservatives, they want people to "obey the dictates of religious authority."

Around the world there are spokesmen for journalism who would view such a premise as absurd, seeing the press as basically pluralistic and generally weak and splintered, virtually powerless as an agent of change or of oppression. This view is more that of Aristotle, the second main tradition: the pluralist nature of society. Aristotle posited that there is a point "at which a state [or a press system in our day] may attain such a degree of unity as to no longer be a functioning entity—like 'harmony passing into unison, or rhythm which has been reduced to a single foot'" (Nisbet, 1979, p. 262). Unity versus dispersion, statism or Big Media versus individualism and pluralism—this is the fundamental problem of the global media systems.

Related to this problem is what Novinger (2001) refers to as "high-context" communication societies (usually less-developed countries) that rely principally on nonverbal behaviors rather than on verbal symbols of meaning. These are mainly personal, face-to-face communication contexts. It is more difficult for these populations to relate to or trust impersonalized mass media. Obviously, then, the more nonverbal a society is, the less powerful the dispersed and impotent institutional media are.

Novinger contrasts these high-context communication societies with the word-oriented societies that rely more on nonpersonal, mass-oriented, mediated communication, largely through the mass media. These are found in the First World or developed nations. In these countries the media have more credibility and impact. The media are seen as powerful social agents in themselves or as instruments for plutocratic elite governmental minorities.

In one way or another, in spite of its size and development, is the world's journalism in the service of accumulating and bestowing power? Many critics believe so. According to Robert McChesney (2002, p. 15), a current media observer, journalism has proved to be "a superior propaganda organ for militarism and war." He proceeds (p. 17):

> The historical record suggests we should expect an avalanche of lies and half-truths in the service of power. Journalists, the news media, should be extremely skeptical, demanding evidence for claims . . . and asking the tough questions that nobody in power wants to address. . . . [There is] control of our major news media by a very small number of very large and powerful profit-seeking corporations. [And] most journalists [see their] primary role as stenographers for official sources [and] do not recognize it as a problem for democracy.

The second half of the above quotation, of course, deals with capitalistic press systems, but the first part applies equally (or perhaps more) to the more authoritarian, state-controlled countries. Power in whatever form tends to corrupt—journalists, political leaders, parties, corporations, and individuals. Global journalists, then, must be alert to oppose government power, but at the same time they must realize that media power can be just as harmful to the people.

Global Media Cultures

Media cultures in the world are like a thousand or more flowers blooming (and withering). Certain soils produce some kinds of media cultures and other soils produce quite different ones. One of the main determining ingredients is freedom—or lack of it. Another is national security—or lack of it. Another is economic development—or lack of it. Another is a basic moral philosophy—or lack of it. And another is a democratic proclivity—or lack of it.

Freedom cultures are hard to find. They are, of course, related to individualism and to a desire on the part of the people to impact their society, to lead, to progress, to express their own spirit and creativity, and to converse without inhibition with their neighbors. Generally this kind of culture calls for a high degree of education, a tradition of antipaternalism, a sense of competition, and a respect for diversity. People, generally, are social animals, relating to the group, to the community, to the society, and to the state. They feel a sense of security in escaping from freedom, as Erich Fromm has called it, and retiring into the anonymity of a group, a crowd, a party, an ideology, a religion, a corporation, or a state.

A growing tendency around the world today is a caution in the media for exercising great freedom. In the present atmosphere of terrorist activities, or uncertainty in personal and group safety, the ideal of press freedom is not flourishing. Wars, military skirmishes, destructive incursions, constant threats, suicide (homicide) bombings, nuclear dangers, biological and chemical horrors, and other catastrophes loom up on every side.

The new century, which really began in September 2001 with the airliner terrorist attacks on the World Trade Center and the Pentagon, anticipates ever more dangers leading to ever more restrictions on a free press around the world. Freedom, it seems, must take a back seat to national security.

What are the most repressive nations in the world in this day of national concern for security? It's hard to say, but in 2002, Freedom House, in New York City, a global organization that keeps a close watch on the state of press freedom, published a list of "the most repressive" nations (Freedom House 2002, p. vii) among many denying basic liberties to the media.

The countries thought to be the worst violators of basic rights and freedoms were: Afghanistan, Myanmar, Cuba, Iraq, Libya, North Korea, Saudi Arabia, Sudan, Syria, and Turkmenistan, together with the territories of Chechnya and Tibet. Freedom House pointed out that violations of press freedom and human rights continued to be found in every part of the world. Of nearly 200 countries in the world, only some 85 are considered "free" by Freedom House (Freedom House 2002, p. viii). In at least half of these 85 countries the main newspaper either is a party-controlled paper or has various controls placed on it. So the situation for press libertarianism does not look good.

Other countries listed by Freedom House as "not free" are found in Africa, the Middle East, and Asia, with a scattering in Latin America. Most controlled press systems are clustered in Africa and the adjacent Middle East. According to Freedom House definitions, North America and Western Europe are virtually free of media controls. However, even in mainline libertarian countries such as the United States, there are press controls of more subtle kinds. It might truly be said that, in fact, there are no free-press nations. More will be said about this in a later chapter on press freedom around the world.

Antifreedom or controlled media cultures existed long before the modern spike in international terrorism. Dictatorial governments and strongman leaders have harnessed media systems to their own ends since such systems came into existence. Especially in nonliberal regions such as Asia, Africa, and the Middle East, political and religious elites have exercised firm control over the media. The freedom cultures of these regions are generally unimpressed by democracy and media libertarianism.

And even in countries such as the United States, growing numbers of intellectuals have become skeptical about the older liberal verities such as individualism, the free marketplace of ideas, and the strong emphasis on media freedom. For them, the public or civic journalists among them, social responsibility and the community must take precedence over freedom. So freedom is having a hard time, both among dictatorial egoists in many less-developed countries and among altruistic antiliberals in more-developed countries.

A similar feeling exists in many countries about American-style capitalism. There is a substantial literature on the "cultural contradictions of capitalism," arguing that capitalist development ultimately destroys itself by its norms that are at odds with those necessary for a healthy, viable society. Probably the most famous exponent of this view was the German economist Joseph Schumpeter (1950), who argued in *Capitalism, Socialism and Democracy* that a class of elites was produced by capitalism that was hostile to the very positive elements that made their lives possible, and that in time this hostility would lead to more socialist societies that would sustain a wider democratic base.

Some countries have basically an information culture, based on much raw data and very little interpretation. Others have "entertainment" media cultures in which the populace is kept relatively passive by submerging them in popular culture. And others, being submerged, of course, are mixed cultures floundering in a sea of information and entertainment. Yet others have media cultures that might be called "bulletin board" cultures in which at least some of the citizens receive governmental policy papers and official memos on a regular basis. In all countries, the traditional media do little or nothing to stimulate citizen participation in government. It might be said that, by and large, global media distract people from serious matters and self-rule and transport them into a mediated world of paradoxes, superficialities, conundrums, exciting escapades, atypical people, threatening situations, and unrelated vignettes.

Politics and economics are other important factors in the existence of various media cultures. It would seem that autocratic or nondemocratic national cultures are prone to have much less freedom. We can see this in Latin America, where military regimes seem to succeed one another periodically. And we can also see it in the Third World generally. Politics, perhaps, is more important than economic development. An example might be in legalistic and autocratic (but developed) Singapore. Another highly developed example is in the expanding free-market nation of the People's Republic of China, where the Communist Party keeps press freedom imprisoned. More democratic nations of Europe and North America, on the other hand, tend to have media systems with much more freedom from government controls. And, it might be added, most of these democratically inclined nations with maximum freedom are also capitalistic or free-market countries.

In the modern world, journalists *must* take various cultures into consideration. It makes things difficult for everyone, for example, if a libertarian journalist tries to insert his or her values into an authoritarian society. It is natural to expect trouble. Common sense, it would seem, would militate against such counterproductive attempts, but common sense too often defers to nationalism and personal ethnocentrism. Intercultural scholars, such as Novinger (2001, pp. 156–157), stresses the need for knowing and respecting other cultures and their rules. And for the communicator, she also says there is a need to (1) be motivated to communicate, (2) have a deep desire to overcome ethnocentrism through education, (3) have a knowledge of a culture's communication styles, and (4) be positive, adaptable, and responsible.

Press and Democracy

Around the world there is much talk of democracy today, even in the post-9/11 atmosphere that has spread a cautious fear in government and media circles. But the current world sense of instability has brought a certain cautionary concern about democracy. Protection of the society and community has forced the media to take a more cooperative stance with governments to retrench themselves in an older, more paternalistic position. Government controls in many parts of the world are being justified by the prevalent need for "national security." Governments systems that were opening up to some degree are reverting to older tactics of intimidation, new press laws, jailings, and violence against journalists in order to prevent dangerous excesses and irresponsible acts that endanger social stability.

Along with talk of globalization (a much more realistic goal) of the media, there are collateral mutterings of media democracy and the role of the media in fostering political democracy. But when we look closely at the various press systems in the second part of this book, we will observe that the press is doing little or nothing to bring larger and larger portions of the societies into active participation in governmental decisions (the exception being the growing influence of the Internet with its diverse web sites for NGOs and others working in this field). Governments are run increasingly by plutocratic elites and bureaucracies, with the average citizen being dragged along without any substantial power to change the situation. And it may well be that this is not always bad. Robert Kaplan, writing in *The Atlantic Monthly*, believes that if the citizens of a country are not "in a reasonable health, democracy can be not only risky but also dangerous (1997, pp. 55–80). Other factors, he notes, are needed for democratic development: a solid educational system, national stability, a healthy economy, and good infrastructure and communications.

In the media themselves, giant conglomerates are stretching their fingers around the world, heading toward a truly global media system, placing increasing emphasis on the business side and less emphasis on the purely journalistic (news views) side. Media barons sit farther and farther from the newsrooms, participating in various enterprises and even, in many countries, in government itself. Journalists the world over are adjusting to group-related media and the community-oriented press, and are adapting to the proclaimed need for social responsibility and national development. Stock prices and social restraints are dictating the editorial policies of media everywhere. Even in the more libertarian countries the older concept of the press as "a watchdog of government" is turning into a "lapdog of government."

Stuart Loory, editor of *The Global Journalist*, maintains that in the current crisis period in the world, five main problems inhere for journalists everywhere (in all media systems). According to Loory (2002, p. 32), these problems are:

1. Dedication to accuracy and perspective in these days of "political correctness"
2. Participation in factual reporting and not simply spouting opinions and unverified information from "debriefings"
3. Covering substantial, significant stories and not frivolous and unimportant ones
4. Determination to keep reporters out of harm's way in pursuing dangerous stories that threaten their lives
5. Allowing news audiences to provide feedback in a manner that is respected

Loory believes that the world's press must combine the values of the "old journalism" with the more participatory values of the "new journalism." He writes, "If modern journalism is to prosper it can only be by combining long established traditions with new technologies and making sure they are not compromised as the formats and interrelationships of the business change."

One might add to Loory's points this one: If democratization is really important in today's media world, the media will begin to stress ways that people can have greater impact on governmental decision making, and also how the media can share their own decision making with the public. However, it may well be that media (and governments), especially in these trying times, do not really care about expanding democracy and may even be anxious to limit it for security, financial, and political reasons. Talk about egalitarianism, a handmaiden of democracy in the eyes of many governments and journalists, implies a giving up of media and state power and a special elite status.

No equality exists today, in or out of the press, and there is no reason to expect it to emerge in the future. It is interesting to note, however, that many serious thinkers are accepting and encouraging that possibility. John Rawls, a Harvard philosopher, is one such person. His influential *Theory of Justice* is a landmark work for those who are proponents of egalitarianism. Rawls, at least for some like sociologist Robert Nisbet (in Templeton 1979, p. 191) equate justice with "fairness," and then concludes that justice and fairness are *equality*. Rawls indicates that he believes in equality, not only equality of opportunity. He contends

that all men of reason and good will, when liberated from the misconceptions and prejudices of the social order they live in [illustrated by Rawls' technique of putting them into what he called "the original position" or behind "the veil of ignorance"], will easily reach the conclusion that society is built on the rock of equality. . . . (p. 191)

Rawls and the interpretation given by Nisbet may well be wrong. "Equality" is one of the most semantically difficult of terms, "a word so wide and so vague as to be by itself almost unmeaning," as James Fitzjames Stephen, a nineteenth century contemporary of John Stuart Mill, put it (in Templeton 1979, p. 130). We do know, however, that for the strict democrat, the concept of equality is logically important. However, it is difficult to understand how in government or in journalism, equality (before the law) or equality (of opportunity) can be a realistic expectation.

The big problem with the media's democratization is that journalists like to think they are the determiners of news and the distributors of views. That is why they are in journalism. And as for governments' democratization ambitions: they are spokespersons and action agents *for* the people. The people cannot make these difficult political decisions (they are not inclined to or qualified to), so the political elite (a plutocratic oligarchy) must do it for them. Of course, official rhetoric from government and the press would not say anything so blunt as the above. For a free press's necessary relationship to democracy is well ingrained in modern thought, despite the critics of liberalism. Even Karl Marx in his younger days saw press freedom as "the pre-requisite for a democratic way of life" (Hardt 2001, p. 26).

Today such optimism is not so strong, largely due to the authoritarianism that Marx and his followers spawned. But one big hope thrown out by new journalists around the world is the potential of the Internet and other electronic marvels (including satellites) to involve increasing masses of people in global communication. Now, it is said, we can all be journalists. But it should be remembered that any meaningful democracy must be based on sound, verifiable information, and information coming from unchecked sources on the Internet is hardly that. Also, electronic communication can be manipulated by elites, and is to a large degree already being manipulated by those who have the power and predilection to do it.

Overly optimistic media leaders should remember the story of Prometheus, who, in his argument with Zeus, provided his people with a kind of blind faith that kept them from foreseeing their own destruction. Listen to Darin Barney (2000, p. 6) in his *Prometheus Wired*:

> The story of modern technology is the story of Prometheus's people writ large: the story of humanity blindly wielding instruments to command and transcend that which is given, in hope of creating its own future.

Because computers are mainly calculating machines, Barney believes that they are devoid of "philosophical thought, ethical action, and, ultimately, wisdom itself" (p. 220). And he concludes that network technology as aiding democracy is problematic. In fact, he says, "If computer networks are to be involved in democracy at all, they are likely to be instruments of democracy at its worst, rather than at its best" (p. 267).

In *Republic.com*, a book on the subject in 2002, the legal scholar Cass Sunstein, like Barney, questions the value of the Internet and warns that web technology to tailor the news may indeed cause democracy to suffer, owing to the proliferation of idle chatter, unchecked information, and a multitude of personal biases.

Barney's and Sunstein's thoughts about computer journalism are not shared by all. Many see this new technology as a way for more direct democracy to take place, for more people to have input into the communication system, for pluralism to increase, and for the state to lose some of its power over citizens. This, of course, is based on two main assumptions: (1) that information put on the Internet by the average citizen will be accurate and worth sharing with others, and (2) that the information will be of the kind that will give citizens more political power and impact.

The argument is strong for the benefit of the Internet. Anthony Kuhn, the *Los Angeles Times* correspondent in Beijing, maintains that in China, the Internet is changing the face of the news, making it easier for people to express themselves and harder for the government to censor (Kuhn 2001). Other regions of the world have reported the same sentiment. But it is more complicated than that. Even in China, for example, there are provisions against "subversive material" and endangering national security and stability. Also, it should be noted that in China, commercial web sites are not permitted to report, only to distribute news from official sources. This situation does help get news to more people, but it is questionable that it permits greater freedom of the press.

The sterile and outward signs of pseudodemocracy (simply voting is equated with democracy) around the world are quite discouraging to true democrats. In spite of much rhetoric and proliferation of technology, the future does not look bright for significantly enhanced "people participation" that would permit greater numbers of people to really have a part in their government or their media. Talking to one another and even voting is one thing; having a part in the actual business of the media or the government is another thing.

Increasing critical attention in the next decade or two is likely to be given to the part the press of the world actually plays in democratization. During the twentieth century there was little more than the assumption that media play a large role. Perhaps in the twenty-first century there will be some kind of systematic grading of the media's performance in this area. And beyond that, the press may help to suggest some new kind of participatory government that goes beyond an authoritarian plutocracy.

Media Accountability

Should global media systems and individual media be accountable for their messages? A basic and simple question. But it is one that requires more than just a yes or no answer. Most (but certainly not all) journalists the world over would say that, of course, media should be accountable. But accountable to whom? For which of their messages? And, most important, *how* will they be accountable?

Since about 1950 we have heard a lot of talk, coming from national press systems and from global organizations such as UNESCO, about the media's social responsibility. If the press is to be responsible to society, then it must in some way be accountable. Mechanisms of accountability are lodged (in authoritarian countries) with the government, the military, and sometimes with rebel armed forces. And in more libertarian countries such mechanisms are found in public opinion, audience acceptance or rejection, pressure groups, and certain laws (such as libel law) that hold media accountable.

Theoretically the freer and more open a country is, the fewer accountability mechanisms there are. Or at least, those that do exist are rather vague, seldom used, and in need of interpretation. As a country inclines toward authoritarianism or dictatorship, its accountability mechanisms become more blunt, brutal, and bellicose. Laws are more specific and unambiguous, and they are used more frequently to control the media.

International organizations such as the International Press Institute, the World Press Freedom Committee, the Inter-American Press Association, and Freedom House in New York keep a wary eye on several of these accountability mechanisms and their use globally. The picture is not a pretty one from the viewpoint of freedom. A continual stream of brutal, blunt, and bellicose actions by governments to control the press is emphasized with every issue of their publications.

One communication educator at the University of Paris, Claude-Jean Bertrand, has probably given more attention to accountability mechanisms than any other scholar. He has developed what he terms "a strategy for democracy"—a rather exhaustive list of ways in which media can be held accountable. He calls his list M*A*S—Media Accountability System—in which he maintains that a journalist's "moral conscience is not enough."

Bertrand (2002) refers to various internal and external accountability mechanisms. Internal ones would include a common creed or code of ethics, correction boxes, in-house critics, readership surveys, and self-regulation. External accountability mechanisms are such things as alternative media, journalism reviews, press councils, ethics courses, critical books and articles, and opinion surveys on the media.

In addition, Bertrand mentions "cooperative" mechanisms, such things as letters to the editor, ombudspersons, ethics coaches, continuing education, and prizes and rewards. Of course—and Bertrand says this himself—the main objection one might find with his accountability system is a possible loss of freedom. In the case of Bertrand's instrumentalities, this loss of freedom would apply only to *voluntary, media-accepted* accountability mechanisms. It would not apply to methods of restriction of the more blatant and brutal kind.

Media *responsibility*—what the media should do—is quite subjective and semantically difficult to define. *Accountability* is more objective and operational. It is not always fair but can open the media to criticism and more direct action that can, but not always will, cause the media to reevaluate their policies and actions with the aim of bettering them.

Quality Journalism

Even if people generally had the desire and power to substantially have an impact on their government, would it mean that global populations would live in more efficient and safer societies? Perhaps. But it would assume that wisdom accompanies the public input. At any rate, it is simply academic, for there is little evidence that the masses of the world's people have a deep desire for quality journalism. One can look at the global scene today and detect only a handful of truly serious, sedate, and sophisticated media of high quality. The "advanced" Western journalists, of course, contend that there can be little quality in journalism unless the media system is capitalistic. Less-developed countries see this as arrogance and believe that quality is largely culturally defined. In spite of such disparate contentions, there is a virtual consensus that quality in media systems does, in fact, depend on the degree of national development. And, what's more, a number of media scholars believe that most of the world's media are spreading their superficial, popular, lurid sensation and negative messages to audiences that seem basically satisfied with the fare. At least no hard evidence has come forth that populations (other than sections of populations, such as intellectuals) are demanding a more serious approach by the media.

Typical of recent criticism of media is *Good Work: When Excellence and Ethics Meet*, by Howard Gardner and colleagues (2002). Based on completed questionnaires from journalists, the authors concluded that the integrity of journalism has been compromised in recent years and good reporting has declined. A reviewer of the book for *Nieman Reports* (Carey 2002) summarized the basic media faults developed in the book as these: Journalists work for a market share rather than for the truth and significance; there is a decline of values and ethics; there appears to be a need to play to "vulgar" audience interests; and the media are filled with entertainment and sensationalism disguised as news. And there are many more. Carey, CBS Professor of International Communication at Columbia University, sees some signs of improvement here and there, but they are few and not so bright.

The calls for better journalism, although well articulated and numerous, are like voices crying in the wilderness: they seem to have no effect. International journals like *IPI Global Journalist, Gazette, Journalism, Ecquid Novi, European Journal of Communication, Index of Censorship, Publizistik, Asian Journal of Communication, Freedom Forum News*, and many others provide more than enough examples of poor or low-level journalism. People are hooked on entertainment. One need only look at the media in whatever country to see this opiate of the masses at work. Of course, one can find small oases of quality in the midst of the vast desert of blandness, but a BBC, a PBS, an NPR, a *National Geographic*, a *New York Times*, a *Neue Zuercher Zeitung*, a *Le Monde*, or an *El Pais* is not easy to find among the strident and shallow voices of the world's media.

Obviously different concepts of journalistic quality (in newspapers or other media) exist in the world, but underneath the nationalistic and ideological variations exists a rather firm sense of media significance and value. I have long been interested in global concepts of quality newspapers and have found as a result of several studies (Merrill 1968, 1999; Merrill and Fisher 1980) that there is a common core of requisites for a quality newspaper, and a general conception of what the highest-quality newspapers of the world are at a particular time.

Enduring criteria that I have identified for a "great" or quality international newspaper are the following:

- Read by opinion leaders globally
- Found in leading libraries of the world
- Read by diplomats in various countries
- Quoted in journalistic and literary circles
- Used in speeches of world leaders
- Good and effective typography and makeup
- In-depth and serious content
- Emphasis on international relations and politics
- Emphasis on economics, science, religion, and ideas
- A cosmopolitan and interconnected approach to news
- Audience feedback and guest essays
- Emphasis on social criticism, literature, art, and music

Little wonder that elite newspapers don't reach mass audiences. Populations the world over are either illiterate or "attitudinally illiterate" and, if they do read, they avoid such serious and heavy journalistic fare. In the United States (and probably elsewhere), young adults and the younger part of the baby-boom generation show the greatest decline in newspaper reading of any kind. And what they do read is not politics, economics, religion, and international and cultural affairs—the big items of the quality newspapers. Surveys show that young people, when they read at all, preferred (in order) crime, community items, sports, and health. No more than 25 percent were interested in such serious subjects as international news, Washington news, science-technology, religion, and business.

Although this does not bode well for elite or quality journalism in the early decades of the twenty-first century, there are some notable examples of serious international newspapers around the world that provide hope and direction for both journalists and readers seeking a journalism of substance and dignity.

What are some of these papers? Following are the names of the world's top quality or elite dailies by year (in the three Merrill studies mentioned earlier). In order, they are:

1999: *Asahi* (Japan); *El Pais* (Spain); *Frankfurter Allgemeine* (Germany); *Independent* (U.K.); *Le Monde* (France); *Los Angeles Times* (U.S.); *Neue Zuercher Zeitung* (Switzerland); *New York Times* (U.S.); *Sueddeutsche Zeitung* (Germany), *Washington Post* (U.S.)

1980: *ABC* (Spain); *Al Ahram* (Egypt); *Ashahi* (Japan); *Christian Science Monitor* (U.S.); *Frankfurter Allgemeine* (Germany); *Guardian* (U.K.); *Le Monde* (France); *Miami Herald* (U.S.); *Neue Zuercher Zeitung* (Switzerland); *New York Times* (U.S.)

1968: *ABC* (Spain); *Borba* (Yugoslavia); *Guardian* (U.K.); *Osservatore Romano* (Italy); *Le Monde* (France); *Neue Zuercher Zeitung* (Switzerland); *New York Times* (U.S.); *Osservatore Romano* (Italy); *Pravda* (U.S.S.R.); *Times* (U.K.)

Other global dailies, of course, are regularly named in various lists among the world's great newspapers. And there is a rather consistent listing of these papers. A few of the other elite papers, mainly European, are the following: *Le Figaro* (France); *Corriere della Sera* (Italy); *The Times* (U.K.), *Globe & Mail* (Canada), *Excelsior* (Mexico), *Mainichi Shimbun* (Japan), *The Wall Street Journal* (U.S.), *Dagens Nyheter* (Sweden), and *The Independent* (U.K.).

In spite of the generally dismal or pessimistic picture of the global press given in this chapter, these quality or serious papers offer a hope for better journalism, however dim.

These papers, typical of the well-informed elite "saving remnant" of the world's journalism, are proof that journalism can meet high standards if there is a journalistic will and a growing desire by populations to raise their sights. Serious journalists and concerned citizens can only hope that this will come about. These elite papers do serve as examples of good journalism, and should inspire journalists—even if out of sense of envy—to raise their standards.

Although envy is usually thought of as negative and harmful to a person or a journalistic medium, it can be a positive influence. It can challenge a monopoly of power; it can have a part in innovation; it can be a significant motivating factor for quality. The envious publisher or journalist might well strive to bring his medium onto an elite level. Envy can, according to Helmut Schoeck (1966, pp. 416–417) turn into "an agonistic impulse, endeavoring to 'outdo' the others" and is thus value enhancing.

The fact is that future and current journalists *should* envy the quality media of the world and aspire to participate in that kind of journalism. Only then can global media improve. In spite of those who say that the media should simply provide what the people want, there is a basic feeling that journalism must fill a deeper need. This, of course, may be only my Western ethnocentrism talking, but there are examples of journalistic quality to be found, rising like mountains above a dry and intellectually suffocating media desert. And these mountains must call all serious journalists to their lofty, though often dangerous, heights, especially international correspondents who have a great responsibility to report on foreign places and events for the people "back home."

Bibliography

Barney, Darin. *Prometheus Wired: The Hope for Democracy in the Age of Network Technology*. Chicago: University of Chicago Press, 2000.

Bertrand, Claude-Jean. "A Strategy for Democracy." *Media Ethics* 13, no. 2 (Spring 2002): 18–23.

Carey, James W. "What Does 'Good Work' in Journalism Look Like?" *Nieman Reports* 56, no. 1 (Spring 2002): 79–81.

Chunder, Pratap Chandra. *Kautilya on Love and Morals.* Calcutta: Jayanti, 1970.

Cooper, Thomas W., et al., Editors. *Communication Ethics and Global Change.* White Plains, N.Y.: Longman, 1989.

Freedom House. *The Annual Survey of Press Freedom 2002,* edited by Leonard Sussman and Karin Deutsche Karekar. New York: Freedom House, 2002.

Freedom House. *The World's Most Repressive Regimes, 2002* (Special Report). New York: Freedom House, 2002.

Fukuyama, Francis. *The Great Disruption.* New York: Simon and Schuster (Touchstone), 1999.

Gardner, Howard, et al. *Good Works: When Excellence and Ethics Meet.* New York: Basic Books, 2002.

Hardt, Hanno. *Social Theories of the Press.* Lanham, Md.: Rowman and Littlefield, 2001.

Holmes, Stephen. *The Anatomy of Antiliberalism.* Cambridge, Mass.: Harvard University Press, 1996.

Kaplan, Robert. "Democracy Just for a Moment." *Atlantic Monthly,* December 1997, 55–80.

Kuhn, Anthony. "China: Internet Boom Changes Face of News." *IPI Global Journalist,* 3rd Quarter, 2001, 8.

McChesney, Robert W. "The US News Media and World War III." *Journalism* 3, no. 1 (April 2002): 14–21.

Merrill, J. C. *The Elite Press: Great Newspapers of the World.* New York: Pitman, 1968.

———. "Global Elite: World's Best Newspapers Reflect Political Changes." *IPI Global Journalist,* 4th Quarter, 1999, 13–15.

———. *The Princely Press: Machiavelli on American Journalism.* Lanham, Md.: University Press of America, 1998.

Merrill, John C., P. Gade, and F. R. Blevens. *Twilight of Press Freedom: The Rise of People's Journalism.* Mahwah, N.J.: Lawrence Erlbaum, 2001.

Merrill, John C., and Harold Fisher. *The World's Great Dailies.* New York: Hastings House, 1980.

Nisbet, Robert. *Twilight of Authority.* Indianapolis, Ind.: Liberty Fund, 1975.

Novinger, Tracy. *Intercultural Communication: A Practical Guide.* Austin: University of Texas Press, 2001.

Schoeck, Helmut. *Envy: A Theory of Social Behavior.* Indianapolis, Ind.: Liberty Fund, 1966.

Schumpeter, Joseph A. *Capitalism, Socialism and Democracy.* New York: Harper, 1950.

Sunstein, Cass. *Republic.com.* Princeton, N.J.: Princeton University Press, 2002.

Templeton, K.S., Jr. (ed.). *The Politicization of Society.* Indianapolis, Ind.: Liberty Fund, 1979.

Trueblood, D. Elton. *General Philosophy.* Grand Rapids, Mich.: Baker Book House, 1963.

3

Global and National News Agencies: The Unstable Nexus

Terhi Rantanen and Oliver Boyd-Barrett

Prologue

For over 150 years, this chapter argues, news media around the world depended largely on the major worldwide news agencies (including, almost from the beginning, Associated Press and Reuters) and the news-exchange practices that they controlled for their supply of world news. By the year 2003, however, the business models that sustained these operations experienced multiple sources of threat. Profits for the wealthiest agency, Reuters, had been hammered by a combination of factors, namely, the economic downturn of 2000–2003, a leveling off of corporate demand, and intensifying competition from New York–based Bloomberg News and other players. In this climate, the advantages of the media-cooperative *model of ownership of news agencies—best represented by AP—grew more apparent. The chairman of AP was even quoted by Lucia Moses in* Editor and Publisher *(2003) as declaring the not-for-profit agency to be in a "very sound financial position." Yet, although AP's budgeted annual revenue for 2002 totaled $500 million, Reuters earned $5,761 million. And while 23 percent of AP's revenues now came from commercial services, for Reuters the corresponding figure was in excess of 95 percent. Cooperative ownership, furthermore, had its own problems, relating in part to the divergent interests of owners and managers on such questions as how best to raise revenue and innovate new services, including services delivered by the Internet. A third business model, represented by Agence France Presse (a public agency managed by government and media interests), had long shown itself vulnerable to client perceptions of possible pressure on its news services from political powers and to restraints imposed by public status on its ability to raise new money and innovate new services. Many national agencies of the developing world, most of them owned or significantly controlled by their respective governments, had experienced acute difficulties resulting from the combination of local and international pressure to become economically self-sustaining (in highly challenging market conditions) and reduced government subvention. Many agencies of the developed world had become more entrepreneurial, even as others* *barely covered the costs of their operations, if at all. All agencies were confronted by the challenges of market deregulation, media concentration and conglomeration, and technology (particularly the Internet). Deregulation had removed protections of national agencies against local and international competition. Media concentration and conglomeration often reduced the number of clients available, while increasing the power of large clients to dictate the operations of news agencies. The Internet was seen to be a boon, in that it could reduce costs of news gathering and news distribution (at least where clients possessed appropriate technology). But it was also the source of more competition, including the web sites of client news media and a wide range of new Internet-only news and information services.*

Since their appearance over 170 years ago, news agencies have exhibited recurring patterns of change and crisis. Our analysis of continuities and discontinuities in news agency history identifies four discrete epochs. A defining theme that emerges is the changing relationship between the "global" and the "national" news agencies. A disciplined network of news exchange arrangements once constituted a multifaceted and interconnected system for the gathering and dissemination of world news. Now, the exclusive cord between the national and international agencies has been ruptured, and the once-integrated agency backbone of international news gathering has collapsed. In this chapter we explore the factors that account for this rupture, and its implications.

The Rupture

The rupture between global and national was foreshadowed in the dialectic between communications media and the processes of globalization as these pertained to constructions of national identity. Many media once identified as national were absorbed into multinational concentrations of capital. These included media that were state-owned or controlled but then privatized or deregulated to enhance their accessibility to international capital. Such trends reflected a deregulated transnational movement of capital and products; the disengagement of governments from activities they could transfer to the private sector; and new technologies that expanded media capacity for regional or global service extension. News agencies faced a changing world in which previous missions of "national" service, nation-building, or development were no longer self-evidently meaningful or worthwhile objectives, where both owners and clients were increasingly transnational, less committed to local public service ideals, more interested in *a la carte* principles of news service and pricing structure, more likely to compete directly with agencies for custom.

News Agencies from Early to Late Globalization

News agencies constitute the oldest electronic media, contributing to processes of globalization from the mid-nineteenth century. They started transmitting news from every corner of the globe with the speed of electricity, and thus contributed to the compression of time and space that is the hallmark of globalization (see Rantanen ["Struggle"] 1998). As we have noted earlier (Boyd-Barrett and Rantanen 1998), the relationship between global and national agencies is of profound importance in the constitution of modernity:

> Part of this has to do with the territorial bonding of "nation states" and the dialectic at the very heart of modernity between national and global formation. The agencies were vital components in the armory of the nation state; then as now, the agencies were among the range of institutions which new nation states came to feel they had to establish in order to be seen to be credible as nations and in order to project or to control the dissemination of their "national image" on global markets. (5)

Significant interdependency between global and national agencies developed with the early, emergent division between the small number of agencies that operated "globally," gathering news in most (known) countries of the world and selling news in most countries of the world, and those that principally operated "nationally," gathering news in single countries and distributing news within those same countries. There were always a few "national" agencies that engaged in significant global activity; included in this category today are the Spanish agency, EFE, and the German agency, dpa. These have constituted a "second tier," a status between global and national agencies.

In the nineteenth century, during the period of the cartel, an international agency would typically sell cartel news on an exclusive basis to a national agency, and a national agency would give without charge or sell at a nominal price its national news on an exclusive basis (after satisfying its own domestic clients) to the international agency (see, for example, Rantanen ["Struggle"] 1998). In later years, national agencies increasingly subscribed to a range of international agencies and sold their national news to one or more such agencies, but the principle of interdependency between international and national was preserved. There are very few examples of regional news exchange without the intermediary role of an international agency before the 1970s. The structure of global news exchange remained more or less intact until the last decades of the twentieth century.

The balance of power between global and national agencies, established in the nineteenth century, tilted ever more definitively in favor of global agencies, such that by the end of the twentieth century, some national agencies had collapsed, while the survival of others was in doubt. This is indicative of transformations in the apparatus and manner of image construction that has long been thought essential to the reproduction of the nation-state, reflective of processes of neoliberal dismantling of barriers to trade and investment flows, regional concentrations of political identity (as in the case of the European Union), and the almost forcible concentration of the interests of OECD (Organization for Economic Cooperation and Development) countries and their allies behind the leadership of the United States.

The period dating from the late 1990s to the early twenty-first century represents a time of change in a global news system that was an interdependent, systemic arrangement (*system* may now be too strong a term) toward something less systemic, less predictable. At the same time, we must also ask whether the global agencies themselves are in crisis, both on their own account and from the perspective of their worldwide clients. At least two scholars of news agencies, Pigeat (1997) and White (1998), have addressed such problems.

The division of industrial interest between news wholesalers and retailers, and the assumption of interdependency between them, was fatally undermined when global broadcasting companies like Cable News Network (CNN) appeared, gathering news from client broadcasters and selling news to them, all the while operating as broadcast news stations available directly to the public by cable television or satellite (and now with web sites directly accessible, free of charge, to individual users worldwide). Press syndication, an earlier manifestation of this phenomenon, had not been sufficiently widespread or international as to pose as great a threat. The web does not merely add new sources of competition but also threatens older principles of news value and organization with new, multimedia, hyperlinked modes of news presentation.

Press syndication did not have the benefit of Internet technology. This has made agency news directly available to the public without the mediation of "retail" news and broadcasting media. The Internet has opened up new markets for the agencies, markets that may increasingly replace older markets but that are also more competitively challenging than their "wholesaler-retailer" predecessors for establishing unique brand identity. In place of the more orderly, systemic, and comprehensive arrangement of yesteryear, a handful of global news organizations (including traditional news agencies, global news broadcasters, and electronic news sites) autonomously gather news worldwide, mainly privileging Western demand and Western need, selling that news to other news media ("wholesale"), including news-related web sites, and incorporating it within their own news products for mass audiences ("retail"). The global news organizations may or may not have exchange arrangements with their clients. They may or may not collaborate with any of the many national and regional news agencies (whose purpose is to gather news within their respective national and regional territories for domestic and international distribution).

The number of agencies that can be described as global has diminished: at one time, some scholars spoke of the Big Five, to include Agence France-Presse (AFP), Associated Press (AP), Reuters, TASS, and United Press International (UPI). These were headquartered in London, Moscow, Paris, and New York. By the mid-1990s it was clear that there were only two powerful agencies, Reuters and AP, headquartered in London and New York, respectively, and even one of these, AP, was operating at a loss (and, by 2002, Reuters also faced a period of business crisis). These two were followed by a third, the French AFP, while both TASS and UPI had significantly reduced the scale of their operations, struggling well behind the others. In the field of news agency television news, by 1998 there were only two significant contenders, Reuters Television News and Associated Press Television News (the result of a merger between AP's APTV and Disney's WTN), both headquartered in London (Boyd-Barrett ["Global"] 1998).

We may conclude that in the world of news agencies as in the world more generally, globalization has worked to exacerbate inequalities and concentrate power. The next section explores how the dialectical interplay between monopolization and cartelization of agency markets, on the one hand, and the competing interests of governments and media corporations, on the other, have destabilized the global news system in a four-stage process.

Constructing and Dismantling the Global News System

News agencies are the oldest electronic media, having survived as a genus since 1835, when the world's first news agency, the French Havas, was established. It was followed by Associated Press in the United States in 1848, Wolff in Germany in 1849, Tuwora in Austria in 1850, and Reuters in the United Kingdom in 1851. Establishment of these agencies was subsequently followed by a national news agency in almost every European country.

Outside Europe, however, the pace of development was much slower. The development of national agencies was critically determined by the evolution of the global agencies, and in each of four developmental periods the relationship between the national and the global has shifted. The periods are:

1. The hegemony of the European news cartel, 1870–1917
2. The dissolution of the European news cartel, 1918–1934
3. The hegemony of the Big Five, 1940s–1980s
4. The dissolution of the Big Five, 1980s–

The Hegemony of the European News Cartel, 1870–1917

The first period was marked by the birth of the earliest news agencies. The European agencies—the French Havas, the German Wolff, the British Reuters—became the first global agencies and soon divided up the world's news market among them by signing cartel agreements. The U.S. Associated Press joined the cartel only in 1927, but earlier had expanded its markets to South America by extracting a concession from the cartel as early as the late nineteenth century (Cooper 1942; Rantanen 1990, 1992). These four agencies, with the exception of Reuters, started as national agencies. Even Reuters worked in close partnership with the British national agency, the Press Association, which would later become, for a period, joint owner of Reuters with Roderick Jones before World War II, and again, with the Newspaper Proprietors' Association, after World War II. The major agencies served national markets that were rich in newspapers and other clients. To better serve those clients they expanded their activities to global markets (after a considerable delay in the case of AP). This factor explains much of their success. Even if their home markets were relatively large, it was their foreign activities, facilitated by the vast imperial and trade activities of their host countries, that essentially marked the distance between them and solely national agencies that operated exclusively on domestic markets, regardless of market size (Boyd-Barrett 1980). The respective size of its global market explains the success of Reuters in relation to its German and French counterparts: the British Empire was bigger than either the French or the German, and British trading activity exceeded that of France or Germany (Boyd-Barrett 1980).

The essence of the relationship between national and global agencies, one in which national agencies provided their news to international agencies without charge and bought the news from global agencies, lay in its exclusivity in two different ways. First, the market was exclusive: only one agency in one country could receive the global agencies' news, their news could only be used by its clients. Second, with the telegraph, speed became a key feature in the nature of news. Only the first users of news could enjoy the commodity exclusivity of news, since it could only be used once before losing its value (Rantanen 1997). Exclusivity often became a significant factor in establishing national monopolies that were either based on cooperative structures or on state subsidy (see, for example, Rantanen ["Struggle"] 1998). The choice as partner by a global agency sometimes determined the eventual success of the local agency in achieving recognition as the official national agency. Even in the nineteenth and early twentieth centuries, therefore, the global agency could determine the local agency, and not infrequently then proceeded to instruct the local agency how to operate to the standards of the global agency (see Palmer 1998).

The emergence of the first agencies was succeeded by the development of national agencies in every European country (UNESCO 1953). In this sense, news agencies became institutions that symbolized the awakening of nationalist sentiments (yet paradoxically, sometimes the national agency was owned by a global agency—the Spanish Fabra, for example, was acquired by the French Havas, and some early Scandinavian agencies were owned by the German Wolff). Although many of the first agencies carried the name of their founder, they mostly soon acquired country titles, such as Suomen Sähkösanomatoimisto (Finland's Telegraph Agency, founded in 1887), thus emphasizing their status as national institutions. The first non-European agencies (after AP) were established in that period (such as the Japanese Shimbun Yotatsu Kaisha, in 1886, the Argentine Agencia Noticiosa Saporitii, in 1900, and the Canadian Associated Press, in 1903). All such agencies were born as junior members of the cartel controlled by Reuters, Wolff, and Havas.

In what senses was this first period a time of change and crisis? The dominance of a few major agencies quickly became a problem for some of the subordinate agencies, even though they felt compelled to work within the cartel structure. There were notable attempts to try to escape or undermine that system, sometimes taking the form of alliances between a national agency and a single global agency (such as Stefani, Wolff and Korrespondenz Bureau in 1889) (Boyd-Barrett 1980; Rantanen 1991). The cartel system made it difficult for newcomers to achieve access to global markets. United Press Associations (UPA; later renamed United Press International, UPI) tried and achieved some early success, partly by establishing links with minor agencies in the countries of the cartel agencies (such as Central News in the United Kingdom; see Boyd-Barrett 1980), and its success was an important factor in motivating Associated Press to be more aggressive in overseas markets (Boyd-Barrett 1980; Rantanen 1992, 1994, ["After Five O-Clock"] 1998). A further point of crisis in this period concerns the relationship of agencies to their respective governments, and even where there was no formal link, it is clear that in almost all cases, news agencies big and small, for temporary (such as in wartime) or more sustained periods, either solicited or succumbed to direct or indirect government support or subsidy, for revenues as for sources. At this level, then, one can say that both global and national agencies grew out of and were supported by nation-states, that global and national were determined by the national.

The Dissolution of the European News Cartel, 1918–1934

The second period started in 1918, when the U.S agencies, AP and UPA (1907), started expanding into South America. As a result of World War I, the German Wolff lost its position as a member of the news cartel. This period witnessed growing dissatisfaction of national news agencies with the power of global agencies. It ended in the dissolution of the cartel in 1934, mainly caused by the two U.S. agencies (AP and UP/UPI) with other national agencies (especially the Japanese and the Soviet) (Rantanen 1994). As a result, national agencies were free to contract with any global agency they liked, but in some cases gradually lost exclusivity on their home markets once competing agencies and media could make direct contracts with different global agencies. This period marked the end of the hegemony of European agencies. In this way, the collapse of the cartel potentially introduced a new, more equitable era in relations between national and global agencies.

It was a time of crisis: survival through war, the introduction of new wireless technology, and the collapse of one form of control of a global news market in favor of a less regulated and more competitive system. In the meantime, the finances of the European global agencies, Reuters and Havas, grew decidedly shaky. Havas was dependent both on government subscriptions and on sale of advertising space for newspaper clients. Reuters restructured its ownership to involve the British national news agency, the Press Association, and looked with increasing interest at possible sources of state support (Boyd-Barrett 1980; Read 1999). These developments raised further doubts about the ability and will of such organizations to maintain independence of government.

The Hegemony of the Big Five, 1940s–1980s

U.S. agency international expansion, which had started prior to World War II, was first delayed by the war, and then accelerated with the peace, as the agencies moved in to capitalize on the market opportunities in war-ravaged countries of Europe as these returned to peacetime conditions (Boyd-Barrett 1980). A new French agency, Agence France-Presse (AFP), was founded as a cooperative agency, managed by a board of media, government, state broadcasting, and staff representatives, and whose most important and wealthiest clients were ministries and other departments of state at home and in French overseas territories. Following the tradition set by its predecessor, Havas, AFP soon gained the status of world agency. The Soviet news agency TASS extended its activities in the new communist countries of Eastern Europe. Across other continents (the Middle East, Africa, and Asia), where countries were achieving political if not financial independence from old colonial masters, successive waves of new national agencies appeared.

By the beginning of the 1970s, more than a hundred countries had national news agencies (Carlsson 1981). The excitement of liberation in the new postcolonial countries quickly gave way to tensions between developing and developed countries, when it became clear that political independence did not guarantee economic independence. One area of contention was the perceived imbalance of news flow and the power of the developed world to determine global media representation of the developing world. There was growing critical realization of the emergence of an international media system that was largely controlled by North American and Western European interests.

For the established agencies, this represented a moment of threat, which the Western powers were quick to rebuff through their withdrawal of support for UNESCO, which had done much to legitimize the critique of what some scholars had labeled "media imperialism" (Boyd-Barrett 1977, ["Media"] 1998; Boyd-Barrett and Thussu 1992). Ironically, the U.S. agencies found themselves in a position they themselves were earlier critical of: the dominant position of the few. To the established global agencies, this debate was something of an irrelevance in their daily battle for survival: AFP was heavily dependent on government support, and neither Reuters (at that time) nor AP easily fit the UNESCO image of Western news agencies as ruthless, capitalist predators. However, this is the period in which Reuters pioneered the digitization of economic and financial news services, a process that was to convert it from the role of amiable, rather stuffy institution to that of multi-billion-dollar, state-of-the-art, internationally aggressive core player in the inner dynamics of economic globalization.

The Dissolution of the Big Five, 1980s

The fourth period, up to the present day, began in the early 1980s. This was the post-NWICO era, instituted by neoliberal economics of media de/re-regulation, conglomeration and convergence, digitization, commercialization and "competitivization" (Hamelink 1994; Boyd-Barrett 2002). Processes of conglomeration hastened the further diminution of UPI (for a time owned by Saudi interests, then acquired by the *Washington Times*), and WTN (finally bought by APTV). The collapse of communism brought about the relative demise of TASS (which became ITAR-TASS—a Russian national agency without the status of global agency) in favor of more commercial operations. The end of communism also weakened or destroyed the old East European national agencies, which have been succeeded by new or reformulated enterprises that must struggle hard to find sources of revenue to make up for the loss or reduction of state subsidies (Rantanen ["From Communism"] 1998).

Although three major agencies may be said to have survived, they survived in a very competitive environment (in general, broadcast and financial news). The deregulation movement undermined state-supported broadcast institutions (important clients for national news agencies) and intensified competition between ever fewer but larger media conglomerates (which became more questioning of the services they received from national agencies). The Internet was perceived as a significant threat because it had the power to reduce competitors' costs of access to news and to clients, although longer experience may suggest that it is still the major players who have the resources that are necessary to attract large audiences.

The Big Three

The major agencies of today, Reuters and AP, have survived as members of the "inner club" for many decades, stretching to well over 100 years in the case of Reuters. The third major agency, AFP, is in many respects a direct successor to Havas, another agency with nineteenth century roots. There is no doubt that Reuters was the leading global agency in the world at the start of the millennium. Figures presented in Table 3.1 show convincingly that Reuters was number one in terms of size, wealth, clients, profits, and so on. What factors explained its dominance?

First and foremost, Reuters had been a global company from its beginning and never operated solely as a national agency. In the latter half of the twentieth century, it increasingly distanced itself from its British identity. By the late 1980s, staff were drawn from 160 nationalities, although British and Americans were overrepresented in senior management (Boyd-Barrett 1980; Read 1999). Fenby (1986), an ex-Reuters executive, remarked that AP and UPI were not international at all in terms of their priorities: "the home market dominates their activities . . . their essentially American nature has been disguised by their worldwide organization and reach." Read (1999) points out that by 1977, Reuters was earning $78,356 in foreign revenue, compared with AP's $19,879 and UPI's $17,190. AP's foreign income amounted only to some

TABLE 3.1 *The Biggest News Agencies*

Agency	Subscribers	Bureaus	Employees	Countries	Budget (U.S. $)	Words per Day
AP	15,000	236	3,374	112	418 million	20 million
AFP	12,500	95	2,000	165	235 million	1 million
UPI	2,000	57	300	75	24 million	—
Reuters	54,000	212	14,600	158	5 billion	1 million
dpa	2,500	107	1,886	75	136 million	335,000
Ansa	957	109	854	60	113 million	300,000
EFE	1,235	77	1,000	70	8.5 milllion	500,000

Source: From White, P. *Le Village CNN: La Crise de agences presse.* Montreal: Les Presses de l'Université de Montreal, 1997.

20 percent of its revenue, whereas Reuters, by contrast, was earning only 16 percent of its revenue from the United Kingdom. In this way, Reuters was the only global agency whose home market revenues had become insignificant compared to its foreign markets.

Second, Reuters secured its financial base by becoming independent of media. An overwhelming majority (over 93 percent in 1997) of its revenues derived from financial news. In 1997, media and professional products accounted for 202 million British pounds sterling (£), transaction products for £828 million, and information products for £1,852 million of Reuters' revenues. Unlike other agencies, global or national, it did not have to compete on its domestic market with its own clients to find new sources of revenue. It could ignore the traditional media market, since its revenues were secured elsewhere, but its success depended in part on the interdependency of general and financial news throughout its operations. Many of its media initiatives in recent years had been internally controversial, as in the case of the establishment of Reuters Television. Suspicions that Reuters was not really interested in the media market encouraged its major competitor, AP, to boast that AP was now the leading global news agency for media, as opposed to Reuters, which saw itself as an information agency for nonmedia clients. In the recession of 2001–2003 Reuters downsized its staffing significantly in response to severe pressure on its revenue position, arising from strong competition from Bloomberg and stagnant market conditions.

In contrast to Reuters, AP has experienced an intensifying financial struggle. By 1995 its losses totaled $25.8 million. White, a Reuters' journalist (1998), argued that those difficulties reflected a declining position as a global agency and the loss of revenue from overseas. He argued this was due to two main factors: competition from Reuters and AFP (which became very active in Asia during the 1990s), and competition from newspaper syndicated services such as those of the *New York Times* and *Los Angeles Times*. As a cooperative agency that had become almost a monopoly on the U.S. market, AP enjoyed the relative luxury of being able to lift member assessments to help it pay its way. By 1994, 94 percent of U.S. newspapers received AP's service, while only 11 percent took UPI's (White 1998). UPI had relinquished its aim to become a global agency and to provide a full-scale national service: instead of transmitting full-scale news, it aimed to interpret it, and it concentrated on certain niche areas such as health care or strategic arms (Richie 1999). Both agencies had faced a situation in which daily newspapers were themselves struggling with financial difficulties, diminishing circulations and, after 2000, diminishing advertising revenues.

The third member of the big league, the French AFP, was behind AP in every way except in the number of countries served (see Table 3.1). Although it continued to depend heavily on subscriptions from state agencies (accounting for over 40 percent of revenue and 46 percent of clients), this was a reduction from over 60 percent dependence on the state for revenue in the 1970s. As many of its clients were foreign as were domestic, so that it had a fairly strong identity as an international agency. It was the only major non-Anglo-American news agency, and devoted significant resource and space to its coverage of Asia, Latin America, and Africa (White 1998).

Hence the three global agencies have developed three different strategies in their struggle for survival. Reuters has been the most successful but has shifted most of its energies toward providing financial information for nonmedia clients. It has proved vulnerable to times of severe economic recession. AP is heavily entrenched in the domestic U.S. market. The arrival of UP earlier in the century had been a significant factor in pushing AP toward a more aggressive international role; the demise of UPI boosted AP's domination of the domestic market and perhaps relieved it of some of the pressure to compete internationally. AP's cooperative structure has provided a robust support during difficult economic periods, even if at times this exercised a conservative restraint on business improvisation. AFP has secured its financial position by continuing reliance on the state, which has enabled it to maintain and even expand its foreign coverage. However, the state has not been as sympathetic to the agency's need for technological transformation as the institution's own executives have wished.

National Agencies

If the global agencies have gone through significant changes, many national news agencies throughout the world appear to be experiencing difficulty. This is especially apparent in the developing world and in Central and Eastern Europe, but also in parts of the developed world. For example, Scandinavian news agencies, which operate in one of the richest media markets in the world, encountered serious financial problems during the latter half of the 1990s. The Swedish news agency, TT, converted from cooperative to private status in 1999. Scandinavian news agencies, like many other news agencies, typically receive most of their revenues from media clients (80–91 percent), and have difficulties in finding new sources of revenues. Where news agencies have been customarily supported by media cooperatives, tendencies toward concentration of ownership and the conglomerization of newspaper chains have encouraged some member newspaper groups to withdraw support and to compile alternative, more competitive, and sometimes cheaper group news services. In countries with a strong national press and national broadcast institutions, there is diminishing public expectation that local media will devote much space to out-of-area news.

The situation in Central and Eastern Europe reveals the difficulties the formerly state-owned and fully state-subsidized agencies face in a new competitive environment in which the state is eager to maintain control but wants to reduce substantially the amount of subsidy (see, for example, Rantanen and Vartanova 1995; Rantanen 2002). Although there have been attempts to establish news agencies controlled by Parliament (for example, in the Czech Republic, Hungary, and Poland) instead of the government, governments still like to maintain their influence over the agencies (Boyd-Barrett and Rantanen 2000). National agencies in Central and

Eastern Europe (CEE) have been forced to cut down their expenses, services, and the number of their staff. Some of them also have to compete with private or foreign agencies in their own home market (Rantanen ["From Communism"] 1998). Global agencies have found it advantageous to sell directly to retail media and other clients in national markets, where before they distributed indirectly through national agencies because of the latter's monopoly position. Now the monopoly is gone, there is less incentive to use national agencies as intermediaries between themselves and retail media. As a result, national agencies increasingly serve small and local media that often belong to larger chains, which can gather their own news of the capital city.

News agencies in developing countries share some of the problems as nations in the CEE. For example, SHIHATA, the Tanzanian news agency, had practically no operations in June 1996, and finally closed in 1999. Reuters had previously interrupted its services because of unpaid fees; only one telephone was in operation, and none of the regional bureaus. Fax and telex lines were also cut for the same reasons (Kivikuru 1998). National news agencies of several other African states either disappeared in the 1990s or became moribund. Many of their problems relate to collapse in confidence in the desirability of state support for news agencies, a trend that has undermined many that had hitherto relied heavily on such support. Even intergovernmental or non-governmental organization (NGO) support for such ventures has declined in the wake of the end of the cold war. Further, the combined forces of deregulation, commercialization of media operations, and democratic forms of government have weakened enthusiasm for state protection of news agencies. As a result, national news agencies in developing countries face serious difficulties. These and other challenges facing national news agencies were the focus of a UNESCO-sponsored workshop in 2001 whose recommendations urged the cultivation of a more entrepreneurial climate within national news agencies to help them compete against other news suppliers and to identify new market opportunities; the elaboration of structures of separation between agency operations and political authorities; and the preservation of a mission to serve the information needs of the nation as a whole (Boyd-Barrett 2001).

Conclusion

The history of both global and national news agencies demonstrates how the gathering and distribution of news is governed by institutional structures and alliances between the agencies, their clients, and governments. Study of these structures and alliances reveals significant continuities over time, as well as important disjunctures. One question that has concerned us in this article is whether at the beginning of the twenty-first century we are witnessing a radical disjuncture in relations between global and national agencies, and in their respective roles.

With respect to global agencies, we can say that there is evidence of greater concentration among the big players. While there is a proliferation of broadcast and electronic media, some with their own news-gathering resource, there are few organizations, to our knowledge, which command anything like the scale of human resource dedicated to worldwide news gathering and distribution as is committed by Reuters, AP or, for that matter, AFP. (The few "retail" organizations that do compare, such as the *Wall Street Journal*, the BBC, or CNN, are all mainstream Western media). The spread of correspondents distributed by other media is typically much smaller and much more limited in geographical and topical range. We conclude that the global agencies, though fewer in number, exercise a profound importance in the distribution of knowledge of current human affairs, although this role is not always very visible in retail media. We recognize the usefulness of the Internet in providing direct access to national media and other sources of "raw" news, but we suspect that this is more useful as a news-gathering tool for journalists than it is for the general public.

We do not want to exaggerate the power of the global agencies, however. Their annual revenues are easily dwarfed by other media industries, such as those of the leading film, cable, and telecommunications industries. The leading news agency, Reuters, earned $5.4 billion sales revenues in 2000. Yet this was modest by comparison with the 2000–2001 sales of corporations like News Corporation ($13.4 billion), Bertelsman ($15.8 billion), Disney ($25.4 billion), or AOL-Time Warner ($214.5 billion) in 2000–2001. Mergers of telecommunications companies frequently involve transfers of money that range up to $50 billion and above (for example, AT&T bought TCI for $32 billion in 1999, and Comcast bought MediaOne for $47 billion). Microsoft, the world's fourth largest corporation, had a market value in 2001 of $258 billion, with annual revenues of $23 billion and assets of $52 billion (Boyd-Barrett forthcoming). News agencies remain relatively small by comparison, and it is remarkable that they have sustained the degree of independence that they do.

With respect to national news agencies, we are inclined to think that these institutions, as a group, do indeed face a severe crisis of survival and identity. The precise nature of the crisis varies by nation and by political system. The rationale of "development" that inspired many national agencies has not provided a philosophy sufficiently coherent to generate a product that has sustained the loyalty of state and non-state clients. Many developing country governments find themselves under pressure from the International Monetary Fund (IMF) to relinquish their involvement in activities that the IMF considers can be performed equally well by commercial operations. In areas of the world such as Europe that have been subject to increasing regionalization (for example, the European Monetary Union), there may be declining interest by clients in "local" news as this has been defined by national news agencies previously, in favor of a broader, less nationalistic remit.

More generally, sources of funding have been undermined by reductions in state subsidy, reductions in aid from NGOs, the cooling of loyalty of media groups that have set up independent news-gathering networks, reductions in subscriptions by global agencies where these now have sufficient local resource to meet their own requirements, competition from global agencies where these have set up financial news services which undermine the nationals' scope for entrepreneurial diversification or where they have even set up competing domestic general news services.

Both state-owned and cooperative modes of national news agency ownership have been threatened by one or more of these tendencies. Many agencies find it difficult to reconcile the clashing interests, first, of the state, which often wants a vehicle for the dissemination of announcements from state ministries, second, of national and global clients in receiving a service that is free of state pressure and responsive to their news agendas, and third, of the agencies' need for dependable sources of revenue.

Relations between global and national agencies, meanwhile, are undermined by the growing weakness (overall, with some significant exceptions as we have seen) of the national agencies and the growing concentration of the global agencies, by the inclination of the global agencies to compete with nationals in the nationals' own markets, and by the proliferation of web and other electronic media as alternative sources of national news. Overused as the terms may be, we conclude that this is indeed a period of change and crisis in the world of news agencies. This may amount to a destabilization of what hitherto had been a fairly stable and therefore well understood system of global news flow; if so, it follows that there are implications for global news quality and for global security.

Bibliography

Boyd-Barrett, Oliver. "Media Imperialism: Towards an International Framework for the Analysis of Media Systems. In *Mass Communication and Society,* edited by J. Curran, M. Gurevitch, and J. Woollacott, 116–135). London: Edward Arnold, 1977.

———. *The International News Agencies.* London: Constable, 1980.

———. "Global News Agencies." In *The Globalization of News,* edited by Oliver Boyd-Barrett and T. Rantanen, 19–34. London: Sage, 1998.

———. "Media Imperialism Reformulated. In *Electronic Empires. Global Media and Local Resistance,* edited by D. K. Thussu, 157–176. London: Arnold, 1998.

———. *Final Report of the Workshop on News Agencies in the Era of the Internet.* Paris: UNESCO, 2001.

Boyd-Barrett, O. "U.S. Global Cyberspace." In *Shaping the Network Society,* edited by D. Schuler and P. Day, Cambridge, Mass.: MIT Press, forthcoming.

Boyd-Barrett, Oliver, and Terhi Rantanen. "The Globalization of News." In *The Globalization of News,* edited by Oliver Boyd-Barrett and Terhi Rantanen, 1–14. London: Sage, 1998.

———. "European National News Agencies: The End of an Era or a New Beginning." *Journalism: Theory, Practice and Criticism* 1 (2000): 86–105.

Boyd-Barrett, Oliver, and D. K. Thussu. *Contra-flows in Global News: International and Regional News Exchange Mechanisms.* London: John Libbey, 1992.

Carlsson, U. *Nyheterna och Tredje Världen: En Översikt av Det Internationella Nyhetsflödet.* Lund: Studentlitteratur, 1981.

Cooper, K. *Barriers Down: The Story of the News Agency Epoch.* New York: Kennikat Press, 1942.

Fenby, J. *The International News Services.* New York: Schocken Books, 1986.

Hamelink, C. *The Politics of World Communication.* London: Sage, 1994.

Kivikuru, U. "From State Socialism to Deregulation." In Moses, L. "Changing of the Guard at AP." *Editor and Publisher,* 25 April 2003. *The Globalization of News,* edited by Oliver Boyd-Barrett and Terhi Rantanen, 137–153. London: Sage, 1998.

Palmer, M. "What Makes News." In *The Globalization of News,* edited by Oliver Boyd-Barrett and Terhi Rantanen, 177–190. London: Sage, 1998.

Pigeat, H. *Les Agences de presse. Institutions du passe ou medias d'avenir?* Paris: La documentation française, 1997.

Rantanen, Terhi. *Foreign News in Imperial Russia. The Relationship Between International and Russian News Agencies, 1856–1914.* Helsinki: Suomalainen Tiedeakatemia, 1990.

———. *Mr. Howard Goes to South America: The United Press Associations and Foreign Expansion.* Roy W. Howard Monographs in Journalism and Mass Communication Research, no. 2. Bloomington: Indiana University School of Journalism, 1992.

———. *Howard Interviews Stalin: How the AP, UP and TASS Smashed the International News Cartel.* Roy W. Howard Monographs in Journalism and Mass Communication Research, no. 3. Bloomington: Indiana University School of Journalism, 1994.

———. "The Globalization of Electronic News in the 19th Century." *Media Culture & Society* 4 (1977): 605–620.

———. "The Struggle for Control of Domestic News Markets." In *The Globalization of News,* edited by Oliver Boyd-Barrett and Terhi Rantanen, 35–48. London: Sage, 1998.

———. "From Communism to Capitalism." In *The Globalization of News,* edited by Oliver Boyd-Barrett and Terhi Rantanen, 125–136. London: Sage, 1998.

———. *After Five O'Clock Friends. Kent Cooper and Roy W. Howard.* Roy W. Howard Monographs in Journalism and Mass Communication Research, no. 4. Bloomington: Indiana University School of Journalism, 1998.

———. *The Global and the National: Media and Communications in Post-Communist Russia.* Boulder, Colo.: Rowman and Littlefield, 2002.

Rantanen, Terhi, and E. Vartanova. "News Agencies in Post-Communist Russia." *European Journal of Communication,* 2 (1995): 207–220.

Read, D. *The Power of News: The History of Reuters,* 2nd Edition. Oxford: Oxford University Press, 1999.

Richie, I. "MBC, an Arabic Global TV Satellite Service." Paper presented at Green College, Oxford, March 5, 1999.

UNESCO. *News Agencies: Their Structure and Operation.* Paris: UNESCO, 1953.

White, P. *Le Village CNN: La Crise des agences de presse.* Montreal: Les Presses de l'Universite de Montreal, 1998.

4

Barriers to Media Development

Paul Parsons

News, photography, movies, and even music died in Afghanistan when the Taliban seized control in 1996. The fundamentalist regime, claiming it was creating the world's purest Islamic state, gave residents 15 days to throw out their television sets, videos, and satellite dishes to rid themselves of "moral corruption" ("Afghanistan" 2001). To show their fanaticism, the Taliban publicly hanged TV sets and burned stocks of films.

Afghanistan spent the next five years as the most media-restrictive country in the world. All kinds of barriers were placed in the way of media development. Newspapers were shut down. Music could not be played on the radio. Afghans were prohibited from having Internet access. The Taliban even banned photography of any living person or animal. Eighteen journalists and aid workers, including Christiane Amanpour of Cable News Network (CNN), were arrested for trying to film women at a Kabul hospital. In another example, photographers from the United States, Brazil, and Pakistan were arrested for attempting to take photographs of a soccer match in Kabul.

Media restrictions, though, merely mirrored the great upheaval that swept through Afghan society. Women could not step outside their homes without wearing a full-body veil. All men were ordered to grow beards. Within their homes, Afghans were told to destroy all pictures of living beings (although shops in Kabul remained open for passport photographs).

The only radio station allowed was the Taliban's Radio Sharia, beaming propaganda 24 hours a day. But from outside Afghan borders, the British Broadcasting Corporation (BBC) and Voice of America offered special radio programming in the Afghan languages of Pashto and Dari.

Foreign journalists, if permitted entry into the country at all, were prohibited from entering private houses, and they could not hire taxis or private cars. In 2001, when the hunt began in the mountains of Afghanistan for Osama bin Laden and his terrorist network, and war threatened the Taliban's grasp on the country, foreign journalists became targets. Two Spaniards, an Australian, and an Afghan-born photographer for the British news agency Reuters were pulled from their car and shot to death on a road leading to Kabul. In all, eight journalists were killed in 2001 while covering the war.

Once the war ended and the Taliban lost power, the reconstruction of Afghanistan's media had to start anew. The Afghan nation had suffered 23 years of civil strife since the first fighting began in 1978, and following a generation of warlords, poverty, bandits, and propaganda, UNESCO estimated that literacy in Afghanistan had declined to a dismal 31 percent. Yet Afghan media are coming back. In 2002, the independent *Kabul Weekly* published for the first time since the Taliban shut it down in 1996. The tabloid is published in Pashto, Dari, English, and French (Scott 2002). Kabul University reopened in 2002, with journalism in its curriculum. Radio Afghanistan is back on the air and broadcasting music again, and satellite dishes are reappearing in the countryside.

Besides the reemergence of newspapers and broadcast stations, magazines have returned to the street stalls of Kabul. A satirical magazine, *Zanbil e Gham*, is no longer an underground publication. The first magazine for women, *Malalai*, was launched in 2002 with an editorial that decried "the past five years of darkness, fear, tyranny" for women in Afghanistan and rejoiced that "freedom has replaced captivity" and women can now have "knowledge instead of ignorance" (AINA 2002). The executive director of the World Press Freedom Committee, Marilyn Greene, nevertheless offered a sobering perspective on Afghanistan: "It would be unrealistic to believe that a strong, independent, and economically viable system for print and broadcast news providers will be possible for quite some time" (Scott 2002).

Afghanistan faces extraordinary barriers in reinvigorating its media system. Besides poverty, barriers include a low literacy level, the many languages spoken in the country, cultural and religious beliefs, economic costs, transportation, technology, and government intervention.

But all nations, from the struggling to the mighty, experience barriers to media development. Back in the late 1970s, when Afghanistan was just beginning its decades of civil strife, American scholars Ray Hiebert, Donald Ungurait, and Thomas Bohn were erecting a media systems paradigm on the theory that the relationship between media and societies is reciprocal: "a country creates a national media system, and this media system in turn modifies that society" (Hiebert, Ungarait, and Bohn 1979, p. 35). They identified six social factors that influence the development of a nation's media system: (1) physical/geographic characteristics, (2) technological competencies, (3) cultural traits, (4) economic conditions, (5) political philosophies, and (6) media qualities. The authors contended that the interaction of these six factors, rather than their independent effects, is crucial in the evolution of a media system.

Updating their paradigm for the twenty-first century, this chapter reclassifies and expands on those six barriers to media development. But let's first define what is meant by the words *media, development*, and *barriers*.

Media is defined as means of communication and comprises the technology for sending and receiving messages and the organizations for gathering, processing, and transmitting news and information to a mass audience. Global news agencies, newspapers, magazines, broadcast stations, and satellite networks are commonly identified as the media. However, means of communication also include books, pamphlets, billboards, and computer sites. Taken together, these mechanisms supply the informational needs of a society. Important in this process is the ability of the media to identify, create, manipulate, and spread public opinion. The media are the institution in society that not only informs the public but also can help move the masses in collective, purposeful, and productive action.

Development is defined as increasing the quantity and improving the quality of the available means of communication. Media development refers to improving the availability, diversity, and quality of news and other information to meet the needs of the audience. Development also includes improved individual access to the channels of communication for the purposes of sending and receiving messages from the mass audience. In short, *media development* facilitates the flow of information among and between individuals and institutions in any given community or society.

Barriers to media development occur in six broadly conceived forms. This chapter defines them as (1) physical barriers, (2) cultural barriers, (3) economic barriers, (4) governmental barriers, (5) media barriers, and (6) technological barriers. These barriers often account for observable differences in the level of development or sophistication among the media systems in the world. In fact, no media system—not even the world's most advanced media system, which is found in the United States—can accurately claim to be without any of these barriers that hinder the ideal conditions for communication.

Barriers may be too pessimistic a word, since it implies an almost insurmountable obstacle. Although some barriers to media development do seem insurmountable—think of communicating across the Sahara, or publishing in a nation of illiterates—other barriers related to government policies and economic systems are more like major challenges that in time can be overcome for the good of a nation and its media.

Physical Barriers

We begin with Earth's topography. In many parts of the world, mountains and other inhospitable terrain prevent the installation of telephone lines and block the reach of broadcast signals. For instance, Peru is a media-rich nation of newspapers and broadcast stations, yet that is true only for the 60 percent of the population who live within 100 miles of the Pacific Ocean. For people who live in the Andes or in the plains to the east of the mountain range, radio signals sent via mountain transmitters are the only means of mass communication.

Geography is an overwhelming obstacle in building a national media system. The vast distances between media centers and media audiences make communication difficult or impossible. This is the case in Russia, with its land mass spanning

11 time zones. News in the afternoon in Moscow is news in the dead of night in eastern Siberia. For the island nation of Indonesia, the ocean presents a physical barrier to convenient communication in a nation spread across 13,700 islands. If economically feasible, satellites and repeater stations provide the solution to bridging some of these distances, waterways, and obstructing terrains.

Other physical barriers include the lack of basic infrastructure such as roads for the transportation of printed communication and the equipment for broadcasting. In the West African nation of Mauritania, for example, the quickest way to travel from the capital of Nouakchott to the northern part of the country is to drive 100 miles along the beach at low tide—"and that's the easy part," according to a U.S. State Department spokesman, because that must be followed by almost 200 miles over sand dunes (U.S. State Department 2002). It is an overnight trip by truck or four-wheel-drive vehicle to reach the nearest population center, if the tide is just right.

Even climate and soil conditions can be a physical barrier to media development. Film stock tends to deteriorate faster in the tropics than in temperate zones, so film companies in tropical areas must take this into consideration when setting up film production and distribution facilities (Hiebert, Ungarait, and Bohn 1979, p. 37). Some nations, like those in sub-Saharan Africa, are unable to grow the trees necessary for producing their own newsprint, so they must rely on newsprint produced in Europe and North America. This physical barrier hampers the development of their domestic print media and keeps them in a constant state of dependency on imported newsprint.

Cultural Barriers

Every society has its own norms, taboos, values, and unique ways. Sexual content in the media that is accepted in Amsterdam would outrage the people of Tokyo. The freedom to analyze and criticize religious institutions in the United States would infuriate Iran. The cultural barriers to media development are perhaps the most difficult to overcome because the solutions often require a change in a nation's attitudes and deep-seated beliefs about religion, society, education, and culture.

Illiteracy is a prime cultural barrier to media development. In India, almost half of the people cannot read and write a short, simple sentence about his or her everyday life, which is the United Nations definition for being literate. The UN's 2000 adult illiteracy rates are even worse in Egypt, Haiti, and Iraq (UNESCO 2000). In Afghanistan, half of the men and 78 percent of the women are illiterate. Clear disparities exist between adult men and women all around the world. In China, the illiteracy rate is 8 percent for men and 24 percent for women. In Saudi Arabia the figures are 16 percent for men and 33 percent for women. In Ethiopia and Bangladesh, a staggering two-thirds of adult women are illiterate. By contrast, the illiteracy rate in South Africa is 14 percent for men and 15 percent for women, and Western nations have almost negligible illiteracy rates for both men and women.

The inability to read and write limits a person's capacity to communicate, and just as important, it limits the ability to learn and grow. Lack of knowledge of the world profoundly influences attitudes and beliefs, often in a negative manner. Literacy opens up the world to the individual and drives the desire for more and better communication content. Literate individuals are much more likely to make demands of the media that will force the media to a higher level of development. The printed media can flourish only to the degree that a domestic population is literate.

Multilingualism in a nation is another cultural barrier because it complicates the logistics of serving the information needs of audiences from different language and ethnic groups. In many African nations, three or four languages are used for daily communication. The mass media are therefore faced with the challenge of providing content in each of these languages to meet the needs of the entire population. This is particularly true where the media are owned by the government and operate on a fixed budget that does not allow expansion of service for all those who need it.

In nations with privately owned commercial media, it is common for media outlets to focus on the information needs of the largest or most profitable segment of the audience, whether that segment is defined by language or by other unique interests. If media organizations do not have the money or the will to cater to specific language or cultural groups, that segment of the population will go without daily communication. Multilingualism makes Singapore a fascinating case study. When it became a nation in the 1960s, Singapore decided to create a multilingual society. The small island nation, tucked between Malaysia and Indonesia, has four official languages: English, Mandarin Chinese, Malay, and Tamil (southern India), with media existing in all four languages. Singapore's leaders had the foresight to declare English the official backbone of a multilingual society, and Singapore has since become a business and technology leader and one of the world's richest nations by being able to converse so fluently with the British and Americans in the West and the Chinese and Indians in the East.

Meanwhile, China is aggressively seeking to educate its young in English. But this country, the most populous nation in the world, faces significant language barriers of its own. The nation shares a written language, but the spoken Mandarin in the north of China and the spoken Cantonese in the south of China are quite different, and some 23 dialects exist in the Chinese countryside. As a result, while Singapore has made multilingualism work to its benefit, multilingualism serves as a barrier to the strengthening of a national media system in China.

Another potential hindrance to media development is the reliance on interpersonal communication and public opinion leadership in some societies. Where the population is geographically removed from the institutions of government and lacks contact with the larger society, mass media have little or no effect on the daily life of the ordinary citizen. Local authority figures such as village elders or wealthy individuals tend to dominate communication and control public opinion. These social hierarchy and community decision-making practices are particularly common in African and Islamic nations. What these opinion leaders and their circle of associates have to say is what matters in the absence of mass media and the diversity of views that the media tend to contribute. These information elites have little or no incentive to foster development of the mass media because it would usurp their power and diminish their status.

Religious beliefs also may result in diminished reliance on mass media and less desire to improve it. In the United States, religious groups such as the Amish or Christian fundamentalists shun or disapprove of their members being heavy media users, because they consider the media to have corrupting or immoral influences on the audience.

Whether rooted in religious beliefs or broader cultural concerns, the fear of negative influences from media content is not confined to any single country or region of the world. This concern is at the heart of what is called *cultural imperialism.* Asian nations in particular have erected barriers against imported media content. Malaysia, for example, limits the amount of Western television programming on its channels for fear that Western content could decimate the indigenous culture and replace domestic attitudes and practices with those embedded in the foreign media. Western entertainment is often the target for exclusion because many of the products, services, and practices it promotes—for instance, violence and sexual innuendo, or the use of alcohol, tobacco, and birth control devices—are anathema to the cultural norms of non-Western societies.

But it is not merely West versus non-West. Western European nations also make the same cultural imperialism argument in taking steps to limit or exclude American and other foreign-produced content from their domestic media. No nation wants to become home to U.S. news and entertainment to the detriment of developing its own media system.

Economic Barriers

Whatever the physical and cultural barriers to media development may be, money is a necessity too. A sophisticated media system cannot thrive in economically impoverished nations. India, for instance, has a telephone density of two for every 100 persons, and its waiting list of over 2 million Indians wanting telephone service will not be satisfied for years (*World Factbook* 2002). A poor country faced with starving people will support a media system only to the extent that it is an asset to the nation's economic improvement, and capitalist countries are more likely to allow profit-oriented media.

Nations with strong national economies, stable monetary systems, and educated workforces tend to be the nations with well-developed media systems. The global economic order has a tremendous impact on the world's media. Unequal economic and trade relations hinder the development, or at least the equal development, of the media in many nations. In some countries, political and economic instability retards development of the media by preventing the enticement of much-needed foreign capital. Across Africa, AIDS is devastating the workforce; in Botswana, for instance, 36 percent of the adult population has HIV/AIDS, the national life expectancy is a mere 37 years, and half of the people live below the poverty line (World Press Review Online 2001). It is hard even to think about developing a strong media system in the face of such catastrophe.

Thus, poverty and inequality in the allocation of the world's resources play a major part in blocking the development of the media in many countries. Even if the media are privately owned rather than government owned, and the owners have an economic incentive to improve the media in order to capture the largest possible audience, it still requires money to buy a color printing press or to install a transponder to relay broadcast signals or to start an Internet café. On a large scale, the cost of national telecommunication systems and communication satellites puts a well-developed media system out of reach for all but the wealthiest nations. Only a handful of nations have the money and technical capability to build, buy, or launch their own communication satellites. These satellites have proven to be tremendous enablers of national broadcast networks, remote printing for newspapers, and individual communication via telephone, fax, and personal computers. Through the cooperative Intelsat organization, most of the world's nations gain access to satellite communication by leasing transponders and accompanying frequencies on orbiting satellites. But without the resources to purchase and operate their own full-time satellites, these nations operate on whatever time and services they can lease.

Meanwhile, those nations with satellite technology can earn additional money to further develop their capabilities and thus keep outdistancing the poor nations with increasingly sophisticated means of communication. The U.S. space program is a prime example. Only a few nations have the economic and technical ability to launch satellites, but the United States is the leader in maintaining them once they are in orbit. The success of NASA's "search-and-repair" missions will help the United States to maintain leadership in the world information economy for a long time.

For developing nations, the cost of building infrastructure to enable significant development of national media is indeed a formidable barrier, even after the decades of debates, diatribe, and development projects aimed at changing the old information order. Competition from imported programming and the increased availability of international broadcast media content weaken development of the indigenous media in many parts of the world. A University of Cyprus report calls international broadcasting "a major competitive source" in news and sports for the Cypriot stations (Mallouppas 1998). Singapore wishes to limit the amount of programming secured from neighboring Malaysia in order to develop its own television and film industry. Because of economies of scale, efficiency, and expertise in production and marketing, larger nations can provide almost unlimited quantities of higher-quality media content at a lower cost than producers in smaller or developing nations. This economic barrier makes it difficult, if not impossible, to develop indigenous entertainment programs by local production companies in a competitive situation.

A new barrier in the West is the emerging trend toward the consolidation of media ownership and control in the offices of a few multinational corporations.

Media consolidation reduces the diversity of voices. For example, 14 newspapers in Canada's major cities were required to publish the same editorial at least once a week because all of the newspapers now belong to a media giant (IFEX December 2001). This trend threatens the criteria for freedom to communicate and for gaining access to communication channels mentioned in our opening definition of media development. In the East, as William Hachten noted in *World News Prism* (1992), media globalization has helped to bring communication infrastructure and investment capital for private ownership to many of the former communist countries of Eastern Europe. But the influx of capital and investors has now meant giving up ownership and control of these domestic media outlets to media barons and corporations in distant and foreign lands. Control over communications content accompanies ownership of media channels, and absentee owners are less likely to sacrifice economic profits to support the social good derived from a civic-conscious media system.

On a smaller scale, the cost of starting a media operation or purchasing an existing one is prohibitively high for individuals in any nation, and more so for those in poor nations. The cost of radio and TV sets also limits individual access to receive communication. Even the cost of a subscription or a single issue of a publication puts mass media out of reach for many people in the poorer nations. In South American countries hit hard by recession, some newspapers in Argentina and Chile are being distributed for free, with the intent of recovering costs through higher advertising rates due to increased circulation.

Then there are scarcities. Many nations do not have the presses and other technology for printing mass copies of publications. They often lack the equipment for photographic reproduction, for printing in color, and for other advanced production processes that add to the quantity and quality of printed materials. The scarcity of available electromagnetic frequencies for broadcasting and of geosynchronous orbital slots for satellites are barriers to developing telecommunications systems. On a daily basis, poorer nations also face a scarcity of electricity, gasoline, spare parts, and other necessities of transportation that hinder media development.

Governmental Barriers

Freedom of the press and broadcasting has gained momentum in the twenty-first century. Freedom House (2002), a nonprofit organization based in New York, declared that 21 percent of the world's people now live in a nation with a free media (examples include the United States, Norway, South Africa, Israel, and Thailand), 43 percent live in nations with some media restrictions (Russia, Brazil, Indonesia, Uganda, Jordan), and 36 percent live in nations with state control or other barriers to a free media (China, Iraq, Cuba, Egypt, Cambodia).

Freedom House notes that the twentieth century began with not a single nation granting the right to vote to all citizens, male and female, and ended with three-fifths of the world's population having democratically elected governments. Despite two world wars and the Holocaust in the past 100 years, Freedom House chairman Bette Bao Lord said, "In the end, this has been democracy's century. If the world's community of established democracies embraces freedom as a major goal, the next century will be freedom's century" (Freedom House 2002).

Media freedom is nearly universal in Western Europe, North and South America, and the Pacific region. Asia and Eastern Europe are in transition, with about half of the nations having free or partly free media. Africa and the Middle East remain heavily tilted toward state control or other barriers to media freedom. Herbert Altschull (1984) theorized that the media serve as agents of power to maintain and perpetuate the sovereign. To maintain political power, the sovereign often finds it effective to suppress, stunt, and otherwise stifle the means of communication for fear that they would be used to usurp him. In such instances, the sovereign resorts to making the mass media part of his dominion. In China, the media have served as the official "eyes and ears" of the Communist Party since the Communist Revolution in 1949. Across Eastern Europe, Africa, and the Middle East, governments control radio and television stations as a way of controlling the flow of information.

Where government does not own the means of communication, it sets up barriers to control the private or independent press. Censorship, licensing, and the use of "insult laws" are common practices used by governments around the world who fear that free expression in an open media system could galvanize public opinion to change the status quo. Because of this potential for the media to promote or instigate political change, journalists are often jailed, beaten, or killed by political leaders attempting to control communication and hold on to power. Organizations such as Amnesty International, the Committee to Protect Journalists, Freedom House, and other international organizations regularly document and publicize the human rights abuses, media suppression, and the killing of journalists around the world.

Threats to life and limb are serious political barriers to media development, but so too is the self-censorship that often results from these threats. Journalists in Central and South America have been under the greatest pressure of practicing quality journalism in the face of unstable regimes, would-be leaders in guerrilla movements, and drug cartels. Although media self-censorship is psychological in nature, the very real consequences of being victimized by political violence are a significant barrier to media development, causing some journalists and media organizations to remain silent at times and to serve as the mouthpieces of government at other times.

Political leaders also may disenfranchise opposition parties and minority groups to maintain power and privilege. These political tactics amount to barriers to media development because political parties and minority populations often sponsor organs of communication that augment and enrich the flow of information in any media system. These suppressed groups, in fact, may provide the only means of mass communication for a significant portion of the population in some countries.

Threats to media freedom come in many guises, from death to defamation, from intimidation to licensing. Some despots shoot or beat the messengers; others use legal means. Here are a variety of examples:

- *Intimidation.* Many African governments have a deep-seated antagonism toward the media. Nations such as Liberia, Malawi, and Cote d'Ivoire all make use of their police and military to intimidate and harass journalists.
- *Tax investigations.* South Korea's president blamed the media for his unpopularity and sought retribution by instigating a tax investigation of media outlets (Associated Press 2001).
- *Defamation.* In Latin America, so-called "*desacato*" or insult laws protecting the honor of public officials remain on the statute books and are used to punish media criticisms. In Cuba, a media executive went to prison for six years for "insulting" President Fidel Castro. In Zambia, four journalists, including a student, were charged with defamation for reporting that the president was suffering from Parkinson's disease, an incurable brain disorder (IFEX June 2002).
- *Licensing.* After permitting the first privately owned newspaper in Syria in 40 years, the government grew frightened and introduced press licensing as a way of maintaining government control. In Zimbabwe, the government announced it would issue only one license to a national radio broadcaster and only one license to a national television broadcaster, effectively maintaining a media monopoly (Bafana 2002).
- *Censorship.* At least 43 newspapers and magazines in Iran were shut down in the aftermath of a scathing speech by Ayatollah Khamenei when he accused the media of "undermining Islamic and revolutionary principles" ("CPJ Chronicles" 2001).
- *Seizure.* The government of Mauritania seized an issue of an Arabic-language newspaper because of an article that criticized political Islam. Security forces in Nigeria impounded newspapers that reported regional violence resulting from the adoption of an Islamic legal system by some states.
- *Travel restrictions.* The governments of Thailand and Myanmar—neighbors on less than friendly terms—each have implemented travel bans on reporters from the other country in order to suppress critical reporting. In the United States, the Washington correspondent for the Arab television network al-Jazeera was detained on his way to cover President Bush when, according to the BBC, police told him al-Jazeera's credit card had been linked to activities in Afghanistan (Freedom Forum November 2001).
- *Jailing.* More than 200 journalists in Ethiopia have spent three months or more in prison. One of the latest was a newspaper editor sent to Addis Ababa Prison for defaming the head of government.
- *Death threats.* In Yugoslavia, a hand grenade was thrown into the house of the director of Radio Paracin but did not explode. In Mexico, a newspaper executive refused a governor's insistence that he support a certain political candi-

date. Water and electricity to his home were cut off, and police officers surrounded it. When the governor threatened his life, the editor fled to the United States (IFEX January 2000).

- *Lack of protection.* In Indonesia, less than 5 percent of the cases of violence against journalists are brought to trial. The absence of prosecution can lead to the perception that such violence will go unpunished.
- *Death.* An editor in Colombia was shot five times in the head after his newspaper published an editorial alleging mishandling of public funds by local government. His death caused a number of media organizations in the interior of Colombia to suspend operations out of fear of reprisals. In 2000, Colombia was the most dangerous place to practice journalism. In 2001 it was Afghanistan ("Waging War" 2001). In 2003, obviously, it was Iraq.

Besides drug wars and shooting wars and political wars, *legal barriers* exist to media development. Guaranteeing human rights, including the right to communicate, is a moral belief. Where human rights are elevated, liberty and creativity of the human spirit abound, and so too do the need and the desire for well-developed channels of communication.

An essential component of the ideal media environment is a legal right for the public and the media to have access to documents and information held by the government. Those nations that have laws guaranteeing access to public records and public meetings provide a great advantage for their media to develop and thrive. In the United States, the First Amendment guarantees freedom of speech and of the press, while public access is mandated through the federal Freedom of Information Act and similar state open meetings and open records laws (called "sunshine" laws because they require governments to operate in the light of day). The media in nations without such laws are usually devoid of the rich and important content that characterizes a quality information system. Sunshine laws create a climate that facilitates news gathering. Government officials and bureaucrats are more likely to cooperate with journalists when there is a presumption of openness and the right of the public to information. In many countries, journalists face a significant barrier in gathering the news because government sources refuse to talk to them and to explain public policy.

While many governmental barriers remain to a well-developed global media, good news abounds in many countries. Mongolia has prohibited government control of broadcasting. Romania is liberalizing its harsh defamation laws. Chile is seeking to eliminate the *desacato* or insult laws. And in China, home to one-fifth of the world's population, a most remarkable development occurred in late 2001. Just a few weeks after China formally issued a list of media taboos, nicknamed the "Seven No's" (no. 7 on the list warns the news media not to violate party propaganda), *People's Daily*, the 2-million-circulation bible of Marxist-Maoist orthodoxy, published an editorial that endorsed the citizen's "right to be informed" by an honest and factual media system (Zeitlin 2001). The march toward a freer media, while inexorably slow, continues one step at a time across the globe.

Media Barriers

Newsrooms around the world have their own shortcomings, such as poorly trained reporters and editors, lack of objectivity, greed, loss of credibility, and self-censorship. Lack of journalistic training is a significant barrier to media development in many nations. Formal journalism education is embryonic or nonexistent in most of the newly independent and developing nations, where on-the-job training is the norm. Journalists in the former communist nations needed retraining before they could work in the media with a new philosophical and ideological approach. Those who could not be retrained were purged to improve the credibility of the "new" media in the eyes of the public. A shortage of journalists resulted, and with the end of communism, the field was suddenly open to anyone who wanted to have a go at it. The experience of press freedom for the first time, or liberation after an era of suppression, led to a surge in the number and variety of media outlets. Experience in Eastern Europe and elsewhere has shown that the newness wears off quickly. New and inexperienced journalists often then turned their attention to partisan reporting with the newfound tool of a powerful press.

Some settings are so volatile that professionalism is extraordinarily difficult. Palestinians living in the Israeli-occupied territories of the West Bank and Gaza were long prevented by Israel from establishing their own media. When Israel and the Palestine Liberation Organization (PLO) formally recognized each other in 1993, the PLO quickly moved to begin the development of a media system operated by Palestinians to meet the information and entertainment needs of Palestinians.

In 2002, Israel strenuously objected to obituaries in Palestinian newspapers that honored suicide bombers. The death notice of a Palestinian man who blew himself up, killing an Israeli woman and her 10-year-old daughter, glorified the man and concluded, "We pray that Allah will grant a haven for the heroic Martyr with His plentiful mercy" (Palestinian Media Watch, quoting *Al Ayyam*, 10 Feburary 2002). Similarly, the media watch group criticized a Palestinian TV children's program for showing a young girl running with a schoolbag over her shoulder. Suddenly, real footage is shown of an Israeli helicopter firing a missile, and then the TV drama shows the young girl falling dead, with her books scattering. The media watch director observed, "One prominent objective of the Palestinian print and broadcast media is to promote hatred and fear by presenting Israelis, even to the youngest viewers, as monstrous, ready and willing to kill them at any time. I do not think it is possible to prevent this kind of programming. After all, we have allowed the Palestinian Authority control over its own media" (Palestinian Media Watch 2001).

On the other hand, a pro-Palestine media watch group attacked news coverage by CNN, the Associated Press, Knight-Ridder, and other Western news agencies as highlighting Israeli suffering while downplaying Palestinian suffering (Palestine Media Watch 2002). As an example, the Palestinian media watch group criticized CNN for having on its web site a memorial listing Israelis who had died at the hands of suicide-bomb Palestinians, but not of Palestinians who had died at the hands of aggressive Israeli military forces.

In 2002, the U.S.-based Committee to Protect Journalists listed the West Bank as the world's worst place to be a journalist because both the Israeli military and Palestinian militants hamper the work of the media. The rest of the top 10 worst places to be a journalist were Colombia, Afghanistan, Eritrea, Belarus, Myanmar, Zimbabwe, Iran, Kyrgyzstan, and Cuba.

A barrier to media development in Russia is manifested by the selling of favorable news stories. The practice is called "hidden advertising" because it goes under the guise of being an honest news story. Two-thirds of the journalists responding to a survey by the Institute of Sociology of the Russian Academy of Sciences in St. Petersburg said they had sold favorable news stories more than once. A senior researcher lamented, "These figures indicate how easy it is to manipulate journalists in Russia. It is difficult for them to resist financial temptations because, just like most people, they have rather modest incomes" (Mater August 2001). The practice, known as *zakazukha* in Russian, involved "price lists" that are discreetly circulated to public relations firms. Former Communist Party mouthpiece *Izvestia* reportedly raised $310,000 in "hidden advertising" in one month alone.

Beyond the corruption of "hidden advertising" is the political power of real advertising. The World Bank reported that Bangladesh newspapers are captives of state patronage because a newspaper's profitability, even its survival, heavily depends on the allocation of government advertising. As a result, a newspaper that turns critical of the Bangladesh government may be quickly disciplined by the withdrawal of state advertising (IFEX July 2002). This potential co-opting of the media may produce a self-censorship that robs the public of necessary information that any well-developed media system should provide.

These barriers to quality journalism feed the low status of journalists in society and the lack of prestige ascribed to the media in general. Accuracy and fairness are measures of professionalism that can add to the quality of news coverage and can generate credibility and trust in the eyes of the public. However, these elements are not found in media systems that practice partisan, advocacy, or sensationalist journalism. In a Eurobarometer public opinion survey by the European Commission, the sensationalist-driven British newspapers were found to be the least trusted by their readers. Their trust level was a dismal 20 percent. The next worse result (39 percent) was in Italy, where the media were dominated by the billionaire prime minister. Trust was highest in Belgium, Finland, and Luxembourg, at roughly 60 percent each.

The practice of journalism in the United States is closely watched around the world. When the United States asked its TV networks not to broadcast excerpts of Osama bin Laden via the Qatar TV station al-Jazeerah, other countries took note. Singapore praised the "healthy guided censorship" it saw in the new U.S. information policy. Zimbabwe sought to justify its repression of independent journalism by noting, "If the most celebrated democracies in the world won't allow their national interests to be tampered with, we will not allow it too." In response, the World Association of Newspapers (WAN) criticized the United States for justifying its call for censorship and noted, "It is no accident that bin Laden operated out of a country which had totally outlawed free expression, information and debate, nor that the regimes most supportive of his and other terrorism networks are among the most repressive in the world" (IFEX May 2002). WAN President Roger Parkinson said, "The international community should put all its political weight and money behind every effort to bring down the barriers and obstacles to the free flow of information and ideas."

Technological Barriers

Technology is both a barrier to media development and a potential destroyer of barriers. Technology is a barrier in the world of established media because newspapers, magazines, radio stations, television stations, and cable systems are expensive to start and to distribute. When technology is transferred from media-rich nations to the media-poor, that transfer usually means sending soon-outdated equipment to the poorer nations. Although this practice does help the recipient nations, the technological gap between rich and poor nations keeps increasing. There are obvious disadvantages, if not dangers, in this growing disparity, but it takes money to close the gap.

The Internet does not share the enormous startup and distribution costs of established media, although its use does require a literate population with access to a computer. As a result, the Internet serves, and will long serve, as a communication forum for elites and the educated young.

The Internet transcends geographical boundaries, which makes its potential to destroy existing barriers so intriguing. The nonprofit Freedom House organization noted that many repressive governments—among them Iran, Pakistan, Syria, and Saudi Arabia—place fewer restrictions on Internet access than they do on print and broadcast media. A Freedom House scholar observed, "The Internet's relative openness in some closed societies reflects the dilemma posed by the opportunities on the web for economic development, international trade, and cultural advances" (Freedom House 2002).

The Freedom House study found that 46 percent of the world's population live in nations with the least restrictive access to the Internet (examples include the United States, Germany, Taiwan, Australia, and South Africa), 40 percent live in nations that are moderately restrictive (Mexico, South Korea, Turkey, India, Lebanon), and 14 percent live in nations ranked as the most restrictive (China, Russia, Laos, Cuba, Algeria). Those nations with the most restrictive access generally allow only state-run Internet service providers to operate, and they block access; for instance, China blocked access to the google.com search engine. Ukraine is listed as moderately restrictive, but its president called the Internet a tool for political warfare and muckraking. Ukraine's biggest political scandal erupted when an on-line newspaper reporter who had been a government critic disappeared and his headless corpse was found two months later. Thousands of Ukrainians took to the streets demanding the president's resignation after audiotapes surfaced on which a voice identified as the president's was heard ordering aides to "deal with" the reporter. The president denied involvement, said the tape was doctored, and concluded, "The Internet has become a killer. People can write whatever they like without signing their names, and then it appears in the mass media" (Freedom Forum online November 2001).

As a harmonized measurement of the international Internet community, the A. C. Nielsen NetWatch (2000) tracking study of 16 countries showed the greatest growth rates in China and the Philippines. Canada had the largest percentage of users, at 38 percent, thanks to its mature economy, excellent telecommunications structure, and a supportive government environment. The United States had the largest population of Internet users (projected to be 55 million by the year 2000, representing 25 percent of the population). Others in the 25 percent range were Singapore, Australia, and New Zealand. At that same period, Great Britain was at 15 percent, France 11 percent, the Philippines 8 percent, and China 4 percent. Nations buffeted by severe economic problems, such as South Africa and Thailand, at 2 percent, and Indonesia, at 1 percent, were far behind other countries in the Internet revolution.

Technological barriers, then, while inexorably tied to a nation's economic underpinning, also are connected to culture, politics, and even computer literacy and access.

Conclusion

Afghanistan has a long road ahead to rebuild its media system. Physical barriers include its harsh terrain and decimated communications infrastructure caused by 23 years of war. Cultural barriers include a low literacy rate, a history of religious strife, and the backlash of cultural imperialism. Economic barriers include rampant poverty, the disintegration of a national economy or international trade, and a scarcity of resources such as radios and printing presses. Governmental barriers include efforts to revive democracy amid assassination attempts and feuding tribes; Afghanistan adopted a new press law in 2002 that bans pen names on published essays, punishes insults, and makes it a crime to blaspheme Islam and other religions. Media barriers are enormous, with *Kabul Weekly* being published using just one computer, a printer, and a scanner; residents of Kabul paid the price of a loaf of bread to buy their first newspaper in five years (UNESCO, 24 January 2002). Meanwhile, the technological gap between rich and poor nations keeps increasing.

Despite these enormous barriers, journalists are at work in Afghanistan, trying to make their nation and their media system better each day. Physical and economic barriers are often the easiest to overcome because all it takes are resources, whereas the barriers erected by human attitudes and actions remain steadfastly immovable until a society and its people are ready to take the next step.

Hiebert, Ungurait, and Bohn's media systems paradigm is based on a reciprocal relationship between a society and its media system, each having a direct impact on the other. Rather than any single factor being the determinant, the evolution of a nation's media system is based on the interaction of physical, cultural, economic, government, media, and technological barriers. Every society is a mixture of stability and change, and the resulting tension between the two involves and affects the development of the media in that society.

Bibliography

A. C. Nielsen Media Measurement Services. "An International Survey of the Internet." Available: http://acnielsen.com/products/reports/netwatch/index.htm, 2000.

"Afghanistan." World Press Freedom Review on-line, International Press Institute. Available: http://www.freemedia.at/wpfr/afghanis.htm, 1997–2001.

AINA. "Publications and Projects: Malalai." Available: http://www.ainaworld.com/en/publication_malalai.html, 2002.

Altschull, J. Herbert. *Agents of Power.* New York: Longman, 1984.

Associated Press. "Kim Dae-jung's Uneasy Relations with South Korean Press." Freedom Forum on-line. Available: http://www.freedomforum.org. Accessed 20 August 2001.

Bafana, Busani. "Zimbabwe: Broadcast Blues." World Press Review Online. Available: http://www.worldpress.org/Africa/113.cfm. Accessed 31 July 2002.

"CPJ Chronicles Crackdown on Iran's News Media." Freedom Forum on-line. Available: http://www.freedomforum.org. Accessed 16 November 2001.

Freedom Forum on-line. Web site: http://www.freedomforum.org.

Freedom House. "Survey of Press Freedom." Available: http://www.freedomhouse.org/pfs2001/pfs2001.pdf, 2002.

Hachten, William. *The World News Prism,* 3rd Edition. Ames: Iowa State University Press, 1992.

Hiebert, Ray, Donald Ungurait, and Thomas Bohn. *Mass Media II.* New York: Longman, 1979.

International Freedom of Expression Exchange (IFEX). Web site: http://www.ifex.org.

Mallouppas, Andreas. "Cyprus Media Profile." Euromedia '98, Vienna, Austria, 26 June 1998.

Mater, Gene. "Most Russian Journalists Sell Favorable Stories as Hidden Advertising." Freedom Forum online. Available: http://www.freedomforum.org. Accessed 29 August 2001.

Palestine Media Watch. Web site: http://www.pmwatch.org. [pro-Palestinian]

Palestinian Media Watch. Web site: http://www.pmw.org.il/bulletins-191101.html. Accessed 19 November 2001. [pro-Israeli]

Scott, Byron. "Reviving Afghan Journalism." Global Journalist Online magazine. Available: http://www.journalism.missouri.edu/globalj/index.html, 1st Quarter, 2002.

UNESCO [on-line news portal]. Web site: http://www.unesco.org.

U.S. State Department. Telephone interview with State Department spokesman Callie Fuller, 1 August 2002.

"Waging War on the Media." World Press Freedom Review, International Press Institute. Available: http://www.freemedia.at/wpfr/intro_wpfr.htm#top, 2001.

World Factbook 2002. Washington, D.C.: U.S. Government Printing Office, 2002.

World Press Review Online. Available: http://www.worldpress.org/profiles/Botswana.cfm.

Zeitlin, Arnold. "Is the Stranglehold Easing?" Freedom Forum on-line. Available: http://www.freedomforum.org. Accessed 10 September 2001.

5

Freedom of the Press Around the World

Robert L. Stevenson

Everyone is in favor of freedom of the press, but there is disagreement about what it is, and even in a globalized world, it remains surprisingly rare. Since the collapse of communism, with which the cold war also ended, the problem is less about the general definition of freedom of the press and more about how it can be established and sustained in countries that are new to Western market-based democracy. By the definition we will use here, press freedom remains an elusive goal as well in many of the countries in the old Third World that continue the struggle to develop stable political and economic institutions.

Press freedom is closely related to technical innovation. The current communication revolution, which has produced the global communication system of the twenty-first century, also influences press freedom, usually for the better, but not always. In this chapter we will consider the history of press freedom and several alternative definitions, then compare different interpretations within the now dominant Western concept, and finally examine some of the issues that have arisen as a product of globalization.

History

Western democracy, including the key element of freedom of speech and of the press, is a product of the European revolution that was set off by the invention of printing with movable type in the late 1400s. The explosion of knowledge that followed led to modern European languages, literacy, popular government, and newspapers. As governments and media developed the symbiotic relationship that continues today, governments tried to maintain control over information about their activities.

Newspapers—and usually the public—wanted to know what governments were doing. The struggle between the two forces remains a part of the twenty-first century world.

The history of that struggle includes several important milestones. Certainly the most famous—and possibly the most influential—was the inclusion of a strong statement of press freedom in the U.S. Constitution, the famous First Amendment, which states flatly, "Congress shall make no law . . . abridging the freedom of speech, or of the press. . . ." In a skeptical assessment of the hyperbole surrounding the First Amendment, J. Herbert Altschull nevertheless acknowledges its continuing influence:

> No doctrine announced by the new republic has been more widely cheered around the world than the declaration of free expression. The declaration has fueled the fires of every revolutionary movement for two centuries. (Altschull 1995, p. 8)

Virtually every national constitution now includes some reference to press freedom, even though the principle of free expression is frequently honored in the breach more than in the observance. It is also enshrined in documents, such as the Universal Declaration of Human Rights, that sketch the outlines of an emerging global understanding of press freedom. But even in the nations with the common Western heritage that serves as the model for the rest of the world, there is agreement neither on the details of what press freedom means nor on the relative importance of this right when balanced against other freedoms that define a modern democracy.

In most Western democracies, the collective good of the nation can take precedence over the rights of the individual. Some argue that the political and civil rights of individuals enumerated in the Bill of Rights are only part of an expanded set of individual and collective rights appropriate for the twenty-first century. A United Nations commission in the 1970s affirmed this position when it argued that the American and French revolutions established individual political rights. It then argued that the Bolshevik revolution in Russia established a second generation of individual economic rights, such as work and housing, followed by a third generation of collective or national rights that defined a new ideal of national sovereignty. These rights included a national right to communicate that comprised a right to determine what information entered the country and what information was reported about the country as elements of an information sovereignty (International Commission for the Study of Communication Problems [MacBride Commission] 1980). Efforts to implement this newfound collective press freedom were part of a broader call to restructure global communication that was known as a New World Information and Communication Order (NWICO).

However, the drive to define a new level of press freedom appropriate for a NWICO largely disappeared along with communism's claim to be a legitimate political ideology and with the NWICO debate itself. Now, after more than 200 years, the simple and uncompromising formulation of the First Amendment remains a model for the world. But what does it mean?

Definitions

Even cursory attention to international media reveals a surprising variety of form, content, and purpose despite nearly universal homage to freedom of the press. The first effort to make sense of this diversity a generation ago identified four distinct "theories" of the press (Siebert, Peterson, and Schramm 1963). Later, William A. Hachten modified the four theories into five "concepts" (Hachten and Scotton 2002). J. Herbert Altschull concluded that global media consisted of a three-part "symphony" (Altschull 1995, Parts III, IV). In all classification schemes, press freedom is a key variable but also a reminder of the lack of a single definition of press freedom and even greater differences in practice. In most formulations, press freedom is defined by the relationship between mass media and government and is key to understanding the country's media system. To highlight differences and similarities among the world's diverse media, we will consider a three-part classification, using Altschull's terms of *market, communitarian,* and *advancing media systems.*

Market

Even among the Western democracies, there is no agreement about the fine points of press freedom. To the American observer, our fellow democrats accept restrictions on free expression that are both surprising and disconcerting. However, a reasonably general definition common to market-based media systems (that is, Western democracies) might go something like this:

> Freedom of the press is the right to speak, broadcast, or publish without prior restraint by or permission of the government, but with limited legal accountability after publication for violations of law. It may also encompass legal guarantees of (1) reasonable access to information about government, businesses, and people; (2) a right of reply or correction; (3) a limited right of access to the media; and (4) some special protections for journalists.

The use of words such as "limited," "reasonable," and "some" is a reminder of the differences within even Western democracies. In all countries, press freedom is balanced against other social values, such as a citizen's right to privacy and justice and the nation's security.

If press freedom is defined simply as freedom from government control, the United States has the freest system in the world, but even there, the right is not absolute. It stops at the law. No one can break a law, criminal or civil, in the name of press freedom. Lawyers and journalists argue endlessly about where the fine line between free press and permissible restriction is (or should be), but most agree that it exists. The First Amendment does not allow anyone to destroy a person's reputation, sell pornography, or give away the nation's defense secrets. Probably the key element of our definition is that the government cannot act in advance to stop a citizen from saying, printing, or broadcasting, but it can hold that individual accountable afterward.

Outside the United States, the first principle of absence of prior restraint or censorship gets less attention, while the ancillary aspects get more. Most democratic governments can, in fact, prevent publication, and some do so routinely. It is done in the name of national security, protection of privacy, or maintenance of social order. The European Union—by any definition a democratic organization with a strong commitment to press freedom—recognizes a right of the "dignity" of the individual that can be used to rein in the worst excesses of intrusive European tabloid journalism. But these same governments also frequently protect reporters from testifying in court or identifying sources. A few countries, notably Scandinavia, guarantee reporters unusual access to government offices and documents. In the U.S. tradition, rights belong to individuals, and distinctions are rarely made between journalists and nonjournalists. In Europe, legal recognition as a journalist brings with it certain special privileges as well as responsibilities. Laws protecting the privacy, reputations, and dignity of individuals are stronger in Europe than in the United States. Penalties for abuse are often modest, a symbolic slap on the wrist for the journalist and return of the victim's good name. The principle of emphasis on the public good is extended to government power to withhold information and to stop publication of embarrassing revelations. In most Western countries, this is accepted as essential to cultural survival and good order. Even where the laws give special protection to journalists, investigative reporting of the kind we expect from *60 Minutes* and the *Washington Post* is rare. Some things, it is argued (sometimes even by journalists), are better left unreported because of the overriding importance of privacy and dignity of the individual, the good name and solidarity of the group, and the stability and even survival of the nation.

A number of specific elements of free expression in the American tradition are quite different in other democracies. They include libel of the dead, group defamation, rights of dignity, prohibitions on insulting officials or nations (not much enforced in Western democracies but copied in authoritarian countries), and blanket secrecy in many areas of government activities, usually in the area of national security or the private lives of public officials. Whether these restrictions lead to a less open society and to less democracy is a question for debate. Advocates of a more active role for governments point to the limitations of private media whose owners are concerned more with bottom lines than with social responsibility, and to the narrow range of opinions that are given voice in mainstream U.S. media. An argument is often made that public debate is more vigorous and journalism contributes more to it when government takes an active role. Where to draw the line between what is public and what is private, how to balance the freedom of the press with the common good of the society, where the public world ends and the private world begins—these are the areas where open democratic governments differ. Whatever the differences among the Western nations' theory and practice of press freedom, they are shades of gray compared with the black-and-white differences between the Western or "market" theory and its main twentieth century competitor for the hearts and minds of journalists, communitarianism. (It should be noted that as used by Altschull, *communitarianism* is broader than the concept defined by Amitai Eizioni [1993]).

Communitarian

Communitarian is a broader concept than Marxist or communist, which most media theorists (including Altschull in an earlier edition of his book) use. The change in terminology from communist to communitarian was based on the emotional baggage attached to communism as well as its vagueness, and suggests the growing divide between the United States, on one hand, and the most democratic Western nations on the other. As we have seen, some recognition of the importance of the broader social structure and some individual responsibility for the greater social good are built into most Western media systems. Canadian law has been governed since the 1867 British North America Act of 1867 by the principles of "peace, order, and good government" rather than the core U.S. concepts of "life, liberty, and pursuit of happiness." Press freedom as a right of individuals and a restraint on government is balanced against individual responsibilities and collective rights that can be enforced only by government action, not constraint. The differences among Western nations, however, should not obscure the essential distinction between a Western definition of press freedom and a communitarian—or Marxist—definition.

For most of the twentieth century, journalists from East and West talked past each other about what press freedom was and why the other side's definition was spurious. Karl Marx produced the intellectual framework for communism but wrote relatively little about journalism itself or press freedom. His occasional impassioned defenses of freedom, which were written in response to suppression of his radical newspaper by German authorities, must be juxtaposed against his intolerance of press dissent or even open discussion during his later tenure as head of the Communist International and part-time journalist in London.

The real Marxist definition of press freedom belongs to Vladimir I. Lenin, who compared the press to the scaffolding used in construction of a building. He extended the analogy to the construction of the socialist state. His statement of the press's function as collective agitator, propagandist, and organizer is well known. A Leninist definition of press freedom is more difficult to piece together, but he clearly rejected the market media definition as "freedom for the rich, systematically, unremittingly, daily, in millions of copies, to deceive, corrupt and fool the exploited and oppressed mass of the people, the poor" (Lenin 1972, p. 187). Instead, he called for state control of the press—including advertising, newsprint, and printing facilities—which would increase access to the press by various citizens' groups.

Lenin and those who carried forward the banner of communism emphasized freedom of the press as the right of access to the media. Soviet newspapers developed a reputation for modestly encouraging readers' letters and using the media as a watchdog on local government bureaucrats and party leaders—but within narrow limits. Until Mikhail S. Gorbachev introduced the policy of *glasnost* ("openness") to support economic restructuring (*perestroika*), government and party maintained the right to a monopoly of information. The only media permitted by law were those authorized by the government or party.

Authors of unauthorized media that challenged the unitary official view—the *samizdat* ("self-published") periodicals, and later audio- and videotapes—were vigorously persecuted and prosecuted, although never with complete success. Unwanted radio voices from the outside were jammed, also with limited effectiveness, and the Soviet government at one time claimed the right to destroy any satellite that could broadcast uninvited television signals to Soviet TV sets.

Of course, communist regimes maintained the same centralized monopoly on information Lenin decried in the capitalist press. Limited access to the media for the purpose of supporting the regime is not a satisfying definition of press freedom. It is, of course, a negative image of the Western view. In one, distance between government and journalism is the heart of freedom; in the other, any crack of light between the government and the journalist is a threat to freedom.

At this point, the Marxist interpretation of press freedom belongs mostly to history, although some of its principles—notably a government monopoly on information—are found in a number of regimes today. The difference between now and the decades when communism was presented as a legitimate alternative to Western press freedom is that there is now rarely an effort to justify press control or to argue that it represents an "authentic" non-Western definition of freedom. One argument justifying government control is found in the relatively large number of authoritarian governments that restrict press freedom but allow some independence and room for maneuver. The dividing line is always hazy. From the minimalist government-shall-not perspective of the United States, even democratic Western countries come under suspicion. By any Western perspective, a lot of the post-cold-war world is undemocratic; its media systems can be described by any of several terms, including Altschull's definition of "advancing" media.

Advancing

The idea of "advancing" media embraces authoritarianism, included in both the original four theories and Hachten's separate concept of development media, which came to prominence in the 1970s. The development concept acknowledged that governments in the Third World frequently justified mobilizing national media to promote national development. Development media originally were used in relatively innocuous projects in areas of agriculture, rural health, education, and family planning. Then national development became synonymous with the political fortunes of those in power, and the media became mouthpieces of the government, very much in the tradition of authoritarianism.

According to Fred S. Siebert, one of the co-authors of the original "four theories" formulation, authoritarianism was the theory of journalism that evolved along with mass media. It is still the most common theory of journalism practiced in the world and embraces some countries we consider Western. In fact, most Western countries practice some of the elements of authoritarianism.

The key element of an authoritarian media system is that media are allowed to flourish as long as they present no challenge to the government. This means that authoritarian media are often privately owned and are often rich and powerful. They tend to stay aloof from the affairs of government, sometimes because they are intimidated by the government, sometimes because they are part of the governing oligarchy.

The relationship between government and journalists is complex and varied. In some countries, government uses its considerable power openly to prevent critical reporting or embarrassing disclosures. In others, the threats to press freedom come from other powers that render governments themselves powerless. In almost all countries, journalists chafe under restrictions and constantly test and challenge the limits. In many authoritarian countries, journalism is a dangerous profession.

A good example of the first situation is Singapore, where, despite unparalleled economic growth and prosperity, the government is still intolerant of critical reporting from either domestic or foreign media. Over the years, foreign media, including the *Economist, Asian Wall Street Journal,* and *Far Eastern Economic Review,* have had their circulation reduced or suspended, have been ordered to apologize or to pay heavy fines, or were forced to close news bureaus over squabbles with the government about the reporting of Singaporean events. As late as 2002, the upstart Bloomberg information service was fined and forced to apologize to Singapore former Prime Minister Lee Kuan Yew for a story that suggested nepotism. The word from the government is straightforward: Enjoy the convenience and efficiency of a Singapore base but don't do anything local media cannot do.

Domestic media are tame. The Freedom House 2002 report on press freedom classifies the information system as "not free" and describes it as "one of the best in the world, but . . . also one of the most centrally controlled" (Sussman and Karlekar 2002). Two privately held corporations control virtually all newspapers and electronic media with close ties to the near-monopoly, People's Action Party (PAP). Government-linked companies also provide the only Internet and cable TV services. Tough enforcement of tough laws about criticism of government has an effect as well. According to Freedom House, "official intimidation motivates self-censorship by many domestic journalists, although some commentary in newspapers has been more outspoken in the past year."

Singapore was one of the leaders in developing techniques to control the Internet. It is important because of widespread access—in 2001, well over half of the population logged on—and because it quickly became a political outlet not directly controlled by the government. In 2001, according to the Committee to Protect Journalists (CPJ), organizations promoting free expression and democracy were forced to register as political organizations, denying them foreign funding (this information is available on the CPJ web site). Organizations not affiliated with the PAP were prohibited from posting information about national elections. An early product of the regulations was the arrest of a free-lance journalist who had posted material critical of the government on an unofficial web site. He was ordered to undergo a psychiatric examination in preparation for a trial. Several of the outside sites, stripped of outside funding, closed. Curiously enough, the Singapore government created a large Internet presence and promoted a program to bring the country on line. Under control, of course.

The other version of authoritarian media can be found in Algeria, Colombia, and Russia, as well as in other countries. In the decade from 1992 to 2001, 60 journalists were killed in Algeria, 34 in Russia, and 29 in Colombia. If the Balkans are treated as a whole, the toll there was also 29. In these countries, there is a common pattern of a deadly three-way tug of war. On the one hand, the government is caught up in a war against some kind of insurgency—Islamic extremism in Algeria, drug warlords in Colombia, a combination of a rebellion and business oligarchs in Russia. On the other, the governments themselves are usually corrupt and intolerant of independent, critical reporting. The journalists get caught in the middle, sometimes ending up in the crosshairs of both forces. By the end of September 2002, CPJ had documented 10 murders of journalists that year, and another 13 whose deaths were confirmed but the circumstances were not (documented on the CPJ web site). Journalism in countries caught up in internal violence is always a dangerous business. It is one thing when reporters are caught in the crossfire of a war but quite another when they become the targets. In many of the world's trouble spots and under many authoritarian regimes, governments do not offer protection to journalists. Sometimes they cannot; often they do not want to.

One positive facet of the picture of authoritarian press systems is that the number of journalists killed around the world dropped from a high of 66 in 1994 to 24 in 2000 and 37 in 2001. The attacks in New York and Washington on September 11, 2001, and the war on terrorism that they ignited did not have an immediately debilitating effect on press freedom. Professional organizations that monitor the state of press freedom documented a growing concern for civil liberties, including free expression, in the United States and other Western countries, but nothing comparable to the restrictions that accompanied previous wars. Freedom House noted that the attacks and aftermath tested conditions for mass media in most countries but concluded that "press freedom emerged intact by the end of 2001." Indeed, it noted small gains for press freedom over 2000.

During the 1970s, the authoritarian principle that journalism should not challenge governments was expanded to include mass media as an active tool of government. Hachten defined it as a separate media system, the development concept of the press. The idea was not new, of course. It was, and is, a key element of Marxist-Leninist press theory, but the development concept of the press also borrowed from Western experience. The United States especially had a history of incorporating mass media into programs of rural development. They included the federal agricultural extension service and educational radio and television that evolved into public broadcasting.

From the widespread use of mass communication in Third World social and economic development programs, it was a small leap to redefine development goals in political terms. That gave journalists the new responsibility of actively supporting the nation or, more commonly, the regime in power. Altschull acknowledges the importance of subordination of press freedom to interests of the nation (or regime in power) in advancing countries with these three summary statements of press freedom: "A free press means freedom of conscience for journalists; press freedom is less important than the viability of the nation; a national press policy is needed to provide legal safeguards for freedom" (1995, p. 435).

"Advancing" media—whether called that or by the more familiar terms of "authoritarian" or "development"—are still the most common. In the old communist countries of Central and Eastern Europe, media tended to evolve from the communist concept to authoritarianism rather than to Western. Even as the NWICO lost its legitimacy, Third World media tended to reflect old-fashioned authoritarian control rather than Western independence. Were "advancing" media en route to the Western model or stuck in permanent authoritarianism? As the new century progresses, we'll find out.

Freedom Today

The last years of the twentieth century were a triumph for market-based Western democracy, and for the principles of journalism associated with it. The most dramatic event, of course, was the collapse of communism in the Soviet Union and Central Europe and the loss of legitimacy in the few remaining outposts of Marxism. Independent, critical journalism from both inside and outside was given part of the credit. The triumph of independent (that is, Western) journalism belongs to Fukuyama's famous "end of history" argument and has been noted as one of the global trends of communication in the opening decade of the new century (Stevenson 1994).

While most attention was fixed on the extraordinary events taking place from Berlin to Moscow, something similar to *glasnost* was taking root in most other parts of the world. Latin American countries, which traditionally swung from fragile democracy to military dictatorship, moved almost uniformly toward democracy. Even Mexico, where corruption and control of the press were part of a long authoritarian tradition, moved toward critical reporting.

In Africa, too, multiparty democracy, which goes hand in hand with Western-style journalism, gained a small foothold. The Pan-African News Agency (PANA), which had been built on the principles of the NWICO and development journalism, announced a course change to independent reporting. In several African countries, independent papers—economically weak, politically insecure—began to challenge government authority.

A curious exception to the wave of democracy sweeping the "advancing" world was seen in parts of Asia. The extraordinary economic success of the "four tigers" (Singapore, South Korea, Hong Kong, and Taiwan) and the second tier of little tigers right behind them (Indonesia, Thailand, Malaysia, and maybe the Philippines) ought to have been preceded by or led to a flourishing of Western freedoms. As we have seen in the example of Singapore, it did not.

The juxtaposition of Asia against Central and Eastern Europe raises the interesting and long-debated question of whether press freedom is a force promoting economic development or a product of it. In the lexicon of the 1990s, the question is which comes first, *glasnost* or *perestroika*? The global test currently under way favors the development-first-then-freedom side advanced by many governments in the old Third World, but a single pattern equally applicable to the cultural diversity and histories of the world's nearly 200 countries may not exist. At best, we can look at the experiences of individual countries as a global laboratory and hope that they can learn from one another while moving collectively toward a common goal of press freedom.

Another exception to the broad trend favoring expanding press freedom is the Arab world. Attention shifted to that part of the world after a series of attacks on the West that reversed initial optimism for the new century, but pointing to problems within the Arab world itself was hesitant and restrained. By chance, an important report appeared in 2002 and called attention to the "freedom deficit" of that important part of the world and linked it to the dismal state of other facets of development. The report was important in part because it was written mostly by Arabs and in part because it was published with the authority of the United Nations. Among various geographic and political regions of the world, the Arab countries rated lowest in composite measures of freedom and of "voice and accountability," falling even below sub-Saharan Africa. Here is what the report said about the "freedom deficit":

> There is a substantial lag between Arab countries and other regions in terms of participatory governance. The wave of democracy that transformed governance in most of Latin America and East Asia in the 1980s and Eastern Europe and much of Central Asia in the late 1980s and 1990s has barely reached the Arab States. This freedom deficit undermines human development and is one of the most painful manifestations of lagging political development. While de jure acceptance of democracy and human rights is enshrined in constitutions, legal codes and government pronouncements, de facto implementation is often neglected and, in some cases, deliberately disregarded. (*Arab Human Development Report 2002*, p. 2)

This is strong criticism of an important part of the world and an equally strong call for change. For most of the world, however, the recent record is at least hopeful, sometimes even warranting optimism.

Recent Changes

Freedom House collapses its detailed 100-point assessment of press freedom in every country and territory into three broad categories: free, partly free, and not free. Despite the gloomy headlines that chronicled a global war on terrorism after September 11, 2001, the Freedom House report for 2001 was upbeat. It noted that 40 percent of the 187 countries surveyed were classified as free, more than at any time in the preceding decade. One-third (33 percent) of the world's countries were rated as not free, the lowest proportion since 1996. By population, the numbers are less positive, but still an improvement over the years following the collapse of communism. Less than a quarter (22 percent) of the world's population lived in countries with a free press, while more than a third (38 percent) were in countries classified as not free. The report could not find a clear pattern in changes:

> Countries where press freedom markedly improved during 2001 represent diverse regions of the world. What most of them had in common, however, were recent changes in regime, in some cases effected at least in part by the work of independent journalists, that ushered in governments with a greater respect for civil liberties and the rule of law.

Cape Verde, Ghana, Peru, and Vanuatu moved from partly free to free, and Congo (Brazzaville) and Niger moved from not free to partly free. On the other side of the equation, Mongolia fell from free to partly free, and Bangladesh and Haiti fell from partly free to not free. Media in North America declined slightly in specific ratings but remained firmly in the middle of the free category. The report noted a modest reduction in media access in the United States following the terrorist attacks and increased concentration of media ownership in Canada as a basis for concern.

Given the tumultuous change in many parts of the world that has accompanied globalization and even the rise of global terrorism as a threat to the stable and democratic West, the progress in the first years of the twenty-first century is remarkable. Has the end of history arrived, with global press freedom triumphant?

Challenges Today

Modern communications technology, we hear repeatedly, has made the world smaller and brought its people closer together. Well, sometimes. President Bush's proclamation of a new world order after the collapse of communism faded quickly in the face of Huntington's "Clash of Civilizations" and the global war on terrorism. A counterpoint to the fragmenting of the familiar cold war world was a slow movement to bind the fractious nations of the world into a global legal system that included elements of press freedom. The movement was slow and bumpy for several reasons: press freedom is traditionally part of national sovereignty, not of international law; despite widespread acceptance of the Western definition of freedom at the theoretical level, big differences exist in practice, even, as we have seen, among the democratic Western nations; most aspects of international law have few enforcement mechanisms.

Global Regulation

A global freedom of the press operates at different levels. At the most general are sweeping principles such as the Universal Declaration of Human Rights that includes a statement on freedom of speech and the press. It sounds a lot like the provisions in most national constitutions, including the U.S. Bill of Rights. There is, however, no systematic mechanism for enforcing the declaration, and, as we have seen, most countries whose presses fall under the Freedom House definitions of partly free and not free have signed on to the United Nations declaration. Other broad statements, such as the one that came out of the NWICO debate, fall into the same category. They do represent some kind of global standard or ideal but are unenforceable and often have no influence on what signatory nations do at home to their own journalists.

At the opposite extreme are a series of technical agreements and a small but important group of international regulatory agencies that enforce them. Among them are the International Telecommunications Union (ITU), which exercises some control over broadcasting and telecommunications; the International Postal Union (IPU), which on rare occasions gets involved in political controversy; and the relatively new World Intellectual Property Organization (WIPO), which works primarily in areas of patent, trademark, and industrial design protection. The United Nations Educational, Scientific, and Cultural Organization (UNESCO), from which the United States, Britain, and Singapore withdrew over claims of mismanagement after the long, bitter NWICO debate, claims to act as the conscience of the world community and works in the area of media development and promotion of press freedom. Britain rejoined UNESCO in 1997, and President George W. Bush announced in 2002 that the United States would also return. Intelsat, originally formed in 1964 as an intergovernmental consortium to develop and maintain the global system of communication satellites, was privatized in 2001 and became less important to global communication—and less controversial. At one point in the NWICO debate, parking spaces for geostationary satellites over the equator appeared to be limited, and some countries on the equator claimed that their sovereign air rights extended to the orbit. They also wanted to reserve space even though they had no current need for it or ability to launch a satellite to fill it. Like most of the earlier political issues that focused on allocation of spectrum resources—frequencies for shortwave broadcasting, for example—technical innovations overcame political problems.

Looming on the horizon for future confrontations is the World Trade Organization (WTO), which will have to deal with issues that have a special impact on the information-based economy of the United States. Already major disagreements with a number of countries involve pirating of software and entertainment products known to international organizations as "audiovisual materials." The audiovisual sector is especially important to the United States for economic reasons, of course, but unregulated trade in pop culture and sometimes software raises alarm signals in democratic countries that are concerned with the ideological baggage that accompanies U.S. exports. Differing views of privacy and control of business practices between the European Union and the United States also are likely to appear on the WTO agenda as sources of conflict in the future. Complicating all of the issues in global regulation of communication is the explosion of the Internet.

The Internet

By design, the Internet is chaotic. It has no center and functions with virtually no oversight. An argument can be made that with the Internet, national sovereignty as we know it is threatened. Since control of communication, especially press freedom, is traditionally an element of national sovereignty, the growth of the Internet presents new challenges to all national governments. Most threatened are undemocratic governments that claim the right to control the media, of course, but there are challenges for democratic regimes as well.

A handful of governments go to great lengths to limit access to the Internet. It is probably impossible to exercise effective control, just as it was impossible for totalitarian governments to maintain a monopoly of information when the challenge came from foreign shortwave radio, smuggled newspapers, and homegrown underground media. Now as then, access to unauthorized information is often restricted to elites with curiosity, knowledge of foreign languages, and access to technology, but it is usually small bands of elites that foment revolutions. Authoritarian governments have reasons to be worried. And, of course, the Internet functions as part of the exploding global digital system that all nations need if they are going to participate in international trade, politics, or tourism. The alternative to dealing with the Internet is to mimic North Korea. However, several important nations try.

China and Saudi Arabia are in the news regularly for their oversight of the Internet, but other countries—Singapore and Cuba come to mind—do some of the same things. In most cases, control starts with limiting the points where the Internet can be accessed and its use monitored. Traditional telecommunication is limited enough that an Internet café is the usual venue for web surfing, and the few private modems can be monitored. Specific sites can be put on a banned list that is supervised and updated by government censors, but through a variety of techniques such as use of mirror sites, anonymous postings, and circuitous access, determined surfers usually can find what they are looking for. When access through traditional telecommunications channels is unsatisfactory, it is sometimes possible to gain access through other links. Private satellite dishes and satellite telephones fall into this category, although in most parts of the world they are prohibitively expensive and controlled to the same degree as direct access through the national telecommunication system. A tactic that dates to earlier eras of press control is to allow greater access to unofficial outside information for small numbers of elites with knowledge of languages and experience outside the national information cocoon. An unwritten code that allows discrete use of rooftop satellite dishes in some countries in the Middle East is that information—whether adult movies, Hollywood's latest hit, or news critical of the regime—will not be widely shared or used to threaten the regime. This jousting between censor and user is similar to that between the two when the weapons were shortwave radio and pamphlets, and access to an alternative view of the world was a powerful incentive not to challenge the power of the state.

Now some governments are more open. In Saudi Arabia, a request to access a banned URL at one point returned a page that explained why the page was not accessible, and the government even cooperated with a Harvard University study to test its effectiveness. For a period in 2002, the Chinese government blocked use of the Google search engine; an attempt to use it or to access a banned page resulted in a 20-minute time-out that presumably cooled enthusiasm for seeking out information the government thought was dangerous or inappropriate.

For open governments, the Internet also presents problems. Some are limited to specific countries. In Germany, for example, Hitler's autobiography *Mein Kampf* is still publicly banned, along with organizations that promote traditional Nazi ideology or its modern-day neo-Nazi reincarnation. The German government did order the German subsidiary of Amazon.com to drop *Mein Kampf,* but it is still available on other Amazon sites. Nazi propaganda could be partially controlled when it had to be produced outside Germany and smuggled into the country, but with web sites originating anywhere, control of access in Germany is effectively eliminated. All Western governments, including the libertarian United States, prohibit child pornography, but they face the same problem: When the material emanates from outside your borders, how can you enforce national laws without adopting the methods of China or Saudi Arabia? Even if some global agreement was approved—and the record of enforcement of international treaties is not encouraging—it is unlikely that Internet-based child pornography would disappear. The Internet adheres to the weakest-link principle. If it is possible in any country, that becomes the standard around the world. In most cases, we applaud because it puts the authoritarian government on the defensive and makes censorship difficult. But sometimes the weakest link becomes a global standard to the detriment of free expression as we define it.

The small but growing number of cases underscored the difference between the United States and most of the other Western democracies in dealing with the Internet. One was whether Internet service providers like CompuServe, Yahoo, and even universities that host discussion groups and massive web sites are responsible for the content of people who use them. In the United States the answer is no; in other democracies the answer is yes. At least sometimes. The second is whether traditional free expression takes precedence over privacy and dignity of individuals. In the United States the answer is clearly in favor of free expression, even in issues involving child pornography or national security. In most other countries it is usually the privacy and good name of individuals and the stability and order of the nation that take priority. The law of the weakest link says that if it is legal in any country, it can be posted on the Internet and will be available anywhere—unless, of course, the other government has the technical skill and will to control access. The opposite side of the weakest link is that material posted on the Internet may be challenged in any other country. As a result, you may find yourself defendant in a lawsuit in a country you have never visited over material you never intended to publish there. Journalists and academics are especially vulnerable because their work now depends so much on the Internet.

The Internet is likely to become even more the center of global issues surrounding freedom of the press as its reach and influence grow.

Annoyances

When assessing the state of press freedom in different countries and particularly when evaluating threats to free expression, it is important to differentiate between serious limitations and minor problems. In the United States, an annual report documents banned books, but most of the cases involve books removed from local school libraries after parents or local groups objected, and most of the books were about sex or religion. Compare that to Britain, where the national government has the arbitrary authority to ban a book that touches on national security, along with any public mention of it. American critics may complain about less than rigorous enforcement of U.S. freedom of information laws (Britain has an Official Secrets Act, not an FOI law), but publication of classified information is routine in the United States and almost never punished. Compare that to Western democracies, where prior restraint is routine and publication of restricted information is punished routinely and severely. And these are the democracies, not the majority of countries where the press is partly free or not free. And where journalists can find themselves in prison or, worse, "disappeared."

The point is that some restrictions on press freedom are serious and some are less so, if not outright trivial. Two issues may produce disagreement on whether they belong in one category or the other.

In the name of constitutionally protected "commercial speech," advertising in the United States operates with very few limitations and minimal government oversight. In Europe it is different. In 1989, two officials from J. Walter Thompson described the problem of promoting a theoretical low-fat diet candy bar, "Jupiter." A commercial designed for TV use across Europe would emphasize three points: "Your waistline will like it, and you get a free tape measure to prove it"; "It's an after-school treat that won't spoil your evening meal"; and "When your doctor says cut down, reach for Jupiter, with one-third of the calories of other chocolate bars." As Martin Mayer (1991, p. 204) points out, here are some of the obstacles the campaign would encounter:

> In Belgium, commercials may not refer to dieting. In France, premiums can't be worth more than one percent of the sale price, which rules out the tape measure, and children can't give endorsements, which means no child eating a Jupiter after school. In West Germany, any comparisons with another candy bar would be illegal; in Denmark, ads can't make nutritional claims; in Britain, candy must be presented as only an occasional snack—and no doctors in the commercial.

A similar trans-Atlantic difference is apparent in rules about publication of election polls. In the United States, it is impossible to prevent publication of last-minute predictions or projections based on Election Day exit polling, even though projections are often made in the East before polls close in the West. Though never demonstrated, the concern is that last-minute polls or election-night projections could influence turnout as well as the outcomes of local races in other time zones.

That issue applies only to a handful of countries that cross several time zones, but a number of countries in Europe restrict publication of polls for a week or two before the election. The curious argument is that democracy works better when citizens vote in isolation from their fellow citizens and in ignorance of public opinion. It is also curious because the argument for restricting publication of polls for a specific period before an election is based on the assertion that information should be withheld not because it is false but because it is accurate. In some Western legal systems, truth is not a full defense against a charge of defamation, but it would be odd to see a pollster in court challenging a charge of publishing poll results illegally with the defense that the results were patently false and, therefore, allowed ("The Freedom to Publish Opinion Polls," 1997).

Outlook

A UN document, *Human Development Report 2002: Deepening Democracy in a Fragmented World,* was a remarkable witness to the universal appeal of freedom of the press and to the link between it and a better human world. Equally remarkable was the source of the document, the UN Development Program (UNDP), which for years either had avoided discussing political and civil liberties or had dismissed the Western concept of press freedom as inappropriate to the rest of the world or, worse, as a mere fig leaf covering postimperial global political ambitions. The UNDP began calculating a numerical Human Development Index (HDI) and extended the measure back to 1975 as well as forward each year. From the beginning, UNDP officials acknowledged the importance of democracy as an element of development but avoided including it in the HDI because of lack of data and lack of agreement on a definition of democracy. Use of Freedom House measures would have provoked an outcry from those who had complained for years about bias in narrowly ethnocentric Western definitions and measures.

The about-face evident in the 2002 report represented more than a victory for those who had argued that press freedom as measured in Freedom House data was universal rather than narrowly Western. In the report, democracy was placed at the center of human development and discussed in just about every chapter. The report even included Freedom House ratings along with others that were equally "Western" in concept. Press freedom as a component of democracy was offered as part of a virtuous circle that would lead to greater development and, in turn, to more democracy. The attention to "free media," unique in development literature, deserves to be quoted at length:

> Perhaps no reform can be as significant for making democratic institutions work as reform of the media: building diverse and pluralistic media that are free and independent, that achieve mass access and diffusion, that present accurate and unbiased information. Informed debate is the lifeblood of democracies. Without it, citizens and decision-makers are disempowered, lacking the basic tools for informed participation and representation.
>
> Free media play three crucial rules in promoting democratic governance:
> - As a civic forum, giving voice to different parts of society and enabling debate from all viewpoints.
> - As a mobilizing agent, facilitating civic engagement among all sectors of society and strengthening channels of public participation.

- As a watchdog, checking abuses of power, increasing government transparency; and holding public officials accountable for their actions in the court of public opinion. (*Human Development Report 2002*, pp. 75–76)

The statement is a powerful endorsement of the value of freedom of the press, an encouraging pat on the back for countries that are still struggling to achieve it, and an admonition for the regimes that proclaim the rhetoric but reject the practice.

Bibliography

Altschull, J. Herbert. *Agents of Power: The Media and Public Policy,* 2nd Edition. New York: Longman, 1995.

Arab Human Development Report 2002: Creating Opportunities for Future Generations. New York: United Nations Development Program, 2002.

Article 19 Freedom of Expression Manual: International and Comparative Law, Standards and Procedures. London: Article 19, 1993.

Atkinson, Rick. "German Muckraker Sets Off an Uproar." *International Herald Tribune,* 9 November 1993, p. 2.

Coliver, Sandra, Editor. *Striking a Balance: Hate Speech, Freedom of Expression and Non-Discrimination.* London: Article 19, 1992.

Committee to Protect Journalists. Web site: http://www.cpj.org. Accessed April 2003.

Etzioni, Amitai. *The Spirit of Community: Rights, Responsibilities, and the Communitarian Agenda.* New York: Crown Publishers, 1993.

Evans, Harold. "The Norman Conquests: Freedom of the Press in Britain and America." In *The Media and Foreign Policy,* edited by Simon Serfaty. New York: St. Martin's Press, 1991.

Freedom House. *Freedom in the World: The Annual Survey of Political Rights and Civil Liberties, 1992–1993.* New York: Freedom House, 1993.

"The Freedom to Publish Opinion Polls." Report published by the World Association of Opinion and Marketing Professionals (ESOMAR) and the World Association for Public Opinion Research (WAPOR). Web site: http://www.wapor.org. 1997.

Hachten, William A., and James F. Scotton. *The World News Prism: Global Media in an Era of Terrorism,* 6th Edition. Ames: Iowa State University Press, 2002.

Huffman, John L., and Denis M. Trauth. "Global Communication Law." In *Global Communication,* edited by Yahya R. Kamalipour, 73–96. Belmont, Calif.: Wadsworth, 2002.

Human Development Report 2002: Deepening Democracy in a Fragmented World. New York: United Nations Development Program, 2002.

Humana, Charles, Editor. *World Human Rights Guide,* 3rd Edition. New York: Oxford University Press, 1992.

International Commission for the Study of Communication Problems. *Many Voices, One World.* Paris: UNESCO, 1980.

Kamalipour, Yahya R., Editor. *Global Communication.* Belmont Calif.: Wadsworth, 2002.

Lahav, Pnina, Editor. *Press Law in Modern Democracies: A Comparative Study.* New York: Longman, 1984.

Lenin, V. I. "How to Guarantee the Success of the Constituent Assembly." In *Lenin About the Press,* 187. Prague: International Organization of Journalists, 1972.

Mayer, Martin. *Whatever Happened to Madison Avenue? Advertising in the '90s.* Boston: Little, Brown, 1991.

Nimmo, Dan, and Michael W. Mansfield, Editors. *Government and the News Media: Comparative Dimensions.* Waco, Tex.: Baylor University Press, 1982.

Press Law and Practice: A Comparative Study of Press Freedom in European and Other Democracies. London: Article 1993.

Restricted Subjects: Freedom of Expression in the United Kingdom. New York: Human Rights Watch, 1991.

Siebert, Fred S., Theodore Peterson, and Wilbur Schramm. *Four Theories of the Press.* Urbana: University of Illinois Press, 1963.

Silverman, Debra L. "Freedom of Information: Will Blair Be Able to Break the Walls of Secrecy in Britain?" *American University International Law Review* 13 (1997): 147.

Stevenson, Robert L. *Global Communication in the 21st Century.* New York: Longman, 1994.

Sussman, Leonard R., and Karin Deutsch Karlekar, Editors. *The Annual Survey of Press Freedom 2002.* New York: Freedom House, 2002.

6

International Journalism Ethics

Dean Kruckeberg and Katerina Tsetsura

In a postmillennial, post-September 11 world, communication technology has become the primary intervening variable influencing the ethical norms of mass communication. Hardt (1979) says the study of mass communication must begin with a theory of society:

> [T]he study of mass communication can make sense only in the context of a theory of society; thus, questions of freedom and control of expression, of private and public spheres of communication, and of a democratic system of mass communication must be raised as part of an attempt to define the positions of individuals in contemporary industrialized Western societies. (p. 35)

This need for a theoretical foundation extends to the study of mass communication ethics; that is, journalism ethics must be predicated on a morally defensible theory of social ethics that is consonant with the normative moral fabric of the societies in which journalism is practiced. These societies must themselves be based on morally defensible normative theories of social ethics, because ethical journalism can only be practiced within societies that recognize ethically valid norms.

While global society is inherently multicultural, communication technology places tremendous pressures on indigenous societies at the regional, national, and local levels to become increasingly pluralistic. Those societies include societies that are not actively seeking modernity for perceived economic, political, or cultural benefits and indeed may be actively resisting such modernity.

Modernity requires pluralism, a social structure that assures multiple messages and identification of alternatives (Barney 1986). In contrast to the monism of traditional societies that are dominated by a single value system and the suppression of dissent, Barney says, a pluralistic society requires a tolerance that is based on discussion and deliberation. Communication technology has allowed for and indeed has by and large created pluralistic societies, although the majority of citizens in many pluralistic societies may not be especially tolerant of or prone to discussion and deliberation to address their intolerance.

Nevertheless, communication technology has become the most influential and powerful intervening variable that simultaneously permits and encourages a global society through the compression of time and space while paradoxically exacerbating social conflicts that are caused by the increased multiculturalism of globalization forces, both in the world at large and in its regions, nations, and localities.

Already the twenty-first century has experienced an extraordinary amount of tension and conflict between modernity and traditionalism, between pluralism and monism, and between nationalism and tribalism, whether this tribalism is in its old familial form or in its new corporate forms. Kruckeberg (1995–96) observes that cold war dichotomies of the twentieth century, such as capitalism versus socialism and democracy versus communism, have become passé in a McLuhanesque "global village" in which the values and beliefs of peoples throughout the world will ideologically confront one another. These contemporary social phenomena have profound implications for the practice of journalism and most certainly for journalism ethics. A host of questions related to communication technology must be examined and satisfactorily resolved, especially as they relate to twenty-first century journalism ethics:

- As in centuries past, when emerging Protestant religions declared that everyone could become his own priest and now could read his own Gutenberg Bible, is today's communication "revolution" more accurately a "reformation" in which each person can be his or her own journalist within a global milieu of interactive multimedia?
- Will "professional" journalism, always ill-defined, exist in the future other than as a handy descriptor for a type of research about current events? In the future, will the possibly "deprofessionalized" craft of journalism be best prepared for through education in computer-based information retrieval, perhaps with limited practice in mining information from primary personal sources? Moreover, will "professional" journalism schools and the "professional" practices and ethical values that they espouse become passé?
- For that matter, will the concepts of news—and any sense of "news values"— still have operational meaning in an era when readily available computerized information will overwhelmingly exceed its reasonable and useful consumption for global audiences having differing concepts of news and news values?
- Will the agenda-setting role of the traditional mass media worldwide be continually eroded because of the surfeit of ungraded news and information selected from myriad electronic channels, with no one to suggest to consumers what is and what is not news?
- Relatedly, will the pervasive, increasingly consolidated, and seemingly all-powerful *mass media,* having increased power in the global economy as a result of international mergers, diminish politically in their importance as news gatherers and providers and as influencers of public opinion? That is, will an erosion of concentrated power and influence result in an era of cacophonous

500-channel "narrow-casting"? Will a loss of power and influence among the mass media result from an Internet-based information superhighway whose tentacles extend to anyone and everyone worldwide who shares this technology?

- And, if such will be the case, who will buy all these people their telecomputers, and what will peasants in less-developed countries, with unfulfilled needs for food and fiber, have to say to one another electronically? One might assume that their immediate and primary concerns will transcend sustained deliberation about the relative merits of microcomputer software. Will twentieth century divisions between political and economic systems be realigned in the twenty-first century between technological haves and have-nots?

- As unseen engineers work for market-driven computer and telecommunication companies and contribute to what Carey ("Space" 1989) calls a "high communications policy" (that is, a policy aimed solely at spreading messages further in space and at reducing their cost of transmission), will a new age of "communitarianism" result from it?

- Or will there be only increasing alienation and anomie between those who avail themselves of communication technology and a global underclass of people in general who cannot or will not accept telecomputers, powerbooks, electronic note pads, digital computer-linked cameras, portable facsimile machines, cellular telephones, and satellite uplinks?

These are indeed weighty questions, ones for which precise definitions of concepts and constructs are required.

What Is Journalism?

Any cogent discussion of journalism ethics requires an operational definition of journalism. At one level, and particularly from a global perspective, we can be no more precise than to argue that journalism is what journalists do.

News reporters in the free press of the Western media, both for print and for broadcast, rightly call themselves journalists. However, many of the most commonly cited distinctions used to define journalism are insufficiently precise for any meaningful discussion about journalism ethics. For example, the plenitude of advice columnists and similar information providers fill a substantial amount of the new range of contemporary media. They are those whom Harris (1992) calls "expert" contributors. Who are they if not journalists reporting for televised tabloid news and feature programs and interviewing guests on the plethora of talk shows?

Another issue to consider is interpretation of the news. Are those reporting and ideologically interpreting "news" in the "propagandistic" media that are owned or sanctioned by authoritarian government regimes not to be considered journalists?

Finally, what about those using "controlled" media within countries having "free" press systems, such as public relations practitioners, marketing communicators, and ideologues who produce sundry journalistic-appearing messages for the media that are owned and controlled by their respective organizations? Can these special-interest mass communicators be called journalists, even though they may disavow themselves or their media of any pretense to objectivity or impartiality? Are such media to be considered part of a nation's press system?

Scholars Typecast Systems, Not Journalists

Western mass communication scholars readily designate a place in their typologies for journalists in authoritarian press systems, although it must be emphasized that these scholars, not actual journalists, typecast the respective systems.

Fred Siebert, Theodore Peterson, and Wilbur Schramm's venerable 1956 volume, *Four Theories of the Press,* included the authoritarian, libertarian, Soviet communist, and social responsibility theories.

Ralph Lowenstein (Merrill and Lowenstein 1971; Mundt 1991) modified this typology, identifying ownership types as well as proffering a somewhat different five-category typology of press philosophies that included private, multiparty, and government ownership.

Merrill (1974) proposed a relatively complex but highly functional political–press circle to distinguish the different press systems. Other scholars have developed additional typologies.

Confusion sometimes results from which media and messages are to be included as part of a nation's press system, particularly when considering special-interest messages and media in nations whose institutionalized free press systems claim objectivity and fairness in their news coverage. Here, the identification of a predominant *general* news orientation of qualified media as a uniform and consistent threshold criterion is helpful. Public affairs reportage of governments' activities is a strong definitional component of this journalism as it is practiced in the *general* news media. Journalists have to closely work with governments to access much of information and thus are exposed to public affairs materials presented by a press secretariat. Moreover, after covering political issues for many years and working with the same public affairs practitioners, journalists tend not only to develop strong professional relationships with those practitioners but also to become strong advocates for mutual collaboration of public affairs and mass media.

Special interest media are often controlled by public relations practitioners, marketing communicators, and the like, so that public relations materials that appear as news in media should *not* be considered journalism.

Such a distinction, although perhaps not entirely defensible, is ultimately correct and appropriate. Public relations practitioners and marketing communicators, as well as a range of other purposive mass communicators who use controlled media to report specialized information in a country that has a commercial press and claims objective and fair news coverage in a free press system, cannot reasonably be considered journalists in any rigorous context relating to journalism ethics.

Rather, these special-interest mass communicators have their own unique ethical concerns and professional identities that are substantively different from those of journalists. Likewise, their concerns and deliberations predominantly are those that journalists in free press systems should not consider.

As noted, however, such a distinction is not entirely defensible. Differences between purposive mass communicators and journalists often can be blurred, particularly when purposive communicators in free press systems are compared with journalists who work for propagandistic media in authoritarian press systems.

Although the jobs of purposive mass communicators require considerable application of journalistic knowledge and skills, they nevertheless are not practicing journalism per se. Their role is not the one considered here, that is, as an occupational specialization of those who gather and report on general interest news in the *general* news media or who editorially comment on such news appearing in media.

Today's practice shows that, nevertheless, the warning must be issued to distinguish between journalists and a range of nonjournalistic purposive mass communicators. The discussion is often anything but clear-cut, especially when purposive mass communicators are compared with their journalistic counterparts in authoritarian, state-owned, or state-sanctioned press systems, which have strong ideological and propagandistic components.

These blurred lines become important to stress in the modern world, and not only because of the increasing and confusing proliferation of "infotainment" and "infomercials" on television channels and the growth of substantial desktop publishing enterprises by sundry special-interest groups.

Rather, these questionable distinctions are particularly important to note because of the increasing inclusion in the global mass communication milieu of overwhelming amounts of computer-accessible news and information from a myriad range of perhaps questionable and frequently highly biased sources. The emerging use of telecomputer technology as a news medium will significantly add to the confusion, not only about what constitutes news, but also about who reasonably may be considered a bona fide and credible journalist.

The Role of the Journalist Is Not in Jeopardy

Despite significant changes brought about by increasingly sophisticated communication technology and despite oft-heard prognoses to the contrary, the role of the professional journalist will be secure in the future. In addition, despite the certainty of massive innovations in media technology, neither will the press be in any appreciable jeopardy as an institution.

The specialized occupation of media will not be substantively threatened and most likely will be further entrenched as a highly needed professional occupation in the new global communication technology.

However, this role may well be ensured because of journalists' ability to *digest*, that is, to condense and to grade overwhelming amounts of information that already may be computer-accessible to consumers in raw form. The journalist's function may decrease in its need to present substantial amounts of new information otherwise unavailable to consumers of news. Of course, news gathering from primary sources will remain, but in an increasingly technological world the exercise of news gathering may not be as dependent on personal sources as has been the case historically.

Just as the Reformation's emerging "priesthood of believers" and Gutenberg's inexpensively reproduced Bible did not threaten the need for an organized church as an institution, extensive and immediate computerized information entry and retrieval in an information society will not threaten journalism as an occupational specialization nor the press as an institution.

Such technology, however, may well threaten journalists' individual well-being as well as that of their sponsoring media organizations within their press systems. Both the role of the journalist and that of the press as an institution are destined to change in significant ways, with accompanying ethical ramifications.

It seems almost certain that an overwhelming majority of people will continue to rely on journalists as experts and on news media (perhaps in the future only in telecomputed, rather than in newsprint, form) to gather and to report the news. This majority will depend on the gatekeepers of an established press to set news agendas, to grade news, and to provide informed comment about current events.

People will rely increasingly upon journalists to make sense of the overwhelming amount of information available to them. News, as gathered and reported by such professionals, will continue to be a valued commodity, either to be sold and consumed as such, as is common in the market-driven free press, or to be presented to support ideology, as in authoritarian press systems.

Journalists Will Lose Their Monopoly on Knowledge

The most significant change to be wrought by the new global communication technology will be the inevitable loss of the monopoly on knowledge on the part of journalists and the press in all types of press systems.

Carey ("Technology" 1989) notes that the concept of the free press consolidates the position of mass media's monopoly on knowledge. He argues that, through newspapers' dependence on both advertising and news, the free press is instrumental in spreading the values of commercialism and industrialism.

Of course, authoritarian types of press systems historically have relied on this monopoly to preserve the status quo by attempting to limit the agendas both about what people knew and about what they thought.

However, O'Neill (1992) argues this is true even in a free market press. Such a press will tend to work against the idea of an informed and critical citizenry simply because it cannot afford to confront its consumers with information, beliefs, and knowledge that do not conform to their preexisting preferences.

Merrill, Bryan, and Alisky (1970) remind us that each nation's press system and philosophy are usually very closely in step with that nation's basic political and social system and ideology. Thus, they conclude, each country's press system is usually truly a branch of the government, or at least a cooperating part of the total national establishment.

However, new global communication technology at least will ensure the *potential*, and arguably will encourage the *likelihood*, of massive fragmentation of communication audiences because of audience members' ample, indeed virtually unlimited, opportunities to use alternative journalistic news and information sources. The only defense for mainstream journalists and their media organizations will be to strive for a comparatively higher-quality product as their commodity of news.

For the commercially dependent free press, competition will be intense among competing professional journalists and their media organizations for a significant and financially viable share of the consumer market for news and information. The same competition will exist within authoritarian-type press systems that previously were accustomed to a controlled monopoly of news.

Simply put, those consumers who are dissatisfied with the perceived quality of a media organization's news and information commodity will have ample opportunities to access other media news and information. Most likely, little effective recourse will be available to prohibit consumers from such choice in news and information access.

With intense competition both for subscribers of the news as well as for an advertising base in a free-market economy, the economic challenges resulting from such audience fragmentation may be financially devastating to at least some of those media organizations in free press systems. Such fragmentation is already being bemoaned by Western advertising agencies, which have increasing difficulty in reaching their markets via the mass media. Indeed, some media organizations may be driven out of business.

Press Systems Will Lose Agenda-Setting Abilities

Although such economic concerns may not be considered of paramount importance for the state-owned or state-sanctioned press of authoritarian governments, such press systems will to a great extent lose their exclusive agenda-setting abilities and their abilities to singularly dictate media content.

Charges of cultural imperialism and of propaganda in its most pejorative sense will continue to be forthcoming, only with heightened concern and accompanying hysteria. Many charges will have considerable validity. Conversely, this same global communication technology will allow those who see themselves as part of the new world information order to have ample opportunities to attempt to compete head to head with First World news media.

Loss of Monopoly Will Have an Impact on Ethics

This loss of monopoly by the press in all types of press systems will have a tremendous and paradoxical impact on any sense of journalism ethics on a global scale.

Bernard Rubin (1978) reminds us that no ethical standards are built into the mass media. Those who are associated with free press systems (with their traditional and much revered news values, including their ideal of objectivity, as well as their sense of "fairness" in presenting all sides of a story and their vehement appreciation of First Amendment rights) often lose sight of this fact.

With the potential for virtually infinite numbers of accessible channels within the worldwide mass communication media milieu, tensions will increase between commercially driven free-market journalists and their media organizations within free press systems, not only competitively among themselves, but also with the counterbalancing efforts of those who consider themselves to be part of the new world information order as well as those presuming to be part of any remaining vestige of the former Eastern bloc press.

Tensions will increase in Western-style free press systems as demarcations become blurred between journalists and such purposive mass communicators as public relations practitioners, marketing communicators, and advertisers, as well as a range of ideologues, because, paradoxically, a free press system allows the freedom to have a controlled press as a subsystem.

Demands Will Be Made for "Ethics" in Journalism

What people and their respective governments cannot meaningfully and effectively legislate and prohibit as *illegal,* they will quickly pronounce *unethical.* A renewed and reinvigorated cry will burst forth for "ethics" in journalism by those who feel they, their cultures, their values, and their beliefs are being wronged! And John C. Merrill's advocacy in *Existential Journalism* (1977) and *The Imperative of Freedom* (1974) may prove victorious in the ensuing melee. Merrill, who eschews journalism professionalism and decries journalism schools' increasing concern with standardized mechanisms, methods, forms, and techniques, argues that the struggle for autonomy, freedom, and authenticity in journalism is a personal struggle.

Relatedly, he submits that press *responsibility* is in the eye of the beholder. He makes compelling arguments against any responsibility of the press as it is described in the social responsibility theory of Siebert, Peterson, and Schramm and as it was championed in the 1947 Report of the Commission on Freedom of the Press, headed by Hutchins. Merrill (1974) observes:

> Increasingly one hears reference to the responsibility of the press and less and less about its freedom to react independently in a democratic society. Not only has the concept permeated the authoritarian countries, where it is an expected development, but also in recent years it has made notable incursions into the press philosophy of the United States and other Western libertarian countries. (p. 88)

In the emerging mass communication milieu, with its potential for virtually infinite numbers of communication channels throughout the world, professional journalists within their respective press systems as well those uncounted numbers within an emerging "priesthood of journalists" participating in a communication "reformation" will be part of a highly libertarian, or *free*, press system, which will be virtually impossible to regulate. In a future era of electronically inexpensive and pervasive media on a global scale, pluralism will be ensured, and so, undoubtedly, will a massive diffusion of power in controlling news and information.

Professional journalists and their media organizations, as well as a highly diverse priesthood of journalists in the communication reformation, will be as ethical as they want to be according to what *they* perceive to be ethics and ethical conduct.

Bibliography

Barney, Ralph D. "The Journalist and a Pluralistic Society: An Ethical Approach." In *Responsible Journalism*, edited by Deni Elliott. Beverly Hills, Calif.: Sage Publications, 1986.

Carey, James W. "Space, Time, and Communications: A Tribute to Harold Innis." In *Communication as Culture: Essays on Media and Society*, edited by James W. Carey. Boston: Unwin Hyman, 1989.

———. "Technology and Ideology: The Case of the Telegraph." In *Communication as Culture: Essays on Media and Society*, edited by James W. Carey. Boston: Unwin Hyman, 1989.

Commission on Freedom of the Press. *A Free and Responsible Press: A General Report on Mass Communication: Newspapers, Radio, Motion Pictures, Magazines and Books*. Chicago: University of Chicago Press, 1947.

Hardt, Hanno. *Social Theories of the Press: Early German and American Perspectives*. Beverly Hills, Calif.: Sage Publications, 1979.

Harris, Nigel G. E. "Codes of Conduct for Journalists." In *Ethical Issues in Journalism and the Media*, edited by Andrew Belsey and Ruth Chadwick. London: Routledge, 1992.

Kruckeberg, Dean. "The Challenge for Public Relations in the Era of Globalization." *Public Relations Quarterly* 40, no. 4 (1995–96): 36–39.

Merrill, John C. *Existential Journalism*. New York: Hastings House, 1977.

———. *The Imperative of Freedom: A Philosophy of Journalistic Autonomy*. New York: Hastings House, 1974.

Merrill, John C., Carter R. Bryan, and Marvin Alisky. *The Foreign Press: A Survey of the World's Journalism*. Baton Rouge: Louisiana State University Press, 1970.

Merrill, John C., and Ralph L. Lowenstein. *Media, Messages, and Men: New Perspectives in Communication*. New York: David McKay Co., 1971.

Mundt, Whitney R. "Global Media Philosophies." In *Global Journalism*, edited by John C. Merrill. New York: Longman, 1991.

O'Neill, John. "Journalism in the Market Place." In *Ethical Issues in Journalism and the Media*, edited by Andrew Belsey and Ruth Chadwick. London: Routledge, 1992.

Rubin, Bernard. "The Search for Media Ethics." In *Questioning Media Ethics*, edited by Bernard Rubin. New York: Praeger, 1978.

Siebert, Fred, Theodore Peterson, and Wilbur Schramm. *Four Theories of the Press*. Urbana: University of Illinois Press, 1956.

7

Global Advertising and Public Relations

Doug Newsom

More truly global markets and economic systems have greatly expanded the integrated use of advertising and public relations techniques. The greatest increase in advertising and public relations activity throughout the world is in the financial section, owing to the greater interlocking global economy. If anyone ever doubted that, the demise in 2002 of the 89-year-old accounting firm Arthur Andersen should have eliminated any questions about a global financial community. Andersen had global accounting and consulting branches in 84 countries.

A second area for emphasis is issues management and crisis communication. Satellite broadcasting and the Internet create global awareness in times of crisis and are a major factor in the way crises are handled. Instant messaging across time zones occurs and the world gets a mix of verified or verifiable information about events, along with the sheer fiction of an international version of urban myths.

Crisis or not, technology places organizations and governments all over the planet, even if they don't intend to be there. Fax and phone, satellite broadcasts, and all of the electronic tools of the computer have indeed wired the world. In a crisis, those involved post news releases on their web site first because that takes some of the international media calls off their cell and line phones. Additionally, the crisis-struck organization gets out e-mail messages to individuals in distant offices and posts information on the organization's intranet so employees have the facts about the crisis first hand.

The existence of global media systems, mass and specialized, means that it is not possible to think in terms of restricting messages, commercial or otherwise, to particular audiences. Global access to messages is occurring at a time when organizations of all kinds are trying to more narrowly focus their messages to specific people or groups. While the original focus may be short-range and sharp, the effect is likely to be broad and diffused. Messages get through the clutter of competing media or ineffective delivery systems only through individual choice.

Recipients of mass media messages are all volunteer readers, listeners, or viewers. If something gets their attention, they may opt to receive the message. The problem is that what is received may not be a message intended for them, such as commercials and ads that come with imported media when the products or services are not available in that market. Or recipients' cultural experience may not give them the same frame of reference for the message, such as the romance and fantasy that surrounds much media content, especially advertising.

The effects of either are usually negative. Frustration occurs when products are not available or are too costly, perhaps because of import duties or the differences in monetary exchange rates. There is bewilderment, sometimes, at not understanding the context of messages or themes for both editorial and advertising content. A good example of confusion over news pictures occurred during and after the September 11, 2001, terrorist events in the United States of America. The reactions of some individuals in other countries apparently "celebrating" the catastrophes further incensed U.S.A. audiences. In at least one portrayal, though, a 10-year-old photograph shown had nothing to do with the U.S.A.'s disasters. Another problem is that digital photography puts scenes on the Internet sometimes as they were and sometimes "enhanced."

The Internet is both an information source and communication tool, and as such is the principal influence for changes in advertising and public relations management. Advertising and public relations efforts rely on carefully crafted messages and graphics designed for specific audiences to persuade them to accept a product or service or to support an idea. The haphazard global media system in global marketplaces considerably complicates such communication. It can create problems for the most conscientious communication efforts. One of the reasons is that appreciation of "foreign" media content is usually limited to cultural elites, and not just in First World cultures. A good example is the lack of understanding of some audiences about web sites that appear to be connected to an organization but really are critics of the organization, its products or services or policies (Hill, Hill, and White 2000; Guntarto 2001).

Thus, global responses to crises and global campaigns are not exactly that. They are concepts that are adapted to the media and the cultures where the communication effort is being made. What public relations and advertising practitioners have relied on for years is a local contact, someone to guide the communication effort safely through the culture, which often includes religious and legal traps for the unwary. Lacking that help can cause serious cultural clashes and, in a crisis, some serious misunderstanding. In the Bridgestone-Firestone tire crisis that began in 2000, the Japanese-owned company sent a Japanese executive to testify before a U.S.A. congressional investigator committee in September. His testimony went around the world. Unfortunately, his lack of understanding of the process and the culture did more harm than good, although his intent was to apologize. Bridgestone replaced him the next month with an American, since the crisis was essentially being aired in the United States of America, although other nations were unquestionably involved. Handling crises and campaigns in a global environment requires culturally astute, careful, and committed practitioners.

The spread of large advertising and public relations companies has a significant impact on the increasing sophistication of practice, and not just in the business of these firms and agencies. It was these earlier connections with individuals and agencies or firms that often led multinational advertising and public relations companies to buy existing local firms with which they previously had an alliance or to found a branch in the city where some contact had been made. Although global economic downturns often cause the closing of offices in some areas, the result has not been the demise of the practice. Local practices have matured and even had an impact on government communication practices. Campaign strategy is a good example of what is occurring.

There are three strategic models for planning global campaigns: standardized, adaptive, and country-specific. In the standardized model, strategy is formed at the global headquarters and implemented in all operating areas. In the adaptive model, a basic strategy is adapted appropriately for each country where it will be implemented. In a country-specific model, the strategic planning is shaped to fit one country.

From research, it is clear that the standardized model is seldom used. Although that might seem strange in an increasingly global environment where nations are exposed to campaigns in other countries, exposure doesn't mean first-hand experience with the implementation. What it does mean is that campaigns have to be certain their messages are consonant when adapted for different countries. Increased sophistication of audiences from global exposure indicates that they recognize why one approach is used in certain parts of the world although they know it wouldn't be suitable for their own country. Particularly is this true when audiences connect religious or cultural differences to the approach. Instead of a truly country approach, what seems to be the trend is a regional approach, indicating that some recognition is now being given to the reality that separation by borders is more political than cultural. What is curious is that while intentional messages, such as advertising and the more overt public relations messages seem to be "filtered" by global audiences, that don't always happen with news. It is in news interpretation, rather than in intentional messages, that misperceptions seem to occur most often.

Generalizations are risky, but in many countries the communication function seems to have developed with a public relations emphasis in governmental and non-governmental organizations (NGOs) that have social missions. The communication function takes on a marketing emphasis when focused on an industrial or commercial enterprise. In some, though, perhaps because of media structures, the lines between advertising and public relations blurred into a general communication function. This began in government-directed social campaigns that used all media and a mix of advertising, publicity, and promotion. Because some advertising agencies were involved in these social campaigns, many developed a public relations segment. The size of some of these accounts has attracted transnational and multinational advertising or public relations groups that have opened offices abroad to service these accounts. These new offices then attracted other clients from the commercial part of the economy. Adding to this has been the use of such firms by political candidates in democracies around the world.

The proliferation of advertising and public relations people employed around the world had an impact on professional organizations and on education. Professional organizations for advertising and public relations are found in virtually every country and there are international organizations too. Because these organizations began some professional upgrading and continuing education, they had an impact on education in their countries. Also, as multinational and transnational companies began looking for employees, they turned to the educational systems in these countries for graduates ready to come directly into the firm knowing what to do. There is little time today for on-the-job learning.

Whereas previously most universities outside of the United States of America preferred the European model of teaching disciplines, not professions (with the exception of law and medicine), many have now added courses in advertising and public relations and even majors. In nations where a tradition of teaching journalism already existed, such as India, the addition of public relations and advertising seemed to come easily. Giving support to these fledgling academic endeavors have been resident practitioners and their companies.

Growth in education for advertising and public relations is in universities around the globe, and even governments that used to look at their development communication as a journalistic or information campaign now recognize that this activity is really public affairs, and they best understand that when they have a crisis. Government web sites are accessed by global audiences and greatly affect tourism, international business, public perceptions of their nation, and much more.

Looking at the world by regions, as this book does, makes it easy to identify major trends and find specific countries where more profound changes are occurring. These observations have been drawn from public relations and advertising practitioners living and working abroad, most of them nationals (see Chan 2002; "PR Week Global Rankings" 2002; Sutherland 2001; Warren 2002).

Asia and the Pacific

In Australia, New Zealand, Hong Kong, and Singapore, the maturity of advertising and public relations practice provides models for countries where, for a variety of reasons, the practices are less developed. India also offers one of the more sophisticated regions for advertising/public relations practice, all the more so now with two high-tech states, Kerala and Andhra Pradesh. Indonesia and Thailand are moving forward, although the development is mostly in large cities. Much of this is driven by the explosive growth in the use of the Internet, especially by the young. Pakistan is caught up in its own government turmoil, exacerbated by the conflict in neighboring Afghanistan. Indonesia, like Malaysia, is paying attention to education for its practitioners, as is China (see Ang 2001; Ayaz 2002; Rananand 2001).

China, with its growing regional markets, is the awakening giant in the area. A somewhat reluctant government has to deal with advertising and public relations issues that come in from the Internet, although China, more than Thailand, polices the pervasive medium. China is less effective in its patrol of Hong Kong, which, like the Philippines, has a long history of advertising and public relations practice. Government difficulties in both the Philippines and China have been a constraint. Nevertheless, Hong Kong remains a significant marketplace for consumer goods, so focus there is mostly on trade. Singapore, on the other hand, is striving to be a knowledge-based economy and is technology driven. Business-to-business trade has increased significantly, with a corresponding impact on both advertising and public relations. Information technology (IT) continues to expand despite the economic impact of some high-tech corporate failures. Education in advertising and public relations is growing in Singapore, which benefits from being the base for a number of multinational advertising and public relations companies as well as many local firms with a long history. Furthermore, support comes from strong professional organizations that facilitate continuing education (Goonasekera 2002; Liang 2002).

Singapore and China are places to watch for significant growth in advertising and public relations practices, as well as education. China's potential as a market has tempted traders for centuries, and no less so today. Growth there has increased with the location of major international advertising and public relations companies in Beijing, Shanghai, and Guangzhou. With World Trade Organizaiton (WTO) status for China, Beijing has a new focus with technology companies and with financial public relations. However, cultural and political land mines require a good guide. The media system too is a challenge, because it takes weeks or even months to buy advertising space and to buy the services of journalists through the China News and Culture Promotion Committee to get publicity. Public relations education, though, continues to grow. The first program opened in 1985 at Shenzhen University, just north of Hong Kong, where the real practice of public relations began in 1981. One interesting facet of public relations practice in both nations that confounds other practitioners is something called *guanxi*. The practice involves using sometimes secret personal connections in a strategy. Some Western practitioners see it as not much more than networking or calling in favors, but it is different because it is tied to Confucianism. *Guanxi* is sometimes seen as being unethical. Another difficulty is created by what is sometimes referred to as Asian values, also of Confucian origin. The values are often seen, even by Asians, as an excuse for authoritarianism (Wu 2002; Huang 2000).

These two cultural manifestations, which do have an impact on public relations and advertising as well as the news media, are not as prevalent in "the other China," Taiwan. In Taiwan, most of the books used for education in universities for teaching public relations and advertising are Western texts. The practice, too, has a strong Western influence and has had since political democracy came to the country in the 1980s. Today, several international advertising and public relations firms are based in Taiwan, and the industry is growing rapidly (Wu 2001). Although Korea gained political democracy too, the growth of advertising and public relations has been inhibited by its following the Japanese model. That, however, seems to be changing with changes in ownership of the news media and the growth of technology.

Japan has a few public relations firms but the advertising agencies have public relations capabilities to offer clients within the 15 percent media commission system and are not now charging extra for public relations services. This structure makes charging for public relations work separately more difficult. One respondent to the survey noted, "In Japan, the advertising business is independent and highly qualified; however, public relations is not necessarily a profitable business." Although public relations and Western-style advertising were introduced to Japan after World War II, the acculturation process has changed the practice considerably. Western-style approaches conflicted with the Japanese distaste for confrontation and braggadocio. Furthermore, there is respect for the creation of long-term relationships, especially with government and the media (Watson and Sallot 2001). Advertising is subtler, and publicity is disseminated through press clubs, some of which are industry related. Others are government oriented, and some are for political parties. Establishing relationships with the press clubs is the only way to get information to the news media unless reporters choose to take it from a company's web site. News is generally announced through authorities, although this has not worked very well when Japan has had major crises. Economic troubles and events such as the terrorist attack that released gas in a subway and the massive earthquake that cause much loss of life needed a prompt response. The government's slowness to act, especially with the earthquake, caused much international criticism. Negative public opinion hit a nerve in the government.

South Korea is showing a great deal of public relations activity. The demand there is for public relations and advertising technicians because the idea of public relations as a management function is slow to develop (Park 2001).

Public relations and advertising as industries are growing but still relatively small in Indonesia and Thailand and are likely to remain limited primarily to Jakarta and Bangkok, although Indonesia seems more poised for development with its significant growth of the Internet, including on-line advertising. In Malaysia growth seems even more likely, perhaps because of its proximity to Singapore. The constraints in Malaysia originate with government regulation of media content and restrictions requiring the use of Malay firms, which is more of a control issue than protectionism. Because of the high involvement with government, public affairs practices are significant. The positive aspect is that increasing attention is being paid to education in the fields. Indochina reflects little development or growth, although technology may change that (Ahmad 2001; Almatsier 2001).

An increase in technology within the Philippines may be driving a growth in advertising and public relations. If so, that would be a welcome change for a country that could lay claim to being the Pacific birthplace for public relations and a climate where advertising always has played an important role. The Philippines dates its "beginnings" for public relations practice to the 1940s, and by 1955 it had a national public relations association. Constraints on corporate speech during the period of martial law were a setback, but by 1977 the government had authorized a bachelor of science degree in public relations. Universities that could support the degree were allowed to offer it. Also in 1977, an institute was formed to serve as a liaison between education and practice. A weak economy has strapped growth, but the technology sector is offering new possibilities. In the Philippines, public relations is growing faster than there are educated practitioners and senior practitioners to fill jobs. There is a strong professional group, which has instituted a university degree in public relations. Public affairs is a major focus (Panol 2000).

Although education for public relations began in Australia about the same time as in the Philippines, that nation is clearly the front-runner in the Pacific for both advertising and public relations practice. The country has major international firms that have been there since the 1980s, and a substantial number of well-developed local companies are doing well despite several economic recessions. Additionally, the communication function appears in many companies contrary to some of the Asian neighbors, where it exists primarily in government or in advertising/public relations firms. Australia's educational institutions offer doctoral degrees in public relations. Undergraduate education has been available in public relations and advertising since 1970. The Public Relations Institute of Australia has been a significant factor in the spread of public relations education and also in setting standards for education and practice in the field. Public relations associations were first established in Australia in 1949 and 1952. Many of the same influences that have affected Australia have influenced neighboring New Zealand. And New Zealand, like Australia and the Philippines, reflects more of a Western-like practice of advertising and public relations (Singh and Smyth 2000).

Westernized advertising and public relations practices also have been the model for India, although the nation's practitioners have been struggling to develop a more appropriate model for their nation, which still has a large rural population. Globalization and India's own national directive from Vision 2020 have emphasized communications, especially the transparency aspect. Communication is becoming a strategic function as this world's largest democracy positions itself for global leadership. Aiding the nation has been its economic reforms of 1991, but a serious distraction has been the continuing trouble with Pakistan over Kashmir. India has a long history of public relations activity, according to Dr. C.V.N. Reddi who has written much about its development in the Indian Public Relations Foundation magazine for which he is responsible, *PR Voice*. Dr. Reddi maintains that until India develops its own code of ethics and revamps education and continuing education for public relations practice, it will miss an opportunity to claim a place in world leadership in the field. The country's very active Public Relation Society of India (PRSI) has conducted continuing education seminars for decades. Also, India does have transnational public relations and advertising firms, and many of its own local firms. Services remain mostly in the area of public affairs, business-to-business, corporate communications, and international communications (Sagar 2002).

India has also been caught up in difficulties with Sri Lanka, which, like Pakistan, has transnational corporations practicing public relations and using advertising. In fact, local public relations practice in Sri Lanka remains a part of ad agencies and not highly professionalized (Kundra 2002; Singh 2000). In Pakistan, the business sector is struggling under military rule imposed on this once democratic nation. Although many local public relations and advertising agencies there do have international affiliation with global firms and agencies, transnational companies with internal advertising or public relations staff have used very little public relations or advertising within the country. Government, the impact of conflict, and a media that expects compensation for publicity hamper communication in Pakistan.

In the Asian Pacific region, the real unknowns are North Korea, Vietnam, and Laos. Laos seems the most likely to develop its areas of advertising and public relations because of the strong influence from Thailand. Government constraints in the other two, detailed in other chapters of this book, suggest a less promising climate. Technology is the driving force in this entire region for e-government and commerce. Asian Pacific on-line ads are expected to exceed $1 billion by 2004. In e-government rankings, Singapore is second to Canada and ahead of the United States of America. As a whole, Asia is expected to lead the world in use of the Internet by 2012 (also see "Trends in the PR Industry Across the Asia Pacific Region," 14).

Latin America and the Caribbean

The growth of advertising and public relations in Latin America and the Caribbean has much to do with the merging of economic initiatives into a more unified market (Starlach 2001; Hirsch 2001). This is not to say that all countries involved here are equal. Some are suffering from economic and political strife and others are struggling to build a sufficient infrastructure. Nevertheless, Latin America and the Caribbean are increasingly getting global attention. The region is the fastest growing place for U.S.A. exports and is expected to be the primary export market for the United States of America soon. Venezuela, despite its political and economic stresses, has a valued resource in its oil. Also, Latin American trade may be the key to untying the Cuba knot for the United States of America.

Most of the other countries in this area have reestablished normal relations with Cuba, including all 15 nations constituting a 1975 market organization called the Caribbean Community and Common Market (CARICOM). There is a possibility for the development of a more united marketplace for all of the Americas, facilitated by the 1994 North American Free Trade Agreement (NAFTA). Another part of this market picture is the Southern Cone Common Market (Mercosur), which involves South American countries in the free-trade pact. Central America has had the Central American Common Market (CACM) since the 1960s. CARICOM is making a difference in the economy of its member nations and could be a major player in the future. In 1998, at the second Summit of the Americas, a step was taken to develop by 2005 a Free Trade Area of the Americas (FTAA). This would create the world's largest free trade area.

All of this bodes well for the further development of advertising and public relations, as does improvement in telecommunications. Telecommunications is important for the whole area. In addition to holding the key to a unified market concept for the continent, it is also necessary for economic and structural reforms that are the key to social development and business development. A significant part of the Caribbean's efforts are still tied up in government campaigns to improve social conditions, attract investments, and interest tourists, a hard sell after September 11, 2001, although some travelers have been looking for holidays closer to home, and that has helped.

In Mexico, the dramatic change in political parties has opened up both internal and external communications, which has been a boon to public affairs and to commercial communication involving advertising and public relations (Diaz 2002). Mexico has a long history of being a home for international public relations and advertising companies. Some have been there since the 1950s. Others joined them in the 1960s, and in the 1970s Mexico began to have substantial local agencies and firms. As host to the first Inter-American Conference on Public Relations in 1960, Mexico facilitated the development of the Inter-American Public Relations Federation, which provides a framework for research on the growth of public relations activities in the area. More recently, the entry of more international public relations and advertising firms, the growth of business media, more cause-related marketing, and the public affairs activities of NGOs has stimulated the advertising/public relations field.

Chile is a thriving place for advertising and public relations with its combination of democracy and a solid market economy. Another nation to watch in this area is Brazil, the first to license public relations (in 1967) and require university education for practice. Although one of the first universities to offer public relations courses in Latin America was Peru's Pontifical Catholic University, many now offer courses, and some have majors. Peru is another country where public relations practice is regulated, as it is in Panama.

Many of these countries offer an array of advertising and public relations services, as is certainly the case in the Central American country of Costa Rica and even more so in the Caribbean country of Puerto Rico. In South America, economic and political turmoil has upset the advertising and public relations business in Argentina, Bolivia, Paraguay, and Uruguay. Some of Ecuador's problems are a spillover from neighboring Colombia, but its economy and political development are on track. The communication industry's focus there has been on public affairs and business-to-business public relations, largely due to the oil industry. The oil and gas industry is also important to Bolivia but its major customer is Brazil, which has also had its own share of political and economic difficulties. The political and economic challenges in Paraguay have been increased by social problems, although the nation did host the 2001 Mercosur meeting, and it was one of the Latin American countries pledging support for the U.S.A.-declared war on terrorism. (Mexico is the other.) South America's general economic crisis had a serious impact on Uruguay and tourism was down, all bad for the communications industry. However, both Paraguay and Uruguay have professional advertising and professional associations and a sound base for development.

Mexico, Central and South America, and the Caribbean are all connected in one way or another through trade confederations and professional associations. Furthermore, many professional advertising and public relations people are members of larger, international educational and professional organizations. Interaction is likely to improve communication relationships and skills, although each practitioner has to accommodate the political and economic vagaries of the nations in which each is working.

Sub-Saharan Africa

Drought, health issues, political turmoil resulting in flights of refugees, corruption, and international scandals, especially about child labor, have created a host of internal and external problems for the countries of sub-Saharan Africa (Kraft 2003). The economic impact of these problems has disrupted tourism and trade, which, of course, affects the advertising and public relations industries. Universities have also been affected, as have communications facilities, creating yet more problems for the practice of advertising and public relations. Bright spots are Botswana, ranked as the least corrupt state in Africa and 26th in the world and where the economy seems to be improving, with resulting progress in the infrastructure. Nigeria has a strong emphasis on public relations education, with graduate programs at its universities. The Nigerian Institute of Public Relations was incorporated into the country's laws. In Nigeria, a full array of advertising and marketing services is available as well as research in the areas of market and opinion research and media analysis and evaluation. Public relations exist at the strategic level in some companies and the practice is offered as a specialty. Also, there are specialties such a financial public relations, integrated business communications, issues and crises management, lobbying and political communications, and government communications. International public relations and international media relations are included in the special services available in Nigeria.

The climate is improving for advertising and public relations in the Democratic Republic of the Congo, where Tanzania-reared President Joseph Kabila is providing some stability. In Ghana, stability has come with the now proven transfer of power in a democratic process. The nation got experience in crisis management when in 2001 hundreds of people who died in a soccer match riot made it the scene of the worst sporting disaster in Africa's history. Kenya, trying to work with Tanzania and Uganda in an East African economic community, faced several setbacks during the 2001–2002 recession.

With all of these problems, it is no wonder that much of the advertising and public relations activities that occur in most of this region are government initiatives. Some of this comes from increasing demand for more accountability on the part of government. Those that are trying for more transparency are using advertising and public relations talents, but often find the need to redirect such efforts to crisis communication. Increased literacy in the area and the presence of the Internet have made public relations a more compelling need. However, much of the education for public relations still is "on-the-job" training, although some schools, especially *technikons,* are making an effort. After three years, *technikon* students can graduate with a national diploma in public relations. Students in Laos at the Enugu State

University can get a master's degree in public relations, and other universities are offering some courses.

Much of the training and continuing education in the area still comes from the oldest and most sophisticated public relations organization, the Public Relations Institute of South Africa (PRISA), which began in 1952. PRISA established an accreditation and ethics council in 1986 and has two certificate programs, one for public relations practice and the other for public relations management. PRISA also is the national external examiner for those who study three years for a diploma in public relations through distance learning. Political problems in Zimbabwe have affected the free-market economy, and thus the advertising and public relations fields as well. Harare, the capital, has been the center of most professional work in the commercial and industrial sectors.

The private sector, on the whole, has more professionally experienced advertising and public relations people who generally are trained abroad. These counselors and managers usually are the one who are able to work across the cultures in this vast continent and cope with the increasing communication technology. Although technology has increased awareness and the ability to connect across the continent, cultural misunderstandings and power struggles provide serious barriers to professional performance.

Middle East and North Africa

Despite the turmoil in the Middle East, some advertising and public relations has continued to develop, especially in Turkey, Egypt, the United Arab Emirates, and Jordan, and to some extent in Saudi Arabia, Kuwait, and Israel. Smaller nations with some advertising and public relations activity include the Sudan, Qatar, Bahrain, and Cyprus (see Shuriedeh 2000).

The secular government in Turkey has attracted transnational advertising and public relations firms and has encouraged the growth of local communication companies. There is a full array of services in Turkey, including strategic counseling in public relations and advertising and marketing services as well as integrated business communications. As might be expected, research is important, and there is an emphasis on marketing and opinion research. Other special areas include financial, health care, the environment, arts and culture, education, entertainment, investor relations, public affairs, sports, sponsorships and fundraising, issues management, and crisis communication. These are in addition to the more traditional specialties of community relations, consumer relations, corporate communications, investor relations, media training, and public affairs.

Egypt is the founding place of the Arab Public Relations Society, which began in 1966. Founder Dr. Mahmoud El Ghary also established the Public Relations Institute. Until the 1970s, most of the public relations practice there was public affairs because most of Egypt's business was in government hands. After the commercial sector began to grow, so did communications, as well as efforts to educate students for careers in public relations. Research has grown there and also includes market and opinion research. Advertising and marketing services have flourished, and in public relations there has been a growth in consumer relations as well as corporate communications. In neighboring Sudan, the public relations emphasis is on international communication, community relations, employee communications, and issues management. Poverty, lack of literacy, and strict government control of media are negative influences on the development of advertising and public relations, although there is a professional Sudan Public Relations Association.

In the United Arab Emirates, advertising and public relations have developed within the confines of the culture, and most of the communication comes from the government. In the commercial sector, marketing efforts usually involve the press agentry and publicity aspects of public relations. The Internet and satellite television stimulated all communications activity in the area. Public relations began being taught in the universities in the 1990s. Public relations at the corporate level came earlier with transnational businesses and with the location of major advertising and public relations firms and agencies. Even with a long history of advertising and public relations practice in the area, since the 1930s, communication is still very much a one-way communication effort and not a strategic function. Neighboring Qatar's focus is mostly on public affairs and government campaigns rather than commercial efforts. In Jordan, the government's use of public affairs has increased, and so has that by business management. As democratizing and privatizing activities continue, there will more demand for skilled advertising and public relations talent.

Saudi Arabia's public relations efforts primarily entail public affairs and corporate communications, although there are sectors of international public relations, issues management, community relations, and consumer relations. Advertising is local and national. The Internet has increased focus on this area, especially the petroleum industry.

Kuwait has been involved in advertising and marketing communications for some time, as well as corporate communications. It now offers market and opinion research, financial and investor relations, and community relations.

Israel has been so caught up in conflict that its advertising and public relations efforts have been limited. Tourism, which affects both, is down, and many transnational corporations have called home expatriate employees. Peace, when it comes, should resurrect what was a large advertising and marketing industry and a comprehensive public relations complement with a wide range of specialties.

In the island nations of Bahrain and Cyprus, most advertising and public relations activities are either corporate or government.

Eastern Europe

This area, which includes East Central and Southeastern Europe, Russia, and the countries and regions of the former USSR, has an unevenness in its development of advertising and public relations, but growth is apparent almost everywhere (McLeish 2001).

Russia has launched an impressive effort at education for these fields, including offering Russian-language editions of major U.S. public relations textbooks for use in its classrooms. Advertising took off right away with the advent of the market economy. Large transnational public relations and advertising firms opened offices in Moscow, and there is a professional public relations association based in Moscow. Professionals and students, now free to travel, are joining international professional associations and studying abroad in significant numbers. Public affairs no longer dominates the field of public relations practice in Russia, which offers as wide an array of specialties as most western nations. That is not to say that the practice is Western. It has been adapted for Russia. The transparency that is being called for in most Western, Asian, and Latin American practice remains something of an issue in Russia, but is emerging as policy. Another problem is the pay for publicity practice. Some of changes occurring, however slowly, are due to the efforts of two professional public relations organizations, the Russian Public Relations Association and ICCO-Russia. The latter is offering instructors to teach public relations practice to second-year MBA students (Maslov 2001).

East Central Europe has made impressive gains both in the practice of advertising and public relations and in education. Hungary and Poland began their efforts almost immediately after being released from communist domination. While Hungary has continued to develop, Poland has experienced a slowdown, with some of the major international advertising and public relations agencies pulling out. Public relations as a discipline is not understand very well in Poland, but some of the international agency–trained people opened their own shops when the parent firms pulled out and are doing well (Laszyn 2001). In some situations they still engage in partner activities with the former "parent" firm. Hungary is a whole other story. Many multinationals and some international advertising and public relations firms have moved their offices to Budapest, now considered a regional headquarters, like Vienna, for business in this region. The news media create problems for public relations practice by wanting money for stories, and often try to politicize simple things like promotional events.

Both the Czech Republic and Slovak Republic are also moving forward, helped to some extent by affiliation with and representation of some global transnational public relations and advertising companies. The Czech Republic has benefited from the presence of multinational companies with Western-trained young managers receptive to the idea of strategic as well as tactical use of advertising and public relations. The Slovak Republic is a bit behind the Czech Republic due to the lack of as much foreign investment and a concentration of the advertising and public relations sector on promotion and publicity (Stransky 2001; Taylor 2001).

In Southeastern Europe, three nations have come to the forefront: Slovenia, Croatia, and Romania, followed in a close fourth by Bulgaria. Advertising and public relations practices in Slovenia are much like those in neighboring Austria. Croatia too has a history of experience in the fields, which was interrupted by conflict but is now on the mend and developing. Romania has been slow to recognize its potential, but some seasoned professionals founded a public relations association and are guiding the practice. The commercial sector is still limited, but public affairs offers many opportunities. Bulgaria was one of the first to celebrate its liberation by a spurt of private enterprise. High-tech and business-to-business as well as financial public relations practice are growing (Karadjov, Kim, and Karavasilev 2001; also see Benova 2001). Commerce in this region of Southeastern Europe is growing despite some disruptions caused by workers protesting privatization in very forceful ways, discouraging investments from abroad. Nevertheless, many of these nations have forged strong educational ties to the United States. For example, Sofia University is now offering a master's degree in public relations.

Among the countries and regions of the former USSR, the Baltics are the fastest developing in both the practice of advertising public relations and in education for the fields. On the educational level, Latvia has been somewhat more aggressive, but only a little. Estonia and Lithuania have been almost as busy. Estonia is a full member of the WTO and has experienced very rapid economic growth, always good for advertising and public relations. The state is also committed to IT (Past 2001). In all, the Baltics seem to be rushing to reconstitute their precommunist markets quickly and move forward. Most of the firms and agencies in the Baltics are local, perhaps because of their languages. Although most know Russian and some speak German, they prefer to use their national languages. Although the Ukraine has potential, it seems slow in developing the marketplace that encourages advertising and public relations practice. The other states are having difficulty with the infrastructure necessary for communications-related fields.

Western Europe

An assumption that all public relations practice preceded by "Western" means homogeneity is not the case. Although the United Kingdom began to practice public relations much on the U.S.A. model, that is not true now. Maturity has given a different path to the practice, so that a London public relations model is not a twin of a New York model.

It was here, in Western Europe, that the definition of public relations as "relationship management" began, the reason being that fit the organizational model (Verčič, van Ruler, Buütschi, and Flodin 2001). Another title frequently used for public relations in Western Europe is communication management, a title that also has been exported to other parts of the world. At a time when U.S.A. practitioners were still resisting research, the British delved into it, perhaps because of the diversity of their European neighbors. Also, in many of these countries an integrated communication model has always been the case. Public relations practice typically has been related to advertising and marketing because the practice was likely to be publicity and media relations, which morphed into branding. Although branding is strategic planning, it does not include what became a critical communication need. The increased impact of global media, especially the Internet and satellite television, has heightened sensitivity to issues and crises, especially in terms of global public opinion.

Much of public relations practice in Western Europe is business to business, with the EU as a major factor in that. The founding of the EU increased the need for public affairs in terms of business to government relations, although public affairs in terms of government public relations is by far the oldest and most traditional public relations model in all of these countries.

Public affairs and business-to-business practices are less costly than consumer contact operations, but there is a growth in that area as well, as many of these countries emphasize tourism. The cost of pan-European campaigns is due to adjusting the presentation to the differences in culture, language, media, and national laws. An earlier solution of locating the most effective agency or firm in each country now most often results in selecting the firm with the best connections to ensure linguistic, legal, and cultural acceptance.

Even though the EU has been the single biggest factor in the growth of public relations practice in Western Europe, standardization of public relations practice is far from the result. Education for the field also differs country by country, but continuing education is usually through professional organizations. Although few European universities have public relations majors, increasing numbers offer courses. In Scotland and Finland, doctorates in public relations are available.

Finland has one of the largest and oldest (dating from the 1970s) individual membership public relations organizations. (In Europe, members may belong as individuals to professional associations or may participate in trade associations to which the major agencies belong.) Public relations and advertising expenditures in this media-rich country are high. As might be expected, with Belgium being the focal point for the EU, public relations practice is well developed and supported by two professional organizations. Neighboring Netherlands calls public relations communication management. The practice there usually involves more editorial work, which keeps the practice at a technical, rather than managerial, level. However, many companies there do offer specialties, such as investor relations and crisis management. The Netherlands also has two professional organizations to offer continuing education and offers practical and theoretical education for the field (de Lang 2000; van Ruler 2000). As in most of the European nations, command of several languages is necessary in these three countries. Greece has a long history of public relations and, with its proliferation of media, offers ample publicity and advertising opportunities. Public relations firms in Greece offer an array of specialties, including integrated communication that combines advertising and public relations (Papathanassopoulos 2002).

Germany and France began public relations associations at about the same time, in 1958. Germany, because it is the financial center for the EU, has a wide array of public relations services and has traditionally attracted offices of the world's major public relations and advertising firms. The practice in France has always been less structured and more individualistic, as has Italy's. In the latter, the personality of the corporate owners and clients is reflected in the advertising and public relations style. Spain shares this style to some extent. The practice is really publicity and is subsumed under the marketing function. Most practitioners not educated on the job come to the field from marketing, commerce, or journalism. The educational experience is the same in Norway, although public relations courses at the university level began in the Norwegian School of Marketing in 1982. Norway offers a number of specialties, including financial, environmental, and crisis communication.

In Austria the educational ties are to management rather than marketing, which puts the field more into the "strategic" area of practice. The preparation is reflected in the practice, which centers on issues management, crisis communication, corporate communications, and such. Their system is more like that in the United States of America, as is Portugal's. A strong influence for Portugal was the fact that multinational Mobil has had public relations in house there since 1959. Portugal also has close ties to Britain as one of the founding members of the 1958 European Free Trade Association.

Of all the Western European nations, Britain's advertising and public relations practices, though not the same, are most like those of the United States of America. The greatest difference in education from that in the United States of America had been the strict separation of vocational training from university education. After 1992, however, the only way to qualify for membership in the Institute of Public Relations in the United Kingdom was to pass an examination to receive the industry-controlled and industry-regulated Diploma in Public Relations. That training is offered through distance learning produced by the Open University for the Public Relations Education Trust. Britain now has university public relations courses at the undergraduate and graduate levels. In Scotland, university-level courses began at Stirling in 1987, largely due to the late Sam Black's IPRA Gold Paper on education of public relations, which has been a model for many nations.

On the whole, it is not realistic to talk about standards of practice for advertising and public relations throughout Western Europe. What is happening is the sophistication of an integrated model focused now on what is called "branding," to give instant identity to a company, and a greater strategic role for the whole corporate communications function due to issues and crises, which can get global attention in a nanosecond.

North America: The United States and Canada

The Internet has strongly influenced the practice of advertising and public relations in North America, which, as of August 2002, had the highest concentration of Internet users in the world, at 182.67 million. The rapid growth of all new technology offers both opportunities and challenges. Perhaps the greatest challenge is just keeping up (e.g., see Vollrath 2002).

Another major influence has been the significant growth in advertising and public relations activities around the world, which has increased ties to major firms and agencies in North America. These firms and agencies, for their part, have been consolidating and restructuring as a result of changes in the global economy and the use of media, especially electronic media.

Disasters of all kinds, terrorist activities, and the failure of global giants such as WorldCom, Enron, and Arthur Andersen focused attention on investor relations, public affairs, and the style and tone of advertising. Other major issues influencing practice are public health and climate concerns, such as global warming. A benefit of this is greater emphasis on issue monitoring to anticipate crises, to take advantage of opportunities, and to place more emphasis on strategic thinking for longer-range goals and objectives.

Trends that have become staples in the practice are litigation public relations and more integrated communication approaches. The latter is interesting, because what doesn't seem to be working is the purchase by advertising agencies of public relations firms. Both industries have been hurt by the economy and have been busy consolidating offices. Apparently, few really understand the complexity of serious communication integration, which involves internal restructuring and rethinking problem solving with an array of tools from both advertising and public relations. The reality is that the lines between advertising and public relations continue to blur, not only in North America but also in other countries with which North American practitioners interact.

What does seem to be improving is the use of research before, during, and after projects, with greater emphasis on education for the field and continuing education for practitioners. Another change is increased requirement to know at least one other language. Many Canadians, especially in the eastern part of the country, know both English and French. In the United States, many, especially in the South and Southwest, know Spanish. The influx of Asians into both countries has created an awareness of the need for other language skills, and having clients abroad has emphasized the need for additional language skills. More advertising and public relations practitioners are getting experience abroad to give depth to the planning and counseling they need just to function at home (Hackley and Dong 2001).

Both Canada and the United States have benefited from their own diverse populations, which has created a particular affinity for global interaction and an awareness of cultural differences. Both also have a long history of trade with other countries and with each other. NAFTA emphasized these opportunities with its intent to create a total marketplace for the whole continent. Implementation has been challenged because of problems with illegal drugs and the need to consider security in light of terrorist activities. However, both issues actually offer the opportunity for greater interaction and enhanced relationships to fight common problems.

Technology makes a global environment unavoidable. Nevertheless, the local climate for the growth of advertising and public relations is directly tied to the type of government, the freedom of expression, literacy, the place of religion in the culture, and education.

Bibliography

Ahmad, Julia. "Malaysia's Changing Face." *IPRA Frontline* 23, no. 2 (June 2001): 22.

Almatsier, Renville. "Indonesia's Struggling Image." *IPRA Frontline* 23, no. 2 (June 2001): 23.

Ang, Peng Hwa, and Lora Lee. "Small Bang in the Singapore Media." *Media Asia* 28, no. 4 (2001): 204–207.

Ayaz, Babar. "Pakistan's Expanding Marketplace." *IPRA Frontline* 24, no. 1 (March 2002): 24–25.

Benova, Verislava. "Bulgaria's PR Landscape." *IPRA Frontline* 23, no. 3 (September 2001): 22.

Chan, Joseph Man. "Media, Democracy and Globalisation: A Comparative Perspective." *Media Development* 49, no. 1 (2002): 39–44.

de Lang, Rob. "Public Affairs Practitioners in the Netherlands: A Profile Study." *Public Relations Review* 26, no. 1 (Spring 2000): 15–29.

Díaz, Flavio. "Impressive Rate of PR Growth (Mexico)." *IPRA Frontline* 24, no. 2 (June 2002): 15.

Guntarto, B. "Internet and the New Media." *Media Asia* 28, no. 4 (2001): 195–203.

Goonasekera, Anura. "Communication Issues and Problems in the Asian Region." *ICA News* 30, no. 1 (January–February 2002): 9, 13.

Guth, David W. "The Emergence of Public Relations in the Russian Federation." *Public Relations Review* 26, no. 2 (2000): 191–207.

Hackley, Carol Ann, and Qingwen Dong. "American Public Relations Networking Encounters China's *Guanxi*." *Public Relations Quarterly* 46, no. 2 (Summer 2001): 16–19.

Hill, Laura, Newland Hill, and Candace White. "Public Relations Practitioners' Perception of the World Wide Web as a Communication Tool." *Public Relations Review* 26, no. 1 (Spring 2000): 31–52.

Hirsch, Vivien. "A Continent Playing PR Catch-Up (South America)." *IPRA Frontline* 23, no. 4 (December 2001): 17–18.

Huang, Yi-Hui. "The Personal Influence Model and *Gao Guanxi* in Taiwan Chinese Public Relations." *Public Relations Review* 26, no. 2 (Summer 2000): 219–236.

Karadjov, Christopher, Yungwook Kim, and Lyudmil Karavasilev. "Models of Public Relations in Bulgaria and Job Satisfaction Among Its Practitioners." *Public Relations Review* 26, no. 2 (Summer 2000): 209–236.

Kraft, Dina. "African Leaders Launch Alliance." *The Fort Worth Star-Telegram*, 10 July 2002, 7A.

Kundra, Siema. "A Teardrop in the Ocean (Sri Lanka)." *IPRA Frontline* 24, no. 1 (March 2002): 25.

Liang, Q. C. "Practicing Public Relations in China." *tips & tactics,* supplement of *pr reporter,* 40, no. 4 (15 April 2002): 1–2.

Laszyn, Adam. "Poland's PR Slowdown." *IPRA Frontline* 23, no. 3 (September 2001): 16–17.

Maslov, Michael. "Russian PR Grows, Somtimes at a Price." *IPRA Frontline* 23, no. 3 (September 2001): 19.

McLeish, Alistair. "East of the EU." *IPRA Frontline* 23, no. 3 (September 2001): 14–15.

Panol, Zenaida Sarabia. "Philippine Public Relations: An Industry and Practitioner Profile." *Public Relations Review* 26, no. 2 (Summer 2000): 237–254.

Papathanassopoulos, Stylianos. "The Media in Southern Europe: The Case of Greece." *ICA News* 30, no. 6 (July–August 2002): 6–7.

Park, Jongmin. "Images of 'Hong Bo (Public Relations)' and PR in Korean Newspapers." *Public Relations Review* 27, no. 4 (Winter 2001): 403–420.

Past, Aune. "A Happy Return (Estonia)." *IPRA Frontline* 23, no. 3 (September 2001): 26.

"PR Week Global Rankings." *PRWeek ,* 29 July 2002, 15–33.

Rananand, Priorgrong Ramasoota. "The Internet in Thailand: Towards a Culture of Responsibility." *Media Asia* 28, no. 4 (2001): 183–194, 203.

Sagar, Prema. "The Need to Nurture Talent and Add Value (India)." *IPRA Frontline* 24, no. 1 (March 2002): 20–21.

Shuriedeh, Mohammad Jihad. "Public Relations in Jordan as an Expanding Field." *AUSACE* [Arab-US Association for Communication Educator] *Newsletter* 6, no. 2 (October 2000): 4.

Singh, Raveena. "Public Relations in Contemporary India: Current Demands and Strategy." *Public Relations Review* 26, no. 3 (Fall 2000): 29–313.

Singh, Raveena, and Rosaleen Smyth. "Australian Public Relations: Status at the Turn of the 21st Century." *Public Relations Review* 26, no. 4 (Winter 2000): 387–401.

Stransky, Marek. "Czech Republic and Slovakia." *IPRA Frontline* 23, no. 3 (September 2001): 20.

Starlach, Jeffrey. "The Reunification of Latin America." *IPRA Frontline* 23, no. 4 (December 2001): 20–21.

Sugár, Róbert. "PR in Hungary Struggles for a Role." *IPRA Frontline* 23, no. 3 (September 2001): 21–22.

Sutherland, Aladair. "Metrics for Ethics." *IPRA Frontline* 23, no. 4 (December 2001): 34.

Taylor, Maureen. "Media Relations in Bosnia: A Role for Public Relations in Building Civil Society." *Public Relations Review* 26, no. 1 (Spring 2000): 1–14.

"Trends in the PR Industry Across the Asia Pacific Region." *IPRA Frontline* 24, no. 1 (March 2002): 14.

van Ruler, Betteke. "Communication Management in the Netherlands." *Public Relations Review* 26, no. 4 (Winter 2000): 403–423.

Verčič, Dejan, Betteke van Ruler, Gerhard Buütschi, and Bertil Flodin. "On the Definition of Public Relations: a European View." *Public Relations Review* 27, no. 4 (Winter 2001): 373–387.

Vollrath, Kathleen. "Issues and Trends in Healthcare PR (Canada)." *IPRA Frontline* 24, no.2 (June 2002): 12–13.

Warren, Annabelle. "Positioning for a Big Transformation." *IPRA Frontline* 24, no. (June 2002): 30–31.

Watson, David R., and Lynne M. Sallot. "Public Relations Practice in Japan: An Exploratory Study." *Public Relations Review* 27, no. 4 (Winter 2001): 389–402.

Wu, Ming-Yi, Maureen Taylor, and Mong-Ju Chen. "Exploring Societal and Cultural Influences on Taiwanese Public Relations. *Public Relations Review* 27, no. 43 (Fall 2001): 317–336.

Wu, Xu. "Doing PR in China: A 2001 Version—Concepts, Practices and Some Misperceptions." *Public Relations Quarterly* 47, no. 2 (Summer 2002): 10–18.

8

Continuing Media Controversies

Paul Grosswiler

Negative media content, monopoly control of communication technologies, and an imbalanced global information current have been three continuing controversial issues in international mass communication, beginning with the creation of the European telegraph system in the mid-1800s until today. In the early 2000s, these controversies are resurfacing at places like the World Summit on the Information Society (WSIS), initiated by the United Nations (UN); in countries such as Canada and France that are concerned about media imperialism, in advocacy organizations such as Voices 21; and at worldwide protests against the neoliberal globalization policies of the World Trade Organization (WTO) and the Group of 8 (G-8) nations, such as those that shook Seattle in 1999. The governments, organizations, and media have changed, but these three themes have persisted in various incarnations and developments throughout nearly two centuries of international mass communication.

At a preparatory meeting of the WSIS, Cees Hamelink (2002) noted that the summit is the third attempt since World War II to address global media issues. First, in 1948, the UN, despite crafting the Declaration of Human Rights, unsuccessfully attempted to draft global treaties on freedom of information. Second, in the 1970s and 1980s, the United Nations Educational, Scientific and Cultural Organization (UNESCO) engaged in a highly charged and politicized debate over the merits of a new global media structure, often referred to as the New World Information Order (NWIO).

NWIO led to the acclaimed but unimplemented MacBride Report (1980) and the withdrawal from UNESCO of the United States and Britain in 1985. NWIO proponents included Third World countries, socialist countries, and Western media critics. Opponents included Western nations and their media, which vigorously resisted any attempt to change the structure of the Western-dominated global media system. Scholars studying the aftermath of the NWIO debate found both biased U.S. media coverage of the debate (Giffard 1989) and distorted information presented in communication textbooks in the United States (Roach 1993).

Hamelink characterized the new WSIS challenge as encompassing issues such as equitable access, cultural diversity, the digital divide, rural communication, e-commerce, e-government, data protection, security, gender, and education issues. Initiated by the UN in late 2001, the WSIS faces the political challenge of fostering a democratic information society, the social challenge of creating an information society based on dialogue and conversation, and the regulatory challenge of adopting a universal declaration on the right to communicate, Hamelink argues in presenting his vision of communication societies that are inclusive, open, and democratic.

Global Media Controversies Today

Media Neoliberal Globalization

The state of global media content, control, and current today underscores the steep challenges faced by movements like the WSIS. The increasing neoliberal globalization of media under the control of a few Western media industries raises serious concerns about global democracy. The list of the 10 media corporations that own most media globally changes as mergers and acquisitions continue apace, the latest being the merger of AOL and Time Warner in 2001 and that of Vivendi, Seagram's, and Universal in 2000. These transnational corporations are among the handful that control most media: AOL-Time Warner, Disney, Viacom-CBS, Bertelsmann, News Corp., and Vivendi Universal.

Before globalization, media giants stayed within limited boundaries. Disney, for example, produced cartoon films and built theme parks. With globalization, Disney owns ABC, 10 television stations, 30 radio stations, Disney Channels in the United States and across the globe, ESPN, A&E, the History Channel, sports networks worldwide, and shares of television companies globally. In other media, Disney owns Touchstone Pictures, Miramax Films, Buena Vista Home Video, Hyperion Books, Hollywood Records, Internet versions of ABC and ESPN, resorts on several continents, more than 700 stores worldwide, and a Major League Baseball team.

Decades before Disney's globalization, the negative cultural impact of Donald Duck and other Disney cartoons in Latin America was critiqued by Ariel Dorfman (1983) and Dorfman and Armand Mattelart (1975). Ben Bagdikian (2000) has been alarmed by the negative impact of media monopolies on public discourse in the United States for several decades as corporate media monopolies have increased inexorably. In print media globally, newspapers and magazines such as the *International Herald Tribune, Newsweek* and *Time,* the *Economist, BusinessWeek, Fortune,* the *Wall Street Journal,* and *Reader's Digest* demonstrate U.S. and British dominance.

Two U.S. and British news agencies, Associated Press (AP) and Reuters, also dominate global news and information. Agence France-Presse rounds out the Big Three, which provide 80 percent of news globally. Associated Press Television News (APTN) and Reuters, both of which narrowed global television news sources after

AP bought Worldwide Television News from ABC/Disney in 1998 and Reuters bought Visnews, also dominate television news. Cable News Network (CNN), which reaches a billion people in 200 counties, and the British Broadcasting Corp. (BBC) are the leading international television news channels.

Media globalization is amply evident in television, which relies on U.S.-based networks as the world's primary provider. Hollywood continues to dominate movie screens as it has since World War I and the video market, as U.S. television programs like *Star Trek, Baywatch*, and *Sesame Street* spread U.S. popular culture to more than a hundred countries apiece. Advertising is dominated by U.S. agencies and offers global services to the major conglomerates, of which the media are now part.

Media Neoliberal Globalization Concerns

Daya Thussu (2000) argues that Western media domination is more pronounced today than during the NWIO debates, promoting Western lifestyles and values through private global media and a market system that cooperate with governments to present a Westernized geopolitical view of global events. Robert McChesney (2001) asserts that global media do not represent U.S. cultural imperialism. Instead, these few corporate media owners globalize corporate and commercial values in a neoliberal global media system that is stacked in favor of these giants and against small, independent, and local media. McChesney also identifies a second tier of 40 to 50 regional media giants, including Globo in Brazil and Televisa in Mexico, that support the dominance of the top Western media corporations and promote pro-business politics.

Thussu (2000) cites the proliferation of regional, licensed versions of U.S. television programs like *Wheel of Fortune*. Editing out sex and nudity in programs like *Dallas* in Muslim countries allows programs to be broadcast and remain popular. TNT, CNN, Star TV, the *Wall Street Journal*, and *Time* all offer regional services in other languages. In China, Rupert Murdoch's Star TV has become the exclusive foreign media provider, with Phoenix TV reaching 45 million Chinese, but it appeases the Chinese government by focusing on business news and omitting sensitive news topics such as Falun Gong (Yun Ding 2001). Despite localization, Thussu contends, the media still bring a Western view of the world, along with messages of a global popular culture that erode local cultural values and reinforce the assertion that there is no credible alternative media system.

James Lull (2000) is more sanguine about the impact of media globalization, arguing that local audiences exert their own cultural power in making meaning from media messages, regardless of ownership or content. Also, media scholars agree that people everywhere prefer their own media, in their own language, for their own culture. The new digital, satellite, and computer technologies that helped to create neoliberal globalization are also helping to revive cultural identity in many Third World regions. Thussu (2000) offers as examples the role of Indian media, such as Zee TV, in the revival of Hinduism, and China's adaptation for television of the classic *Journey to the West*. Beyond state borders, diasporas of culture create audiences for local media from their home countries (Lull 2000).

Internet Problems and Promises

The rise of the Internet raises the stakes of neoliberal globalization and provides potential alternatives. The Internet is a decidedly U.S. and Western medium. Estimates in the early 2000s indicate that about half a million people use the Internet, which is less than 10 percent of the world's population, providing clear evidence of a "digital divide" between rich and poor. Governments seek ways to censor the Internet, and corporate interests work to commercialize it. But the Internet has proved effective in promoting communication among organizations such as human rights groups, environmental activists, churches, labor unions, and political networks, including a worldwide network of activists coordinated by the Association for Progressive Communication (Straubhaar and Larose 2002).

In this way, technology is aiding an emerging social movement opposing the neoliberal globalization policies pursued by the WTO, the G-8, and others. Centering on issues of environment, agriculture, labor, and peace, the anti-neoliberal globalization protests that have shaken the global economic planners since the late 1990s have used the Internet to communicate and bypass the corporate global media.

The stage appears to be set for a new struggle over the global media system's control, content, and current. In the neoliberal corner, the global media corporations, supported by the United States, the WTO, and the G-8 nations, will seek to preserve the status quo of unregulated global communication that favors the existing giants. In the other corner, the EU, the ITU, and the UN, allied with a host of Western and Third World countries, as well as a wide variety of advocacy groups, desire to reverse the corporate control of global media, democratize globalization, and preserve local media. The latter is described as the humanitarian regime (Hamelink 2002) and the human rights framework of globalization (Siochru 2002). Perhaps at no other time since the rise of the old world information order has so formidable a challenge been mounted. But to assess this newest media controversy requires an understanding of the serious challenges the global media system has undergone in the last two centuries. (For a historical overview, see Merrill, 1995.)

UNESCO and the New World Information Order

Calls for a New International Order

Third World countries took issue with the international economic order in the early 1970s and then included cultural and communication issues. These objections were expressed primarily in UNESCO, but also in the UN, ITU, and Non-Aligned Movement. Third World countries had reason to be concerned with the imbalanced flow of media messages and the inability to stem the flow of television, film, news, and recordings from the West. In the face of this dominance, countries responded by setting up alternative news agencies, mostly after the NWIO debate began in the early 1970s, but the impact of these regional or southern news services remained negligible.

Western countries and media generally did not deny an imbalanced information flow or technology gap between the North and South, but they focused on technical aid through the World Bank and the ITU, while maintaining the free flow of information (Fortner 1993). Third World countries found supporters in socialist countries that wanted to control the flow of information across borders for different reasons. Western media argued that state control of information was anathema, while the socialist and Third World countries argued that Western-dominated media did not provide free flow but served only Western media and audiences. The West saw information as a commodity; the socialist and Third World countries saw information as a social good. As a commodity, information flow prevented Third World countries from attaining independence. To balance the flow, suggestions ranged from alternative news systems to reserving satellite slots for future use and licensing journalists.

First Calls for NWIO

In 1970, UNESCO heard calls for a two-way information flow for Third World countries to preserve their cultures, and for national communication policies. UNESCO initiated research on news flow, cultural autonomy, and isolationism. UNESCO experts identified problems of "cultural neocolonialism" caused by new communication technologies (Galtung and Vincent 1992). In 1973, the Non-Aligned Movement led to the establishment of a Third World news agency, the Non-Aligned News Agency. By 1976, the group had articulated the need to change the global communication system to decolonize information and create a new international information order.

In 1974, UNESCO called for a two-way flow of information and for a "free and balanced flow," and in 1976 UNESCO called for "liberating the developing countries from the state of dependence" (Mehra 1986). In 1978, UNESCO unanimously adopted, with U.S. support, the Mass Media Declaration. This document affirmed freedom of expression and information, called for access and protection of journalists, and asked the media to help give a voice to the Third World. It asked the media to report about all cultures and peoples, exposing the problems that affected them, such as hunger, poverty, and disease. It asked the media to include the opinions of those who found the media prejudiced against them, and it sought correction of the imbalance in global news flow. The declaration also asked media professionals to include its ideas in their codes of ethics. UNESCO sought to promote "a free flow and a wider and better balanced exchange of information between the different regions of the world." In 1980, a resolution was adopted to implement the declaration, and a global congress was set for 1983.

The MacBride Commission

In 1976, UNESCO set up the 16-member MacBride Commission, headed by Ireland's Sean MacBride, to look at problems relating to the free and balanced flow of information and the needs of Third World countries. In 1980, the MacBride Commission issued its report, *Many Voices, One World,* containing 82 recommendations, of which 72 were unanimous. The remaining ones were opposed, with the West against anti-commercial media suggestions, the Soviet bloc opposed to the abolition of government controls, and Third World countries seeking more balanced flow. UNESCO did not adopt the MacBride Report. Instead, in 1980 it created the International Program for Development Communication (IPDC) to help develop media systems in the Third World.

The MacBride Report called for "a free flow and a wider and better balanced dissemination of information." It also called for a "new, more just and more effective world information and communication order" (Galtung and Vincent 1992). With recommendations on media economics, administration, technological uses, training, and research, the report also dealt with journalistic standards, but rejected the idea of licensing. It called for U.S. journalists abroad to receive language and culture training, and for gatekeepers in the West to be familiar with Third World cultures.

Among its other recommendations, the MacBride Report condemned censorship as well as the use of journalists for spying, and supported the need for national communication policies. It emphasized the media's role in helping oppressed peoples gain independence and the right to expression and information. It also called for reducing media commercialism. The report encouraged UNESCO to take a crucial role in carrying out the recommendations (Frederick 1993).

Western Opposition to NWIO

By the late 1970s, Western media had united against NWIO by associating it with government control of media. The World Press Freedom Committee was formed before the 1976 meeting on the Mass Media Declaration in order to disrupt its progress (Frederick 1993). Opposition intensified after the MacBride Report was issued, with the gathering of more than 50 representatives of private media from 20 countries in Talloires, France, in 1981 (Hachten 1987). The private gathering, arranged by the World Press Freedom Committee and the law school at Tufts University, formulated a declaration that called press freedom a "basic right" and urged UNESCO to drop attempts to restrict the press in violation of the Declaration of Human Rights and other international covenants. The group opposed plans to license journalists and an international code of ethics. The group also reiterated the MacBride Report's call for the end of censorship and the journalists' right of access to all news sources.

The response to the Talloires Declaration was nearly unanimous in the United States, with the *New York Times, Newsweek,* and other major U.S. media opposed to NWIO. The Reagan administration abandoned the flexible policies of President Jimmy Carter in the late 1970s that had led to the creation of the IPDC in the UN. The ultraconservative Reagan policy attacked the UN and UNESCO (Frederick 1993). The United States announced in late 1983 that it would withdraw from UNESCO in 1985 because the Reagan administration felt UNESCO held an anti-US. bias. The U.S. withdrawal silenced the debate about NWIO (Hachten 1987).

New Efforts to Address Global Media Controversies

The confluence of several forces appears to be driving renewed efforts to address the recurrent problems of global media content, control, and current in the 2000s. The much greater visibility of neoliberal media globalization raises social awareness far beyond the level of earlier decades. The shift of concerns about cultural imperialism from the Third World to developed Western nations brings these problems closer to home. Resistance to neoliberal media globalization has found an official home in the approaching World Summit on the Information Society, representing a resurgence and convergence of efforts undertaken in the UN, UNESCO, the ITU, and other organizations.

The coalescence of socially activist professional and scholarly groups brings a new dimension, the voice of civil society, which was muted in earlier attempts. The rising movement of neoliberal globalization protests also contributes to dissatisfaction with the global media as representatives of the neoliberal world order that is opposed. The enormous potential for democratic media change posited by the Internet helps connect all these forces. This network of new technologies empowers opposition voices to join together globally and provides a vision for democratic communication.

Concerns in the West

The cultural impact of neoliberal global media on industrialized countries has caused increasing concern since the NWIO movement faded. In 1989, the European Union (EU) set domestic content quotas for its member states' media. In 1993, France succeeded in an attempt not to include audiovisual media in the GATT trade agreement. In 1998, groups of Western and Third World countries met in Ottawa and Stockholm to recommend ways to resist U.S. media influence and to exempt cultural products from WTO agreements. A number of countries throughout the world have instituted film subsidy programs to offset Hollywood imports. France and Canada have emerged as leading examples of Western efforts to combat U.S. media imperialism.

The WTO succeeded the GATT in 1995 as the arbiter of global trade, including trade in culture, knowledge, and communication. The umbrella term used for trade involving the media is "intellectual property, " which the WTO describes as the important value of new technology products (World Trade Organization ["Trading"]). The WTO's 1995 agreement on intellectual property rights attempted to create international rules to protect ideas and knowledge. Among the types of intellectual property added in 1995 were international copyright, trademarks, geographical indications, and patents. But as WACC notes, copyright and patents are Western concepts that run counter to traditional values of collective ownership of resources. Also, WTO support for liberalized trade in audiovisual products is allowing further consolidation of global media ownership (World Association for Christian Communication ["Key Issues"]).

It was at France's urging that the EU passed the 1989 television quota measure that required a majority of programming in member countries to be European (Gordon and Meunier 2001). It was again France that led opposition to a U.S. attempt to apply free trade to goods in cultural goods in GATT talks. The result was that GATT did not explicitly include cultural goods, so the EU in effect had the right to include them in its protectionist "Television Without Borders," Gordon and Meunier concluded.

Gordon and Meunier note that between 1995 and 1998, Canadian and U.S. consumer groups, along with French media artists, opposed an effort in the Organization for Economic Cooperation and Development (OECD) to make it illegal to protect cultural investments in Europe in the Multilateral Agreement on Investment (MAI). The MAI was defeated in 1998 after France left the talks, marking the first victory for the anti-neoliberal globalization movement combining cultural groups with others, such as farmers and intellectuals.

France's resistance also is evident in its negative response to Disney's efforts beginning in 1985, to build a theme park near Paris. The project was dubbed a "cultural Chernobyl" to express the widespread fear of cultural invasion (Packman and Casmir 1999). The authors concluded that Disney's cultural insensitivity and negative strategy resulted in a loss of time, money, and reputation, although Disney overcame these initial hurdles to make Disneyland Paris Europe's top vacation spot in the late 1990s.

Polls cited by Gordon and Meunier (2001) point to a majority perception in France that the United States has too much influence on French television and cinema, with 75 percent of the 15–24 age group believing U.S. influence is excessive. The authors also cite the relative strength of France's subsidized film industry, which produces 100 to 150 films a year and accounted for nearly 40 percent of ticket sales in 1999. In the rest of Europe the percentage of local ticket sales ranged from 10 percent in Spain to 24 percent in Italy. Despite this success, U.S. exports still dominate the French movie market, with 91 percent of summer 2000 tickets sold for U.S. films, compared with 7 percent for French movies.

The French also represent global reaction to the threat presented by the spread of English. The author of a 1994 French law that mandates the use of French in advertisements, public announcements, and scientific conferences called English a "new form of colonization" (Gordon and Meunier 2001). Although France also banned many English business words, such as "e-mail" and "start-up," in 2000, the French language continues to fall in the global hierarchy as English advances.

On the other side of the Atlantic, the French have a powerful ally in Canada, where more than 90 percent of movies in cinemas and on television, 75 percent of the music on radio, 80 percent of the magazines, and 60 percent of the books are imported, primarily from the United States ("Culture Wars" 1998). Canada has been formulating Canadian content (Cancon) rules since the late 1950s to protect and stimulate Canadian cultural production (Media Awareness Network 2002). The 1958 Broadcasting Act set a 45 percent quota for television Cancon, which was upped to 60 percent in 1968. The Canadian Radio-Television Commission (CRTC), created in 1968 to oversee Canadian broadcasting, extended Cancon quotas to other broadcasting stations, including a 35 percent quota for radio in 1998. As of 1999, private television stations were required to achieve an overall 60 percent Cancon quota and at least 50 percent from 6 P.M. to midnight. For the public Canadian Broadcasting Corp., the Cancon level is 60 percent overall and during evening hours.

Negotiating the Canada–U.S. Free Trade Agreement (FTA) in 1988, Canada gained an exemption for its cultural industries, which the United States also may claim. The cultural exemption was included in the North American Free Trade Agreement (NAFTA) in 1994. Despite these protections, Canada organized a meeting in Ottawa in 1998 on U.S. cultural dominance, with 19 countries, including Brazil, Mexico, and Britain, attending ("Culture Wars" 1998). With the view that free trade threatens national cultures, the Ottawa meeting examined ways to exempt cultural goods from free trade agreements. Earlier in 1998, a UN-sponsored meeting in Stockholm resolved to press for exemptions to cultural goods in the MAI trade pact.

Beyond North America and Europe, fears of U.S. cultural goods eroding national identities prompted a study for the Asia-Pacific Broadcasting Union (ABU) in 1999. A review of measures the ABU's seven member countries have taken to safeguard their broadcasting found content regulations, tax incentives, and subsidies in place to manage the tensions between cultural autonomy and neoliberal global trade policies (Asia-Pacific Broadcasting Union 1999). Australia, India, Indonesia, and South Korea have domestic television content requirements, while South Korea, India, and Indonesia have policies to protect domestic films. Domestic broadcast advertising is required by Australia, Malaysia, and Indonesia, while Australia, South Korea, and Japan provide some financial assistance to television or film industries. As individual countries and regions intensify their attempts to block cultural imperialism through these methods, though, the ABU report predicted that neoliberal trade policies dismantling domestic safeguards would be more strongly demanded in the future.

The World Summit on the Information Society

The role of international government organizations since UNESCO debated the NWIO at first suffered a setback but has reemerged in several initiatives in the UN, ITU, and UNESCO in efforts that appear to be converging in the upcoming UN World Summit on the Information Society. After 1985, UNESCO redirected its energies to avoid the politically sensitive issue of communication and reaffirmed its commitment to the freedom of the press, focusing on building infrastructures and training and education in Third World media systems. The goal of these technical programs is a balanced flow of information that attains a free flow of information (Galtung and Vincent 1992).

But UNESCO has not fully recovered from the NWIO debate that led the U.S. to withdraw from and not rejoin UNESCO (Siochru 2002). UNESCO continues to support progressive media initiatives and lower level debates, although its initiatives concerning a tax on the broadcast spectrum to fund noncommercial programming made at its 1995 World Commission on Culture and Development were not ratified and its questioning of media globalization was not discussed at a follow-up meeting in 1998 (Siochru 2002).

The NWIO debate first resurfaced outside of UNESCO in the ITU, which in 1985 issued the Maitland Report, or the *Missing Link,* which framed the ITU's task as political and declared that the gap between the developed world and the Third World should be closed. Radically departing from its previous role as a technical, engineering group, the ITU became a more activist organization, calling for a New World Telecommunications Order (Frederick 1993). But at its quadrennial 1998 meeting, in Minneapolis, the ITU gave way to increased rights for industry even as it proclaimed its importance in the global marketplace by harmonizing national policies, bridging technologies, and fostering interconnectivity (ITU 1998). Even as industrial groups criticized the ITU, its value was acknowledged in a deregulated and privatized global environment.

Siochru (2002) suggests that the WSIS may provide an opportunity to test the global governance structure's strength. Together with the ITU, the UN at the end of 2001 initiated a call for the WSIS to address the whole range of relevant issues related to the information society (Hamelink 2002). In mid-2002 in Geneva, the ITU took a lead role in the first of a series of preparatory meetings that will lead to the first phase of WSIS at the end of 2003 in Geneva and the second phase in Tunis in 2005 (ITU ["Global"] 2002).

Focusing on the digital divide, ITU Secretary-General Yoshio Utsumi told the UN in New York that action is needed to keep the information gap between haves and have-nots from growing (ITU ["World"] 2002). Noting that 61 countries represent less than 1 percent of Internet use, Ustumi urged world leaders to create a more just, prosperous, and peaceful world. Calling on the WSIS to draw up an action plan for improving access to information technologies, Utsumi cited e-commerce in a Peruvian mountain village and an on-line African shopping mall as signs of positive applications. He counted among the WSIS goals guaranteeing the right to communicate and focusing on information technologies being used to eradicate poverty.

In Geneva, Utsumi called on governments, UN agencies, civil society groups, and the business sector to work together to develop national policies, to represent diversity and development and to create material networks to benefit all people (ITU ["Global"] 2002). The agenda, themes, and outcomes of the WSIS suggested at the meeting include: freedom of expression and the media; the needs of the developing world; access to information; the role of government, the private sector, and civil society; intellectual property rights; bridges between digital media, radio, television, the press, and the Internet; wireless technologies; consumer protection and privacy; affordability; gender; empowerment and democracy; e-health; and economic, social, and cultural development.

Civil Society Advocacy Groups

The inclusion of civil society groups in the WSIS debate may signal the emergence of media advocacy groups such as the People's Communication Charter, the Platform for Communication Rights, the World Association of Community Radio

Broadcasters, the World Association for Christian Communication (WACC), the MacBride Round Table, the Association for Progressive Communication (APC), and many others (Siochru 2002).

As the information order debate shifted in the 1980s after the demise of the NWIO, some of these groups filled the breach. For example, the media and international law were debated at a 1989 meeting of the Union for Democratic Communications and the National Lawyers Guild (Galtung and Vincent 1992). Also in 1989, the WACC adopted a declaration focusing on communication as an individual right. The First MacBride Round Table was held that year, sponsored by the International Organization of Journalists, the Media Foundation of the Non-Aligned, and the Federation of Southern African Journalists. In 1989, the Round Table found that NWIO topics were more relevant, including concern over expanding technologies, and its statement called for a free and responsible press, echoing the Hutchins Commission. At its meeting in 1991 in Turkey following the Persian Gulf war, the MacBride Round Table called for new coalitions of media professionals, activists, consumer groups, women, minorities, and labor and environmental groups to regain participation in cultural policy for peace and security.

Other groups meeting with NWIO as a central topic included an Institute for Latin America and WACC seminar in 1990; an Intercontinental Journalists Conference in 1990; a Gannett Foundation Media Center conference in 1991; and an International Press Service Council on Information and Communications meeting in 1991. In the scholarly community, the International Association for Mass Communication Research has provided strong support for NWIO since the mid-1970s.

Many of these groups have become affiliated with the Platform for Cooperation on Communication and Democratization, which formed in 1995, and a second umbrella organization, Voices 21, which formed in 1999. The first group emerged from a meeting in London of the APC, Article 19, the Catholic Media Council, PANOS London, the People's Communication Charter, Communication for Social Change, the International Women's Tribune Center, the MacBride Round Table, Videazimut, WACC, Worldview International, and Zebra (International Telecommunication Union 1999). The platform agreed to work for the right to communicate to be guaranteed as a human right needed to democratize society. The platform also emphasized the democratization of communication structures, institutions, and processes.

Voices 21 called for an international alliance of groups to spur a new social movement based on an awareness of the growing importance of media and concerns about concentration of ownership and control of media, as well as a concern that government censorship is being overtaken by subtle corporate censorship and a lack of public participation. Voices 21 suggested organizing activities around themes including media access; the right to communicate; diversity of expression; security and privacy; and the cultural environment (Voices 21 1999). The fears expressed about current neoliberal global media trends by Voices 21 include a threat to media diversity from homogenized programming, a threat to public understanding of the democratic process from the influence of media moguls and the corporate influence, a threat to economic development from the growth of global advertising, and a threat to cultural and social forms from the domination of English and the corporate shaping of media content.

Seeking to target the WTO, the EU, the OECD, governments, the global media and their CEOs, and Internet providers, Voices 21 bases its concerns on voluminous academic research. Its mix of academics and advocacy organizations includes Videazimut, Deep Dish TV, the People's Communication Charter, the MacBride Round Table, the APC, the Platform for Democratic Communication, WACC, Eco-News Africa, George Gerbner and the Cultural Environment Movement, Robert McChesney, and Mark Raboy.

The Internet and the Anti-Neoliberal Globalization Movement

Whether the Internet will follow patterns of neoliberal globalization or forge a new structural alternative to help alleviate problems of global information control over content and current remains to be seen. The liberating potential of the Internet is served by the difficulty of corporate and state control of Internet content and access, as well as the ability of anyone with a computer to produce and distribute content globally and the myriad currents of information flow, which was part of the design of the original U.S. ARPANET to guarantee its invincibility against enemy attack. Meanwhile, corporate colonization of the Internet continues, including the creation of Internet versions of traditional mass media, along with efforts to marginalize nonprofessional Internet media.

Regardless of the outcome of this struggle for control, the Internet's existence draws global public attention to political, economic, social, and cultural communication issues and to the stark realities of various media divides that have existed for centuries. Pippa Norris (2001) identifies three aspects of the digital divide. The global divide refers to Internet access differences between rich and poor countries. The social divide is that between socioeconomic groups within a nation. The democratic divide separates those who use the Internet for public participation and those who do not.

Creating a global divide, the Internet is American, as two-thirds of Internet traffic comes from the United States (Flynn 2000). The Internet reached only 5 percent of the world's people in late 2000, and there were twice as many users in Sweden than in all of sub-Saharan Africa (Norris 2001). Norris noted that the global divide has caused alarm among international organizations such as the OECD, UNESCO, the World Bank, the EU, the UN, and G-8, all of which have highlighted the problem of exclusion from the knowledge economy. Governments in Finland, Germany, Canada, and Sweden have formulated programs to deal with Internet access.

Despite the digital divide, activist groups effectively use the Internet to demonstrate the democratizing potential of all media. Norris (2001) found that the Internet facilitates social movements protesting WTO policies, landmines, and sweatshop manufacturing by Nike. Opposition movements in Myanmar, Norwegian environmentalists, Australian labor union advocates, and European human rights organizations also use it. U.S. citizens mobilizing in opposition to President George W. Bush's intention to wage war against Iraq in late 2002 used the Internet as a key component of organization national demonstrations (Tucker 2002).

Anti-neoliberal globalization groups have employed the Internet as a foundation for organizing WTO and G-8 protests, and producing movement media. John Downing (2002) details how the Internet was particularly effective for debating and organizing protests at the WTO meeting in Seattle in 1999. Media projects including Paper Tiger Television, Deep Dish Television, and Radio for Peace International were involved. Movement media laid the groundwork and enabled the movement to bypass corporate media to inform global audiences about the event. The Seattle Independent Media Center, Downing found, was at the heart of the demonstrations, as were independent media centers that emerged during protests against the World Bank, the Organization of American States, and the International Monetary Fund in 2000. Aided by the Internet, demonstrations were organized in 1999 meetings of the WTO and G-8, as well. These followed on the heels of earlier protests, such as one in 1998 at the WTO ministerial conference in Geneva, staged by People's Global Action, representing farmers, workers, and consumers.

The corporate global media have also become targets of opposition as they fail to cover anti-neoliberal globalization protests adequately. The mainstream media were unable to explain the protests in Seattle because they were unaware of the extensive preparations by many groups, from U.S. steelworkers to farm, church, environmental, and peace groups (Downing 2002). The media concentrated on a propaganda campaign for a trade system favoring multinational corporations, according to alternative journalists (McQuinn, Wheeler, and Munson 2000). The *Columbia Journalism Review* also argued that the media had missed the story of Seattle (Giuffo 2001). A study of major news media coverage of protests in Seattle, Prague in 2000, and Quebec City, Sweden, and Genoa in 2001 revealed misrepresentation of underlying issues. The media presented the protests as antiglobalization when in fact the many participants wanted a different type of globalization with democratic rather than corporate control. The mainstream global media are easily recognized as heavily favoring the corporate side of the debate editorially. Global media such as CNN, Fox, ABC, the *New York Times*, the *Washington Post, Time*, and *Newsweek* were included in the study.

The G-8 summit in Genoa in 2001 witnessed the first death among protesters when an Italian was shot by police and run over, leading to more media coverage of anti-neoliberal globalization and drawing editorial comment around the world (Yurkovsky 2001). In Washington, D.C., riot police responded to protests against the annual World Bank and IMF meetings by arresting 650 people later in 2002 (Agence France-Presse 2002). G-8 leaders, however, met in distant Calgary, Canada, for their 2002 summit, as a way to escape protesters (Harrington 2002), whose relative absence was approvingly reported by media such as the *New York Times* and *Newsday* (G-8 Economic Summits 2002).

The difficulty of predicting the ultimate outcome of renewed opposition to neoliberal media globalization may be appreciated by what political economist and sociologist Immanuel Wallerstein (1998) calls "utopistics" as a way to engage in the serious assessment of historical alternatives. Wallerstein has argued that the world is experiencing the collapse of the capitalist world system of the last 500 years, and predicts that a new historical system will emerge after a 50-year "Black Period" of intense cultural and political struggle. During this period, he predicts, the privileged will attempt to preserve their interests through historically proven methods of repression and concession. Some ways of protecting privilege in the transition to a new world system in the twenty-first century will be adopting the terms of the discontented, such as ecology, multiculturalism, and feminism. The oppressed will respond, Wallerstein predicts, with a variety of means, from violence to electoral challenge, theoretical development in institutions of knowledge, and public appeals. He suggests that the only viable option is a rainbow coalition.

The current range of responses by global governmental organizations, Western and Third World governments, activist groups, and others aided by the Internet to the latest media controversies over control, content, and current of the global information flow may be viewed as emblematic of the struggle Wallerstein presents. The privileged global media owners and the powerful corporations and governments that they represent have in the past responded with concessions rather than systemic change. Challenges to the current order of neoliberal globalization appear to be more globally widespread, better organized, and better communicated to global audiences than were the cloistered responses to media controversies in the past. The outcome could be a new historical system that will bring with it a global media system, with democratic control, content, and current.

Bibliography

Agence France-Presse. "Activists Decry Police Intimidation in Anti-Globalization Protests," 2002. Available: http://commondreams.org/headlines02/1001-01.htm.

Amin, Hussein, and Zureikat, Dana. "Roundtable on Culture and Communication in the Global Information Society." *TBS Reports* 2 (1999). Available: http://www.tbsjournal.com/archives/spring99/documents/amman.html.

Asia-Pacific Broadcasting Union. *Trade Liberalisation in the Audiovisual Services Sector and Safeguarding Cultural Diversity.* Paper commissioned by the Asia-Pacific Broadcasting Union, Sydney, Australia, 1999.

Bagdikian, Ben H. *The Media Monopoly,* 6th Edition. Boston: Beacon Press, 2000.

Bullion, Stuart J. "The New World Information Order Debate: How New?" *Gazette* 30 (1982): 155–165.

Center for Democratic Communication of the National Lawyers Guild. "About CDC." Available: http://www.nlgcdc.org/about.html.

Cooper, Kent. *Barriers Down.* New York: Farrar and Rinehart, 1942.

"Culture Wars." *Economist,* 12–18 September 1998. Available: http://marshallinside.usc.edu/mweinstein/teaching/fbe552/552secure/notes/economist.hml.

Dorfman, Ariel. *The Empire's Old Clothes: What the Lone Ranger, Babar, and Other Innocent Heroes Do to Our Minds.* New York: Pantheon Books, 1983.

Dorfman, Ariel, and Armand Mattelart. *How to Read Donald Duck: Imperialist Ideology in the Disney Comic.* New York: International General, 1975.

Downing, John D.H. "The Seattle IMC and the Socialist Anarchist Tradition." In *Global Media Policy in the New Millennium,* edited by Marc Raboy. Luton, England: Luton University Press, 2002.

Flynn, Mary Kathleen. "Nations Fear English Language Dominance on Net," 2002. Available: CNN.com.http://www.cnn.com/2000/tech/computing/01/12/world.without.borders.

Fortner, Robert S. *International Communication: History, Conflict, and Control of the Global Metropolis.* Belmont, Calif.: Wadsworth, 1993.

Frederick, Howard H. *Global Communication and Internatonal Relations.* Belmont, Calif.: Wadsworth, 1993.

G-8 Economic Summits. "Corporate Party Line at G-8 Summit: June 2002," 2002. Available: http://gnp.org/g8.htm.

Galtung, Johan, and Richard C. Vincent. *Global Glasnost.* Cresskill, N.J.: Hampton Press, 1992.

Gerbner, George. "Global Media Mayhem." *Global Media Journal* 1 (Fall 2002). Available: http://lass.calumet.purdue.edu/cca./gmj/new_gerbner.htm.

Giffard, Anthony C. *UNESCO and the Media.* New York: Longman, 1989.

Giuffo, John. "Smoke Gets in Our Eyes: The Globalization Protests and the Befuddled Press." *Columbia Journalism Review,* 2001. Available: http://cjr.org/year/01/5/giuffo.asp.

Gordon, Philip H., and Sophie Meunier. "Globalization and French Culture Industry." *French Politics, Culture and Society* 19, 1 (2001): 22–41.

Hachten, William A. *The World News Prism,* 2nd Edition. Ames: Iowa State University Press, 1987.

Hamelink, Cees J. *Cultural Autonomy in Global Communication.* New York: Longman, 1983.

———. "Keynote at the Opening Session of the Civil Society Sector Meeting at the Prepcom 1 for the World Summit on the Information Society." Geneva, Switzerland, 2002. Available: http://www.geneva2003.org/home/events/documents/gen_hamelink_en.htm.

Harrington, Carol. "Protests Loud But Peaceful." *Canadian Press,* 2002. Available: http://cgi.canoe.org/cnewsg8/0627_protest3-cp.html.

Hutchins, Robert, and the Commission on the Freedom of the Press. *A Free and Responsible Press.* Chicago: University of Chicago Press, 1947.

International Telecommunication Union. "Enhancing the Capacity of the NGOs to Achieve Development Aims, Through the Use of Telecommunication." Document 2/085-E, Geneva, Switzerland, 1999.

———. "Global Strategy for the Information Society Takes Successful First Steps." Geneva, 2002. Available: http://www.itu.int/newsroom/press_releases/2002/17.html.

———. "Minneapolis Conference Gives Way to Increased Rights for Industry." Minneapolis, 1998. Available: http://www.itu.int/newsarchive/press_releases/1998/30.html.

———. "World Leaders Must Shape the Direction of the Information Society." Geneva, 2002. Available: http://itu.int/newsroom.

Kerner, Otto, et al. *Report of the National Advisory Commission on Civil Disorders.* New York: Bantam, 1968.

Khor, Martin. "WTO Party Marred by Anti-Globalization Protests." *Synthesis/Regeneration 17,* 1998. Available: http://web.greens.org/s-r/17/17-07.html.

Lull, James. *Media, Communication, Culture: A Global Approach,* 2nd Edition. New York: Columbia University Press, 2000.

MacBride, Sean, et al. *Many Voices, Ones World* (MacBride Report). New York: Unipub, 1980.

McChesney, Robert. "Global Media, Neoliberalism, and Imperialism." *Monthly Review* 52, no. 10 (2001): 1–15.

McQuinn, Jason, Tom Wheeler, and Chuck Munson. "Media Lies in Seattle." *Alternative Press Review* 5, no. 1 (2000). Available: http://www.altpr.org/apr12/apr12_edit.html.

Media Awareness Network. "Canadian Content Rules (Cancon)," 2002. Available: http://www.media-awareness.ca/eng/issues/cultural/issues/cancon.htm.

Mehra, Achal. *Free Flow of Information: A New Paradigm.* New York: Greenwood, 1986.

Merrill, John C. *Global Journalism: Survey of International Communication,* 3rd Edition. White Plains, N.Y.: Longman Publishers, 1995.

Norris, Pippa. *Divide: Civic Engagement, Information Poverty, and the Internet Worldwide.* Cambridge, England: Cambridge University Press, 2001.

Packman, Holly Muir, and Fred L. Casmir. "Learning from the Euro Disney Experience: A Case Study in International/Intercultural Communication." *Gazette* 61, no. 6 (1999): 473–489.

People's Communication Charter. "About the People's Communication Charter." Available: http://www.pccharter.net/about.html.

———— . "People's Communication Charter Text." Available: http://www.pccharter.net/charteren.html.

Roach, Colleen. "American Textbooks vs. NWICO History." In *Global Media Debate: Its Rise, Fall and Renewal,* eduted by George Gerbner et al. Norwood, N.J.: Ablex, 1993.

Schiller, Herbert I. *Culture Inc.: The Corporate Takeover of Public Expression.* New York: Oxford University Press, 1989.

Siochru, Sean O. *Social Dimensions of the Globalization of the Media and Communication Sector.* Paper presented at a meeting of the International Labor Organization, Geneva, Switzerland, 2002.

Staubhaar, Joseph D., and Robert Larose. *Media Now: Communications Media in the Information Age,* 3rd Edition. Belmont, Calif.: Wadsworth, 2002.

Thussu, Daya Kishan. *International Communication: Continuity and Change.* New York: Oxford University Press, 2000.

Tucker, Typhanny. "U.S. Groups Protest Iraq War Plans." *Yahoo News,* 2002. Available: http://www.dailynews.yahoo.com/news?tmpl=story2&cid=514&ncid=514.

Uriarte, Mercedes Lynn de. "Educators Do Little to Prepare Students for Multiculturalism." *Quill* (April 2002): 12–14.

United Nations. "Universal Declaration of Human Rights." Available: http://www.un.org/Overview/rights.htm.

Voices 21. "A Global Movement for People's Voices in Media and Communication in the 21st Century," 1999. Available: http://www.communica.org/v21/statement.htm.

Wallerstein, Immanuel. *Utopistics: Or, Historical Choices of the Twenty-First Century.* New York: New Press, 1998.

World Association for Christian Communication. "Key Issues in Global Communication." Available: http://www.wacc.org.uk/our_work/global_study_prog/resources/world.

———— . "WACC's General Objectives." Available: http://wws.wacc.org.uk/info/aims_and_principles/aims.html.

World Trade Organization. "Trading into the Future: The Introduction to the WTO." Available: http://www.wto.org/english/thewto_e/whatis_e/tif_e/agrm6_e.htm.

Yun Ding. "The Dragon and the Phoenix." *New Internationalist 333,* 2001. Available: http://www.newint.org/issue333/dragon.htm.

Yurkovsky, Andrew. "A Death in Genoa." *World Press Review,* 2001. Available: http://www.worldpress.org/europe/236.cfm.

9

Global Journalism Education

Mark Deuze

Fast-paced developments in a changing social and professional economical environment, media-technological advancements, and the ever increasing "corporate colonization," coupled with declining prestige and credibility in the eyes of the public, are the main causes of concern and unrest within journalism worldwide. The heavy or high modernistic and rather self-congratulatory view of journalism as being intrinsically objective, free, fair, and thus legitimate in itself is waning, particularly in well-established elective democracies (Hallin 1992). Global journalism education has many different faces, but programs, schools, and courses in journalism across the globe face similar developments. This chapter tackles some of these issues in terms of their impact on contemporary debates regarding challenges and changes in vested journalism education practices worldwide.

Global Journalism

In discussing global journalism education, it is first important to address what is meant here by *global*. As Morgan (2000) argues, ways of training and teaching journalists depend on culture and should be seen as a function of time and place. On other hand, Reese and Cohen (2000) make a strong case for addressing issues in journalism education on a worldwide scale, claiming that in particular, the U.S. model of journalism education, in which journalism is taught as part of the university curriculum, more so than, for example, continental-European polytechnics or Anglo-Saxon on-the-job training traditions, has been widely adopted in schools often staffed by graduates of U.S. universities. Furthermore, international comparisons of journalist populations suggest that even though reporters and editors all over the world disagree on many issues, journalists in many if not most democratic countries share a history of continuing professionalization, culminating in a growing body of knowledge, a deeply felt commitment to autonomy in their work, and a strong awareness of the fundamental role journalism plays in the formation and sustenance of society (Weaver 1998; Deuze 2002). Research and education are connected to the ongoing professionalization of journalism internationally as the training of journalists evolves in formal and structural journalism education—a process that can be observed in widely differing stages of development across the globe (Sparks and Splichal 1989; Gaunt 1992).

What makes a discussion of issues facing journalism and thus journalism education global, however, is not so much a debate about curricular matters—what to teach—or pedagogical matters—how to teach. What makes global journalism education truly global is analysis and discussion of how the various ways to organize the training and education of journalists are or can be interconnected with developments in society at large. This understanding is based on the assumption that journalism cannot exist independently of *community*; it is a profession that interacts with society in many, not entirely unproblematic ways, thereby influencing and operating under the influence of what happens in society. Although many developments are particular to the country and region involved, global media saturation caused by the proliferation of network technologies (satellites, cabling, digital telecommunications) and the corresponding globalization of media industries have brought international issues to everyone's doorstep, and thus to the doorstep of journalism and its education. Comparing the demographic and occupational characteristics of journalists in different countries, German scholars have suggested that the professional group of journalists is similar, regardless of different political and social structures (Weischenberg, Loeffelholz, and Scholl 1998, p. 236). Several authors share this view, observing an increasing homogeneity of news and news professionals worldwide (Gaunt 1992; Splichal and Sparks 1994). In a comparison of journalists in 21 countries, however, David Weaver concluded there is too much disagreement about professional norms and values to claim an emergence of "universal occupational standards" in journalism (1998, p. 468). It should be noted, however, that a plurality of answers does not necessarily reflect disagreement among journalists on what the more or less global standards of journalism are, but rather represent a variety of views on the importance of certain universal standards and what their meanings can be in country-specific circumstances and different cultural contexts. As argued in the seminal work of Philip Gaunt (1992, p. 2) on international journalism training: "Indeed, whatever the geographic area or sociopolitical context, journalism educators and media professionals have had to come to terms with the same problems."

Worldwide Challenges

The four main changes or challenges facing education programs in journalism worldwide are widely recognized to be the following:

- Increasing recognition and awareness of cultural diversity in society
- The merging of entertainment and media industries, genres, and formats

- The convergence of digital media technologies (multimedia)
- The internationalization of media, journalism, and news flow

Gaunt (1992) adds to this list a practical issue: a general lack of resources in Latin American, East European, African, and Asian countries. I would like to suggest that this is a problem of all countries, regions, and places around the world, if by resources one understands the array of preconditions available to students and educators alike, guaranteeing them professional training and education from multiple perspectives and based on different approaches, acknowledging that journalism is dependent on community and on changes and challenges in society, economy, and technology (Deuze ["Educating"] 2001; Holm 2002). In this view, *all* schools, departments, and programs of journalism training and education can suffer from a lack of resources. This is *not* necessarily a problem of countries and regions outside of the dominant First World hemisphere.

Even though there seems to be some kind of consensus on these developments and their potential impact on the way journalism functions in society, their attributed meaning in local contexts varies widely. This suggests that it can be useful to consider some broad approaches to each of these trends, as long as one acknowledges the particulars of the locality.

Multiculturalism

Recognition of cultural diversity is generally seen as a function of multiculturalism, even though the normative implications for thinking about societies consisting of a plurality of cultures vary in different parts of the world (Parekh 1997). Whether it functions as a celebration of migrant communities, and thus challenges journalism in a particular country to become more "international" in its outlook, or whether it operates as an acknowledgment of the rural in an otherwise extremely "urbanized" program of journalism education, the influence of multiculturalism is felt at all levels of editorial decision-making processes. Multiculturalism particularly challenges any notion that journalism could ever operate "outside" of society (Cottle 2000).

The discussion about the media and multiculturalism centers on three core concepts: the knowledge of journalists about different cultures, issues of representation (i.e., pluriformity, diversity), and the social responsibility of journalists (Deuze ["Journalism"] 2001). Multiculturalism can therefore be seen as one of the foremost issues in journalism where media professionals are confronted by their real or perceived responsibilities in contemporary society, whether such a society is seen as a melting pot of supposedly inherently different cultures or as a society where culture is understood as actively (re-)negotiated, shared, and diversified over time (Baumann 1999, p. 81*ff*). The multicultural society indeed shifts the focus and news values of today's media professionals: "Orientation points for journalists are now the multicultural society, in which the position of minorities will have to be redefined. Race, language, ethnic background, religion, all these factors are present and potential battlegrounds and generate a constant stream of events" (Bierhoff 1999).

Media Conglomeration

One of the most powerful forces behind the culture industry is commercialism, sometimes dubbed the "corporate colonization" of the newsroom, or the emerging worldwide media monopoly of culture and entertainment industries (Bagdikian 2000). Regardless of whether critics applaud or loathe commercialization of the media—and most authors are cynical about the effects of the development—the impact thereof on journalism and education in particular is cause for concern (McManus 1994; McChesney 1999; Reese 1999). The blurring of the lines between information and entertainment in the news media can be seen as a trend developing hand-in-hand with media conglomeration worldwide (think NewsCorp, think AOL-Time Warner). The global concern regarding these developments suggests that it used to be clear where the dividing line between journalism—the profession, its practices, its education—and "media"—the industry—could be drawn. This distinction has blurred beyond the seemingly clear-cut demarcations of the past (Dahlgren and Sparks 1992). The concerns about media conglomeration and the rise and establishment of infotainment in contemporary journalism show that further commercialization has an impact on the way to do journalism, and thus on the way to learn and teach journalism (Hallin 1996; Loennroth 1997; Megwa 2001).

Multimedia

Computerization has taken place in all sectors of society, with effects on the way the economy and society operates. Network technologies such as Internet and the proliferation of the World Wide Web have inspired training programs all over the world to develop courses, curricula, or even entire institutes devoted to the teaching and study of journalism in a "new media" environment (see, for example, Kennedy 2002). The literature on the impact of technology on the practice and education of journalism is expanding rapidly. Whether it's a program in on-line journalism in Latin America by the CIESPAL institute in Quito, Ecuador, or a program at Rhodes University's New Media Lab (home of the yearly *HighwayAfrica* conference on African media and information technologies) in Grahamstown, South Africa; whether it's the U.S.-modeled curriculum of the Indian Institute of Journalism and New Media in Bangalore, India, which opened its doors in January 2001; the tailored courses on new media, on-line journalism, and digital newsroom management offered regularly by the European Journalism Centre in Maastricht, the Netherlands; or the widely acclaimed New Media Program of the Columbia University Graduate School of Journalism in New York, digital media and, more recently, multimedia newsrooms are transforming the training and education of journalists worldwide. Professional experience and the literature clearly suggest that new media technologies challenge one of the most fundamental truths in journalism, namely, that the professional journalist is the one who determines what the public sees, hears, and reads about the world (Singer 1998). An "old media" way of training journalists perhaps ignored the flourishing alternative journalisms on the World Wide Web; an example here is the success of Independent Media Centers (Indymedia) across the globe (Deuze ["Online"] 2001). The combination of mastering news-gathering and storytelling techniques in all media formats (so-called "multi-skilling"), the integration of digital network technologies, and a rethinking of the news producer–consumer relationship tend to be seen as the biggest challenges facing journalism and media education in the twenty-first century (Pavlik, Morgan, and Henderson 2001; Teoh Kheng Yau and Al-Hawamdeh 2001; Bardoel and Deuze 2001).

Internationalization

The news media bring the world to everyone's doorstep, whether people want or need it or not. It is almost impossible to imagine any industrial center in the world today that is not connected to (and partly dependent on) the worldwide flow of news. Recurring news themes such as poverty, democratization, immigration, and access to water are relevant to the farmer in Tajikistan or Guatemala as much as to the CEO of a multinational corporation in Germany or the United States. Holm (1997, 2002) therefore argues, "Journalism education has to break out of the national mold in which it has been traditionally cast." Tomorrow's journalist should be able to connect the local to the global, and this ambitious claim has obvious consequences for the way one teaches and contextualizes journalism. On a different level, it has to be noted that internationalization in journalism education also translates into the transfer of Western notions of journalism and its core values to countries all over the world, particularly in Southeast Asia, Africa, and Latin America, because many educators there received their training in North America (Reese and Cohen 200). This may result in a training program that does not reflect the wants and needs of local communities, or in the forceful rejection of the possible neocolonial effects of this development (Gaunt [1992] mentions as an example the predominance of dependency theorists in Latin America). Either way, internationalization has an impact on the way journalism education functions and is perceived by students, scholars, and practitioners alike.

Global Models of Training and Education

Although change in journalism is nothing new, the threats and challenges to contemporary journalism have caused scholars, publics, journalists, and journalism educators to reconsider their approaches, definitions, roles, and function in community and society. Journalism education in most countries around the world has traditionally covered the ground of practical skills and standards training, on the one hand, and general contextual education and liberal arts courses on the other hand. Although the specific needs and demands of the media system differ from region to region and are largely determined by (and are a reflection of) the particular culture and foundation in law and history, the delicate balance between practical and contextual knowledge has always been the main area of attention within journalism programs worldwide (Gaunt 1992). From analyses of programs and discussion about change in several countries and regions in the world regarding journalism (studies and education), three general conclusions can be drawn. First, it seems that much of the debate about journalism training issues takes place within the different national contexts. This is in contrast to the nature of contemporary media innovations and developments, which is distinctively international. Second, almost everywhere one can observe a heightened awareness and range of initiatives regarding journalism (further) training and education, a sense of urgency or even immediacy, which seems to be a sign of the times, particularly when it comes to reconnecting journalism with developing or established democracy (another system in turmoil) and when it comes to the implementation of new media strategies. A third and most troubling conclusion must be a certain confusion and lack of focus regarding the overall pattern of media change, and little systematic response to media innovation in the professional (training) world. Changes and challenges abound, but at the same time, there seems to be a lack of vision, of strategies to master the current situation and work out a sustainable change model.

These three conclusions connect to a reevaluation of what journalism education in fact is or should be in the context of fast-paced developments and trends in society. Such concerns are articulated worldwide by national audits of journalism training and education programs and an almost feverish increase in the volume of more or less scholarly work in the field of journalism education.[1] Such audits generally assess the state of the art in a given national setting, contextualizing the report with one or more societal developments: new media technologies, further training wants and needs, globalization, convergence, and media differentiation. Some examples of such recent audits or studies (in alphabetical order) follow.

Australia

Mapping the field of communication and media studies in Australia, scholars concluded that particularly "newer" universities were innovating their curricula in order to meet the demands of a rapidly restructuring, broadening, and fracturing labor market (Putnis, Axford, Watson, and Blood 2002). The journalism education model in Australia has evolved out of competing Anglo-European and American paradigms—generally framed as a culturist/positivist divide—and now includes a sprawling variety of course titles, job descriptions, and range of discipline areas drawn on. "Communication" is increasingly becoming a central organizing category for a variety of fields, including journalism, which development is similar to the one in the United States. Scholars like Carey (1996) blame this "colonization" of journalism by larger university departments of communication for the disconnection of journalism education and society. The Australian authors call for a clearer articulation of the skills that are being taught in the various areas of communication and media studies and an assessment of likely employment destinations of students. Their core concern seems to be the following question: Yes, we are all innovating and diversifying our fields and disciplines, but what are we training our students to be(come)?

Canada

Although Canadian journalism programs have emerged and developed largely similar to U.S. programs, a distinct difference has been the fact that the curricular line between journalism and other forms of media education such as public relations or advertising is much stricter in Canada (Johansen, Weaver, and Dornan 2001). What the models in both countries share is an emphasis on three core components: news production practices, courses in media history and politics, and education in the liberal arts. The authors argue that although there is greater curricular diversity in Canadian journalism programs than, for example, in the United States, what seems to be lacking is a rich tradition in journalism research.

Germany

Meyn and Chill (2001) offer an overview of journalism schools and training programs, concluding that most roads into the open profession in Germany focus heavily on down-to-earth practical skills. Their report singles out the increasing need for media companies to make a profit and the influence of the Internet (notably regarding the emergence of on-line journalism as a more or less distinct field) as developments having a particular impact on journalistic training and awareness. Although Germany has its fair share of journalism departments in universities and a range of specific training institutes offering short-term programs, the bulk of the journalistic workforce enters the profession via a *Volontariat* (internship) of approximately two years. In an earlier book, Mast (1999) concluded that in recent years media companies have become increasingly specific regarding the qualifications they expect from newcomers to the profession. This has resulted in a wide variety of rules and ways of training within German media companies. Thus, one could argue that a particular problem for the student is choosing the best way into the profession.

Great Britain

Herbert (2000, p. 113) writes: "British journalism might have been at the root of the western and colonial tradition of newspapers and broadcasting, but its imperialism didn't extend to journalism education." The British media tend to rely on in-house training and a system of apprenticeships that could be considered to be similar to the German model, as in both countries roughly two-thirds of journalists enter the profession through on-the-job training. But in both countries growing numbers of journalists train through university journalism courses, which is a sprawling field of education particular to the second half of the twentieth century. This has resulted in many B.A.- and M.A.-level programs in new fields such as journalism ethics, or multimedia, or digital media journalism. According to Herbert, what is particular to this emerging field is a strong base in academic research, but without any direct involvement or collaboration with the industry for which these students are preparing. A significant difference between British and U.S. programs is the main criterion for hiring new faculty: one has to have at least five years' practical experience, while in the United States one's academic degree (notably the Ph.D.) can be the decisive qualification (see also Dickson 2000).

Europe

At the 2002 annual meeting of the Forum for European Journalism Students (FEJS) in Helsinki, Finland, Koskinen and Sederholm (2002) presented results of a survey of students in 51 educational institutions in 28 countries, concluding that most journalism schools have not innovated their programs to meet future demands of new media convergence, multimedia, and multiskilling of journalists. An earlier report by the European Journalism Centre showed that in Denmark, Sweden, the Netherlands, Austria, and Switzerland, widely varying approaches to journalism education and innovation persist, indicating a north–south divide (Bierhoff, Deuze, and De Vreese 2000). Scandinavian countries seemed to be farthest along in adapting to a new media environment in contemporary newsrooms, while central European countries were much more reticent in restructuring their curricula or in-house training projects. But, as shown in a 1997 survey of 56 schools belonging to the European Journalism Training Assocation, if schools do develop new teaching methods or programs, it is in areas having to do with new technologies (Loennroth 1997). European schools for journalism tend to be very practically oriented, as the implicit consensus seems to be that journalism training is a vocational rather than an academic activity (Stephenson 1997). Another characteristic of these programs is that they are almost exclusively oriented toward their domestic base, although that is slowly changing in countries like Denmark, the Netherlands, and Wales (Holm 1997).[2]

The Netherlands

In a critical overview of media trends and developments linked to the status quo at Dutch vocational training schools (similar to recent publications in, for example, South Africa and the United States), Drok (2002) concludes that communication skills, ethics, analytical skills, and an unequivocal commitment to "the democratic mission" should guide any and all journalism education efforts. Although he signals technology and cultural diversity as important trends in society, Drok maintains that these emphasize core journalistic skills, rather than calling for a reconsideration or rethinking of additional skills for the contemporary media professional. Hagen, Manders, and Van Ruler (1997), in a historical overview of the Dutch system of vocational and academic journalism programs, write that the future particularly holds promise for lecturers to engage in more "applied research" and programs to engage in more cross-disciplinary collaboration. Because all the EU member states will cross over to the Anglo-Saxon system of bachelor's and master's degrees in tertiary education, more fertile ground may become available for such initiatives.

South Africa

Two of the most striking conclusions of the 2002 South African National Editor's Forum (Sanef) National Journalism Skills Audit in South Africa are a call for more "life skills," such as communication skills, motivation, professional commitment, and ethics, in tertiary training, and an awareness that hierarchical, top-down styles of media management are counterproductive in today's newsroom (Steyn and de Beer 2002). South Africa has a split system, comparable to that of the Netherlands, of journalism education programs at so-called technikons (offering vocational training) and at universities. The Sanef report explicitly mentions the fact that most news media in South Africa lack the resources, time, or training policies to manage in-house training programs (such as is the case in Germany and Great Britain, for example) or to have more structured involvement in the technikon and university programs.

Southern Africa

In an assessment of media training needs in Southern Africa—Malawi, Mozambique, Namibia, Lesotho, Swaziland, Tanzania, Botswana, Namibia, and South Africa—Lowe Morna and Khan (2001) find that the entry level for journalism training is gradually increasing everywhere. As the media industry booms, so are media training institutions in the region. There exists a wide variety of in-service training opportunities offered by existing national training institutions and by regional organizations such as the Johannesburg-based Institute for the Advancement of Journalism (IAJ; partnering with the U.S.-based Poynter Institute) or the Maputo-based Nordic SADC (*Southern Africa Development Community*) Journalism Centre (NSJ). A specific problem for the region is the history of apartheid and colonialism, as until the 1980s and 1990s, journalism training was restricted to a small, generally white elite. In recent years training programs for journalists have emerged all over the region, resulting in a sprawling field of journalism education. The report concludes that the standard of education in all these programs, courses, and institutes is not very high, that the university courses tend to be too theoretical, and that most of these programs do not match the needs of the working environment, particularly when it comes to, for example, community media reporting. On the other hand, the media industry does not seem willing to invest in courses in content knowledge on issues particular to the region, such as covering AIDS/HIV or environmental issues. Lowe Morna and Khan also mention the effect of international (non-African) donors for these programs: donors want to influence course content, which results in programs that meet the needs of the international journalism community instead of the one in Southern Africa (see also Bos 2001).

United States

A major study has been the report *Winds of Change,* by the Freedom Forum, in which Medsger (1996) writes, "Though its roots in American universities are more than a century old, journalism education has the characteristics of an experiment—not a dynamic, evolving experiment, but a fragile, unsure, endangered experiment. Journalism is being de-emphasized, submerged or threatened with elimination on many campuses." This pessimistic discussion refers to the trend of journalism programs being incorporated into larger communication departments, a trend that is seen by many as a potential threat, particularly regarding the skills-based training of journalism students. Medsger makes a strong case for demanding extensive professional experiences from print and broadcast journalism faculty. In a critical response to this report, Reese (1999) argues that the Freedom Forum report simplifies all issues facing journalism education to a "professional–academic" antagonistic dichotomy. He further criticizes the report for being based on an unproblematized view of "the" profession, its mission, purpose, and its skills. In 2001 the Association for Education in Journalism and Mass Communication (AEJMC) released a series of reports on various challenges facing journalism education. Two crucial elements these reports focused on were the implications of multiculturalism and information technology for journalism education. The conclusion regarding the convergence of digital media technologies was that medium-independent training of journalists indeed leads to a renaissance of so-called across-media skills: critical thinking, storytelling, and ethics (Pavlik, Morgan, and Henderson 2001). The report on inclusivity and multiculturalism found that "few departments of journalism in the US are developing multicultural courses or are acquiring materials on multicultural issues for use in classes" (Bealor Hines 2001, p. 32). Of 107 accredited journalism education programs in the United States, 38 contain indirect references to multiculturalism and six offer direct references to courses explicitly on multicultural reporting, a situation not that much different from the one in Western Europe and Australia (Deuze ["Journalism"] 2001).

In a special issue of the authoritative U.S.-based journal *Journalism and Mass Communication Educator* (issue no. 3 of 2001), nine professors and professionals discuss journalism education "at the crossroads," although the journal does not make explicit what the crossroads stand for. Recurring themes in this debate are the importance of understanding diversity and social complexity; journalism ethics; globalization and the global village; interdisciplinary or cross-departmental teaching; establishing internal quality assessment tools; and, as Lana Rakow writes, the need to "look for the enduring principles of service to the public's right and need to speak and be heard, to hear and be informed, to discuss and decide."

Worldwide

To conclude this overview of current debates in various countries and regions around the world, mention should be made of a special issue of the scholarly journal, *Journalism Studies* (issue no. 2 of 2001), where educators from South Africa, India,

Slovenia, and the United States write about the issues they face in their countries. Interestingly, all authors call for more research to be done in the field of journalism, research that would be applicable to better journalism education. Furthermore, these educators critically address the notion of public service in journalism, as they invariably call into question the widening gap between the teaching and practice of journalism and its publics, the communities it intends or pretends to serve. This disconnect from segments of the public is a concern voiced by professional educators across the globe and most certainly relates to increased awareness of social complexity and the (re-)introduction of "life skills" into the journalism education curriculum.

Discussion

Contemporary changes on the level of society, economy, and technology are well documented and apparent in most, if not all, elective democracies. Individualization, commercialization, fragmentation, and disintermediation are some of the key concepts used in this context to signal challenges to the way one defines journalism. What matters is not who a journalist is but who acts "'journalistically" in the context of a local, national, or international news culture (Kovach and Rosenstiel 2001; Deuze 2002). The act or attitude of journalism is generally defined ideologically, using terms such as objectivity, ethics, public service, immediacy, and autonomy. But what do these terms mean for a journalist covering underprivileged communities? Or a journalist facing political or commercial pressures? When your colleagues only see the color of your skin instead of your individual talents and competencies? How, in other words, can a journalist learn to cope with the myriad influences on daily work and still make a personal contribution to solving the issues of contemporary society and thus democracy? As Megwa (2001, p. 283) writes, "…journalism education has too important a part to play in deepening and broadening the country's democratic processes for it not to be multisectoral, multicultural, and multiperspectival." Particularly internationalization and the increasing (awareness of) cultural complexity demand of journalists a critical-reflective awareness and sensitivity toward issues of representation and diversity, while maintaining professional and ethical standards of (multimedia) news gathering and storytelling.

As journalism and democracy have developed and professionalised, journalism education must now act correspondingly. Professionalization brings organization, increased public self-criticism, constant evaluation, and standards for assessing quality. We must be aware of our own vocabulary and discourse as scholars and educators, which both enables and constrains us when we are considering what can or must change in our ways of doing things. Not only must the journalists of today work in a constantly changing setting and context, the educators must also evolve to cope with a new and changing news culture as well. This is not a skills versus theory debate but a cultural and ideological debate. Journalism education has national particularities, but as journalism and its practice of training and learning becomes professionalized, some more or less global issues arise that need international attention and exchange. To engage the changes and developments interrogated by national and international audits, one needs global awareness of best practices, identification of common problems, and an overview of practical implications from across the field. The biggest challenge worldwide seems to be to find ways to educate and train tomorrow's media professionals based on the need to regain, reconnect with, and join hands with a fragmented, disengaged, and increasingly critical public in the context of contemporary democracy.

Notes

1. See in particular English-language scholarly journals like the U.S.-based *Journalism & Mass Communication Educator,* the British *Journalism Studies,* the South Africa-based *Ecquid Novi,* and the Australia-based *Asia Pacific Media Educator.* Some prolific contemporary authors in the field include Frank Morgan (Australia), Jan Bierhoff (the Netherlands), John Herbert (United Kingdom), Arnold de Beer (South Africa), Tom Dickson, Jeremy Cohen, and Stephen Reese (United States), and Claudia Mast (Germany).

2. Expect an update of the situation in Europe and North America in late 2002 with the publication of Froehlich and R., Holtz-Bacha, *Journalism Education in Europe and North America.* This book was not available at the time of writing.

Bibliography

Adam, G. S. (2001). "The Education of Journalists." *Journalism* 2, no. 3 (2001): 315–339.

Bagdikian, B. H. *The Media Monopoly,* 6th Edition. Boston: Beacon Press, 2000.

Bardoel, J., and M. Deuze. " 'Network Journalism': Converging Competencies of Old and New Media Professionals." *Australian Journalism Review* 23, no. 2 (2001): 91–103.

Baumann, G. *The Multicultural Riddle: Rethinking National, Ethnic, and Religious Identities.* London: Routledge, 1999.

Bealor Hines, B. *Into the 21st Century: The Challenges of Journalism and Mass Communication Education* [on-line]. Report of the AEJMC Subcommittee on Inclusivity in the New Millennium. Available: http://www.aejmc.org/pubs/2001.html. Accessed 12 August 2002.

Bierhoff, J. *Journalism Training in Europe: Trends and Perspectives.* Paper presented at a conference, Media Minority's Message, Universitat Autonoma de Barcelona, 11–13 June 1999.

Bierhoff, J., M. Deuze, and C. De Vreese. *Media Innovation, Professional Debate and Media Training: A European Analysis* [on-line]. European Journalism Center Report. Available: http://www.ejc.nl/hp/mi/contents.html. Accessed 5 June 2002.

Bos, B. "Daggeld, Donoren en Eendagsvliegen: Journalistieke Training in Zuidelijk Afrika" [on-line]. *Media News Media Southern Africa* 3. Available: http://www.niza.nl/nl/media/. Accessed 21 August 2001.

De Beer, A. S. "The 'Professional Teaching of Journalism as a Science' Approach: An Introduction." *Ecquid Novi* 16, no. 1 (1995): 3–40.

Carey, J. *Where Journalism Education Went Wrong.* Presented at the 1996 Seigenthaler Conference at Middle Tennessee State University, Murfreesboro. Available: http://www.mtsu.edu/~masscomm/seig96/carey/carey.htm. Accessed 30 August 2002.

Cottle, S., Editor. *Ethnic Minorities and the Media: Changing Cultural Boundaries.* Ballmoor, U.K.: Open University Press, 2000.

Dahlgren, P., and C. Sparks, Editors. *Journalism and Popular Culture.* Thousand Oaks, Calif.: Sage, 1992.

Deuze, M. "Educating 'New' Journalists: Challenges to the Curriculum." *Journalism and Mass Communication Educator* 56, no. 1 (2001): 4–17.

———. "Journalism Education and Multiculturalism: Enhancing the Curriculum." *Asia Pacific Media Educator* 10 (2001): 127–147.

———. "National News Cultures: Towards a Profile of Journalists Using Cross-National Survey Findings." *Journalism and Mass Communication Quarterly* 79, no. 1 (2002): 134–149.

———. "Online Journalism: Modelling the First Generation of Newsmedia on the World Wide Web" [on-line]. *First Monday* 6, no. 10 (2001). Available: http://www.firstmonday.dk/issues/issue6_10/deuze/index.html.

Dickson, T. *Mass Media Education in Transition: Preparing for the 21st Century.* Mahwah, N.J.: Lawrence Erlbaum, 2000.

Drok, N. *Drift en Koers: Trends op de Journalistieke Arbeidsmarkt.* Utrecht, the Netherlands: TUZE, 2002.

Froehlich, R., and C. Holtz-Bacha, Editors. *Journalism Education in Europe and North America: A Structural Comparison.* Cresskill, N.J.: Hampton Press, 2002.

Gaunt, P. *Making the Newsmakers: International Handbook on Journalism Training.* Westport, Conn.: Greenwood Press, 1992.

Hagen, P., H. Manders, and B. Van Ruler. "Nieuw Perspectief voor de Opleidingen Communicatie en Journalistiek." *Cahier* 8 (1997).

Hallin, D. "Commercialism and Professionalism in American News Media." In *Mass Media and Society,* 3rd Edition, edited by J. Curran and M. Gurevitch. London: Arnold, 1996.

———. "The Passing of the "High Modernism" of American Journalism." *Journal of Communication* 42, no. 3 (1992): 14–25.

Herbert, J. "The Changing Face of Journalism Education in the UK" [on-line]. *Asia/Pacific Media Educator* 8, (2000): 113–123. Available: http://www.uow.edua.au/crearts/journalism/APME/contents8.morgan.htm. Accessed 5 December 2000.

Holm, H. "Educating Journalists for a New Europe." In *European Journalism Training in Transition,* edited by J. Bierhoff and M. Schmidt, 47–50. Maastricht, the Netherlands: European Journalism Centre, 1997.

———. "The Forgotten Globalization of Journalism Education." *Journalism and Mass Communication Educator* 56, no. 4 (2002): 67–71.

Johansen, P., D. H. Weaver, and C. Dornan. "Journalism Education in the United States and Canada: Not Merely Clones." *Journalism Studies,* no. 2 (2001): 469–483.

Kees, B. "Newsroom Training: Where's the Investment?" [on-line]. Poynter Institute "Today's Centerpiece," posted 9 April 2002. Available: http://www.poynter.org/centerpiece.newsroomstraining.htm. Accessed 10 April 2002.

Kennedy, H. *Postgraduate Multimedia Education: Practices, Themes and Issues* [on-line]. Infonomics report, April 2002. Available: http://cmd.infonomics.nl/reports.htm. Accessed 20 April 2002.

Koskinen, P., and E. Sederholm. *Survey on Journalism Education in Europe* [on-line]. FEJS Report. Available: http://www.sockom.helsinki.fi/fejs/archives/00000082.htm. Accessed 13 June 2002.

Kovach, B., and T. Rosenstiel. *The Elements of Journalism.* New York: Crown Publishers, 2001.

Loennroth, A. *Journalism Training in Europe.* Maastricht, the Netherlands: European Journalism Training Association, 1997.

Lowe Morna, C., and Z. Khan. *Assessment of Media Training Needs in the Southern African Region: Preliminary Findings.* Maputo, Mozambique: Nordic SADC Journalism Centre (NSJ), 2001.

Mast, C. *Berufsziel Journalismus.* Opladen/Wiesbaden, Germany: Westdeutscher Verlag, 1999.

McChesney, R. *Rich Media, Poor Democracy: Communication Politics in Dubious Times.* Urbana: University of Illinois Press, 1999.

McManus, J. *Market-Driven Journalism: Let the Citizen Beware?* Thousand Oaks, Calif.: Sage, 1994.

Medsger, B. *Winds of Change: Challenges Confronting Journalism Education* [on-line]. Freedom Forum Report. Available: http://www.freedomforum.org/freedomforum/resources/journalism/journalism_edu/winds_of_change/. Accessed 14 July 1999.

Megwa, E. R. "Democracy Without Citizens: The Challenge for South African Journalism Education." *Journalism Studies* 2, no. 2 (2001): 281–285.

Meyn, H., and H. Chill. "Journalistic Training in Germany." *Bildung und Wissenschaft* 4. Bonn: Goethe-Institut Inter Nationes, 2001.

Morgan, F. "Passing the Torch: Professional Education for Communication and Media Worldwide" [on-line]. Address to the IAMCR 20th General Assembly and Scientific conferences of 18–22 August 1996 in Sydney, Australia. Available: http://www.dfat.gov.au/intorgs/unesco/iamcrmor.html. Accessed 19 August 1999.

———. "Recipes for Success: Curriculum for Professional Media Education" [on-line]. *Asia/Pacific Media Educator* 8 (2000): 4–21. Available: http://www.uow.edua.au/crearts/journalism/APME/contents8.morgan.htm. Accessed 5 December 2000.

Parekh, B. C., Editor. *Rethinking Multiculturalism.* Basingstoke, U.K.: Palgrave, 1997.

Pavlik, J., G. Morgan, and B. Henderson. *Information Technology: Implications for the Future of Journalism and Mass Communication Education* [on-line]. Report of the AEJMC Task Force on Teaching and Learning in the New Millennium. Available: http://www.aejmc.org/pubs/2001.html. Accessed 8 May 2001.

Putnis, P., B. Axford, L. Watson, and W. Blood. *Communication and Media Studies in Australian Universities.* University of Canberra, Australia: Lifelong Learning Network, 2002.

Reese, S. D. "The Progressive Potential of Journalism Education: Recasting the Academic vs. Professional Debate. *Harvard International Journal of Press/Politics* 4, no. 4 (1999): 70–94.

Reese, S. D., and J. Cohen. "Educating for Journalism: The Professionalism of Scholarship." *Journalism Studies* 1, no. 2 (2000): 213–227.

Singer, J. (1998). "Online Journalists: Foundation for Research Into Their Changing Roles" [on-line]. *Journal of Computer-Mediated Communication* 4, no. 1. Available: http://jcmc.huji.ac.il/vol4/issue1/singer.html. Accessed 10 November 1998.

Sparks, C., and S. Splichal. "Journalistic Education and Professional Socialization. *Gazette* 43, no. 1 (1989): 31–52.

Splichal, S., and C. Sparks. *Journalists for the 21st Century: Tendencies of Professionalization Among First-Year Students in 22 Countries.* Norwood, N.J.: Ablex, 1994.

Stephenson, H. "Journalism Education and the Groves of Academe." In *European Journalism Training in Transition,* edited by J. Bierhoff and M. Schmidt, 23–27. Maastricht, the Netherlands: European Journalism Center, 1997.

Steyn, E., and A. de Beer. *2002 South African National Journalism Skills Audit.* Sanef/ETC Report. Noordbrug: South African National Editor's Forum (Sanef) and the Sanef Education and Training Committee (ETC), 2002.

Teoh Kheng Yau, J., and S. Al-Hawamdeh. "The Impact of the Internet on Teaching and Practicing Journalism" [on-line]. *Journal of Electronic Publishing* 7, no. 1. Available: http://www.press.umich.edu/jep/07-01/al-hawamdeh.html. Accessed 12 September 2001.

Weaver, D. H., Editor. *The Global Journalist: News People Around the World.* Cresskill, N.J.: Hampton Press, 1998.

Weischenberg, S., M. Loeffelholz, and A. Scholl. "Journalism in Germany." In *The Global Journalist,* edited by D. H. Weaver, 229–256. Cresskill, N.J.: Hampton Press, 1998.

10

Journalists: International Profiles

David H. Weaver

Comparing journalists across national boundaries is difficult. Many characteristics, attitudes, and behaviors depend on a specific setting. Yet there are also similarities that cut across the boundaries of geography, culture, language, society, religion, race, and ethnicity.

This chapter points out similarities and differences in the basic characteristics and professional values of journalists from 21 countries and territories. (For more details, see *The Global Journalist,* edited by David Weaver, Hampton Press, 1998). These include Algeria, Australia, Brazil, Britain, Canada, Chile, China, Ecuador, Finland, France, Germany, Hong Kong, Hungary, Korea, Mexico, New Zealand, the Pacific Islands, Poland, Spain, Taiwan, and the United States. The surveys were conducted between 1988 and 1996, mostly by mail and telephone, and included interviews with more than 20,000 journalists in total.

The point of attempting to draw comparisons of journalists in these different areas of the world is to try to identify some similarities and differences that may give us a more accurate picture of where journalists come from and whether they are becoming more professional as we leave the twentieth century behind and begin a new millennium. The major assumption is that journalists' backgrounds and ideas influence what is reported (and how it is covered) in the various news media around the world, and that this news coverage matters in terms of world public opinion and policies.

Backgrounds and Demographic Profiles

In their 1992 national study of U.S. journalists, Weaver and Wilhoit concluded that the statistical profile of the typical U.S. journalist in 1992 was much like that of a journalist in 1982–1983: a white Protestant male with a four-year bachelor's degree, married, and in his thirties. But there were some changes from the early 1980s, including an increase of four years in median age to 36, more minorities, and more earning college degrees, but no increase in those majoring in journalism in college (about 40 percent). This demographic profile of U.S. journalists is similar in some ways to the profiles of journalists in other areas of the world, but there are some notable differences as well.

Gender

For example, men were more common than women in newsrooms in all 19 countries or territories reporting gender proportions, although in some countries women were almost as numerous as men (New Zealand and Finland), whereas in others women lagged far behind (Korea, Algeria, Britain, and Spain). The average proportion of women journalists across these 19 countries and territories was one-third (33 percent), almost exactly the proportion in the United States (34 percent).

Age

Another similarity uncovered between the United States and the rest of the world is that journalism is a young person's occupation, with most journalists between 25 and 44 years old. The average age ranged from 30 to 40 years in the dozen places reporting it, with the youngest journalists coming from Hong Kong and Algeria, where the average age is 30, and the oldest living in Canada and Finland, where it is 40.

In most places, journalists are younger on average (35 years old) than the workforce in general. In Hong Kong, as in other places, many young people become journalists to earn some experience before leaving for more lucrative and stable jobs in other fields, especially public relations. This seems to be a fairly common pattern in many countries.

Education

Although most journalists in the United States hold a four-year college degree, this is not the case in a number of countries. The countries with the lowest proportions of college graduate journalists are Australia, Finland, and Mexico—all well below one-half. Those with the highest rates are Korea, Spain, and the United States, with Chile and Ecuador nearly as high. Eleven of 18 countries or territories reported more than one-half of their journalists holding a four-year college degree, so it is more common than not for journalists to be college graduates in this group, but the variation is substantial.

It is not typical for journalists to be graduates of journalism programs in college, however. Only three countries reported that more than half of their journalists had concentrated on journalism in college—Spain, Brazil, and Chile. In the other 11 countries or territories reporting this proportion, most did not exceed 40 percent, with the lowest figure reported from Britain (4 percent) and more typical figures hovering in the 30s.

Thus, whatever benefits or evils are attributed to journalism education must be tempered by the fact that most journalists are not graduates of college-level journalism programs in this sample of countries and territories. In fact, the average percentage among the 14 countries reporting was 41.5. Without including the extremes of Spain, Brazil, Chile, and Britain, it was one-third, a bit under the U.S. percentage of 39.

Ethnicity

Less than half of the countries and territories represented in this study reported a figure for racial and ethnic minority journalists. The reported figures are small at best, ranging from 1 to 11 percent, and reinforcing the conclusion of the 1971 U.S. study by Johnstone and colleagues that journalists come predominantly from the established and dominant cultural groups in society. This seems to hold true especially in Taiwan, Britain, and Canada, and somewhat less so in Brazil, China, and the United States.

Thus, in terms of demographics, the journalists from the various countries and territories were similar in average age and proportion of minorities, but varied considerably in gender, level of education, and whether they had majored in journalism.

Professional Values

In *Journalists for the 21st Century,* based on surveys of about 1,800 first-year students in 22 different countries in 1987–1988, Splichal and Sparks (1994) argue that even though there is no strict definition of journalism yet, the occupation seems to be moving from craft to profession (although not yet a true profession) because of changes in the education and specialist knowledge of journalists and an emphasis on autonomy and professional ethics.

The conclusion that journalism is not yet a true profession is similar to that made by Weaver and Wilhoit (1992). At the end of their book on American journalists, they wrote that American journalists are unlikely ever to assume a formal professional status because of their skepticism of institutional forms of professionalism such as certification or licensing, membership in organizations, and readership of professional publications.

Looking across 22 countries, Splichal and Sparks noted that their initial hypothesis was that similarities across countries should prevail if journalism is really becoming a profession. They concluded in their last chapter that their major finding was a striking similarity in the desire of journalism students for the independence and autonomy of journalism. In addition, they didn't find evidence that journalism education and professional socialization were necessarily a function of politics or dominant ideology.

Based on these findings, they argued that some universal ethical and occupational standards were emerging in journalism, but this conclusion seems to contradict the differences in ethical reporting standards found in surveys of journalists in Britain, Germany, and the United States, and it may reflect the lack of specific questions about journalists' roles, reporting practices, or ethical dilemmas in the Splichal-Sparks questionnaire more than the emergence of universal ethical and occupational standards in journalism.

There is probably a universal desire for more freedom among journalists in various parts of the world, although our findings on the importance of this job aspect are mixed, but that does not necessarily signal the emergence of any universal standards in journalism, nor is it necessarily anything new. A look at more specific professional roles or values, as well as reporting practices, may help to more precisely define the areas of agreement and disagreement among the 20,000 journalists of the world represented in Weaver's *The Global Journalist* (1998).

Roles

In their 1992 study of U.S. journalists, Weaver and Wilhoit found that for the most part, their perceptions of the roles of the news media were broadly similar to those they had identified a decade earlier. A majority of U.S. journalists tended to see two responsibilities as extremely important: getting information to the public quickly, and investigating government claims.

Among the 12 countries or territories reporting on the role of getting information to the public quickly, there was also considerable agreement. In most cases, two-thirds or more agreed that it was very important, except in Taiwan and Canada, but even in these places a clear majority agreed.

On investigating government claims (or being a watchdog on government), there was considerably less agreement, however, with journalists most likely to consider this role very important in the more democratic countries of Australia, Britain, and Finland. Those least likely to see this watchdog role as very important came from Taiwan, Algeria, and Chile, where there has not been a long history of democratic forms of government.

But there were exceptions to this pattern. In Germany, which has been a democracy since World War II, there was not any more support for the watchdog role than among Algerian journalists. And in China, which has never had a democratic system of government, there was more support among journalists for investigating government than in France and Canada.

The analytical function of news media—providing analysis of complex problems—remained about the same in the United States during the 1980s, with about half saying it was extremely important. But among the 14 countries or territories where this role was measured, there were considerable differences, with journalists in Taiwan and France least likely to consider it very important and those in Finland and Britain most likely to say so.

Another role about which there was some disagreement was the extent to which journalists should give ordinary people a chance to express their views on public affairs. A little less than half of the U.S. sample said this was an extremely important role, with journalists working on daily and weekly newspapers especially likely to say so. Although only six countries reported the importance of this role, there was some agreement among five—Hong Kong, Britain, Finland, Germany, and the United States—but Chinese journalists were notably less likely to see this role as very important. Compared to other journalistic roles, this one was not seen as important by large proportions of journalists in any location. Only in Britain and Finland did slightly more than half of the journalists consider this a very important role.

There was great disagreement on the importance of providing entertainment among the 14 countries or territories reporting this role. Those journalists least likely to consider this very important were from Canada and France, whereas those most likely were from Germany and Chile. Clearly, this is one role where national differences in journalistic values are in sharp evidence. It seems that journalists from the Far East and North America were least likely to regard entertainment as an important function of journalism, but in Europe there were huge differences by country, suggesting that this is not a universal Western journalistic role.

There was also disagreement on the importance of reporting accurately or objectively, with those journalists least likely to say so from Britain and the Pacific Islands and those most likely from Germany, Finland, and Taiwan.

Thus, there was considerable agreement among journalists regarding the importance of reporting the news quickly, and some agreement on the importance of providing access for the public to express opinions, but considerable disagreement on the importance of providing analysis and being a watchdog on government. There was most disagreement on the importance of providing entertainment, and considerable variance in opinions on the importance of accurate or objective reporting.

Clearly, there was more disagreement than agreement over the relative importance of these journalistic roles considered together, hardly evidence to support the universal occupational standards mentioned by Splichal and Sparks. The reasons for the disagreement are difficult to specify for so many possible comparisons, but a secondary analysis of the data from journalists in China, Taiwan, and the United States by Zhu and others (1996) suggests that political system similarities and differences are far more important than cultural similarities and differences, organizational constraints, or individual characteristics in predicting the variance in perceptions of three roles (timely information, interpretation, and entertainment) by journalists in these societies.

Professional Organizations

Another possible indicator of professionalism is membership in organizations that encourage professional standards and values. Only seven studies reported data on this, but among those there was a wide range, from 18 percent claiming to belong to a journalistic organization in Hong Kong to 86 percent in Australia and 83 percent in Hungary, followed fairly closely by Taiwan, Britain, and Spain, with the United

States in between. Most of these differences are likely explained by the requirement in some countries that journalists belong to a union to be able to work, but the large differences here also call into question whether journalists are becoming more professional around the world.

Ethics

Still another measure of how professional journalists are is which reporting methods they consider acceptable. Weaver and Wilhoit's surveys of U.S. journalists included questions about the acceptability of questionable reporting practices that were first asked in a 1980 study of British and West German journalists and also in public opinion surveys in the United States during the 1980s.

For example, a majority of U.S. journalists in 1992 said that becoming employed to gain inside information might be justified on occasion. But a national survey of 1,002 adults done for the American Society of Newspaper Editors (ASNE) in 1985 found that only one-third of the public approved of journalists not identifying themselves as reporters, as did a 1981 Gallup national survey and a 1989 Indiana statewide survey. The questions were somewhat different, but it is likely there was a considerable gap between the U.S. press and the public on the acceptability of undercover reporting.

Another gap with the public appeared when U.S. journalists' opinions about the use of hidden microphones or cameras were compared with the public's. Less than half of the 1985 national sample of the public and the 1989 Indiana sample approved of using hidden cameras, compared with almost two-thirds of journalists in 1992 who said this practice might be justified. Again, the questions were not identical, but a gap seemed likely.

One practice that was approved by fewer U.S. journalists than the U.S. public was paying for information. Only one-fifth of journalists in the 1992 study said this might be justified, compared with about one-third of the 1985 national public sample and the 1989 Indiana public sample that approved. On this score, then, U.S. journalists seemed less permissive (or more ethical) than the public at large.

If journalists are becoming more professional in a universal sense around the world, we should expect their views on the acceptability of various reporting practices to also become more similar. In an earlier 1982 study of U.S. journalists, Weaver and Wilhoit found considerable differences between U.S., British, and German journalists on whether certain practices might be justified. The Germans were much less likely to approve of badgering or harassing sources, using personal documents without permission, and getting employed to gain inside information than were the U.S. and British journalists. The British journalists were especially likely to say that most of the questionable reporting practices could be justified, with the U.S. journalists in between the British and the Germans on most practices.

What about more recent times? Are journalists' views about which reporting methods are acceptable becoming more similar over time?

In the United States, Weaver and Wilhoit found some large increases from 1982 to 1992 in the percentage of journalists who thought that it might be justifiable to use confidential business or government documents without permission (up from 55 percent to 82 percent) and to use personal documents such as letters and photographs without permission (up from 28 percent to 48 percent). But the percentages approving the other methods stayed about the same.

When journalists from different areas of the world are compared, there are considerable differences, some very large, on the proportions saying that some reporting methods might be justified, as well as some agreement on other practices.

For example, on revealing confidential news sources, which has been the practice of most agreement (as unacceptable) among U.S. journalists from 1982 to 1992, journalists from 13 of the 14 countries or territories measuring this practice were very reluctant to say it might be justifiable (10 percent or less said so in Hong Kong, Korea, Taiwan, Australia, the Pacific Islands, Britain, France, Germany, Canada, the United States, Brazil, Chile, and Mexico), but 39 percent of the journalists in Finland said it might be acceptable. On this practice, then, there was a high level of agreement among all journalists except those from Finland, suggesting a near-universal professional norm of protecting confidential sources.

Given these very large differences in the percentages of journalists who think that different reporting methods may be acceptable, it seems that there are strong national differences that override any universal professional norms or values of journalism around the world, except in the case of revealing confidential sources, where there is strong and consistent agreement that this should never be done.

Aspects of the Job

Another possible indicator of the professionalism of journalists is which dimensions of their jobs they consider most important. Some scholars would argue that salary, job security, and chance to advance are less professional aspects of an occupation than editorial policies, ability to develop a specialty, autonomy, and helping people.

There are wide disagreements among journalists from different countries on which aspects of the job are very important. Journalists in France and the former West Germany were more likely to emphasize freedom on the job than pay, job security, and chance to advance, but this was not the case in Brazil, where journalists were more likely to say that pay was very important, followed by freedom and the chance to help people. Journalists in Algeria were likely to think that almost all job aspects were equally important.

Looking at the "nonprofessional" job aspects, it's clear that Brazilian journalists were most likely to rate pay very important, perhaps because of the very high rates of inflation in that country, followed by former East German journalists. Surprisingly, journalists in Chile and Mexico were least likely to say so. Whatever the reasons for these differences, there is not much agreement across countries on the importance of pay.

In regard to job security, journalists in the United States were most likely to consider it very important, no doubt because of the much more competitive job market and the lack of growth in jobs during the 1980s, followed by those in East

Germany. Those least likely to say so were from Canada and France, most likely reflecting the economic situations in their countries and illustrating a considerable range of disagreement across countries. As for the chance to advance or to be promoted, those most likely to rate it very important were from Brazil and Australia, again likely reflecting the economies of their countries. Those least concerned about advancement were from Finland and Mexico.

Even on perceived freedom on the job, a journalistic norm that Splichal and Sparks identified as strikingly similar among the journalism students from 22 different countries, there were notable differences among the journalists interviewed in the studies reported here. Those from the former East Germany, Brazil, and France were most likely to say that freedom on the job was very important, whereas those in Canada were least likely (although this was the aspect of their jobs rated most highly as compared to others). There does seem to be more agreement on the importance of this aspect of the job than on others, as Splichal and Sparks argued, but there are still considerable differences between countries.

And, finally, on the journalistic norm of helping people, those journalists most likely to consider this very important were from Brazil and Chile. Those least likely were from Canada, again suggesting a wide range of opinion on this indicator of professionalism.

Images of the Audience

A final possible indicator of professionalism of journalists is their view of their audiences. Although only six countries included this measure in their studies, there were some striking similarities and differences. About one-fourth of journalists from Algeria, Brazil, and the United States strongly agreed that their audiences were interested in breaking news. But only one-third of the journalists in the United States strongly agreed that their audiences were interested in politics and social problems, compared with nearly three-fourths of the East German and Mexican journalists. Nearly one-half of the East German journalists strongly agreed that their audience was gullible, or easily fooled, and the U.S. journalists were the least likely to say so (only 3 percent strongly agreed).

Again, on these measures of professionalism, there were some striking differences on two of the three, raising the question of whether journalists are becoming more professional around the world.

Conclusions

Whether one thinks that journalists are becoming more universally professional depends on the definition of professional and the indicators used. But a variety of possible measures of professionalism reviewed here suggest that there are still many differences among journalists from the 21 countries and territories represented in *The Global Journalist* (Weaver 1998). Even though these are not a representative sample of all countries, they do include some of the largest and most influential, and they are located in most of the major continents and regions.

Further analysis is needed to uncover some of the reasons behind the differences reported here. Many of them seem to reflect societal influences, especially political system differences, more than the influences of media organizations, journalism education, and professional norms. The patterns of similarities and differences are not neatly classifiable along some of the more common political or cultural dimensions, however, lending some support to the conclusion of Splichal and Sparks that journalism education and professional socialization are not necessarily a function of politics or dominant ideology. Additional comparative research about journalists, perhaps using in-depth case studies, might uncover other influences on journalists' views concerning their professional roles and ethics, and document these views in more detail.

Bibliography

Beam, Randal A. Professionalism as an Organizational-Level Concept. *Journalism Monographs* 121 (1990): 1–43.

Donsbach, Wolfgang. "Journalists' Conceptions of their Audience." *Gazette* 32 (1983): 19–36.

Gaziano, Cecilie, and Kristin McGrath. "Measuring the Concept of Credibility. *Journalism Quarterly* 63 (1986): 451–462.

Johnstone, John W. C., Edward J. Slawski, and William W. Bowman. *The News People.* Urbana: University of Illinois Press, 1976.

Koecher, Renate. "Bloodhounds or Missionaires: Role Definitions of German and British Journalists." *European Journal of Communication* 1 (1986): 43–64.

McLeod, Jack, and Searle Hawley, Jr. "Professionalization Among Newsmen." *Journalism Quarterly* 41 (1964): 529–538, 577.

Splichal, Slavko, and Colin Sparks. *Journalists for the 21st Century.* Norwood, NJ: Ablex, 1994.

Weaver, David H., Editor. *The Global Journalist: News People Around the World.* Cresskill, N.J.: Hampton Press, 1998.

Weaver, David H., and LeAnne Daniels. "Public Opinion on Investigative Reporting in the 1980s." *Journalism Quarterly* 69 (1992): 146–155.

Weaver, David H., and G. Cleveland Wilhoit. *The American Journalist: A Portrait of U.S. News People and Their Work.* Bloomington: Indiana University Press, 1986.

Weaver, David H., and G. Cleveland Wilhoit. *The American Journalist in the 1990s: U.S. News People at the End of an Era.* Mahwah, N.J.: Lawrence Erlbaum, 1996.

Windahl, Swen, and Karl Erik Rosengren. "Newsmen's Professionalization: Some Methodological Problems." *Journalism Quarterly* 55 (1978): 466–473.

Zhu, Jian-Hua, David Weaver, Ven-hwei Lo, Chongshan Chen, and Wei Wu. "Individual, Organizational and Societal Influences on Media Role Perceptions: A Comparative Study of Journalists in China, Taiwan and the United States." *Journalism & Mass Communication Quarterly* 74 (1996): 84–96. [Reprinted in Michael Prosser and K. S. Sitaram, Editors, *Civic Discourse: Intercultural, International, and Global Media*, Vol. 2, 361–374. Stamford, Conn.: Ablex, 1999.]

11

Journalists Reporting from Foreign Places

P. Eric Louw

Because U.S. power underpins the new world order, the processes whereby Americans make sense of distant places now have real consequences for non-Americans. To a great extent Americans form impressions of distant places, issues, and events from their news media. These impressions often translate into electoral pressure on U.S. politicians to act in certain ways toward distant populations. Hence, in a globalizing world, journalist coverage of foreign places increasingly influences the governance of those places. For this reason it is important to pay some attention to the practices associated with the reporting of foreign affairs.

Gaye Tuchman (1978) has argued that journalists construct a "window on the world" and has explained why this window is always a partial view (that is, a skewed picture). For the consumers of local news, a potential corrective exists for moderating the inbuilt skewing or distortion produced by news practices. In the local context consumers, including politicians, can to some extent carry out their own reality checks by comparing their own lived experiences and understandings with what is reported in the media. But when it comes to the reporting of distant places, such reality checks are not possible. So news consumers become virtually entirely dependent on the news media to help them make sense of those distant places they themselves have no direct access to. Further, when distortions occur, they are generally not redressed because there is no pressure to correct them, because distant audiences do not recognize distortions, and when they do, as Wallis and Baran (1990, p. 231) note, it is difficult for foreigners to redress reporting inaccuracies at a distance. For this reason, the emergence of international governance based on foreign news–driven "mediated realities" has inherent dangers.

Distance and Double Misreadings

Relying on the news media to understand distant places inherently produces a double misreading because journalists generally are not equipped to read distant contexts, and neither are their audiences. The result is a double misreading, as audiences with already limited understanding of distant contexts are forced to rely on partial or skewed journalistic reports to build up any kind of picture of foreign places. These partial pictures acquire a reality which then serves to frame the way the next generation of foreign correspondents and their news editors look at (and hence report on) the distant places. Once a prejudice, whether negative or positive, has rooted itself in a newsroom culture, that prejudice will unconsciously inform future newsmaking about that particular group of people.

In a sense, if distant issues are not reported, they do not "exist," because only that which enters one's consciousness exists. Increasingly, television sets the agenda for what enters the consciousness of people in North America, Europe, Japan, and Australia. And when it comes to foreign contexts, this agenda-setting role is almost absolute. As regards the reporting of distant places, "televisualized" agenda setting generates a particular variety of partiality, one often governed by emotive images. Television is very good at presenting visually sensational and unidimensional material, but it is a poor medium for dealing with complicated issues and contexts that require nonsensational, analytic unpacking of their complexity. Watching television news tends not to leave audiences with a store of knowledge of the details and facts of what is happening but with a blur of images. So watching television news generally leaves audiences with strong yet ill-defined feelings and emotions, but little understanding of the issues underpinning what they saw. Neuman and colleagues discuss how television news creates "common knowledge [which helps] people think . . . and structure their ideas, feelings and beliefs about political issues" (1992, p. 3), and argue that television is good at putting obscure and distant events onto the agenda (p. 86). They are correct that television is good at creating "common knowledge" about distant places; however, such common knowledge is likely to be highly skewed and partial due to the nature of the medium. As Wallis and Baran note, "radio and television are *immediate* and emotional media. The emotional prerequisite for successful communication in the broadcast media means that news, ideally, should be both informative and dramatic if it is to grip" (Wallis and Baran 1990, pp. 246–247). Hence, foreign news selection tends to be geared to the highly visual, dramatic and emotional because such news is more appealing to audiences. This leaves television audiences with a (highly "visualized") reductionist "knowledge" of foreign places that is extremely limited and often devoid of factual detail. This tends to leave audiences with very strong feelings about foreign issues that, ironically, are based on a highly limited repertoire of information. Neuman and colleagues (1992, pp. 63–64) gives the example of intense antagonism toward white South Africans in the 1980s based on U.S. television coverage of the anti-apartheid struggle. A similar antagonism developed toward Serbs in the 1990s as a result of Anglo media coverage of the Bosnian and Kosovo wars.

At its heart, the problem with television reportage of distant places is that television news seeks out the visually dramatic and the emotional. Television news compresses, condenses, simplifies, and eschews complexity and ambiguity. Wherever possible, television news production will reduce complexity to binary oppositions, mobilizing what Hartley (1982, p. 21) calls "hooray" and "boo" words, because this makes for good emotive television that can attract and hold audiences. Foreign situations can be more easily simplified into facile good guy versus bad guy scenarios than local situations because audiences have no way of personally verifying reports about distant places. In this regard, Westmoreland's complaint that television news is simplistic is instructive:

> Television brought war into the American home, but in the process television's unique requirements contributed to a distorted view of the war. The news had to be compressed and visually dramatic. Thus the war that the Americans saw was almost exclusively violent, miserable, or controversial: guns firing, men falling, helicopters crashing, buildings toppling, huts burning, refugees fleeing, women wailing. A shot of a single building in ruins could give an impression of an entire town destroyed. . . . Only scant attention was paid to . . . the way life went on in a generally normal way for most of the people much of the time. (Westmoreland 1980, p. 555)

Sadkovich notes a similar process at work in reporting the breakup of Yugoslavia. He says:

> Television seems able to portray only a limited range of emotions because it lacks linear development and nuance. It homogenizes and reduces complex situations, events and emotions to simple standard items that are almost mythic. . . . Television precludes careful exegesis in favor of simple explanations of group conflict and reality in general. It invokes and evokes, it does not inform or explain.
>
>   If television is a dream, it also decides what is real. . . . As the tube creates and idealizes some groups and ideas by focusing on them, it makes other disappear by ignoring them. Because it is the key source of news for most Americans it has seriously distorted our view of reality. (Sadkovich 1998, p. 60)

Sadkovich also examined how U.S. journalists mobilized "name-calling" (1998, p. 82) or emotion and drama during the Yugoslav conflicts, such as the story of the Serbian boy and Muslim girl killed in each other's arms: "As drama the show was wonderful. As news, it meant nothing" (Sadkovich 1998, p. 68). Yet such visual dramatization has become the stock-in-trade of U.S. televisual coverage of distant places—dramatization which then spills into non-U.S. television. This often generates deep emotional responses among TV audiences, which can, in turn, produce emotion-driven foreign policy formulation. Having recognized the power of negative TV images on foreign policy making, the U.S. military developed a strategy for limiting these (see Louw 2001, Chap. 8).

But it is not only audiences who misunderstand distant places; journalists regularly misread and misunderstand the foreign contexts to which they are sent. When journalists (and news editors) cover foreign contexts, they engage in their task with already existent pictures and discourses in their minds. These existing images determine the questions they ask and the images they seek. Hence, the partiality of news frames tends to be recycled and reproduced, so that discourses about foreigners and foreign places are resistant to change.

Journalistic misreadings occur owing to a number of factors. First, journalists arriving in a new context are foreigners, not rooted in the history or codes of the society they are expected to report on. Journalists necessarily experience real difficulties when sent to cover societies grounded upon unfamiliar religions (such as Anglo journalists in the Muslim world), or to societies that are extremely complex (such as the Balkans, Russia, or South Africa). Van Ginneken (1998, p. 125–126) notes how journalists often read the history and mores of their own societies into foreign contexts when trying to make sense of these places. In the process they simply produce a distorted view of "the other." Karim, for example, notes how the Western media, when confronted with sociopolitical complexities they could not understand in the Caucasus and former Yugoslavia, simply produced a reductionist explanation based on "religious differences" and "irrationality" (Karim 2000, p. 177). Further, when encountering "difficult" and "foreign" places, journalists often herd together into expatriate communities consisting of Western media people, businessmen, embassy and intelligence staffers, and non-governmental organization (NGO) humanitarian and aid workers (Van Ginneken 1998, p. 134). These expatriate communities tend to be cut off from the countries they live in, and so invent "closed-shop" interpretations or "scripts" (Van Dijk in Karim 2000, p. 179) to describe the "difficult cultures" surrounding them. It is these "closed" interpretations the "folks back home" get to hear (via journalists and embassy dispatches). The reporting of post-Taliban Afghanistan is an example of this. Van Ginneken suggests that once created, these scripts or "prime definitions tend to stick" (1998, p. 113) and be recycled.

Misreadings also occur because journalists carry their cultural biases with them when reporting on foreign contexts. Further, they carry by extension the biases of their news editors. In other words, journalists necessarily respond to requests and pressures from their home base to deliver stories conforming to "home needs" (see Cohen, Levy, Roeh, and Gurevitch 1995). In this regard, Karim (2000) and Said (1981) have discussed the anti-Muslim bias in Western media. Van Ginneken (1998, p. 110) argues that journalists effectively judge others in terms of their own cultural biases. So foreigners operating in ways that confirm the journalist's own cultural norms seem sensible and normal, while anyone operating outside these norms becomes incomprehensible or even despicable. Attention is drawn to such "incomprehensible" and "despicable" behavior, while "dark issues" in one's own culture are forgotten and blotted out (Van Ginneken 1998, p. 111). Significantly, Anglo values have become something of a measure of "normalness" (or even "truth") in the global media system due in no small measure to the growing centrality of the U.S. media (such as CNN) within this system, and because of the central position occupied by the United States within the new world order. Consequently, Anglo journalists assume their values to be universally valid truths and uncontestable, partly because the new world order is a de facto Anglo hegemony. Measuring other cultures against

Anglo values is thus taken for granted. So, for example, the American trajectory of socioeconomic development is seen as a valid model for all to emulate, and the Anglo-American model for political modernization becomes a self-evident truth. Greenfeld suggests that Americans have decontextualized their model of sociopolitical organization and transformed it into a "pan-human universalism" (Greenfeld 1993, p. 446). Anglo-American journalists now uncritically apply this pan-human universalism to all situations they encounter. Hence, when Americans believed in the melting pot, that became the measurement criterion for all. When "multiculturalism" replaced the melting pot, the journalistic measurement criterion shifted. Those not adhering to Anglo-American models of societal organization become "despicable" or "incomprehensible." North Korea, Iran, Afghanistan, and Libya have become such "incomprehensible" societies, as have all Muslim fundamentalists. "Muslim fundamentalism" has become a major "boo word" in the Anglo-global media. Generally, black African conflicts, such as in Somalia, Sierra Leone, Rwanda, and Congo, have also been presented as incomprehensible, although the opaqueness of these conflicts is often indirectly explained away by alluding to Western "common knowledge" of the "inherently" despicable nature of "darkest Africa." Similarly, ethnic wars in the former Yugoslavia were seen as despicable by the Anglo-global media, while the Balkan peoples become incomprehensible for failing to behave in a "civilized" (Anglo) way. In an earlier era Afrikaners were deemed despicable for violating the Anglo model of sociopolitical organization. However, Anglo journalists tried to make Afrikaner actions comprehensible by equating apartheid with American white supremacy and slavery (because the Dutch *verzuiling* model that underpinned apartheid was unknown to Anglos, they simply ignored it and mistakenly substituted another explanation for the behavior of Afrikaners). If the global media are to be believed, Anglos fight wars, engage in conflict, and impose their will on others because they have "good reasons" to do so, whereas other people do so because they are despicable or uncivilized or just plain odd. So Anglo hegemonies are routinely normalized while non-Anglo hegemonies are routinely measured (judged) against Anglo norms or in terms of their usefulness to Anglo hegemonies.

A third reason for the misreading of foreign contexts is the journalistic practice of deploying simplistic role labels. This takes place because journalists are often faced with the problem of rendering incredibly complex foreign contexts easily comprehensible for overseas audiences. Although the habit of shorthand labeling pragmatically achieves this, it can also simplify to the point of distortion. In this regard, Wallis and Baran (1990, p. 231) cite the BBC's deployment of race labels to describe 1980s South Africa. Van Ginneken (1998, p. 105–108) looks at similar deployments in the case of Libya, Iran, and Eastern Europe. Ultimately the journalistic practices of labeling, seeking the visually dramatic and sensational, necessarily eschews complexity in favor of decontextualized and dehistoricized reductionisms. For example, the complexity of Kosovo was reduced to the label of "ethnic cleansing," and the complexity of South Africa was reduced to a struggle against "white supremacy." The problem is, such reductionisms, when applied to foreign contexts, can become "reality" because the audiences have no direct knowledge of the context being described. Simplistic labels grow into "truth" for the audiences (and the editors) back home. They also become reality for the next generation of journalists sent to cover these foreign contexts, who then frame their questions in terms of such learned, preconceived labels.

A fourth reason for journalistic misreading is that journalists routinely use binary oppositions when describing foreign contexts. Foreign places are peopled by "good guys" and "bad guys." Some individuals and groups are idealized, while others are demonized and villainized. The process of demonization and idealization is frequently directly related to the foreign policy requirements of one's own hegemonic order. Hence, in an increasingly Anglofied global hegemony, it is the U.S. media's binary oppositions that have generally acquired a universalized naturalism. Not surprisingly, those demonized become pariah groups that one is not just allowed to dislike but supposed to dislike. Over the past decades pariah groups have included Libyans, Iranians, Afrikaners, Serbs, and Muslim fundamentalists.

The binary opposition model often slips into a victim–villain discourse, in which victims are portrayed as needing to be rescued from villains. This villain–victim discourse allows nature to be the villain (in the form of natural disasters), or possibly some ill-defined villains who are discursively portrayed as bringing about climate change, which then causes natural disasters. Since the 1980s, the villain–victim discourse in its various forms has become very influential, and has even produced a whole industry of NGOs and aid and humanitarian agencies that specialize in helping "the weak." Those perpetrating the victimizing are often equated with the Anglo folk devil of "Hitler." Once such a "folk devil" is successfully evoked, aggression against the villain can be easily justified (since it involves saving the "weak" from being victimized). Not surprisingly, Western military planners and political spin doctors have learned to mobilize both the villain–victim and folk–devil discourses. For example, before commencing the 2001 war in Afghanistan, Pentagon spin doctors first popularized the idea of liberating Afghan women from the Taliban. These spin doctors recognized that women's liberation was a useful issue to piggy back on because it has widespread currency and resonates well with many Western intelligentsia gatekeepers (journalists, teachers, and university intellectuals). Pentagon spin doctors understood the propaganda value of this theme in getting anti-Taliban stories picked up with minimal critical scrutiny from many Western journalists. For this reason, the burka was mobilized as iconic of the Taliban's repression of women, a symbol of victimhood that justified a war against the Taliban.

For the global media machine, the most valuable foreign stories are those that can be cast as binary oppositions, in which the weak (or victims) are helped and the villains are defeated. In a sense, such news provides a form of "collective therapy" (Van Ginneken 1998, p. 32). It is as if Western audiences needed "good news stories" to make them feel better. This "news as therapy" is even more appealing if the audiences can be made to believe they have personally helped the victims (via donations to aid agencies or sending their troops to rescue victims). Mandela's inauguration as South Africa's president is a classic example of such a binary opposition/good news/collective therapy portrayal, in which victims were "miraculously" rescued from villains. Coverage of the 2000 Mozambique floods fell into the same news genre. These floods received significant coverage in the global media (when other equally large human tragedies were being ignored) because this story neatly complemented the Western media's binary needs. The floods provided victims to be helped, while those who did the helping were white South Africans. The story could thus simultaneously serve to recuperate white South Africans (now that apartheid was dead), demonstrate that the "South African miracle" was working (and so confirm past "collective therapy"), and provide the sort of images of weak and dependent black Africans so loved by Western media voyeurs of Third World poverty and misery. (This story originally got onto the global news agenda—unlike other African disasters—because the South African Broadcasting Corporation covered it due to strong South African-Mozambican connections. For example, the then head of SABC-News was Mozambican, Mandela's wife is Mozambican, and the flooded area was fortuitously easy to cover from well-serviced South African towns.)

But the binary opposition model also generates "problem groups" for the global media—groups that cannot be unambiguously idealized or villainized. This can happen because they are former pariah groups that now need to be recuperated (such as the Russians after the Soviet Union collapsed, or Afghan warlords who became incorporated into the post-Taliban government). Or they are groups of former allies, who have now become enemies (such as the Iraqis in the Gulf war, or the Indonesians during the Timor war). In such instances, the problem group is often divided into bad guys (supporters of Saddam and the Indonesian military) and good guys (ordinary Iraqis and civilian Indonesians). Another problem group are allies with "dark secrets" (such as Iraq's and Turkey's repression of Kurds, or Indonesia's massacre of communists and its repression in West Papua, Ache, and the Moluccas). These problems produce silence: no TV cameras are pointed in this direction. Then there are problem groups, formerly portrayed as victims, who begin behaving in ways that might call into question the old binary opposition model (such as the repression, corruption, and mismanagement seen in many African states). The discomfort produced when the old binary oppositions unravel causes the media to fall silent; the "uncomfortable" issues "disappear" because they are taken off the television screens. The way in which Africa has generally fallen off the news agenda is an example of this. Similarly, journalists pay scant attention to the enormous post-Soviet social, religious, and ethnic tensions in Russia, as well as the repression of Russians in some former Soviet states, because these get in the way of the preferred postcommunism news agenda. Then there are foreign groups enmeshed in U.S.-issues, which prevents their media portrayal in a binary opposition format. For example, despite some striking similarities between Israeli and white South African aggression and repression, the Israelis were never unambiguously cast into the role of villains because of the strength of the U.S. Jewish lobby and Western guilt over the Holocaust. Further, binary oppositions routinely deployed by the media are sometimes shelved when using them would generate too much discomfort—Karim (2000) argues that attention is always drawn to a religious binary opposition when Muslims can be cast as repressing Christians—but is dropped in favor of "ethnicity" when the reverse is the case.

A fifth reason for journalistic misreadings is that when sent to report on foreign contexts, journalists tend to (subconsciously) select contacts with whom they feel comfortable working, usually contacts who are as culturally close to them as possible, or people who confirm their world views (Van Ginneken 1998, p. 91). For example, in non-Western societies, Western journalists generally cultivate contacts among Westernized elites because it is easier (and more culturally comfortable) to associate with and understand people who broadly mobilize the same discourses as oneself. Such contacts also tend to express views that confirm the cultural biases and prejudices of news editors back home (whom journalists have to please). Choosing foreign contacts who are culturally proximate to oneself necessarily skews the reports produced and can even build in biases that the journalist may not be aware of. An example of this can be found in the way Anglo journalists sent to cover South Africa have done their job: for contacts they have favored white Anglos leaning slightly to the left (such as opposition politician Helen Suzman) or Anglofied/Westernized blacks (such as Anglican Archbishop Tutu). Such people are culturally proximate to Anglo journalists and so confirm their worldviews. Significantly, foreign correspondents based in Johannesburg have generally lived in affluent suburbs (mostly inhabited by white Anglos and some Westernized blacks), socialized with South African Anglos, sent their children to white Anglo schools, and routinely lifted stories from the local English liberal press. Consequently, the perspectives of one (minority) local interest group gained a disproportionate airing on the international stage. This has necessarily skewed foreign news coverage of South Africa by inadvertently incorporating "local struggles" into the journalistic picture presented (in an unconscious and unacknowledged way): struggles associated with an Anglo dislike of Afrikaners for "taking the country away from Anglos in 1948," and Anglo efforts to develop "moderate" and "Westernized blacks" who can be co-opted into an alliance against "radical blacks" and Afrikaner nationalists. Ironically, because of this Anglo bias, the voices of the majority of South Africans have seldom been heard in an unmediated and authentic way. The experiences and views of the non-Anglo majority, black and white, are effectively avoided because they remain "incomprehensible" to global (Anglo) media workers, and became drawing contacts from among the Westernized/Anglofied black elite and white Anglos is so much easier and more comfortable. Similarly, in Russia, the global media have clearly felt more comfortable relying on "liberal reformers" as contacts and "framers." This is partly because their interpretations confirmed what editors back home want to hear, and partly because the worldviews of liberal reformers tended to be more proximate to those of Western journalists than other Russian constituencies, whose perspectives tended to be rather incomprehensible from within a mainstream (Anglo) global media perspective. A similar process unfolded in post-Taliban Afghanistan, where Western journalists relied on the interpretations of those inside the Kabul compound—that is, Westernized members of the new government, aid workers, and UN staffers—while shying away from the majority of Afghans because they behaved in ways that were incomprehensible to Western journalists.

The news skewing that results from overdependence on one section of the population can have serious consequences for foreign policy formulators. For example, a reliance on Westernized Iranians as contacts necessarily skewed reporting on Iran, which left the West unprepared for the Islamic uprising against the Shah's Westernization policies.

A sixth reason for journalistic misreading is that foreign issues are read in terms of "home" understandings and agendas. For example, the U.S. media have read South Africa's race relations as if they were simply equivalent to U.S. racial problems (Neuman 1992, p. 112). Hence, white South Africans have been equated with white supremacists from U.S. southern states, the anti-apartheid struggle has been equated with the struggle for civil liberties of a U.S. minority group, and the U.S. history of race relations (tied up with slavery) has been read into the South African context. In addition, U.S. political battles being fought by African-Americans became conflated with struggles in South Africa. Conflating these two radically different contexts produced journalistic readings that bordered on the mythological. Anglo journalists have also tended to assume that the outcomes of Western struggles over secularization, multiparty democracy, and gender equality have a teleological "naturalness." Once such struggles are seen not as Western, but as "universal," journalists assume they have right to read (impose) their contemporary measurement criteria, their home battles, and their home agendas into foreign contexts. It also means that journalists are licensed to be lazy, because they do not have to seriously engage with the difficulties confronting overseas decision makers but can simply judge them in terms of their home base contexts. For example, much reporting about China's postcommunist reforms avoids mention of the complexities, contradictions, and dangers confronting the reformers. Not only can this produce misreadings of societies with different socioeconomic trajectories from that of the Anglo world, it also produces foreign resentments about "Western misunderstanding" and "interference," as has become evident at various times in locations such as China, Iran, Malaysia, and Indonesia.

Spin-Doctoring "Tourist Journalists"

Because U.S. power underpins the new world order, the processes whereby Americans make sense of distant places now have real consequences for non-Americans. In particular, the impact of TV news on U.S. policy-making means that non-U.S. players interested in having an impact on U.S. foreign policy must now pay attention to how they can influence the journalists collecting information about their countries. Not surprisingly, one now finds groups in zones of crisis explicitly using the media (such as CNN and BBC) to try and appeal directly to Western audiences (Shaw 1996, p. 7). The notion of a passive periphery merely receiving information from the core, or of the south being manipulated by the north, cannot be seen as valid. In the emergent global communication system it is simply wrong to assume that countries on the margins are always passive victims, because players on the peripheries also now actively engage in spin doctoring and manipulation of communication variables in an attempt to impact on decisions being made in the United States and European Union (EU).

Essentially, as the new world order has shaped up, a number of processes have been modified, including the conduct of international politics, information flows and the nature of news reporting. A new form of journalistic practice is emerging, driven by new technologies and a growing professionalization (and public relationsizing) of news contacts. In the arena of foreign news, the relationships between newsrooms based in the Western "core" (U.S./EU) and "noncore" areas have also shifted. New technologies have opened up the possibility of building "newsrooms without walls" in which journalists and camera operators are free to roam widely, collect material relatively easily from remote sites, maintain regular contact with distant home bases, and easily download audio, visual, and written material into home computers from these distant locations. Air travel also means it is now relatively easy to deploy journalists and camera crews to distant locations to cover breaking stories. This means it is becoming less important to base journalists in foreign locations, and so the phenomenon of "tourist journalism" is emerging, in which camera crews and journalists fly in, cover stories and (thanks to satellite hookups) file these stories in real-time with home newsrooms, and then fly out to the next story. Tourist journalism overlaps to some extent with "parachute journalism" from an earlier era; however, tourist journalists are in constant contact with their home bases (they virtually take their newsrooms with them) and piggyback on the comfortable infrastructure built for global tourism. So the new style is more voyeuristic than the old parachute journalism because increasingly contemporary tourist journalists jet into foreign locations for very limited periods; spend much of their time in sanitized, air-conditioned hotels (where one can also watch CNN); and, except for working with an organized industry of local spin doctors and public relations people, hardly interact at all with the local natives or context.

On the one hand, tourism journalism means that news can (and does) now come from anywhere. It also provides even small governments with a potential communications vehicle with global reach. Nonetheless, this global news machine has an Anglo heart and a center that is very much geared to an American audience. After all, those who try and manipulate the global news machine understand where power resides in the new global hegemony—and so they use the global media machine to try and influence those who count, namely those who drive the new world order. Hence, CNN may wish to claim that it is not American and that its staff composition reflects an international focus, but in reality CNN has a U.S. home base, its practices and discourses are Anglo-American, and its influence and importance derive precisely from it being a communicative conduit to the decision-making heartland of the new world order, which is de facto a Pax Americana.

Tourist journalists can be more easily manipulated than local journalists because they spend short periods of time in unfamiliar places. And given the impact news images can now have on foreign policy formulation in the United States and

EU, tourist journalists necessarily become key targets for spin doctors and public relations operators. Many CNN staffers, for example, have reported an awareness of how governments around the world use CNN to distribute messages globally (Volkmer 1999, pp. 153–155). Manipulation of the global news agenda is in no way unidirectional, although the center of the global news machine does set the broad parameters for what is considered newsworthy. Certainly players all over the world (large and small) are able to influence this agenda, although to be successful at manipulating the global news agenda (that is, to sell their particular message or to successfully capture the attention of the power brokers of the new world order) requires playing in terms of the rules—discourses and practices—of the Western news machine, especially the Anglo-American machine. Ultimately, it is not only Western communication players (like U.S. military spin doctors) who are able to spin the global news system; the system can be spin-doctored by players on the margins as well.

A good example of spin doctoring from the margins was the creation of the South African "miracle discourse" in 1994 (Louw and Chitty 2000). A television spectacle was choreographed by South Africa's then ruling coalition, consisting of the African National Congress and National Party (the party responsible for apartheid), to sell the idea of a miracle transition to democracy in which the good guys won, the bad guys lost, and justice triumphed. A scripted, stage-managed show was organized (largely by Afrikaner bureaucrats) with tourist journalists in mind and geared to producing the sort of festive television event beloved of global TV news (see Dayan and Katz 1992, pp. 5–12). Ultimately, the key target audience for this public relations spectacular was African-American, because it was hoped that South Africa could use this black constituency (much as Israel used the Jewish lobby) as a conduit to U.S. policymakers. Because most journalists jetted in for a short period, for the elections and Mandela's inauguration, it was assumed they would not be in the country long enough to get on top of the situation, and so could be spin-doctored. The South Africans built an International Broadcast Center (IBC) to supply tourist journalists with quality images of the "miracle transition" and the facilities for each TV crew to personalized these images with their own voiceovers. The IBC actually made it technically possible for tourist journalists to cover the 1994 elections without ever venturing into the conflict-ridden South African community. The outcome was a tremendous spin-doctoring success, with almost the whole world watching the same pooled images and receiving the same public relations message—of a miracle, in which South Africans had found each other through negotiation, and in the process had created a social order worthy of foreign investment (Louw and Chitty 2000, pp. 292–293). Within this media spectacle, Mandela provided wonderful public relations material because he could be constructed as an icon of "liberal reasonableness." For the South African choreographers, attaching to Mandela a saintly aura was invaluable public relations, given the worth of "icons and symbolism within global television news" (Volkmer 1999, p. 106). At the end of the choreographed TV spectacle the camera crews went home, and South Africa's turmoil and transition to one-party dominance disappeared from the global news agenda.

Tourist journalism has become a central fixture of the emerging global media machine and newsrooms without walls. For spin doctors on the margins, this can be a good thing, as it provides them with at least some opportunities for influencing the images reaching the key global cities. However, if nonskewed coverage of distant places is the measurement criterion, then the emergence of tourist journalism, festive television events, the televisualizing of diplomacy (and warfare), the closure of discourse by normalizing one set of discourses and practices (those acceptable to Anglo-Americans), and the widespread public-relationsizing of journalist contacts must be seen as less than welcome developments. But for better or worse, this has become the nature of the new media environment, and by extension it now appears to be one of the given variables within foreign policy decision making.

Bibliography

Cohen, A. A., M. R. Levy, I. Roeh, and M. Gurevitch. *Global Newsrooms, Local Audiences.* London: John Libby, 1995.

Dayan, D., and E. Katz. *Media Events: The Live Broadcasting of History.* Cambridge, Mass.: Harvard University Press, 1992.

Greenfeld, L. *Nationalism: Five Roads to Modernity.* Cambridge, Mass.: Harvard University Press, 1993.

Hartley, J. *Understanding News.* London: Methuen, 1982.

Karim, K.H. "Covering the South Caucasus and Bosnian Conflicts: Or How the Jihad Model Appears and Disappears." In *The Global Dynamics of News Coverage and News Agendas,* edited by A. Malek and A. P. Kavoori. Stamford, Conn.: Ablex, 2000.

Louw, P. E., and N. Chitty. "South Africa's Miracle Cure: A Stage-Managed TV Spectacular?" In *The Global Dynamics of News Coverage and News Agendas,* edited by A. Malek and A. P. Kavoori. Stamford, Conn.: Ablex, 2000.

Louw, P. E. *The Media and Cultural Production.* London: Sage, 2001.

Neuman, W. R., M. R. Just, and A. N. Crigler. *Common Knowledge: News and the Construction of Political Meaning.* Chicago: University of Chicago Press, 1992.

Sadkovich, J. J. *The U.S. Media and Yugoslavia, 1991–1995.* Westport, Conn.: Praeger, 1998.

Said, E. *Covering Islam.* London: Routledge and Kegan Paul, 1981.

Shaw, M. *Civil Society and Media in Global Crisis: Representing Distant Violence.* London: Pinter, 1996.

Tuchman, G. *Making News.* New York: Free Press, 1978.

Van Ginneken, J. *Understanding Global News.* London: Sage, 1998.

Volkmer, I. *News in the Global Sphere: A Study of CNN and Its Impact on Global Communication.* Luton, U.K.: University of Luton Press, 1999.

Wallis, R., and S. Baran. *The Known World of Broadcasting News.* London: Routledge, 1990.

Westmoreland, W. C. *A Soldier Reports.* New York: Dell Books, 1980.

12

News—The Fleeting, Elusive but Essential Feature of Global Journalism

Arnold S. de Beer

The Origins and Definition of News

In the first section of this fourth edition of *Global Journalism* a number of issues have been addressed that affect journalists worldwide. However, at the end of the day, global journalism is all about news. But what does this elusive concept mean? What does it consist of, how can one define it; will there be universal acknowledgment if such a definition should exist? As Mowlana (1997, p. 41) puts it: "The definition of news in many studies falls short of a comprehensive and universally accepted definition. In fact, there is doubt whether there can be a definition of what constitutes news which will be acceptable to all."

The purpose of this chapter is to shed some light on the concept of news and to come to grips with some of the main elements of this elusive term as it is found in international journalism, especially in foreign reporting.

Over the years media scholars and media sociologists have applied their minds to this intangible concept. The approaches range from the functional to the critical, from the biblical (the four apostles being the first great journalists of the present era) to the Marxist (news is produced by the bourgeoisie to enslave the proletariat; see Mowlana 1994, pp. 353–368). Over the past three to four decades a number of scholars have tried to shed more light on the term *news*. There were those who believed that news is made or *manufactured* (Cohen and Young 1973; Roscho 1975; Tuchman 1978), and those who described how news is *discovered* (Schudson 1973), *decided upon* (Gans 1979) or *selected* (Epstein 1981). Although not necessarily dealing with news as such, there were studies showing how difficult it is to *capture* the (news) reality. For instance, news is only the *reflection* or the image of a pseudo-event (Boorstin 1971), and even then it is a question of how *real* or true the reflection is (Watzlawick 1977).

Other authors searched for the basic fundamental principles underlining news, including issues such as *news values* and *news criteria* (Cohen and Young, 1973; Merrill 1997). Almost a century ago the German sociologist Max Weber discussed the role and function of journalists as *disseminators of ideas* in the form of news. A fellow sociologist, Albert Schäffle (1979) studied how people organize the *reproduction of symbols* (the unique feature of human civilization and the external reflections one perceives) in economically feasible and profitable enterprises called newspapers (Hardt 1979).

Media and journalism theorists also tried to explain the idea of news by developing theories of the mid-range. These include Elisabeth Noelle-Neumann's *spiral of silence* (2001) and models such as "agenda setting," "uses and gratifications," "information-seeking," and "gatekeeping" which try to explain how news *works* in society (see McQuail and Windahl 1981).

The question of what news is exactly, and how to define it in precise terms, was still not answered satisfactorily by the turn of the present century, as the special editions of *Journalism Quarterly* ("How News Is Shaped" [2000, 77:2] and "How News Is Constructed" [2001, 78:3]) testify.

On the other hand, all journalists and consumers of news do have a basic, or almost instinctive, notion of what news is, as the following short discussion of the history of news will show. However one looks at news, especially the international version of it, the idea, if not the modern concept, of news can be found throughout the centuries. According to most sources, *news* (new information of topical interest) first appeared on a regular basis in the West when Julius Caesar had a written version of the Senate discussions, called the *acta senatus*, posted on the Forum outside the Senate building for the citizens of Rome to read. At the same time (A.D. 59) Caesar ordered the daily posting of the *acta diurna* (daily acts). The contents of the *acta diurna* was amazingly similar to the news in modern-day newspapers: about Caesar as head of state, about his family, birthdays and funerals of important Romans, trials and executions, wars, and even sports—the outcome of gladiatorial contests. A number of transcriptions were sent to other parts of the Roman Empire, making it the first kind of international newspaper (though it contained only official information).

It was not long before an enterprising Roman named Chrestus began collecting local and international information (from ships landing with merchandise to sell, to bumper crops, to the burning of witches at the stake) and selling these handwritten "newspapers" in local markets. He thus became one of the first journalists (from the Latin *diurnarius,* diary writer). Not unlike today, politicians and other important Romans, such as the writer Cicero (who died in A.D. 43), were very upset about the "sensational" news that Chrestus often "published" in his "newspapers." (For a more detailed description of the early development of international or global news, see Luykx 1978.)

The first regular daily and weekly newspapers with local and international news appeared in the eighteenth century in Germany. As far as can be established, the very first doctoral dissertation on news (and especially international news) printed in newspapers appeared in 1690, when a German student, Tobias Peucer, published his doctoral dissertation *De Relationibus Novellis* ("On News Reporting") at the University of Leipzig. Apart from a cynical (but often correct?) definition of news being information to *satisfy the curiosity of people . . . by* (publishing) *unimportant and downright worthless material* (think about the news of modern-day international celebrities in the tabloids), Peucer also defined news as the *notification of a variety of matters that occurred recently in various places in the world* (see de Beer, Van Ryneveld, and Schreiner 2000, p. 9; see also Atwood and de Beer 2002). People's desire to learn things unknown to them (or *thirst for the latest information,* as Peucer puts it) was such that even 300 years ago, newspapers fulfilled the role of answering the basic question in journalism as researched by Peucer: *Ecquid novi?* ("What is new?" or "What is the news?" For a translation of this part of Peucer's dissertation, see de Beer, Van Ryneveld, and Schreiner 2000, p. 57).

Part of the problem of finding a generally accepted version of what news is has been the trend in journalism circles for the past few decades to regard the practice of journalistic skills as more important and relevant than the development of sound conceptual and theoretical foundations of what actually constitutes news. Sometimes it seemed that journalists who could type fast and reach deadlines under pressure were more valued than those who would first stall the story to consider newsworthy issues on a more abstract and theoretical level (even if this was done for a mere few seconds of reflection; see later the discussion under "News values"). Consequently, since there are no hard and fast rules of exactly what defines news, journalists tend to familiarize themselves with the concept of news and related aspects such as newsworthiness and news values through a process of "osmosis" or newsroom socialization (Breed 1956; Tuchman 1978). The theoretical study of news therefore often becomes quite esoteric, leaving journalists without credible criteria with which to define the concept *news.* (See later the discussion on *news values.*) As a result, although the planning, gathering, processing, distributing, and need for news as a specific variety of information have evolved on a high level over the past few decades, especially on a technical-practical level, academic journalism and the scientific analysis of the fundamental mechanisms of news still need to come to pass.

As foretold by Alvin Toffler in *Future Shock* (1977), Western civilization's most basic activity in the twenty-first century—communication—has been the subject of radical and fundamental transformations and alterations, as the third wave of change, the *Information Revolution,* came into existence (Toffler 1980). The arrival of the agricultural age (the first wave of change) and the launch of the second wave (the Industrial Revolution) paved the way for the third wave, in which the development of electronic superhighways and information applications such as news have an impact on every level of everyday human activity. Naturally, these changes have influenced the media as a primary source of information (e.g., McQuail 2000, Chapter 6). Journalism researchers, teachers, and students, therefore, not only should be versed in the art of technical journalistic competencies (such as finding, writing, and editing the news), but also should contribute to the science of journalism by conceptualizing and confronting communication challenges and problems on theoretical and critical levels. It remains an essential and often elusive ideal to educate potential journalists, and especially foreign correspondents, not only in the practicalities of news but also in the *scientific analysis* of news and all its related complexities. This is what this book purports to do.

One of the main problems media executives struggle with is how to present international news to audiences who are not really interested in news events occurring in countries whose names they cannot even spell. Another problem executives have to deal with is how much "uninteresting" global news they can afford to publish without losing their audiences and profits (see, for instance, Hoge 1997; Seaton 2002; Shaw 2002). For example, researchers at Media Tenor, an international institute for media analysis, cite and analyze which stories are deemed more newsworthy than others, according to frequency in coverage and the tone in which individual stories are written and published. Year after year they find that in most Western countries international news takes a back seat to national and local news (see www.mediatenor.com; Malek and Kavoori 2000; McCombs 1997 on the issue of the media's agenda-setting function).

However, so-called "bad news" (see Glasgow University Media Group 1976) or events of conflict (see Gilboa 2002), such as the attack on the World Trade Center in New York City on September 11, 2001, is always *big* news, especially when they are events that can be described and shown on television in detail (such as floods in Western Europe or the burning of forests in Australia in 2002–2003). On the other hand, trends, such as the HIV/AIDS epidemic or famine, are more difficult to relate as news. This is demonstrated time and again by Media Tenor analyses of different media in countries such as the United States, the United Kingdom, and Germany. Foreign news is placed on the backburner unless it is related to events such as those described above (bad news events) or sporting events, such as the Olympic Games and the Soccer World Cup (see *Media Tenor Quarterly* 2002, no. 2 at www.mediatenor.com).

Even so, news about the societal impact of sex workers, violence, and drugs; the role of the Internet in society and its effect on news; the relationship between news, terror, and conflict; and gender issues are recent trends that have made headlines (Bromley and Bowles 1995; Kamalipour and Rampla 2001; Ojajävari 2001; Schechter 2002). As Fulton (1998, quoting from Neil Postman) argues, it is not so much the topics of news themselves that cause problems but rather the way journalists see and experience news and the way media organizations present news to their audiences. In this regard Postman argues that journalists have not adapted to the world they helped create. In the nineteenth century the problem facing journalism was the scarcity of information. Today the problem is a glut of information. The question is no longer how to get more diverse forms or topics of news in the media but how to decide what is significant and relevant information for the news process and how to get rid of unwanted information that will not make it to the news columns and broadcasts (Fulton 1998).

The Concept: News

As we have seen, defining the phenomenon of news is not an easy task. News does not exist in reality outside of the individual and therefore does not qualify as an occurrence or event *per se*. Within the Western context, news is regarded as the reporting in the media of actual issues and events that occur before, during, or after actual incidents transpire.

However, news as a *concept* is not synonymous with an event. Instead, news can be seen as an attempt by individual journalists and their media organizations to capture the essential framework of particular events and trends by *retelling* them in the form of news reports. Such exercises are usually carried out by journalists working within the context of specific news policies defined by particular cultural, political, economical, ethical, and journalistic frames of reference. The latter are constructed by means of various factors that may include the nature of the publication, the policies of the institution, the policy of what is considered newsworthy or of special news value, the editorial organization of the publication, the quality of competition with other forms of media, the demographic profile of the readers, and the accompanying wants and needs of the publication's audience. All these elements should then again be considered against the background of societal forces, such as the political, economic, cultural, technical, geographic, and general media setup of a particular country (Hiebert, Ungurait, and Bohn 1991; see, for instance, Wilson and Gutiérrez 1995 on the way race and culture have an impact on what becomes news and what does not).

Clearly, news cannot be reduced to a one-dimensional formula of practical knowledge and practices (such as the "definition" of news being that "when a dog bites the mailperson it is not news, but when the mailperson bites the dog, it is"). Our presence within the information age demands solid practical training in journalism, as well as journalistic scholarship with appropriate academic-theoretical approaches. Consequently, scholars of news often view the topic from their own specific paradigmatic point of view and treat it within a particular context, such as the Glasgow University Media Group's range of projects on *bad news* (see also Eldridge 2000).

One rather easy way to solve the problem of what exactly one means by the word "news" is to consult a dictionary. *The South African Oxford Pocket Dictionary* (Branford 1994, p. 640) defines news as "information about important or recent events, when published or broadcast." This seems simple enough, but it does not address all the questions raised by such a definition. The *Dictionary of Communication and Media Studies* (Watson and Hill 1997) defines news as the construction of reality by means of a production process providing "a familiar discourse, based on common sense and precedent."

Newspaper people also have their own versions of what news is. The British press baron Lord Northcliff once declared, "News is what somebody somewhere wants to suppress; all the rest is advertising," while a news scholar, such as Dennis MacShanj, sees news as "conflict; hardship and danger to the community; the unusual (oddity, novelty); scandal and individualism based on the latter attributes of news" (Watson and Hill 1997).

Or perhaps news can be defined by a very simple notion: "News is what newspaper men make it," as Gieber (1964, p. 180) wrote. But—and this is an important point in our quest for more knowledge about the concept of news—Gieber concludes that while news might be what newspaper people make it, "Until we understand better the social forces which bear on the reporting of news, we will never understand what news is" (Gieber 1964, p. 180).

We will now discuss a few of the approaches used by media scholars to understand and describe news.

Objectivity and Reality

One way to describe news is to aver that it is an "objective" account in the media of a recent newsworthy event or trend. The Western journalistic tradition is one that, for the past century, has prided itself on practicing a custom that is based purely on objective news analysis and presentation. It is the journalistic claim that professionalism is seated within the ability to objectively judge and report on newsworthy events (Janowitz 1975, p. 618). According to this traditional perspective of objectivity, the journalist is an impartial observer who gathers, processes, and imparts news in such a manner that it can be vividly and concretely verified by the sensory capabilities of his or her readers (Atkins 1977, p. 27).

Although objectivity developed into the foremost trait to empower journalists (Tuchman 1978, p. 123), it is notable that journalists (and others) show very little awareness of what the concept truly entails. Objectivity in journalism has not necessarily established itself as a professional standard per se, but rather has developed as a kind of organizational imperative or belief by which journalists are required to perform their work. In reality, objectivity does not equal a professional tradition. Instead it frequently involves a routine post hoc rationale by which journalists justify their professional behavior and activity.

For practical as well as academic journalism, the problem of objectivity presents two cumbersome questions: How do journalists evaluate news within reality, and what are the impact and the degrees of influence within reality that impinge on such evaluations?

Within the science of communication (and for a large part also within practical journalism) it has been suggested over the years that objectivity in journalism cannot qualify as a positivistic, verifiable concept (Drew 1973; Atkins 1977). As proposed by Cillié (1967, p. 5), journalism does not exist as a neutral or objective mirror image of reality as it often chooses to claim: "The newspaper, seen in its totality, is far more related to a portrait, an impressionistic portrait, than a mirror or a photo image. We select and accentuate; we cannot do otherwise."

For this reason researchers (Rivet 1976, p. 96) have concluded that objective journalism is not possible—that in fact it is a myth (Sigelman 1973, p. 133)—indicating that journalists move between two antagonistic poles (Hemánus 1976, p. 102). On the one hand, there exists the inclination to report on reality in compliance with each individual journalist's value system (De Fleur 1973, pp. 155–172). On the other hand, the pressures of factual circumstances influence the value systems and world views of journalists as they present themselves within the reality in which the journalists find themselves, and vice versa (Snyman 1994). Therefore, one can assume that each journalist's interpretation of a news event is just as subjective as the reader's version of an article at the time it is read (Rosengren 1978, p. 42). One reason for this is that the journalist essentially decides what should and should not be perceived as news but always within the news policy of the media he/she works for and the circumstances surrounding the story (e.g., being in a war zone or working under political pressure). It is suggested, then, that the arrangement (and omission) of facts on a news page or news broadcast reveals its author's opinions and intentions, as well as those of the news medium and the society in which the journalist operates.

Another basic difficulty in the process of structuring news is that the words used to convey and symbolize meaning are by nature haphazard. As stated by Richards (1936, p. 69) and Brooks (1978, p. 64), words themselves do not have meaning, but humans as communicators attribute meaning to words according to social and psychological factors. Each reader of a news article will also assign his or her own interpretation of its content—the principle of the so-called "active audience" such as encapsulated in Hall's (1981) model of the encoding and decoding model, later applied in a classic study by Morley (1980) on the British program *Nationwide*.

For the disciplines of journalism and mass communication, the issue of objective, impartial reporting on the one hand and subjective, partial treatment of news events on the other thus involves an especially delicate and problematic situation.

News Values

Another way to look at news is to identify the different news values that constitute news. These "values" are the "professional codes used in the selection construction and presentation of news stories in corporately produced press and broadcasting" (O'Sullivan, Hartley, Saunders, and Fiske, 1983, p. 153). As the old adage says, "Old news is no news." Therefore, in journalism variables such as time and distance play significant roles in what does and does not constitute news. As Christians (1981, p. 64) puts it: "In reporting there is a premium on rapid decisions rather than on extended deliberation, on response rather than reflection. The person (journalist) of action is valued; the intellectual is frequently suspect." From this, one could conclude that Christians advocates that journalistic practices be orientated toward systematically investigating substantive issues, so as to gain more informed insight into the prevalence of such realities. The practice of merely processing information into news before a certain deadline is reached should be abandoned.

The German sociologist Albert Schäffe already wrote in 1881 (see Hardt 1979, p. 68) that the typical journalist lives only for day-to-day news and often feels and ponders on issues as the result of routine and mechanistic requirements of the trade, rather than critically developing and materializing intellectual thoughts. "News values such as its other *sister concept—new—are ambiguous."* As Hall (1973, p. 181) stated: "News values are one of the most opaque structures of meaning in modern society. All journalists are supposed to possess it; few can or are willing to identify and define it." Yet, Hall argues, of the millions of events that occur around the world, only a very tiny portion become salient as "potential news stories." Of this small portion, a smaller fraction is actually produced as news.

A number of authors of journalism textbooks have made lists of news values that they believe constitute news. An example is that given by Harriss, Leiter, and Johnson (1992, pp. 27–33). According to these authors, the intrinsic characteristics of news values are:

> Conflict (tension, surprise)
> Progress (triumph, achievement)
> Disaster (defeat, destruction)
> Consequence (effect of individuals or community)
> Prominence (the well-known or famous)
> Novelty (the unusual or emotional)

In their groundbreaking work on foreign news, Galtung and Ruge (1965) identified nine elements or news factors that make up news selection, and these are still applicable today. These are:

> *Time span*: The event should best fit the time schedule of the news medium.
>
> *Intensity or threshold value*: Magnitude or sudden increase in the normal level of events.
>
> *Clarity/lack of ambiguity*: A story with clear facts would rather be published.
>
> *Cultural proximity or relevance*: The closer the event, the better.
>
> *Consonance*: Stories that are "expected"—for instance, corruption in certain countries—are more likely to be selected.
>
> *Unexpectedness*: The more unusual or unpredictable (also the reverse of consonance) will add to a story's news value.
>
> *Continuity*: Once a story is "running" there will be some momentum to carry it further.
>
> *Composition*: News stories should normally fit the overall balance of the medium.
>
> *Sociocultural values* of the society and the gatekeepers at the particular news medium.

These news values should be tied with the traditional journalistic 5 Ws and the H, or as Peucer showed 300 years ago (de Beer et al., 2000, p. 17):

> The character in the event (who)
> The event itself (what)

The cause (why)
The place (where)
The time (when)
The manner (how)

Elsewhere, de Beer (2000, p. 257) has combined the different news values cited in journalism textbooks in a Distance-Intensity Scale: the nearer the news event and the higher the intensity of the event, the bigger the news value would be:

Distance Scale
Time (the closer to the event, the higher the news value)
Proximity (ditto)
Sociopsychological (ditto)

Intensity Scale
Status quo (the bigger the impact on the status quo, the bigger the news value)

Magnitude (single/plural; for example, one important politician versus many people dying in an accident)

Novelty (human interest, unusual events)

The higher the event scores on all or a number of these values, the more likely will the event "become" news. For instance, Iraq is quite far from the United States, but when loved ones are sent off to war in that region, it becomes very close in terms of the sociopsychological scale for people living in the United States. One general dying in such a war will be big news, bigger than the death of one GI. But a thousand GIs dying in one clash is likely to overtake the "story" of the general's death in terms of news value. And if one GI dies or saves a number of fellow GIs in an unusual event, this might also outstrip the death of the general on the news value scale. Fowler (1991, pp. 15–19, applied to the South African apartheid context by Oosthuizen 2001, p. 455) has pointed out that these news values are not ideologically neutral but can lead to a divisive view of society based on a distinction between "us" and "them," as was clear, for example, in the way different nations, organizations, media, and individuals viewed the U.S. stance on the war or invasion—depending on one's point of view—against Iraq in 2003 (see, for instance, McGuire 2003).

News Preferences

The quantitative [and empirical] evaluation of news [elements] is a potentially fertile field for journalistic investigation to get closer to this elusive concept. Whether the professional actually addresses the reader's news preferences is a particularly worthwhile inquiry. Are journalists aware of what their readers want to know? More often than not there appear to be disparities between what the professional journalist deems an appropriate view on reality and what the reader perceives as a suitable explanation of reality (Bagdikian, 1974, p. 134).

Reading Habits

Regardless of how the definition of news changes over the next few decades, the question that remains is whether people will in the future still satiate their informational hunger by getting "their news" through traditional media such as newspapers, news magazines, television, and radio.

The electronic age has introduced new modalities of communication, and the human activities that surround these innovations may also alter drastically (McQuail 2000). One of the biggest threats to the survival of the printed media is readers' lack of motivation to engage in the "trouble" of reading or their inability to do so. Edwin Yoder (1981, p. A18), senior editor of the *Washington Star*, wrote more than two decades ago that one of the main reasons for the death of this renowned institution was the public's increased inability to read. This condition has nothing to do with the fact that electronic media such as television package news in a more attractive form, but rather stems from the fact that these media present news in an ever-increasing condition of pseudo-knowledge (Boorstin 1971). In light of McLuhan's (1973) conception of *the medium is the message*, the illusion is created that by getting news from television one becomes more knowledgeable by looking at visual news images and listening to audio versions and that the need to read about these news events is becoming more and more obsolete.

Related to this phenomenon is the increasing tendency among children to spend time in malls or at home playing video games rather than reading. In fact, Yoder (1981, p. A18) believes that the *Washington Star* probably perished because of the growing number of cultures in which reading is performed without comprehension. Therefore, it is of the utmost importance to research such issues as reading habits in order to ascertain whether news presented in the traditional media still has a place within modern-day society.

New News Concepts

If we accept that in the modern industrialized age news can still be regarded as a particular form of information, which modern humans need for their survival, there is still the open question of whether the concept of traditional news will remain the conventional standard in the decades to come, especially in international news. Such is the case with so-called *good news*, which is still commonly regarded as non-newsworthy. Instead, the focus of newspeople and news organizations, with regard to foreign news as well, still seems to center on conflicts, the negative, and the abnormal.

This above-mentioned tradition has its roots in the custom of qualifying news according to longstanding news values, such as timeliness, changes in the *status quo*, and the peculiarity of events that make it potentially newsworthy. Often the end product, when it finally reaches the receiver, is an incomplete, summarized, and superficial representation of reality. It also remains an open question whether the "bad news syndrome" will continue its reign. In a period in which the individual is overwhelmed by enormous amounts of information (Toffler 1980), it is essential to know whether the concept of conflict, rather than cooperation and harmony, will spur the making of a *good story*. Clearly, then, not only do news values need to be scrutinized, but also those themes that the profession considers newsworthy must be studied.

Training and Education in Journalism

An issue often mentioned when news is discussed is the training and education of journalists. South Africa offers a very clear example of this at the University of Natal, where Keyan Tomaselli and his group work very close to the lines taken by the Birmingham group. They consider news quite differently from, say, Potchefstroom, where for a number of years news was seen and dealt with in a very functional, pragmatic, and eclectic paradigm. In the same fashion, Rhodes's journalism department is very much a part of transformation processes in the country, and during the apartheid years news was not necessarily considered within an Anglo-American objective "style" (de Beer and Steyn 2002; de Beer and Tomaselli 2000; Steenveld 2002). In other words, students schooled in an anti-apartheid and transformational environment will have different views on news than those schooled within the apartheid or racist dogma (Jackson 1993; Louw 1993; Sanders 2000; Switzer and Adhikari 2000; see the special editions of *Rhodes Journalism Review* on racism in the media [2000] and the Internet [1995]).

But nowhere is a journalist's concept of news influenced more than in the way he or she is taught what is right and wrong, what is truthful and what is a plain lie. How far can one stretch the limits of one's own conscience (e.g., stealing a picture from a bereaved family in order to scoop competition with a front page photo)? At a weeklong seminar in the United States on media ethics, attended by the author of this chapter, one senior media ethics scholar produced what he called "the tool box of journalism ethics." One of his tools was the lie, which he argued could be used very successfully under certain circumstances. Obviously, his students will approach his concept of news differently from students who are taught always to seek the truth and never to knowingly lie. The problem with this issue is that journalism ethics research receives very little attention at most universities. However, Starck (2002, p. 142) shows that research supports the idea that students might think "more extensively and deeply" about ethical issues but that instruction does not change their moral values. The fact that journalism ethics receives relatively little attention at universities would also affect this.

Further complicating the issue is the question of whether there are ethical journalistic principles that may be universally applied when deciding on what is news and what is not. For instance, does the principle of truth-telling (see above) necessarily "resonate across cultures" (Starck 2002, p. 140)? For example, Starck (2000, p. 140) describes how leading journalism and ethics scholars struggled with this concept when Thomas Cooper came up with three potential ethical elements as "candidates for universal status": the quest for truth, the desire for responsibility, and the call for free expression. Over the years, media ethics scholar Clifford Christians (Christians, Ferré, and Fackler 1993) developed the idea of a community-based approach to media ethics. The basis of his argument is that the journalist should be led by a love for the human community in the form of *caritas* (*agape*) in searching for news. "We . . . are governed not by autonomous rationality, but by what we love most with our whole heart as whole persons" (Christians, Ferré, and Fackler 1993, pp. 194–195).

Snyman (1994) elaborates on this idea in his deontological approach to media ethics and in the concept of the *liefdevolle persoonsbehartiging* (in German, *personen detreuing*). There is no easy and direct translation for this concept, but in general it relates to concepts such as caring for the other, looking after the other, showing concern or having consideration for the other, and even promoting, serving, or furthering the needs and interests of the other. Even though it is not exactly the same, *persoonsbehartiging* closely relates to the concept of *personhood* (Christians, Ferré, and Fackler, 1993, pp. 194–195). However, Christians and his co-authors warn that a "communitarian" approach to journalism (based on personhood) might become "Orwellian at the point where other institutions so constrain the press that it ceases to bear its own fruit and merely shades another pasture" (Christians, Ferré, and Fackler 1993, p. 7).

Media ethics scholar John Merrill (1997) devised a definition that journalists could apply when reporting on their own country or other countries. According to Merrill (1997, p. 76), from a deontological departure of ethics and based on the TUFF outline, news stories should be Truthful, Unbiased, Full, and Fair. But this is not as easy as it seems. As Fuller (2001, p. 8) quotes Kovach and Rosenstiel, truth is the "first and most confusing principle of journalism." What might look like light at the end of the tunnel for one journalist might be an oncoming train for another, and in war, as in international news about wars, truth is often the very first casualty.

In fact, it is not only journalists working in the "real world" who struggle with what is news and what is not. Journalism teachers, researchers, and authors face the same problem. Academic research journals around the world also struggle with the concept of news and present to their readers updated results of the elements that are argued to make up the news. In this regard *Journalism and Mass Communication Quarterly* 2000 (vol. 77, no. 2) dealt with the topic of how news is shaped, while in 2002 (vol. 79, no. 1) the journal explored news content and consequences as special issue topics. Although coverage of international news can be traced back to the seventeenth century, unfortunately, relatively few research projects were turned into books (see, for instance, Fascell 1979; Hachten 1999; Malek and Kavoori 2000; also see the special edition of *Ecquid Novi*, 1997 [vol. 18, no. 2] on news flow).

One can also learn more about the content of news in a global or international context by looking at publications dealing specifically with news reporting from different continents and countries. (For example, see Harrison and Palmer 1986; Mkhondo 1993; Peterson 2000). Many of these studies relate to news flow projects (e.g., Malek and Kavoori 2000).

In the long run, international reporters and foreign correspondents will ask themselves (mostly by instinct), How does this event score on the news level scale?

Will my news medium, given its news policy (e.g., will it help sell the publication?) be interested in this story? Will other media carry the story or is it a scoop? Will it be possible to get the story out (of a war zone) in time to reach a deadline? And even with these questions answered in the positive, we have not yet touched on issues such as media freedom, media ethics, and media controversies dealt with earlier in this section in different chapters. That's the fascinating and elusive nature of news.

Bibliography

Atkins, G. In search of new objectivity. In *Mass Media Issues,* edited by L. L. Sellers and W. L. Rivers, 203–243. Englewood Cliffs, N.J.: Prentice-Hall, 1977.

Atwood, R. A., and A. S. de Beer. "The Origins of Academic News Research: The Case of Tobias Peucer's '*De relationibus novellis*' (1690)." *Journalism Studies* 2, no. 1 (2002): 485–496.

Bagdikian, W. H. "Professional Personnel and Organizational Structure in the Mass Media." In *Mass Communication Research: Major Issues and Future Directions,* edited by W. P. Davison and F. T. C. Yu, 122–141. New York: Praeger, 122–141.

Boorstin, D. J. *The Image: A Guide to Pseudo-Events in America.* New York: Athenaeum, 1971.

Branford, W., Editor. *The South African Pocket Oxford Dictionary of Current English.* Cape Town: Oxford University Press, 1994.

Breed, W. "Social Control in the Newsroom." *Social Forces* 33 (1956): 323–335.

Bromley, R. V., and D. Bowles. "Impact of Internet on Use of Traditional Media." *Newspaper Research Journal* 16, no. 2 (1995): 14–27.

Brooks, W. D. *Speech Communication.* Dubuque, Ia.: Brown, 1978.

Christians, C. G. "Journalism Ethics in a Double Bind." *Ecquid Novi* 2, no. 2 (1981): 61–68.

Christians, C. G., John P. Ferré, and P. M. Fackler. *Good News: Social Ethics and the Press.* New York: Oxford University Press, 1993.

Cillié, P. J. "Koerante en Koerantmense Vir Ons Tyd" (Newspapers and Newspaper People of Our Time). Unpublished paper, journalism seminar. University of Stellenbosch, 1967.

Cohen, S., and J. Young. Editors. *The Manufacture of News: Deviance Controversies, and Alternatives.* Englewood Cliffs, N.J.: Prentice-Hall, 1973.

de Beer, A. S. "The Professional Teaching of Journalism as a Science Approach: An Introduction." *Ecquid Novi* 16, nos 1 and 2 (1995): 3–52.

de Beer, A. S. "New Mirror in a New South Africa? International News Flow and News Selection at the Afrikaans Daily, *Beeld.*" In *The Global Dynamics of News: Studies in International News Coverage and News Agenda,* edited by A. Malek and A. P. Kavoori, 249–276. Stamford, Conn.: Ablex, 2000.

de Beer, A. S., and E. F. Steyn. "Towards Defining News in the South African Context: The Media as Generator or Mediator of Conflict." *South African Journal of Sociology* 27, no. 3 (1996): 90–97.

de Beer, A. S., and E. F. Steyn. Editors. "Focus on Journalism Skills." *Ecquid Novi* 23, no. 1 (2002). (Special issue)

de Beer, A.S., & K. G. Tomaselli. South African Journalism and Mass Communication Scholarship: Negotiating ideological schisms. *Journalism Studies* 1, no. 1 (2000): 9–35.

de Beer, A. S., L. F. Van Ryneveld, and W. N. Schreiner. "Leipzig: From Tobias Peucer's '*De relationibus novellis*' (1690) to *Ecquid Novi.*" *Ecquid Novi* 21, no. 1 (2000): 6–61.

De Fleur, M. L. *Theories of Mass Communication.* New York: David McKay, 1973.

Drew, D. G. "Attitude Toward a News Source, Expected Reporter–Source Interaction and Journalistic Objectivity." Ph.D. diss., Indiana University, Bloomington, 1973.

Eldridge, J. "The Contribution of the Glasgow Media Group to the Study of Television and Print Journalism." *Journalism Studies* 1, no. 1 (2000): 113–129.

Epstein, E. J. *News from Nowhere.* New York: Vintage, 1994.

Epstein, E. J. "The Selection of Reality." In *What's News: The Media in American Society,* edited by A. Abel, 119–132. San Francisco: Institute for Contemporary Studies, 1981.

Fascell, D. B. *International News: Freedom Under Attack.* London: Sage, 1979.

Fowler, R. *Language in the News. Discourse and Ideology in the Press.* London: Routledge, 1991.

Fuller, J. "Making the Truth an Idea That Journalists Can Believe Again." *Nieman Reports* 55, no. 2 (2001): 8.

Fulton, K. "A Tour of Our Uncertain Future." In *What's Next in Mass Communication?* edited by C. Harper. New York: St. Martin's, 1998.

Galtung, J., and M. H. Ruge. "The Structure of Foreign News." *Journal of Peace Research* 2 (1965): 64–90.

Gans, H. J. *Deciding What's News: A Study of CBS Evening News, NBC Nightly News, "Newsweek," and "Time."* New York: Vintage, 1979.

Gieber, W. "News Is What Newspapermen Make It." In *People, Society and Mass Communications,* edited by L. A. Dexter and D. M. White. New York: Free Press of Glencoe, 1964.

Gilboa, E., Editor. *Media and Conflict: Framing Issues, Making Policy, Shaping Opinions.* Ardsley, New York: Transnational, 2002.

Glasgow University Media Group. *Bad News.* London: Routledge and Kagan Paul, 1976.

Hachten, W. A. *The World News Prism: Changing Media of International Communication.* Ames: Iowa State University Press, 1999.

Hall, S. "The Determinations of News Photographs." In *The Manufacture of News: Deviance Social Problems and the Mass Media,* edited by S. Cohen and J. Young, 176–190. London: Constable, 1973.

Hall, S. "Encoding/Decoding." In *Culture, Media, Language,* edited by S. Hall, D. Hobson, A. Lowe, and P. Willis. London: Hutchinson, 1981.

Hardt, H. *Social Theories of the Press: Early German and American Perspectives.* London: Sage, 1979.

Harrison, P., and R. Palmer. *News Out of Africa: Biafra to Ban Aid.* London: Hilary Shipman, 1986.

Harriss, J., K. Leiter, and S. Johnson. *The Complete Reporter: Fundamentals of News Gathering, Writing, and Editing.* N.Y.: Macmillan, 1992.

Hemánus, P. "Objectivity in News Transmission." *Journal of Communication* 26 (1976): 102–107.

Hiebert, R. E., D. F. Ungurait, and T. W. Bohn. *Mass Media VI. An Introduction to Modern Communication.* New York: Longman, 1991.

Hoge, James F. "Foreign News: Who Gives a Damn?" Available: http://cjr.rog/year/97/6/foreign.asp. Accessed 1 October, 2002.

Jackson, G. S. *Breaking Story: The South African Press.* Boulder, Colo.: Westview Press, 1993.

Janowitz, M. "Professional Models in Journalism: The Gatekeeper and the Advocate." *Journalism Quarterly* 52 (1975): 618–626, 662.

Kamalipour, Y., and K. R. Rampal, Editors. *Media, Sex, Violence and Drugs in the Global Village.* Oxford: Rowman and Littlefield, 2001.

Louw, P. E. *South African Media Policy: Debates of the 1990s.* Bellville: Anthroppos, 1993.

Luykx, T. *Evolutie van de communicatie media.* Brussels: Elsevier, 1978.

Malek, A., and A. P. Kavoori. Editors. *The Global Dynamics of News: Studies in International News Coverage and News Agendas.* Stamford, Conn.: Ablex, 2000.

McCombs, M. "New Frontiers in Agenda Setting: Agendas of Attribute and Frames. *Mass Communication Review* 24 (1 and 2): 32–52.

McGuire, S. "What, Me Worry?" *Newsweek,* 3 March 2003, 10–14.

McLuhan, M. *Understanding Media: The Extensions of Man.* London: Sphere, 1973.

McQuail, D. *McQuail's Mass Communication Theory.* London: Sage, 2000.

McQuail, D., and S. Windahl. *Communication Models for the Study of Mass Communications.* London: Longman, 1981.

Merrill, J. C. *Journalism Ethics: Philosophical Foundations for News Media.* New York: St. Martin's, 1997.

Mkhondo, R. *Reporting South Africa.* London: James Currey, 1993.

Molotch, H., and M. Lester. "News as Purposive Behavior: On the Strategic Use of the Routine Events, Accidents, and Scandals." *American Sociological Review* 39 (1974): 101–112.

Morley, D. *The Nationwide Audience.* London: British Film Institute, 1980.

Mowlana, H. "International Communication Research in the 21st Century: From Functionalism to Postmodern and Beyond." In *Mass Communication Research on Problems and Policies. The Art* of Asking the Right Questions in Honor of James D. Halloran, edited by C. J. Hamelink and O. Linn. Norwood, N.J.: Ablex, 1994.

Mowlana, H. *Global Information and World Communication: New Frontiers in International Relations.* London: Sage, 1997.

Noelle-Neumann, E. *Journalism and Mass Communication Quarterly* 78 (Spring 2001).

O'Sullivan, T., Saunders D. Hartley, and J. Fiske. *Key Concepts in Communication.* London: Methuen, 1983.

Ojajävari, S. "From Talking Heads to Walking Bodies: Challenging the Masculinity of News. In *Contesting the Frontier Media and Dimension of Identity,* edited by U. Kivikuru, 209–225. Göteborg: Nordicom, 2001.

Oosthuizen, L. M. "A Critical Assessment of News." In *Media Studies,* edited by P. J. Fourie, 447–468. Lansdowne: Juta, 2001.

Peterson, S. *Me Against My Brother: At War in Somalia, Sudan, and Rwanda.* London: Routledge, 2000.

Richards, I. A. *The Philosophy of Rhetoric.* New York: Oxford University Press, 1936.

Rivet, J. Ecriture et journaliste: De l'opinion—événement, à l'opinion. *Communication et Information* 1, no. 2 (1976): 75–96.

Roscho, B. *Newsmaking.* Chicago: University of Chicago Press, 1975.

Rosengren, K. E. "Vertrekking in Het Nieuws: Methoden en Begrippen." *Massacommunicatie* 6, no. 2 (1978): 37–47.

Sanders, J. *South Africa and the International Media 1972–1979: A Struggle for Representation.* London: Frank Cass, 2000.

Schäffle, A. "The Nerves of Society." In *Social Theories of the Press: Early German American Perspectives,* edited by M. Hardt, 41–74. London: Sage, 1979.

Schechter, D. *Media Wars: News at a Time of Terror. Dissecting Media Coverage after 9/11.* Bonn: Innovatio, 2002.

Schramm, W. "The Nature of News." *Journalism Quarterly* 26 (1949): 259–269.

Schudson, M. *Discovering the News: A Social History of American Newspapers.* New York: Basic Books, 1973.

Seaton, E. "The Diminishing Use of Foreign News Reporting." Available: http://asne.org/ideas/seatonmoscow. Accessed 13 October 2002.

Shaw, D. "Foreign News Shrinks in an Era of Globalization." Available: http:///www.common-dreams.org/headlines, 2002. Accessed 13 October 2002.

Sigelman, L. "Reporting the News: An Organizational Analysis." *American Journal of Sociology* 79 (1973): 132–151.

Snyman, P. G. "Media Ethics: A Deontological Approach." *Ecquid Novi* 15, no. 1 (1994): 43–70.

Steenveld, L. Editor. *Training for Media Transformation and Democracy.* Grahamstown, South Africa: South African National Editor's Forum/Independent Newspapers Chair of Media Transformation, 2002.

Switzer, L., and M. Adhikari. "South Africa's Resistance Press: Alternative Voices in the Last Generation Under Apartheid." *Freepress* 24 (2000).

Toffler, A. *Future Shock.* New York: Random House, 1977.

Toffler, A. *The Third Wave.* London: Collins, 1980.

Tuchman, G. *Making News: A Study in the Construction of Reality.* New York: Free Press, 1978.

Watson, J., and A. Hill. *A Dictionary of Communication and Media Studies.* London: Arnold, 1997.

Watzlawick, P. *How Real is Real? Confusion, Disinformation, Communication. An Anecdotal Introduction to Communications Theory.* New York: Vintage Books, 1977.

Wilson, C. C., and F. Gutiérrez. *Race, Multiculturalism, and the Media: From Mass to Class Communication.* Thousand Oaks, Calif.: Sage, 1995.

Yoder, E. M. "Reasoned Dialogue of the Printed Word Remain Essential for Democracy. *The Washington Star,* 7 August 1981, A18.

Part II

The World's Regions

13

Western Europe

Lianne Fridriksson

Background and Historical Notes

While diversity remains a hallmark for the media of western Europe, several trends are evident. Along geographic lines, the nations of the north tend to have higher levels of readership, newspaper circulation, and penetration of new technologies than do the nations of southern Europe. (A map of western Europe is shown in Figure 13.1.) Although newspaper circulation is on the decline overall in western Europe, the nations of Scandinavia find levels remaining fairly stable. Effects of the European Union (EU) on the region's media are yet to be fully understood, but a number of EU initiatives are already in play. Broadcast deregulation in a number of western European nations has brought about a lively if sometimes chaotic challenge on the airwaves.

Concentration of media ownership remains an important and pressing concern. In a speech on World Press Freedom Day in 2002, Czech President Vaclav Havel warned that conglomeration might have serious and adverse effects. "Fifty years from now," he said, "the globalization process may be the biggest threat to freedom of expression. . . . There will be no direct political oppression and censorship, but there might be more complex issues, especially at the economic level, that may affect freedom of speech" (Hargreaves 2002). The media of Europe operate under the libertarian system, which was born in Europe between the time of the Reformation and the French Revolution. European nations rank among those with the highest levels of press freedom.

Many of the world's most respected newspapers and magazines are published in western Europe. *Le Monde* of France, *El Pais* of Spain, *Svenska Dagbladet* of Sweden, *Frankfurter Allegemeine Zeitung* of Germany, the *Times* of London, and the *International Herald Tribune* have long been global leaders in print news.

In most European nations, television developed as a public service rather than as a commercial industry, and therefore was viewed largely as an educational tool

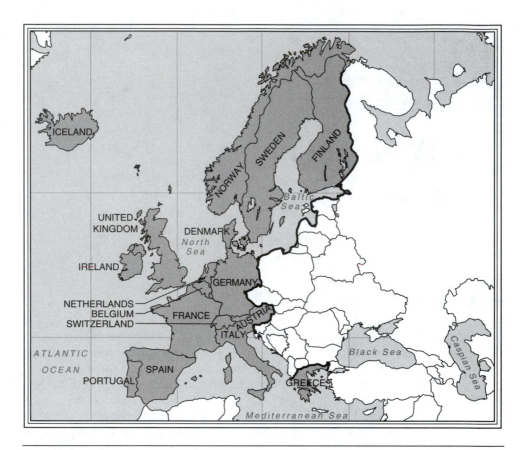

FIGURE 13.1 *Western Europe*

and as an information provider. Later, deregulation brought in commercial channels aimed largely at entertainment. European viewers generally are required to buy a television license, with costs ranging from country to country and with the revenues of those licenses funding public stations. European television overall saw one of its worst recessions in history at the start of the twenty-first century. Television advertising revenues at ITV in Great Britain, for example, fell 12 percent in 2002, the worst decline since commercial television broadcasting began in the country in the 1950s.

This downward trend has been evident in Germany and France as well, prompting some discussion as to whether traditional mass audience commercial television will continue to be a viable medium in the face of mounting competition from digital and cable ventures. Britain's ITV also had stiff competition from the British Broadcasting Corporation (BBC), the country's public service broadcaster, which is financed through license fees and therefore not dependent on advertising revenues to remain viable.

One possible outcome of a continued advertising revenue downturn would be more consolidation of media outlets. RTL, for example, based in Luxembourg and operating commercial television and radio channels in all of Europe's major broadcasting markets, is unique in its pan-European approach and is expected to continue to be a major player. Varying and complex national and regional broadcast regulations are significant barriers to further consolidation, however.

The clear leader in pan-European print journalism is the *International Herald Tribune*, founded in 1887 and headquartered in Paris. Begun by James Gordon Bennett, Jr., as the European edition of his *New York Herald*, falling profits and fierce competition have not diminished its reach (Balter 1996). Jointly owned by the *New York Times* and the *Washington Post* since the late 1960s, the *International Herald Tribune* has long enjoyed a strong reputation in journalistic integrity and excellence. The *Wall Street Journal Europe* was redesigned in 2000 and added color (as did its U.S. paper) in hopes of capturing more of Europe's business readership.

Newspaper publishers in the United Kingdom were looking into opportunities to establish a strong pan-European presence as well (Knox 1999). Although media mogul Robert Maxwell's *The European* newspaper folded in 1998, that did not inhibit Britain's Guardian Newspapers from launching *The Guardian Europe* in 1999 in an attempt to find a pan-European outlet. Published simultaneously in France and Germany, it offers a condensed version of its domestic newspaper product. The *Financial Times* also launched a German-language edition in 2000, a joint venture between the Financial Times Group and the mostly Bertelsmann-owned Grüner and Jahr.

European Initiatives

The Council of Europe has addressed four areas of concern with regard to mass media: (1) media and democracy; (2) pan-European mass media; (3) conflict and the media, including such topics as the protection of journalists and violence in the media; and (4) mass media and tolerance, including racial tensions (Goldberg, Prosser, and Verhulst 1998). Among the council's priorities concerning media are freedom of expression in audiovisual as well as print media, the development of pan-European policies and legal instruments, and seeing that media law and policies keep up with changes in technology and regulation. Goldberg and co-authors note that the European Convention on Human Rights has provided Europe with a media charter, and "through its protections for freedom of expression and privacy performs the role undertaken by constitutional principles and court decisions" in several national jurisdictions (p. 41).

Also addressing matters of press freedom, democratization, and broadcasting policy are the European Broadcasting Union, the Organization for Security and Cooperation in Europe, the European Platform of Regulatory Authorities, and the European Radiocommunications Office. In late 1997, the so-called "Green Paper" on telecommunications convergence sparked discussion on the regulation of European broadcast media in the twenty-first century. Its principles include limiting regulation to achieving necessary, clearly stated goals; considering the needs of media users; the existence of a clear and predictable framework to dictate possible regulatory decisions; the equitable and full participation of the public in an information society; and the use of effective, independent regulators (Goldberg, Prosser, and Verhulst 1998). The EU is discussed later in the chapter.

Government Subsidies

Subsidy schemes in a number of West European nations have sought to provide financial stability and assistance for media outlets as well as a competitive base for the diversity of news and opinion. Murschetz (1998) noted, however, that public austerity programs, increasing commercial challenges, changing tastes on the part of audiences, and inherent weaknesses in national programs have forced Austria, France, Norway, and Sweden to rethink their subsidy schemes. Most European nations, according to Murschetz, give some concessions on value-added taxes (VAT) or tariffs to their newspaper industries. While transportation assists are less frequent, postal breaks on mass communication are fairly common among European countries. Further information on subsidies by individual country is given later in the chapter.

Satellites

As original signatories to the agreement creating the 1964 International Telecommunications Satellite Organization (INTELSAT), the nations of Denmark, France, Italy, the Netherlands, Spain, and the United Kingdom, along with Vatican City, the United States, Japan, Australia, and Canada, were part of the world's first global satellite system. Four of the first five INTELSAT Earth stations were located in Europe as the world's first satellite, Early Bird, was launched in 1965. From these beginnings, Europe has maintained a high profile in numerous satellite systems. The European Commission confirmed that all private individuals in the EU should have the right to use satellite dishes without undue technical, administrative, urban planning, or tax obstacles (also see Higgins 2001).

Internet and Mobile Phone Penetration

In 2001, for the first time, Internet usage in western Europe surpassed that of the United States. Predicted increases in the number of European Internet users were expected to continue to surpass the United States through 2005. The number of on-line users in Europe is expected to reach more than 200 million, or 67 percent of the population, by the start of 2007, with the Scandinavian nations continuing to have the highest levels of on-line penetration. It is expected that Italy and France will see the most dramatic number of new users by 2007. Most European Internet users connect from either Germany or the United Kingdom, the two largest on-line populations in Europe. And most regular on-line users in Europe connect from home, with only about 13 percent of users having access from work alone. About half of the nearly 120 million European Internet users in 2002 were aged 35 or younger. The council formally adopted the .eu domain name in 2002.

Under the auspices of the EU, the Telecommunications Council has addressed the likelihood of trans-European telecommunications networks and the European Parliament continues to examine protections against what it terms illegal and harmful content on the Internet. The infrastructure for such an information society and the necessary regulatory frameworks continue to be high on the council's agenda.

The use of personal computers (PCs) and mobile phones also has grown across Europe. According to the International Telecommunication Union (ITU), the number of PCs in use in EU nations increased to 108 million users in 2000, while the proportion of mobile phone subscribers was 63 per 100 inhabitants.

The Business and Culture of Film

Europe's film industries fared well in the late 1990s and into the early twenty-first century, despite fierce competition from Hollywood. The top ten films in Europe in 2001, in terms of audience size, all were U.S. productions or coproductions, although 2001 was considered a healthy year for European filmmakers since overall, Hollywood accounted for only two-thirds of the EU market. In 2000, for example, European films accounted for only one-quarter of the EU market. France continues to be Europe's leading filmmaker, with a roughly 50 percent share of the domestic market, and such success has some impact on other European nations. As Waterman and Jayakar's (2000) economic model implies, "Increases in any one country's domestic consumer spending on theatrical films will increase the potential market for film producers in all countries" (p. 522). Europeans, however, do not see each other's films (Kemp 2002).

Experts have credited Europe's film resurgence since 2001 with the high quality of productions. But films such as the Franco-German production *Amelie of Montmartre* face an increasingly difficult challenge from Hollywood. Smaller, independent European films face an ever-increasing number of multiplex cinemas with distribution links to the major Hollywood studios, as well as increased concentration of U.S. ownership. Europe's filmmakers and distributors often cite the lack of an overall, pan-European distribution system, and the challenges of cultural and language fragmentation. In 2001, European film and audiovisual industries were given €1 billion in aid by the European Commission and the European Investment Bank Group. European films had met a steadily declining audience since the mid-1950s, a trend that began to reverse in the 1990s. The slump in the 1950s began with the introduction of television to the continent. Cinema box office receipts increased 80 percent between 1990 and 1998.

The Italian movie industry enjoyed moderate success in the 1960s and 1970s in the United States and abroad, and although Italian films lagged from the 1980s until about the mid-1990s, cinematic ventures from the country have shown signs of resurgence (Waterman and Jayakar 2000). Critics point to the successes of films such as 1998's *Life Is Beautiful,* which netted several Academy Awards and accounted for some of the highest box office receipts for any foreign film in U.S. history. In a study of spending by consumers in the United States and Italy on theater tickets, pay television subscriptions, videocassette rentals, and videocassette sales, Waterman and Jayakar found that U.S. successes were dependent on the country's rapid and sustained media development and attendant financial strengths, components found lacking in the Italian film industry. A joint venture between Bertelsmann and Arnoldo Mondadori Editore of Italy, which is part of the Italian Fininvest Group, combines the companies' Spanish-language distribution and book publishing in Spain and Spanish-speaking Latin America.

Dangers for European Journalists

Europe became a more deadly place for journalists trying to do their jobs in the 1990s and into the twenty-first century. One of the highest-profile murders of a journalist was that of Veronica Guerin, who reported on organized crime for Ireland's best-selling newspaper, the *Sunday Independent*, in Dublin. Famous throughout the country for her reporting about Dublin's underworld, she was the target of numerous death threats and attempts on her life. In 1996, a gunman linked to an organized crime boss pulled alongside her car on a motorcycle at a traffic signal outside Dublin and shot her six times, killing her.

In late 2001, Martin O'Hagan, an investigative reporter for Dublin's *Sunday World*, was shot to death outside his home. A Protestant paramilitary group claimed responsibility. Colleagues said that O'Hagan, an Irish Catholic, was targeted because he exposed their narcotics trafficking network and involvement in extortion and murder. In 1989, O'Hagan was kidnapped by the Irish Republican Army, which attempted to get him to reveal his news sources. He fled Dublin in the early 1990s following continuing death threats, and did not return until 1995, when most paramilitary groups had declared ceasefires. His death was the first reported fatality of a journalist covering the conflict in Northern Ireland. The Committee to Protect Journalists has noted that though physical attacks on journalists are rare in Northern Ireland, death threats and intimidation are common.

The killings and violent attacks against journalists and newspapers in Spain have garnered condemnation from the European Commission and other organizations. Those killings included the murders of several Basque journalists in Spain by the Basque terrorist group ETA, which has murdered more than 830 people in its 30-year campaign for Basque independence. ETA also has claimed responsibility for parcel bombs sent to prominent Spanish journalists in 2002. Although none of the journalists was injured, the European Commission said it was clearly an attack against freedom of the press in the country.

During the 2002 Group of Eight (G-8) summit meeting in Genoa, Italy, police and demonstrators attacked and beat journalists in several incidents. Nearly 85 police officers raided and ransacked the Independent Media Center, which was helping independent journalists file stories about the demonstrations, in which several journalists were beaten. A British reporter was seriously injured in the raid. The following day a group of demonstrators attacked journalists and television crews from Germany and Japan.

The work of European journalists outside the region continued to be dangerous. One of Spain's most famous war correspondents, Julio Fuentes of *El Mundo*, along with Maria Grazia Cutuli, who worked for the Italian daily, *Corriere della Sera,* were killed in late 2001 in an ambush in Afghanistan. The safety and freedom of journalists is high on the agenda of several European-based organizations. France, for example, is home to Reporter sans Frontiers (Reporters without Borders), an organization working to ensure fair treatment and protection of journalists around the world.

Historical Aspects

From the Greek science of rhetoric to Iceland's strong literary tradition to Gutenberg's printing press to the global reach of the Internet and burgeoning digital capabilities, the history of communication in western Europe has been one of innovation and determination. Europeans made many of the advances in the field of mass communication. The printing of books prospered in Europe after Johannes Gutenberg's 1450 invention of the printing press made mass publication and the circulation of literature possible. By the year 1500, an estimated 20 million books had been published for a largely illiterate population of 100 million. Public demand for books, the availability of paper, and new technological discoveries led to increased printing in Europe (Frederick 1993). By 1600, typical printing output was about 2,000 to 3,000 copies per title, but the cost of books was high, and it was mostly Europe's wealthy who could afford them. This trend continued into the early nineteenth century, when such inventions as the metal press, the foot-operated cylinder press, and the steam press made printed matter more affordable (Frederick 1993). Early information sheets were published in several German cities after Gutenberg's press, and by the seventeenth century, a number of other European cities had such circulars.

A strand of coated copper wire laid underwater between Dover, England, and Calais, France, in 1842 allowed American Samuel Morse to test the sending of electric impulses via a dual-wire device. Within nine years the device allowed the London and Paris stock exchanges to be connected (Cherry 1978). German Johann Philip Reis built the first telephonic instrument in 1861, although credit for the invention of the telephone more commonly is given to Alexander Graham Bell (Frederick 1993). Italian Guglielmo Marconi is credited with sending the first wireless radio signals in 1894, a system he patented in 1896 in London. By 1901, he was able to send a telephonic message across the Atlantic from England to Newfoundland. By the mid part of the nineteenth century, Germans Julius Reuter and Bernhard Wolff and Frenchman Charles Havas had each established news agencies. Reuter and Wolff worked for Havas at his Paris news service, founded in 1835—the world's first news agency. Eventually, the men agreed to pool their services to exchange news on a global basis, in essence dividing the world into three news regions.

Radio broadcasting began to flourish in Europe in the 1920s, with most radio outlets being run by national governments. These public service stations provided mostly informational and educational programming and were financed by government subsidies and radio set license fees. The same approach was taken with television, which began in Europe in the 1950s, also as state-run enterprises, with similar funding structures. Commercial, private radio and television stations, with entertainment-focused content, entered national markets as broadcasting was deregulated.

The European Union and Mass Media

The European Union and the process of European integration began in 1950 as a French initiative. This effort has raised the standard of living in member nations, built an internal market, and launched the euro currency. The six original members—Belgium, Germany, France, Italy, Luxembourg, and the Netherlands—were joined by Denmark, Ireland, and the United Kingdom in 1973, Greece in 1981, Spain and Portugal in 1986, and Austria, Finland, and Sweden in 1995. In 2002 the EU was preparing for the accession of 13 eastern European and southern European nations.

Michalis (1999) has argued that the EU has faced difficulty in creating regulations regarding European media content and culture, and instead has concentrated on the financial side of telecommunications and broadcasting. This framework will have far-reaching effects on the balance of power in the EU as well as implications for the development of the EU and its citizens. Michalis states that EU telecommunications policy has developed in three areas: (1) technological issues and industrial policy concerns; (2) the creation of an equitable playing field via an internal market; and (3) program initiatives that support the telecommunications industry. As well, the issue of European identity is a prime concern of the EU's research and policy agendas. The Economic Commission for Europe in 1987 recognized the importance and impact of digital communications when it indicated that investment in digital infrastructure was important as earlier investments in railways and electricity (Economic Commission for Europe 1987).

The EU's eEurope 2005 action plan aims to involve public and private sectors of member nations in an integrated trans-European information society. The eEurope 2005 plan is considered crucial for turning Europe into the world's most competitive and dynamic knowledge-based economy by 2010, otherwise known as the Lisbon Goal, according to Erkki Liikanen, Enterprise and Information Society Commissioner. The EU's eEurope 2002 plan focused on extending Internet connectivity across Europe, while the 2005 plan focuses on translating connectivity into improved economic productivity and improved quality of life for Europeans via better and more widely accessible broadband services. A 2002 agreement between the EU and China provided shared technology resources and gave Chinese researchers access to Europe's high-speed data-sharing network, GEANT. Media convergence, however, has largely been ignored by the EU, which has instead concentrated on telecommunications regulation with regard to broadcasting.

The adoption of a single European monetary unit, the euro, was expected to help not only the whole of the European market, but also advertisers. The differences between countries' broadcast advertising costs would account for ranges of success, however. Robertson (1999) said that television outlets in Spain, Italy, Portugal, and the United Kingdom would probably gain more advertisements than stations in Belgium and Austria because those four countries charge less for ads. At the start of the twenty-first century, the variance in charges to reach 1,000 consumers was broad, ranging from 6 euros in Portugal to 23 euros in Austria.

The European Commission, the EU's executive body, in 2001 proposed new directives to outlaw tobacco advertising in print, on the radio, on the Internet, and in the sponsoring of cross-border events, such as sporting competitions. Most EU members already have far-reaching prohibitions against the advertising of tobacco products.

The EU established daily radio broadcasts in the languages of Dari and Pashtu of a program transmitted to Afghanistan in 2002. Called *Good Morning Afghanistan,* the two-hour program is accessible to about 80 percent of the Afghan population. A coproduction of the Baltic Media Center, the European Commission, and Radio Afghanistan, the program is run by about 20 young Afghan journalists.

The European Institute for the Media, a nonprofit research organization based in Dusseldorf and Paris, studies the impact of the media's role in the process of European integration, in addition to media convergence, public interest aspects of new media, and the future of an information society. The notion of a European identity has yet to be engaged by European media, according to Cebrian (1999), who said that very few daily or weekly newspapers in Europe openly express a sense of European identity. "The only paper [that] could aspire to do so, with any chance of success, because of its global vocation, is, paradoxically, an American paper: the *International Herald Tribune,* published in English, naturally enough" (p. 39). The promotion of understanding between European natives and immigrants of different ethnic, religious and cultural groups is a responsibility of European media, Cebrian, publisher of Spain's *El Pais,* said.

National Media Profiles

The following summaries of each European nation's print and broadcast media reveal a number of trends, including (1) an overall decrease in the circulation of newspapers and general interest magazines; (2) an increase in the circulation of numerous special-interest magazines; (3) private and public ownership of broadcast outlets; (4) strong traditions of freedom of the press; (5) high readership levels in northern Europe and lower readership levels in southern Europe; and (6) increasing Internet, cable, satellite, and digital broadcast penetrations. With regard to digital television, agreements to merge competing digital platforms that have struggled to attract subscriptions were forthcoming in 2002. Old systems in numerous European companies were upgraded to digital at the start of the twenty-first century, with Spain, Sweden, and Finland at the forefront.

Austria

More than three million newspaper copies are circulated daily to Austria's 8 million residents, with more than one million of those distributed by *Neue Kronen Zeitung,* one of the country's two largest newspapers. Along with *Kurier,* these two dailies reach more than half the country's population. Concentration of ownership since World War II has left the country with a relatively small but stable number of newspapers at the start of the twenty-first century. Though regional newspapers are financially viable and continue to be strong contenders on the media market, regional editions of the *Neue Kronen Zeitung* either have taken the circulation lead or are as strong as regional competitors. *Neue Kronen Zeitung* has garnered attention "with an almost dadaist collage of stories fanning fears that Vienna is being swamped by undesirable refugees, editorials tinged with anti-Semitic innuendo, and articles trivializing the Holocaust," and has become "required reading" by the European Union's Monitoring Center on Racism and Xenophobia (Wise 2002). The tabloid staunchly defended former President Kurt Waldheim against charges of Nazi war crimes in the 1990s, and critics have called it "the house organ of the Austrian anti-Enlightenment" (Wise 2002). Since 1975, government subsidies have been granted to all daily newspapers at their request. The country tightened its cartel law in 1993, and according to Murschetz (1998) introduced obligatory controls over mergers, with some consideration for media, in that mergers must be declared to cartel authorities that can forbid mergers should they strengthen dominant market positions.

Strong regulations with few self-regulatory options characterize Austria's broadcast media. The Austrian Broadcasting Corporation, ORF, has no competition in television, with private TV channels limited to localities. Various federal institutions share control of the country's highly concentrated media markets, the most powerful being the Federal Chancellery, which is responsible for federal press subsidies, the licensing of private radio operators, membership on ORF boards, and participation in film and audiovisual production. ORF operates two television channels and four radio stations. Attempts at introducing more Austrian music content on radio have met with mixed results. A member of parliament as well as a petition by Austrian musicians, for example, in 1997 called for a 25 percent local quota system on ORF's radio station 03, the country's only national top-40 outlet. 03's programming director said that kind of percentage would be tough to meet, considering that Austrian labels were not producing enough material to increase local ratios on the station (Schuhmayer 1997). Beginning in about 1990, the market share of Austrian-produced music has been increasing.

Among the media organizations based in Austria are the International Press Institute (IPI), which chronicles violations of press freedom around the world, and the Association of United Nations Journalists. Austria has no institution or university program for the training and education of journalists, although theoretical courses in communication exist at several universities. For this reason, most journalists in Austria have degrees in fields other than journalism and generally are trained in journalistic skills on the job.

Belgium

Belgium is the most heavily cabled country in the world: about 95 percent of Belgian households with televisions also have cable. But unlike cable's success, newspapers have a low subscription rate, at about 35 percent of all households, and at the start of the twenty-first century, circulation figures were declining, though slightly. Ownership concentrations since the 1960s have left the country with fewer newspapers, and only 10 of the nation's 26 newspapers are independent. Of total circulation, Flemish-language newspapers account for about 65 percent of sales and French-language papers for about 35 percent. Recent trends show a decreasing readership among young people, and newspapers that have mounted circulation successes in recent years have done so by moving toward more sensational news coverage. Critics note that Belgium's media policies have been largely laissez-faire, with numerous media laws ambiguous and most policies ignoring increasing media ownership concentration. Direct media subsidies for Flemish newspapers ended in 1999, with only indirect assistance still in place.

Three public television broadcasters in Belgium serve three language audiences: VRT in the Flemish-speaking region of the north, RTBF for the French-speaking region in the south, and BRF for the German-speaking area. The country also has five public radio networks in Flemish as well as networks in French and German. Private television channels include VTM (news, games, and documentaries), Kanaal-2 (series and films), VT-4, from the United Kingdom, and TMF, a music channel. Private regional television and radio can be found in most provinces of the country. But Belgian television has lost numerous French-speaking viewers to French and Luxembourg channels and Dutch-speaking viewers to channels from the Netherlands. Pay TV is relatively untapped, with only one channel offering services in 2001. The number of personal computers and the rate of Internet access are low in Belgium compared with the rest of Europe.

Denmark

Continuing the high quality of their media products is foremost on the agenda of Danish media organizations at the start of the twenty-first century, in particular seeing that quality is ensured without foreign ownership, especially in cable and satellite broadcasting industries. The Danes' strong interest in international and national news has not helped to curb steadily declining newspaper readership, which surfaced shortly after World War II. Only 35 newspapers remain in the country, with three of these being large national broadsheets and two national tabloids. The country's largest newspaper is *Morgenavisen Jyllands-Posten*, with a circulation of about 180,000. Local and regional newspapers also have steadily declined in circulation. Newspapers were traditionally associated with political parties, and flourished until shortly after World War II. From a high of 155 newspapers in 1920 and 122 in 1945, Denmark lost nearly a quarter of its newspapers in the 1950s. As newspapers declined, so did party affiliations, and remaining newspapers were largely independent products. And, although the number of newspapers has fallen off sharply, overall circulation of the remaining papers has increased, leading to an extremely competitive newspaper market at the start of the twenty-first century. Only indirect subsidization of the press by government is available in Denmark, including postal breaks and tax exemptions. Training in print and broadcast journalism is available at the university level, most notably at the University of Aarhus, and through several institutes.

Danmarks Radio (DR), a public broadcasting organization, is the Danish version of the BBC—a dominant player in television and radio. But challenges have come from several other channels, including TV-2, which began in 1988 and is funded 80 percent by advertising and 20 percent by license fees. DR added a second satellite-only channel in response to competition. Several commercial, private channels, including Kinnevik's TV-3 and TV-3+, and TVDanmark, now operate. Foreign satellite channels account for less than 15 percent of Danish viewing, leaving Danish channels highly successful. Competition is nonexistent in Danish radio, with DR holding a terrestrial monopoly. Bondebjerg (1996) divided Danish television development into three distinct phases: first, a paternalistic period from 1951 to 1964, when information and education were emphasized; second, a public service period from 1964 to 1980, otherwise known as the golden age of television in the country, when DR developed into the country's central cultural and journalistic institution; and the final phase, which began in 1980 and is considered by Bondebjerg to be a mixed-culture period that began with the breakup of DR's monopoly. A commercialized and privatized media landscape marks this third phase.

Finland

With a circulation rate of 455 copies per 1,000 citizens, Finland ranks third in the world in newspaper readership. Although Finland is officially a bilingual country, Finnish speakers account for about 94 percent and Swedish speakers for 6 percent of the 5.2 million population. And, though its newspaper market is considered stable, it is also saturated, meaning the possibility for growth and for new publications is limited. Daily newspapers number 26 in Finland, the highest number in Scandinavia, with the highest circulation being that of *Helsingin Sanomat* in Helsinki at about 500,000 copies. An additional 75 or so newspapers publish between three and six issues per week. Conglomeration has been evident since the 1990s, and daily newspaper publishing is primarily the domain of three chains—Sanoma-WSOY, Alma Media Group, and Intermediate-Finland Media. About 2,750 magazines and periodicals were published in the late 1990s, with consumer magazines and trade or professional magazines representing the lion's share. Freedom of the press in Finland has been constitutionally guaranteed since 1919. Journalism education is available in Finland, with the University of Tampere offering a specialization in public relations as well.

The Finnish Broadcasting Company (YLE), owned almost wholly by the government, had a monopoly on television broadcasting when TV was introduced in Finland in 1955. The first radio broadcast was in 1923, and Finland's first national commercial radio station began in 1997. Reforms to television structure in the country occurred in 1993, creating a model of broadcasting characterized by the regulated competition of two broadcasters, one public and one private (YLE and the commercial MTV Finland).

One of Finland's telecommunications success stories has been that of Nokia, born in 1967 of a merger of a papermaking business, a cable manufacturer, and a rubber works company. The world's leader in mobile communications, its net sales in 2001 totaled $28.15 billion in more than 130 countries. Nokia manufactured the first car telephones for NMT, the first international cellular mobile phone network, which was introduced in 1981 in Scandinavia. In 1987 it produced the first hand-portable cell phone, but it was the introduction of digital technology to Europe in 1991 that accounted for its ultimate global success.

France

Even though one of the world's elite newspapers, *Le Monde,* which is edited in Paris, is located in France, the country has one of western Europe's weakest newspaper markets and a low per-capita readership. Nine out of ten adults in France do not read a national daily, and only about half read a local or regional daily (McMane 1994). The majority of French dailies publish in the morning, though *Le Monde* is an afternoon paper. Before World War II, most daily papers were aligned with political parties or ideological stands, but that no longer is the case. The combined circulations of *Le Monde* and the two other major dailies, *Le Figaro* and *Liberation,* total one million, with a readership of five million, but that is still much lower than figures in most of the rest of Europe. The country's second most popular national daily is *Le Parisien-Aujourd'hui,* with a circulation of about 500,000. The regional newspaper industry has fared better than the dailies, with a combined annual circulation of 2.2 billion and more than 400 titles. One of the few outright newspaper success stories in France was the arrival in the mid-1990s of free commuter publications (one owned by a Swedish company, the other by a Norwegian firm) aimed at Metro riders, which, along with daily newspapers, now account for 70 percent of Parisians reading while riding on the subways. France also has one of the highest levels of magazine readership in the world, with publications such as *Paris Match* and *L'Express* enjoying healthy circulations.

At the start of the twenty-first century, however, it was unclear whether France's broadcast industry was faring much better than its print media. In 2000 French citizens were watching television for an average of three hours and 20 minutes a day, but were spending only 30 minutes reading newspapers or magazines. Commercial television began in France in 1982, and within 10 years, the number of channels had grown from three to more than 30. But by 2002 three of France's leading commercial television stations had issued profit warnings, with net incomes expected to fall about 10 percent from the previous year. And after telecommunications revenues peaked in early 2000, the profits of Vivendi Universal and France Telecom, then the country's largest business, fell dramatically, and by mid-2002, the two companies were facing a growing lack of investor confidence. Recession left most media outlets suffering setbacks in 2002, with national daily press profits falling 21 percent, film profits by 11.4 percent, radio down by 8.5 percent, and television down nearly 6 percent. Reality television programming also has been a success, with programs such as *Loft Story*, the French version of *Big Brother*, garnering huge audience shares since it debuted in 2001. A French version of *Survivor* also has captured large viewing numbers. Vivendi's $372 million acquisition of the U.S. firm MP3.com, the Internet music portal, in 2001, followed its agreement with Japan's Sony to create an on-line rival to Napster, which has formed an allegiance with Bertelsmann (Barnard 2001). Vivendi's chief executive stated that the acquisition was part of the company "becoming the world leader in on-line music distribution" (Barnard 2001).

Digital terrestrial television is in its infancy in the country, having begun in 1996. French President Jacques Chirac pressed the need in 2002 for a major French-speaking international news organization capable of competing with the likes of CNN or the BBC. Cable and satellite television programming accounts for about 10 percent of overall viewing in France. Canal Satellite, a multichannel package from Canal Plus, had nearly 800,000 subscribers in 1999. Canal Plus, begun in 1984, is the oldest of the independent television channels. By 2001 it had nearly eight million subscribers. Radio also has been popular in France, where there are now five national stations, 30 regional commercial stations, and 350 stations run by voluntary organizations. To protect French culture, the February 1994 law requires that a minimum of 40 percent of songs broadcast be sung in French. The world's most successful videotext system, French Minitel, which began in 1985, was the subject of concern over the rise of sexually explicit video services in the mid-1990s. Dupagne (1994) noted that, based on judicial precedent against the applicability of press legislation to broadcasting in France, French courts applied criminal laws in their efforts to penalize providers of allegedly pornographic message services.

The Conseil Superieure de Audiovisuel (CSA) performs a number of functions with regard to France's television industry. Most important, CSA functions as the manager of the French quota system, in which 50 percent of airtime (for fictional shows) is allotted to programs produced in France (Feigenbaum 1998). Through the Television Without Borders directive of the EU, France has advocated an EU quota of 60 percent for European-produced products. CSA also manages frequency spectrum allocations and has the power to impose sanctions on broadcasting networks that violate CSA regulations. Some scholars have noted that the CSA increasingly resembles the operations of the Federal Communications Commission (FCC) in the United States.

Journalistic exposés of corruption in the French government during the mid-1990s shook the "political elite and the news industry to their roots" (Hunter 1995, p. 40). A series of nearly monthly reports on political scandals possibly led to the suicides of two of then President François Mitterand's close associates, as well as to illegal wiretaps on a French reporter and to a trend of using anonymous sources. Former Prime Minister Pierre Beregovoy reportedly committed suicide in 1993, after he was implicated in a court case for which Mitterand publicly blamed the "dogs" of the press (Hunter 1995, p. 41). Media critics in the country have blamed the fact that the government owns four of the seven French television networks for the increasing difficulty in practicing investigative journalism in the country.

One of the earliest French press exposés concerned the direct involvement of the French government in the bombing of the Greenpeace flagship *Rainbow Warrior* in New Zealand in 1985, and the death of one of the organization's photographers in the blast. Greenpeace had been protesting French nuclear testing in the South Pacific at the time and was evacuating civilians from possible contamination in Moruroa Atoll when French government agents attached two bombs to the ship.

Hunter cited an alarming trend in the 1990s in which French courts and the French political elite changed the journalistic legal climate in France. But political criticism and satire can be traced to earlier publications, including *Le Bavard*, a weekly satiric publication, which, despite heavy criticism, successfully lampooned French politicians and government officials (Collins 1996).

Germany

As is the case with most of Europe, Germany's newspapers have declined in number and circulation since the 1990s, although many regional and local publications have remained stable. Several national newspapers, including the widely respected *Suddeutsche Zeitung* and *Frankfurter Allegemeine Zeitung,* account for about 1.6 million of Germany's 31 million circulation. Axel Springer Group accounts for the largest newspaper market share, at nearly 24 percent. Nearly 800 general magazine titles circulate about 127 million copies in the country. Bertelsmann's liberal and investigatory *Der Stern* remains a leader, although circulation has dipped since the start of the twenty-first century. Both public and commercial concerns compose Germany's broadcasting structure, and the states of the republic are responsible for broadcasting within their borders, with the exception of Deutschlandfunk (DLF) and Deutsche Welle (DW), whose responsibilities are to provide non-German audiences with news and information. Each state offers three to five radio channels. Commercial concerns in broadcasting began in the mid-1980s. German commercial television has been controlled primarily by two media conglomerates, KirchMedia and Bertelsmann.

The collapse of KirchMedia in 2002 reverberated across Europe, although the long-term effects of the failure were unclear. In operation for nearly five decades, Kirch held broadcasting rights for such telecasts as the German soccer league, Bundesliga, and Formula One car racing. The Center for European Policy Studies in Belgium stated that the bankruptcy would have a deep and lasting impact on Germany's media landscape, in particular in the area of media management practices. Rupert Murdoch and Silvio Berlusconi, Italy's prime minister and largest media owner, were looking into buying Kirch's media assets after the collapse, and if either is successful, it will mark the first time a non-German mogul would be a prominent player on the German media market. Murdoch's BSkyB pay-TV enterprise already held a large stake in Kirch pay TV.

Bertelsmann, which began in 1835 publishing Christian hymnals, quickly expanded to produce newspapers and general literature, and later LP records. It branched out into the United States in the 1970s when it acquired Arista Records and the Parents Magazine publishing group. By 1986 Bertelsmann had acquired RCA Records and Doubleday publishing, and in 1998 it purchased Random House. Nearly 70 percent of its business is conducted outside of Germany. It employs 82,000 people in 56 countries, and its annual revenues are about $18 billion (Martin 2002).

Greece

A steady decline in the annual number of newspaper copies sold per person in Greece left that average at about 24 copies at the start of the twenty-first century, with the majority of these being political newspapers. Diversification has been the hallmark of the Greek magazine scene, with general-interest magazines falling behind special-interest publications. By the mid-1990s the number of Greek magazines had doubled to 800, although magazine sales per person had fallen to about nine issues per person at the start of the twenty-first century.

Deregulation of the broadcast industry in the late 1980s led to both public and private ownership and control of multiplying television and radio outlets. Papathanassopoulos (2001) noted that Greece's rapid deregulation and attendant commercialization had some adverse implications for journalism in the country. One of those effects, he said, was diminished coverage of government news, foreign news, and investigative stories and an increase in coverage of police and crime news.

Greek media came under critical fire throughout the 1990s when, in attempts to increase their audiences and readership, they published or broadcast waves of stories dealing with rising crime rates, particularly violent crimes committed by immigrants (Mitropoulos 1999). Sensational prime-time coverage more resembled entertainment series than news, with the inclusion of "ominous music, reenactments and special effects imported from American television" (Mitropoulos 1999). Broadcasters subsequently tamed their coverage of crimes by immigrants, although the sensational nature of evening news programs remained.

The first two private television channels, Mega and Antenna TV, began broadcasting in 1989, to compete against the country's two national channels, ET-1 and NET, and the single regional channel, ET-3. By 2002 approximately 160 private TV channels were operating in the country. A burgeoning number of unlicensed private radio stations have created a state of chaos on the airwaves. Public stations include four national radio channels, one world service station, and 19 regional channels, with competition from about 1,600 private local and regional stations. Legal frameworks and policies regarding broadcasting have helped bring some organization to the disarray. But higher pay and improved working conditions for the nation's reporters have remained a problem, prompting widespread protests and nationwide strikes by Greek journalists. By mid-2002 journalists and newspaper owners had reached an agreement for salary increases and a five-day instead of a six-day working week. National debates concerning broadcast media focused on media concentration of ownership at the start of the twenty-first century. Papathanassopoulos (2001) said the audiovisual market in Greece now resembles its print media in that "there are too many stations for such a small market" (p. 509). All television stations, he said, face severe financial problems.

In 2002 the National Council for Radio and Television in Greece attempted to suspend broadcasts of two popular reality television programs appearing on Antenna and Mega, including *Big Brother,* for violating laws of public decency, although critics charged that both shows were tame compared with Greece's lurid television soap operas, soft porn films, and partial nudity in advertising (Quinn 2002). The organization's head, Vassilis Lambridis, resigned after the board refused to ratify his decision to ban the programs. One of the first successes on Greek radio in the twenty-first century was that of three Greek monks, known collectively as Eleftheroi (the Free), whose profits from album sales are given to their monasteries (Paravantes 2002).

Iceland

Morgunbladid, a daily associated with the Independence Party, continues to lead the field of Icelandic newspapers. Widely respected throughout the country and considered fair and balanced in its political coverage, *Morgunbladid* has a circulation of more than 55,000 in a country with a population of just over 280,000. Although the number of Icelandic newspapers, most of which are associated with political parties, decreased during the 1990s, Iceland still enjoys its status as one of the world's leaders in newspaper readership and rank as highest per capita in book readership. Iceland's rich literary tradition includes Halldor Laxness, who won the Nobel Prize for literature in 1955. Three national dailies, numerous local newspapers, nine terrestrial television stations, and about 26 public and private radio stations operate in the country. About 1,600 book titles and more than 1,000 periodicals publish annually. Political parties administer government subsidies to the press, which are based proportionately on the number of party members.

The Icelandic State Broadcasting Service or Rikisutvarpid (RUV) began radio programming in 1930, financed by license fees and later by advertising revenues as well. RUV began transmitting television in 1966, also financed by license feeds and advertising, although Icelanders had been able to pick up television signals from the country's NATO base since 1960. Private ownership of television and radio began with a 1985 broadcasting act, and television station Stod-2 began subscription transmissions the following year. Two additional channels began broadcasting in 1995, with one of those closing several years later.

Nearly 98 percent of households in Iceland are equipped with television sets, and more than 99 percent with radios. About 80 percent of homes have video capability. RUV operates two national radio stations, both highly successful in competition with several commercial radio stations, most broadcasting out of Reykjavik. Concentration of ownership is evident in both print and broadcasting arenas. Cell phone penetration and Internet use in Iceland are among the highest in the world.

One of the first debates regarding U.S. cultural hegemony in Europe began in 1951 in Iceland, when American NATO forces introduced a radio service at the NATO base in Keflavik, about 50 kilometers from the capital of Reykjavik. Icelanders in the southwestern part of the country could pick up the broadcasts, mostly consisting of popular music. When U.S. television broadcasting was added several years later at the base, it, too, could be received in Icelandic homes, although reception was poor. By 1960, however, when the transmission capability was boosted, the issue of uninvited U.S. television (and radio) broadcasting became a heated political debate in the small nation—so serious, in fact, it was called "one of the most significant political and cultural rows in Iceland's postwar era" (Bjarnason and Broddason 1997, p. 57).

The Iceland Television Service was begun in 1966, years ahead of schedule, in an effort to dissuade Icelanders from watching the NATO base broadcasts (Bjarnason and Broddason 1997). Still, watching the U.S. programs remained popular, particularly among young people. Iceland's television programming amounted at first to only about a dozen hours per week. And for almost 20 years, RUV did not broadcast during the month of July, when RUV employees took summer vacation, and it did not broadcast on Thursdays for nearly 25 years. The hegemonic debate has not ceased as RUV continues to broadcast mostly non-Icelandic–produced programming.

Ireland

Ireland's economic boom, beginning in the mid-1990s and continuing into 2001, has led to growth along several media lines, including an overall increase in daily newspaper readership, unlike the rest of Europe. However, by late 2001, advertising revenues for the media industry had dipped by about 5 percent. Because all media outlets in Ireland, including Radio Telifis Eireann, or RTE, the public service broadcaster, are dependent on ad revenue, that decrease led to a number of staff layoffs in 2002. Four national daily newspapers, two national evening newspapers, five national Sunday editions, and about 64 local and regional newspapers compose the newspaper landscape. The *Irish Independent,* with a circulation of about 168,000, and *The Irish Times,* at about 119,000, are the leaders among the dailies, and the *Evening Herald,* at about 104,000, leads the evening circulation.

About one out of every four dailies sold in Ireland is British, as British newspapers are widely available throughout the country. Independent Newspapers PLC wholly or partially publishes about 80 percent of all Irish newspapers, including the *Irish Independent.* Led by Tony O'Reilly, former chairman of H.J. Heinz, the U.S.-based multinational corporation, Independent Newspapers also publishes papers in Australia, New Zealand, South Africa, and the United Kingdom. Foreign ownership of Irish newspapers and magazines is small.

A freedom of information act implemented in 1998 has given journalists in Ireland unprecedented access to previously confidential government documents and has led to a greater degree of openness by government offices. The 1997 end to a ban on journalists' ability to interview members of the Irish Republic Army (IRA) and other organizations has allowed Irish citizens more access to information on the ongoing peace process in Northern Ireland.

Broadcasting has long been led by RTE, which operates three national channels, including RTE-1 and Network 2, which broadcast about 16 hours a day. TG4, a channel devoted mostly to programming in the Irish language, was begun in late 1996. RTE-1 broadcasts the main news programs as well as a variety of other entertainment programming. TV3, a private commercial channel, began broadcasting in 1998, receiving 45 percent of its financial base from CanWest Global in Canada, which also owns about 30 percent of Ulster Television. Since late 2000, the British media group Granada also has a 45 percent share of TV3. Programming on TV3 consists primarily of television series produced in the United States, the United Kingdom, and Australia. RTE also operates four national radio channels, and 43 licensed radio stations were in operation in the country in 2002. The Broadcasting Act of 2001 meant a number of changes to the framework of broadcasting in the country, including digital terrestrial television, the promotion of multimedia services, and the later introduction of broadcasting codes and standards. Residents along Ireland's east coast can watch British land-based channels, such as the BBC, which also are available throughout the country via cable.

Italy

The two highest circulating newspapers in Italy are *La Repubblica*, published in Rome since 1976, and considered an elite, serious industry leader, and *Il Corriere della Sera*, which began in Milan in 1876. The majority of Italy's newspapers are published in the northern and central areas of the country.

Recent mergers of pay-TV platforms in Italy have helped cover financial losses in that industry. Italy's vast number of free channels has made it a difficult market for pay services. Competition between Canal+ and News Corp/Telecom Italia's Stream service inflated programming costs, and their merger was expected to help stem those costs. The state broadcasting leader is RAI-Television. Six other nationally broadcast channels and one regional channel are owned by Prime Minister Silvio Berlusconi, who has been the subject of criticism for his media holdings and de facto control of state-run broadcasting. He resigned as chief of Fininvest, the multimedia giant, upon taking office for the first time in 1994, but his critics note that his nearly 50 percent ownership of Italy's print and broadcast media gave him unprecedented political and ideological advantages. The week following his election, *Panorama*, his weekly news magazine, ran a cover story titled, "How He Wants to Change Italy" (Shugaar 1994). According to Italian diplomat Sergio Romano, "If Ted Turner were to run for president, the news staff of CNN would . . . be worried that the quality of their . . . news might be contaminated and compromised. Unfortunately, Italian journalism does not . . . even consider this to be a problem" (Shugaar 1994, p. 16).

Critics now say that Berlusconi's control of media extends to 90 percent of Italian television and 65 percent of its advertising market (Hargreaves 2002). Mediaset, owned by Berlusconi, and the public broadcaster RAI account for 95 percent of Italian television advertising revenues and 90 percent of Italy's television viewing audience. Mediaset owns three of the four private national television channels.

The prime minister's political opponents have charged that his level of ownership and control over Italian media is undemocratic. Several incidents in which

Berlusconi was displeased with what he considered critical media coverage under-lined his opponents' concerns. In one of those incidents in 2002, Berlusconi accused journalist Enzo Biagi, "the acknowledged dean of Italian journalism" (Henneberger 2002), of "criminal use" of state television when actor Roberto Benigni, as a guest on Biagi's television program, *The Fact,* said shortly before the national election that he planned to vote for Berlusconi's opponent. The International Press Institute denounced Berlusconi's government for later dropping the show from RAI's pro-gramming lineup. The Organization for Security and Cooperation in Europe (OSCE) also criticized Berlusconi, noting that "Some voices in Italy, including that of the Italian journalists' union, have called this . . . a 'political move' " (Agence France-Presse ["Press Group Denounces"] 2002).

OSCE had earlier in the year urged the European Union to act to ensure EU principles were not violated by Berlusconi's ownership of media. Reporters Without Borders' secretary general Robert Menard said, "Italy is the only country in the European Union to have all its radio and television media, private as well as public, directly or indirectly controlled by the government in power" (Agence France-Presse ["Press Group Urges"] 2002). Berlusconi later cosigned a letter to parliament with Italian President Carlo Azeglio Ciampi calling for legislation to ensure free expression in the country by making "holding public office incompatible with running a company, but not with owning one—terms that [opponents say] are insufficient" (Rachman 2002). That legislation, passed in late 2002, limits a single media operator's market share to 20 percent, including subscription income, adver-tising, pay TV, newspapers, and other media formats. It also included measures that would allow for the eventual and gradual privatization of RAI. Critics of the bill, however, said it did nothing to end conflict of interest, and instead not only left Mediaset unchallenged but gave Berlusconi even more control.

An exception to the rule in Italy is Radio Popolare, which is neither directly nor indirectly controlled by Berlusconi. Thanks to its financing structure, which is based 50 percent on voluntary audience subscriptions and 50 percent on advertis-ing, Radio Popolare has been able to remain independent. Its editor, Piero Scara-mucci, who worked for RAI for 30 years, said that because Berlusconi controls most of the broadcast industry in the country, media in Italy are "in a condition of near monopoly" (Cataldi 2002). Based in Milan and considered left wing, Radio Popolare was founded by Scaramucci in 1976. One of its more popular programs is *Open Microphones,* during which audience members can call the station to voice opinions on various daily topics.

Luxembourg

Links to political parties and trade unions characterize the country's print media. Luxembourg's largest circulating daily newspaper at 80,000 copies is *Luxemburger Wort,* owned and operated by the Catholic Archbishop of Luxembourg, with links to the dominant Christian Social Party. *Tageblatt,* with a circulation of 26,000, is operated by several socialist trade unions and is linked to the Socialist Party. Newspapers in this small country are published in one of three languages—German, French, or Portuguese. Public broadcasting continues to dominate the television and radio airwaves at the start of the twenty-first century, although the private sector has made some inroads. A flourishing number of pirate radio stations, however, made evident a need for more local broadcasting outlets. Radio Luxembourg, begun in 1931, was an early commercial success in the country.

Luxembourg's media powerhouse is RTL Group, Europe's leading broadcasting and production company. RTL has financial stakes in 23 television channels and 17 radio stations in 11 European countries. It also owns Pearson TV, the world's leading international independent production company, which distributes such programs as *Baywatch* and a number of U.S. game shows. RTL, however, is owned largely by non-Luxembourg interests, including Bertelsmann.

The Netherlands

While national daily newspapers in the Netherlands have seen about a 3 percent growth in circulation, overall that circulation has stabilized. About 4.7 million copies are sold daily, including eight national newspapers and 29 regional papers. The single largest daily is *De Telegraaf,* with a circulation of about 850,000. Until the late 1960s, newspapers were aligned with one of four interests, Catholic, Protestant, Socialist, or Liberal, and therefore were primarily used as a means of disseminating political or ideological messages. More than 200 magazines are published, with the largest circulating being *Elsevier,* a news and opinion publication with a circulation of about 133,000.

Radio frequencies in the Netherlands, much like newspapers, were first distributed to associations with political or religious affiliations. Television, introduced in the early 1950s, also was aligned along these association divisions. Funding was made by the associations and by a government tax on radio or television set ownership. In the 1960s, "pirate" stations broadcasting from ships just off the Dutch coast in the North Sea and funded by advertising became very popular. Parliament eventually handed down laws prohibiting the broadcasts, but debate about changing the Dutch broadcasting system continued into the 1980s. It wasn't until Luxembourg's RTL started transmitting programming into the Netherlands (and elsewhere in Europe) that the Dutch government allowed commercial broadcasting in the country, in 1991.

An annual license fee, combined with membership fees from TV and radio outlets and advertising revenues, funds the Dutch broadcasting system. Three national television channels and five national radio stations operate at the start of the twenty-first century. Several foreign-owned commercial stations via satellite and cable interests entered the Dutch market in the mid-1980s, and in 2002, seven Dutch-language commercial stations broadcast nationally. Thirteen regional and more than 275 local broadcasting entities operate in 2002. Cable companies are legally bound to offer all television channels to customers, and nearly every Dutch home has cable access.

Freedom of the press is guaranteed in the Netherlands' Constitution in the statement, "Nobody needs previous permission to publish thoughts or feelings by use of the printing press, excluding everybody's responsibility in the face of the law." An independent Journalism Council reviews complaints against journalists or the media but does not pass down legal consequences. A number of educational and training programs for journalists exist in the Netherlands, including one that specifically trains Catholic journalists.

The Netherlands-based media company Endemol Entertainment registered numerous successes in the late 1990s and, in 2001, doubled its revenues. A subsidiary of Spain's Telefonica, it was formed in 1994. One of its largest advances came with the sale in 2000 of the *Big Brother* television program format to CBS, making its inroad into the U.S. market, and it is that program that has accounted for its global reputation. The company also has liaisons with several Latin American media companies, such as Admira, which wholly owns Argentine channel Telefe and half of TV Azul. In 2002, Endemol launched a 50/50 joint venture with TV Globo of Brazil and another 50/50 deal with Mexico's television giant Televisa in order to form a Brazilian-Mexican production house. The company also owns 65 percent of the Argentine television production company that produces that country's edition of *Big Brother*. (In fact, *Big Brother* has been something of a European phenomenon. The program's premise is the fly-on-the-wall observance of a group of people residing together, a sort of mediated view of the mundane. The Dutch television station that aired the first edition of the program more than doubled its viewer share, and viewer numbers were near record levels as well in the United Kingdom, Germany, Spain, Italy, Belgium, Switzerland, and Portugal.)

Norway

With one of the highest newspaper readerships in the world, at about 600 copies per 1,000 residents, Norway also boasts one of western Europe's highest numbers of newspaper entities, with about 220 newspapers for a population of about five million. About 65 newspapers operate daily, and 15 are published four or five times weekly. Five regional newspapers account for about one-fifth of total sales, with *Aftenposten* (288,000) and *Bergens Tidende* (94,000) leading. Most local newspapers operate outside of partisan lines and are mostly operating as monopolies, with true competition evident only in about 20 markets. Conglomeration characterizes newspaper ownership in the country, with three major media owners controlling almost 60 percent of total circulation. While special-interest magazines have seen some increases, general-interest weeklies have been on the decline.

Norsk Rikskringkasting (NRK) is the state-run public service broadcasting monopoly and is financed mostly by license fees. Local television and radio interests began in 1981, with only radio stations showing substantial profits. In 2002 two national television channels, NRK-1 and TV-2, accounted for more than 95 percent of television audiences. NRK's radio monopoly ended in 1993, when the first private radio station was begun. NRK now operates four national radio channels. Norway's parliament passed legislation in 1998 to prevent conglomeration, although by 2002, no clear moves had been made to lessen concentration of ownership. Commercial broadcast outlets have challenged the print media for advertising dollars.

Norway's media conglomerate Schibsted joined Sweden's media company Sandrews in the late 1990s to combine their distribution, production, and video assets into a single film giant. Hence known as Sandrews Metronome, the company is the largest "vertically integrated film and video acquisition, distribution and exhibition company in the Nordic territories" (Edmunds 1998). Schibsted, along with TeleDenmark, had earlier also acquired Metronome in Denmark. The film companies' merger is part of a larger trend of viewing the Scandinavian nations as one entity or market, according to Sandrews's chief. Even before the merger, Schibsted and Sandrews had teamed up to build multiplex theaters across Scandinavia and into the Baltic states.

Portugal

Although Portuguese newspapers have seen a steady decline in overall readership, circulation figures show that Portugal has registered the largest circulation increase (at 12.5 percent) in the EU. The irony of the situation is due primarily to a reduced market size, a lowered literacy rate, and the lowest concentration of television and telephone among EU nations. *Jornal de Noticias* (106,000 circulation) and *Correio da Manha* (89,100) are daily circulation leaders, with the weekly press dominated by *Expresso* (136,900). In terms of magazine publishing, *Maria,* a women's magazine with a circulation of 315,000, enjoys the market's lead at the start of the twenty-first century. Media conglomeration centers on press and broadcast ownership by four main media groups, in addition to that owned by the Catholic Church and public concerns. The church runs several successful radio stations, having sold its sole television interest in 1998.

The European Commission opened an investigation in late 2001 into Portugal's aid to national television broadcaster Radiotelevisao Portuguesa, or RTP, specifically looking into tax breaks, payment facilities for network use, debt payment rescheduling, and the state's forfeiting the right to interest on repayment delays. In mid-2002, Portugal's new center-right government, led by Prime Minister Jose Manuel Durao Barroso, decided to stop funding RTP's second television channel as part of its effort to control spending. A new public broadcaster was to be created by 2003 to administer the remaining RTP channel. Also suspended was Portugal Global, which ran RTP, RDP Radio, and the Lusa news agency. Portugal's television market is considered underdeveloped compared to the rest of Europe, although it experienced substantial expansion in the late 1990s. Advertising revenues grew by more than 32 percent in 2000. Still, the Portuguese government found it difficult to rationalize the need for taxpayers to subsidize state-owned television when private channels were readily available.

One of those is the commercial channel SIC, begun in the mid-1990s, which became a quick and lucrative success. Broadcasting such programming as soap operas and variety shows, SIC also launched angry debates in the country about its level of quality. Critics noted that competing private television station TVI, recognizing the loss of viewers, began pandering to a lower common denominator as well. SIC has moved into numerous international markets, including agreements with Globo TV of Brazil, various U.S. independent film producers, Spain's Morena Films, and others.

Portugal's PT Multimedia, owned mostly by Portugal Telecom, has been one of Europe's more successful media ventures. Its consolidated earnings in 2001 were $549 million, more than twice what it earned the previous year. Most of its success has come from its foray into pay TV, but it also owns print media and online concerns. Through its company, Lusomundo, PT Multimedia owns *Jornal de Noticias*, the leading daily, as well as *Diaro de Noticias*, with a circulation of 61,300. Competing companies are gaining ground, however. Cabovisao for example, operates cable companies in more than 230 suburban and regional Portuguese markets, reaching nearly 600,000 homes in 2002. And smaller media companies such as Ono, Plurica-nal, and Bragatel are expanding as well.

Spain

Privatization and liberalization have dictated media development in Spain in recent years. More than 100 newspapers are published in Spain, with the circulation leader being *El Pais*, at about 450,000 copies. Several national dailies devoted to sports news also enjoy healthy circulations. *Marca,* for example, a national sports daily, is the country's second highest circulating newspaper, with 417,000 copies. But low circulation continues to be a problem for Spanish newspapers at the start of the twenty-first century, and concentration of ownership also has been a trend. *Diario 16,* a respected left-wing newspaper that began publishing in 1976 as Spain was beginning its transition to democracy following the death of dictator Francisco Franco, folded in late 2001, after suffering steady losses for four years. Newspapers are read by only 12.3 million of Spain's 40 million citizens.

About 350 magazines attracting about 18.6 regular readers are published in Spain, and, like the country's newspapers, are owned by private interests. Traditional gossip magazines, such as *Hola!* and *Pronto,* attract nearly six million readers weekly. A merger between media owners Grupo Correo and Prensa Espanola in late 2001 created strong competition for Prisa, Spain's most important media group, which owns *El Pais* and the country's most popular radio station, Cadena 40, with 2.6 million listeners. Although Spain has seen less media consolidation than other European nations, one digital megamerger in mid-2002 between Telefonica and Sogecable, which could net 2.5 million pay-TV subscriptions and a $1.2 billion budget, was still awaiting government and EU approval.

Television and radio stations are owned by both private and public concerns. Radiotelevision Espanola, or RTVE, operates two public national television channels, TVE-1 and La2, and several digital channels. Three private national television stations began broadcasting in 1989. Radio Nacional de España, or RNE, runs about 100 AM stations and 350 FM stations. Local radio stations number about 500. Advertising revenues, not license fees, account for the income of both private and public broadcasting outlets, but after years of sustained growth, Spanish television advertising lost about 7 percent by late 2001, a loss that was attended by a wide downturn in finances in all Spanish media, with the possible exception of magazines.

Football matches and films are the most popular programming on Spanish television, but it was the impact of Telecinco's airing of *Big Brother* in 2000 that garnered some of the country's largest audiences and boosted its advertising revenues. More than 25 percent of Spanish households have access to digital television channels. The merger of digital operations between Spain's largest media group, Prisa, and telecommunications giant Telefonica, and the subsequent merger with the television conglomerate Sogecable, created Spain's largest pay-TV operator in 2002 "in a deal that would not so much reshape as replace the local TV landscape" in Spain (Hopewell 2002). Prisa focused its business in 2002 on local television, specifically its 60 stations, grouped under Localia TV, that target small towns as well as Spanish cities. This type of local approach is inevitable, according to Hopewell and De Pablos (2002), because "the Catalans around Barcelona and the Basques in the north think of themselves as separate nations."

Sweden

The media in Sweden are among the freest media in the world, with freedom of the press having been constitutionally protected since 1766. Subsequent protections have included, for example, the right of Swedish journalists to protect the identities of their sources. Local and regional newspapers flourish in the Swedish market, with only three newspapers having a truly national audience. Nearly all morning daily papers are sold by subscription and are home-delivered. Most of the country's 160 newspapers are no longer affiliated with political parties. Of these 160 papers, about 50 publish once or twice a week. The three highest-circulation broadsheets are morning dailies: *Dagens Nyheter* in Stockholm, with a circulation of 361,000; *Goteborgs Posten*, in Gothenburg, with 262,000 copies; and *Sydsvenska Dagbladet*, in Malmo, with 128,000. Leading the evening tabloid field is *Aftonbladet*, with a circulation of 412,000, and *Expressen*, with 327,000, both published in Stockholm. Circulation declines have concentrated on the evening tabloids, while circulations of the morning dailies have remained stable. But these declines also have characterized the general-interest, family, and women's magazine markets in Sweden, whereas special-interest periodicals have seen circulations grow. Direct government subsidies account for about 3 percent of total revenues of the Swedish press and primarily benefit local and regional papers that publish periodically. In terms of state support for newspapers, the Swedish Press Support Board is responsible for allocating government subsidies and grants. And as circulations fall and advertising revenues shrink, even the national newspapers are becoming more dependent on state subsidies.

Regular television broadcasting in Sweden began in 1956 and rapidly gained in popularity. Bjork (2001) noted that by the end of 1956, there were 8,900 paid licenses for televisions in the country, increasing to 75,000 in 1957, 244,000 in 1958, and nearly 600,000 in 1959. But that popularity was "all the more remarkable in light of how little (the Swedes) had to watch," Bjork said, noting the low number of broadcasting hours per week (p. 310). Sveriges Television (SVT), which is owned by a foundation funded by the government, operates two channels, as well as a Swedish-language channel for Finland, a satellite channel, and a 24-hour news channel. Private television channels first appeared in the late 1980s. Concentration of ownership has garnered much attention since the 1990s. The Bonnier Group is the largest media conglomerate, with interests in newspapers, radio, television, film, books, and magazines. Sweden's system of journalism training and advanced university degree programs in the field is extensive.

According to International Data Corporation (IDC), Sweden maintained its position as the world's leader in information technology in 2001. In its study, the Information Society Index (ISI), countries are ranked according to computer, information, Internet, and social infrastructures, by which a score for each is produced, enabling a global ranking system. The index tracks data from 55 countries that together account for 98 percent of the global gross domestic product and 99 percent of information technology expenditure. In 2001, after Sweden, were the following nations: Norway (2nd), Finland (3rd), the United States (4th), Denmark (5th), the United Kingdom (6th), Switzerland (7th), the Netherlands (10th), Germany (13th), Austria (14th), Belgium (15th), Ireland (20th), France (21st), Italy (23rd), Spain (24th), Portugal (25th), and Greece (26th). Iceland and Luxembourg were not among the countries examined in the study.

Switzerland

Several official languages, primarily German, French, and Italian, compose the Swiss media scene. German-language newspapers are circulation leaders, the largest of which are *Blick* (309,000), *Tages Anzeiger* (268,200), and *Neue Zurcher Zeitung* (170,000). These and other dailies with circulations of more than 100,000 are owned by media conglomerates, most notably Ringier, the largest. About 230 newspapers are published in the country, but the print media of Switzerland were hit by a 7 percent decline in advertising revenues in 2001. Recent mergers include the 2001 creation of *Mittelland Zeitung,* a combination of four separate newspapers, which then became the country's third largest circulating paper. Freedom of the press is constitutionally guaranteed. Journalists' skills education in Switzerland is limited to post-hire training at one of several institutions, although theoretically based communication courses are offered at some universities.

The Swiss Broadcasting Corporation (SBC), a nonprofit association with a public service mandate, produces programming in accord with the Swiss Constitution, which states radio and television should inform, educate, and entertain, in that order. One of the challenges the SBC and commercial broadcast enterprises face is the country's language diversity. Financed by license fees and advertising, SBC also is required to promote understanding and cultural diversity among the various linguistic areas of the country. The 2001 failure of Tele-24, one of Switzerland's first national commercial television stations, focused attention on the future of the Swiss television industry, which has been dominated by SBC since its first transmission in

1953. Experts have pointed to viewer loyalty as the biggest challenge for commercial broadcasters in the country. Switzerland's radio broadcasters have largely favored Anglo-American music on-air, although Swiss record companies would like to see a bigger share for locally produced fare. Among the obstacles facing a larger local share of airtime is the composition of Italian speakers, German speakers, French speakers, and speakers of Swiss dialects. This multilingualism has made the Swiss market particularly difficult in which to market a successful local release.

United Kingdom

Home to some of the most reputable and respected print media in the world, the United Kingdom also boasts some of the world's most flamboyant and sensationalist tabloids. The print media of Great Britain comprise about 130 daily and Sunday newspapers, more than 2,000 weekly newspapers, and about 7,000 periodicals, constituting more national and daily newspapers for every British citizen than in most other developed nations. Traditionally divided into qualities and populars, or broadsheets and tabloids, 13 national morning newspapers appear daily in Britain and nine appear Sundays. The *Times*, the *Daily Telegraph*, the *Guardian*, and the *Independent* are among the world's most respected newspapers. Free to comment on matters of public interest, and subject to national laws, including libel, British newspapers are almost all financially independent of political parties, although most ascribe to political leanings. The United Kingdom adopted the European Convention on Human Rights in 2000, which guarantees British subjects freedom of expression.

The print media of the United Kingdom are self-regulating. Set up in 1991, the Press Complaints Commission was established at the suggestion of a government-appointed committee to promote more effective press self-regulation and to prevent invasions of privacy. An independent organization, the PCC completed investigations into more than 3,000 complaints in 2001, with the majority of those dealing with accuracy in reporting.

British broadcasting comprises three public bodies that are responsible for television and radio throughout the country: (1) the British Broadcasting Corporation (BBC) broadcasts radio and television; (2) the Independent Television Commission (ITC) licenses and regulates all non-BBC television services, including cable and satellite; and (3) the Radio Authority (RA) licenses all non-BBC radio services. Traditionally a public service accountable to the public through parliament, British broadcasting has expanded to include formerly competing services. Television viewing has become Britain's most popular leisure activity, with more than 95 percent of households having at least one color television set. The government is not responsible for programming content, but broadcasters are required not to offend good taste.

The BBC, known in Britain as "the Beeb," operates two national television channels, a number of cable and digital television channels, and five national radio services. The BBC also runs 39 local radio stations and regional radio in Northern Ireland, Wales, and Scotland. BBC World Service Radio has about 120 million regular listeners and transmits in 38 languages worldwide. BBC World Service Television, set up in 1992, provides a subscription channel in Europe, a 24-hour news and information channel available throughout Asia, and a news and information channel in Africa. The BBC's domestic services are financed almost exclusively by the sale of annual television licenses. BBC World Service Radio is financed from a government grant, while BBC World Service Television is self-funding. BBC television programming is now widely available throughout the United States via BBCAmerica and throughout the world via BBCWorld. BBC's nine new digital television and radio channels are subject to public service obligations, and the funding of them does not constitute state aid, which would violate EU rules. The total cost of the new channels, estimated at GBO 90 million, were of concern to competing European broadcasters, who felt the state financing would give unfair advantage to the BBC and distort trade.

In 2002 the British media market was braced for becoming "one of the most liberal and television radio markets in the world" after the British government proposed to end ownership bans that had prevented buyers from the United States and non-EU countries from entering the British market (O'Connor 2002, p. 1). Harding (2002) said the Parliament's decision "crossed a line" (p. 18) in that Tony Blair's government was treating media "more like widget factories." The bill, he said, "takes a far more dispassionate and economic view of the industry than any previous legislation." The government provided some monopoly safeguards in the legislation, including the barring of the owners of British's largest newspapers from owning the largest commercial television broadcaster, which would keep, for example, Rupert Murdoch, as owner of *The Times* and *The Sun,* from buying ITV.

At a 2001 meeting of Le Marche International de Contenus Interactifs (MILIA), more than 7,000 media professionals from 52 countries acknowledged that Europe is a prime proving ground for digital media. And the United Kingdom is seen as the most likely market for digital interactive television (Kavanaugh 2001). MILIA pointed to BSkyB's completion of digital replacement of more than five million analog direct-to-home subscriptions. Rival company ONdigital marked more than one million digital subscriptions by 2001. In 2002 AOL Time Warner acquired IPC Media, one of the United Kingdom's leading consumer magazine publishers, for $1.7 billion. AOL Time Warner chairman Steven Case predicted that half of the company's earnings would come from non-U.S. sources by 2010.

Twenty-First Century Challenges

Profound changes throughout the European media landscape continue into the twenty-first century. Print media in Europe will continue to run the risk of diminished revenues, and more newspaper failures are predicted. Government subsidies will help to offset serious declines, but the general expectation is that profits will not be healthy enough to offset large losses. However, the delivery of information will more than likely continue toward a more interactive format via the Internet, digital media, and convergence, all of which will pose challenges to journalists, audiences, EU regulators, governments, and media groups. Mergers and alliances between and among disparate newspapers also may help to curb closures. Most promising would be long-term strategies, although large financial commitments to implement them may pose difficulties. And, as newspapers more frequently produce on-line editions, European journalists may find it necessary to adopt a broad range of new skills, including the use of audiovisual on-line formats, graphics, interactivity, and databases. With an expected 720 million Internet users worldwide by the end of 2005, on-line sources of news, information, and advertising seem a likely area for profit making.

Among European broadcasting's challenges are ongoing deregulation and the sometimes staggering financial commitments to digital platforms. According to the European Audiovisual Observatory (2002), net losses for all EU television companies surpassed €1.5 billion in 2000, with nine out of 15 national television systems in deficit, the most serious in Portugal. Only Austria, Belgium, France, Germany, and Greece systems showed a profit. An examination by the EAO of the balance sheets and annual accounts of about 350 European Union media companies showed an average annual growth rate of 11.9 percent, but the transition to digital from analog and increased programming competition have drained pre-1998 profits. EAO's research showed that private media companies financed through advertising were the only ones that fared well financially overall. Their profit margins increased nearly 16 percent in 2000, although 2001 saw a depression in the advertising market. Digital platforms' diminished financial health has not helped matters. These include the bankruptcy of ITV Digital in the United Kingdom and the financial woes of Premiere Medien in Germany, and Telepiu and Stream's problems in Italy. Pay-TV channels have continued to lose money since 1997 as well. The EAO concluded that large investments into digital technology have caused a general loss of profit margins, a point of concern for the future of all of Europe's audiovisual industries.

The notion of a European "identity" may be troubled as well, given the variety of languages and cultures among member nations, and the diversity presented by continuing immigration. As the nations of the EU move toward a common cultural policy, any attempts at creating a common European identity may come at the expense of existing cultures and languages. The countries of France and Germany, for example, have officially stated they want development of a common European culture and identity, but without an emphasis on Anglo-Saxon popular culture. Some scholars have noted that cultural differences among the nations and regions of Europe will indeed inhibit true European political integration, but that a common culture would be difficult, if not impossible, to develop and direct (Zetterholm 1994). If any resemblance of a pan-European culture exists today, it is largely via U.S.-produced music, television and film. As such initiatives as the EU's Television Without Borders become important contributions to the liberalization of broadcasting in Europe, they will also continue to face criticism and reevaluation.

The challenges facing European nations and their integrated identity within the European Union were succinctly summarized by Varis (1998): "In an intercultural world, communication necessarily mediates different values and cultural behaviors. Great civilizations and cultures have very different patterns of communication and use different senses in a different way. In consequence ... more attention should be given to the diversity of cultures and the co-existence of different ... cultures" (p. 68)

Bibliography

Agence France-Presse. "Press Group Denounces Italy for Banning Critical TV Shows." 1 July 2002. Available: http://www.afp.com.

——. "Press Group Urges Berlusconi to Maintain Media Pluralism." 3 July 2002. Available: http://www.afp.com.

Balter, Michael. "Shake-Up in Paris: At 109, the *International Herald Tribune* Is at a Crossroads." *Columbia Journalism Review* 35–36 (1996): 36–38.

Barnard, Bruce. "France's Vivendi Universal Acquires MP3.com." *Europe* (Delegation of the European Commission) (June 2001): 54.

Baugh, Christopher. "Dishing Out Broadband Success in Europe." *Satellite Broadband* 2, no. 11 (2001): 44.

Bjarnason, Hilmar Thor, and Thorbjorn Broddason. "Mass Media in Iceland." In *Media Trends 1997 in Denmark, Finland, Iceland, Norway and Sweden,* edited by Ulla Carlsson and Eva Harrie. Göteborg, Sweden: Nordicom, 1997.

Bjork, Ulf Jonas. " 'Have Gun, Will Travel': Swedish Television and American Westerns, 1959–1969." *Historical Journal of Film, Radio and Television* 21 (2001): 309–321.

Bondebjerg, Ib. "Modern Danish Television: After the Monopoly Era." In *Television in Scandinavia: History, Politics and Aesthetics,* edited by Ib Bondebjerg and Francesco Bono. Luton, Bedfordshire, United Kingdom: University of Luton Press, 1996.

Cataldi, Benedetto. "Analysis: Italy's Alternative Voice." BBC Worldwide Monitoring, 19 August 2002.

Cebrian, Juan Luis. "The Media and European Identity." *New Perspectives Quarterly* 16 (1999): 39–41.

Cherry, Colin. *World Communication: Threat or Promise?* Chichester, United Kingdom: Wiley, 1978.

Collins, Ross F. "A Battle for Humor: Satire and Censorship in Le Bavard." *Journalism and Mass Communication Quarterly* 73 (1996): 645–656.

Dupagne, Michel. "Regulation of Sexually Explicit Videotext Services in France." *Journalism Quarterly* 71 (1994): 121–134.

Economic Commission for Europe. *The Telecommunications Industry: Growth and Structural Change.* New York: United Nations, 1987.

Edmunds, Marlene. "Film giant forms in Norway." *Variety* 369/10 (1998): p. 29.

European Audiovisual Observatory. "The Deficit in the European Television Sector has been Growing Since 1998." On-line press release, 9 April 2002. Available: http://www.ibs.coe.int.

Feigenbaum, Harvey. "Regulating the Media in the United States and France." *Journal of Arts Management, Law and Society* 27 (1998): 283–292.

Frederick, Howard H. *Global Communication and International Relations.* Belmont, Calif.: Wadsworth, 1993.

Goldberg, David, Tony Prosser, and Stefaan Verhulst. *EC Media Law and Policy.* London: Addison Wesley Longman, 1998.

Harding, James. "Watch This Space." *Financial Times,* 9 May 2002, 18.

Hargreaves, Ian. "Threat to European Media Regulation Is a Muddle." *Financial Times,* 21 May 2002, 18.

Henneberger, Melinda. "Italian Leader Warns Critics on TV to Toe the Line." *The New York Times,* 21 April 2002, 5.

Higgins, Jonathan. "Draw Your Sabres: The Impact of Satellite on Cable." *Satellite Broadband* 2, no. 4 (2001): 22–24, 26.

Hopewell, John. "New Reign in Spain: Media Giants Plan to Merge Digital Payboxes." *Variety* 386, no. 13 (2002): 21.

Hopewell, John, and Emiliano De Pablos. "Prisa Banks on Local Heroes." *Variety* 386, no. 5 (2002): 20.

Hunter, Mark. "The Rise of the Fouille-Merdes." *Columbia Journalism Review* 34 (1995): 40–43.

Kavanagh, Michael. "Europe: Earth's Digital Proving Ground." *Electronic Media* 20 (2001): 13, 15.

Kemp, Stuart. "U.S. Films Dominate Growth in European Admissions." *The Hollywood Reporter,* 25 June 2002.

Knox, Tom. "UK Papers Eye Euro Openings." *Marketing,* 13 May 1999, 46.

Martin, Terry. "The Bertelsmann Empire." *Europe* (May 2002): 16–17, 19.

McMane, Aralynn Abare. "A New French Recipe." *Editor and Publisher* 127 (1994): 10–11.

Michalis, Maria. "European Union Broadcasting and Telecoms: Towards a Convergent Regulatory Regime?" *European Journal of Communication* 14 (1999): 147–171.

Mitropoulos, Dimitri. "Immigrants Ignite a Media Maelstrom in Greece." *Nieman Reports* 53, no. 2 (1999): 36.

Murschetz, Paul. "State Support for the Daily Press in Europe: A Critical Appraisal." *European Journal of Communication* 13 (1998): 291–313.

O'Connor, Ashling. "Media Bill Heralds TV Free-for-All." *Financial Times,* 8 May 2002.

Papathanassopoulos, Stylianos. "Media Commercialization and Journalism in Greece." *European Journal of Communication* 16 (2001): 505–521.

Paravantes, Maria. "Greece's rocking monks use media to deliver message." *Billboard* 114, no. 20 (2002): 65.

Quinn, Patrick. "Greece Suspends Two Reality Shows." *Associated Press Online,* 21 March 2002.

Rachman, Tom. "In Unusual Step, Italy's President Sends Message to Parliament on Free Media." *Associated Press Worldstream,* 23 July 2002.

Robertson, Andrew. "Emerging Euro Will Change the Rules for Media." *Marketing,* 18 March 1999, 21.

Schuhmayer, Susan L. "Austrian Biz Wants Radio Quota." *Billboard* 109, no. 22 (1997): 57.

Shugaar, Antony. "Italy's New Hall of Mirrors." *Columbia Journalism Review* 33 (1994): 15–16.

Varis, Tapio. "Media Culture and Communication Competence in Europe." *Nordicom Review* 19 (1998): 59–68.

Waterman, Davis, and Krishna P. Jayakar. "The Competitive Balance of the Italian and American Film Industries." *European Journal of Communication* 15 (2000): 501–528.

Wise, Michael Z. "Austria's Troubling Tabloid." *Columbia Journalism Review* (January–February 2002): 12.

Zetterholm, Staffan. "Why is Cultural Diverstiy a Political Problem? A Discussion of Cultural Barriers to Political Integration." In *National Cultures and European Integration: Exploratory Essays on Cultural Diversity and Common Policies,* edited by Staffan Zetterholm. Oxford: Berg, 1994.

14

Eastern Europe, the Newly Independent States of Eurasia, and Russia

Catherine Cassara, Peter Gross, Dean Kruckeberg, Allen W. Palmer, and Katerina Tsetsura

The evolution of mass media in eastern Europe, the newly independent states of Eurasia, and Russia during the postcommunist transition period has been uneven and, at times, turbulent and chaotic. As reported by Human Rights Watch in 2002, respect for media freedoms in the region has followed "a rough path of ups and downs." The legacy of communist-style governance continues to haunt those working for media reforms. In many places, threats and intimidation pose a threat to journalists' lives and independence. More often, they work without adequate economic support, which leaves them vulnerable to bribes, extortion, and other forms of payoffs.

Although some states in the region have remained authoritarian and largely unchanged, others have confronted many of the legal, economic, and political obstacles to democratic expression. Private media in eastern Europe are now considered to be relatively free, as assessed by agencies such as Freedom House and Human Rights Watch, but governments increasingly have sought to impose serious legal limitations on the exercise of these freedoms. The new media are inventing themselves, searching for ways to build economic and political independence in difficult times. In Russia, the media are caught in the wild swings of public and political favor. Most media in the region exist in the shadow of political and economic threat, corruption, or intimidation. Many observers wonder how these societies can break out of old ways of thinking and cultivate a healthy and transparent relationship between government and the media (Gross 2002).

The arrival of venture capital from Europe and North America has been accompanied by sensationalized tabloid treatment of the news. More generally, the press there has seen a sharp decrease in circulation since the early 1990s, because of economic distress and because of lack of consumer confidence. The infrastructure of the print media (equipment, facilities, distribution systems) remains generally inadequate.

Although many nations have enacted civil codes consistent with Western standards, the ambiguity of codes addressing "defamation," "libel," "ridicule," "derision," and "insults" allows courts the wide latitude. This has the potential "chilling effect" of curbing bona fide reporting of malfeasance by elected or appointed public officials, civil servants, and politicians.

Some observers of democratic developments in the region now ask whether a single model of reform and media development is reasonable. Those who track rapid changes point to the uneven and unpredictable evolution.

Media Developments in Eastern Europe

Development of the press, television, and radio remains key to a civil society in most of the countries of eastern Europe (Figure 14.1). They all share histories of aristocratic rule, colonial struggle, authoritarianism, and an uncertain and halting path toward democratic reform.

Prior to political reform in the late 1980s and the 1990s, censorship and self-censorship dominated the media. A lingering suspicion of democratic ideas and institutions made it difficult for people to embrace change.

There was, however, considerable progress in most eastern European countries, where parliaments expanded the independence of both public and private media through laws on free access to information. Partisanship, politicization, advocacy, and a literary bent were the shared tradition of most journalists in eastern Europe, where the profession was practiced mostly by the intellectual and political classes.

The communist era, which began shortly after World War II, harnessed the newspapers, radio, and television to serve the one-party Marxist-Leninist systems that the Communist party controlled. The communist systems disappeared in 1989, and along with them the journalism of advocacy practiced in the service of only one political party.

Media growth in the 1990s defied commercial rationale, was divorced from a rich civil society that it could claim it directly represented, and was primarily politically motivated. By the mid-1990s, circulation figures had fallen drastically, and many newspapers ceased publication. At the same time, however, new ones came into existence.

Former Yugoslavia and the Balkan States

In the Socialist Republic of Yugoslavia, the media were expected to operate according to state-mandated policies, but generally were more abundant than in other socialist states. Throughout the 1980s, Yugoslavian audiences had access to "a much greater content variety than anywhere else in Europe" (Robinson 1977, p. 213).

FIGURE 14.1 *Eastern Europe*

Strong political control was exercised, if indirectly, through the League of Communists of Yugoslavia in the six republics, Bosnia-Herzegovina, Croatia, Macedonia, Montenegro, Serbia, and Slovenia, and the two autonomous provinces within Serbia, Kosovo and Vojvodina. By 1989, when a federal law allowed private media operation in Yugloslavia, there were nine TV stations and 202 radio stations. There were also 27 daily newspapers, with about three-fourths printed in Serbo-Croatian, Serbian, or Croatian languages. Yugoslavia also had a thriving book publishing industry, and outside books and publications were generally circulated without ironclad restrictions, unlike in most other socialist countries.

Under Slobodan Milosevic, Serbia's radio and television network, RTS, was heavily politicized. "RTS is not media. It's full of government employees who are paid to produce propaganda and lies. To call it media is totally misleading" (Online News Hour 1999). Serbian journalists were accused of portraying "Serbs as the chosen race, creating an atmosphere in which genocide and other war crimes were justified as acts of the state" (Freedom Forum, 1 July 2001). NATO bombed RTS headquarters in Belgrade on April 23, 1999.

In 1999, when North Atlantic Treaty Organization (NATO) forces arrived in Kosovo, there were no functioning radio or television outlets in the province. To remedy this problem, UN Interim Administrative Mission in Kosovo and the Organization for Security and Cooperation in Europe (OSCE) established Radio Television Kosovo in 1999. The station was a recreation of Radio Television Pristina, a provincial broadcasting station that was taken over by Serb authorities in 1990, when all Albanian employees were replaced by Serb journalists.

The October 2000 revolution in Yugoslavia brought to an end tight government control of the media and offered the hope of democratic media reforms, yet progress has been uneven. Old regulations, such as the Law on Public Information, a restrictive measure passed in 1998, still remain in place. In addition, many journalists working for state publications seem unable to shake off innate deference to authorities. The regulation of broadcast media, including the Radio Television Serbia Act and federal regulations for the allocation of frequencies, remains unchanged. The Ministry of Telecommunications announced a moratorium on the redistribution of frequencies and the allocation of new ones until new regulations were adopted.

Elsewhere in the region, Bosnia-Herzegovina adopted the Stability Pact Charter for Media Freedom in 2001, acknowledging that freedom of the media and the free flow of information should play a role in the development of the new democracy. The Bosnian government issued a formal statement saying it was obligated to promote principles of the charter. The Stability Pact is a multinational document that pledges cooperation in guaranteeing a free and independent media.

Critics of media in such states as Macedonia complained that public trust in media performance reached its lowest point in 2002 during outbreaks of violence along the Kosovo border. At that time, a Swedish study found that only 15 percent of Macedonians and less than 10 percent of ethnic Albanians in Macedonia believed the media were operating free of political influence. Complaints about unverified reports issued by the government were cited as examples of weak media performance by the Balkan Report, issued by Radio Free Europe/Radio Liberty. Yet some analysts argue that "Macedonian society is taking the right direction to establish a democratic media landscape . . . [and] reflects the social pluralism within civil society" (Trajkovski and Trpevska 2001).

In Croatia, the media are governed under the national constitution, which liberally guarantees freedom of thought and expression, in line with western European standards. However, constraints to media freedom are hidden in penal codes, which have a deleterious effect on the work of most journalists.

Czech and Slovak Republics

The first Czech newspaper was launched in 1719 (*Cesky postylion nebolizto noviny Ceske*); the first Slovak newspaper began publishing in 1783 (*Prespurske noviny*). Modern-era Czech and Slovak presses were established during the time of the Austro-Hungarian Empire. Czech newspapers were established in the 1860s and Slovak newspapers around 1990, helping to create national identities. They practiced a journalism that was partisan, subjective, and opinionated. When the Republic of Czechoslovakia was established in 1918 after the collapse of the Austro-Hungarian Empire after World War I, newspapers took it upon themselves to contribute to building the new nation. Until the breakup of the new democracy in 1939, Czech newspapers were partisan contributors to a vigorous political life.

In the Czech Republic by 2002, among the 60 dailies published, eight are national newspapers. *Mlada fronta Dnes* is the leading newspaper in the country, with a 22.3 percent market share, reaching 1.3 million readers every day. The tabloid *Blesk* has 16.3 percent of the market, followed closely by *Pravo,* which has a little over 13 percent share of the media market. German publishing chains dominate the Czech print media market, as they do Slovak publishing.

When the Slovak Republic became a sovereign state, in 1993, there were 753 publications (up from 326 in 1989), and by 2000, 1,465 publications were officially registered, among them 451 newspapers. By 2002 there were fewer than 20 dailies (half of them with a national reach, six regional, and three local). The most popular newspapers are *Novy cas, Sport, Pravda,* and *Sme,* with a daily circulation of 140,000, 70,000, 60,000, and 53,000, respectively.

Poland

Poland's first newspaper was launched in 1661, only to cease publication after a few issues. The second newspaper survived for more than 60 years (1729–1790). For a few short years after 1790, the Polish press multiplied and offered energetic and relatively free journalism, but the breakdown of centralized political control also led to Poland's dissolution by 1500. For the next 130 years the Austrian, Prussian, and Russian empires divided Polish territories among themselves and instituted stringent press controls and censorship. When Poland was reborn as a sovereign state in 1918, its press evolved into a highly diverse system, with the partisan, political press dominating the dailies and the commercial press leaning toward sensationalism.

Today, Poles can choose from among 5,500 periodicals, including 16 national dailies. The most widely read daily newspaper in Poland is *Gazeta Wyborcza,* established in 1989 by the Solidarity movement and now partly owned by a U.S.-based Cox Communications. It has a circulation of about 600,000, or 17 percent of the daily readership market. The second most popular daily is *Rzeczpospolita*, with a circulation of about 260,000, 7 percent of the market, followed by the tabloid *Super Express*, 500,000 (14 percent of the market). There are also 78 regional dailies and a plethora of magazines, the major ones owned by foreign companies. In addition there are approximately 1,500 to 2,500 regional and local publications.

Hungary

The first newspapers in Hungary were published in Latin and German. The first Hungarian-language newspaper (*Magyar Hirmondo*) was published in 1780 in Pozsony (today's Bratislava, the capital of the Slovak Republic). Censorship dominated the Hungarian press scene until 1859, when the three-month-long Austro-French-Italian war marginalized censorship and journalism became more interesting. When Hungary became a sovereign state in 1918, a lively, highly politicized, literary press fed the fires of a rich political and intellectual life until fascism snuffed out both in the 1930s.

Twenty-one percent of Hungarians do not regularly read either a daily or weekly newspaper, up from 10 percent in 1990. Whereas there has been a decrease in readers of political/quality newspapers, readership of the tabloid press went from almost zero to 665,000 by 1998. There are about 1,600 registered publications available to Hungarian readers, 33 of them daily newspapers.

Journalists in Hungary have legal access to government information as long as the documents don't compromise state security, but there is a prevailing "mindset" of security that prevents government transparency. The Hungarian parliament debated a law in 1999 that would have required media outlets to publish corrections to false statements of fact and also opposite opinions. The International Helsinki Foundation called the proposal "the first step to censorship." The proposal was later dropped.

Romania

In Romania, a repressive penal code, persistent corruption, political and economic pressures, and low journalistic standards are all significant obstacles to genuine press freedom. After the demise of the Nicolae Ceausescu dictatorship in late 1989, Romania's press freedom blossomed in the early 1990s, only to decrease to "partly free" through 1999. A Romanian law on state secrets, passed by the Romanian parliament in March 2001, could result in a further decline of media freedoms. Nineteen cases of legal and physical harassment of journalists were investigated by the Committee to Protect Journalists during 2000–2002.

Two Romanian daily newspapers, *Adevarul* and *Romania Libera*, reached 1.5 million circulation shortly after democratization began. Today there are hundreds of privately owned publications. However, financial and political pressures undercut the general independence of most private newspapers. One critic noted recently that advertising is often used as a tool for political bargaining or even blackmail. A report by the European Journalism Center criticized the sensationalized approach of many Romanian newspapers, which tend to focus on entertainment and novelty at the expense of investigative reporting. Media credibility has dropped among Romanian institutions, behind the church and the army.

Bulgaria

Hundreds of private radio and television stations began operation after government changes in 1989, but there was a litigious climate in the Bulgarian courts and parliament that affected the accountability of almost every journalist. The number of legal charges against journalists averaged about 100 each year. Because of efforts of journalists' organizations and human rights groups, a Bulgarian penal code relating to media libel and insult was changed in 2000, limiting the scope of criminal prosecution of journalists. The maximum punishment for libel and insult was changed to a fine of €7,000, instead of prison.

After 1989, the Bulgarian print media were free of overt government control. The two largest daily newspapers, *Trud* and *24 Chassa*, were owned by the German media group Westdeutsche Allgemeine Zeitung. Two other newspapers are party organs. Pluralism of views and criticism of government are apparent in the Bulgarian press, but many believe that influence peddling persists in more subtle forms. Bulgarian journalists prefer to focus on sensationalism and report only negative stories. Many rumors, persistent but unsubstantiated, connect newspapers with the former state security apparatus of Bulgaria, the Russian mafia, or other secretive groups.

In 2000 the Bulgarian Helsinki Committee published the results of a survey about the ethnic press in Bulgaria. Between May 1999 and May 2000, it analyzed 19 ethnic publications—seven Roma, three Armenian, two Wallachian and Romanian, two Jewish, two Russian, two Turkish, and one Macedonian—and outlined how these publications played an important role in helping to integrate communities into the broader society and promote national consolidation.

Albania

The Albanian government generally respected freedom of speech and of the press provided by the Law on Fundamental Human Rights and Freedoms. There were reports, however, of police assaults on journalists who were covering news, and of journalists being attacked by unknown assailants. Defamation trials against the media and political interference with allocation of state-funded advertising to media outlets also appeared as obstacles to media performance. The ability of Albanian journalists to initiate significant media reforms or to protest attacks on their colleagues remained limited by professional disunity.

Unresolved Tension Between Government and Mass Media

While they are hesitant to admit overt interference in news decisions, many eastern European government officials award incentives to compliant journalists. Government ministries reportedly offered the "most deserving" journalists money, gifts, or holidays at resorts.

A vexing problem facing the media in eastern Europe is the inclusion of defamation laws in the penal codes. Journalists found guilty of any infractions under a penal code could serve time in prison. In the Czech Republic, however, nearly all libel cases since 1990s have been adjudicated according to the civil code. And in Hungary, thanks to a 1994 constitutional court ruling judged libel to be unconstitutional, it is difficult for libel laws to be used to harass journalists who criticize government officials. Poland's penal code includes punishment for those who "insult, ridicule and deride the Polish nation, the Polish Republic, its political system or its principal organs." Criminal libel suits in Poland are rare, however. Similar provisions are found in the Slovak and Hungarian penal codes. In the Czech Republic the statute on defamation of the president was revoked in 1997, but the statute addressing defamation of the republic remains in effect.

The 1996 penal code in Romania makes it a crime to insult public officials and defines penalties for libel and slander. After Romania was invited to join the European Union in 1999, there were significant media reforms, but parliament then considered various laws to limit rather than promote press freedoms. The Romanian constitution prohibits defamation of the nation, attempts to instigate wars of aggression, incitement to discrimination and public violence, and obscene conduct contrary to morality.

In many regions of eastern Europe, free press advocates are concerned about the influence of organized crime in the operation of the mass media. Physical intimidation and attacks on journalists have occurred throughout the region. The Freedom Forum issued a statement early in 2001 saying investigative journalism in Serbia is an increasingly dangerous job. Serbian journalists are the most consistent critics of corruption.

Elsewhere, influence and intimidation of journalists are also recognized as a problem. Slovenian journalist Miro Petek, a writer for the daily newspaper *Vecer*, was covering corruption in Slovenian government and politics. He was attacked outside his home on February 28, 2000, and suffered serious injuries. The South East Europe Media Organization complained about lack of action in investigating the attack.

Growing Popularity and Influence of Electronic Media

Hungary has 35 television stations, according to the International Journalists' Network (IJNet). The most important among them are three publicly owned stations, two privately held terrestrial stations, and four cable channels. Publicly owned MTV1 reaches 97 percent of households yet attracts only 7 percent of the audience. Privately owned RTL-Klub and TV2, both owned by foreign consortiums, each reach 86 percent of TV households. There are 77 radio stations in Hungary, three of which are shortwave.

The Czech Republic has 120 radio stations, according to the IJNet, the most important being a three-channel public radio network and two nationwide radio stations. The Czech public radio has a 33 percent share of the radio market, whereas private radio stations take up about 60 percent of the market. A U.S.-owned company owns the most popular regional radio station.

Czech audiences can access 150 television stations, among them a two-channel public television network and two commercial stations with national reach. TV NOVA, the first commercial television station to be introduced in the former Soviet bloc (1994), attracts roughly 46 percent of Czech viewers. The two channels of Czech public television have about a 34 percent share of the market. Cable and satellite channels attract over 6 percent of the audience.

Slovak television is dominated by privately owned TV Markiza, which covers over two-thirds of the country, and is followed in popularity by public service Slovak Television, private JOJ, and NOVA. In addition, there are 78 terrestrial and cable television stations spread around the country. There are 94 commercial radio stations competing with public service radio stations.

There are approximately 200 national, regional, and local radio stations in Poland according to IJNet. Public Radio has four national channels, one shortwave broadcast channel for international transmission, and 17 independent regional radio stations. National commercial stations such as RMF FM Radio and ZET Radio provide the biggest competition for public radio. The Catholic Church in Poland is also engaged in broadcasting, with the most controversial of its stations, Maryja Radio, a network broadcasting from over 30 local frequencies.

Poland has a rich television landscape, with 24 mostly local and regional television stations, according to IJNet. Poland's public service television offers two national channels with 11 regional offices broadcasting local programs. TV Polonia is a special satellite channel that broadcasts abroad. In addition, Poles access popular satellite channels such as MTV, Eurosport, RTL, and the Cartoon Network.

East Europeans also access foreign radio and television transmissions, particularly broadcasters from contiguous countries, from other West European nations, and broadcasts by stations with a specific international profile such as the BBC and Radio Free Europe/Radio Liberty.

In Romania, there are more than 50 private television stations and 100 radio stations. Romania's meager market economy has limited commercial support. Advertising totaled $13 per capita in 2001, and most of the nation's advertising revenue, about 70 percent, is channeled to TV. A dual broadcasting system was introduced in 1992 that led to the creation of the Romanian Broadcasting Corporation and, in 1994, the Romanian Television Corporation, which transformed the state system into an independent, public service institution. Both private and public stations are regulated by the National AudioVisual Council, which awards broadcast licenses and regulates the airwaves.

Romanian TV programming is dominated by imported programs for entertainment, especially programs originating in the United States. The collapse of communism created a craving for Western ideas and products, which is filled through the vicarious experience of TV fantasies in imported programs.

Even in the Balkan countries such as Macedonia, the airwaves are crowded. Two private national TV channels broadcast in Macedonia, along with 44 regional

TV channels. There are three public broadcasting channels, all operated by the Macedonian Radio and Television. The first TV channel is a national service, the second broadcasts in minority languages, and the third transmits only foreign satellite programs. There is one national radio outlet and about 70 local radio stations in Macedonia.

In Poland, a number of news agencies offer news and photo services. In the Slovak Republic there are three news agencies, TASR, SITA, and the Slovak Information and Press Agency. Hungary has MTI, and the Czech Republic has the public Czech News Agency, the Prague News Agency, and an Internet news agency.

The Bulgarian News Agency has a network of journalists and correspondents that serve as information sources for most media outlets. The agency is partially funded by government funds and is generally considered to be a quasi-public organization, raising questions about its leadership and the credibility of its work. Parliament was reworking a new law in 2002 to designate the news agency as "autonomous" and to define its role in distributing government information to media outlets.

Authoritarian Roots Persist in Government–Media Relations

Postcommunist governments in eastern Europe retain authoritarian habits and tendencies and continue to politicize decisions on media policies, laws, and regulations, and attempt to control or at least manipulate public broadcasting media.

In the first few postcommunist years, the most notorious attempts to manipulate and control occurred in the public service media. Hungary's "media wars," which pitted reform-minded public service media leaders like Elemer Hankiss and Csaba Gombar against the government and parliament, were emulated in Poland and the Czech Republic. In the Slovak Republic, the authoritarian Meciar government (1992–1998) was successful in controlling, manipulating, and intimidating the media.

In 2002 the Polish government tried to change regulations so as to limit media concentration, a move that many media owners and parliamentarians considered to be an attempt to strengthen the control of the ruling party over public media. In the Czech Republic in 2001, an alleged political appointment to the directorship of Czech Television sparked a revolt at the television station that led to the resignation of the newly appointed general director, the dismissal of the Czech Television Council by the Czech parliament, and a change in media legislation that shifts the nomination of council members from the Chamber of Deputies to civic associations. The new law, however, allows the chamber to assume the television council's responsibilities and to appoint a new temporary director, thus leaving the future of Czech Television in political hands.

In Hungary, the appointment of a new National Television and Radio Board in February 2000 by the ruling coalition government brought thousands of protesters into the streets of Budapest demanding the establishment of a truly independent board. In the Slovak Republic, the heads of Slovak TV (STV) and radio were dismissed for failing to guarantee objective and independent broadcasting, and in 1999 STV became editorially independent.

Despite continued attempts at controlling and manipulating the media, there has been considerable resistance from journalists, journalism associations, civic groups, and opposition parliamentarians.

Hammering Out Equitable Media Laws

Postcommunist laws addressing various aspects of the media system and of journalism are sources of continuing controversy. With the enactment of their respective broadcasting laws, the Czech Republic in 1991–1992, Hungary in 1995, Poland in 1992, and the Slovak Republic in 1992–1993 established councils and boards to distribute licenses and regulate broadcasting. One of the immediate and most serious political controversies arose over who was to appoint the members of the national councils or boards: the parliament alone, as in the Slovak Republics, or the parliament and the president of the country acting together, as in the Czech Republic and Poland, or the government and opposition parties, as in Hungary. The potential ability of these broadcast councils or boards to control or micromanage the private commercial television field for partisan political purposes remains great.

Because East European governments often equate society with the state, thus demanding that public broadcasting represent the state, the mission of public television and radio to serve society is not fulfilled. The short history of postcommunist public service television in particular is filled with incidents of resistance and revolts against the overt politicization of public television on the part of its personnel, unions, and members of governing councils, or on the part of parliamentarians and political parties.

Ultimately, the crisis in east European broadcasting has "deep roots in the unresolved contradictions" of political culture (Szekfu 2002). In Poland, broadcasting law stipulates that all broadcasts respect the religious feelings of the audiences, although the law has not been used.

Access-to-information laws and laws protecting journalistic sources have been enacted, but slowly, and there is no uniformity in their interpretation and application by the courts. A new Data Protection and Freedom of Information Law was passed in Hungary in 1992 and strengthened in 1995 when a parliamentary commissioner to oversee its implementation was elected that year; it forces government agencies to respond to requests for information within eight days. In 1998, a law prohibiting recordings of government meetings, except for recording a summary containing the names of the participants and the agenda, put a damper on Hungarian journalists' access to information. A law similar to the Hungarian one went into effect in the Czech Republic on January 1, 2000, and provides freedom of access to information under the control of the state and local authorities, as well as under other institutions affecting the rights of citizens. A new Access to Public Information Law was approved by parliament in September 2001, and the Czech Press Act gives journalists the right to protect their sources unless the sources are involved in a criminal act.

The Slovak Republic adopted a comprehensive Freedom of Information Act in 2000 that grants all citizens access to almost all unclassified information. Poland does have laws on access to information, but not a clear legal act ensuring full public access.

Concepts of Media Freedom and Accountability

East European constitutions provide for freedom of speech and of the press, and in general the governments respect these rights, but not without some reservations. The notion that the media are far too important to be left to their own devices and that public service broadcast media, in particular, are to serve the elected governments is still strongly held.

Politicians are inclined to emulate Italy's Silvio Berlusconi when they become media proprietors, as the case of TV Markiza in the Slovak Republic illustrates. Pavel Rusko, chairman of popular Markiza TV and the founder of a new political party in 2001, has used the station to promote the party and his own political ambitions.

The manipulation of print media is far less obvious, partly because journalism is defined as a political weapon and partly because commercial interests cannot be satisfied without attention being paid to political interests in highly politically charged societies. By the end of the 1990s, however, overt partisanship had lost currency and a few media outlets had asserted their independence. The notion of accountability to the public has slowly been suggested as a replacement to a "social responsibility" defined in the 1990s almost exclusively in terms of politics, ideology, subservience to owners, and personal political and economic ambitions.

The definition and application of media freedom concepts and accountability have until recently been left to people and institutions outside the media systems. That is slowly changing, partly with the help of stronger professional organizations. Codes of ethics have been formulated in all four east Central European countries, but the enforcement of journalistic ethics is at best uneven. Nevertheless, the professional organizations that have been formed (and re-formed) since 1989 are part and parcel of the media's postcommunist evolution and an important part of the slow processes of professionalization.

Journalism Education and Training

The demise of communist regimes brought an explosion of journalism education and training programs, partly because of increased interest in journalism once it was no longer related to the state and the Marxist-Leninist ideology, and partly because Western media aid packages invariably contained educational and training elements.

Under communism, university-level journalism education in Czechoslovakia and Poland was of doubtful practicality and little academic standing, and was supplemented by training carried out by professional associations, themselves under Communist party control. There were no journalism programs in Hungarian universities. Instead, the Hungarian Association of Journalists, a government-subsidized organization, provided journalism training that essentially consisted of Marxist-Leninist indoctrination. East Central Europe's underground press served more or less as a recruiter of nonstate journalists and as an informal training ground for new journalists, who came from a variety of professions and educational paths.

The Future of East Central Europe's Media

The future of the region's media, and with it the future of their journalism, depends in large measure on economic factors, but even more fundamentally on the evolution of political culture and politics. That is, economic development, important in supporting a wide range of media outlets, does not guarantee independence from political pressures. Instead, what readers, listeners, and viewers will demand of the media, and the direction in which journalism will develop, will be determined by their practical definitions of democracy and citizenship. Publishers, editors, directors, and journalists have to play a central role in determining the nature of journalism's development in the region. Thus, there is a need for continued support for journalism education and training and journalistic associations, as well as collaboration between Western and East Central European journalists and journalism educators.

The Future of Media in the Region

The spread of the Internet in eastern Europe, as in most regions of the world, has opened new horizons for dialogue and dissemination of information. The Internet is generally not regulated and is subject to no control by governments in the region, perhaps because some still underestimate its scope and reach. Hundreds of "Internet cafés" have appeared in urban settings throughout the region, even in relatively spartan places like Kosovo and Albania. Government efforts to regulate or monitor Internet services to date have generally been unsuccessful. The Bulgarian government sought to impose a 20 to 40 percent fee on Internet service providers in new regulations adopted in November 1998. The proposed licensing provision was struck from the regulation after protests from the fledging Bulgarian Internet Society.

Media in the Newly Independent States

The story of the media in the newly independent states of Eurasia (Figure 14.2) is the story of the struggles, successes, and failures of postcommunist democratization. More than a decade after the collapse of the Soviet Union, optimism about the ease of such a transition has given way to a recognition of the complex challenges such transitions present. For all these nations, democratization has been a struggle, and the development of both independent media and the civil and cultural climates to support it has been fraught with difficulty.

One of the most noteworthy aspects of the transition to life after communism in the newly independent states is the difference in the experiences of the regional groupings. Whereas all the nations of the former USSR have encountered challenges along the path to self-governance, there are qualitative differences between the experiences of the Baltic states, the central European states, the Transcaucasian states, and the central Asian states. These differences arise out of the different cultural and political differences that held, and hold, sway in these countries before, during, and after communism.

The Baltic states had long considered themselves something apart from the Soviet Union, and their transition to life after its collapse has been relatively smooth. In the new nations of Ukraine, Belarus, and Moldova, the transition has been much more traumatic. Although these countries had some sense of an independent identity prior to the collapse of the former USSR, they were nonetheless Slav and less inclined to see the Russian empire as something distinct from themselves. For them, the transition to new nationhood has been the struggle between entrenched forces from the old days and forces that would radically change governance. The countries of the Transcaucuses were more prepared for transition than others of the new nations. Given their established tribal and geopolitical identities, they were psychologically prepared for existence apart from the Soviet Union. Unfortunately, the very origins of such fierce independence have also meant that each of the three countries now faces tribal and territorial disputes that sap their resources, deflect their political energies, and preoccupy their media. In Central Asia the fights are first for the right and ability to publish independently.

The very complicated challenges faced by the newly independent states, and especially by the smaller group of nations that are also members of the Commonwealth of Independent States, have prompted political scientists to question whether paradigms of democratization drawn from noncommunist countries are relevant to the study of postcommunist political change.

Under Soviet rule, media were viewed as instruments of the state, and criticism or discussion was to be aimed at correcting the course of communism, not challenging the system or those in power. Under Gorbachev's control, the USSR and its republics were introduced to the concept of *glasnost*, which was intended to reinvigorate the Soviet Union by allowing freer public comment about issues of importance to modernization of the country. While *glasnost* opened windows and then doors to media coverage of formerly taboos topics, it did so without providing the rule of law or civil institutions necessary to support press freedom over the long haul.

Thus, while each of the newly independent states has provisions for free speech and media independence written into its constitution, and many of those constitutions include provisions for due process in the courts should media behavior overstep the bounds, those laws are not recognized in practice. Investigative journalists in Ukraine are killed for pursuing stories the government does not like, journalists in Kazakhstan are sentenced to hard labor for insulting the president or his wife, and newspapers in Azerbaijan must check every fact they run—simply quoting someone is not enough. Outside organizations like the International Freedom of Expression Exchange, the Committee to Protect Journalists, PEN, Article 19,

FIGURE 14.2   *The newly independent states of the former Soviet Union*

Reporters sans Frontiers, and PEN keep track of and call attention to these incidents. There are is now also the Center for Journalism in Extreme Situations, which provides the journalists of the former Soviet Union with an opportunity to keep their own records of their struggles for independence.

The struggles of the media in all of these countries have been carried on with extensive support from organizations in western Europe and the United States. These include government-sponsored organizations, such as the Organization for Security and Cooperation in Europe, Radio Free Europe, and the U.S. State Department, as well as regional and international non-governmental organizations (NGOs), such as the European Institute for the Media, the International Federation of Journalists, Human Rights Watch, and the Soros Foundation.

The Baltic States

The Baltic states—Estonia, Latvia, and Lithuania—are still troubled by lingering issues from the past, but they are ahead of the other newly independent states, particularly in the area of media independence. While each of the Baltic countries has a mix of public and private media ownership, most of the broadcasting and newspaper outlets across the three countries are privately owned and free of government intervention. The problems that challenge Baltic journalists tend to cluster around issues of ethics and professional practice.

Estonia, Latvia, and Lithuania all rank high on the list of democratic countries and have enviable scores in both the political rights and press freedom categories. All three countries have actively engaged in the economic and democratic reform necessary to make them eligible for admission to the European Union.

Estonia. Estonia has stable political and economic systems and respects basic civil liberties, including freedom of the press. Corruption is not pervasive, and there is an active campaign to eradicate it.

All Estonian language dailies are privately owned and receive no financial assistance from the government. There are seven daily newspapers, of which five publish in Estonian and two in Russian. In addition, there are dozens of weekly papers. Although the government still owns the nation's printing facilities, they are managed privately without official interference. There are two news agencies.

Estonia has three national television stations that are private and one state-owned television station which has the largest audience. There are 30 private radio stations in addition to the state radio. Russian-language broadcasting is popular in Estonia.

More than 40 Estonian-language papers have united to form the Estonian Newspaper Association, which lobbies on behalf of its members' interests, defends member newspapers, and champions the interests and rights of Estonian media again violations of freedom of the press.

Fifty percent of Estonia's advertising expenditures are spent on newspapers. Television follows, with 20 percent. Magazines and radio each get 12 percent.

Estonia has the highest Internet penetration of any of the countries of eastern Europe or the former Soviet Union. Twenty-eight percent of Estonians between the ages of 17 and 74 use the Internet, and projects are under way to make 80 public access sites available. The only constraint on Internet access remains the high cost of computers and connections.

In general, unethical reporting is less of a problem in Estonia than in either of the other two Baltic states. However, Estonia has not been exempt from press trauma. An Estonian publisher of the country's largest Russian-language daily and weekly was shot in 2001, a year after his son had been killed in the same manner. No suspects were identified in either case.

Latvia.   Latvia is a functioning market economy with a democratic constitutional system. In general, the government respects freedom of speech, and the press and Latvian media express a wide range of critical views. Latvia has no legal penalties for irresponsible journalism, and legal penalties are the same for libeling private and public people.

Most newspapers and magazines in Latvia are privately owned. The two most popular dailies have circulations of 70,000 and 65,000. A Russian-language paper comes in next, with a circulation of 15,000. There is one state-owned weekly and a second state-owned paper that come out four times a week. All major cities have their own privately owned papers. Private companies handle the bulk of newspaper distribution.

The country has two state-owned television networks and nine privately owned stations. The station with the largest audience is the privately owned Latvian Independent Television, which has nearly twice as many viewers as its closest state-owned competitor. Ten percent of Latvian viewers turn to satellite television. There are a large number of independent radio stations broadcasting in both Russian and Latvian, and 10 of those stations are located in the capital, Riga. The radio station with the most listeners is the major public radio station, Latvijas Radio 1.

Television gets the largest share of Latvian advertising expenditures, with 43 percent, while newspapers get 35 percent, radio gets 6 percent, and magazines get 4 percent.

Latvian media problems tend to center around language issues, particularly as they impact the Russian-language press; the professional performance and ethics of journalists, particularly with regard to libel and slander; and the impact of Latvia's corruption problems on journalists who investigate them. This is illustrated by the death in 2001 of a journalist who had written stories about smuggling through Latvian ports by the Russian mafia and was investigating alleged involvement of local officials in an illegal alcohol business.

Latvian journalists are subject to in-house pressures from owners and, as a result, tend to engage in routine self-censorship. In 2000, research suggested 2.9 percent of the population used the Internet regularly and all of the major news outlets had their own Internet sites.

Lithuania. Lithuania continues to struggle with weakness in its judicial system that undermines the rule of law.

The mass media in Lithuania inspire more confidence than all other institutions. Nonetheless, in 2000 lawmakers passed legislation that would have created a national ombudsman to control the media. Although the president vetoed that provision of the bill, it was replaced with measures to beef up an existing commission charged with investigating journalism ethics.

Most of the Lithuanian media are privately owned, although the state still owns part of the dominant news service and all of the National Radio and Television Public Broadcasting Company. Private media are doing well, but state broadcasting has had a harder time paying its creditors.

Lithuania has three major daily newspapers and three major broadcasting operations. Newspaper distribution is privately owned, and few publications use the state-owned postal system. Two percent of Lithuanians are connected to the Internet; 5 percent of the population report that they use it.

Journalists working for state-owned radio and television face frequent pressure and intervention from the government. Russian-language journalists are more likely to feel beleaguered. All journalists have problems with access to government information, particularly information relating to military and security issues.

Lithuanian journalism has a reputation for sensationalism, scandal mongering, and focusing disproportionately on violent juvenile crime. In addition, Lithuanian media are prone to periodic outbreaks of inflammatory content, whether nationalistic, anti-Semitic, or pornographic. Lithuania has the harshest libel laws of all the Baltic countries, and penalties can include jail time, hard labor, or fines. In the mid-1990s Lithuanian journalists experienced personal attacks and office fire bombings, which were thought to be related to newspaper coverage of crime and local government connections to criminals.

Ukraine, Belarus, and Moldova

Ukraine. September 16, 2002, was the second anniversary of the disappearance of Georgy Gongadze, an investigative journalist and founder of *Ukrajinska Pravda,* an on-line paper which specialized in exposing government corruption. The anniversary was marked by mass protests in most large Ukrainian cities.

The journalist's body was found six months after he disappeared, and Ukrainian officials showed no great eagerness to solve the case, even turning away FBI agents who had come to Ukraine with an official invitation. Police and security services made numerous attempts to muzzle publications that carried coverage critical of the Gongadze scandal, generally laid at President Kuchma's door.

Kuchma's crackdown on the opposition and the press began in the months leading up to the 1999 presidential election and did not let up. Opposition newspapers were harassed or suspended. Tax police, fire brigades, and printing houses all harassed media critical of Kuchma. Television broadcasts were suspended. In both

1999 and 2001, Kuchma was listed on the Committee to Protect Journalists list of the "Ten Worst Enemies of the Press."

By 2000 there were 8,000 media in Ukraine, although only 2,600 appeared regularly. Seventy percent of print media were privately owned, with the true owners hiding from public view behind claims that ownership was in the hands of the editorial staff. Printing houses were state-owned and newspapers were distributed by various means, including the state-owned postal service, state-owned kiosks, and private distribution services.

Ukraine has several major private television broadcasters whose signals reach nationally, as well as four major FM radio stations. Given the hard economic times, television was many people's only source of information. A 1999 survey found that 90 percent of the population watched television every day, and that viewers were fairly evenly divided among the four top stations (McCormack 1999). However, research conducted a year later indicated that the broadcast outlets with the most credibility in Ukraine were the BBC and Radio Svoboda, sponsored by the United States.

While some influential, independent media outlets had begun to appear on the World Wide Web, only 1 percent of all Ukrainian homes had web access.

Numerous layers of Ukrainian legislation include language to protect press freedoms, but the word of the law and the practice diverge. However, there is one area in which the laws are followed to the letter. Ukrainian legal provisions make no distinction between rights to privacy for private individuals and public officials, and these laws have been used repeatedly by politicians, who have sued the media for massive amounts of money. Efforts by journalists to get the parliament to limit a newspaper's liability for damages failed.

Belarus. A free and fair election in 1994 brought Aleksandr Lukashenko to the Belarus presidency, and with him a return to the authoritarian government. Under Lukashenko's administration, censorship was reintroduced, independent trade unions were banned, and restrictions were introduced on who could run for election. Opposition politicians and journalists have disappeared. Leaks from within the government indicate that the president's security force was behind their murders.

The Belarusian government has done away with many civil liberties now taken for granted in the newly independent states. The government strictly constrains civil liberties, including freedoms of association, assembly, religion, movement, speech, and the press.

The neo-Stalinist philosophy of the Lukashenko government extends to economics. Belarus has attempted none of the economic reforms under way in many of the newly independent states. Instead, it continues to function with a centrally planned economy that is hostile to private enterprise and inhibits foreign investment. The country's borders are closed to print, audio, and video imports, and the independent media, which moved to Lithuania when they were denied the opportunity to publish in Belarus, have been forbidden to transport their papers across the border.

With the return to Soviet-style government, political information officers have been assigned to all state enterprises and offices. Official youth groups and trade unions have been reestablished, and even entry to university is under the president's control. In 1997 the Council of Ministers introduced strict regulations that held foreign correspondents responsible for any critical remarks made about officials of the regime and forbade them to report anything negative about Belarus.

Although the country's constitution and various amendments provide for a free press and free access to information, the provisions are not borne out in reality, and restrictions were tightened in 1998. The legislation includes a prohibition against defaming the president, senior government officials, and other members of the ruling elite. It also allows the State Committee for Press to suspend a publication for a year without a court ruling. This is the law that banned imported publications.

The country's nine state-owned large publications receive government subsidies, in addition to subsidized printing, paper, and distribution. As a result, state media support government policies and attack the opposition.

While the constitution allows for independent media and half of the Belarusian press is privatized, public officials are not allowed to give them any information or any advertising. In addition, independent media are subject to assorted official harassment, from visits from tax police and unannounced fire inspections to threats that their operations will be suspended or their issues confiscated. Local press tends to focus on entertainment and social issues and to avoid politics. High printing costs, high postage, and high taxes make it difficult for readers to afford the 10 independent newspapers, which account for less than 15 percent of the nation's official circulation figures.

Belarus has 165 licensed television operations and 40 radio stations. The largest are controlled by the state. All of them are in competition with Russian media, which broadcast into Belarus. Some stations have been suspended for critical coverage of the regime. But while the regime controls all Belarus broadcasting, it has no impact on Radio Liberty, which provides independent coverage of Belarusian news.

Belarus has two organizations of journalists, the state-run Belarusian Union of Journalists, with 2,000 members, and the independent Belarusian Association of Journalists, which has 750 members and is itself a member of the International Federation of Journalists. In October of 2000 the Belarusian Association of Journalists tried to hold a festival celebrating the non-state-owned media, but the government put a stop to it. Other organizations in Belarus that are concerned with the media include the PEN Center, the Law Center for Media Protection, the Association for Belarusian Editors and Publishers, and the Association of Regional Press.

Moldova. In 2000, Moldova voted to become a parliamentary democracy—the first in the CIS—but its future is uncertain, because while the western portion of the country is a oriented toward the West and interested in reform, the eastern, industrial region has formed a breakaway republic that is oriented toward Russia and even provides a foothold for Russian troops. Whereas the Moldovan government in Chinisau is a democracy, Transnistria, or the Dnestr Moldovan Republic (DMR), is an authoritarian state that restricts civil liberties.

Moldova has a robust press, with a wide variety of newspapers and television outlets. Most media are affiliated with a party or political coalition. And, although most of the independent papers publish in Romanian, the state issues one paper in Romanian and one in Russian. All Moldovan media are supposed to be licensed, but to avoid the tax, some publications are issued as "supplements" of already licensed organizations. The government runs its own news service, but it is outdone by several private services.

Teleradio-Moldova, the state-owned broadcasting operation, is the country's main source of television and radio programming, although there are private television and radio stations that broadcast in local markets.

Moldovan press law protects press freedom, but no distinction is made between defamation of public or private individuals. Journalists accused of libel must prove the veracity of their statements, and if they are found guilty and have not already retracted the statement, they can be fined amounts of money equal to 100 to 200 times the average monthly salary.

In the DMR, the state owns the two major newspapers. The neo-Stalinist government in Tirasol restricts press freedom and harasses or closes the small independent papers. No papers from one side of the country are allowed to circulate in the other side.

Both parts of Moldova have language issues, like many of the newly independent states. After independence, a law in Moldova proper required that 65 percent of all programming be presented in Moldovan, essentially Romanian; however, it is much easier for stations to use Russian programming.

There are 15 active Internet providers in Moldova, but most Internet hookups are found in schools, Internet cafés, foreign companies, and offices of NGOs with foreign backing.

Transcaucasia (Georgia, Armenia, Azerbaijan)

Georgia.   Georgia has had an uphill fight to establish itself as an independent state, as the result of both territorial and political battles that drained its resources and challenged its stability. Two regions, Ossetia and Abkhazia, have broken away after bloody fighting, and a third territory, Ajaria, has claimed autonomy but has not seceded.

President Shevardnadze has managed to stabilize the country and restore civil order and ethnic peace, and generate economic reforms.

While all government agencies are required to subscribe to the state-owned Georgian newspaper, independent newspapers dominate the market. Major dailies have circulations just below 10,000, but the largest-circulation papers are 35,000 for a weekly digest and 23,000 for a tabloid newspaper. Small papers outside the capital struggle to survive. Some find help from grants from foreign foundations.

All print media are private; however, the papers that have evolved from formerly communist media have a privileged existence. They continue to get subsidies from the state, the president appoints their editors, and they serve as outlets for government propaganda. A news service, also controlled by the government, has privileged access to information and acts as the president's press center.

A number of private news agencies compete in the market. Media distribution is also a mix of state-controlled and privately owned operations.

Most of the population gets its information from television. Two national television channels provide official viewpoints, but the addition of competition from the independent Rustavi-2 has forced them to begin to attempt somewhat more balanced coverage. The independent channel survived government attempts to force it out of business and gets most of the nation's viewers as well as more than half of the national advertising expenditures. Other independent television stations compete in Tbilisi, but without strong business or political support they lack viability. Radio tends to concentrate on music although a radio channel in the capital had begun to explore the potential of political satire.

Public officials often use libel and defamation provisions against journalists, although cases tend to get dropped or else get snarled up in court proceedings. Police and justice officials periodically harass journalists trying to get information, which led to rallies and public demands for change until Shevardnadze came out in favor of the media position.

Georgian media are free of censorship, but the dire economic conditions open them up to financial pressures of all sorts. Papers have even been known to run stories commissioned by rival local clans. In general, observers suggest that Georgian media lack professionalism, credibility, and financial stability. Authorities control most of the media in Ajaria, South Ossetia, and Abhazia.

A number of journalism organizations and NGOs promote media issues in Georgia. One of the most aggressive at promoting legislation, organizing protests, and so forth is the Liberty Institute.

While there is robust competition among Internet providers, only two-tenths of a percent of the Georgian population has Internet access.

Armenia.   Armenia was credited with free and fair elections in 1999, but in December of that year a deranged former journalist led a team of gunmen into the parliament, where the prime minister, the speaker, and six others were murdered. The upshot was six months of political finger pointing and uncertainty. In the end, President Kocharian, whose side had lost in the election, won the power struggle, and the country stabilized and began to make progress toward membership in the Council of Europe.

Armenian media offer a wide array of opinions; however, they face serious professional and economic challenges. Most news operations are privately owned and funded. Of the more than 900 operations registered by the state in 2000, only 150 newspapers and magazines were active. Ten percent of all newspapers are owned by the state. There are six privately owned national dailies. Most newspapers were distributed by a state-owned operation that also controlled most of the kiosks; the operation was intended for privatization early in this decade.

Because Armenian living standards are so low, print media sales are also low. The largest paper in the country has a circulation of less than 10,000. Thus, newspapers are not attractive to advertisers and are generally unprofitable; they depend on backers with economic or political motives of their own, and are also susceptible to pressure to accept subsidies in place of earned income. To the extent that journalists exercise self-censorship, it is usually from economic rather than political motives.

Broadcast media get the largest Armenian audiences and are profitable and attractive to advertisers. Armenia has 30 national and local television stations and six FM stations. Most television operations concentrate on talk shows and entertainment and offer little news. Only state-run television is accessible every in the country. Daily programs by Radio Free Europe/Radio Liberty and the Voice of America are rebroadcast by state radio.

Press law in Armenia is inadequate and actually violates many of the international human rights instruments the country has signed, although according to Armenian law, international agreements supersede national regulations.

Authorities generally don't interfere with the media, but the government has been known to jail opposition journalists for slander. Editorial independence varies from media outlet to media outlet, but as a rule, although the media will not attack their own owners or patrons, everyone else is fair game, including their political enemies, even the president. However, there is little in-depth reporting or investigative journalism.

Several press associations are active in Armenia, although none represents the majority of journalists, who tend to be young and untrained. The Journalists Union of Armenia is an artifact of the Soviet era and represents older journalists. The Yerevan Press Club is a watchdog group that provides training and calls attention to challenges to press freedom.

Poverty has put the Internet beyond the reach of most Armenians. The estimated 1 percent of the population with access gets it through universities or NGOs.

Azerbaijan. With its strong president form of government, Azerbaijan depends for progress on President Heydar Aliyev, whose health has been uncertain for the last several years.

Azeri oil reserves have attracted Western investment and involvement, which has propped up the country through tough economic and political times. Although the government has passed a lot of reform legislation, the results have not shown up in institutional reform. Azerbaijan also faces problems because of its unresolved war with Armenia.

Oil profits from a new pipeline have begun to turn the economy around, but the results have yet to reach the population, which was reduced to poverty by the war and the resultant economic turmoil. International aid agencies that initially showed up to address the crisis how focus on development, but it is not clear that reforms will be transparent, effective, or sustainable. What small gains have been made toward democracy and openness are tenuous and will wither without continued commitment to difficult economic, social, and political reform.

Public confidence in the media is high, but most people cannot afford newspapers and get their information either from broadcast media or by word of mouth.

Audience research suggests television is considered the most credible source of information and radio is considered the least credible.

There are 151 newspapers in Azerbaijan, of which 141 are in Azeri and the rest are in Russian and English. Newspapers are generally outlets for political or business interests, although the Russian-language paper *Zerkalo*, which relies on advertising revenues, is truly independent. It publishes daily and weekly editions as well as an on-line version. The most popular independent paper, which is linked to the Musavat party, has a circulation of about 20,000, while the next most popular paper, also political, has a circulation of just under 10,000.

Some small papers publish in English for the expatriate community in Baku, and there are also some niche magazines, the most successful of which tend to deal with business. The state operates a distribution company, which competes with five private companies and street vendors.

Because of the poverty of the country, the independent press finds itself in dire circumstances. Companies that used to advertise have been forced to close, and with fewer advertisers, newspapers have had to raise their advertising rates.

Azerbaijan has a number of news agencies and many journalist organizations. One, Yeni Nesil, or New Generation, has 550 members and reports that 70 percent of all journalists in Azerbaijan have little or no journalism education or training, and as a result they can't do objective, balanced reporting. The organization developed an ethics code, organizes training programs, and provides seminars on topics such as how to attract advertising. The Baku Press Club provides a neutral, central place for press conferences. A new press club called Ideal was organized in 2001 and hopes to be able to offer journalism prizes.

There is one functioning state television channel in Azerbaijan that provides music, information, and features on the president and his son. There are also several independent broadcasting operations and one cable channel. At least one of the "independent" channels is operated by Ilham Aliyev.

The most powerful station in the country, which reached most parts of Azerbaijan, began broadcasting Russian television in 1999 and had begun developing local programming when it was suddenly closed in 2001. The announcement came on the second anniversary of the station's founding when the owner announced that he would seek asylum in the United States after repeated tax investigations and other interferences from the Aliyev regime.

Residents of Baku can get foreign television stations via cable, but the service is too expensive for all but foreign residents to afford. Satellite dishes are cheaper and, thus, prevalent.

The Ministry of Press and Information and the Ministry of Communications regulate the media. The former handles regulation and licensing and the latter is one of several ministries involved in allocating frequencies. For the most part frequencies are available only to those with connections to the president.

Censorship was officially outlawed in 1998, but journalists censor themselves and the government is quick to launch prosecutions for libel against newspapers that insult the president or members of the government. A 1999 press law requires that media must verify all facts before they run them or face prosecution.

The Internet is increasingly used as a source of news and information. Azeri Internet cafés are open 24 hours a day, and both public and private universities have added computer labs. NGOs and foreign governments both support Internet access and training centers for professionals. Dial-up services are too expensive for most homes, but businesses have it, and Azeri journalists are more and more connected to the web.

Central Asia (Kazakhstan, Krgyzstan, Tajikistan, Turkmenistan, Uzbekistan)

Kazakhstan. From his "the one and only official Kazakhstan website" to the legislation that gives him lifelong oversight over future presidents and governments of the country, it is clear that Nursultan Nazarbaev is Kazakhstan. In fact, the Kazakh calendar has a month named after Nazarbaev and one named after his mother.

Vast mineral and oil reserves make Kazakhstan attractive to the West, and Nazarbaev described his country as an "oasis of stability," a feature investors find reassuring. However, the resultant petro dollar income highlights the poor living conditions of Kazakh citizens and has triggered corruption and bribery scandals, which have caused massive capital flight.

Kazakhstan offers the rhetoric of democratization and political reforms, but rhetoric bears little resemblance to reality. Control of all strategic resources and political power is concentrated in Nazarbaev, his family, and clan. Those strategic resources include the media. In 1996 Dariga Nazarbaev, the president's oldest daughter, took over the state-owned news agency. This change led to closure of many of the country's media.

The Kazakh press experienced a brief spell of freedom in the mid-1990s. At that time, the country had a popular, professional newspaper that had its own broadcast operation. The company was driven out of business by raids, intimidation, tax audits, and arson. In the end, the company paper was purchased by a business with close ties to Nazarbaev's son-in-law.

Since 1996 the government has cracked down on press freedom, and conditions for the media have worsened. In 1998 Nazarbaev-handpicked legislators passed a media law that restricted media independence officially. Then in 1999 a law was passed that made it a crime for anyone to disclose or publish any information about the president and his family, their economic interests, or investments.

While there are 45 individual broadcasting outfits—17 television, 15 radio, and 13 combined—all of them are now required to use facilities owned by the state. Business groups finance most existing newspapers with close ties to the country's leadership. Since the national security law limits foreign ownership of Kazakh media to 20 percent, what little independent media there is tends to get some support from Nazarbaev's political opposition. The president has accused the media of distortion and warned against use of the media to settle old scores or discredit the state.

Human Rights Watch has identified four means used by the government to intimidate the media during the 1999 elections: assignment of massive libel damages in favor of government officials; disruption and intimidation by state agencies, such as tax, customs, printing, and distribution offices; formal and informal censorship of and unwritten orders to journalists; and, finally, violence and terror.

Several organizations work to protect press freedom in Kazakhstan. Edil Soz is a public foundation for the protection of free speech that gets funding from the United States Agency for International Development (USAID). The foundation speaks out for press freedom and is represented on a state committee on pornography and the media. USAID also helped with the formation of the Kazakhstan Press Club, which supports journalists' professional development, while avoiding run-ins with the state. Independent Electronic Mass Media in Central Asia guides journalists seeking legal representation. In the mid-1990s U.S. funding helped create exchanges that sent Kazakh journalists to spend time with American newspapers, and then offered them a workshop at home on American-style journalism. Other Western countries have also developed contacts intended to help Kazakh journalists learn the ropes of democratic media.

Opposition activists and independent journalists without a voice in Kazakhstan have resorted to the Internet to disseminate their views. The Kazakh opposition helps fund a web presence in Moscow that exposes corruption of the Nazarbaev regime. The Kazakh government blocks citizens' access to the Eurasianet site.

Regular assaults on the independent media in Kazakhstan have prompted mounting expressions of concern from Washington and watchdog organizations concerned about antidemocratic developments in the country. Another well-known reporter was beaten up earlier in August, allegedly by three police officers, in what was described by his colleagues as "an intimidatory attack." In May, the offices of the independent newspaper *Respublika* were destroyed in an arson attack just days after a headless dog was sent to its journalists with a note warning "there will be no next time." Two staff members of another critical newspaper were beaten and their offices were raided.

Kyrgyzstan. Kyrgyzstan was once considered an oasis of democracy in a region of autocrats. In the early 1990s the West viewed the Kyrgyz as the most democrat people in Central Asia. The country had diverse representation in their parliament; their president hadn't been a Communist party leader under the old regime; the president tolerated media criticism, if not investigation of high-level corruption. In the intervening decade, however, President Askar Akayev has done his best to bring his country into line with its neighbors.

Although Kyrgyzstan is still more liberal than some of the surrounding countries, it is beginning to demonstrate the hallmarks of a Central Asian autocracy. Media covering topics unpopular with the president found themselves at the mercy of tax auditors or burdened by crippling criminal libel judgments. However, not all of the characteristics that gave Western observers hope are gone. There is still a vigorous civil society. There is still a multiparty system, and independent media still exist.

Most of the Kyrgyz media are state-owned. They include seven national, regional, and local papers. There are 50 private newspapers and magazines, most in the capital of Bishkek and two in the Osh region.

The Kyrgyz media take different approaches to the country's political situation. The state media praise the president lavishly. Most of the private media try to provide balanced coverage, but there are outspoken critics among the private media, and they face harassment. Journalists routinely engage in self-censorship.

Advertising is restricted by law to 20 percent of print media space. Newsstands and kiosks were privatized in the early 1990s, but they still get all their publications from the state distribution operation. The government owns the printing plant for the state media, and a businessman who is close to the president owns the private publishing center. The government controls all newsprint, and newspapers that get on the wrong side of the president have experienced paper shortages.

There are 114 independent television and radio stations, which also are mostly located in the capital. Although broadcast services reach much of the country, their equipment is not powerful enough to make it possible to reach the more mountainous regions. The law limits advertising in broadcasting to 25 percent of airtime. Broadcasting stations are required to pay for all the supervisory functions of the National Agency for Communication. That agency and the Minister of Justice and the president's office must approve all broadcast licenses.

The country has legal guarantees of press freedom, but there are many constraints and limitations. It is illegal to print government secrets. Media are not allowed to print false information, even in a direct quote. It is illegal to damage someone's honor, or to publish articles that encourage war or incite ethnic or religious antagonism.

Res Publica, which has a circulation of 10,000, has repeatedly challenged the president and as a result has faced repeated court cases. Its reporters, copy editors, and even its chief editor, have been imprisoned for their roles in producing "anti-state" stories. Other journalists have been jailed for writing the wrong kind of stories, and several journalists charged with printing state secrets were jailed and interrogated by government security forces. Papers that interviewed opposition politicians faced fines for tax code violations and the repeated attentions of tax investigators.

In 1998 Akayev set up a Morals Commission made up of illustrious citizens and academics. The commission suspended three newspapers. All of them revised their approaches to the practice of journalism and reopened in 1999. Observers suggest that it is only fair to note that Kyrgyz journalists do tend to report stories based on rumor and unsubstantiated reports.

Independent Kyrgyz media faced considerable political and financial constraints during the 2000 election. Local officials filed libel suits in response to critical articles, the presidential administration triggered tax audits and criminal investigations, and while most private media got off without excessive trouble, the treatment of outspoken members of the press provided a clear warning to the rest.

Internet use is limited both because the citizens of Kyrgyzstan are poor and cannot afford service and because the infrastructure of the country does not make it possible for people who live in rural areas to get service. Internet use is estimated at 0.4 per 1,000. There are no government restrictions on Internet use or access.

Tajikistan.   The end of the 1990s brought Tajikistan some recovery after five years of civil war. President Imomali Rakhmanov stuck to the terms of the military part of the agreement but was less gracious about providing the opposition access to media and a role in government.

The Tajik constitution provides for freedom of both speech and press, but these freedoms are more recognized in the breach. As a matter of practice, Tajikistan restricts freedom of speech and press. Journalists and citizens who disagree with the administration are rarely allowed to voice their opinions. The media are licensed, and journalists routinely get friendly advice about what they should and should not cover. Editors practice self-censorship out of fear of retaliation.

Tajikistan has 245 registered newspapers. Four papers are run by the state and 21 papers belong to political parties. There are 64 regional, city, and district papers. Three independent papers are published in the capital, Dushanbe. There are no dailies because the economy is too bad to support anything beyond weeklies.

During the recent election campaigns the range of views covered was limited in both print and media coverage. The state-owned press gave the opposition only negative coverage. The major Russian-language paper gave 90 percent of its election coverage to the president and the ruling power. Several independent papers did try to balance coverage of all candidates.

The government controls all printing facilities and newsprint supplies, and subsidizes nearly all publications. Because of the government stranglehold on production and distribution, even independent papers are extremely dependent on the central government, and because of short supplies of newsprint and high prices they can't always publish. When uncertain conditions are coupled with low salaries, the result is low morale particularly among experienced journalists who are leaving the business for more certain employment.

Television and radio are the most influential media in Tajikistan. Both are state-owned. The state also controls all broadcast licenses and subsidizes all broadcasting facilities. Under pressure from the Organization for Security and Cooperation in Europe, the state-owned television gave limited airtime to opposition candidates during the 1999 parliamentary campaign, but the result fell far short of balanced or objective coverage. The only alternative media from outside are Russian, and a reported 78 percent of Tajiks watch Russian television.

Internet access in Tajikistan is growing, in part because of the efforts of the U.S.-funded Central Asian Development Agency. There are five Internet service providers in Tajikistan, but most of their customers are foreigners, since the cost of subscription is the equivalent of $20 dollars, and monthly fees are $4 to $6 an hour—the equivalent of a Tajik's monthly salary. Government operations and research institutes also provide access to a small elite. The exact number of Internet users is unclear, but it may be three-hundredths of 1 percent of the population.

Independent journalists are routinely exposed to intimidation, harassment, and violence. Reprisals are frequent, particularly punishment for investigative reporting into government connections with narcotics trafficking. The head of the Ministry of Interior Press Center was shot and killed near Dushanbe, apparently because of his investigation into the regime's involvement in the drug trade.

Owners and editors avoid criticizing the ruling party out of fear that their newspapers will be shut down.

Turkmenistan.   No private print or broadcast media are allowed in Turkmenistan. The several autonomous publications that existed under Soviet rule were closed. In 1996 President Niyazov declared himself the founder and owner of all newspapers and magazines. Two nominally independent papers were created, but they were founded and are run by the state.

There are 23 state-owned magazines and 14 newspapers. Of those, one magazine and two newspapers are published in Russian and one newspaper is published in Turkish. Almost all print publications are based in the Ashgabat Press House in the capital. Government agents often seize Russian papers from travelers landing at the Ashgabat airport, but Russian and Western newspapers are often available at hotels in the capital.

Turkmen journalists are civil servants, and their work is subject to Niyazov's whims. The government budget funds all newspapers. Ads and sales provide little income. The government imports and restricts access to newsprint, equipment, and supplies. Party functionaries hold most key posts in Turkmen radio, television, and newspaper operations.

The state-owned National TV and Radio Broadcasting is the only domestic broadcaster. It operates two television channels. The first broadcasts in Turkmen and Russian. The second, in Ashgabat, broadcasts in Turkmen. The state broadcasting operation delays, censors, and rebroadcasts content from the Russian Public Televison and the Russian radio station Mayak. The only independent broadcast content available to Turkmen comes from Radio Liberty's shortwave operation. The stringers who work for Radio Liberty have been harassed, detained, and beaten. Most of those who continue to string for Radio Liberty work under pseudonyms.

The media are forbidden to cover opposition views. Broadcast news generally consists of the activities and speeches of the government. The president is generally presented as the wise, benevolent father of the country. The only criticism allowed on the news is the president's criticism of government officials.

Few foreign journalists are allowed to enter the country, and those allowed in are monitored and their movements are restricted.

All independent journalism organizations were dissolved by presidential decree. Several new organizations are state run. They include a Turkmen branch of a Central Asian broadcast association, an organization for women journalists, and an organization for young journalists. In 1999 police broke up a gathering of journalists planning to form their own organization.

There is very low Internet usage in Turkmenistan both because there is little access and because the state has few resources. In May of 2000 the government closed what few Internet service providers the country had. Since then it has been hard for businesses and NGOs to access the Internet. Usage in 2000 was estimated at 4.5 per 10,000. Server facilities are donated by the international Internet registry in London.

The Organization for Security and Cooperation in Europe's Representative for Media said in 1999 that Turkmenistan had a virtual absence of media freedom and that there are no independent media, nor is there any debate on issues.

Uzbekistan.   Uzbekistan is still run by its Soviet-era leader, President Islam Karimov. While the country's constitution and laws provide for civil rights and good governance, in reality it is an extremely authoritarian state in which human and political freedoms are restricted.

The Uzbek political environment presents challenges for press and media. State-sponsored media dominate the country, and active and passive government censorship on a daily basis serves to chill expression and limit access to information.

The country has 477 newspapers, 136 magazines, and four information agencies. Several minor independent papers publish in Tashkent. They tend to focus on business and have small circulations. The government controls all print distribution. Both print and broadcast media are subjected to multiple levels of government oversight. They are also subject to annual inspections by government agents.

Exile groups publish papers in Moscow and Istanbul and smuggle them into the country.

The country has 25 television studios and two radio stations. Broadcast media are subject to a highly bureaucratic annual re-registration process. More progressive stations have been shut down, ostensibly over licensing issues.

Libel, public defamation of the president, and irresponsible journalism, especially reporting falsehoods, are all crimes under the 1997 Law on Media. They carry stiff fines and possible prison time.

The Uzbek government has criticized foreign journalists—mostly Russian-based reporters for newspapers like *Nezavisimaya Gazeta* and *Izvestiya* and the news service Interfax—for reporting libelous stories. Journalists have been pressured to leave Uzbekistan.

Homegrown journalists are also targets. In 1997 a popular Uzbek journalist known for his satirical work and his criticism of corrupt officials was arrested. He was held for more than a year before he was found guilty and sentenced to 11 years in jail. A popular writer was arrested and charged with having links to a banned political party.

In 1999 the Ukrainian government arrested two men who had gone there to pick up copies of a paper for distribution in Uzbekistan. The men were extradited and stood trial in Tashkent on charges that included distributing a banned paper containing slanderous criticism of the president, participating in a banned political association, and attempting to overthrow the government. The pair was sentenced to 8 to 15 years in jail.

Contemporary Russian Journalism's Problems and Opportunities

Journalism in Russia has changed rapidly in the past two decades, reflecting the country's political, social, and economic changes. Today, Russian journalism has a new philosophy that is heavily rooted in the long tradition of this profession. The major turning points of Soviet and post-Soviet history of Russia as well as this country's political and economic turnaround have directly influenced the character of journalism in Russia at the beginning of the twenty-first century.

The development of journalism in Russia can be divided into three major parts: the pre-Soviet period, which includes the early days of journalism, nineteenth century journalism, and journalism in the early twentieth century; the Soviet period, from 1917 until 1985, which includes the Soviet period as well as changes during *perestroika* and *glasnost*; and the Gorbachev and post-Soviet period, from 1985, when the Soviet Union collapsed, to the present. We present a brief overview of each of these periods. Much has been written about all three periods in Russian journalism, so those who are interested can access cited sources for more comprehensive information on the subject (see McNair 1991; McReynolds 1991; Murray 1994).

Censorship has existed in Russia as long as journalism itself. Since the government brought the media to Russia, it had to guard the press content, so that the press could serve the government. Censorship had a complex structure: government officials of many levels had to read newspapers and journals regularly and were required to report on ambiguous or potentially harmful materials. Then the authors would be investigated and often prosecuted. Many newspapers and journals were shut down as a result of censorship activities. Most of the Russian writers and publicists of the pre-Soviet era were exiled from the capitals, Moscow and St. Petersburg, at some point in their careers; many were sent to Siberia for their freethinking, and all were carefully watched by the censors.

Contemporary Russian journalism is very diverse. Today's Russian journalism took over a gigantic media system, divided it into parts, and made independent media out of these pieces. One of the major characteristics of post-Soviet Russian media is its human and material resources, which have allowed fairly easy restructuring of the media. New Russian media did not have to start from scratch: a journalism tradition and infrastructure were already available. At the same time, many media, such as the Internet, developed as a result of political and technological changes in Russian society. In this section we present general information on Russian media—print, broadcast, and the Internet—and then discuss journalism education in Russia.

Print Media. Even though many independent newspapers that were created in the early 1990s had to use grants from Western organizations to begin to publish and many editors and journalists of national newspapers split up to create their own media organizations, Russia had arrived at its independence with a strong foundation of diverse forms of journalism. If readers in the Soviet Union were active subscribers to major national and local newspapers (often it was a sign of a good party citizenship to subscribe to *Pravda, Izvestiya,* and others) as well as many special-interest media (young Russians read at least *Komsomolskaya Pravda* and *Rovesnik*; teenagers had to follow news in *Pionerskaya Pravda* and *Pioner*; and even elementary schoolchildren had their own magazines, such as *Murzilka*), readers of post-Soviet Russia have been not only economically disempowered, but also highly selective in their choice of media.

Segmentation of the audience is a central feature of modern Russian media. In the last ten years, even though the annual circulation of Russian newspapers has declined by about 35 percent, the number of newspapers being published grew by 20 percent (Shkondin 2002).

The frequency and times when newspapers are published have also changed. In 1989, 11 (32.4 percent) of the 34 national newspapers were published daily and 15 (43.1 percent) were published once or twice a week; in contrast, of the 333 newspapers that were published in 2000, only 20 (6 percent) were published daily; 100 (30 percent) were published once or twice a week, and the majority, 183 (54.95 percent), of newspapers were published up to three times a month. In 2000, 5,425 regional newspapers were published, and their circulation totaled 14.9 million copies, or 27.2 percent, and covered 94% of the total number of newspapers in Russia. Although the number of daily newspapers declined by only a small amount, their total circulation was cut by 2.8 times (Shkondin 2002).

Russian periodical media have kept the structure that was created during the Soviet period. Until now, Russian newspapers have been divided into national, regional, city, *raion* (county), and other local, internal (usually factory-owned) newspapers, and specialized (such as economic and professional and leisure interest) newspapers. Many of them have changed their focus and now publish strictly informative or tabloid materials as well as reprints from national and newspapers. This is especially true for local newspapers, such as city- and *raion*-oriented newspapers, because of the lack of professional staff and financial flexibility required to cover local current events.

Magazines have suffered economic crises the most. If in Soviet times magazines of general and special interest were extremely popular and were successful in promoting the image of Soviet women, today most magazines are just Russian versions of popular Western magazines from leading publishing houses.

Broadcast Media. As with print media, broadcast media were also a part of a larger Soviet system, and thus their dissemination throughout the country as well as their structure that was built under the Soviet regime helped Russia to keep broadcast media well and alive, even after the collapse of the Soviet Union.

Historically, television set ownership has been high in Russia, and it has remained so since the collapse of the Soviet Union. In a Gallup survey of eight regional cities, 73% of households have had a color TV set since 1993, and around 43% have two or more televisions (Internews 1999).

At least 500 registered TV stations are located throughout Russia today (Internews 1999). Among the most popular newscasts are *Vremya*, which is state-controlled and has an estimated audience of 14 million viewers nightly, with about a

26% rating; *Vesti,* on the second national channel, RTR; and *Sevodnya,* on the commercial channel NTV. However, because neither RTR nor NTV reaches as many viewers as ORT, *Vremya* has a much broader overall reach, mostly because of transmitter availability (Kagan World Media 1996).

The majority of broadcast media in today's Russia, specifically television, is state-owned. Most administrative regions in Russia have their own government-run TV stations as well as at least one independent station. Independent stations suffer financial shortages and for the most part exist through grants from Western independent associations and private businesses. Because TV is the most successful medium to influence Russian publics (International Center for Journalists [ICJ] 2000), federal and local governments pay particular attention to the content of state-run and independent TV stations. Even though they cannot dictate a specific political view anymore, they find other ways to influence what and how events are reported (the phenomena of self-censorship and economic dependency will be explained later in this chapter). Radio broadcasting also continues to be dominated by state-owned and state-operated stations, but more and more local independent radio stations are emerging. Among independent media that have emerged, the most popular are *Ekho Moskvy* (Moscow region), *Mayak,* and *Radio Rossiya* (both national), as well as Europe Plus, a national radio that mostly broadcasts music and has virtually no informative programming.

These stations have the highest ratings, with "an estimated 180 million potential listeners in the Commonwealth of Independent States (CIS), although surveys indicate that local stations together have the highest percentage of listeners, at 41%" (Kagan World Media 1996). Research by the former U.S. Information Agency claimed that 92% of the former USSR population could receive radio on an estimated 208 million sets in 1994, and this number has substantially increased (Kagan World Media 1996).

Internet. In 1997, Russia had about 600,000 Internet users, according to the Russian Committee for Communications and Information (Goskomsvyaz), and this number has grown substantially since then. The European Media Institute (2000) cites the Institute for Social and Political Research, which estimates that if present trends continue, the Russian Internet audience (only 9 million in 2000) should reach 27 million by the end of 2002. Still, many problems of access to the Internet remain for a broad range of Russian publics. Internet cafés are the most popular places for Russians to surf the Internet, since the vast majority of Russians does not have any type of Internet connection at home. Public institutions, such as universities and libraries, often do not have a fast and reliable Internet connection either because of their inability to pay for continuous use of the Internet (despite national programs funded by the Open Society Institute of the Soros Foundation, which has helped to establish initial computer classes having Internet connections). Thus, universities and nonprofit organizations cannot fully take advantage of the Internet's potential because they do not have access to the Internet.

Major media organizations have invested in existing Internet-based publications and have also established their own. Politics remains the major theme of these publications. Internet media are divided into government and non-governmental media. Many websites are mirror publications of already existing print or broadcast media (*Komsomolskaya Pravda, Izvestiya, Kommersant,* and others); others are original Internet media (*Gazeta.ru, Lenta.ru*).

Journalism Education in Russia.   The Soviet form of higher education in journalism, which has a solid, comprehensive foundation, remains in post-Soviet Russia. The ideological core of Russian journalism—coverage of news events in accordance with the Communist party's view of the world—required a comprehensive liberal education with in-depth study of works by Russian writers and publicists; such education helped to prepare journalists as well-educated thinkers, not just as skilled technicians. As Murray (1994) puts it: "The role of the Soviet press . . . was not simply to report in accordance with Marxist-Leninist logic. The journalist also had a duty actively to participate in the construction of the future society" (p. 88).

During the Soviet period, the most famous universities for journalism education were Moscow State University and Moscow Institute of International Relations, which mostly prepared journalists for work in national media. The capital city of each republic of the former USSR, as well as major cities in several Russian regions, also had large state universities that offered journalism majors. Among the most competitive and popular were St. Petersburg State, Ural State, Voronezh State, Far-Eastern State (all in Russia), as well as Kiev State (Ukraine), Minsk State (Belarus), and Tartu University in Tallinn (Estonia). They all had a rich journalistic and literary tradition and the best faculty available. At the same time, these universities were watched closest by Glavlit and other party representatives and thus were highly conservative in their curricula.

When *perestroika* and *glasnost* came, Russian journalism education went through an exciting period of reestablishing and rethinking its educational practices. This was a great time to study journalism at a Russian university because faculty members inspired by open discussions of previously banned publications and other materials were hurrying to share their thoughts and enthusiasm with their students. Many faculty members engaged in extremely interesting debates about modern journalism issues as well as the state of higher education, and students were witnesses of these debates as they listened to lectures and participated in seminars. The first author of this chapter was studying at Voronezh State at that time, and she remembers the excitement and richness of each seminar and lecture as professors and students together progressed in their thinking and reconceptualization of their worldview.

In the beginning of the twenty-first century, however, journalism education in Russia faces several challenges. First, many faculty members have left the universities in search of better-paid jobs. If in the Soviet Union professors could be placed in the higher than middle-class salary range, by the end of the 1990s they hardly managed to make enough money to cover the basic needs of their families. Today, faculty members, in addition to full-time teaching, usually work in the Russian media or in advertising and public relations to be able to support themselves.

Furthermore, professors of the "old school" have retired, and many undereducated professionals and young scholars who have very little graduate training have taken their place. Moreover, many people who work for today's Russian media come from a various backgrounds and do not know the rich tradition of Russian journalism, nor do they have any solid training in journalism writing. As a result, informational genres occupy the press and broadcast media, and a shift to a Western model of journalism has become more evident. A Westernized press has replaced the Soviet model of journalism, bringing a new ideology to Russian media, according to Murray (1994).

Some even point out that editors sometimes prefer to hire people with no professional education because such employees are not familiar with "old-school" journalism and thus can actively use the Western informational model of journalism (McNair 1991). Although this may have been a popular view in the early days of *glasnost*, it seems rather unreasonable to claim that editors today are not seeking professionally trained journalists.

Nevertheless, more and more journalists who are working in Russian local and regional media have never received extensive training and have not studied a Russian model of journalism. Instead, they are following a Western model of purely informative reporting without providing any analysis of the events. Often, sensational tabloid journalism replaces quality writing on current subjects of political and economic importance.

In addition, the concepts of freedom of speech, independence, and the principles of investigative journalism are not well understood by Russian journalists. And, even if they do understand these concepts, they do not know how to use them to empower themselves. Formal training at the university level does not solve the problem completely, precisely because of Russia's lack of tradition in studying and examining the principles of freedom of expression and press. Media marketing is also an underdog in journalism higher education: traditional liberal arts schools of journalism have a hard time finding faculty members who are properly trained and who completely understand media marketing and the principles of publishing in the new economic context.

A series of special training seminars and workshops, as well as internships in Western media, are constantly offered to Russian journalists by independent organizations that guard freedom of speech worldwide. Among them are the International Federation of Journalists, the International Journalists Network, the Open Society Institute of the Soros Foundation, and many others. Also, Fulbright grants encourage U.S. journalism professors to come to Russia to teach a Western view of journalism (Aumente et al. 1999).

Contemporary Problems of Russian Journalism

Among important contemporary issues of Russian journalism are political influence, economic dependency, ethical challenges, and self-censorship. Each of them is discussed in this section of the chapter.

Political Influence.[1] Freedom of speech, widely celebrated and acknowledged in the early 1990s, established 1989 through 1992 as a golden era of Russian journalism (ICJ 2000). However, by the middle and late 1990s, the euphoria of freedom of speech was overcome by the political influence that government officials tended to have over the media, working from the old assumption that journalists should follow the party line. Many representatives of the Russian administration, especially at the local levels, still had a communist approach, even though now they called themselves democrats.

Russian President Vladimir Putin, who has been actively criticized by international organizations for limiting opportunities for freedom of speech for Russian media and who was even named one of the "10 Worst Enemies of the Press for 2001" (Dine 2002) nevertheless has a quite realistic view of the current status of the media. In his interview in the Russian newspaper *Izvestiya,* he pointed out the inability of the majority of the press media to financially support themselves; thus, he argued for state subsidies to guarantee media independence, arguing, "The media must be made truly independent, so that it can then reflect real life rather than the one its master would like presented" (Dine 2002).

Sanctions such as cuts in governmental subsidies and isolation from printing presses, which sometimes are also concentrated in the hands of local government officials, are effective means for government officials to exercise economic influence over the media. Often officials would use other sanctions, such as closing newspaper offices because they did not immediately meet updated fire requirement standards, and not renewing media licenses (some of these examples are reported in the publications of International Federation of Journalists and International Journalists Network).

A question of editorial freedom is raised every time a newspaper is forced to stop publication, leave an occupied building, or pay substantial fees that may result in media bankruptcy.

Economic Dependency. The economic problems of Russian media began in the early 1990s, when the economy of the Soviet Union began to fail. Mass media faced the greatest challenge of how to stay alive during this financially unstable period. Many newspapers, for instance, were not in a hurry to obtain independence from official administration for purely economic reasons: "Newspapers that were registered with official bodies were still entitled to a greater allocation of state-subsidized paper from the state publishing committee" (Murray 1994, p. 51).

Independent newspapers had to buy paper at much more expensive prices, and this was one of the methods of indirect influence the party-state apparatus used on rebel media (Murray 1994). Another problem that outspoken Russian print media faced in the 1990s was the refusal of the state-owned retail distribution organization Soyuzpechat' to distribute the newspapers (Tolz 1990). Hiring independent distributors rather quickly solved this problem. Some national newspapers organized their own circulation organizations, which were later used to sell many newspapers and magazines that were printed by publishing houses that were created by the newspaper leaders. The best example is a publishing house of one of the leading Russian newspapers *Komsomolskaya Pravda*, which now has own distribution offices in almost every region of Russia.

Economic methods are still used by Russian oligarchs and the government to control or silence media. Ketter (2001) observed that officials still indirectly control the economy of the Russian media. More and more media in Russia are in the hands of oligarchs, and many scandals have risen around media and their editors directly from the scandals and disputes among oligarchs. In the 1990s, Russian oligarchs Gusinsky and Berezovsky were engaged in so-called informational wars that became a central issue for Russian national media. The leading national TV channels in Russia, including NTV (Independent TV) and ORT (All-Russian TV), as well as the biggest national newspapers, continue to be central figures in these informational wars.[2] Together with oligarchs, governmental officials often are also involved in the information war.

A Question of Ethics.   The question of ethical conduct among Russian journalists is often raised in relation to the economic dependency that individual journalists face today. Often, professional ethics are questioned when a journalist who works for one newspaper, magazine, or broadcast channel also works for an advertising or public relations agency. *Zakazukha* is a Russian slang word that can be translated as "pay-for-publicity." Holmes (2001) explains that this is "the payment to newspapers and individual journalists for media coverage" (on-line). In Russian media, *zakazukha* simply is bribery that is offered to, or demanded by, journalists. This practice, prevalent in Russian television and print media, is in violation of Russian Federation Law 108, "On Advertising," signed on July 18, 1995, which states, "Media information organizations are not permitted to take payments for placing advertising in the guise of informational, editorial, or authored material." *Zakazukha* became a popular word in the Russian journalistic lexicon because the practice of *zakazukha*, unfortunately, has become more and more popular.

The problem of demanding and accepting money for news coverage has developed as a result of the unprofessional publicity policies of uneducated advertisers who label their media advertising tactics as publicity. Much has been written about this problem in Russian public relations (Tsetsura 2000, 2002; Tsetsura and Kruckeberg in press), but the problem has not been substantially addressed in journalism research. Even though many Russian media have ethical codes of professional conduct and the Russian Association of Journalists has initiated its own code of ethics, they often remain on paper, but are not enforced. One of the major reasons cited by Russian journalists in regard to why this practice occurs is the economic dependency of journalists. An average salary of a Russian journalist in regional newspapers hardly ever exceeds $200 a month and often is less than $100. Many journalists live in poverty and are forced to work in advertising and write *zakazukha* materials. However, Moscow journalists working for national media make much more money, and their salaries are often comparable with the salaries of business and account managers of successful companies. Yet the problem of *zakazukha* also occurs in Moscow media. Many argue that the practice will not disappear soon because of both poor economic conditions and low ethical standards.

National and international organizations are helping prevent unethical journalistic practices. For instance, the project Media Transparency International, conducted by the International Public Relations Association in collaboration with the Institute for Public Relations and journalism leaders worldwide, aims to minimize the existence of "cash for news coverage." Russian journalists and public relations professionals are excited about the project, but so far no concrete results or decisions have resulted.

Self-Censorship. Self-censorship is a phenomenon that came to play in post-Soviet Russia in the late 1990s, when political and economic sanctions as well as criminal charges were leveled against journalists and editors who tried to investigate corrupt officials and lucrative business. Self-censorship became quite popular among editors who did not want to get their media "in trouble."

Self-censorship stops journalists before they even begin investigations or news reports on certain subjects because of their fear of economic problems that their media could experience later, such as cuts in subsidies from the government or financial support from publishers. And the weak Russian economy has made truly independent journalism onerous not only on economic grounds; today, journalists often fear criminals' retributions against them if they investigate subjects or persons having criminal connections. The lives of journalists who dare to investigate governmental or business wrongdoings can also be threatened. In the last decade, several famous journalists who worked for national media, including Dmitry Kholodov, were killed as a result of such investigations.

Today, many journalists and editors in Russia do not investigate or write materials that may potentially bring harm to their media and themselves. They most often fear economic sanctions and criminal retributions. As recently as 1997, 15 journalists were killed in Russia (murder can be considered the most extreme form of censorship), and 71 were harassed, according to the report of Glasnost Defense Foundation (GDF 1998). Furthermore, the numbers are not declining: 17 journalists were killed in 2001, according to a GDF monitoring report (GDF 2002), and 64 journalists were physically attacked because of their professional activities (Center for Journalism in Extreme Situations 2001). Most of these crimes were not properly investigated, several cases were closed as a result of unproven accusations, and many of these crimes were not even filed. Filed cases usually used the Criminal Code of the Russian Federation (in cases of murder or harassment). However, civil cases on these grounds have not yet been filed (GDF 1998). In cases where media rights were violated, courts were not active in analyzing the cases and making recommendations.

Many newspapers today have turned into a tabloid-like press, publishing scandal materials about Russian movie stars and singers, crimes, and disasters, as well as reprinting similar publications from the Western tabloid media. Some claim that the *glasnost* campaign was interpreted by many media as "an opportunity to indulge in forms of media sexism" previously associated with capitalist societies (McNair 1991, p. 203).

Tabloid-like materials have a huge success among a Russian public that is tired of reading stories about corrupt officials and the country's socioeconomic problems, which make no difference to Russians' reality and provide easy and fun reading. Instead, tabloid stories are actively promoted by newspapers and magazines that are formatted after popular Western mass media, such as *Cosmopolitan* and *Esquire*. Articles also are reprinted with permission of Western publishers, who have seen a big potential for such media. For several years, the country has been filled with Russian editions of *Maxim, Cosmopolitan, Playboy*, and Russian newspapers (like *Speed Info*) and magazines (like *Karavan Istorij*), modeled after Western tabloids. Regional media have followed this path and have come up with their own local versions of *Elle* and the *New York Post*. For instance, newspapers *Moe!* and *Efir*, published in Voronezh, are typical examples of the Russian tabloid press.

It is a sad fact that many nationally recognized newspapers have also turned to tabloid materials and now have less and less quality journalistic publications. Among these media is a newspaper *Komsomolskaya Pravda*, which was the major newspaper for a young audience during the Soviet regime and for a long time was considered one of the most progressive and high-quality newspapers during the glasnost period. Now, *Komsmolskaya Pravda*, unfortunately, is becoming more of a quality tabloid rather than a quality professional newspaper, expanding its tabloid empire (both ideologically and physically) to regional publications such as *Komsmolskaya Pravda-Voronezh* and *Komsomolskaya Pravda-Don*.

Many researchers cite a rapid growth in the number of media and, at the same time, a formal decline in journalists' responsibility for publications as the major reasons for low professional standards (Kazhikin 2002). A crisis of trust has been progressing dramatically in the past ten years. A low level of professionalism and journalists' widespread "sell-off" (a formal word for *zakazukha*) are obvious to readers and lower media consumers' loyalty to Russian media in general. Among the most trusted media today are television (even though the problems discussed earlier are vivid there) and Internet media.

Freedom of Speech in Russian Mass Media

Freedom of speech is a relatively new phenomenon in Russia with a short but very rich history that is associated with events of the twentieth century. All the aspects of freedom of speech in Russia would not fit into a large book; however, a detailed analysis of some aspects of this phenomenon can be presented here to understand its nature and modern state of existence. It is extremely important to study freedom of speech in a country that has a long history but a brief democratic tradition. Those who study the concept of freedom of speech worldwide can benefit from examining how freedom of speech in Russia has helped to shape democratic principles of that country and what obstacles freedom of speech faces today.

Freedom of speech has always been associated with freedom of expression in the mass media. Some research has been done on the Soviet mass media and the particularities of the freedom of speech in the former Soviet Union (Bittman 1985; Pehowski 1978; Schreiberg 1978). Several works have been written on freedom of speech in contemporary Russia (Anderson 1997; Dawson 1995; McNair 1991; Murray 1994). Usually, such works combine a discussion of issues related to freedom of speech with an analysis of Russian journalism and post-Soviet mass media. However, researchers have failed to closely examine the legal basis of freedom of information in Russia (Tsetsura 2002).

Legal Aspects of Freedom of Information.   The Russian Constitution meets European standards of human rights, including the right to have freedom of information. Article 29 of the Constitution states, "Freedom of mass information is guaranteed. Censorship is prohibited." Articles 41, 42, and 55 also provide sets of instruments to defend citizens' freedoms such as freedom of expression. However, these rights, supported by international laws, have never been applied in practical terms to court proceedings that involve freedom of information disputes (Simonov 2000).

The very democratic Media Law of the Russian Federation, which is a main federal document that guarantees freedom of speech in mass media, has a number of provisions that form the legal grounds for freedom of speech. Several aspects should be considered when freedom of speech in mass media is discussed. First, the Media Law confirms that censorship is prohibited (Article 3). Second, Article 43 says that any citizen or organization has a right to request a denial in the media if false information concerning someone's honor and dignity has appeared. As one can note, honor and dignity are used here in relation to a person as well as to an organization.

The next point reflects a crucial difference from the American legal tradition in solving disputes between journalists and plaintiffs. The same Article 43 states that the burden to prove that statements are true first of all lies with the media: "If the editors of a mass medium do not have evidence to demonstrate that distributed information is true, they are obligated to refute such information in the same medium." This differs significantly from the ways in which such cases are presented in the United States, where the burden to show falsity is almost always on the plaintiff (Tedford 1997).

Another article of the Media Law elaborates on the rights of journalists, specifically saying that any journalist has a right "to state his/her personal opinions and evaluation in materials to be distributed under his/her name" (Article 47). As the analysis shows, sometimes this statement is not take into consideration and is bypassed in court.

Article 49 declares, "The state guarantees protection of journalist's honor, dignity, health, life, and property in relation to his/her professional activities." This statement is too vague and has not been cited in any of the decisions related to the cases of infringements of media rights. Many times this right is neither cited nor addressed in legal charges.

The penalties for violating the Russian laws in relation to freedom of information are identified according to the legislation of the Russian Federation, the Civil Code, and the Criminal Code. They usually involve filing other civil cases as a result of violations in relation to freedom of information (in successful cases, in which it is proved that the media were offended, journalists can continue filing cases as individual citizens) or in publishing a denial and paying some compensation (in cases in which it is proved that the media offended the plaintiff).

Public Aspects of Freedom of Information.   Freedom of information also struggles to find its place in public debates. First, Russians question the right to freedom of information that they have now, at the beginning of the twenty-first century. If at the beginning of *perestroika* the public was active and enthusiastic about promoting freedom of information and defending its rights (the public's protests in August 1991 and the support of Yeltsin at that time support this claim[3]), today the public is less and less involved in the debates on freedom of speech. Some governmental actions have contributed to the public's disappointment and withdrawal. Media law often is not enforced and not supported in practice. Moreover, mass media stay uninvolved in public debates because of the self-censorship phenomenon.

According to a recent study conducted by the Glasnost Defense Foundation (GDF 1999), several factors have contributed to the decline of public interest in issues of freedom of speech as well as increasing concern among media representatives about media rights to accessing information. Political pressure on the media, confusion in legal documents, and the media's economic dependency on their political orientation are among the factors identified.

Another big problem addressed in the GDF study is a poorly interpreted notion of media being "the fourth branch of power" in Russia, with no mechanisms to express and promote diverse opinions and defense the public's interests. Media, not having actual power to pressure administrators and influence opinions, have lost readers' trust. A disappointed public does not have an interest and confidence in freedom of information that is essential for successful public debates in the media (Simonov ["Law"] 2000).

Conclusion

Russian laws are riddled with contradictions in relation to freedom of speech. The lack of fair judgments and consistency in rulings only adds to the problem.

Freedom of the press and economic achievements are closely related to each other. Silencing the media through political and economic means impedes a country's economic and democratization progress. As some Western observers have noted, "We should remember that while Russia may have a free market it still does not have a free press" (Dine 2002). The greatest problem of the Russian economy today is corruption, for which media serve as a good check. As long as Russian media exercise self-censorship or are silenced by government, the country's free-marketplace economy will function improperly. More important, democratic principles that have been long advocated by the post-Soviet government in Russia are now in danger because of threats against the country's freedom of speech.

Notes

1. For more information on political influence, see Murray (1994) and Vachnadze (1992) as well as IJNet newsletters of ICFJ and RFE/RL, available on-line.

2. It is beyond the scope of this chapter to analyze these ongoing wars, partially because the process is still very much alive and continues to influence all Russian media to a bigger or lesser extent. For more information on these wars, please see Murray (1994), Vachnadze (1992), and updated articles in digests of Russian press and Western media, as the events develop rapidly.

3. For more information on Russian media during the events of 1991, see, for example, Hosking (1992); Miller (1993); Murray (1994).

Bibliography

Adrounas, E. *Soviet Media in Transition*. Westport, Conn.: Praeger, 1993.

Alexandrova, P. "Media, Mafia, and Monopoly in Bulgaria" (on-line). *World Press Review*, 2001. Available: http://worldpress.org.

Anderson, R. D., Jr. "Speech and Democracy in Russia: Responses to Political Texts in Three Russian Cities." *British Journal of Political Science* 27, no. 1 (1997): 23–45.

Aumente, J., P. Gross, R. Hiebert, O. V. Johnson, and D. Mills. *Eastern European Journalism. Before, During and After Communism*. Cresskill, N.J.: Hampton Press, 1999.

Bittman, L. *The KGB and Soviet Disinformation*. Elmsford, N.Y.: Pergamon, 1985.

Braun, A., and Z. Barany, Editors. *Dilemmas of Transition: The Hungarian Experience*. Oxford: Rowman and Littlefield, 1999.

Center for Journalism in Extreme Situations (CJES). *A Dangerous Profession: Monitoring of Violations in 2000 of Journalists' Rights in CIS Countries*. Moscow: CJES, 2001.

"Czech Republic." *Post-Soviet Media Law and Policy Newsletter* (15 May 1998): 28.

Dawisha, K., and B. Parrott. *Conflict, Cleavage, and Change in Central Asia and the Caucasus*. Cambridge, U.K.: Cambridge University Press, 1997.

Dawson, M. "Free Speech and the Mass Media in Russia: Lessons from the December 1993 Election and Constitutional Referendum." *Cardozo Arts and Entertainment Law Journal* 13, no. 3 (1995): 881.

Dine, T. A. "Free Russian Economy Needs a Free Press: President Putin's Media Crackdown a Major Problem." *Chicago Tribune*, 16 July 2002, Section 1, p. 19.

Drobyshevsky, A. G. *The History of Russian Journalism: Course Lectures in the History of Russian Journalism*. Unpublished manuscript. Voronezh State University, Voronezh, Russia, 1997.

Drucker, J. "The Ongoing Struggle for Freedom of Information." *Transitions-on-Line* (August 1998).

European Journalism Center. "European Media Landscape: The Russian Media Landscape" (on-line), 2002. Available: http://www.ejc.nl/jr/emland/russia.html.

European Media Institute. *Newsletter* (on-line); July 2000. Available: www.eim.org.

Federal'nyj zakon RF ot 18 iulya 1995, N 108-F3 "O reklame" (Federal Law of the Russian Federation, no. 108-F3, "On Advertising") 1995.

Federal'nyj zakon RF ot 27 dekabrya 1991 N 2124-1 "O sredstvax massovoj informatsii (s izme-neniyami ot 31 janvarya, 6 iunya, 27 dekabrya 1995, 2 marta 1998, 20 iyunya, 5 avgusta 2000)" (Law of the Russian Federation no. 2124-1, "About Mass Media," 1991, amended in 1995, 1998, and 2000).

Fossato, F. "Russia: Russian Journalists Not United to Defend Press Freedom" (on-line). *RFE/RL Newsline* 4 (12 July 2000): 132. Available: www.rferl.org/newsline/2000/07/120700.html.

Freedom Forum. (On-line), 1 July 2001. Available: http://www.freedomforum.org/templates/document.asp?documentID-14307.

Freedom House. *Media Responses to Corruption in the Emerging Democracies: Bulgaria, Hungary, Romania, Ukraine.* (on-line), 2000. Available: http://freedomhouse.org/reports/mediatxt.html.

Giorgi, L. *The Post-Socialist Media: What Power the West?* Aldershot, 1995.

Glasnost Defense Foundation. *Ponyatie chesti i dostoinstva, oskorbleniya I nenormativnosti v tekstah prava i sredstv massovoj informatsii* (Notions of Honor and Dignity, Insulting and Abnormality in Legal and Mass Media Texts). Moscow: Prava Cheloveka, 1997.

———. *Sredstva massovoj informatsii i sudebnaya vlast' v Rossii* (Mass Media and the Judicial System in Russia). Moscow: Galereya, 1998.

———. *The Silent Regions.* Moscow: Sashcko Publishing House, 1999.

———. "General Resolution of all-Russia Extraordinary Congress in Defense of Human Rights." (on-line), January 2001. Available: www.gdf.ru/arhiv/info007e.html.

———. Archive: "Journalists Killed in 2001" (on-line), 2002. Available: http://www.gdf.ru/arh/mort/2001.shtml.

Gleason, T. *The Watchdog Concept.* Ames: Iowa State University Press, 1989.

Goban-Klas, T. *The Orchestration of the Media: The Politics of Mass Communications in Communist Poland and the Aftermath.* Boulder, Colo.: Westview Press, 1994.

Gross, P. *Entangled Evolutions: Media and Democratization in Eastern Europe.* Washington, D.C.: The Woodrow Wilson Center Press/Baltimore, Md.: Johns Hopkins University Press, 2002.

Holmes, P. "IPRA moves swiftly on Zakazukha; PRSA stays out of the Nike fray." *Holmes Report* 2 (12 March 2001).

Horga, I., and R. de La Brosse, Editors. *The Role of the Mass-Media and of the New Information and Communication Technologies in the Democratisation Process of Central and Eastern European Societies.* Brussels: International Institute of Administrative Studies, 2002.

Hosking, G. *A History of the Soviet Union,* 3rd Edition. London: Fontana Press, 1992.

Human Rights Watch. "The Cost of Speech." (on-line), 2002. Available: http://www.hrw.org/reports/2002/albania/index.htm.

International Center for Journalists. "Regional Russian Journalists Publish Book on Mass Media." (on-line). International Journalists' Network (IJNet), 12 April 2000. Available: http://www.ijnet.org/Archive/2002/4/12-12271.html.

———. "Russia: Press Overview. A Profile." (on-line). International Journalists' Network (IJNet), 2002. Available: http://www.ijnet.org/Profile/CEENIS/Russia/media.html.

———. "Independent TV Broadcaster in Azerbaijan Closes Station, Goes Into Exile." International Journalists' Network (IJNet), 2001.

International Federation of Journalists. "IFJ Supports Russian Media Protest and Calls for Charter for Editorial Freedom at NTV." Media release (on-line), April 2001. Available: http://www.ifj.org/publications/press/pr/202.html.

International Journalists' Network (on-line). Available: http://www.injet.org.

International Press Institute. *Waging War on the Media: World Press Freedom Report 2001.*

Internews. "A Survey of Russian Television" (on-line), 1999. Available: http://internews.ru/report/tv/tv1.html.

Jusi, T. "Towards Modern Education of Journalists in Southeast Europe." *Media Online,* 2002. Available: (http://217.75.196.2/mediaupitE/tekst.html?sifra=4726).

Kagan World Media. *The Future of Media in Eastern Europe and Russia, 1997.* London: Kagan World Media, Ltd., 1996.

Karatnycky, A. *Nations in Transit, 2001: Civil Society, Democracy and Markets in East Central Europe and the Newly Independent States.* New Brunswick, N.J.: Transaction Publishers, 2001.

Ketter, W. B. "Russia's New Media Struggles for Freedom." *American Society of Newspaper Editors newsletter* (on-line), August 2001. Available: http://www.asne.org/kiosk/editor/01-ian-feb/ketter1.htm.

Kratovak, K. "Tough Times for Yugoslavia's Media" (on-line). Available: http://www.balkaw-peace.org/hed/Archive/Octoo/hed1028.shtml.

McCormack, G. *Media in the CIS: A Study of the Political, Legislative and Socio-Economic Framework.* Dusseldorf: European Institute for the Media, 1999.

McNair, B. *Glasnost, Perestroika and the Soviet Media.* London: Routledge, 1991.

McReynolds, L. *The News Under Russia's Old Regime: The Development of a Mass-Circulation Press.* Princeton, N.J.: Princeton University Press, 1991.

"The media: Leading Journalists Discuss State of Freedom of Speech in Russia Today." *Current Digest of the Post-Soviet Press* 52, no. 12 (2000): 17.

Miller, J. *Mikhail Gorbachev and the End of Soviet Power.* New York: St. Martin's Press, 1993.

Mills, R. D. "In the Communist World." In *Comparative Mass Media Systems,* edited by L. J. Martin and A. G. Chaudhary, 167–186. New York: Longman, 1983.

Milton, A. K. *The Rational Politician: Exploiting the Media in New Democracies.* Aldershot: Ashgate Publishing, 2000.

Murray, J. *The Russian Press from Brezhnev to Yeltsin: Behind the Paper Curtain.* Brookfield, Vt.: Edward Elgar, 1994.

Naegele, J. "Macedonia: News Media Under Fire for Poor Reporting, Government Manipulation." Radio Free Europe/Radio Liberty, 3 May 2002.

Online News Hour. (on-line), 4 May 1999. Available: http://www.pbs.org/newshour//bb/media/jan-june99/seebTV_S-4.html.

Paletz, D. L., K. Jakubowicz, and P. Novosel, Editors. *Glasnost and After: Media and Change in Central and Eastern Europe.* Cresskill, N.J.: Hampton Press, 1995.

Pehowski, M. *Problems in International Communication: China and the Soviet Union.* Paper presented at the annual meeting of the Association for Education in Journalism, Seattle, Wash., August 1978.

Press Research Centre, Jagiellonian University, Krakow. Website: www.media.onet.pl.

Ratinov, A. R., and G. Z. Efremova. *Mass Media v Rossii* (Mass Media in Russia). Moscow: Prava Cheloveka, 1998.

Robinson, G. *Tito's Maverick Media: The Politics of Mass Communication.* Chicago: University of Illinois Press, 1977.

Schreiber, E. S. "The Rise and Fall of the Soviet Underground Press." *Communication Quarterly* 26, no. 3 (1978): 32–39.

Simonov, A. "Anatomy of Freedom of Speech." Glasnost Defense Foundation (on-line), 2000. Available: http://www.gdf.ru/publications/simonov10.html.

Simonov, A. "Law Pressed Hard by Lawlessness." Glasnost Defense Foundation (on-line), 2000. Available: http://www.gdf.ru/publications/simonov09.html.

Smid, Milan. "History of the Czech Press Law: A Missing Definition of Public Interest—The Obstacle to the New Media Legislation in the Czech Republic?" *International Journal of Communication Law and Policy* 2 (Winter 1998/99): 1–9.

Smolla, R. A. *Free Speech in an Open Society.* New York: Knopf, 1992.

Sunstein, C. R. *Democracy and the Problem of Free Speech.* New York: Free Press, 1993.

Sussman, L. R., and K. Deutsch. *The Annual Survey of Press Freedom 2002.* New York: Freedom House, 2002.

Szekfu, A. "The Crisis in Hungarian Public Service Broadcasting: Margin Notes on Two Reports." *South-East Europe Review* 1 (2002): 83–92.

Tedford, T. L. *Freedom of Speech in the United States,* 3rd Edition. State College, Penn.: Strata Publishing, 1997.

Thomas, B., and T. Michaela, Editors. *Medien und Transformation in Osteuropa.* Wiesbaden, Germany: Westdeutscher Verlag, 2001.

Thompson, M. *Forging War: The Media in Serbia, Croatia, Bosnia and Hercegovina.* Luton, U.K.: University of Luton Press, 1999.

Tolz, V. *The Impact of New Press Law: A Preliminary Assessment.* RFE/RL Report on the USSR, 9, November 1990.

Trajkovski, I., and S. Trpevska. *Country Reports on Media: Republic of Macedonia,* 2001.

Tsetsura, K. *Development of Public Relations Theory and Practice in Russia: A Geopolitical Perspective.* Paper presented at the 5th PRSA Educators Academy International Interdisciplinary Conference, Miami, Fla., March 2002.

Tsetsura, K. *Understanding Public Relations Terms: "Evil" Nature of Public Relations as it is Seen by Some of the Russian Publics.* Paper presented at the 3rd PRSA Educators Academy International Interdisciplinary Conference, Miami, Fla., March 2000.

Tsetsura, K., and D. Kruckeberg. "Theoretical Development of Public Relations in Russia." In *International Public Relations,* edited by D. J. Tilson. Boston, Mass.: Allyn and Bacon, in press.

Ulmanu, A. "The Romanian Media Landscape." *Media Online,* 2002. Available: (http://217.75.196.2/mediaupitE/clanak_print.html?sifra=5492).

Vachnadze, G. N. *Secrets of Journalism in Russia: Mass Media Under Gorbachev and Yeltsin.* New York: Nova Science Publishers, 1992.

Varbanova, L., and A. Dimitrova. "Is There Any Social Cohesion in the Bulgarian Multicultural Society?" *Canadian Journal of Communication* 27 no. 2 (2002).

15

The Middle East and North Africa

Orayb Aref Najjar

The changes in the media landscape in the Middle East and North Africa (Figure 15.1) make the media almost unrecognizable from what they were only a decade ago. Many media organizations have embraced new technology, challenged sole government ownership of all means of communication, reduced their reliance on Western news agencies, and diversified their content. These changes have accelerated the pace of communication and enriched it, allowing people of the region to read each other's media, and, via the Internet, hear it and see it. The changes have also made internal and across-border censorship difficult and have prompted many countries to reconsider their information policies. Arab satellite channels, with their pan-regional fare, also have united the fragmented Arab news and advertising market. But most important, they have reversed the direction of news flow about themselves, which used to travel mostly from West to East and from North to South.

The acquisition of new technology, however, has favored those who can afford it, shifting and rearranging influence between and among geographical areas within the Middle East and North Africa. Despite these changes, the most important issue facing the countries of the region has remained the same: how to adopt new technologies necessary for advancement while preserving their traditional values and culture. Each country has handled this issue differently, but not a single country has managed to avoid it.

Historical Highlights

The Ottomans ruled the Middle East and parts of North Africa for 400 years, until World War I, when they lost their empire to Western powers. Britain, in effective control of Egypt and the Arabian Gulf since the turn of the twentieth century, gained

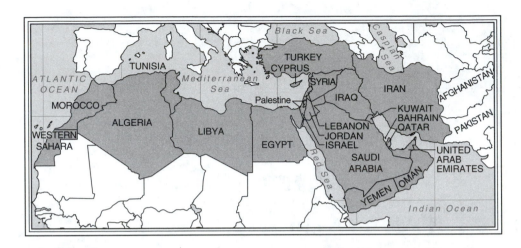

FIGURE 15.1 *Middle East and North Africa*

control over Palestine, Trans-Jordan, and Iraq through a League of Nations mandate. France, already with colonial control over Morocco, Tunisia, and Algeria in North Africa, was granted mandatory powers over Syria and Lebanon. Although the mandate powers were supposed to shepherd the countries to independence, some powers were reluctant to leave, forcing Arabs into years of struggle to oust Britain and France from the Middle East and North Africa (Ismael and Ismael 1999, pp. 131–133). Algeria earned the nickname of "the country of the million martyrs" for the number of Algerians who died fighting for freedom from France.

Modern Turkey was founded in 1923 from the ashes of the Ottoman Empire. First elected president in 1923, Kemal Atatürk admired the West and secularism and forcibly reduced the influence of Islam by attempting to turn Turkey into a secular Westernized country. The Turkish military exercises substantial but indirect influence over politics to protect the secular nature of the state. But Turkish nationalism and secularism have not yet replaced Islam in the hearts and minds of many Turks, as evidenced by the November 2002 elections, in which Islamic-affiliated parties were returned to power. The suppression of the 1925 Kurdish uprising still haunts Turkey today (Goldschmidt, Jr., 1988, pp. 211, 228).But the Turkish parliament's vote of August 2002, allowing radio and TV broadcasts in Kurdish, promises to ease relations between the government and the Kurdish minority (Parsons 2002). This Turkish liberalization coincided with the media liberalization that Kurds in northern Iraq started to enjoy under the protection of the United States.

In Iran's more recent history, the U.S. Central Intelligence Agency (CIA), in cooperation with British intelligence, plotted the military coup that returned the Shah of Iran to power and toppled Iran's elected prime minister, Mossadegh, an ardent nationalist. Both countries were fearful of Iran's plans to nationalize its oil industry. President Eisenhower had approved the plan also because of his fear of communism. The *New York Times* reporter in Tehran during the coup wrote, "The only instance since I joined the *Times* in which I have allowed policy to influence a strict news approach was in failing to report the role our agents played in the overthrow of Mossadegh" (Risen 2000). To Iranians, however, meddling in internal Iranian affairs was a major U.S. failing that continues to haunt U.S.-Iranian relations.

Iranian cleric Ayatollah Khomeini, exiled after his arrest for speaking out against the Shah's relationship to the United States, returned to Iran in 1979 and established a government in the wake of the Iranian Revolution that forced the Shah out of Iran (Goldschmidt, Jr., 1988, pp. 216–221). Iran is still ruled by clerics who are suspicious of the West and of Western influence, especially in the press. But Iranians elected a reformist-dominated parliament on May 27, 2000, for the first time since the 1979 Iranian Revolution. The outcome of the struggle between conservatives and reformists has not yet been determined.

The founding of the state of Israel in 1948 was seen by Israel and most Western countries as a fulfillment of the nationalist-religious Zionist dream of return and as a refuge for European Jews fleeing the Nazis. But Palestinian history books call that same event "the disaster" because they say it led to the dispersal of an estimated 520,000 to 850,000 Palestinians and the creation of their refugee problem. The founding of the state of Israel in the middle of the Arab world also has resulted in a profound Arab public reaction to Western sponsorship of Zionism. Anti-Zionist and anti-imperialist rhetoric unified the Arab media and continues to do so. As Susan Sachs writes, "The Palestinian 'problem' has driven policy in the Arab world for nearly as long as there have been independent states. More than a preoccupation, it has had the force to undermine rulers, incite revolutions, circumscribe development and define patriotism" (Sachs, 2000). Since Egypt and Jordan signed peace treaties with Israel, and after the Palestinian National Authority entered into negotiations with it, the total boycott against talking to Israelis has been breached, exposing viewers to the Israeli point of view from Arab satellite stations for the first time since 1948.

By the early 1960s, most of the Arab states were governed by nationalist military regimes that had wrested control from the overly pro-Western elite set up by Western powers. Even though the Arabs had not been united since the fall of the Omayyad Dynasty in 750 A.D., they began to feel that people who speak one language should unite. Egypt's skillful use of its media, most notably *Voice of the Arabs* radio in the 1960s, gave concrete expression to that Arab nationalist longing. Pan-Arab nationalism became a dominant theme in regional political dynamics despite tensions between several countries (Goldschmidt Jr., 1988, p. 277). That same longing for unity is now being rekindled by pan-Arab satellite broadcasting.

Several recent events and trends have changed the dynamics of societies in the Middle East and North Africa and have had a profound impact on their media:

1. The disintegration of the Soviet Union and the retreat of the Arab Left
2. The change in media economics and content as a result of globalization and privatization
3. The rise of religious fundamentalism

4. The onset of the Palestinian-Israeli peace negotiations, which, despite their failure, changed the Arab world's media relations with Israel
5. The accession to power of new young leaders relatively more open to freedom than their predecessors
6. The growth of non-governmental organizations that monitor government–press relations
7. The fallout of September 11, 2001, and the media's reaction to it, as well as to the coalition's invasion of Iraq in 2003

Print Media in the Arab World

Because of the liberalization of print media in some Arab countries, it is no longer possible to write about "the Arab media" as if it were one entity. There are 22 Arab countries, and their media differ in physical infrastructure, technical capability, and content. The level of freedom of speech each government allows, or each press body extracts through struggle, varies from one Arab region to the next. All of these countries, however, have one thing in common: All have witnessed the slow erosion of state power vis-à-vis the media. As Dale Eikelman notes, the "[a]uthority to suppress or 'guide' the printed and spoken word in the Middle East has become inherently vitiated by social and technological developments that are reaching full force in the 1990s" (Eickelman 1999, p. 29). Following is a description of each region's media (in alphabetical order) and the forces that drive them.

Print Media in Iraq, Jordan, Lebanon, Palestine, and Syria

Iraq. Iraq is a prime example of what happens when one party monopolizes political power as well as the press. Iraq closed all private daily newspapers in 1967. Saddam Hussein's regime, which started in 1979, banned all political parties operating in Iraq at that time, including the Communist Party. Although the Iraqi government invited the public to form political parties in 1991, no one took the invitation seriously. A renewed call in 1999 to form "supportive" parties to the one allowed party, al-Ba'ath (Renaissance), resulted in failure to get the 150 signatures needed to register them because those parties are not allowed to enter the elections (HR Report 2000, p. 39).

Until the fall of Baghdad to the coalition forces, Iraq's ministry of information and the journalists' union controlled the six daily and one dozen weekly newspapers. Uday, the son of President Saddam Hussein, headed the committee of editors-in-chief and owned Babel, the highest–circulation newspaper. *Al-Thawra* (Revolution) was the official mouthpiece of the Ba'ath Party (Russell 2003). Media censorship was extensive, and the penalty for disobedience was harsh. The daily adulation of Saddam Hussein in the Iraqi press was evidence of government control and a throwback to older times, when all Arab papers looked that unsophisticated and controlled.

The British-American coalition's occupation of Iraq led to a scramble among various local and diaspora forces for the control of the hearts and minds of the conquered/liberated Iraqi people (according to differing perceptions of what happened to Iraq). The actors on the new media scene include returning Iraqi exiles, British and American officials, Iraqi former political parties, and various indigenous Iraqi secular and religious groups. But the party that beat the whole lot turned out to be the Iraqi Communist Party, or as Reuters correspondent Rosalind Russell put it, "It would not be Washington's first choice, but the long-banned Iraq Communist Party on Sunday won the race to publish the first newspaper in Baghdad. . . . 'Collapse of a Dictator' read the headline under the hammer and sickle on the front page." On April 20, 2003, the eight-page weekly, *People's Path,* distributed thousands of free copies in several Iraqi cities (Russell 2003).

The Worker Communist Party of Iraq (WCPI) web site explained that the majority of Iraqis "want neither the USA and British presence nor a religious, ethnic and tribal government. . . . This Party has resolutely stood up to the Ba'ath regime, Kurdish nationalist parties and Islamic groups, has opposed economic sanctions and the war against Iraq and is the defender of the most extensive rights, freedoms, prosperity and dignity for the people." Iraq now has 150 newspapers (al-Jazeera). The largest is *Azzaman*—circulation 75,000—published by a former Hussein aide who escaped in 1992 (Oppel 2003).

Jordan. Jordan, the host of Palestinian refugees in 1948 and 1967, always felt the need to shield itself from the fallout of the Israeli-Palestinian conflict with tough press legislation to curb hostility to its alliance with the West. The government tightened press regulations every time the country faced a major internal or external crisis. After the start of the Palestinian Uprising in December 1988, for example, the government forced the two main dailies to sell it shares (62 percent of *Al-Ra'i* and 31 percent of *al-Dustour*) (Ni'mat 2000). The government's appointment of editors of some papers further strained its relations with the journalistic profession. Journalism did not flourish, however, until the country resumed its parliamentary life in 1989 (Najjar 1998, 2000).

Today, Jordan has a variety of publications that range from leftist to Arab nationalist to Islamist. The country also publishes two English-language newspapers, a daily and a weekly. Press liberalization prompted the Arab Organization for Human Rights to name Jordan as the country that has made the most far-reaching changes to its press freedom because its amendments to the press law on September 7, 1999, decreased the "forbiddens" from 14 to six, reduced monetary penalties, did away with Article 37 (which forbade criticizing the king or the royal family, criticizing Arab governments, revealing information about the armed forces, or harming national unity), and deleted Articles 50 and 52 (which allowed suspending publications).

The regulations introduced after the September 11, 2001, attacks on the World Trade Center and the Pentagon have reversed most of those changes. The Jordanian prime minister argued that Jordan's old code, amended on October 8, 2001, did not cover the current need "to face up to terrorist acts and punish them." The amendments to the code provided for the closure "permanently or temporarily" of publications with items that are "defamatory, false, harmful to national unity or the state's reputation" or that carry news that incite holding illegal public meetings or disturbing public order, or news instigating acts of religious and racial fanaticism. The code imposed prison sentences from one to three years instead of fines for insulting the royal family. Furthermore, the ministry of information continued to coexist with the council (which has no executive powers). The Jordanian government continues to believe that it is unable to depend on the union-dominated Jordanian Press Association to express the government's point of view; thus its reluctance to allow freedom of the press (El Sharif 2002). Despite that control, the private Jordanian press often writes about media restrictions and depicts them in cartoons.[1] It also parts ways with the government on the state's policy of normalization with Israel. The Jordanian Press Association ignores government directives and threatens to expel any member who visits Israel.

Years of journalistic lobbying have convinced the government to sell all but 15 percent of its press shares. Jordan, however, no longer censors foreign publications and has adopted the slogan, "From the airport to the bookstore," to express that new attitude.[2]

Lebanon.   The early arrival of printing in Lebanon enabled it to develop its press and export its journalistic expertise to several Arab countries. Lebanese journalists founded *al-Ahram* newspaper of Egypt and, later, publications in Sudan, Morocco, and Qatar (Abu Zaid 1985). The period from 1943 to 1962 saw the proliferation of a vigorous political press which turned Lebanon into the capital of Arab journalism. Because of the wide margin of freedom Lebanon enjoyed, Arab leaders waged their political battles in the Lebanese press they directly owned or subsidized in the 1950s (Al-Alawi 1981). To put an end to that trend, the Lebanese government stopped issuing licenses for new political publications in 1953 in an attempt to reduce the number of daily political papers to 25, and the number of weekly and monthly papers to 20. Yet during the chaos of the civil war, newspapers multiplied. Today, those who wish to start papers still are required to buy the licenses of two existing publications to get one license (Al-Ghareeb 1978, pp. 70–71). Lebanon has 12 major newspapers and 60 magazines ("Courtesy Profile, Lebanon").

The Israeli invasion of Lebanon in 1982 to oust the PLO, and the 16-year Lebanese civil war, which ended in 1991, destroyed the infrastructure of Lebanon and reduced the influence of the Lebanese press in the Arab world (Ellis 1999). During the civil war years many regular publications either stopped publishing because of the difficulty of distribution or published outside the country. Since then, says *As-Safir* columnist Ibrahim Amin, the press has lost its pan-Arab appeal and has become local.

Jihad al-Zein, op-ed editor of *al-Nahar* daily, says, however, that even though the Lebanese press had lost some of its pan-Arab appeal, it contributes trained cadres to the Arab media as well as ideas for debate (al-Zein [Interview] 2000).

The press in Lebanon continues to have a much wider margin of freedom than many other countries "because press institutions are strong and have a long tradition of freedom," says al-Zein (2000).

The Palestinian National Authority. The Palestinian case is interesting because the ongoing power struggle between the liberal Palestinian Ministry of Information and the repressive Palestinian security services will determine which type of system the future Palestinian state will have. The Ministry has applied the 1995 press law it enacted (Najjar 1997) in consultation with journalists in the most liberal way: When the law asks for licensing, it makes the process akin to registration. When the law stipulates that books get import permission, ministry employees give permission without reading the political books (but censor pornography and antireligious books). When the security forces, who have no legal jurisdiction over the press, detain journalists anyway, the ministry intervenes to free them and encourages them to complain in writing and even sue (Masri 2000). Yet the clout of the secret services has had a chilling effect on journalism and encourages self-censorship. Inter-Palestinian censorship also takes place when Palestinians attempt to keep out articles or photographs that embarrass them abroad or when it prevents the public from seeing members of the outspoken Legislative Council criticize government practices or call for reform.

The Palestinian territories have 13 newspapers, which range from the leftist *al-Masar* to the Islamist *al-Risalah*. Government subsidies to the official paper, *al-Hayat al Jadida,* do not prevent it from criticizing government officials. In fact, the publisher of the paper was appointed minister of information in April 2003. The red line for the three dailies, however, is personal criticism of Yasser Arafat and criticism of members of security services by name. The magazines range from the serious and political publications that discuss human rights to entertainment magazines. Newspapers continue to post their issues on the Internet (http://www.amin.org).

Syria. The establishment of the Ba'ath (Renaissance) Party in 1944 determined the political course of Syria. The party has secular, socialist, and Arab nationalist goals. Hafez al-Assad, who became president in 1970, signed a 20-year cooperation agreement with the Soviet Union in 1980, putting Syria at odds with the United States. The demise of the Soviet Union left Syria without strong allies (Lancaster 2000) and made it more vulnerable to pressures to liberalize. Syria outlaws fundamentalist Islamists and has expelled their leaders following their struggle with the regime in 1982 (Jarrus 2000).

Early signs indicate that the new ruler of Syria, Bhasar Al-Asad, will be more open to freedom of the press than his father, but that it will take time before old Syrian habits of censorship die.

The Syrian government controls the press. The media receive their news from the Syrian Arab News Agency (SANA). Until recently, political parties were allowed newsletters for internal distribution but not newspapers, despite repeated applications since 1970. Only the Communist Party was allowed two newspapers that were not sold to the general public.

In December 2000, parties were allowed to have their own newspapers after decades of banning. The Syrian Communist Party, accordingly, launched a general circulation newspaper on January 4, 2001. Ali Farzat, a cartoonist, published the satirical weekly *Addomari* in February 2001 and was distributing 60,000 copies. He decided to close it in January 2002 over a dispute with the government over distribution rights. The cartoonist wanted to retain distribution rights the government usurped despite the Syrian press law (Reporters Without Borders ["The Only"] 2002).

Paradoxically, the presence of Syrian troops in Lebanon has made Syrian journalism slightly more free, and Lebanese journalism less free. Some independent journalists edit articles in Syria, print them in nearby Lebanon's magazines, and then import them as Lebanese publications to circumvent restrictions (Jarrus 2000, p. 174).

Syria is taking cautious steps toward privatization in two areas: the Internet and advertising. Bashar al-Assad, who used to oversee the Internet before his father's death, has increased Syrian access to the Internet by increasing the number of phone lines available to the population and dropping cell phone rates. Syria's Internet subscribers are projected to grow by a compound annual growth rate of 43 percent between 2001 and 2006, and user penetration is expected to reach 3.17 percent by 2006 (Syria Live Net 2002). The rate is low compared to the Emirates (30 percent) (Al-Jazeera 2003), because of Syria's recent entry into the field and its lack of resources.

Syria, with a population of 17 million, has only 15 advertising agencies, whose proceeds go directly to the treasury. In contrast, Lebanon, with a population of only 4 million, has 150 agencies. Lebanon, which hosted the International Association of Advertisers in 2001, is expected to help Syria make its advertising viable (Moubayid 2000).

Print Media in the Gulf States: Bahrain, Kuwait, Qatar, Saudi Arabia, and United Arab Emirates

The whole Arabian Gulf area was on the fringes of the Arab world because most countries were British protectorates until 1971 and were late in developing any type of media. Those countries were thrust onto center stage during the oil boycott following the 1973 Arab–Israeli war, a period in which the Gulf area became visibly linked to the Palestinian problem, and during the Iraq–Iran war and the Gulf war, when they became important as oil producers (Zahlan 1998). Gulf countries have caught up in terms of physical infrastructure and state-of-the-art equipment, but with few exceptions, they did not make very much progress in freeing the press from government control.

The Kingdom of Bahrain. It is important to understand Bahrain's political history to realize why it took the country so long to start on the road to reform that is bound to free its long-controlled press. The Kingdom of Bahrain, called the state of Bahrain until it became a constitutional monarchy on February 14, 2002, was deprived of its real independence by a series of treaties with Britain.

The "Perpetual Truce of Peace and Friendship," concluded in 1861 and revised in 1892 and 1951, between Britain and the ruling family of Bahrain specified that the ruler could not dispose of any of his territory except to the United Kingdom and could not enter into relationships with any foreign government without British consent (a move that kept the Soviet Union and others at bay). In 1967, Britain moved its main regional naval base from Aden to Bahrain. Bahrain gained its independence from Britain in August 1971. It is a member of the Gulf Cooperation Council, established on May 26, 1981.

Based on its 1971 constitution, Bahrain drew up its constitution on May 12, 1973, and elected its first parliament that year. Just two years later, in August 1975, the emir (prince) disbanded the National Assembly because the Parliament attempted to legislate the end of Al-Khalifa hereditary rule (there since the late eighteenth century), and the expulsion of the U.S. Navy from Bahrain (there since 1948). The constitution was suspended in 1975.

Even though Bahrain was nominally independent, a Britisher continued to determine who gets into politics internally. Colonel Ian Henderson, a colonial police officer who used to be stationed in Kenya, was head of state security for some 30 years until 1998. He was instrumental in ruthlessly suppressing prodemocracy unrest in Bahrain, along with his deputy Adel Felaifel. The vice chair of the parliamentary human rights group, Lord Avebury, described the investigation started against Henderson in Britain in 2000 as "by far the strongest U.K. torture case we have seen, and yet the police investigation seems extraordinarily leaden-paced."

Bahrain and the United States signed a Defense Cooperation Agreement in October 1991 granting U.S. forces access to Bahraini facilities and ensuring the right to pre-position matériel for future crises. Bahrain has built an advanced infrastructure in transportation and telecommunications, making it a regional financial and business center.

The move toward a more open society did not come until 1999, when a generational change brought Shaykh Hamad bin Isa Al Khalifa to power after the death of his father. The constitution was amended and ratified on February 14, 2001. Parliamentary elections were held in October 2002, the first for nearly 27 years. Women were allowed to run for office (State Department Notes: http://www.state.gov/r/pa/ei/bgn/5301.htm; "Timeline: Bahrain"; Silverman 2003).

The Bahraini opposition expressed its disappointment when the king of Bahrain gave the appointed consultative council the same legislative powers as the elected parliament. Critics admit, however, that the changes at least pave the way for a more independent press ("Bahraini Opposition Accuses the King" 2002; "Bahrain Replaces the Intelligence Services" 2002). The press is attempting to show some independence, but it is still hobbled by the fact that various officials and institutions that have traditionally wielded power unopposed still are not used to receiving direct criticism from the new more assertive press. It is expected, however, that as banned political parties are allowed to function, the press will feel free to criticize the political and religious establishments.

United Arab Emirates. In the United Arab Emirates, the Consultative Council confrontations erupted between the deputies, on the one hand, and the ministers of information and interior on the other, triggered by the disclosure of a list of names banned from writing in the press or speaking on the radio or the television. Both ministers denied any involvement in the preparation of the blacklist (Arab Freedom Watch: http://www.apfwatch.org). The print media in the Emirates continue to be dominated by the government.

Two of the Gulf countries, Kuwait and Saudi Arabia, are compared for contrast.

Kuwait.   Kuwait, one of the few monarchies in the Gulf with an elected parliament, enjoys a vigorous private press with technical capabilities and experienced reporters who are respected in the Arab world. Five Kuwaiti papers are in Arabic, two in English. Kuwaiti journalists have a margin of press freedom other Gulf states do not enjoy. This difference can be explained by the fact that some Kuwaitis had flirted with leftist and Arab nationalist parties and ideas in the 1950 and 1960 while other Gulf countries remained shielded from the intellectual currents of that era. The inability of women to vote still mars Kuwaiti democracy, but women were poised to sue again in order to take part in the 2003 elections.

In 2000, however, Kuwaiti attempts to replace prison sentences by fines for journalists who ignored press law restrictions on publishing "opinions that include sarcasm, contempt or denigration of religion" or that "soil public morals" failed. Nonetheless, there are at least two camps in Kuwaiti society, both with a presence in parliament. Islamists would like to muzzle the press and introduce Saudi-like controls on the Internet, while the less conservative others want to continue the present Kuwaiti practice of being one of the few Gulf nations to criticize its officials in the media.

While some in the government continue to censor the press or to imprison journalists, there are countervailing forces in parliament, within the legal system, and among intellectuals, who continue to fight restrictions. Kuwait has a press association.

Saudi Arabia.   The state was created in 1932 as an absolute monarchy. The kingdom follows the Wahhabi sect's strict interpretation of Islam, making it the most conservative Arab state. Unlike Kuwait, Saudi Arabia does not allow political parties. Although it has one of the most sophisticated media scenes in terms of equipment, it is also the most restricted in terms of content ("Country Profile, Saudi Arabia" 2002). Control is achieved through government input on who gets into journalism. Only press organizations, not individuals, are allowed to publish. The organizations are run by government-approved boards of directors. A censorship committee reviews and censors all national and foreign publications according to the policies of the state. A Saudi government policy statement of 1982 that forbids criticizing the government, the royal family, or the clergy and heads of state of friendly countries (Rampal 1994, pp. 245–246) still applies. Saudi Arabia has ten dailies, one per major region. The Kingdom publishes the *Daily News* in English. The government owns the Saudi Press Agency (SPA), and newspapers tend to follow SPA's lead on whether or not to publish news on sensitive subjects. Observers have noted that the Saudi press has been able to publish informative articles that would have been censored in the past, for example, articles about rising unemployment or the outbreak of Rift Valley fever in 2000. But those revelations are not an indication that the media are about to be free.

Saudi Arabia sponsors several Arab newspapers in European capitals, where Saudi moguls dominate the market. The high profile *Al-Sahrq al-Awsat* (Middle East) daily newspaper is only one of H.H. Saudi Research and Marketing Ltd.'s 16 London-based publications. These papers have a wider margin of freedom than Saudi papers but are not very critical of Saudi policies (IPI ["Saudi Arabia"] 1999).

One of the latest positive developments concerning the formation of unions in the Gulf states was the decision by the Saudi cabinet on April 2, 2001, to approve the right of workers to organize themselves in the workplace. The new labor regulation allows workers in firms employing more than 100 employees to form "workers committees," a measure Arab human rights activists hope will eventually promote the formation of trade unions in the Gulf states (www.apfwatch.org).

Qatar. The government abolished the ministry of information and lifted controls over the press in 1995, paving the way for press freedom. The press has not yet established itself on the Arab scene. Qataris approved their permanent constitution by referendum on April 30, 2003, opening the way to democracy.

Print Media in North Africa: Algeria, Egypt, Libya, Morocco, and Tunisia

Countries formerly ruled by France, such as Algeria, Morocco, and Tunisia, were left with a legacy of French culture, expressed daily in the French-language press, which still carries a lot of weight and, some charge, gets the lion's share of government advertising.

Algeria. After a century of rule by France, Algeria became independent in 1962. Algeria is an interesting case of what happens when democratic reform is not inclusive. The first-round success of the fundamentalist Islamic Salvation Front (FIS) party in the December 1991 balloting caused the army to intervene, crack down on the FIS, and postpone the subsequent elections. Islamists resented being kept out of power unfairly when the government allowed elections featuring pro-government parties and what it considered moderate religion-based parties to run for office.

After a long civil war in which more than 100,000 rebels, soldiers, and civilians were killed by both sides, FIS's armed wing, the Islamic Salvation Army, dissolved itself in January 2000, and many armed insurgents surrendered under an amnesty program designed to promote national reconciliation. But that period took a big toll on the press. Fifty-seven journalists were murdered between 1993 and 1996.

The Algerian press started to enjoy some freedom only after the Algerian constitution in 1989 introduced political pluralism and information diversity. Sixty-five political parties sprang up as soon as it was permissible, a fact that attests to the Algerian thirst for political participation. The 630 daily and weekly publications that rushed to appear were finally reduced to 30. Algerians responded by avoiding the official press in favor of the new private publications. Six dailies in Arabic and French are owned by the state. Of the main papers, the Arabic-language daily *al-Akhbar* has the largest circulation, with close to 400,000 copies. *Liberté*, the *Quotidien d'Oran*, and *Le Matin* have a circulation of over 100,000 copies each. The total Algerian press distribution is about $1.5 million copies a day (N. Abdul Rahman 2000). In 2001, Algeria had 18 dailies that offered a wide range of previously taboo subjects, such as AIDS, sex, corruption, and politics (IPI ["Algeria"] 2001). Algerian journalists take great risks when they publish hard-hitting news, but continue to do so.

Journalists have organized in a union that is taking professional issues seriously. Areas of concern are the official control of the press through licensing, printing, and advertising. The weight of the public sector in advertising, 65 percent, remains decisive in the success of publications. Some claim that the government does not hesitate to financially "strangle" publications with "wrong ideas" (http://www.ifj.org/regions/med/rep98.html). One quantitative study showed that government favors French papers with subsidies even though they distribute fewer copies than the Arabic papers. This favoritism, they say, creates tension because it isolates the French-educated elite from the masses and delays the Arabization of Algeria (Diliou 2000, pp. 58–61). Five printing presses belong to the state. Furthermore, a state-owned company imports newsprint. Sometimes, news does not get printed for "technical reasons." Some attempts to create alternative printing presses have been thwarted, but efforts continue. Also of concern is the severity of the press law. On May 16, 2001, in response to strong criticism of the government and the army, two senior representatives of the state criticized the private-sector press. The general assembly then passed an amendment to the penal code. Article 144 provides for jail sentences of two to 12 months and heavy fines for any "attack on the state president in terms containing insult or defamation, whether in writing, drawing or speech, irrespective of the medium used: sound, image, electronic or computer, or any other." The prosecutor can now institute proceedings directly, without first filing a complaint. In cases of a second offense, jail sentences and fines are doubled. All these sanctions are also applicable to offenses against "parliament or one of its two chambers, the ANP [the army], any public institution or any other constituent body." Since then several journalists have been sentenced to jail. As in previous years, journalists with the foreign press have had problems obtaining visas (Reporters Without Borders ["Algeria's Annual Reports"] 2001, 2002). The most important issues now being debated in Algeria are the role of Islamists in the country and the public acknowledgment of past human rights abuses.

Egypt.   The Egyptian press is not as influential as it used to be at the pan-Arab level because satellites now provide up-to-the-minute news from numerous other sources. There is, however, a vigorous tradition of investigative reporting and lively dialogue on internal Egyptian affairs not found in the rest of North African countries. For example, the press thoroughly investigated charges of corruption in the process of privatization under President Sadat and continues to do so.

The degree of freedom enjoyed by the Egyptian press has always been tied to the strength and diversity of Egyptian political parties, as the following brief background information on parties illustrates. In 1952, Egyptian President Gamal Abdel Nasser overthrew the Egyptian monarchy, under which there was a combination of private and party press. Nasser dissolved political parties in 1953 and closed four of their publications as well as 42 others appearing irregularly. The 1960 Law for Reorganizing the Press made it illegal for individuals, corporations, or political parties to own or run papers. Newspaper ownership was given to the Arab Socialist Union, which established three dailies. Although the papers sometimes published dissenting views, only a few trusted editors dared criticize the regime. Censorship was imposed on and off during that period (A. Abdul Rahman 1989, pp. 18–38). Despite these restrictions, the regime enjoyed wide popular support. Pan-Arab nationalism, which stressed political unification, anti-imperialism, and non-alignment, became personified in Nasser's leadership. *Al-Ahram*'s column "Frankly Speaking," written by Nasser's confidant Mohammad Hassanein Heikal, was read and analyzed by world politicians and Arab masses (Al-Shalabi 1999).

President Sadat showed his pro-Western orientation shortly after coming to power in 1970. Sadat lifted the direct censorship imposed since 1967. The 1977 Law No. 40 for organizing political parties allowed parties to issue papers without licensing. But Sadat closed some publications and transferred the staff of others in 1974 and 1977. Especially targeted were leftist publications that criticized his overtures to the West. Law 148 for the year 1980 restricted freedom of the press.

President Hosni Mubarak came to power after Sadat's assassination by Islamists in 1981. He continued allowing most political parties to publish their own papers, and he also allowed some leftist publications suppressed under Sadat to return. But the imposition of martial law after the assassination gave the government wide powers over the press (A. Abdul Rahman 1989, pp. 18–38, 67–72). Today, the Egyptian media are owned either by the government, or by political parties, or by the private sector.

Although the constitutional high court affirmed in 1993 that the right to criticize public officials was one of the requirements of a democratic system, and Article 4 of the 1996 press law prohibits censorship, the government's pressure on journalists is constant. The Egyptian press also is subjected through diplomatic channels to U.S. and Israeli pressure to curb the anti-Israeli sentiment of the press ("U.S. Ambassador to Cairo" 2002). Islamists also attempt to censor the press.

September 11 has had a negative effect on freedom of expression in many countries. The Egyptian People's Assembly on February 23, 2003, renewed the state of emergency in Egypt until 2006 even though it was not due for renewal until May.

Libya. Libya gained its independence in 1951. Since 1969, when Muammar al-Qaddafi came to power, Libya has been closed to the outside world. A few foreign journalists are occasionally granted permission to visit the country and may function with "escorts," but no permanent foreign correspondents are allowed in Tripoli. Libya has only three newspapers, all government-owned. There is one monthly that addresses some topical issues with relative freedom. One newspaper publishes in English.

After September 11, 2001, Qaddafi cracked down on Islamists and forbade anti-Western preaching in mosques. Islamists also happen to be among those who oppose his rule (IPI ["Libya"] 2001). In October 2002, he announced his intention to withdraw from the Arab League (established in 1945) because of his disappointment in the way the 22-Arab-country consortium has handled Palestine and Iraq, but President Hosni Mubarak convinced him to postpone that decision. He then turned his attention to African matters. It remains to be seen whether his press will orient itself to Africa or the Arab world.

Morocco.   King Mohammad VI, crowned in July 1999 at the age of 37, has tried to reconcile with communities that were at odds with his father and liberalize the economy and the country. Many argue, however, that he has not gone far enough, despite the fact that the September 2002 parliamentary elections were thought to be honest. Even though elections were presented as part of the "democratic transition," journalists were summoned for interrogation or fined over articles they wrote.

The government is still able to exercise censorship because the new press law passed by the House of Representatives on May 6, 2002, did not go far enough. Even though the law imposes fewer controls over starting publications and lighter penalties and smaller fines for journalists, it retains jail terms for insulting the king and the royal family (three and five years in prison, compared with between five and 20 years previously). Article 29 retains the government's right to ban Moroccan or foreign newspapers if they are deemed to "undermine Islam, the monarchy, national territorial integrity or public order." The Islamist fundamentalist media was also targeted.

Tunisia.   Tunisia shook off colonial rule in 1956, but a French-language press continues to coexist with the Arabic press. The press, both private and official, is characterized by its uniform tone. All dailies, without exception, publish the president's picture on their front pages almost daily, and headlines hardly differ from one newspaper to the next. Every edition has to be submitted to the interior ministry for registration before publication. Refusal by the ministry to register it amounts to a ban. The government prevents the entry of foreign publications that do not meet its approval. Despite repeated promises of reform, both the private and the government press continue to receive instructions from above on what not to publish. The government also uses advertising to pressure publications into compliance. Reporting on human rights abuses in Tunisia continues to be off limits. The first newspaper seizure since 1991 was prompted by the inclusion of a manifesto of the National Conference on Freedoms and Democracy, which was held in Tunis on July 1, 2000, as well as articles on some recent prosecutions of human rights activists (IPI ["Tunisia"] 2001). The 1993 amendments to the press law gave journalists the right to use truth as a defense even if writing about a member of the government. Other changes forbade the administrative suspension of whole newspapers but kept the right to suspend the offending issue. The impetus for this proposed liberalization is the realization that "the opening of the market has led to sharp competition between local and Arab and foreign papers and television channels" and to a decrease in circulation (Hamdan 2000, p. 19).

The April 2001 reform to the press code disappointed many journalists, who were hoping for "an end to the existing paradox of official liberal discourse and continued censorship."

Print Media in Iran, Israel, and Turkey

The Islamic Republic of Iran.   Press freedom and state regulation of the press have emerged as crucial issues in the struggle for power between reformists and conservatives. In the absence of legally recognized opposition, independent newspapers raise public awareness about alternative viewpoints and are the major mobilizing tool of Iranian reformists. The issue of freedom did not come to a head, however, until conservatives lost the election on May 27, 2000, for the first time since 1979 (Human Rights Watch ["As Fragile"] 1999). Conservatives believe that the culmination of the Islamic Revolution in 1979 was itself a political, social, and cultural reform based on Islamic principles. So conservatives want to guard against the press becoming "a gateway for cultural invasion" ("Iran" 1999). Reformers want to see greater openness. Says Minister of Culture and Islamic Guidance A. Mohajerani, "I am in favor of cultural tolerance.... We must create a climate in the Islamic Republic in which individuals will be able to express their views on various issues" (Human Rights Watch ["The Press"] 1999). The freedom of the press fostered by President Khatami and his supporters, however, exists only within the limits drawn by the clerical leadership. Those opposed to clerical rule still have no place in public debate in Iran. Nonetheless, the new administration restored licenses to a number of banned publications. The press was beginning to insist that powerful state institutions should be accountable for their actions and carry out their functions in a transparent manner. But while the Iranian press courageously debated contentious issues, it lacked the protection of basic legal safeguards and was vulnerable to the shifting currents of Iranian politics.

Conservatives passed amendments to the Press Law on July 7, 1999, that extended the control of the clergy over every aspect of press production and publishing. Legal issues in contention are the role of the jury in press courts, the ability of the Supervisory Press Board to close newspapers by administrative order, and the use of courts other than the press courts to punish writers (Human Rights Watch ["As Fragile"] 1999). When some reformers in parliament introduced a bill to deregulate the press in August 2000, the intervention of Ayatollah Ali Khamenei, the country's top Muslim cleric, prevented the bill from being debated or voted on ("Two" 2000). The parliament revisited that bill in November 2000 despite conservative clerics' objections and insisted that intelligence services and the ministry of interior should not oversee publications. This, amid student demonstrations asking for freedom of the press (Nun 2000). Since April 2002, 80 publications have been suspended (Reporters Without Borders ["Conservatives"] 2002).

Israel.   The Israeli press has passed through several stages of development in terms of ownership, political control, and content. The early Israeli press was financed and controlled by political parties that also appointed their editors. The party press gave way to the private press in the 1980s and 1990s (Caspi and Limor 1999, pp. 67–68). A dozen Hebrew newspapers appear in Israel. Three of those are intended for religious readers who feel that the secular press does not fulfill their needs or reflect their values. Several hundred other local papers, mostly weeklies, are published, mostly on Fridays (Limor 1999).

Israel since its founding in 1948 has been a country of immigrants. This immigration profile is reflected in its press. Israel has 12 foreign-language dailies, with the largest number, four, in Russian, two in Romanian, and one each in Arabic, English, German, Hungarian, Polish, and Yiddish (Caspi and Limor 1999, pp. 65–66). There are also dozens of periodicals published in Russian. Some newspapers and periodicals are published in Arabic, but those are subjected to more restrictions than those published in other languages because of Israel's conflict with the Arab world.

The political content of the Israeli press has grown more sophisticated over time. During the early years of the Israeli occupation of the West Bank in 1967, the Israeli press was too dependent on the Israeli army spokesperson for its news and interpretation of events (Halabi 1981, p. 56). But the surprise Egyptian crossing of the Suez Canal in the October 1973 war and, later, statements made by Israeli spokespersons about Lebanon convinced Israeli editors that they should no longer allow "army assurances, army assumptions, and army censors to deter our pens," as former editor of the *Jerusalem Post* Erwin Frenkel put it (1994, p. 76). The press was strengthened by a 1982 ruling in Tel Aviv District Court upholding a *Ha'aretz* reporter, Uzi Benziman, in a libel case brought against him by Ariel Sharon. The Israeli press has been strengthened by reporters like Amira Hass, who insisted on covering the West Bank and Gaza by living there among Palestinians (rather than among settlers). She, along with Palestinian journalist Daoud Kuttab, were among the 50 recipients of the World Press Freedom Hero Award. Hass's dispatches from the Palestinian territories are honest and courageous despite the fact that she is monitored by Palestinians and Israelis alike. Kuttab insisted on broadcasting the Palestinian Legislative Council deliberations, even if it meant going to jail for a week in the process. Those changes in coverage improved the level of objectivity of news transmitted to the foreign press, whose members depended heavily on Israeli sources (Najjar 1995).

Although Israel did not abolish the 1945 British regulations that imposed press censorship, the government signed an agreement on military censorship with Israeli editors in 1949. A three-member "censorship tribunal" was set up to resolve the disputes that arise between the chief censor and the Israeli press, which received general guidelines on the topics the government considered sensitive (Gavron 1987). In 1989, the High Court of Justice ruled that censorship may be applied only when the item in question would harm public safety (Limor 1999). That ruling embold-ened the Israeli press. The International Press Institute (IPI) noted that the weaken-ing of the once stringent Israeli military censorship was dramatized in 1997 in the coverage of two fiascos involving the Mossad, the country's secret service (IPI ["Israel"] 1997).

Israel has come under international criticism for its handling of the press since the beginning of the uprising starting September 2000. According to an April 2002 report by the Vienna-based IPI, six journalists have been killed and 59 have been injured by gunfire or shelling ("Country Profile: Israel").

Turkey.   Turkey has a diverse and lively press. Aside from the nationally circulated newspapers, there are more than 700 local newspapers published either daily or periodically. Their daily circulation varies between 500 and 10,000.

Advanced technology and specialization have helped the magazine industry. The circulation of weekly political magazines varies between 10,000 and 50,000. While overall readership of the local press is not large for a country of that size, the newspaper business is intensely competitive. Despite the government's restrictions, the media criticize government leaders and policies daily. The Constitution provides for freedom of speech and of the press; however, the government sometimes limits these freedoms.

The 1991 repeal of the law prohibiting publications or communications in Kurdish legalized private spoken and printed communications in Kurdish.

Reporters Without Borders charged that "[d]espite the announcement of democratic reforms within the framework of Turkey's candidacy for membership in the European Union, prosecutions for beliefs and opinions are still systematically and severely punished by virtue of a repressive legislative arsenal aimed at protecting the state against demands by the Kurds, Islamists and the far left" (Reporters Without Borders ["Turkey"] 2002). That legislative arsenal was removed by the Turkish parliament when it voted in August 2002 to allow broadcasting in Kurdish. Turkey appears to be moving toward giving its journalists more freedom in law, if not yet in practice.

Broadcasting in the Arab World

Until recently, broadcasting in the Arab world was under the thumb of various governments, with the exception of Lebanon.[3] Current trends suggest that broadcasting is entering a new era characterized by channel and program diversity, technological sophistication, and sweeping commercialism. Apart from the presence of less traditional broadcasting, liberalization has also been manifest in the restructuring of broadcast organizations. In Jordan, Bahrain, the United Arab Emirates, Lebanon, and Kuwait, new more autonomous corporations have been established. Ridding the stations of old bureaucratic practices and streamlining management have improved programming (Ayish 1998). Yet while those countries have privatized entertainment for fear of losing the members of their audience to widely available satellite stations from several countries, many have not privatized news or political opinion. Ali A. Mazrui, then Senior Scholar in Africana studies, Cornell University, observed that the cold war was globalization-friendly in global politics but hostile to globalization in terms of the world economy (Mazrui 1999). The demise of the Soviet Union, however, has eroded barriers to full-throttled economic globalization. Governments realized they cannot ignore vital technology sectors that are the entry to the Internet-driven global economy. Countries of the Middle East and North Africa know that most cannot afford to invest what it takes

($30 to $50 billion each year over the next five years) to bring their telecommunications systems up to global standards. Faced with these huge demands for capital, many state monopolies have been compelled to cede a significant role to technology-rich private sector consortia.

Not everyone in the region is accepting the inevitability or desirability of privatization and globalization. Some insist that focusing too narrowly on efficiency criteria ignores fundamental questions about "the nationality of capital" (Pripsten-Posusney 1999). Many fear returning their countries' strategic assets to foreign hands. But more important, some fear the erosion of their own values. Jordanian columnist Hussein al-Rawashdah laments the effects of the spread of foreign culture "that refuses all types of freedom except the freedom of commercial speech, and wages war on all values except the value of consumption" (Al-Rawashdah 1997).

Broadcasting in Iraq, Jordan, Lebanon, Palestine, and Syria

Iraq. Until it was occupied by the United States of America, Iraq had two channels: the official channel of Iraq Television and Youth Television, a private channel headed by Uday Hussein, the son of the former Iraqi president. Although Iraq was the first Arab country to have television in 1956, it was the last to have satellites, first because of censorship, and then in 1996, because American sanctions against it prevented the importation of satellites. In July 1998, Iraq launched its first satellite channel ("Satellite" 1999).

Although Iraq now has a prolific press, Iraq's broadcasting is less diverse. TV stations are being run by the United States and Britain. The United States set up an AM and FM radio station, a TV station, and a daily paper, *Al-Sabah*, all funded and supervised by the U.S.-controlled Iraqi Media Network. "The network's role was envisioned to be an information conduit, and not just a rubber-stamp flacking for the C.P.A.," said Don North, a television producer who returned to the United States after serving as an advisor to the network but grew frustrated by orders to run programs that were not sound journalism, as well as by a slim budget. Officials counter that some form of propaganda was always part of the plan (Oppel 2003).

Reporters Without Borders (RSF) urged the United States to replace the restrictive regulations it imposed on the media in early June with "clear and coherent laws." A decree dealing with "inimical media activity" issued by the country's U.S. civilian administrator, Paul Bremer, bans incitement to violence against the U.S. and British forces, as well as incitement to "ethnic and religious hatred," phrases RSF called "vague terms whose interpretation by U.S. authorities could be used to crack down on the local media." The organization also criticized the detention of journalists of Al-Jazeera while filming an anti-U.S. demonstration. Another Al-Jazeera reporter described on Al-Jazeera how he was detained for 24 hours and had his video confiscated after photographing the remains of a family in a burned car hit by American forces responding to attacks against them from elsewhere (RSF 2003).

In contrast to the restrictions under the old regime, however, Iraqis now can use satellite dishes, and they are selling briskly to Iraqis who were unable to tune to other Arab satellite stations under Saddam Hussein. Internet cafes are also flourishing. Broadcasting has not yet been privatized, but days after the regime fell, volunteers in the city of Karbala took over an abandoned 100-watt television substation and began broadcasting over a range of about 12 miles. Karbala TV mixes Koranic verses with pirated satellite news broadcasts, cartoons, and local news segments about the city's electrical and water problems. Najaf TV broadcasts eight hours a day from a tiny one-kilowatt substation once used to strengthen broadcasts. Again, they stress local fare, including city council elections and the gas shortage (Daragahi 2003).

Jordan. Despite partial privatization of television and the appointment of a Jordan Radio and TV board, the media, especially the channel that transmits news, remain under government control because entertainment, rather than news, was partly privatized. Critics charge that privatization *cum* capitalism defeats the original goal of privatization: to liberate news and public affairs programs from government control.

Television transmission began in April 1968 from one studio, with three hours of black-and-white programming. Channel 1 continued to promote local production. Channel 2 was added in 1972 to broadcast news and programs in English. Color was introduced in 1974, and French programming was added in 1978. Jordan Radio, established in 1956, merged with TV to form Jordan Radio and Television Corporation. In January 2001, the corporation underwent major restructuring. Channel 2 specialized in sports and in transmitting sessions of parliament (but to the chagrin of viewers, it cut transmission when discussions got heated). Channel 3, which is operated with the private sector, has a morning cartoon channel and an evening movie channel, according to the JTV web site.

The appointment of a JRTV board in accordance with the new Radio and TV Law of October 1, 2000, was seen as a positive step that would lead to the increased participation of the private sector. But critics note that when the eight-member board was reshuffled, its appointed head was the minister of information. The new board also included representatives from the Ministry of Religious Affairs as well as the armed forces, making it less likely to be as liberal as it would have been had its members been mostly media professionals (Najjar 2003).

Lebanon. Radio broadcasting in Lebanon, which started in 1938 under the French Mandate, remained a government monopoly until the beginning of the civil war in 1975 (Dajani 2003).

As a result of the failure of Radio Lebanon to satisfy the needs of the Lebanese during the civil war, different warring groups established their own illegal radio stations. The abundance of funds available to the warring groups allowed these stations to produce programs that were professionally and technically more advanced than Radio Lebanon. With time, nonpolitical, extralegal stations specializing in music and talk shows began to operate. By the end of the war, these stations declared themselves commercial and sought official recognition. Several years of deliberations produced the 1994 audiovisual law, which ended the monopoly of Radio Lebanon over radio broadcasting. Subsequently, the government issued licenses to nine radio stations authorized to broadcast all types of programs, including news and political programs, and to 13 other stations authorized to broadcast specialized programs but not news or political programs. Some unlicensed radio continues to operate, with the government ignoring them to avoid confrontations with the influential backers of these stations (Dajani, 2003).

Lebanon is the only country in the region that saw television as a business from the start. Lebanon's view of the media as a private enterprise ensured its primacy in entertainment television, if not in political broadcasting. Private control created a freer climate for political criticism than that found in other countries with government-controlled media, but at the same time, it also led to government pressure to reduce critical reporting for fear of driving away potential investors.

When the government got involved in television, it was at the request of the two private stations that had started broadcasting in 1956 and 1959. A 1977 legislative decree legalized the official merger in a new company, the Lebanese Televison Company (Tele Liban), licensed it for 25 years, and gave it monopoly until 2012. Tele Liban was to be managed by a 12-member board of directors, six representing the government, with the chair to be appointed by the government (Dajani 2003).

The weakening of the central government in the mid-1980s ensured the failure of the idea of monopoly and encouraged some warring factions to establish their own pirate stations because they felt that Tele Liban was not doing them justice.

The government legalized the existing stations in 1989. Many rushed to form new ones before the regulations took effect. Forty-six were set up in a few months, and 10 were on the air by the end of 1991 (Dajani 2003). The new Audio-Visual Law adopted by the parliament gave 16-year licenses and classified television stations according to their content (news and politics, no news and politics, coded signals to subscribers, international satellite).

In September 1996, the council of ministers restructured private broadcasting on the recommendation of the National Council of Audio-Visual Media. Radio stations were reduced from 150 to 10. TV stations were reduced from 60 to four (in addition to Tele-Liban) ("Lebanon" 1996). Lebanon's permitted TV channels reflect sectarian and boss interests. Those include Lebanese Broadcasting Company International (LBCI, formerly LBC), which represents the Maronite Christians and whose shareholders include prominent members of the government; Future TV, which represents the Sunni Muslims and is owned by the former prime minister; Murr Television (MTV), which represents the Greek Orthodox Christians and is owned by the family of the former Minister of the Interior; and the National Broadcasting network (NBN), which represents the Shiite Muslims and is owned by the family and supporters of the Speaker of the Parliament. Unlicensed stations continued broadcasting, although the government closed a few (Dajani 2003; Kraidy 1999). Al-Manar station, belonging to Hizbullah (the Party of God), was allowed to stay open. The station was established on June 3, 1991, while Israelis were still occupying 20 percent of the south of Lebanon. According to its web site, it was not unusual for the south and Bekaa Valley to be under Israeli fire "while singers chant on numerous TV channels simultaneously. There had to be a TV that committed itself to put in images the suffering of our people in the occupied territories." But its effectiveness lay it waging a "psychological warfare against the myth of the invincible Israeli" (Muhsen 1998, p. 63). Hizbullah statistics after the April 1996 conflict with Israel show that 1,200 journalists visited Hizbullah's information center. Hizbullah also issued 474 briefings and distributed 200 videos to news agencies (Muhsen 1998, pp. 66–67).

A Catholic station, Tele Lumiere, continues to broadcast without a license, but with tacit government approval. The Holy Koran TV does the same. When a new Lebanese government took over, it reconsidered the applications rejected by the previous one, and granted three more licenses: the New Television (NTV) in June 1999 (12 percent of its shares belong to the Communist party), the Independent Communication Channel International (ICNI), and United Television (UTV), both in September 1999 (Dajani 2001).

Despite the sectarian nature of the origin of some of those stations, commercial self-interest has led them to reach out beyond their original constituencies. For example, the Lebanese Broadcasting Corporation, in addition to having been a mouthpiece for the now disbanded Lebanese forces with a declared Christian Lebanese nationalist agenda, runs special Ramadan programming during Islam's holy month and fasting season (Kraidy 1999, p. 498). Similarly, Future TV caters to its Christian audience by broadcasting a Sunday mass. But the need for commerce prompts the government to pressure Lebanese satellite stations not to spread alarmist messages about the state of the Lebanese economy, in an attempt to get Lebanese expatriates as well as other Arabs to invest in Lebanon. This has led to the rare situation in which the government is less concerned about critical reporting on government officials inside Lebanon, but is very sensitive about the image projected abroad via satellite TV (Kraidy, 1999, p. 490). The attitude of the Lebanese government contrasts with the attitude of other governments that are very concerned about public criticism of their policies or persons. The low cost of cable in Lebanon enables the Lebanese to receive some 70 channels, including most of the Arab satellite stations as well as CNN and the BBC. In some heavily populated areas, this subscription could be as little as US $5 a month. Unlicensed satellite television distribution companies mushroomed in the past few years and had penetrated almost two-thirds of Lebanon's households by 1999 (*The Daily Star*, 1999).

Lebanon has eight earth stations, seven satellite stations, and more than 30 radio stations. Two attempts at censorship were met with determined resistance by the media, as well as the professional unions. In September 2002, Murr TV, known for its opposition to the presence of Syria in Lebanon, was closed ostensibly for broadcasting election propaganda during elections, and in early 2003, New TV was closed for four days to prevent it from broadcasting a program uncomplementary to Saudi Arabia. Although both resumed operation, their closure led to calls for the discussion of the media's main problem, namely, "the presence of a number of red, unannounced moving lines that contract or expand according to determinations made by those in power" ("Problems of Politics" 2003).

Palestinian Radio and Television. The West Bank provides an example in which media privatization has led to more local production rather than to corporate ownership. This local production persists at a time when the use of satellite TV has been extended to 40 percent of TV-owning households in 2000 (Palestine Survey Research Center 2000), and when international and regional Arab satellite broadcasts are available. The government-owned Palestine Broadcasting Corporation (PBC) operates Palestine TV from Ramallah and Gaza. Listeners can hear the news every hour on the hour in Arabic, Hebrew, English, and French, in that order. The PBC also operates Palestine Satellite Channel. But a development unique in the Arab world has been the establishment of 40 private radio and TV stations alongside PBC. Private TV stations include Al-Quds Educational TV, Al-Mahd TV, Al-Majd TV, Al-Nawras TV, Al-Sharq TV, Amwaj TV, Bayt Lahm TV, Shepherds TV, and Watan TV ("Country Profile: Israel and the Autonomous Palestinian Areas" 2002).

When the Palestinian authority, headed by Yasser Arafat, entered Gaza on July 1, 1994, it asked broadcasters who had worked at various PLO radio stations around the Arab world since 1965 to return and establish the official radio in the West Bank and Gaza ("History" 2000). But even before the autonomy was extended to the West Bank in September 1995, several Palestinian citizens had already established unlicensed small radio or TV stations starting in December 1993.[4] The broadcasters came from all sectors of society: the physics university student who experimented with the first transmitter that broadcast only around his house; the penniless print media veterans who found the new medium promising for hard-hitting documentaries on public issues and solicited funds from business people who wanted to make money off advertising; and the leftist political party that wanted a voice in the political process (Farraj 2000). The stations live on ads for regular products, as well as cheaper ads of birthday, high school, wedding, and other greetings sent by families.

Historically, Palestinian newspaper publishing has always been strong in the middle of the country (East Jerusalem and, later, Ramallah).

A few attempts to start papers in the north were aborted by Palestinian security services in the mid-1990s. It is not surprising, then, that the north and the south of the West Bank took to the new medium of broadcasting quickly and established radio and TV stations that became popular. According to the Palestinian Human Rights Monitor's report (1994–1999), when there were 27 TV stations and seven radio stations, the distribution of those stations showed that 17 of them were in the north of the country, four in the center, and six in the south. The introduction of TV to badly served towns made broadcasting much more central to the lives of people in those areas than the centrally located print media whose concentration remains national.

To save money, stations depend on inexperienced volunteers and on family members. Othman Al-Hamshari, of Al-Salam (Peace) TV, Toulkarm, says he is willing to borrow $1.5 million but would not risk it with a one-year license.

The Palestinian security services close the stations from time to time, a fact that encourages some to practice self-censorship, but leads others to take risks to broadcast what they think is important: investigations of corruption, investigative reporting of local issues outside large cities, and taboo sexual subjects no government station dares touch. Israelis accuse both government and private stations of incitement when they show demonstrations and funerals of suicide bombers. When pressure to change the content of the stations failed, Israel destroyed the government-owned Ramallah Radio and TV building of the PBC after confiscating its equipment (Committee to Protect Journalists 2002). The station quickly shifted to local FM private stations that came to the rescue. In April 2002, Israeli soldiers destroyed the equipment of various private TV stations. Donations have been solicited to replace equipment, and most stations are back in operation.

Syrian Radio and Television. The first official Syrian radio station launched during the French Mandate in 1941 was taken over by the Syrian government in 1946 after the French withdrew from Syria. A series of military coups beginning in 1949 increased the importance of radio for the different regimes, which strengthened its operation. By 1951, its service covered all the Syrian provinces as well as the neighboring countries, the Mediterranean region, and parts of Africa. Syria transmits programs in Arabic, French, Hebrew, Turkish, Spanish, and Russian (Dajani 2003).

The Syrian Arab Television is financed directly by government, which also controls its political content, as well as by advertising. It operates within the General Directorate of Radio and Television whose board is chaired by the Minister of Information (Dajani 2003). Syrian Arab TV commenced operations on July 23, 1960. By 1967, television stations in different regions were connected by a microwave link and transmission links. Consequently, all the Syrian provinces started receiving simultaneously the same programs transmitted from Damascus. Television studios that were set up in most of the Syrian provinces contributed to the direct broadcast operations of Syrian television. By 1980 all broadcasting was in color. In 1985, Syrian television started a second channel that concentrated on cultural programs (Syrian Arab News Agency [SANA] 2002, quoted by Dajani 2003). Paradoxically, Syria's refraining from importing Western TV series, unlike its neighbor Lebanon, gave its own TV industry a boost by forcing it to rely on the active Syrian cultural scene (theatre and dance troupes). Syrian historical drama and political satire shows are very popular in the Arab world for their good scripts and biting social commentary. Its *Ghawwar al Tosheh* program, a comedy that indicts Arab bureaucracy, ran in many Arab countries for years and is now broadcast on satellite. Syrian drama is not afraid of treating gender and class issues in a serious but entertaining way. On the other hand, Syrian political and news talk shows have not distinguished themselves in the pan-Arab debate scene because political censorship prevents Syrian satellite TV from inviting guests whose views are radically different from its own. Syria does not restrict its citizens' use of satellite dishes, and Syrian callers and experts frequently participate in Al-Jazeera satellite TV call-ins.

The Arab News Network (ANN), a Syrian satellite channel owned by the estranged nephew of the former president of Syria, can be received in Syria.

Broadcasting in the Gulf Countries: Bahrain, Kuwait, United Arab Emirates, Saudi Arabia, and Qatar

While Gulf countries have lagged in terms of print press freedom, they have distinguished themselves on the Arab information technology and media scene, in part because of their financial resources, but also because of a conscious commitment to move away from having oil as their only product. Dubai, which in the early 1970s depended on oil for 87 percent of its economy, now depends on it for only 17 percent and hopes to reduce that to only 2 percent in 2010 ("Dubai" 2002). Qatar and Abu Dhabi have distinguished themselves in satellite broadcasting, and Dubai by luring Internet and communication technology to a special media zone it set up.

Bahrain. Bahrain government-owned Radio and TV Corporation operates five terrestrial TV networks. Those consist of a general program in Arabic, a second program featuring cultural and local programs, a *Koran* program, a sports service, and the English-language Radio Bahrain. The long absence of elected government until October 2002 resulted in a press used to self-censorship or exile. The media have not yet developed as institutions capable of policing government. The recent elections may put them on the path of reform.

Kuwait. The Kuwaiti Ministry of Information controls the radio and four terrestrial TV stations. Kuwaiti media are currently involved in a power struggle with Islamists who want them to be more conservative, especially in entertainment. The tide turned against the liberal Kuwaiti Minister of Information, Sa'ad Al-Ajami, who resigned after occupying his position since July 1999 after enduring severe criticism by Islamist members of parliament for not applying a conservative policy to the state TV and radio ("Kuwaiti Minister" 2000). Despite that setback, Kuwait has a strong constituency for freedom of expression.

There are no private radio stations in Kuwait. Radio Kuwait is controlled by the Ministry of Information and broadcasts programs in Arabic and English.

Saudi Arabia. Saudi Arabia is an example of country whose strict media policy is being eroded by the various Arab satellite programs that are picked up in the kingdom. But it is also a country that has created and funded a media empire for itself outside its borders, thus making itself an important media player in the Arab world (although not in political broadcasting until the establishment of Al-Arabiyah).

The state-owned Broadcasting Service of the Kingdom of Saudi Arabia (BSKSA) is responsible for all broadcasting and is directly controlled by the Ministry of Information. Satellite dishes are banned, but people use them freely without fear of prosecution.

The Saudi-owned Orbit Satellite Television and Radio Network is the world's first fully digital, multichannel, multilingual, pay television service. Orbit news offers daily coverage that includes ABC, CBS, NBC, and MSNBC news. It also offers its viewers the choice to see the BBC in Arabic or English. Orbit is now translating into Arabic all its English-language fare (such as *The West Wing, Le Femme Nikita*, and the History Channel). How much of a competition Orbit will be for Al-Jazeera remains to be seen. After all, it is news and public affairs programming (rather than *La Femme Nikita*) that keeps Arabs watching Al-Jazeera, and others worrying about it.

United Arab Emirates. The United Arab Emirates is a federation of seven states formed in 1971: Abu Dhabi, Dubai, Ajman, Fujairah, Ras Al-Khaimah, Sharjah, and Umm Al-Qaywayn. The UAE is one of the most liberal countries in the Gulf region.

Abu Dhabi. Abu Dhabi TV consists of three channels: the Emirates Channel, which focuses on the Gulf region; the Abu Dhabi Sports Channel, a pay channel, and the Abu Dhabi Satellite Channel, which is making its mark on the Arab media scene by competing with Al-Jazeera by presenting political talk shows that draw large audiences. Even though Abu Dhabi TV does not get much coverage in the West, in the Arab world it is followed with attention. During the 2003 U.S. war with Iraq, all U.S. stations heavily used Abu Dhabi's coverage, as well as Al-Jazeera's.

The station employed Zogby International poll (April 11, 2002) to determine the feelings of the Arab audience toward the United States instead of just speculating about them. The station also interviews Israelis, despite protest calls from Arab viewers. The minister of foreign affairs, Sheikh Hamdan, rejected pressure from Secretary of State Colin Powell to pull a 30-episode TV series making fun of Israeli prime minister Ariel Sharon ("This" 2002).

A Lebanese media critic described one of Abu Dhabi's satellite programs as a seamless performance in which the station interviewed the editor of *Oriental Studies* in Paris, then cut to its own correspondent in Bethlehem, then to its correspondent in Ramallah, West Bank, then to the United Nations, then to Tehran, then to Ramallah to interview some politicians, then to Damascus to cover demonstrations. The critic said that the Lebanese satellite stations, which dazzled Arab viewers when they first appeared, are now behind Gulf stations and should reconsider their coverage (Yaghi 2000). Radio is owned by the government.

Dubai. Dubai is a perfect example of a country that adopted capitalism and globalization with a Middle Eastern twist that befits the country's background as the home of traders and seafarers. Unlike Abu Dhabi and Qatar, Dubai has shunned political broadcasting to avoid controversy, but has turned itself into a media hub by attracting 194 world-class computer companies to its Dubai Internet City (DIC) and the Oasis for electronic projects, and for inducing Arab companies that had migrated to the West to set up shop in Dubai alongside Western companies it attracted through tax breaks ("After" 2000).

Dubai Media City, launched on November 4, 2000, like DIC, accepts 100 percent foreign ownership and offers a 50-year corporate and personal tax exemption to "individual media people" as well as corporations. The vision is of a media community that will bring broadcasters, TV production companies, publishers, ad agencies, and public relations companies as well as individual journalists together in one 500-acre landscaped "media ecosystem."

Dubai has invested approximately $800 million in Media City, slightly more than its investment in Dubai Internet City. It provides cutting-edge technology, including production and transmission facilities. The strategic position of Dubai at the crossroads of the Middle East, Africa, and South Asia enables it to serve as a media hub for the region and target an audience of nearly two billion people. The list of residents include Indian channels like UNI TV, AsiaNet, the Iranian Soroush Multimedia, and Zen TV, a channel targeting teens.

Most of the space in Dubai Media City has already been taken by local, regional, and multinational companies, among them TV producers, record companies, postproduction studios, and freelance service providers. DIC has already reportedly leased out 95 percent of its space, with IBM already breaking ground in DIC for a regional headquarters and with Microsoft, Oracle, Compaq, Master-Card, Sun Microsystems, and Hewlett-Packard among the more than 190 companies already licensed to operate in DIC.

MBC, the largest Middle East, pan-Arab broadcaster, has relocated to Dubai Media City from London. Other clients include Middle East Business News, producing for CNBC. CNN started operating out of Dubai Media City early January, doing two things: incorporating a regional news bureau there, and launching CNNArabic.com out of Dubai Media City. Reuters has relocated its operation and expanded it at Dubai Media City. Reuters is a major "anchor" client for Dubai Media City and, like MBC, has a building named for it.

But while Duabi calls its zone "Free Media Zone," an Arab comedian might define "free" as relating only to the tax breaks companies get.

Qatar. Qatar's state television runs three channels: one main Arabic service, a Koran channel, and one English channel. Qatar has one private station, Al-Jazeera, run by an independent board.

Al-Jazeera Satellite TV: A Pan-Arab Voice in Qatar. The most important recent development for the Arab media was the establishment of the Al-Jazeera satellite station in Qatar in 1996. That station put Qatar on the map of Arab politics. Qatar (population 565,000) has also replaced Egypt (population 67,884,000) as the media leader in the Arab world. A cover story in a political magazine crowns Al-Jazeera as the most-watched station in the Arab world (Darwish 2000). When asked about their favorite news satellite channel, 78.2 percent of the Palestinians interviewed in a national census listed Al-Jazeera.[5]

Al-Jazeera has introduced a new form of "Global Arab Village" not seen since the days of "Voice of Arabs Radio" from Cairo in the 1950s and 1960s. The station's most famous talk-show programs, *More Than One Opinion, The Opinion and the Other Opinion,* and *The Opposite Direction,* pit people from different political camps or countries against each other and invite listeners to call in, and they do—from every Arab country as well as from Iran, Pakistan, Europe, and the United States. Sparks fly and "red lines" imposed by governments are crossed because all the "forbiddens" are ignored (criticism of rulers and regimes, religion, and women's status). Al-Jazeera is the only station that has a women's program that does not deal with cooking, childcare, or fashion. *For Women Only* discusses gender and work issues, as well as women's education and political participation. Satellite TV has enabled that program to tap the expertise of Arab feminists in different countries. A program on May 12, 2003, for example, pitted the opinion of an Iraqi feminist and member of the Iraq Communist Party who demanded full equality for women, against the opinion of a Muslim Shi'ite cleric who had other plans for them. He criticized the West for objectifying women and "using semiclad women as a name brand" to advertise all types of commercial products. The feminist wondered whether the rising power of Islamists and tribal leaders will adversely affect the gains women made in Iraq in the last two decades.

Al-Jazeera is constantly fielding protests from different countries. Iraqi officials condemned the station for suggesting that birthday cakes and celebrations on Saddam Hussein's birthday were inappropriate while Iraq was under siege. Saudi Arabia protested when the station broadcast a Saddam Hussein speech in which he urged Arab governments to overthrow their leaders if they were allied to the United States. Kuwait banned Al-Jazeera after an Iraqi viewer insulted the Kuwaiti prince during a call-in program. Libya recalled the head of its diplomatic mission because participants in a debate said Libya's system of people's committees was a mere facade, behind which the country's leader Mua'mmar al-Qaddafi made all decisions. Bahrain resented Al-Jazeera's airing footage of anti-American demonstrations when Bahrain's media ignored them. In August 2002, Jordan shut down the offices of Al-Jazeera after it broadcast a program about the Jordanian royal family in which it criticized its relations with the West and Israel over the years. (Jordan reopened the office in early 2003.) The Palestinian authority has, from time to time, censored the station. Israel accuses Al-Jazeera of glorifying the Intifada, while some viewers accuse the station of being an agent of the Israeli Mossad (intelligence service) for breaking the Arab tradition of not interviewing Israelis. The United States has unsuccessfully attempted to pressure Qatar to clamp down on Al-Jazeera, and has asked U.S. media not to broadcast the full bin Laden tapes the station supplied. All that has failed, leading U.S. government officials like Donald Rumsfeld, Condoleeza Rice, and Colin Powell to conclude that the best way to get their point of view across is not by advocating censorship, but by being interviewed by Al-Jazeera. British Prime Minister Tony Blair has also been interviewed. Saudi Arabia has denied Al-Jazeera permission to cover the Pilgrimage to Mecca and refuses to let it establish a permanent office in the Kingdom. All this outspokenness is affecting Al-Jazeera's bottom line. Several Gulf states threatened to "halt cooperation with Al-Jazeera offices, presenters and employees" and urged the public and private sectors to stop commercial cooperation with the station if it failed to stop "insulting and slandering" Arab leaders (Ahmed 2002).

Al-Jazeera says it has been the victim of an advertising boycott. It was bailed out by the ruler of Qatar in 2003 after racking up losses of £19 million. Hamad Ibn Khalifa, prince of Qatar, refuses to censor the station. Qatar had agreed to fund it for the first five years starting in November 1996, but continues to help fund it because Qatari rulers believe that it offers Qatar clout abroad that is worth more than any financial profit. Al-Jazeera is a lean operation by Western standards, with 755 employees worldwide—compared with CNN's 4,000 and BBC News's 3,300. Its plans for expansion include a semiautonomous English-language service in 2004, plus a documentary channel and a sports channel. Its planned training college for Arab media, which is being developed with help from the BBC, promises to be a moneymaker. The station has begun to exploit the Al-Jazeera brand on T-shirts, sunglasses, and even cosmetics. Its employees are very optimistic about its future (Wheeler 2003).

Al-Jazeera made its name in the west during the war in Afghanistan as the only television station with a permanent base in Kabul that could provide exclusive footage other channels around the world were eager to buy. In the process, it earned the enmity of the U.S. administration. Its office in Kabul was destroyed by American "smart" bombs two hours before the Northern Alliance took over the city. The station clinched its place as a pace-setting news organization in Iraq. Al-Jazeera, whose viewer base has been estimated at anywhere from 35 to 65 million viewers, broadcast blood-and-guts images from the invasion of Iraq, photos many Western news organizations would consider too shocking to publish. One showed the head of a child, aged about 12, that had been split apart, reportedly in the U.S.-led assault on Basra. On March 23, 2003, Al-Jazeera relayed footage of Iraqi television's interviews with five captured American soldiers, infuriating the Americans. Ali Kamal, the marketing director of Al-Jazeera, defended the station's right to show pictures of dead bodies because the media have a duty to show the bloody price of war. He added that Arab media are under attack because they now have the "upper hand" over Western broadcasters. Kamal was in England receiving the Index on Censorship Freedom of Expression Awards for circumvention of censorship (Whitaker 2003; Tryhorn 2003). The New York Stock Exchange ejected Al-Jazeera's financial reporters and has since reinstated them. Then the network's English-language Web site debuted, only to be hit by computer hackers (Carlson 2003). Saddam Hussein himself, when he was still in power, asked Al-Jazeera to replace its Iraqi correspondent in Baghdad. Al-Jazeera insisted that he either stay there, or no one will replace him in Baghdad. Hussein relented. During the invasion, the Iraqi Minister of Information, Mohammad al-Sahhaf, asked Al-Jazeera to replace two of its correspondents. Al-Jazeera announced on air on April 2, 2003, that it "froze" the reporting of all eight of its correspondents in Baghdad (but said it will continue broadcasting live images of the invasion). The minister relented, and the station quietly resumed its operations. Francis Hasso said both Arab and American attacks on the station show that "al-Jazeera's approach to covering the war—both critical and multidimensional, with an ideological commitment to democracy, openness and pluralism—has seriously threatened the political projects of the world's most powerful." She added that Al-Jazeera's coverage has contradicted American and British claims that the war was "bloodless, costless and clean." At the same time, the coverage "has reflected the Arab recognition that the Saddam Hussein dictatorship was a tragedy," even while it questioned the claim that Iraq was invaded to bring about democracy and liberation (Hasso 2003).

Some criticize the station for harming Qatar, others for being soft on Qatar. Al-Jazeera is just starting to touch on Qatar's allowing United States to have bases in Qatar, a subject it had avoided going into at length. Admirers of the station note that Al-Jazeera is selling a rare commodity: freedom from censorship and an opportunity for the Arab world to discuss crucial issues without government interference. Al-Jazeera reaches people because satellite TV makes traditional sovereignty in which states enjoy communication monopoly over their territories impossible. The fact that Al-Jazeera's reporters and producers are drawn from various Arab countries adds to the station's pan-Arab appeal, enriches the station's programming, and makes it earn its slogans, "The Opinion and the Other Opinion" and "All the Colors of the Rainbow."

Broadcasting in North Africa: Algeria, Egypt, Libya, Morocco, and Tunisia

Only Egypt has opened up broadcasting to private investors, and those investors have so far not threatened the status quo because they are more interested in broadcasting as a business than a political tool.

Algeria. Algeria has three national radio stations and two television channels, all state owned. The broadcasting sector has not been touched by the "liberalization" the government has boasted about. In the framework of the Organic Law, a broadcasting regulatory authority will be created and will consider opening radio and television to the private sector. But, officials said, those plans "will initially exclude news bulletins."

Egypt. President Nasser understood the oral culture of nonelite listeners and distributed radios to rural areas. He used radio most effectively for developmental purposes, but also to spread the idea of pan-Arabism and nonalignment as he cooperated with Asian and African leaders, among them Jawaharlal Nehru, prime minister of India, and Kwame Nkrumah, prime minister of the Gold Coast (later Ghana). Afro-Asian states hoped to strengthen their independence from Western imperialism while keeping the Soviet bloc at a comfortable distance. This strategic bloc was the beginning of what came to be known as the nonaligned movement and the Third World (Quest no date). During that period, Egypt expanded its radio services to many countries, especially in Africa, and transmitted in several languages. Egyptian radio, "The Voice of the Arabs," however, lost its leading role after the 1967 Arab–Israeli war, when listeners criticized its lack of credibility in war reporting and Arabs turned to the BBC to learn of their defeat at the hands of Israel. The Egyptian place in political Arab media was further eroded after President Anwar Al-Sadat signed a peace treaty with Israel in 1979 and Egypt was expelled from the Arab League until 1989. The pan-Arab leadership in political media went unfilled until 1996, when Qatar established its satellite station, Al-Jazeera, and Abu Dhabi established its satellite station.

The Egyptian Radio and Television Union (ERTU) which controls TV is state owned. Television started in Egypt in 1960. It has two national terrestrial channels and six regional channels. ERTU launched its first satellite channel in 1990 ("Country Profile: Egypt"). Egypt was the first Arab country to acquire its own satellite (Nilesat 101). It now runs Egyptian Space channels ESC1 and ESC2, plus Nile TV International, which broadcasts some programs in English and Hebrew. Egypt is the leading television producer in entertainment in the Arab world because it is able to rely on its huge library of old Egyptian films. By announcing on January 17, 2000, that it was creating a free media zone, it was serving notice that it intends to capitalize on its TV production infrastructure to preserve that preeminence (Feuilherade 2000). Egypt offers a variety of news talk shows and cultural entertainment, but its news still has the official look and concentrates too much on the comings and goings of the Egyptian leaders, although not to the same extent as the Saudi station.

In November 2001, Egypt launched the first private satellite network, Dream TV, targeting young viewers and Dream 2, a film and variety channel. Dream 3 is in the planning stages. Contracts were signed to establish private stations, including Al-Mihwar in June 2000 and Misr in March 2001, and they are both functioning.

Libya. Libya's radio and TV are controlled by the government.

Morocco. Both radio and TV in Morocco are controlled by the government. Following the dismissal of the Interior Minister, Driss Basri, in 1999, King Mohammed VI replaced the directors of the official news agency (MAP) and the main public television channel (TVM). These changes on the media scene were considered as a "slackening" of official control over public media. But broadcasting has not yet provided alternatives to government-issued fare.

Tunisia. Tunisia has four domestic terrestrial channels. Tunis 7 and Canal 2 are both national public service channels operated by ERTT, which produces about 30 percent of its programming locally. Tunis 7 also transmits by satellite to Europe and neighboring countries. Tunisia's domestic pay TV, Canal Horizons Tunisie (launched in 1992), is uncensored. The fourth channel is the Italian RAI-Uno. Tunisians can also receive by agreement Canal 2 of France, although Tunisians have in the past suspended relays (for example, during the 1999 elections). Two London-based opposition satellite TV channels can be received in Tunisia, Al-Mustaqillah, The Independent, and the Islamist Zeitouna (Olive Tree) ("Country Profile: Tunisia"). The state maintains monopoly of radio stations.

Radio and Television in Iran, Israel, and Turkey

Iranians rely on television and radio because newspapers and print media a have a limited circulation outside the main cities. Iran's radio and four-channel television are controlled by the state. Starting in 1993, and within a short period of time, satellite dishes started to proliferate in Iran. The ban on the installation of satellites, ratified on February 12, 1995 (*Official Journal*, no. 14468, 6 March 1995) slowed down but did not prevent satellite acquisition because of the difficulty of practical implementation. By 1994, about 500,000 dishes had been installed ("Cultural Satellite" 1995). Iranians, however, manufactured their own dishes in Iran and made smaller ones that avoid detection but get fewer channels (Arjomandi 1999, pp. 4–13 *passim*). The 1995 ban had largely been ignored since the 1997 election of President M. Khatami. In 2001, Iran once again enforced the law and confiscated thousands of dishes. Reuters quoted Defense Minister Ali Shamkhani as saying, "Bankrupt elements abroad are trying to use the satellite network to launch a political challenge

("Iran Cracks Down" 2001). He was referring to several expatriate TV channels, run by West-based dissident groups, who were exhorting Iranians to riot after soccer matches ("Police" 2001). There are five Iranian-American TV stations in Los Angeles, which is the home of the largest Iranian population in the world outside Iran. The decision to ban dishes engendered a great deal of discussion, with some officials arguing that it is better to adopt of policy of "cultural immunity" rather than ban the technology because of some benefits on satellite TV ("Iran Confiscated" 2001). Some worry that, with the closure of newspapers, the bans and propaganda against reform by the state broadcast monopoly controlled by hard-liners could prepare the ground for a further crackdown. State radio and television chief Ali Larijani said he will expand official satellite, radio, and television networks to provide an alternative to foreign sources ("Iran Intends" 2000).

Israel. "The Voice of Israel," established in 1948, had its origins in the Palestine Broadcasting Service established by the British in 1936. In 1951, Israel's foreign-language broadcasting was extended to cover several languages to serve its immigrant population and Jews abroad. Initially, the government was determined to keep its monopoly of broadcasting. In the mid-1960s, the government controlled the Israeli army radio and the educational TV, while state radio and television became part of the public system. Starting in 1973, however, some challenged government monopoly by resorting to offshore broadcasting. The first such station was the Voice of Peace, 1973–1993. The offshore vessels represent various Israeli constituencies, from music-only stations to religious stations whose purpose was to "return people to religion."[6]

By the 1990s, 50 pirate radio stations went into operation (Caspi and Limor 1999, pp. 125–126). Legal commercial local radio began only in 1995. The parliament legalized pirate stations that had been in operation continuously for at least five years as of January 1, 1999. The two meeting these criteria are Arutz 7 and Shas's Radio 2000, both religious. Petitions were submitted to Israel's High Court claiming that the law "rewarded criminals and discriminated against the legal operations of Israel's existing regional stations," which had to put up large financial guarantees and compete against other bidders in order to obtain licenses. Arutz 7 argues that it had to put up large sums to keep a ship offshore. In the mid-1990s, the Second Authority set up 16 regional radio stations, to be operated by private licenses. Radio 2000 was intended for the Arabs of Northern Israel, and Kol Hay for Jewish religious listeners.[7]

Israeli radio is diversifying its content and using the latest technology. Net-kaing has grabbed the musical niche by providing Israel's dominant digital radio station. Since its debut in early 2000, The Marker.com has become the favorite in business circles because it offers immediate Hebrew translation of the *Wall Street* column, the street.com. The English-language daily, *The Jerusalem Post*, launched Internet radio (JpostRadio.com) in an effort to encourage reporters to tell stories in more than one medium.

Israel started TV broadcasting in 1968 in response to a report that lauded the medium's educational potential as a way of integrating Israel's new immigrants into the culture, as well as a mechanism that would prevent Arabs who remained in

Israel in 1948 and Arabs Israel occupied in 1967 from being exposed only to the televisions of the surrounding Arab countries (Caspi and Limor 1999, p. 146). Television was controlled first by the government, and then by the Israeli Broadcasting Authority (IBA) which is controlled by a board of directors composed of political appointees. TV was initially financed from license fees but now accepts paid ads (Lehman-Wilzig and Schejter 1994, pp. 115–119). The first venture to break away from government monopoly came from the owner of Odelia TV, who started broadcasting in June 1981. By July, the government had prepared a hastily proposed anti-offshore broadcasting law. On November 29 the station was temporarily closed. On November 30 the anti-offshore law came into force. Israel refused to cooperate with offshore broadcasters except in cases of emergency.

There was a great deal of resistance to the introduction of a second TV channel in Israel. Initially, National Religious Party ministers blocked even the discussion of the issue. In 1990, Israel finally accepted the introduction of the second channel, "22 years after the inception of television in Israel, 13 years after the major parties included the demand in their party platforms, and nearly 4 years after the law was first proposed." Experimental broadcasts of the second channel, however, had started in 1986 in order to allow Israel to "seize" frequencies for the second channel before other countries of the region started using them (Caspi and Limor 1999, p. 152). The second channel turned commercial in 1993. Cable television started broadcasting in January 1991. The Cable Television Council divided the country into 31 areas. As a result, Israel is covered well by this local network (Lehman-Wilzig and Schejter 1994, pp. 115–119).

Turkey. Turkish TV had a slow start as a government enterprise, but once it took off, broadcasting flourished and was later privatized. The Turkish government started broadcasting in 1968. Full-color transmission came on July 1, 1984. The single-channel era ended in 1986 when TRT-2 joined TRT-1. In the 1980s, people who had satellite dishes watched foreign channels. In March 1990, a private Turkish TV channel, Star 1, took advantage of a gap in the telecommunications law and started broadcasting from Germany. Another, Show TV, started in Paris in 1992 ("History of Turkish TV": http://www.creatonic.com/tv/history.htm). By 1992, Kamal 6, Flash TV, HBB, ATV, and TGRT had joined the television market. Private television channels debated Alevi religious practices, homosexuality, feminism, Kurdish nationalism, and other formerly taboo subjects. M. Hakan Yavuz observes that "the new communication channels have combined with a wave of Islamic movements to promote sectarian and ethnic minority consciousness by a fusion of local and global identities" (Yavuz 1999, p. 181). This fusion is also true in the case of Turks in Amsterdam (Ogan 2001).

The Turkish audience was receptive to uncensored broadcasting. TRT attempted to compete by establishing its own satellite station in 1990, TRT-INT (TRT-International) to reach the Turkish population living in Germany. The government station expanded in other areas as well. But the floodgates of privatization were opened. The new stations, Kanal 6, HBB, TGRT, Kanal D, ATV and STV were backed by private investors. Municipalities in major cities bought dishes and transmitters and rebroadcast these channels locally. As the perception of state monopoly was weakened, several stations started to broadcast from Turkey, without linking up to a satellite. Hundreds of stations started when people with camera, video recorders, and primitive transmitters got into TV production. The government charged that these unregulated broadcasts were interfering with police and air-traffic-control communications and shut all the pirate channels down in March 1993. Drivers tied black ribbons to their car radio aerials, and many protest campaigns were organized all over the country. The government wisely realized that returning to state control was no longer an option, and ended the state monopoly on broadcasting in April 1994.

Turkish radio and television experienced explosive growth in the years since privately owned broadcasting was allowed in April 1994. Radio stations range from AÇIK Radyo (94.9 FM), identified on the Internet as a "private and independent radio station with news, music, and personality," to Power Radio Bilkent (106.6 FM), which offers "world news, entertainment and joy." There are several sites that offer ham radio as well as on-line radio. Other radio and television stations broadcast without an official license (Yavuz 1999, p. 181).

In 1994, the Turkish parliament passed regulatory legislation making it illegal for broadcasters to threaten the country's unity or national security and limiting the private broadcast of television programs in languages other than Turkish. In response, Pro-PKK Med-TV, based in Belgium and the United Kingdom, started broadcasting via satellite dish in 1995, and can be received in the southeast. Thus, satellite broadcasts bypass the Turkish government's laws and restrictions. MED-TV has made the Kurds the first "satellite" nation. The Medya TV web site identifies it as a station that serves a Kurdish audience in 77 countries and offers Kurdish-language broadcasts to a potential audience of 35 million.

In 1999, 230 local, 15 regional, and 16 national television stations—the majority private—were registered, along with 1,055 local, 108 regional, and 36 national radio stations (Yavuz 1999, pp. 193, 195, 181). Turkey has some 300 private TV stations that compete with the state broadcaster, TRT. Although Kurdish broadcasts were banned for years, a parliamentary vote in 2002 paved the way for their legalization.

Not all satellite transmissions picked up in MENA are political. Sexual fare, or "silicon-enhanced erotica," as one Lebanese TV critic put it, is readily available especially after midnight (Al-Hajiri 2000). Sexually explicit programs have led religious leaders to call on Arab governments to block such broadcasts "that have been successful in promoting new social values that were not, until recently, either common or accepted in society," especially the depiction of violence and consumerism and using women's unclad bodies to sell products. So the battle over who should be the moral arbiter of values continues.

Regional and National News Agencies

Nothing has changed the content and tone of news on the area more than the change in the way news is gathered, and the sources from which it is received. The complete reliance on foreign news agencies for news of the region has given way to news from several sources, including from pan-Arab satellite TV.

Concepts of Media Freedom and Government–Media Relations

Even though the General Union of Arab Journalists, established in 1964, had a committee on freedoms that met for the first time in 1976 (Falhut 1982, p. 285), it was ineffective. After years of acquiescence to press laws that impose prison sentences on journalists for speaking their minds, the General Union of Arab Writers chose the slogan "No to imprisoning journalists!" for its 1999 conference.

The penal code, the emergency laws, and a variety of publication laws and regulations are all part of the legacy of a long history of state hegemony. Many are still in force, with devastating implications for press freedom. What has changed, however, is that the members of the media are collectively dealing with this problem by forming alliances with the legal profession. The Arab Journalists' Union and the Arab Lawyers' Union cooperated on the draft of a press law for the Arab world, to ensure that it avoids the pitfalls of existing laws. The draft of that law, presented to Arab leaders at the Amman summit in March 2001, proposed abolishing prison terms for press "offenses" and called for freedom of publishing, printing, and distributing for individuals and corporations and the abolition of the require-ment of administrative licenses; the abolition of the practice of the suspension of publications by any authority other than the judiciary and the termination of any role played by political and administrative agencies in this regard; and recognition of the right of journalists to access information as well as the imposition of sanctions against individuals illegally obstructing this right or withholding information.

The media in most Arab countries gave censorship unprecedented press coverage. Satellite stations now broadcast weekly programs about freedom of the press. Abu Dhabi TV has *The Censor's Scissors,* and MBC TV has *The Fourth Estate,* in which the latest issues in press freedom are discussed. This new activism bodes well for freedom of speech in the coming years.

A number of freedom-of-speech issues have galvanized the media in different Arab countries. The most famous were the trial in Lebanon (and later acquittal) of the singer Marcel Khalifeh on charges of "disrespecting religious rites"; the banning in Egypt of a Syrian political novel reprinted by the Egyptian Ministry of Culture, *A Feast for Sea Weeds,* in response to demonstrating Islamists; and the trial (and acquittal) of two Kuwaiti female novelists for writing what the censor considered sexually explicit novels.

The Israeli press continues to be more independent of the government than it used to be because of the decrease in the role of political parties, professionalization of the press and the competition that resulted from commercialization.

The Turkish media, which enjoy freedom in theory, have now more legal leeway to publish on controversial issues. The push toward joining the European Union means the government will be more careful about suppressing Kurdish, leftist, or Islamist speech. And while Iranian journalists still struggle with media law and practice, they have a long way to go to make a dent in the restrictions now in force.

Journalism Education

Journalism education is thriving in countries that enjoy a certain margin of freedom, countries in which the local press is willing to accept journalism students as interns, and areas in which private academic institutions or NGOs have been allowed to function. The American University of Cairo's Al-Adham Center is among the best in the Arab world. Its strong hands-on media program enables it to export media talent to different Arab countries. Its concern for freedom of speech issues also has enriched its program and produced reporters and administrators who are now working for Arab media in several countries.

The American Lebanese University, Beirut, is a leader in new technology. The course offerings include 3-D, cartoon production, video production and digital editing, and web authoring, along with the traditional journalism and communication courses. The Jesuit College program in Lebanon cooperates with the Sorbonne University and visiting French journalists to enhance journalism education. Students who do well are assured internships in Lebanon or abroad. The department runs its own audiovisual studios on campus.

The West Bank's Birzeit University's expanded journalism curriculum leading to a bachelor's degree in journalism has thrived after it received funding and expertise from several countries and from progressive NGOs that wanted to decrease top-down communication. The university is the only one in the region to have a student-operated radio station that broadcasts to the local community, and to allow grassroots organizations public access to broadcasting. This outreach was made possible by funding from the German Green Party's H. Boell Foundation in 1996.

In addition to offering traditional journalism courses in their universities, several Gulf countries are involved in staff training. The Kuwaiti News Agency's (KUNA's) Center for Training and Development of Media Skills, for example, runs a series of five-day seminars on topics that range from covering economic news, to election news, to oil and energy. The courses are meant for professionals already working in the press (KUNA 2000).

A 500-page Iranian report notes that people's enthusiasm for the press is not in proportion to the literate population (72 percent of the population over the age of 6) and that radio and TV are the media of choice. Even though 68 percent of Iranian journalists have a university education, only 4.6 percent have received academic education in communication, and about 93 percent of graduates in media communications have not been recruited by the press in the past 20 years. Authors of the report find that the curriculum of journalism courses, in most cases translation of Western academic texts, is not suitable for Iran and is incompatible with press practices and job requirements in Iran (Mohsenian-Rad and Enterzari 1994, p. 75).

The Koteret School of Journalism and Communications in Tel Aviv offers journalists training in print and electronic media in a two- to three-year program.

Departments for communication at four institutes of higher education also hold practical workshops in journalism.

Prospects for the Future

Most rulers of the region have a different set of problems from the ones they had with the old media they easily controlled: how to keep their grip on power while some of the control of communication is out of their hands and beyond their borders (Reporters Without Borders ["Enemies of the Internet"] 2000). Some governments have adapted by liberalizing the media (e.g., Qatar). Other governments are facing the prospect of having their state-run media become irrelevant because of competition from pan-Arab and regional satellites (Sakr 2002).

Some countries are establishing their own news channels to directly compete with Al-Jazeera (e.g., Al-Arabiya, a joint Saudi-Lebanese-Kuwaiti venture); others are enhancing their credibility by merging with respected newspapers (e.g., Lebanese Broadcasting Corporation's merger with *Al-Hayat* Arabic daily newspaper of London). LBC was tops in entertainment, but weak in news (Schleifer 2002). Some satellite stations have gone into niche programming for groups not previously served in the Arab world—for example, the hip Zen TV for teenagers and young adults; Khalifa TV, a French-Arab venture designed to cement ties to Europe and to the large immigrant Arab population there; Al-Majd 2 TV, devoted to the presentation of Islamic perspective in English; and Al-Mehwar TV, designed to give a voice to the maligned private sector and civil society in Egypt (*TBS* Editors 2002). And yet others are offering a dizzying array of choices in English and in translation (e.g., Orbit). In the meantime, media professionals everywhere appear determined to remove impediments to free communication and have formed associations that promise to achieve that purpose. September 11 and the occupation of Iraq, however, have given some Arab governments the excuse to clamp down on anti-U.S. free speech in the name of security.

What is certain is that there are more media, more choice, and more outreach from and to the Middle East and North Africa than ever before. There is more radio and TV "chatter" about politics and sex.

In the 1970s, the nonaligned countries criticized the global economic imbalance between the North and the South, the Western monopoly of global news services, and the quality, quantity, and fairness of the news that developed countries produced about the developing countries. The debate resulted in a call for a plurality of sources, and a "New World Information and Communication Order" (Fore 1982, p. 442).

Within this context, the most important thing Arab satellites have done is to provide that alternative to the old flow of information by reversing the flow that used to travel mostly from West to East and from North to South. The Arab world now generates its own news and exports it to other countries. Al-Jazeera has been making deals in Latin America, Africa, and Asia. In translation, Sheikh [Dr.] Qardawi's tapes and videos sell as far away as Indonesia and Malaysia. Qardawi declared September 11 a crime, but said the invasion of Iraq could not be justified (Shahid 2003). Al-Jazeera has seen its European subscriber numbers double from four to eight million since the start of the war in Iraq amid huge demand for an alternative to Western media coverage (Cozens 2003). *Slate* opined, "If you doubt that Al Jazeera is the clear winner of the Iraq war so far (other than U.S. forces), check out the most recent Lycos 50, a tally of the most-searched-for words and phrases on the Lycos search engine" (Suellentrop 2003). Al-Jazeera has reached a deal to transmit its news reports on cable in the U.S. ("Al-Jazeera Broadcasts" 2003).

Michael Wolff concluded that Al-Jazeera is going to be "big to an extent and at a scale that is just dawning on the Al Jazeera folk themselves. The network is being transformed the way Gulf I transformed CNN." Wolff told three Al-Jazeera correspondents that, by the time whole thing is over, "you'll be far and away the dominant media organization in the region—one of the largest in the world! . . . you could end up being Time Warner Al Jazeera." "Al Jazeera Time Warner," said [Al-Jazeera correspondent] Omar, according to Wolff (Wolff 2003). A number of alternative web sites on the media and Iraq have sprung up since the first Gulf war (Electronic Iraq: The Media, http://electroniciraq.net/news/themedia.shtml).

Several nations have responded by attempting to regain their dominance in the field, or to enter it for the first time to broadcast to the Arab world. Israelis are planning to establish an Arabic satellite TV channel to counter the many voices of the Arab media. Britain and France (separately) also are considering establishing Arabic news TV networks as part of the race to win over Arab and Islamic public opinion. The United States has started Radio Sawa, which presents a mix of music and news for young people.

Europemedia.net reported that the Bush administration was so maddened by broadcasts and webcasts delivered by Al-Jazeera that it has put aside a $30.5 million initial cash endowment to finance an alternative, the Middle East Television Network (*Inquirer* Staff 2003).

The most important change that would please those who called for "A New World Information Order" is that the Arab world no longer depends on the West for news about itself. It is the West that is now complaining about other countries' news coverage and attempting to censor or counter Arab reporting on its actions. Furthermore, the number of listeners depending on foreign sources has decreased at an astonishing rate. Radio Monte Carlo in Arabic used to be the number one station for Palestinians in the 1980s. Because of the proliferation of private Palestinian radio stations, Radio Monte Carlo and the BBC stations are now among the least listened to from among a choice of 29 radio stations (Palestinian Central Bureau of Statistics, 2000). The monopoly of news agencies on news of the region has been broken. Different nations are trying to reach each other in different ways and in different languages. The author of this chapter envisions a time when news produced by private independent stations in Africa, Asia, and Latin America will also be exchanged directly with those who collect and produce news of the Middle East and North Africa, without government intermediaries or Western news agencies. That could be dubbed the "New and Ideal Information Order," or the NIIO for short.

Notes

1. For a glimpse of a Jordanian cartoonist's comment on freedom of the press in Jordan, see http://www.mahjoob.com/archive/02/1/23/jan23.jpg. In the cartoon, a newspaper headline reads "Cloudy climate, lack of vision, need for caution, use reflectors, do not shine strong lights." "Weather bulletin?" one reader asks another. "No, it is the new information policy."

2. I would like to thank the Fulbright program for funding my research on Jordan, the West Bank, Syria, and Lebanon.

3. For a history of broadcasting in the Arab world, see Boyd (1999).

4. Information is culled from interviews with TV station owners in the summer of 2000: Issa abu al-Izz, April 30; Omar Nazzal, May 30; Tareq Jabbar and Rimah Kilani, June 8; Hamdi Farraj, June 12.

5. Palestinian Central Bureau of Statistics, "Media Survey 2000," conducted in the period of June 17–July 15, 2000, on a sample of 8,276 households. Available: http://www.pcb.org/press/media_su.htm.

6. Information about offshore broadcasting is available from "The Off-Shore Radio Guide," http://israeliculture.about.com/culture/israel/cs/radio/index.htm.

7. See Douglas Boyd, "Hebrew-Language Broadcasting During the British Palestine Mandates." Available: http://www.israelradio.org/history/pal-clan.html.

Bibliography

Abdul Rahman, Naseema. "The Experience of the Algerian Press . . . Between Freedom and Bullets." *Al-Mashrek al-Ilami,* June 2000, 22.

After the Opening of the 'Internet City' in the Emirates: The Launch of the Dubai Oasis for Electronic [Start-up] Projects." *As-Safir,* 30 October 2000, 20.

Ahmed, Assya. "Al-Jazeera Under Fire Once Again: This Time the GCC Threatens Sanctions." *TBS Journal,* 9, Fall/Winter 2002.

Al-Hajiri, Mohammed. "Televised Sex: Crude Pictures Crush the Imagination." *As-Safir,* 27 January 2000, 17.

Al-Jazeera. The Correspondents, 10 May 2003.

"Al-Jazeera Broadcasts to U.S." BBC, 9 April 2003.

Al-Rawashdah, Hussein. "What Do We Do? What Do They Do?" *Addustour,* 19 May 1997.

Al-Zein, Jihad. Interview, Beirut, Lebanon, 16 October 2000.

Al-Zein, Hassan. "Irawi Satellite Covers the Palestinian Uprising: Nationalist Atmosphere Instead of Breaking News." *As-Safir,* 6 October 2000, 15.

Amin, Ibrahim. Interview, Beirut, Lebanon, 16 October 2000.

Amnesty International. *Amnesty International Year 2000 Report. Kuwait.* _____: Amnesty International, 2000. Available: http://www.amnesty.org/web/ar2002.nsf/mde/kuwait.open.

Arab Press Freedom Watch. "Muslin Fundamentalists Escalate Their Campaign Against Freedom of Thought and Creativity," 2001. Available: http://www.apfwatch.org/en/annual_report/2001/4.

Arjomandi, Gholamreza. *The Impacts of Direct Broadcasting Satellite (DBS) on the Iranian Media Sphere.* Paper presented at the Article 19 International Seminar, Satellite Broadcasting in the Middle East and North Africa: Regulations, Access and Impact, Cairo, 20–21 February 1999.

Ayish, Mohammad. *New Trends in Arab Television Broadcasting.* Paper presented at the Arab Television Seminar, American University of Beirut, Lebanon, 12 March 1998.

"Bahraini Opposition Accuses the King of Reneging on His Promises on Democracy." Al-Jazeera Transcripts, 25 February 2002.

"Bahrain Replaces the Intelligence Services with a National Security Outfit." Al-Jazeera Transcripts, 9 May 2002.

Boyd, Douglas. *Broadcasting in the Arab World.* 3rd Edition. Ames: Iowa State University Press, 1999.

Carlson, Peter. "In the Line of Fire." *Washington Post,* 3 April 2003.

Caspi, Dan, and Yehiel Limor. *The In/Outsiders: Mass Media in Israel.* Cresskill, N.J.: Hampton Press, 1999.

Committee to Protect Journalists. "CPJ Condemns Israel's Destruction of Palestinian Radio and Television Building," 19 January 2002. Available: http://www.cpj.org.

"Country Profile: Egypt." BBC News. Available: http://news.bbc.co.uk/1/hi/world/middle_east/country_profiles/737642.stm.

"Country Profile: Israel and the Autonomous Palestinian Areas." BBC News, 2002. Available: http://news.bbc.co.uk/1/hi/world/middle_east/country_profiles/803257.stm.

"Country Profile, Lebanon." BBC News, 2002. Available: http://news.bbc.co.uk/2/hi/middle_east/country_profiles/791071.stm.

"Country Profile, Saudi Arabia." BBC News, 2002. Available: http://news.bbc.co.uk/1/hi/world/middle_east/country_profiles/791936.stm.

"Country Profile: Tunisia." BBC News. Available:

"Country Profile, Turkey." BBC News, 2002. Available: http://news.bbc.co.uk/1/hi/world/europe/country_profiles/1022222.stm.

Cozens, Claire. "Europeans Flock to Al-Jazeera." *The Guardian,* 25 March 2003.

"Cultural-Satellite: The Fate of Satellite in Iran, Yes or No?" *Gozaresh-e Film* 26 (March 1995): 36–38.

Dajani, Nabil. "Lebanese Television: Caught Between the Private and Public Sectors." In *Journalism as a Mission,* edited by J. Atkens. Ames: Iowa State University Press, 2001.

Dajani, Nabil. "The Media in Lebanon, the Status of." "The Media in Syria, the Status of." In *Encyclopedia of International Media and Communications,* edited by Donald Johnston. San Diego, Calif: Academic Press, 2003.

Daragahi, Borzou. "Rebuilding Iraq's Media." *Columbia Journalism Review,* July/August 2003.

Darwish, Kassi. "Why Are They Afraid of It?" *Al-Hadath* 9, September–October 2000.

"Dubai Internet City (TECOM)." Newsflash, 21 April 2002. Available: http://www.newsflash.org.

Egyptian Organization for Human Rights. "Emergency Laws Oppress the Country" (press release), 0 March 2003. Available: http://www.eohr.org/PRESS/2003/3=0.HTM.

Eikelman, Dale. "Communication and Control in the Middle East." In *New Media in a Muslim World: The Emerging Public Sector,* edited by Dale Eickelman and Jon Anderson. Bloomington, Ind.: University Press, 1999.

Ellis, Kail. "The Struggle of a Small Country in a Regional Content." *Arab Studies Quarterly* 21, no. 1 (Winter 1999): 5–25.

El-Sharif, Nabil. Interview, 18 May 2002, cited in Orayb Najjar, "Jordan: Status of Media in." In *Encyclopedia of International Media and Communications,* vol. 4. San Diego, Calif.: Academic Press, 2003, pp. 310–315.

Farraj, Hamdi. Interview, 12 June 2000.

Feuilherade, Peter. "Censor-Free Zones?" *Middle East International,* 28 January 2000, 13.

Fore, William. "A New World Order of Communication." *Christian Century,* 14 April 1982. Available: http://www.religion-online.org/cgi-bin/relsearchd.dll/showarticle?item_id-1305.

Frenkel, Erwin. *The Press and Politics in Israel: The Jerusalem Post from 1932 to the Present.* Westport, Conn.: Greenwood Press, 1994.

Gavron, Daniel. "Unique or Absurd." *Jerusalem Post,* 6 March 1987, 10.

Goldschmidt, Arthur, Jr. *A Concise History of the Middle East.* Boulder, Colo: Westview Press, 1988.

Halabi, Rafik. *The West Bank Story.* New York: Harcourt, 1981.

Hasso, Francis. "Who Covered the War Best? Try Al-Jazeera." New York *Newsday,* 17 April 2003.

"History of Broadcasting" (radio seminar). Ramallah, Poetry House, 14 May 2000.

Human Rights Watch. "As Fragile as a Crystal Glass: Press Freedom in Iran." Human Rights Watch Report, 1999. Available: http://www.hrw.org/hrw/reports/1999/iran/Iran990.htm.

———. "The Press Under President Khatami," 1999. Available: http//www.hrw/org/hrw/reports/1999/iran990-02.htm.

Inquirer Staff [U.K.]. "Bush Admin to Fund Al-Jazeera Rival," 20 April 2003.

International Press Institute (IPI). "Algeria: World Press Freedom Review," 2002. Available: http://www.freemedia/at/wpfr/Mena/algeria.htm.

———. "Israel: 1997 World Press Freedom Review." Available: http://www.freemedia/at/wpfr/israel.html.

———. "Libya: 2001 World Press Freedom Review." Available: http://www.freemedia.at/wpfr/libya.htm.

———. "Saudi Arabia: 1999 World Press Freedom Report." Available: http://www.freemedia.at/wpfr/saudiara.htm.

———. "Tunisia: 2001 World Press Freedom Review." Available: http://www/freemedia.at/wpfr/libya.htm.

"Iran Closes Down Newspaper." BBC News, 7 July 1999.

"Iran Confiscated Satellite Dishes: Create Cultural Immunity." *Tehran Times,* 3 November 2001.

"Iran Cracks Down Further on Satellite Dishes, Newspapers," 30 October 2001. Available: http://www/freedomforum.org.

"Iran Intends to Put Two Small Telecom Satellites into Orbit Within Next Few Months." Reuters, 5 June 2000.

"Iran Women Get More Divorce Rights." BBC News, 2 December 2002.

Ismael, Jacqueline, and Tareq Ismael. "Globalization and the Arab World in Middle East Politics: Regional Dynamics in Historical Perspective." *Arab Studies Quarterly* 21, no. 3 (Summer 1999).

"Kuwaiti Minister of Information Resigns." *Al-Sharq,* 19 October 2000, 1.

Lancaster, Pat. "Syria Looks Forward." *The Middle East,* July/August 2000, 5.

"Lebanon to Slash Private Broadcasters." Reuters, 7 February 1996.

Lehman-Wilzig, Sam, and Amit Schejter. "Israel." In *Mass Media in the Middle East: A Comprehensive Handbook,* edited by Yahya Kamalipour and Hamid Mowlana, 109–125. Westport, Conn.: Greenwood Press, 1994.

Limor, Yehiel. "The Printed Media: Israel's Newspapers," 1999. Available: http://www.israel-mfa.gov.il/mfa/go.asp?MFAH00n80.

Masri, Maher. Interview, Ramallah, West Bank, Palestine, 20 March 2000.

Mazrui, Ali A. "Globalization and Cross-Cultural Values: The Politics of Identity and Judgment." *Arab Studies Quarterly* 21, no. 3 (Summer 1999): 97–109.

Mohsenian-Rad, Mehdi, and Ali Enterzari. "Problems of Journalism Education in Iran." *Rasaneh* (A Research Quarterly of Mass Media Studies) 5, no. 2 (Summer 1994): 75.

Moubayid, Sami. "Syria Takes Long Hard Look at 'Primitive' Advertising Market." *Daily Star,* 2 October 2000, 7.

Muhsen, Mohammad. *The Information War: Examples of Resistance Media in Lebanon.* Beirut: Dar al Nada, 1998.

"From Enemies to 'Colleagues': Relations Between Palestinian Journalists and Israeli West Bank Beat Reporters." *Gazette* 55 (1995): 113–130.

Najjar, Orayb. "The 1995 Palestinian Press Law: A Comparative Study." *Communication Law and Policy* 2 (1997): 41–103.

———. "The Ebb and Flow of Press Freedom in Jordan, 1985–1997," *Journalism and Mass Communication Quarterly* 75, no. 1 (Spring 1998): 127–142.

———. "Freedom of the Press in Jordan 1927–1998." In *Mass Media and Society in the Middle East: Impact for Political and Social Development,* edited by Kai Hafez. Cresskill, N.J.: Hampton Press, 2000.

———. "The West Bank and Gaza, Status of the Media in." In *Encyclopedia of International Media and Communications,* edited by Donald Johnston. San Diego, Calif: Academic Press, 2003.

Ni'mat, Salamah. "Jordan: Steps Toward Privatization of Government Information." *Al-Hayat,* 25 June 2000, 6.

Nun, Muhammed. "Iran: Crisis Between Reformists and Conservatives." *Al-Hayat,* 6 November 2000, 2.

Ogan, Christine. "Introduction." *Communication and Identity in the Diaspora: Turkish Migrants in Amsterdam and their Use of Media.* Lanham, Md.: Lexington Books, 2001.

Oppel Jr., Richard. "Iraqis Get the News but Often Don't Believe It." *New York Times,* 5 August 2003.

Palestinian Central Bureau of Statistics. http://www.pcb.org/press/media00/tab_23.htm.

Parsons, Claudia. "Turkish MPs Vote for Kurdish TV in EU" (on-line). 3 August 2002. Available: http://english.planetarania.com/content/article/cfm/103052/913640.

"Police Will Not Enter Houses to Seize Satellite Dishes." *Payrant's Iran News,* 15 November 2001.

Pripstein-Posusney, Marsha. "Egyptian Privatization: New Challenges for the Left." *Middle East Report* (Spring 1999): 38.

"Problems of Politics and Information in Lebanon." *Al-Jazeera,* 15 January 2003.

"The Prosecutor Conducts Wide-Ranging Investigation with the Editor-in-Chief." *Akhbar AlKhalee,* 27 May 2003.

Quest, Matthew. "The Lessons of the Bandung Conference: Reviewing Richard Wright's *The Color Curtain* 40 Years Later." Available: http://www.spunk.org/library/pubs/lr/sp001716/bandung.html.

Rampal, Kuldip. "Saudi Arabia" In *Mass Media in the Middle East: A Comprehensive Handbook,* edited by Yahya Kamalipour and Hamid Mowlana, 244–260. Westport Conn.: Greenwood Press, 1994.

Reporters Without Borders (Reporters sans Frontières). "Enemies of the Internet," 2000.

———. "The French Weekly *L'Express* Banned," letters of protest, 5 July 2000. Available: http://www.rsf.fr/uk/cplp/lp/050700.html.

———. "Algeria's Annual Reports," 2001, 2002. Available: http://www.rsf.org/article.php3?id_article=1431.

———. "Egypt Annual Reports," 2001, 2002. Available: http://www/rsf.org.

———. "Conservatives Renew Attacks With the Suspension of Two Reformist Papers," 16 September 2002.

———. "Cyber-dissident Arrested and His Online Newspaper Censored," 5 June 2002.

———. "The Only Satirical Paper Suspends Its Publication," 22 January 2002. Available: http://www.rsf.org/article.php3?id_article=202.

———. "Turkey: Annual Report," 2002. Available: http://www.rsf.org/article.php3?id_article=2002.

———. "The Iraqi Media Three Months After the War: A New but Fragile Freedom," 23 July 2003.

Risen, James. "C.I.A. Tried, With Little Success, to Use U.S. Press in Coup" (in-line), 16 April 2000. Available: http://www.nytimes.com/library/world/mideast/041600iran-cia-media.html.

Rugh, W. A. *The Arab Press,* 2nd Edition. Syracuse, N.Y.: Syracuse University Press, 1987.

Russell, Rosalind. "First Newspaper to Hit Baghdad's Streets Is Red." Reuters, 21 April 2003.

Sachs, Susan. "Arab Leaders' Choice: Unleashed Anger Can Bite Its Master." *New York Times,* 22 October 2000.

Sakr, Naomi. *Satellite Realms.* London: I.B.S. Taurus and Co., 2002.

"Satellite TV Reaches Iraq." Agence France-Press, 11 October 1999.

Schleifer, Abdullah. "Super News Center Setting Up in London for *Al-Hayat* and LBC: An Interview with Jihad Khazen and Salah Nemett, *TBS* 9 (Fall/Winter), 2002.

Shahid, Anthony. "Maverick Cleric Is a Hit on Arab TV." *Washington Post Foreign Service,* 14 February 2003, p. A01.

Silverman, Jon. "Is the U.K. Facing Up to Bahrain's Past?" BBC News, 16 April 2003.

Suellentrop, Chris. "Al-Jazeera: It's Just as Fair as CNN." *Slate,* 2 April 2003.

Syria Live Net, 30 April 2002.

TBS Editors. "New Guys on the Block." *TBS,* 9 (Fall/Winter 2002).

"This Won't Be Limited to Abu Dhabi TV." *TBS Journal,* 8 (Spring-Summer 2002).

"Timeline: Bahrain." BBC News. Available: http://news.bbc.co.uk/2/hi/middle_east/81705.stm.

Tryhorn, Chris. "We Have the Upper Hand in Iraq, Claims Al-Jazerra." *The Guardian,* 27 March 2003.

"Two More in Iran Are Detailed in Crackdown on the Press." *New York Times,* 15 August 2000. Available: file:\\A:/iran-writers-nyt.html.

"U.S. Ambassador to Cairo Takes on Conspiracy Theories in the Egyptian Press." MI-MRI Special Dispatch, no. 423, 1 October 2002.

Wheeler, Brian. "Al-Jazeera's Cash Crises." BBC, 7 April 2003.

Whitaker, Brian. "Al-Jazeera Causes Outcry with Broadcast of Battle Casualties." *The Guardian*, 24 March 2003.

Wolff, Michael. "Al-Jazeera's Edge." *New York Magazine*, 21 April 2003.

Yaghi, Zainab. "'The Event' on Abu Dhabi Station: Another Example of the Development of the Gulf Stations." *As-Safir*, 6 October 2000, 15.

Yavuz, M. Hakan. "Media Identities for Alevis and Kurds in Turkey." In Eickelman and Anderson 1999, 180–199.

Zahlan, Rosemarie. *The Making of the Modern Gulf States*. London, U.K.: Ithaca Press, 1998.

Arabic Sources

Abdul Karim, Ahmad. *The Iranian Press*. Baghdad: Ministry of Information, 1972.

Abdul Rahman, Awatef. *Studies in the Contemporary Egyptian and Arab Press: Current Issues*. Cairo: Dar al-Isha'a, 1989.

Abu Saud, Ibrahim. "Egypt in the Age of the Internet." *Media Studies* 100 (July–September 2000): 116–125.

Abu Zaid, Farouk. *The Immigrant Arab Press*. Cairo: Madbouli, 1985.

Al-Alawi, Hasan. "The Theory of National Investment in the Press and Abdul Nasser's Theory in Defensive Communication." *Al-Siyassa* (Kuwait), 3 March 1981. Reprinted in Bashir Al-Awf, ed., *The Press: Its History, Development, Art and Responsibility*. Beirut: Islamic Office, 1987, pp. 169–174.

Al-Ghareeb, Michael. *The Press: History and Present*. Beirut, Lebanon: Al-Kifah, 1978.

Al-Shalabi, Jamal. *Mohammad Hassanein Heikal: Continuity or Change?* Translated from the French by Hayah Attiyyah. Beirut: Arab Institute for Printing and Publishing, 1999.

Al-Shamikh, Mohammad. *The Press in Hijaz, 1908–1941*. Beirut: Dar al-Amanah, 1971.

Arab Human Rights Organization. "Freedom of Expression and the Condition of Human Rights in the Arab World, 1999." *Media Studies* 100, July–September 2000: 12–54.

Diliou, Fadeel. "The Print Press in Algeria: Between Authenticity and Alienation." *Arab Future* 255 (May 2000): 47–61.

Ismail, Ibrahim. "The Investigative Report and Freedom." *Media Studies* 100, July–September 2000: 55–69.

Izzat, Mohammad. *News Agencies in the Arab World*. Jeddah: Knowledge Library/Dar al Shurouk, 1983.

Jarrus, Suad. "The Party Press in Syria." *Media Studies* 100, July–September 2000: 173–175.

16

Sub-Saharan Africa (East, West, and South)

Minabere Ibelema, Mitchell Land, Lyombe Eko, and Elanie Steyn

The collapse of Soviet-bloc communism and the resulting end of the cold war early in the 1990s became a catalyst for democratization in Africa and much of the developing world. Similarly, the end of apartheid in South Africa had an equally dramatic impact on world events. The effect of these events and the related spurt in economic liberalization and globalization underlie this examination of the sub-Saharan African media.

Political Context

Africa's democratization has continued into the new millennium, but with considerable tension and setbacks. As with the situation in Eastern Europe and the former Soviet republics, most democratizing African countries are struggling to harmonize contending interests, typically along ethnic or religious lines. In countries such as Nigeria, political faults that had remained relatively in check under dictatorships shifted markedly with the introduction of electoral government, resulting in more frequent violent clashes (Dadge 2000).

In general, however, South Africa stands out as an example of a country that went through a peaceful transition from an apartheid government to a full democracy after its 1994 general elections. These changes also resulted in more openness and democracy in the country's media system.

Similar tensions also arose in some countries with a tradition of electoral rule, following the departure of heads of state who had had long tenures. After their death, ouster, or voluntary stepdown, leaders who could not muster the same loyalty or acquiescence replaced them. In Côte d'Ivoire, for instance, the death in 1993 of Félix Houphouet-Boigney after about 33 years as president gave rise to internecine military coups and instability. Meanwhile, other countries, such as Angola, Congo (Kinshasha), Liberia, and Sierra Leone, are struggling to emerge from years of civil war and into true democracies.

Despite the difficulties, the modern democratic ethos is becoming entrenched in Africa. As will become evident in the discussion of the press that follows, such values are transforming the press landscape in sub-Saharan Africa (Figure 16.1).

Many observers believe that a new wave of democracy hit Africa during the late 1990s. By 2002, and with ever increasing regularity, multiparty election systems had materialized in 29 of the 42 sub-Saharan African countries. Pressures from within the continent as well as from the outside world have increasingly forced dictators and warlords to put down arms and declare concord in war-torn African regions. Another reason for optimism was the initiatives taken by Africa itself, namely the formation of the African Union in July 2002 and the formation of the New Partnership for Africa's Development (NEPAD) at the Lusaka summit in 2001. On the South African front, the government has committed itself to creating an agency to promote access to the media by marginalized groups and to enhance media pluralism. This has led to the formation of an independent Media Development and Diversity Agency to help alter the communications environment in a way that builds infrastructure and fosters the emergence of media reflecting the experiences and perspectives of the marginalized (Media Development and Diversity Agency 2000).

Economy, Literacy, and Communications Infrastructure

Sub-Saharan Africa remains far behind most regions of the world in economic development. For instance, the region's 1997 per-capita gross national product (GNP) of $522 exceeded only that of South Asia, at $452 (United Nations Development Program [UNDP] 1999, p. 183). However, sub-Saharan Africa's 1997 per-capita GNP showed a 6.5 percent increase over that of 1990 (UNDP 1993, p. 139). Moreover, "Africa grew faster than any other developing region in 2001, reflecting better macroeconomic management, strong agricultural production, and the cessation of conflicts in several countries" (Economic Commission for Africa 2002). South Africa remains the economic powerhouse of Africa. For instance, the South African magazine printing and publishing sector is highly advanced and competes on par with countries such as Britain, Germany, and the United States. Its broadcasting structure is also better resourced than anywhere else on the continent, and it has been a leader in the field of information technology, becoming the first country in Africa to have Internet connectivity, which has resulted in a mushrooming of Internet service providers. Much of the Internet activity in the southern African region is routed via South Africa (Media Institute of South Africa [MISA] 2002).

Despite economic pressures on sub-Saharan Africa's educational institutions, an increasing proportion of the people are receiving formal education up to secon-

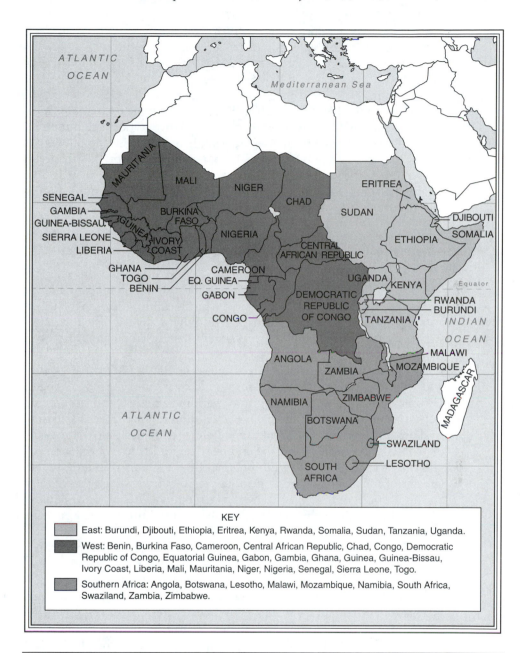

FIGURE 16.1   *Sub-Saharan Africa.* Countries grouped according to East, West, and Southern Africa.

dary school level and beyond. Sub-Saharan Africa's adult literacy rate of 58.5 percent in 1997, for instance, was 24.5 percent higher than in 1990 (UNDP 1993, p. 147; 1999, p. 137). This, of course, is an important factor in the growth of the print press.

In terms of communication infrastructure, the growth of on-line and cell phone technology is of the greatest significance. Not since the advent of radio broadcasting has any technology shown the promise of bridging Africa's gap as much as on-line communication and cell phones do. Telephone line density has been very low in sub-Saharan Africa, and its growth over the past decades has been offset by the growth in population. Although on-line and cell phone use remains meager relative to population (with the exception of South Africa, where cell phone development in particular has taken off to a very high degree and companies are presently expanding into African countries such as Cameroon), growth is relatively rapid and does not face the same logistical and economic hurdles that retarded the growth of telephone services. This augurs well for the overall communication situation in sub-Saharan Africa, especially the practice of journalism.

Press History: The Colonial Period (1800–1960)

Journalism in sub-Saharan Africa is rooted both in colonialism and in traditional African communications. Elements of African communication include the communitarian approach of collective dispute resolution, deference to religious and secular authority, cryptic and subtle expression of dissent, and extensive use of the *double entendre*.

Before the advent of modern mass media, mass communication in Africa took place in various traditional forms and by various means, among them talking drums, totem poles, artistic grave markings, sacred and secular art, itinerant bards, cultural societies, and palaver trees under which open discussions were held and disputes settled. The Adinkra symbolic and ideographic writings of the Ashanti of Ghana and Côte d'Ivoire, the cryptic royal ideograms of the kings of Danhomé, the distinct Ge'ez script of Ethiopia, and the systems of hieroglyphics and ideographs of the Nuba and other peoples of sub-Saharan Africa were the repositories of the wisdom of the region. These rough equivalents of today's journalism were changed dramatically by the arrival of Islam and European colonialism, especially the latter.

Three very distinct press traditions emerged in Africa from the colonial era: the Anglo-American, the French, and the Portuguese. The early press in colonial Africa was generally organized to serve the needs and interests of the colonial administrations and European settlers. In the British colonies, with the exception of newspapers that had been started by freed American slaves, colonial administrations limited the holdings and shares of British colonial publications to British investors. These British colonial newspapers carried out their business more or less within the free press tradition that existed in England.

In the French and Portuguese colonies, most publications were owned either by the colonial administration or the Catholic Church, or by private interests beholden to one or the other. The imprint of these models on contemporary African journalism is very evident.

Anglo-American Tradition

The first European press tradition to be grafted onto traditional African communication systems was the Anglo-American tradition, brought to Africa by African-American slaves who had been freed and allowed to return to Africa. The first African newspaper was started in 1801 in Freetown, Sierra Leone, by freed slaves, who brought with them some of the press traditions of the young American republic.

The early African newspapers vigorously denounced slavery and the slave trade. Freed slaves also started African newspapers in Liberia; Accra, Gold Coast (Ghana); and Lagos, Nigeria (Ainslie 1966). When the British took over Sierra Leone, Ghana, and Nigeria, they found African newspapers that served the ruling African elite (mostly freed slaves and their descendants) and that used the London newspapers as their model.

These newspapers later became the launching pad for political protests against the British colonial administrations. Pioneers such as American-educated Nnamdi Azikiwe of Nigeria borrowed a leaf from the Anglo-American journalistic tradition and quickly launched scathing attacks on colonialism and colonial administrators (Eribo 1997). The British colonial administrations promptly passed laws against such "sedition," and censored offending newspapers in Ghana, Nigeria, and other African countries.

Although several African journalists and writers were prosecuted under these sedition laws, generally speaking, at independence, a homegrown freedom of the press that had African and European elements was part of the journalistic culture of the English-speaking countries. In Kenya, Rhodesia, and Malawi, for instance, the tradition inherited from the colonial administration was that of a privately owned, competitive commercial press. Indeed, newspapers in Lagos, Accra, Nairobi, and other African capital cities under British rule had circulations of up to 200,000 at independence.

In the 1920s and 1930s, the British colonial administration decided to develop radio as a public service in its African colonies. The British formed statutory public broadcasting corporations along the lines of the British Broadcasting Corporation (BBC) in virtually all colonies (Ainslie 1966). These were basically aimed at keeping European settlers in Africa in touch with the rest of the British Empire and at maintaining a ritual connection between them and their British culture. Even today, broadcasting in Africa is not free to follow its own cause regarding policy-making and restructuring. As a result of financial crises and international competition, national broadcasters in Africa are often forced to restructure institutionally along new liberal lines, and not necessarily according to their own developmental needs (see Duncan 2000).

French Colonial Tradition

The development of the press in francophone Africa reflected the French policy of assimilation, the aim of which was to transform all Africans in "French" colonies into black Frenchmen and women (Betts 1961). To help accomplish this goal, the colonial administration was the sole authorized newspaper publisher in most territories. One of the roles of this press, which was strictly controlled from Paris, was to advance the "Frenchification" of Africans (Palmer 1997).

The French government extended the right to publish to all French colonies only in 1881. (By way of contrast, in 1881 newspapers had existed in South Africa for 81 years, and in Liberia and Sierra Leone for 80 years.) Still, all publications were systematically censored.

Broadcast stations in the French-speaking countries were organized along the lines of the French government broadcaster, the Office de Radiodiffusion Télévision de France (ORTF). They had even less autonomy than those in the British colonies. They were highly centralized and run strictly according to directives issued by the colonial office in Paris. They broadcast to Africans only in French. The colonial administration introduced African-language broadcasts in African stations for the first time during World War II, when France was on the verge of military collapse in the face of the onslaught of Hitler's armies, to fight for France in North Africa and Europe (Silla 1994). At independence, the French-speaking countries inherited these overly centralized systems, which were public service broadcasters only in name. They were thoroughly politicized government bureaucracies that received meager advertising revenues.

Portuguese Colonial Tradition

The Portuguese were probably the first Europeans to venture into Africa south of the Sahara. They are also known to have launched the African slave trade in the fifteenth century. Portugal subsequently acquired the following African territories: Angola, Mozambique, Guinea Bissau, Cape Verde, and Sao Tome and Principe. During the heyday of Portuguese colonial rule, the administrations maintained very tight control over information getting into and out of these territories through strict censorship. Although private Portuguese interests owned the press in the Portuguese territories, it was part and parcel of the colonial administrative machinery because it enjoyed government patronage and subsidies (Eribo 1997). Because all newspapers had to be submitted to the administration for prepublication censorship, the owners had to be on good terms with the colonial administration to be allowed to publish.

Post-Independence Press Systems (1960–1990)

When African nations became self-governing in the late 1950s and early 1960s, after long and often bitter struggles against colonial governments, most countries inherited the media setup of the colonial administrations. As a result, their first challenge was to give newspapers, radio, and television (where they existed) an African identity, culture, and accent. Countries set out to "Africanize" or domesticate the mass media (Mazrui 1996).

In radio and television, many countries initially selectively used Western techniques, materials, ideas, and forms to produce original, creative, and culturally relevant programming (Hassan 1996). This was no easy task, considering that post-independence broadcasting in Africa was a mishmash of models inherited from European colonial governments.

This challenge, and the need to harness modern communications to accelerate social and economic development, gave rise to development support-communication policies, including development journalism. As formulated in its early stages by Schramm (1964) and other Western experts, the development communication perspective postulated that developing countries were fragile, fledgling societies with many internal and external threats. They did not have the resources to indulge in the luxury of the liberal, watchdog journalistic model of the West. Striving for national unity and cohesion was considered more important than freedom of the press. Journalists were required, at the risk of arrest or prosecution, to observe "journalistic restraint for the sake of social tranquility" (Kale 1997, p. 279).

The consequence of the development communication policy was the extreme politicization of broadcasting and the print media. Most governments, often one-party or military regimes, became gatekeepers that controlled the production and dissemination of information. There was no question of neutrality, objectivity, political pluralism, or equal access to different political views (Eko ["Jerry Springer"] 2001). Nevertheless, the application of development communication was never uniform throughout Africa.

While Africa was undergoing its freedom from colonialization during the 1960s, South Africa was still in the grip of apartheid. In the 1960s and 1970s the South African press, even though functioning within the confines of the apartheid system, was regarded as one of the freest in Africa. However, the second half of the 1980s witnessed prohibitive emergency regulations that muzzled the local, national, and international press during the last years of apartheid, a time when the country was torn by civil unrest and violence (see de Beer ["Intercultural"] 2002). Within the framework of apartheid (late 1940s to mid-1990s), the South African media were characterized by conflict between the liberal democratic tradition, with its emphasis on the importance of the individual and individual rights, and collective participatory or social democracy—a situation that exacerbated the potential for conflict. During this period, South Africa seemed to experience all five stages of news reporting discussed by Wilson and Gutiérrez (1995).

Press Liberalization (1990–Present)

With the end of the cold war, many African leaders lost the unconditional support of their former superpower backers. They had little choice but to accede to their citizens' demands for reforms that would bring political freedom and better standards of living. In response, leader after leader legalized opposition parties and allowed more civil liberties (Ihonvbere 1997; Eko ["Jerry Springer"] 2001).

One of the consequences of political liberalization was "an explosion of publishing of all types" (Palmer 1997, p. 253). There was an exponential growth of independent newspapers, tracts, pamphlets, handbills, tabloids, and satirical publications containing bold messages critical of the regimes in power (Grosswiler 1997). The anemic, much-muzzled mass media suddenly found their voices. They got into the thick of the struggle for freedom, often spearheading demands for democracy, justice, transparency, and accountability. Government-owned newspapers often faded away.

The new independent newspapers were filled with reports on previously taboo topics, such as the real or imagined misdeeds of political leaders. In many cases, newspapers became outlets for the pent-up frustrations of journalists, publishers, and readers (see Ibelema 1994 for the "steam effect").

Competitive pressures also inspired some excesses. Newspapers tried to outdo themselves to survive. It is inevitable that the excesses would create new tensions even with the most liberal of African leaders.

Broadcasting was also affected by political upheavals. In virtually every country, government monopoly of broadcasting has been broken. In some countries, government-owned broadcasting stations that were intimately associated with vilified regimes were attacked by mobs. In the Democratic Republic of Congo (the former Zaire), for instance, journalists of the Zairian Radio and Television Corporation (OZRT), which had been the mouthpiece for the authoritarian regime of Mobutu Sese Seko, were attacked on the streets of Kinshasa, the capital.

As a result of democratic pressures, press laws were liberalized across the continent, and the media landscape has been revolutionized. However, the greatest changes have taken place in broadcasting. Dozens of private, African-owned radio stations (legal and pirate) broadcasting in several African and European languages sprouted like anthills on the African savanna. Virtually all African countries now have a multitude of private radio and television stations broadcasting side by side with the government stations. This new group of broadcasters is a mixed bag of private, commercial, and community broadcasters (including religious broadcasters) whose mission is public service broadcasting—with the aim of making a profit in most cases.

Indeed, the arrival of independent stations has blurred the line between commercial and public broadcasting in the traditional sense. For example, the French-speaking countries of West Africa have a category of private broadcasters called "association radio." These are nonprofit stations owned by community groups or associations. They are not forbidden from making a profit so long as the profits are not distributed to individual members of the association (Senghor 1996).

Regulatory agencies, which were unnecessary during government monopoly, were created in many countries. These include the Conseil National de Communication (National Communication Council, CNC), in Gabon, the National Broadcasting Commission, in Nigeria, the Conseil National de la Communication (National Communication Council), in Cameroon, and the Communications Commission of Kenya.

These agencies were given the task of managing the electromagnetic spectrum, delivering licenses to new public and private stations, and acting as referees in case of disputes. However, in many countries these agencies either were toothless or never got the funding they needed to carry out their mandates. The result is that privatization of broadcasting in many African countries was not systematic (Silla 1994; Ogundimu 1996).

While African countries were struggling for media freedom after colonialization, the South African media had to resist apartheid impediments. For many observers of the South African political and media landscape during the period 1948–1994 the Afrikaans press and apartheid went hand in hand, whereas the English-language press, the black press, and alternative press struggled against apartheid legislation (see *Ecquid Novi*, "Focus on Media and Racism," volume 21, no. 2, 2000).

A turning point for the media came with the media hearings that were held as part of the Truth and Reconciliation Commission's (TRC's) process to conduct an inquiry into apartheid in 1997. This was followed by the media inquiry into the South African Human Rights Commission (HRC) dealing with racism in the media in 2000. These hearings did not present a real solution to the issue of racism in the media (see de Beer and Fouché 2001). Considered as acrimonious by some (mostly white) commentators and as much-needed by other (mostly black) commentators, this process also did little to bring about clear-cut guidelines for the media to follow.

The press, though freer than ever, has been confronted after the TRC and HRC hearings with a number of crucial issues that would have an impact on a peaceful versus a conflict-ridden transition to a fuller democratic society.

After two successful democratic general elections in 1994 and 1999, the specter of conflict and a feeling of evading peace were still evident in much of South Africa. Much of the negativism in the media originated from a perception that the government was becoming more and more iconoclastic, moving with a steady pace to centralization of power and not heeding any kind of criticism, especially not from the media and intellectuals utilizing the media to air their views on government and society.

The net result was that criticism of government was considered to be "racist and unpatriotic" and was only made public by "those who wish to see the new South Africa flounder" (de Beer and Fouché 2001). Reaction from the government came in the form of President Thabo Mbeki's view that an "erroneous legacy of Afro-pessimism" had pervaded society and the media. This view was fueled, according to Mbeki, by the fact that the ANC government had

to contend with a situation that what masquerades as "public opinion" as reflected in the bulk of our [South African] media, is in fact minority opinion informed by the historical social and political position occupied by this minority: The situation has changed only marginally since we obtained our liberation in 1994. We are faced with the virtually unique situation that, among democracies, the overwhelmingly dominant tendency in South African politics, represented by the ANC, has no representation whatsoever in the mass media. (de Beer and Fouché 2001)

What was of concern at the time during the TRC hearings and the HRC media hearings was thus still very much part of the present debate on the role of the media in a racially divided society. As Paton (in de Beer and Fouché 2001) put it:

> While the ruling party insists that whites must take responsibility for the past if the nation is to move forward, the opposition is adamant that we [South Africans] can only move forward if the past is put behind us.

Even if many Afrikaners may not have wanted to accept it, it could be argued that the TRC has, to a degree, freed them from their past. White English speakers and the liberal English media have also been found wanting. Their ambiguous role during apartheid, according to senior black journalists' evidence before the TRC, as well as black intellectuals, must have come as a shock to many.

By early 2001 the public debate about the effect the TRC process has had on South African society and South African media was still in progress. One Afrikaans author, Dan Roodt, termed the process "the South African *Jerry Springer Show*" (de Beer and Fouché 2001). Another Afrikaans author, Antjie Krog, received honors for her soul-searching analysis of the same commission, called *Country of My Skull*, a book dedicated to "every victim who had an Afrikaner surname on her lips."

The Print Press Today

West Africa

The print press in West Africa has grown dramatically in many respects. The most notable area of growth is the number of independent newspapers and magazines. This trend has been spurred especially by the liberalization of the various polities and the advent of desktop publishing. However, the growth in independent newspapers has not necessarily resulted in significantly higher readership. In many cases the independent press merely drew readers away from the government- or party-owned newspapers, which subsequently declined or folded.

The concept of an independent press, it should be noted, is quite ambiguous. An often unasked question is, independent from whom? Government, political parties/interests, activist groups, advertisers? A useful definition in the context of Africa is offered by Campbell (1998):

> . . . [An] "independent" press refers to daily, weekly, fortnightly, monthly, and irregularly appearing newspapers that are published without direct state or government control. The editorial decisions and policies of such newspapers are established and pursued independently of the state. This definition does not, however, exclude newspapers aligned with or financed by opposition political parties or partisan movements. (p. 3)

Campbell's definition is practical in that it minimizes the element of judgment. The definition is also especially suited to the African context, where the press remains overtly political. However, there is an emerging breed of African newspapers, magazines, and broadcast operations that are striving to be objective and professionally even-handed in their reportage and commentary even when their political sympathies and ideology are evident. This chapter uses the term *independent press* to refer especially to such news media. When there is uncertainty as to such independence, the term *privately owned* is used to distinguish the structure from government ownership.[1]

Nigeria. The trends and realities of the print press in West Africa are especially exemplified by Nigeria. As Kakuna Kerina, then of the Committee to Protect Journalists (CPJ), wrote in 1998: "The 139-year-old Nigerian press is Africa's most prolific and vociferous, setting the standards for media practitioners throughout the continent" (Kerina 1998).

The growth of the independent press in Nigeria began in the early 1980s, a few years after the federal government acquired a majority share of the Daily Times group, then Nigeria's most successful publishing house. The subsequent decline of the Daily Times group spurred the establishment of privately owned newspapers and magazines, among them the dailies the *Concord,* the *Guardian,* and the *Vanguard,* and the weekly news magazine *Newswatch.*

The growth of independent newspapers continued in the 1990s during a period of draconian military rule, spurred in part by opposition to the dictatorship. Among the notable publications established during this period were the daily *This Day* and the news magazines *Tell, TheNews,* and *Tempo* (a sister magazine and sometime reincarnation of *TheNews*). These publications were among the most strident in resisting military rule and defying censorship between 1994 and 1998, Nigeria's most perilous years since the 1967–1970 civil war.

A discussion of the growth of Nigerian newspapers would be incomplete without an acknowledgment of its internal geopolitical structure. A vast majority of Nigeria's major newspapers and magazines are based in the south, especially in the commercial (and former political) capital, Lagos. Thus, the south has a predominance of the mass media, especially newspapers. In contrast, political power until recently was wielded primarily by the north. This de facto separation between press and political power was altered in 1999, when a southwesterner, Olusegun Obasanjo, was elected president. Now the north is scrambling to redress the imbalance in newspaper proprietorship.

For a long time, the daily *New Nigerian* was the authoritative and respectable voice of the north. However, it began a precipitous decline after the federal government acquired it in 1976.

The *Guardian*'s intellectual approach to journalism contrasts with the more populist journalism that has kept the veteran daily, *Punch,* as probably Nigeria's most widely read daily. (As will be noted later, circulation figures are phantoms in Nigeria.) The *Guardian* and *Punch* face competition from the *Vanguard,* which has labor union ties—*This Day* and the *Daily Independent*; these joined the crowded market in 2001. Nigeria's major news magazines are *Newswatch, Tell, TheNews,* and *The Week. Newswatch* lists its weekly circulation as between 70,000 and 100,000.

Ghana. Like Nigeria, Ghana has had a lively press since the years before independence from Britain in 1957. However, it went through a period of severe repression during the revolutionary government of Flight Lieutenant Jerry Rawlings, who came to power in a military coup in December 1981. The Ghanaian press saw little growth until 1991, when Rawlings lifted major restrictions. About 20 independent newspapers were soon established, "most of them critical of the government" (Asante 1996, p. 111–112). "Though primitive in layout and journalistically poor, their arrival marked the end of over a decade of media silence" (Asante 1996, p. 112, quoting a Ghanaian journalist).

The Ghanaian press has since moved increasingly from state ownership and overt control to private ownership and independence. However, in Ghana state-owned newspapers, such as the *Daily Graphic, Ghana Times,* and its sister daily *The Evening News,* remain major voices on the newsstand. The *Ghana Times* (formerly *Guinea Times*) and the *Evening News* is especially of note, having been founded by the government of Ghana's first post-independence prime minister, Kwame Nkrumah. The *Daily Graphic* was for long a top-circulating independent paper (owned by the London *Mirror*) before the Ghanaian government acquired it.

These state-sponsored newspapers face stiff competition from privately owned dailies such as *Accra Mail,* the thrice weekly *Ghanaian Chronicle,* and the weeklies *Public Agenda, Palavar,* and *The Independent.*

Liberia and Sierra Leone. The development of the independent press in both countries has been stunted by the outbreak of devastating civil wars in both countries in the 1990s just as other African countries were democratizing. Still, the forces of press growth in the region did not entirely bypass these countries. Even under the repression engendered by the wars, the independent press is still a presence in both countries.

Among the major newspapers in Liberia are the independent dailies *The News* and *The Inquirer* and the pro-government papers *The Patriot, Newsbeat,* and *New Liberia.* The major papers in Sierra Leone are *Unity* (the People's Party official newspaper), *The Democrat* (a daily), the *Concord Times,* and *The Pool Newspaper.*

Côte d'Ivoire (Ivory Coast). As with other francophone countries in West Africa, the press in Côte d'Ivoire has been less robust than in the anglophone countries, especially Nigeria and Ghana (Hachten 1967). Under the charismatic tenure of President Felix Houghouet-Boigny from 1960 to 1993, the Ivoirean press was relatively stunted in its growth and tame in its content. However, that began to change even before Houghouet-Boigny's death in 1993.

The founding in 1991 of *La Voie,* "a brash, aggressive daily" (Campbell 1998, p. 9), marked a definite change. The newspaper gained particular notoriety because of its critical reporting and scathing commentary about the government. It has been described as "the most punished newspaper in Côte d'Ivoire and perhaps in all of francophone West Africa" (Campbell 1998, p. 9). At least six of its editorial staff served prison terms for supposed journalistic offenses in the paper's first five years (Campbell 2000, p. 138).

Côte d'Ivoire now has about 22 dailies, all but two of which are privately owned and published in French. Among the most notable papers are *Le Jour, Fraternité Matin, Ivoire Soir, Le Patriote,* and *Notre Voie. Le Jour* is described as "perhaps the most sophisticated independent daily newspaper in Côte d'Ivoire" (Campbell 2000, p. 139). In contrast, *Le Patriote* is "often described more as a feisty political pamphlet than a newspaper" (Committee to Protect Journalists 2002).

Benin. Perhaps nowhere else in sub-Saharan Africa has democratization had as profound an impact on the growth of the independent press as in Benin. Following a stretch of Marxist rule from 1974 to 1989, Benin embarked on a democratization process that culminated in a presidential election in 1991. President Ahmed Kerekou, who officially abandoned Marxism two years earlier, lost that election but won the subsequent one in 1996. Benin has since witnessed some of the most dramatic growth in private newspapers, now having as "as many as 18 independent dailies and 40 magazines" (Committee to Protect Journalists [CPJ] 2002).

In its 2002 survey of press systems around the world, Reporters Without Borders ranked Benin the highest in Africa, at no. 21 out of 139 countries. That is a tie with Great Britain and several places ahead of the Western European democracies Austria, Spain, and Italy.

Press freedom and newspaper proliferation in Benin, however, has come at the expense of quality. Some of the papers are more like pamphlets, and inadequate remuneration of journalists has led to incidents of entrepreneurial reporting; or journalists being paid to influence the slant of reporting (CPJ 2002). Among Benin's leading dailies are *Les Echos du Jour, Le Matinal,* and *La Nation.*

Mali. Like Benin, Mali's privately owned press has grown remarkably since 1991, when a popular uprising brought an end to the dictatorship of Moussa Traoré. By 2002, there were up to 40 such newspapers, most of them published in French and some in native languages (CPJ 2002). As with the case in Benin, the proliferation has meant an increase in papers that barely qualify to be so called. Yet the Malian press has grown to be one of the liveliest in the region.

Senegal. Of the francophone African countries, Senegal comes closest to the anglophone African countries (especially Nigeria and Ghana) in having a long tradition of a vibrant press. Under the long tenure of the Poet-President Leopold Senghor, the Senegalese press was allowed considerable freedom, and so the independent press thrived. The tradition has continued since Senghor's retirement and death, despite a guerilla insurgency in a southern province. Some of Senegal's most notable papers are *Le Soleil, L'Equipe Sénégal, Sud Quotidien,* and *Wal Fadjri.*

Togo. Togo has remained one of the most repressive press systems in West Africa. Journalists as well as dissidents are routinely persecuted in this country, which has been ruled with an iron fist by Gnassingbe Eyadema since 1967. Still, it too has experienced a growth of privately owned newspapers. Ellis (1993) notes that in

Togo, 20 newspapers appeared in the capital city Lomé alone within a few months in 1990–1991.

Cameroon. Although not as repressive as Eyadema of Togo, Paul Biya of Cameroon continues to hold on to power, obstructing free and fair elections in spite of the country's multiparty political status. His regime has attempted over the years to silence the independent press, particularly *Le Messager,* but has backed off overt measures in the face of international scrutiny. Still, Cameroon has remained relatively peaceful since independence while suffering persistent and periodic human rights violations.

More than 50 private independent newspapers sprang up between 1990 and 1995. Today that number has been reduced to about 20 newspapers that publish regularly. Among the major papers are *Le Messager* (private) and the *Cameroon Tribune* (state-owned). As is often the case in the competition between the private and the government-owned press in Africa, *Le Messager's* facilities are three generations ahead of those in use at the *Cameroon Tribune.*

East Africa

The East African press reflects much of the journalistic tradition of Britain, the former colonial power. Most East African countries have had a private press since before independence, some of them foreign-owned.

Kenya. The Kenyan press was the most vibrant in East Africa in the post-independence era, although it was controlled for the most part by foreign interests. The largest circulating English-language newspaper in Kenya is *The Daily Nation.* Together with its sister publications *The Sunday Nation* and the Swahili-language *Taifa Leo,* the Nation Group is the dominant media group in Kenya. The group now owns a TV station, Nation TV, and owns shares in the Ugandan newspaper *The Monitor,* among other business ventures.

The *East African Standard, The Sunday Standard,* and *The East African,* which were also owned mostly by foreign interests, belonged to the next largest newspaper publisher in Kenya. The third major newspaper house in Kenya was *The Kenya Times,* which was owned by the ruling party, KANU (Kenyan African National Unity). Under the one-party regimes of Jomo Kenyatta and Daniel arap Moi, these newspapers' major preoccupation was to avoid offending the president and his powerful coterie of political appointees and followers. Another newspaper of note is *The People Daily,* an opposition paper.

The most significant news magazine of the one-party era was *The Weekly Review,* published by Hillary Ngweno. For years, the *Review* carried out investigative reporting, which exposed some of the financial and political misdeeds of the rich—and some of the powerful—always being careful not to ruffle the feathers of the president or powerful cabinet ministers.

Reporters Without Borders ranks Kenya behind Uganda and Tanzania as the freest press systems in East Africa (Reporters Without Borders 2002).

Tanzania. Tanzania is an interesting case study in journalism and political leadership. The country's first president, Julius Nyerere, started his political career as editor of the nationalist, anticolonialist *Sauti Ya TANU* (Voice of TANU), the publication of the Tanganyika African National Union party. Later he started *Mwafrika* (The African), another anticolonialist newspaper. When TANU was dissolved to create the Chama Cha Mapinduzi (Revolutionary Party), newspapers and the radio were expected to toe the official party line (Grosswiler 1997).

In 1967, the Arusha Declaration transformed Tanzania into a socialist country that advocated *ujamaa* (collectivization). In 1970, President Nyerere nationalized *The Tanganyika Standard*, Tanzania's largest newspaper, which had been owned by a British company, and merged it with *The Nationalist*, which was owned by the party. The new paper was called *The Daily News.* President Nyerere became editor-in-chief of the newspapers, appointed the managing editor, and issued the newspaper's working charter.

In a signed front-page editorial, Nyerere said Tanzania's largest daily newspaper could not be left in the hands of foreign, nonsocialist owners. He told the new managing editor and staff of the newspaper that the watchwords of the newspaper would be "the socialist equality and dignity of man" rather than profits (Bhanji 1999). Benjamin Mkapa, who later became president of Tanzania, also served as managing editor of the *The Daily News* under President Nyerere.

Because of the socialist policies, the Tanzanian press was one of the least developed in the region until the polity was liberalized in the early 1990s. Like Benin's in West Africa, the transformation of the Tanzanian media landscape has been one of the most profound in East Africa. By 1997, more than 60 newspapers had started publishing in English, Swahili and several African languages (Grosswiler 1997). Among the notable papers are *The Guardian, The Daily Mail, Nipashe* (Swahili), and *Alasiri* (Swahili). Reporters Without Borders rates Tanzania as the second freest press system in East Africa, after Uganda (Reporters Without Borders 2002).

Uganda. In Uganda, the press tradition inherited from Britain at independence was dealt a near fatal blow by the former dictator, Idi Amin. He shut down all newspapers except one that served as his propaganda vehicle, and jailed, tortured, and killed journalists (Robins 1997). The independent press did not fare much better in the second administration of Milton Obote, after Amin was overthrown in 1979.

The Ugandan press began to grow in numbers and freedom after Yoweri Museveni became president in 1986. Several independent newspapers began to compete freely against the state-owned daily *New Vision* and its local-language sister publications. By 1997, more than 25 daily and weekly newspapers in various languages had been launched (Robins 1997). Among the notable independent papers are *The Citizen* (weekly), *The Star,* and *Ngabo* (in Luganda). Reporters Without Borders lists Uganda as the East African country with the freest press (Reporters Without Borders 2002).

Ethiopia.   For more than 15 years, Ethiopia had one of the most hard-line Marxist-Leninist regimes in the world. The government tightly controlled every aspect of economic activity, including the mass media. All that changed when Colonel Mengistu Haile Mariam fled the country as the ragtag militia of the Tigray People's Liberation Front (TPLF) approached the city of Addis Ababa. The country was caught in the euphoria of the departure of the much-hated junta. The press flourished. Newsstands on the streets of Addis Ababa were full of publications ranging from Amhara nationalist publications championing the restoration of the monarchy to newssheets campaigning for an Oromo state.

The new Ethiopian People's Revolutionary Democratic Front (EPRDF) government, led by President and later Prime Minister Meles Zenawi, tolerated this multiplicity of opinions, as long as it did not contradict its contradictory ideology of "ethnic federalism."

However, the government soon started enforcing a very restrictive Press Proclamation under which journalists could be jailed for criminal libel, incitement to violence, and spreading of false information (CPJ 2001). In no time, tens of journalists were arrested, jailed, or fled the country. Before long, Ethiopia became known again as one of the leading persecutors of journalists in Africa.

Despite the restrictive environment, the independent press (especially weekly newspapers) has continued to grow and thrive. Among the major privately owned newspapers are the daily *Ilete Addis* and the weeklies *Efoyta, Seifenebelbal*, and *Addis Tribune.* The government also sponsors the daily *Addis Zemen.* Reporters Without Borders ranks Ethiopia and Eritrea among the least free press systems in East Africa (Reporters Without Borders 2002).

Southern Africa

Like the other regions just reviewed, Southern African countries have also gone through press liberalization. Some countries, such as Botswana, have a long history of press freedom. Others have only recently emerged from civil conflicts and dictatorships. In virtually all cases, independent media systems are emerging almost daily, from privately owned newspapers and radio stations to cyber cafés, daily facsimile reports, and Internet service providers.

Angola.   Angola is one of the few exceptions so far to the liberalization of the press in sub-Saharan Africa. Almost 30 years of civil war have left this mineral-rich country a host of problems ranging from rampant corruption and press repression to devastating poverty for most of the people.

The government-controlled media dominate the mediascape. The government runs the Angola Press News Agency (ANGOP), *O Jornal de Angola* (the only daily newspaper), and the national television and radio services. ANGOP claims to be editorially independent although it is funded by the government. It was established in Luanda in 1975. Its Web site contains no links to any other media sources. No dispatches criticize the ruling party, the MPLA, or the president. *Jornal de Angola* was founded in 1923 by the Portuguese and prints about 41,000 copies daily.

In addition, the government maintains two sophisticated web sites that report aggressive efforts to build civil society. These efforts include partners other than government (see http://www.angola.org/news/mission/ and http://www.angola.org/news/pensador/). But these media rarely report stories critical of the government. The government employs 80 percent of Angolan media workers, who are punished when they are perceived as reporting too critically.

The Committee to Protect Journalists (2002) observed that in 2001, Angolan authorities sacked journalists from government media for alleged "excessive transparency," banned radio programs for going "against the government," and restricted movements of outspoken independent reporters such as Gilberto Neto of the newspaper *Folha 8.* Reporters from the independent media, such as the Catholic radio station Radio Ecclesia, are routinely summoned to explain stories remotely critical of the government (see http://www.misanet.org/).

Although the Angolan constitution guarantees freedom of expression, the government does not abide by the law, and the few independent media continue to be attacked, harassed, and threatened. Still, several of the independent newspapers and private radio stations have become bold in their criticism of the government.

Among the newspapers of note are the government dailies *Jornal de Angola* and *Diario da Republica,* and the weekly *Correio da Semana.* Major private papers (all weeklies) are *Folha 8, Actual,* and *Agora.*

Botswana.   Botswana enjoys one of the best records of press freedom in the region. In fact, the country was not even a blip on the radar screen of Reporters Without Borders (Reporters sans Frontières) when it published the first-ever worldwide Press Freedom Index in October 2002; it was not listed at all. Still, in May 2001, the government threatened to pull its advertisements from two of the independent newspapers, which accounted for 40 percent of the newspapers' income.

A number of media voices maintain a robust presence in the country. *Mmegi* (*The Reporter*) was founded in 1984 and is now the country's largest weekly, with an average national circulation of 28,000. Some other newspapers of note are the *Botswana Daily News* (government), *Botswana Guardian* (private, also publishes the Sunday *Botswana Gazette*), and *The Midweek Sun* (private).

Lesotho.   Six independent newspapers published freely in the small land-locked country of Lesotho after 1998. This fact was remarkable, considering the political turmoil that characterized the democratic elections that brought into power Bethuel Mosisili of the Lesotho Congress for Democracy (LCD). Media outlets were ransacked, many offices were burned, and journalists were attacked during the riots that followed the election. Although the LCD had won a landslide victory, calm had to be restored by forces from neighboring South Africa and Botswana.

Among Lesotho's major newspapers are *Mopheme News* and *Public Eye.* They maintain a web presence (http://www.lesoff.co.za/ and http://www.publiceye.co.ls/). *Mopheme's* home page provides links to the BBC, CNN, and the United Kingdom's *The Mail* and *The Guardian. Mopheme* is a weekly that is published in English and Sesotho. *Public Eye* provides hyperlinks to ten U.S. newspapers, five

U.K newspapers, and two Canadian newspapers. A hyperlink to Islamic news lists some 30 links to Muslim web sources.

Public Eye evolved from a compilation of freelance stories to a six-page photocopy edition that was produced in the home of Editor-in-Chief Bethuel Thai. The photocopies were sold on the streets of the capital city in 1997. The newspaper was formally established in 1998 during the peak of political turmoil in the country and became popular with the public regardless of political affiliation.

The web site cites the goals of the newspaper: to provide a venue for popular feeling, raise awareness of public concerns, to provide information regarding development plans and methods, to aid the growth of literacy, to report development news—successes and failures—and to act as a watchdog on government and public associations. *Public Eye* is the widest circulating newspaper in Lesotho and is distributed in urban and rural areas, including in South Africa. The paper publishes mostly in English, but 20 percent of its material is written in Sesotho, a local language.

Other newspapers of note (all private weeklies) are *Makatolle*, *MoAfrica*, *Mohlanka*, *Mopheme—The Survivor*, and *The Mirror*. All are published in Sesotho except *The Mirror*, which is published in English. *Mopheme—The Survivor* is published in both Sesotho and English.

LENA, the Lesotho News Agency, maintains a web presence at http://www.lena.gov.ls/. The site offers the latest headlines along with photographs. User-friendly links provide information to members, reporters, and the general public at no charge.

Malawi. Some 40 newspapers have come, and most have gone, since 1996. Although government-controlled media dominated during the 1990s and early 2000s, a growing independent press threatened the state monopoly of media communications. Two daily newspapers, *The Daily Times* and *The Nation*, dared to report the news, often challenging the official line reported in government media. *The Nation* maintained a web site in 2002 (http://www.nationmalawi.com/).

Some other notable newspapers in Malawi are the the weeklies *Business Telegraph*, *Dispatch*, *Enquirer*, and *The Mirror*.

Mozambique. Print and broadcast media operate in the country with little government interference. However, the news media face other threats. An investigative journalist, Carlos Cardoso, was murdered in 2000, and there have been subsequent threats against newspapers.

Bonin (1999/2002) noted in a United Nations Development Program (UNDP) study the impressive range and number of media organizations in the country, which reflects a dynamic Mozambican media sector. About 67 percent of all media organizations surveyed in the UNDP study described themselves as provincial. Only nine of the 66 media organizations interviewed were located in the capital city of Maputo. The rest were in the 10 provinces.

A total of 123 media organizations were registered in 1999 (Bonin 1999/2002, p. 47). The Office of Information at the Eduardo Mondlane University reported that as of 2002, there were 230 media operations in the country. Among them are 26 newspapers, 16 magazines, 10 TV stations operating in association with the state-run television service Televisao de Mozambique (TVM), and 43 radio stations (Namburete 2002).

Mozambique's largest and oldest newspaper, *Notícias de Moçambique*, was founded in 1906. Sociedade Notícias owned the newspaper before 1974. The company's original shareholders included individuals, private companies, and a Portuguese bank, Banco Nacional Ultramarino, which later became Mozambique's central bank. After the company's collapse, the Frelimo government took it over and now controls 15 percent of the shares, with the remaining shares distributed among government and company employees (MISA 2002).

Sociedade Notícias also owns *Domingo,* a weekly launched in the 1980s and currently managed by Editoras Associadas, a publishing company formed in 1994. Notícias owns the weekly sports paper *Desafio,* which is managed by the publishing company Moçambique Desportos Lda. *Diário de Moçambique* is published from the central province of Sofala and thus is the only widely circulated newspaper produced outside Maputo. *Savana* became the first independently owned newspaper when it was launched in 1994. *Mediafax,* an innovative newspaper founded by Carlos Cardoso, was widely distributed to businesses and diplomatic missions during the 1990s. The English-language monthly magazine *Mozambique Inview* and *Savana,* along with *Mediafax,* make up the Mediacoop newspaper group (MISA 2000).

In 2002, new media were launched in the country in both broadcasting and print. The former editor of *Savana* published the first edition of one of two weekly newspapers titled *Zambeze* in September 2002. It is owned by NOVOmedia.new. A second weekly was launched at the same time titled *Demos,* owned by COOPARTS Editors.

South Africa. South Africa's media history has been dominated by entrenched economic and political racial segregation. Whites were at the top of the spectrum, followed by coloreds (people of mixed race), Indians, and black Africans at the bottom. An armed struggle was spearheaded by the ANC, the Pan-Africanist Congress (PAC), and the Azanian People's Organization (Azapo), which were subsequently banned. With simultaneous boycott efforts by the international community, however, and different forms of isolation, States of emergency were announced by the National Party in the 1980s, but then the bans on the various political organizxations were lefted and the first democratic elections were held in 1994. Post-apartheid circumstances such as black empowerment and affirmative action have changed the print media environment considerably.

True to the African background of the country, many aspects of newspapering are unique to South Africa. The wide cultural variety of the country's people and the sheer vastness of the land have played important roles in the presentation and dissemination of information through newspapers. Its historical link with the Western world, together with Western values, gave the South African newspaper its form, with the British and American input being the most visible. (See de Beer 1998.)

South Africa's print media sector is highly concentrated in the hands of five major players (MISA 2002):

- Independent Newspapers owns 15 publications, including *The Star, The Argus, Daily News, The Cape Times, Business Report, Saturday Star, Sunday Tribune*, and *Sunday Independent*. The company also controls more than 60 percent of the national daily newspaper market.
- Times Media Limited (TML), now owned by Johnnic under the leadership of former ANC leader Cyril Ramaphosa, has seven publications, including the high-circulation *Sunday Times, Financial Mail*, and *Business Day*. In its previous guise, TML also published the *Rand Daily Mail* until that paper was closed in 1985.
- New Africa Publications (NAP), a subsidiary of New Africa Investment Limited (NAIL), owns the largest-circulation daily in South Africa, the *Sowetan*. NAP also has a joint venture with TML to publish the *Sowetan Sunday World*, a tabloid that is garnering black readership.
- Nasionale Pers Beperk (Naspers) is made up of *Rapport* (an Afrikaans Sunday newspaper), *Beeld* (a daily Afrikaans paper), and *City Press* (a weekly black paper). Perskor's media ownership includes *Die Volksblad* and *Die Burger*.
- In recent years the Caxton newspaper group has grown and consolidated over 40 regionally based community newspapers, mainly targeting affluent white communities in towns and urban areas. These papers are largely dependent on local advertising. The group also owns *The Citizen* (a large daily newspaper).

Alternative print media in South Africa have a colorful history. Alernative media attempted to provide an alternative voice to the racist and inadequate coverage of black activities in the mainstream press. Unfortunately for these titles, newfound freedom after 1994 also brought about harsh economic consequences. With the "cause" largely something of the past, these publications struggled to secure international funding, and subsequently had to close down. Today's *Mail and Guardian* is the country's only remaining title of the alternative newspapers published in the 1980s.

Zimbabwe. During the days of British rule of Rhodesia and through Ian Smith's illegal regime, legislation was passed to curtail press freedom. The media were prevented from supporting efforts toward independence during British rule and later any resistance to minority rule. Once in power, Mugabe took advantage of draconian laws to keep the media in check.

Under his regime, the media, both state and independent, were hindered at every turn from reporting events fairly and objectively. Indeed, employees of the state-controlled media practiced self-censorship even while their counterparts in the independent press forged ahead courageously to report current events in the face of continuing repression. These legal measures include the Law and Order

Maintenance Act, the Official Secrets Act, the Magistrates' Act, and the Censorship and Entertainment Control Act (see Meldrum 2002, p. 9).

The Media and Information Commission set November 21, 2002, as the deadline for all journalists to submit accreditation applications under the repressive Access to Information and Protection of Privacy Act. Journalists with most independent newspapers decided to comply with the law while they challenged it in court. Most likely the government would judge a journalist's level of patriotism based on his reporting practices.

The main newspapers and all broadcasting from within Zimbabwe were controlled by the government and supported the views of Mugabe and the ruling ZANU-PF party ("Medias" 2002). Mugabe created the Zimbabwe Mass Media Trust (ZMMT) in 1980 to act as a holding company for all public commercial interests in Zimbabwean media. It controlled shares in Zimbabwe Newspapers, which operated *The Herald, The Manica Post, The Sunday News,* and the Community Newspaper Group, which published five regional papers. The national news agency, Zimbabwe Inter Africa News Agency, was also state-controlled.

In 1998, an independent newspaper group led by Geoff Nyarota, the Associated Newspapers of Zimbabwe (ANZ), was founded. Supported by funds from Australian, British, and South African investors, the group published six newspapers, of which five were community papers. ANZ's flagship newspaper, *The Daily News,* was launched in 1999 and soon became Zimbabwe's most popular newspaper (MISA 2002). ANZ's other newspapers are *The Express, The Despatch, The Mercury, The Tribune,* and *The Eastern Star.*

The Zimbabwe Independent is a weekly independent newspaper published by Zimind Publishers Ltd. in Harare. The newspaper reported an average weekly print run of about 40,000. It claimed that an independent media survey estimated its weekly print readership to be around 400,000. It specialized in reporting political and economic news of Southern Africa. Its web edition reported on the Zimbabwe Stock Exchange.

News Agencies

Several African countries operate government-sponsored news agencies. Among them are the News Agency of Nigeria, the Ghana News Agency, the Liberian News Agency, Kenyan News Agency, Agence Ivoirienne de Presse, and Agence de Presse Senegalaise, Zimbabwe Inter-Africa News Agency, and Agencia Informacao Mocambique. Most of these agencies were established by the mid-1980s, during the height of the diplomatic and academic debate over the New World Information Order. (The debate revolved around the complaint by developing countries that global information flow was dominated by and slanted toward the interests of Western countries.)

The Pan-African News Agency (PANA 1987) began operations in 1983 as an umbrella organization for the national news agencies. PANA was established by the Organization of African Unity and is headquartered in Dakar, Senegal.

In its stylebook, PANA acknowledges the particular challenges facing all government-sponsored news media that aspire to credible journalism. On the one hand, "The aims listed in the convention setting up PANA impose on the agency certain political responsibilities such as the promotion of African unity" (p. 9). On the other hand, "A news agency exists to provide news to newspapers, radio, and television stations and it lives on credibility. Those who subscribe to its services have the confidence that its news and features will always be factual, objective and balanced and that it can always be relied upon to provide good quality service promptly" (p. 19). One goal of the stylebook, it states, is "to reconcile these responsibilities with the professional principles which guide all news operations" (p. 9).

In South Africa the South African Press Association (SAPA) has been a long-standing national news agency. It is an independent, cooperative, nonprofit news-gathering and news-distributing organization that is operated in the interests of the public and its own members. It was formed in 1938 by newspaper owners and replaced the Reuter SA Press Agency. SAPA receives and distributes national news all over Southern Africa and has its own correspondents in different countries. It also supplies news by member organizations and foreign news agencies such as Reuters and Associated Press (see de Beer 1998, p. 114).

Newspaper and Magazine Circulation

Circulation figures in Africa are suspect at best. When available, they are based on newsprint use rather than actual circulation. Even otherwise authoritative sources such as *Editor & Publisher International Yearbook* (2002) have dated or wrong information, because sometimes even the newsprint figures are hard to come by.

The evidence strongly suggests that despite the growth of independent newspapers and magazines in Africa, readership remains low. Nowhere is this more pronounced than in Nigeria, the region's most robust press system. As recently as the mid-1980s, the *Daily Times* alone had a circulation in the 400,000 range, and its Sunday edition circulated up to 500,000 weekly (Epku 2002). The *Times* group declined precipitously by the 1990s following years of image and identity problems after the federal government acquired a majority share of the company in 1976. None of the newspapers that overtook the *Times* have come close to the *Times'* peak circulation.

The situation in Nigeria also obtains in other African countries. In preparations to write this chapter, a brief e-mail query was sent to selected newspapers soliciting basic information about them, including circulation. Few responded.

The latest and most authoritative data available show that the overall readership rate in sub-Saharan Africa in 1996 is 12 copies per 1,000 population. Although this is an improvement over the 1970 figure (10 per 1,000), it is still very low. UNESCO estimates that more than 50 countries around the world have daily circulation figures of 50 per 1,000 people (UNESCO 2001). Evidently, the substantial increase in adult literacy in sub-Saharan Africa has not fully manifested in readership.

The reason is primarily economic. There is not enough disposable income to make routine purchase of newspapers possible for most people. As noted earlier, the cost of newspapers and magazines is high even by U.S. standards. For instance, single copies of the leading newspapers in Nigeria cost up to the equivalent of 67 cents, and magazines cost from 83 cents to $1.25. To put these costs in perspective, when the Nigerian federal government mandated a minimum monthly wage of about U.S. $50 in 2000, it was considered a momentous step to help wage earners. Yet several state governments pleaded inability to pay that sum to their civil servants. In that context, Nigerian (and other African) papers are far from the modern-day penny press.

There is also the possibility that the culture of reading is underdeveloped or has even regressed, as people are preoccupied with bread-and-butter issues. Jide Oyewusi, a Nigerian playwright, novelist, and author of primary and secondary school textbooks, is quoted in the Nigerian *Guardian* (7 October 2002) as saying, "At the moment, the reading culture of Nigerians is at the zero level."

However, just as circulation figures are often exaggerated, readership measures based on purchases may also underestimate the reality. Per-copy readership has traditionally been high in Africa. For instance, the Nigerian *Vanguard* estimated in 1998 that on average, 15 people read its daily edition and 16 people read its Saturday and Sunday editions. Cursory observation would support the thrust if not the specifics of the claim with regard to other major African newspapers.

Government and corporate offices tend to subscribe to a handful of newspapers, which the staff is free to peruse. Individual purchasers also routinely share newspapers with family members, friends, and even fellow riders on buses and taxis. News stands in the streets of African cities are also typically crowded with "free readers." Therefore, even with low circulation, there is relatively high readership.

Moreover, Nigerian radio stations have traditionally summarized a sampling of commentary by Nigerian newspapers. (The Newspaper Proprietors Association of Nigeria, which wants to be compensated for the airing of commentaries of their members, contested the practice in 2001.) Newspaper content is also spread by word of mouth, a still potent means of spreading information in a society where communal interaction is still relatively strong.

The Broadcast Press

West Africa

Until recently, broadcasting was virtually a monopoly of the government in West African countries. That too has changed rapidly since the 1990s. However, because of the high cost of initial investment, government control of frequency allocation, and weak advertising support, the growth of private broadcasting has not been as phenomenal as that of the print press. In fact, in several countries, especially with regard to television broadcasting, government stations are still dominant. But in most countries the monopoly has at least been broken. In others, private radio broadcasting has become dominant.

Nigeria. Although broadcasting in Nigeria was for long a monopoly of the government, there was always much greater diversity than in other African countries (Eribo 1997; Lasode 1993). That was because regional and, later, state governments had their own broadcast systems that competed against the federal system and sometimes were even in opposition to the federal government.

In fact, two regional governments established television stations ahead of the federal government. The Western Region established a television station in 1959, and aptly promoted it with the slogan "First in Africa." The Eastern Region followed suit the following year. Federal television broadcasting began in 1962, nearly three years after the Western Region's. This bit of Nigerian television history reflects the considerable autonomy and power of the regional governments at the time.

Military rule and the creation of 12 states out of the four regions in 1967 diluted the regional clout. However, the creation of states also resulted in the proliferation of broadcast stations, as each state government sought to establish its own voice in the airwaves. As the number of states grew (ultimately to 36), so did the number of stations. Thus there are at least two television stations in many states, one affiliated with the federal-owned Nigerian Television Authority (NTA) network and the other with the state government. Most states also own at least one radio station. Several have established FM broadcasting, along with short- or medium-wave radio.

The federal government also owns the Federal Radio Corporation of Nigeria (FRCN), which covers much of the country, with operations based in Abuja (headquarters), Enugu, Ibadan, Kaduna, and Lagos. The Nigerian Television Authority and the FRCN were created from the former Nigerian Broadcasting Corporation. The Nigerian government also sponsors one of sub-Saharan Africa's remaining international broadcast services, the Voice of Nigeria.

Internally, Nigerian broadcasting has become even more diverse now. The airways were opened to private enterprises during the 1990s. The establishment of the 24-hour commercial FM station RayPower in 1994 by DAAR Communications Limited marked a particular milestone in the privatization of broadcasting. RayPower, which commenced broadcasting on Nigeria's independence day (October 1), immediately captivated the Lagos audience. Its success led to the establishment of RayPower 2 in 1999 in Abuja, Nigeria's political capital. Daar Communications subsequently established television broadcasting.

Ghana. As in Nigeria, broadcasting in Ghana has ceased to be the exclusive domain of the government. However, there is a certain irony in the development of private broadcasting in Ghana when compared with that in Nigeria. Nigeria's privatization took place under military rule but was attained without major conflicts. Ghana's privatization took place under democratic rule but only after defiance and street protests, which were met with violence.

Frustrated by the government's refusal to grant him a license, an entrepreneur started broadcasting Radio Eye in November 1994 from a secret location in Ghana. Ghanaian authorities soon located the operation and shut it down in December. By then the station, which played primarily American rhythm and blues and reggae hits, had gained so great a following that hundreds of people staged a street demonstration to demand laws allowing private broadcasting. When the protesters made their way to the parliament to press their case, they were attacked and dispersed by pro-government counterprotesters. Yet their demand was essentially met within months.

Early in 1995, the Frequency Registration and Control Board (Ghana's equivalent of the Federal Communication Commission in the United States) awarded a license to the University of Legon to operate a small radio station. The award of commercial licenses followed this soon after to several stations, including Joy 99.7 FM, which started broadcasting in April 1995 (Kwaku 1997; Sharfstein 1995).

The Ghanaian Broadcasting Corporation (GBC) remains the single largest broadcaster in radio and television. However, by 1997, "the FM radio-scape in Accra [alone had] five 24-hour independent stations: Joy, Vibe, Groove, Sunrise, and Gold" (Kwaku 1997). Other private broadcasters that have since joined the market are Atlantis Radio, Choice FM, Radio Universe, and Meridian FM, a women-oriented station. The GBC also started a commercial service, Radio 2.

In television broadcasting, the monopoly of the GBC's GTV has also been broken by Metro-TV (which the GBC jointly operates with a private company) and TV3, a wholly private enterprise. There are at least three cable services in the country, although penetration is low.

Liberia. Broadcasting in Liberia is still dominated by the government. The two major broadcast systems, the Liberian Communication Network (LCN) and the Liberian Broadcasting Service (LBS), are both controlled by the government of President Charles Taylor. He personally established the LCN; the LBS is government-owned. Most of the few privately owned broadcast operations are also pro-government.

Sierra Leone. The Sierra Leone Broadcasting Service (SLBS) provides the only television broadcasting in Sierra Leone. SLBS is also the dominant radio broadcaster. The government of Ahmad Jejan Kabbah also controls Radio Democracy, which was set up on his behalf while he was in exile after being ousted by a military coup. (A West African military force led by Nigeria later restored him to power.) Other radio stations include KISS-FM, a private station; Believers Broadcasting Network, an FM station operated by a Christian group; and Voice of the Handicapped. The UN radio network also broadcasts in Ghana.

Côte d'Ivoire. The government-owned La Premiere and TV2 are the primary television broadcasters in Côte d'Ivoire. The government also runs Radio Cote d'Ivoire and Frequence 2. Private radio stations include Radio Nostalgie and two Catholic mission stations.

Benin.   Broadcast laws were liberalized in Benin in 1997, and since then there has been a rapid growth of private broadcasting. By 2001, there were about 12 private radio stations and two television stations (CPJ 2002.) The state-owned Television National and Radio Benin remain major voices on the air, but privately owned broadcasters such as the commercial TV station have broken their monopoly, on LC2 and the radio station Golfe FM. The independent broadcasters have joined their print counterparts to make the Benin press one of the most diverse and outspoken in Africa.

Mali.   Liberalization of broadcasting in Mali began in 1992 following a popular uprising that ousted the military dictatorship the previous year. By 2002, there were about 28 private radio broadcasters. In all, there are "about 100 radio stations, one fifth of them unlicensed" (CPJ 2002). The licensing of privately owned television stations was delayed for several years, however, despite their statutory legality. Two privately owned television operations, Multi Canal and Tele-Kledu, are now in operation, along with the state-sponsored Radiodiffusion Television du Mali (ORTM). ORTM also operates a network of radio stations. Some of the major private radio stations are Radio Bamakan, Radio Patriote, Radio Frequence 3, Radio Tabaley, and Radio Guintan.

Senegal.   The Senegalese press has not changed as drastically as others in the past decade because Senegal has had a relatively liberal system for much of its postcolonial history. The state-run Radiodiffusion Television Senegalaise (RTS) remains the dominant voice in television and radio broadcasting. However, there are several privately owned radio stations, including Sud FM Radio Nostalgie, Walf FM, Sept FM, and Radio Dunyaa.

East Africa

Broadcasting was made a part of very tightly controlled government bureaucracies or military regimes, in the case of Uganda. They were quintessentially mouthpieces of the political policies of the governments in power. Development communication was the order of the day. For the most part, these situations have now changed.

Kenya.   The Kenya Broadcasting Corporation (KBC) was a tightly controlled parastatal corporation under the Ministry of Information and Broadcasting. The ideological posture of the KBC was *Harambee* (Swahili for pulling together), the development philosophy of Jomo Kenyatta, Kenya's first postcolonial president. This philosophy was especially manifest in the programming of the Voice of Kenya radio and television. After Kenyatta's death, his successor, Daniel arap Moi, launched a new national development policy called *Nyayo* (which means footsteps in Swahili). This new policy ostensibly followed the footsteps of Jomo Kenyatta but added the motto "Amani, Upendo na Umoja" (peace, love and unity). The KBC routinely lashed out against antigovernment groups.

As early as 1990, Kenya Television Network (KTN), then owned by the Kenya Times Media Trust, the media arm of the ruling party KANU, started broadcasting in Nairobi. When agitation for multiparty democracy began, the station was barred from reporting local (Kenyan) news. KTN was later sold to the *East African Standard* ("Change of Ownership" 1997)

Indeed, when agitation for multiparty politics began to make itself felt, the KBC banned music in all African languages except Swahili from the airwaves. The management felt that "tribal music," especially Kikuyu music, contained hidden subversive messages. The ban only served to make the music popular among Kikuyu speakers. Legal and pirated audiocassette recordings of some of the black-listed music sold like hot cakes in the streets of Nairobi and other Kenyan cities and towns.

Things changed in 1997 when, after five years of unrelenting political pressure, including strikes and demonstrations, President Moi signed into law constitutional amendments making Kenya a multiparty state. The Kenyan parliament passed the Kenya Communications Act of 1998 and created the Communications Commission of Kenya. The commission is given the responsibility of issuing broadcast licenses and generally regulating the broadcast communication sector.

Today there are at least four privately owned television broadcasters and more than nine privately owned radio operations (Kariithi n.d.). Kenya Television Network (KTN) broke the government monopoly in 1990. However, although it is technically considered a private operation, it was started as a joint venture between the ruling party, KANU, and the British firm Maxwell Communications. Other privately owned TV operators that have since joined the field include National TV, Citizen TV, Stella TV, and Family TV. Notable private radio stations include Capital FM, Nation FM, Kiss FM, East FM (which targets ethnic Asians), and Radio Citizen.

Tanzania. Radio Tanzania, Dar-es-Salaam, was the main mouthpiece of Tanzania's *ujamaa* socialist policy. Despite its great contribution in the standardization and popularization of Swahili language and culture, Radio Tanzania operated under the tight socialist policies outlined under the Arusha Declaration. Parliament has since passed the Broadcasting Services Act, which liberalized the airwaves. A national television service, Televisheni ya Taifa, was created to compete with private broadcasters and cable companies. The government of Zanzibar also created the Zanzibar Broadcasting Commission to issue broadcast licenses and regulate the sector. However, private-enterprise broadcasters are not allowed to cover the whole country. That is the territory of national radio and television.

Uganda. Uganda was the first East African country to liberalize its airwaves. Its first private radio station went on the air in 1993. Parliament passed the Electronic Media Statute of 1996, and the Uganda Communications Commission Act of 1997 in order to regulate the sector. The UCC was given the power to issue broadcast licenses as well as establish, manage, and operate Information and Communication Technology training centers ("IT Key to Development" 2002).

This liberalization was driven in part by the economic liberalization demanded by the World Bank and International Monetary Fund as a condition for loans (Ogundimu 1996). So far tens of broadcasting licenses have been issued to religious, communal, and ethnic groups. The news stations compete with the state-owned Radio Uganda and Uganda TV.

Southern Africa

Angola. As indicated earlier, Angola has some of the most restrictive press systems in sub-Saharan Africa, an outgrowth of the country's decades-old civil war. The airwaves remain dominated by state broadcasters, Radio Nacional de Angola (RNA) and Televisao Popular de Angola. However, there are some private broadcasters: Radio Ecclesia, a Roman Catholic FM station that broadcasts only in the capital city, Luanda; Luanda Antena Comercial; and Radio Morena, which is based in Benguela.

Botswana. Since 1999, two privately owned radio stations have been operating in the country. Botswana's first national television service began broadcasting in 2000. A digital satellite service offers multiple television channels with broadcasts from the regions. Gaborone Television, which is funded through advertising, broadcasts only to the capital city of that name.

The government-owned Radio Botswana National Service and Botswana TV are major voices on the airwaves. Among the notable private broadcast services are Gaborone Television (owned by Gaborone Broadcasting Company and funded by advertising) and Radio Botswana 2. Multichoice Botswana provides multiple TV channels via digital satellite television.

Lesotho. The media climate in Lesotho has eased considerably, and the 1998 broadcast reforms made it possible for five commercial radio stations to go on the air that year. State-run Radio Lesotho still remained the only station to broadcast nationally. Radio provides an important source of information to the country because of the high cost of printing and because much of the population lives in remote areas of the Lesotho highlands, which are difficult to reach via convenient transportation systems. Indeed, horseback remains a major means of transportation.

In addition to the government-owned Radio Lesotho and Lesotho Television, there are also the privately held MoAfrika FM, People's Choice Radio FM, Joy Radio FM, Radio Kledu, and Catholic Radio FM.

Malawi. The state-run Malawi Broadcasting Corporation (MBC) dominated the radio market with its two stations broadcasting to major population centers throughout the country. The government benefited from favorable news coverage and editorial content via national radio and television, and used state-owned media to frame the public agenda and marginalize opposition voices.

Seven private radio stations, all FM, were active in 2001, including two commercial stations headquartered in Blantyre. There is also at least one rural community radio station. The Dzimwe Community Radio Station is located in Monkey-Bay District and was licensed in 1997. The station covers a radius of 95 kilometers and reaches 3.2 million listeners. Rural women formed media clubs to listen to the station in groups as a way of widening access for women who could not afford radios and batteries. The Malawi Media Women's Association supported the station. Another major private broadcaster is FM 101 Power.

In May 2001, the Malawi Institute of Journalism launched a private training-commercial radio station, MIJ FM. Three radio stations with religious affiliations broadcast in Blantyre and other major urban center. The state-owned Malawi Broadcasting Corporation (MBC)-TV, Radio One and Radio Two, and Capital Radio are dominant on the airwaves.

Mozambique. State-run Radio Mozambique is the main source of news and information for many Mozambicans, and about 40 community radio and TV stations operate with funding from the government and UNESCO. As in the rest of Africa, the primary source of breaking news is radio. Portuguese state TV's African service, RTP Africa, is available in the parts of the country that can receive the domestic state-run TV. Satellite services bring in a variety of international services, and the BBC World Service is available on FM in Maputo. The independent media have enjoyed moderate growth, and private or commercial radio stations operate in most urban areas.

There are 10 public radio stations—two from the private sector and eight religious radio stations (Bonin 1999/2002). Moreover, 13 community radio stations were counted in 1999. There were two public television stations broadcasting that year. Two new television stations began broadcasting from Maputo in 2002. STV-SOICO Televisao broadcasts to a radius of 70 kilometers. Sociedade Independente de Communicacao (SOICO) owns it. Major television broadcasters are Televisao de Mozambique (TVM) (government), STV- SOICO Televisao (private), and TV Miramar (religious, private). TV Miramar, a religious station, is owned and operated by the Universal Church of God's Kingdom. It retransmits the television programs produced by Record TV in Brazil from the church's headquarters.

South Africa. South Africa has an extremely and highly sophisticated broadcasting system, including television and radio stations. Although television broadcasting in South Africa started only in the mid-1970s, television has grown into an advanced industry. The South African Broadcasting Corporation (SABC) currently owns three television stations (SABC1, 2, and 3), with the independent e.tv and pay television M-Net and Digital Satellite Television (DStv) completing the spectrum. For the 2001 financial year, subscribers to M-Net's pay television increased by 100,000 households to 2.16 million households. The channel recently underwent a transition from analog to digital subscription, resulting in increased turnover of 17 percent (Naspers 2002).

The pay television service provider MultiChoice also provides television and subscriber services to more than 50 countries in Africa and neighboring islands. DStv currently offers more than 48 video channels, six data channels, and 48 audio channels. The total subscriber figure for Africa toward the end of 2001 stood at 1.24 million (Naspers 2002).

With the establishment of the broadcasting regulator in 1993, community radio licenses were issued, leading to a booming community radio sector, with more than 80 stations being licensed thus far. Apart from this, the SABC sold off six radio stations in the mid-1990s, including OFM, Jacaranda 94.2, and 94.7 Highveld Stereo.

Zimbabwe. State-run Zimbabwe Broadcasting Corporation (ZBC) operated two television channels. For a brief period, the ZBC leased the second channel to the private station Joy TV, but the agreement was cancelled in May 2002 because its programs offended the government. No private radio stations were allowed to transmit from within the country. Fearing that independent broadcasters would enjoy a similar popularity, the Mugabe government prevented all efforts at establishing independent broadcasting services, such as Gerry Jackson's attempt to establish Zimbabwe's first privately operated radio station Capital Radio.

The government also took drastic measures against broadcast programming efforts on the part of Radio Dialogue and the Voice of the People. The latter two radio stations broadcast programs from outside Zimbabwe. The Broadcasting Services Act of 2001 required a license for private broadcasting, but no group has been granted a license since the law was passed. Gerry Jackson, who took refuge in the United Kingdom, established SW Radio Africa in 2001 and broadcast programs into Zimbabwe via shortwave and the Internet. Mugabe accused the United States and the United Kingdom of financing the station.

Broadcast Content: Localization and Internationalization

One remarkable feature of sub-Saharan Africa's new airwaves is the trends toward localization on the one hand, and toward internationalization on the other. On the one hand, radio content is being Africanized and localized anew. On the other hand, many of the new, privately owned stations rely extensively on foreign content, and there is an influx of foreign-affiliated stations that are being operated domestically. In effect, competition is giving rise to diversification of programming in all directions.

Some stations have been successful with local programming that is both consistent with traditional cultural practices and relevant to contemporary audiences. Many private radio stations are going back to their local communities and taking over the role of the traditional palaver tree, under which villagers discussed issues and settled disputes. Some radio stations serve as open forums in which villagers gather to discuss issues of interest and participate in storytelling (Mhlophe 1996).

Some West African radio shows replicate real life village situations—hosts and guests use multiple languages and switch dialects in the course of the program. Sometimes language itself becomes the topic of discussion (Senghor 1996). The "palaver tree of the air" is Africa's version of American talk radio. Through local "culture-tainment," radio promotes cultural diversity, gives voice to the hitherto voiceless segments of society, records and enriches African cultures—and increases ratings in the process.

The East African equivalent of the West African "palavar trees of the air" are the *ekeemeza* or *bimeeza,* on-air "street debates." This unique radio genre is especially popular in Uganda. *Ekimeeza* or *bimeeza* (literally bar table) are live, raucous political discussions that take place in bars with names like Club Obbligato and African Village ("Bimeeza" 2002).

When politicians, including President Yoweri Museveni, took to the airwaves to campaign for reelection, radio stations saw an opportunity to increase their ratings. They took their outside broadcast vans, headed for the bars, chose a moderator—usually a lawyer, politician, or other well-known figure—and opened the floor to all and sundry and broadcast the resulting alcohol-fueled debate live. All topics are fair game. Before too long the phenomenon had spread like wild fire across he broadcast spectrum.

Some stations started Ekimeeza in Luganda, the language spoken by a large section of Ugandans ("Bimeeza" 2002). However, Ugandan government officials soon became impatient with the Ekimeeza when debaters started insulting the president and government officials ("Bimeeza" 2002). A jittery Ugandan government has spoken about banning the barroom debates on the grounds that broadcast licenses did not allow such live outside broadcasts.

Many politicians and the press of course see this as an attempt to censor the free-form political debates. It is left to be seen whether the live barroom verbal brawls will disappear as did a similar open-door broadcast experiment in Burkina Faso called *Radio Entrez Parler* (Radio Come in and Speak Your Mind). It should be noted that the *ekimeeza*-type programming is shunned by some private commercial broadcasting stations, which increasingly opt for Western and African pop music formats (Zulu 1996).

Indeed, there is the countertrend toward internationalization of the African airwaves. Certainly the African airwaves were never truly monolithic in the first place, because the continent has always had one of the highest rates of listenership to international shortwave broadcasts. International broadcasters such as the BBC, the Voice of America, Radio Moscow, *Radio France Internationale, Radio Deutschewelle,* and many others, have been broadcasting hundreds of hours of programming to Africa in English, French, German, Arabic, Swahili, Hausa, and many other African languages. The difference is that now international broadcasters have expanded their African services to include direct broadcasting by satellites, relays, rebroadcasts, and the Internet.

Since the liberalization of the mass media, international broadcasters such as the BBC, the Voice of America, and Radio France Internationale have been granted FM licenses to broadcast directly to African audiences. Thus, African countries now have much more liberal policies regarding their airwaves than does the United States. The equivalent would be for the U.S. Federal Communication Commission to assign FM frequencies to the Russian or Chinese government to broadcast into New York, Washington, D.C., and other American cities.

In a bid to take advantage of the historic opening up of the African airwaves, many Western international broadcasters have lined up affiliates and are actively seeking African "surrogates" to rebroadcast their programming to African audiences (Eko 2003). For instance, the U.S. government-owned Voice of America and Worldnet now have an extensive presence in Africa. In order to support the Voice of America's Radio Democracy for Africa project, which is aimed at creating surrogate or affiliate radio operations throughout Africa to promote democracy, the U.S. House of Representatives in 1998 passed the Promoting Independent Broadcasting in Africa Act. The bill provides the Voice of America's African affiliates with the means to relay or rebroadcast American government-funded programming. This is in addition to regular Voice of America shortwave and satellite broadcasts to the African continent.

Programs by the U.S.-based Cable News Network International (CNNI) are also relayed or rebroadcast in a number of English-speaking African countries, and are carried in virtually all MMDS and direct broadcast satellite packages.

Other international broadcasters with domestic operations in Africa include the BBC World Service (radio and TV), Radio Vatican, Radio France Internationale, Canal France International, Canal Horizon, Radio Deutschewelle, and Deutschewelle TV (Voice of Germany Radio and Voice of Germany Television), and Radio Television Portuguès International (RTPI). The BBC is the leader in surrogate broadcasting on the continent (Médias 2000).

Ironically, some governments find foreign programming safer in some respects. For example, former President Daniel arap Moi of Kenya had, on several occasions, banned popular music in certain indigenous languages in order to halt the subtle but strident antigovernment messages that were being communicated through the programming and the music. Moi preferred that broadcasting be done in English and Swahili.

The South African television programming schedule suggests that the country faces similar challenges as other Southern African countries in terms of local content. Most program content currently is being imported from countries such as the United States, the United Kingdom, Australia, Germany, Canada, and India. Regulations issued by the Independent Communications Authority of South Africa (ICASA) prescribe an overall quota of 50 percent local content for public service television (SABC), with a similar percentage of local content required for the pay television channel MNet. As elsewhere in the world, the high percentage of foreign content on South African television raises questions about the relevance of this content for local viewers, the influence of foreign imperialism, the presentation of appropriate role models for local children's audiences, and so on.

Government–Press Relations and Democracy

The forgoing discussion of the sub-Saharan African press makes it clear that press liberalization is the order of the day. However, the tension continues. A major challenge facing the sub-Saharan African press and governments is how to maintain the dynamic of liberalization. The trend toward press freedom can be aborted if the press is not vigilant or if its excesses undermine its independence (Ibelema, Powell, and Self 2000).

The press systems in general are increasingly equipped to ensure that the newly enhanced freedom is not lost. On the one hand, the sub-Saharan African press is asserting its freedom vigorously, aided by new press technologies (Eko ["Jerry Springer"] 2001; Geslin 2002). On the other hand, there is an increasing concern for professionalization and the development of ethics.

Perhaps nowhere in Africa has the departure of censorship regulations to a free and democratic press been so evident as in South Africa. Not only were a number of laws affecting the freedom of the press suspended after the 1994 democratic elections, but the new constitution (considered by many experts to be the most liberal in the world) now also guarantees freedom of the press and speech. With few exceptions, the Bill of Rights enshrined in South Africa's constitution clearly states that everyone has the right to freedom of expression, which includes the press and other media. However, this right does not extend to propaganda for war; incitement to criminal violence; or advocacy of hatred that is based on race, ethnicity, gender, or religion and that which constitutes incitement to cause harm. As part of the process of freedom, both the broadcasting and the print media organized themselves into professional organizations with their own institutional ethical codes, namely the South African Press Ombudsman's office, the Broadcasting Complaints Commission of South Africa (BCCSA), but also media-related organisations such as the Advertising Standards Authority (ASA) and the Public Relations Institute of Southern Africa (PRISA). After discussions between government and the media in 2001, newspapers also undertook to print their own codes by which they could be held accountable. One problem remaining is that not all legislation that was on the statute books prior to 1994 and could be used against the media has been removed. Organizations such as the Freedom of Expression Institute (FXI), Article 19, and the South African National Editors' Forum are involved in efforts to remove these laws from the statute books.

Perhaps the dynamic between the press and democracy in sub-Saharan Africa is best illustrated in Uganda. During elections there, President Yoweri Museveni took to the airwaves in the face of a stiff challenge from his opponent. He went from radio program to radio program answering call-in and e-mailed questions from listeners (Fisher 2000). Through the press, he gave an unrehearsed account of his leadership directly to the people. It was the new democracy in Africa.

Beating the Censors Through the Internet

A major tool with which African journalists are preserving their freedom and pressing for more is on-line technology. Its availability among the African populace is still very limited but is growing, especially among those who need it the most to enhance press freedom and democracy.

In general, less than 3 percent of the world's people participate in cyberspace. For sub-Saharan Africa, the percentage is even lower. Accessing the Internet is expensive, from the cost of receiver equipment to the high cost of telephone lines and server fees. In addition, governments have been slow to share the dominance of PTT services that would stimulate competition and thus lower prices (Thussu 2001).

Nearly two-thirds of the world's nations have their domestic messages regulated by laws inherited from print-press censorship and updated to restrict radio and television. However, to regulate the Internet internationally would require the almost impossible task of framing a treaty signed by each and every country in the world that uses the Internet. On the other hand, domestic controls are already in place, and not only in authoritarian countries. At least 40 countries (including France) now restrict Internet access on the grounds of protecting the public from subversive ideas or violation of national security—code words used by censors since the sixteenth century (Sussman 2001).

Still, there are some encouraging signs, and information technology (IT) development is on the rise in Africa. The 2001 ITU African Telecommunications Report stated that the year 2000 became Africa's banner year for IT development. All 54 countries that make up the African continent became connected to the Internet, and sub-Saharan Africa passed the threshold of one telephone per 100 inhabitants. Most mobile phone providers and telecommunication services became privatized (ITU 2001). In 1999, only two countries in Africa had more cell phone subscribers than fixed-line subscribers. According to the report, that number jumped to 17 by the end of 2001. Mobile telephone usage has surged from 2 million in 1998 to 30 million in 2002. This number is expected to reach 100 million by 2005.

Necessity truly seems to be the mother of invention in sub-Saharan Africa because a number of innovations have helped stimulate wider access to these technologies. For example, people are able to purchase prepaid phone cards to insert into their mobile phones, thereby bypassing dependence on expensive land-based PTT services. Telecommunications operations are being privatized regularly, which brings in multiple cellular operators in many markets. Shared facilities for web access have sprung up everywhere—in cyber cafés, Internet centers, schools, and public libraries.

In addition to shared group access at public venues, each computer with Internet access often serves up to five users. Extrapolating from this estimate (excluding North Africa and the country of South Africa), from five million to eight million people use the Internet. This translates roughly to one user for every 250 to 400 people, compared with a world average of one user per 15 people.

Statistics indicate that shared public access and the use of corporate networks are growing at greater rates than the number of individual dial-up users. This can be seen in the deployment of international Internet bandwidth, which has expanded substantially, at more than 100 percent, from just over 700 Mbps of available outgoing bandwidth in 2001 to 1,500 Mbps in 2002 (African Internet Status Report 2002).

At the beginning of 2001, Africa had about 4.4 million Internet users, 50 percent from southern Africa and 16 percent from northern Africa (ITU 2001). Although only

1.3 million came from sub-Saharan Africa, that number represented twice as many as the year before.

Moreover, the Internet is driving demand for dial-up connections. Africa boasts the highest ratio of Internet subscribers to fixed telephone lines in the world. The ITU speculates that cell phones are siphoning off the market for voice communication, inciting national PTOs to meet market demand, as well as the public's use of fixed-line communication for Internet access.

A new breed of pan-African companies such as MTN, Orascom Telecom, and MSI are competing in the region to provide the wiring and networking infrastructures to connect most of the region's inhabitants to a mobile signal. The French telecom company Alcatel has moved aggressively into the African market. Nigeria and Angola are considered the most important immediate markets for the company, which bought out a former joint venture partner, Allied Technologies, for $33 million in 2002.

Also, costs are falling in those countries that now allow local call charges to the Internet regardless of distance. This innovation makes it possible for rural people to connect to the Internet. At the same time that new communications technologies serve primarily urban elites, declining costs point to the day when the masses will also be able to benefit from technology. Creative accommodations such as these can provide the fuel to sustain African IT development.

UNESCO, which facilitated the creation of national news agencies in Africa, reported in 2001 that the Internet offers the potential of reviving those agencies that have failed for economic or political reasons (UNESCO 2001). These new communication technologies are providing a number of opportunities to national press agencies, newspapers, and even to opposition groups, including subversive media.

The countries in southern Africa benefit from their close proximity to South Africa, which has low tariff policies for international links. South Africa has become a hub for the countries of Lesotho, Namibia, and Swaziland, for example. In addition, some 19 countries of sub-Saharan Africa now boast points of presence in a number of secondary towns, bringing the number of discrete centers across the continent with local infrastructure to about 240 (African Internet Status Report 2002).

As far as the Internet is concerned, South Africa is undoubtedly the most developed country in Africa. According to a World Bank status report on the Internet in Africa, Africa is the world's least computerized continent, even though it is the second largest. By the early 2000s there were about eight million African Internet surfers, most of these being from southern Africa (around three million) and northern Africa.

In terms of its Internet policy, the South African government has gone to great lengths in roll out multipurpose community centers (MPPCs) and public Internet terminals (PITs) in the hope of stimulating Internet use among its citizenry.

In the mid-1990s, the country's then deputy president Thabo Mbeki appointed a task group to investigate the state of government communications within the context of a democratic South Africa. South Africa has set itself on the path of becoming part of the international information highway. The task group envisioned that South Africa would seek to ensure the creation of an equitable information order nationally, regionally, and internationally. It would therefore take into account the undoubted potential of communities at various levels to cooperate, to bridge differences, to work for mutual uplift and the meeting of basic needs, and to use the new media to redress the social imbalances of underdevelopment in the country. One of the consequences was the establishment of a sophisticated system for internal and external government communication. The State Information Technology Agency (SITA) was established in 1999 with the main objective to provide information technology systems, solutions, and related services that would ensure adherence to the government's e-government policy. A case study conducted by de Beer and Otto (2002) at the Independent Electoral Commission of South Africa indicated that a highly sophisticated system was already in place to develop sustainable democracy through access to Internet.

Press Agencies and the Internet

The 2001 UNESCO report acknowledged that with the rapid privatization of media systems in the developing world, national news agencies will have to adopt a more entrepreneurial model to survive. The Internet will likely provide the backbone for any viable regional or national press agency. A web model similar to that of the Associated Press may offer a practical solution, especially if these agencies route public access through their members' web sites.

There is an international proposal to set up an African press network to be called *Reseau africain pour la presse du XX1e siecle,* that is, African Press Network 21 or RAP 21 (Boyd-Barrett 2001). Among the organizations involved in this effort are Reporters sans Frontières (RSF) and the World Association of Newspapers (WAN) in collaboration with the *Union des editeurs de press d'Afrique Centrale* (the Union of Press Editors in Central Africa, UEPAC). This service will be Internet driven and will provide a gateway for publications, press agencies, and private and public radio and TV stations. The Internet offers a low-cost means for gathering and disseminating news compared with the costlier traditional methods of newsgathering.

Subversive Media and Democracy

African journalists increasingly have at their disposal the technologies to subvert government repression. The Nigerian press was especially successful at this during the difficult years of military dictatorship between 1994 and 1999. Despite a determined attempt to silence the press, courageous journalists continued to publish and broadcast critical commentary and reportage, sometimes on the run (Ibelema 2003). From clandestine radio stations, cell phones, and web sites to independent newspapers, journalists and government agents alike are reaching out to their constituent publics in ways never before imagined.

Antigovernment Nigerian groups set the commercial airtime trend in 1996, when Radio Kudirat, funded by the Soros Foundation and a Norwegian human rights nonprofit organization called Worldview Rights, hit the airwaves. It broadcast intermittently for three years via transmitters located in South Africa.

Internet technologies are also an increasingly available option for reaching people inside and outside a given country, whether the government approves or not. Indeed, the fact that most web sites post information in English and other languages suggests that their authors seek to reach audiences beyond their direct constituencies to influence world opinion.

With the exception of Zimbabwe, most subversive Internet sites and clandestine radio stations operating against African governments are based in Europe and North America. The respective Diaspora in Germany and the United States, for example, runs all Ethiopian and Eritrean stations. They also purchase airtime on commercial shortwave transmitters in Europe (Grace 2002).

Between 1997 and 1999 Sudan and Eritrea waged a psychological war over the airwaves. Eritrea funneled covert U.S. funding to a pro-democratic Sudanese organization, the National Democratic Alliance (NDA), and provided the group with a base and a transmitter. The NDA radio station, Voice of Sudan, was extremely powerful and could be heard all around the world (Grace 2002). Realizing the opportunities, the NDA also provided airtime to three anti-Asmara radio stations: Voice of Free Eritrea, Voice of Truth, and Voice of Democratic Eritrea.

The Sudanese stations were taken off the air when relations between the two countries began to improve. Eritrea finally pulled the plug on the NDA station in 2000. The Voice of Democratic Eritrea now broadcasts via a hired transmitter in Germany (Grace 2002).

When Côte d'Ivoire moved to the brink of civil war in September 2002, cell phones and on-line technologies played a major role in the partial success of the rebels' coup d'etat. The Patriotic Movement of Ivory Coast used a web site to call on Ivoireans in Paris to take to the streets demonstrating their opposition to President Laurent Gbagbo's government (O'Brien 2002).

The new technologies are also being used for nonjournalistic subversions. The Ivoirean rebels used their cell phones to coordinate their attacks when they were launched September 19. Even though forces loyal to President Gbagbo immediately cut the lines, the rebels were able to continue communicating via hand-held satellite phones. O'Brien's article quoted Herman Hanekom of Pretoria's Africa Institute: "First you need the satellite phone, second you need to make sure journalists from outside can have access to rebel areas to get the personal touch, then, if you can publicize it widely, the Web site will come in."

Using both mobile phones and the web also provides a link to the vital youth population, which is quickly growing accustomed to these new technologies (O'Brien 2002). Guerilla groups are finding the Internet to provide effective channels of communication to convince young people and elites to support their efforts to overthrow governments in power.

Other groups on the continent have used the web the same way. Samson Kwaje of the Sudan People's Liberation Movement (SPLM) told O'Brien (2002) that the web provides subversive elements with a venue for responding to inquiries made by those who seek documents and other information that can be provided quickly. "We want people to see who we are, our history, events," Kwaje said. The Sudan People's Liberation Movement has struggled for 19 years, O'Brien reported.

Clandestine radio stations with their related web sites also abound on the subcontinent. Two interesting sources track the constantly changing mediascape of both: www.clandestineradio.com and its newsletter, *Clandestine Radio Watch* (see http://www.schoechi.de/crw/crw097.html).

Journalism Professionalization and Education

As sub-Saharan African journalists increasingly assert their freedom, there is an increasing concern for the professionalism and responsibility. This is an important issue as African countries seek to consolidate their democracies. The late Francis Kasoma, who wrote extensively on journalism professionalism in Africa, argued that there is a link between press ethics and democratization (Kasoma ["Independent Press"] 1997).

The issue of press ethics is also of concern among African journalists. In Nigeria, for instance, Dan Agbese and Ray Ekpu, both founding executives of *Newswatch* magazine, have written and spoken often about the issue. Ekpu, who is also the president of the Newspaper Proprietors Association of Nigeria, is concerned that the unprofessional practices and excesses of some news media may undermine the very democracy the press fought so hard to restore.

Ekpu is especially concerned that press commentary that suggests there have been no "democratic dividends" (economic benefits of democracy) may create a backlash that could encourage another military coup (Ekpu 2002). Such speculation is well founded, as military coups in Africa have typically followed (and been attributed to) popular discontent. Ekpu also criticizes reportage that fails to put issues in context, is outright false, or uses debasing and insulting language.

African journalists are under pressure from their governments to check the excesses and unprofessionalism. In many cases there is a push for a press council that would arbitrate complaints or even certify journalists. Despite the popularity of publications that are critical of (even irreverent toward) governments, the African populace is uncomfortable with journalistic malfeasance, especially the use of crude language and pandering of falsehoods (Ibelema 2003).

African journalists are responding to these concerns by establishing watchdog bodies of their own and developing codes of ethics. In Nigeria, for instance, journalism associations such as the Nigerian Union of Journalists and the League of Editors are working to refashion the Nigerian Press Council to ensure that it can facilitate journalism ethics without serving as an agent of government censorship (Ibelema 2002). Similar efforts are going on in other countries, sometimes in cooperation with the governments.

An increasing number of African journalists are now university (or polytechnic) educated. Journalists are also increasingly attending seminars (at home and abroad) on reportage on everything from legislatures to the scourge of AIDS. However, the proliferation of news media also means continued use of some undertrained staff for quite some time.

This was exactly the concern expressed by the South African government during a meeting with the media in 2001. Government representatives felt that media reporting on the government's policies and activities was unfair and unbalanced. Apart from this, the government representatives also indicated an "irritation" with the fact that reporters apparently lacked the experience and skills to accurately report individuals' names, titles, and positions. This resulted in a colloquium for South African journalists, media trainers, and media scholars in the beginning of 2002, based on the expectation that training for the media could facilitate the transformation of society and enhance democracy (see Steenveld 2002 for a complete discussion of the colloquium). Ultimately, these concerns also resulted in a National Journalism Skills Audit in the middle of 2002 (de Beer and Steyn 2002).

Conclusion

The sub-Saharan African press has changed remarkably and for the better in the past ten years. Reporters Without Borders' ranking of 139 press systems worldwide listed 19 sub-Saharan African countries in the top half, with most others following closely behind. Benin and South Africa were ranked ahead of Austria, Spain, and Italy. A few years ago, any ranking of press systems would have placed sub-Saharan countries in a cluster somewhere in the bottom half. These are remarkable changes over a short period of time.

Phenomenal progress has been made despite Africa's ongoing economic difficulties. As African countries continue to democratize and stabilize, the "democratic dividend" of improved economies should bring about further transformation of the press. Countries such as Zimbabwe and Eritrea, which are still suppressing their press with draconian measures, cannot remain exceptions for too long.

Note

1. Data on media growth in Africa have been culled from a variety of sources, most notably the United Nations Development Program reports, UNESCO statistics, the British Broadcasting Corporation's country reports, the International Telecommunications Union 2001 report, TvRadioWorld, the Committee to Protect Journalists annual reports, the British Home Office, and the CIA *World Fact Book.*

Bibliography

African Internet Status Report, July 2002. Available: http://www3.sn.apc.org/africa/afstat. htmhttp://www3.sn.apc.org/africa/afstat.htm.

Ainslie, R. *The Press in Africa: Communications Past and Present.* London: Victor Gollancz, 1966.

Asante, C. E. *The Press in Ghana: Problems and Prospects.* Lanham, Md.: University Press of America, 1996.

Bell, J. "Nyemb Popoli contraint à l'exil" (Nyemb Popoli forced to go into exile). *Le Messager,* 28 December 1998.

Betts, R. F. *Assimilation and Association in French Colonial Theory.* New York: Columbia University Press, 1961.

Bhanji, S. "Mwalimu Remembered by TSN Workers." *Daily News* (Tanzania), 16 October 1999.

"Bimeeza: Uganda Takes to Speaking Out Loud." *The Monitor,* 28 August 2002.

Bonin, M. "Media Pluralism Landscape: An Overview of the Media Sector in Mozambique." United Nations Development Program Media Development Project. UNESCO, 1999. Posted on the Communication Initiative site, 22 March 2002.

Boyd-Barrett, O. *The Future of National News Agencies: Report to UNESCO.* Final Report of the Workshop on News Agencies in the Era of the Internet. Amman, Jordan, 28–31 January 2001.

British Home Office. Web site: http://www.ind.homeoffice.gov.uk, 2002.

Campbell, W. J. *The Emergent Independent Press in Benin and Côte d'Ivoire: From Voice of the State to Advocate of Democracy.* Westport, Conn.: Praeger, 1998.

———. "Freedom Neruda: Struggles for Press Freedom in West Africa." *Media Studies Journal* (Spring/Summer 2000): 136–142.

Celestine, M. "Playwright Bemoans Poor Reading Culture in Nigeria." *The Guardian* (Nigeria), 7 October 2002. Available: http://www.ngrguardiannews.com/news.

"Change of Ownership." *The Weekly Review,* 19 December 1997, 19.

Committee to Protect Journalists. (CPJ). *Attacks on the Press 2002.* Washington D.C.: CPJ, 2002.

———. "Africa 2001." Available: http://www.cpj.org/attacks01/.

Dadge, D. "Hunting the News Gatherers." *IPI Report: The International Journalism Magazine—2000. World Press Freedom Review.* Zurich: International Press Institute, 2000.

de Beer, A. S. *Intercultural Dimensions of News: The Dilemma of the South African Press.* Paper read at the International Communication section of the 23rd Conference and General Assembly of the IAMCR, Barcelona, Spain, July 2002.

de Beer, A. S., Editor. *Mass Media Towards the Millennium: The South African Handbook of Mass Communication.* Pretoria, South Africa: J. L. van Schaik, 1998.

de Beer, A. S., and J. Fouché. *In Search of Truth: The TRC and the South African Press. A Case Study.* Paper read at the annual convention of the International Division of the Association for Education in Journalism and Mass Communication, Washington, D.C., 5–8 August, 2001.

de Beer, A. S., and H. Otto. *An e-Volution: Will African Democracy Do Digital? A South African Case Study.* Paper read at the Euricom Colloquium, *Electronic Networks and Democracy,* Amsterdam/Nijmegen, the Netherlands, 8–12 October 2002. Available: http://baserv.uci. kun.nl/~jankow/Euricom.

de Beer, A. S., and E. Steyn. "Sanef's '2002 South African National Journalism Skills Audit.'" *Ecquid Novi* 23, no. 1 (2002): 11–86.

Duncan, J. *Broadcasting and the National Question: South African Broadcast Media in an Age of Neo-Liberalism.* Johannesburg, South Africa: Freedom of Expression Institute, 2000.

Economic Commission for Africa. *Economic Report on Africa, 2002.* Available: http://www.uneca. org/era2002.

Editor & Publisher International Yearbook. New York: Editor & Publisher, 2002.

Eko, L. "Between Globalization and Democraticization: Government Public Broadcasting in Africa." In *Public Broadcasting in the Public Interest,* edited by M. McCauley, E. Peterson, B. L. Artz, and D. Halleck, 171–191. Armonk, N.Y.: M. E. Sharpe, 2003.

———. "Jerry Springer and the Marlboro Man in Africa: Communication and Cultural Eclecticism." *Ecquid Novi* 21 (2001): 25–40.

———. "Many Spiders, One World Wide Web: Towards a Typology of Internet Regulation." *Communication Law and Policy* 63 (2001): 445–484.

———. "Public Broadcasting in a Changing Regulatory Environment: The Case of Africa." *Ecquid Novi* 21 (2000): 82–97.

Ekpu, R. Personal interview, 25 October 2002.

Ellis, S. "Rumor and Power in Togo." *Journal of the International African Institute* 63 (1993): 462–475.

Eribo, F. "Internal and External Factors Affecting Press Freedom in Nigeria." In *Press Freedom and Communication in Africa,* edited by F. Eribo and W. Jong-Ebot, 51–74. Trenton, N.J.: Africa World Press, 1997.

Fisher, I. "Uganda Must Choose Popular Autocrat or Democracy." *The New York Times*, 8 June 2000, A8.

Geslin, J.-D. "Coups de Griffe á Libreville" (Showing Some Claws in Libreville). *Jeune Afrique L'Intelligent*, 20 November 2001, 63.

———. *L'Info d'abord* (Information First). *Jeune Afrique*, 2 September 2002, 72–77.

Grace, N. E-mail interview, 23 October 2002.

Grosswiler, P. "Changing Perceptions of Press Freedom in Tanzania." In *Press Freedom and Communication in Africa*, edited by F. Eribo and W. Jong-Ebot, 101–119. Trenton, N.J.: Africa World Press, 1997.

Hachten, W. A. "The Press in a One-Party State: The Ivory Coast Under Houphouet." *Journalism Quarterly* 44, no. 1 (1967): 107–113.

Hassan, S. "The Modernist Experience in African Art: Toward a Critical Understanding." In *The Muse of Modernity: Essays on Culture as Development in Africa*, edited by P. G. Altbach and S. Hassan, 37–61. Trenton, N.J.: Africa World Press, 1996.

Horwitz, R. B. 2001. *Communication and Democratic Reform in South Africa.* Cambridge, U.K.: Cambridge University Press, 2001.

Ibelema, M. "The Nigerian Press and June 12: Pressure and Performance." *Journalism & Communication Monographs* 4, no. 4 (2003).

———. "Nigerian Press Ethics and the Politics of Pluralism." In *The Mission: Journalism, Ethics and the World*, edited by J. B. Atkins, 153–168. Ames: Iowa State University Press, 2002.

———. "Professionalism as Risk Management: A Typology of Journalists in Developing Countries." *Journal of Development Communication* 5, no. 1 (1994): 22–32.

Kbelema, M., L. Powell, and Self William. "Press Freedom as a Logistical Notion." *Free Press Yearbook* 38 (2000): 98–115.

Ihonvbere, J. Democratization in Africa. *Peace Review* 9 (1997): 371–378.

International Telecommunications Union. *African Telecommunications Indicators.* Report, 2001.

"IT Key to Development." *New Vision* (Kampala), 27 September 2002, 1.

ITU. "World Radiocommunication Conference Concludes on Series of Far-Reaching Agreements," Available: http://www.itu.int/newsroom/press/releases/2000/13.html. Accessed 10 October 2001.

Kale, M, II. "Deconstructing the Dialectics of Press Freedom in Cameroon." In *Press Freedom and Communication in Africa*, edited by F. Eribo and W. Jong-Ebot, 263–289. Trenton, N.J.: Africa World Press, 1997.

Kariithi, Nixon. "Kenya [Broadcasting]." Available: http://www.museum.tv/archives/etv/K/htmlK/kenya/kenya.htm. Accessed 1 November 2002.

Kasoma, F. P. "The Independent Press and Politics." *Gazette* 59 (1997): 295–310.

———. "Press Freedom in Zambia." In *Press Freedom and Communication in Africa*, edited by F. Eribo and W. Jong-Ebot, 135–156. Trenton, N.J.: Africa World Press, 1997.

Kerina, K. "Free-Press Hopes Fade." *Columbia Journalism Review* (November/December 1998): 24–26.

Kolawole, T. "Challenges of Newspaper Marketing." *The Guardian* (Nigeria), 28 July 2002. Available: http://www.ngrguardiannews.com/news.

Kwaku. "Independent Radio on the Rise in Ghana." *Billboard*, 12 April 1997, 45–46.

Kwame Boafo, S. T. "Supporting Democracy, Good Governance and Peace-Building in Africa: Some Ethical Challenges for African Media." In: *Handbook on Journalism Ethics: Journalism Practice and Training—African Case Studies*, edited by C. Ukpabi. Windhoek: Media Institute of Southern Africa, 2001.

Lasode, O. *Television Broadcasting: The Nigerian Experience (1959–1992).* Ibadan, Nigeria: Caltop Publications, 1993.

Mazrui, A. "Perspective: The Muse of Modernity and the Quest for Development." In *The Muse of Modernity: Essays on Culture as Development in Africa*, edited by P. G. Altbach and S. Hassan, 1–18. Trenton, N.J.: Africa World Press, 1996.

"Media as Freedom Crusader." *The Guardian* (Nigeria) on-line, 1 October 2001. Available: http://www.ngrguardiannews.com.

Media Development and Diversity Agency. *Media Development and Diversity Agency—A Draft Position Paper.* Pretoria: Government Printer, November 2000.

Media Institute of Southern Africa (MISA). *Southern African Media Directory 2001/2.* Windhoek: MISA, 2002.

———. *Southern Africa Media Directory 2000.* Windhoek: MISA, 2000.

"Médias: La BBC tisse sa toile (Media: The BBC Weaves its Web in Africa)." *Jeune Afrique/L'Intelligent,* 13 July 2002, 14.

Meldrum, A. "In and Out of Jail." *The Global Journalist* 8, no. 3 (2002): 9–11.

Mhlophe, G. "Storytelling, a Part of Our Heritage. In *The Muse of Modernity: Essays on Culture as Development in Africa,* edited by P. G. Altbach and S. Hassan, 109–115. Trenton, N.J.: Africa World Press, 1996.

Nakazibwe, C. "How *Monitor* Reopened." *The Monitor* (Kampala), 18 October 2002, 1. Available: http://allafrica.com/stories/200210180129.htm.

Namburete, E. E-mail interview, 19 September 2002.

O'Brien, F. "Ivory Coast Warriors Take War to Web." Story filed by Reuters, 16 October 2002. Available: http://www.cnn.com/2002/TECH/internet/10/16/ivorycoast.war.reut/index.html.

Ogundimu, F.F. "Private-Enterprise Broadcasting and Accelerating Dependency: Case Studies from Nigerian and Uganda." *Gazette* 58 (1996): 159–172.

Olorunyomi, D. "Defiant Publishing in Nigeria." *Media Studies Journal* 10 (1996): 65–74.

Palmer, A. "Reinventing the Democratic Process of Benin." In *Press Freedom and Communication in Africa,* edited by F. Eribo and W. Jong-Ebot, 243–261. Trenton, N.J.: Africa World Press, 1997.

PANA. *Stylebook.* Dakar, Senegal: Pan-African News Agency, 1987.

Paterson, C. "Reform or Re-Colonization? The Overhaul of African Television." *Review of African Political Economy* 2 (1998): 571–584.

Promoting Independent Broadcasting in Africa Act, H. Res. 415, 105th Congress., 2nd Session, 144 Cong. Rec. H7655 (1998).

"Radio Netherlands Radio," 30 November 2001. Available: http://www.rnw.nl/realradio/features/html/zimbabwe000804.html.

"Reporters Without Borders" Press Freedom Index 2002. Available: http://www.rsf.fr/article.php3?id_article=4116. Accessed October 2002.

Robins, M. B. "Press Freedom in Uganda." In *Press Freedom and Communication in Africa,* edited by F. Eribo and W. Jong-Ebot, 121–134. Trenton, N.J.: Africa World Press, 1997.

Rude, J. "Birth of a Nation in Cyberspace." *The Humanist* 56 (1996): 17–22.

Sanders, J. 2000. *South Africa and the International Media, 1972–1979: A Struggle for Representation.* London: Frank Cass, 2000.

Schramm, W. *Mass Media and National Development.* Stanford, Calif.: Stanford University Press, 1964.

Senghor, D. "Radio Stations in Africa: Issues of Democracy and Culture." In *The Muse of Modernity: Essays on Culture as Development in Africa,* edited by P. G. Altbach and S. Hassan, 79–108. Trenton, N.J.: Africa World Press, 1996.

Sharfstein, D. J. "Radio Free Ghana." *Africa Report* (May/June 1995): 46–48.

Silla, M. *Le paria du village planetaire ou l'Afrique à lîjheure de la télévision mondiale* (The Paria of the Planetary Village, or Africa in the Era of Global Television). Dakar, Senegal: Nouvelles Editions Africaines du Senegal, 1994.

Steenveld, L., Editor. *Training for Media Transformation & Democracy: A Colloquium for South African Journalists, Media Trainers and Media Scholars.* Grahamstown: The South African National Editors' Forum and the Independent Newspapers Chair of Media Transformation, 2002.

Steyn, E., and A. S. de Beer. *Sanef's 2002 South African National Journalism Skills Audit.* Final Report Prepared for the South African National Editors' Forum (Sanef) and the Sanef Education and Training Committee (ETC), May 2002.

Sussman, L. R. "The Internet & Press Freedom 2000: Censor.gov." *Free Press,* (May 2001): 22–24.

Thussu, D. "News Agencies in the Internet Age." In UNESCO: Final Report of the Workshop on News Agencies in the Era of the Internet. Amman, Jordan, 28–31 January 2001.

Tomaselli, K. G. "Developing the Region Through Research." *Free Press,* 27 March 2001.

UNESCO. *Facts and Figures 2000.* Paris: UNESCO Institute for Statistics, 2001.

UNESCO. *Final Report of the Workshop on News Agencies in the Era of the Internet,* Amman, Jordan, 28–31 January 2001.

United Nations. General Assembly Committee on Information From Non-Self-Governing Territories: Social Conditions in Non-Self-Governing Territories. Report no. A/AC/35/SR.180. United Nations, 1958.

United Nations Development Program (UNDP). *Human Development Report 1993.* New York: Oxford University Press, 1993.

———. *Human Development Report 1999.* New York: Oxford University Press, 1999.

Wilson, C. C., and F. Gutiérrez. *Race, Multiculturalism, and the Press: From Mass to Class Communication.* Thousand Oaks, Calif.: Sage, 1995.

Zulu, B. "Rebuilding Africa Through Film Video and Television." In *The Muse of Modernity: Essays on Culture as Development in Africa,* edited by P. G. Altbach and S. Hassan, 63–78. Trenton, N.J.: Africa World Press, 1996.

Web Sites

http://unesco-nairobi.union.org/eamwa//mwamalawi.html
http://www.angola.org/news/mission/
http://www.angola.org/news/pensador/
http://www.bbc.co.uk
http://www.cia.gov/cia/publications/factbook/
http://www.clandestineradio.com
http://www.crl.edu/info/camp/malawinews.htm
http://www.freemedia.at
http://www.freemedia.at/wpfr/world.html
http://www.ijnet.org/Profile/Africa/Lesotho/media.html
http://www.ind.homeoffice.gov.uk
http://www.ind.homeoffice.gov.uk/default.asp?pageid=3075
http://www.irinnews.org/frontpage.asp
http://www.misanet.org/samd/MOZAMBIQUE.html
http://www.mtrustonline.com/dailytrust/daily_trust
http://www.rsf.org
http://www.tvradioworld.com

17

Asia and the Pacific

Jiafei Yin and Gregg Payne

Diversity and change define twenty-first century Asia and its mass media. Asia is best known for its large population. It occupies 29.5 percent of the world's land area but supports 60 percent of its population. Of the 10 most populous countries in the world, six are in Asia, and seven metropolises in Asia make it to the top 10 list of the world's most populous cities. Together, China and India account for more than one-third of the world's population, while Indonesia is the largest Muslim country in the world. The U.S. Bureau of the Census predicts that by the year 2050, India will become the most populous country in the world, with 1.63 billion people, while China will drop to second place, with 1.37 billion. A large population provides a mass market for the media but puts enormous stress on the environment. In 2001, about 35 percent of the population was urban. By contrast, some independent countries in the South Pacific, such as Kiribati, Tonga, Vanuatu, and Nauru have populations below 300,000. The discussions in this chapter will therefore concentrate on nations with more than 500,000 people and a media system that can truly be described as "mass."

Economically, Asia presents sharp contrasts as well. Japan is an economic powerhouse and a strong contender in global trade despite its economic slowdown in recent years, while the economic miracle of the "four small dragons"—Singapore, Hong Kong, South Korea, and Taiwan—caught the attention of the world before the financial crash in 1997. Despite the recent economic difficulties, Singapore, Hong Kong, and Japan rank high on the list of world's richest countries, with a per-capita gross domestic product (GDP) of around $25,000 in 2001, while Taiwan has the third largest foreign reserves in the world, after Japan and China. But elsewhere in Asia are some of the poorest countries in the world—Afghanistan, Bangladesh, Bhutan, Cambodia, Laos, Myanmar (Burma), and Nepal—with a per-capita GDP below $900. Such extreme contrasts in wealth come from the very diversified economic systems practiced in Asia, including laissez-faire capitalism, state-guided capitalism, rigid communism and communist systems undergoing major reforms, such as in China and Vietnam. Different levels of economic development help explain the varied pace of media development on the continent.

Asia's political systems are as varied as its economic ones. They range from constitutional monarchy in Japan and Thailand to parliamentary democracies, quasi-democracies, communism, authoritarian governments, and governments with civilian and military leaders taking turns, as in Pakistan. However, the general trend on the continent is toward liberalization, with new democracies appearing, such as in Indonesia, the Philippines, South Korea, and Taiwan, and more countries opening up, such as China, India, Vietnam, and Laos. The political system in any given Asian country determines the level of government control of the media, but culture also plays a big role in the control of news.

Asia has a rich and diverse cultural heritage. Two of the world's four oldest civilizations are in Asia—Chinese and Indian. The Chinese language is the only ancient language still used in the world today, and the ancient Chinese philosopher-educator Confucius still has a strong influence on politics, business, and culture in East Asia and some countries in Southeast Asia. India is the birthplace of Buddhism, which is popular throughout Asia and is spreading to other continents as well. All the major religions in the world today originated in Asia and the Middle East. As a result, different religions coexist on the continent. The ethnic and religious mix adds to the strength and vitality of Asia, but it also poses challenges to stability in the region and to the Asian value of harmony. In some countries, such as Malaysia and Singapore, it is a tough issue for the news media to deal with. The countries of Asia and the Pacific are shown in Figure 17.1. (For the convenience of discussion, the Middle East is presented in Chapter 15.)

Historical Highlights

Print media have existed longer in Asia than anywhere else in the world. Paper was invented in China, with some surviving specimens dating to 49 B.C. The use of ink (for making marks with brushes) began even earlier, at least by 1300 B.C. Early writing, in the form of graphs on pottery, has been dated to about 5000 B.C. The Chinese began using woodblock printing extensively in the 900s A.D., while Koreans perfected metal movable type in the early 1400s.

Although the classical Chinese language united people in Japan, Korea, Vietnam, and other countries in Southeast Asia, only elites mastered it. Even in China itself, a mere 1 or 2 percent could read and write the language in 100 B.C., and only about 5 percent could as late as A.D. 1800. But with a population of about 300 million in 1800, China had about 15 million potential readers.

Beginning in the Ming Dynasty (1368–1644), competing publishers issued court news periodicals for sale to literate officials and merchants. Printed from hand-carved blocks, these gazettes lasted into the 1800s. More popular illustrated newspapers carrying sensationalized news appeared occasionally before 1800 (Bishop 1989, p. 42).

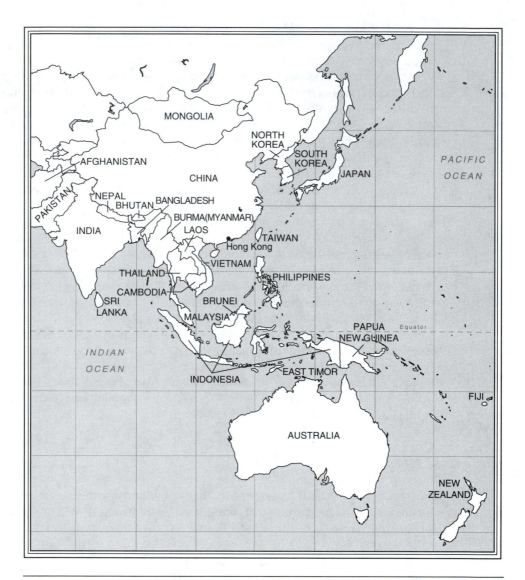

FIGURE 17.1   *Asia and the Pacific*

The Press in the Nineteenth Century

Papers in indigenous languages appeared later than those in colonists' languages. A British missionary began a monthly magazine in vernacular Chinese in 1815. The first newspapers in Afghanistan, Burma, and Korea were also in the native language.

An American missionary established the pioneering *Bangkok Recorder* in Thailand in 1844. Other missionaries active in publishing set up a printing press, which had been "reinvented" by Gutenberg and exported back to Asia, in the important port of Malacca (now Melaka, Malaysia).

The first Indian paper owned by an Indian was the English-language *Bengal Gazette,* established by Gangadhar Bhattacharjee in Calcutta in 1816. Raja Ram Mohan Roy, one of India's greatest champions of political and press freedom, published the country's first non-English-language paper, *Mirat-ul-Akhbat,* in 1821. Sometimes called the "father of modern India," he wrote a noted memorial for the repeal of the press ordinance of 1823.

In South and Southeast Asia, a number of existing publications have nineteenth century roots. Both Singapore's *Straits Times* and Malaysia's *New Straits Times* share a common parentage in the original Straits Times, founded in 1834 and a daily since 1858. The *Times of India,* the country's oldest English-language daily, was established in 1838 as a commercial biweekly and converted into a daily in 1851. Other long-established Indian papers include the *Amrita Bazar Patrika,* a Bengali-language daily in Calcutta (1868); the *Statesman,* an independent liberal English-language daily (1875); and the *Hindu,* an English-language daily published in Madras (1878).

In Japan, the first vernacular newspaper started in 1868. At first the press toed the government line, but by the summer of 1875, the reformist demands of Japanese who had studied abroad were finding their way into the press. Both the *Asahi Shimbun* (Rising Sun Newspaper) and *Yomiuri Shimbun* (Read and Sell Newspaper) were established during this era, in the 1870s. The third of Japan's Big Three, the *Mainichi Shimbun* (Daily Newspaper), is the successor to a paper established in 1870s as well. In the Philippines, journals specializing in commerce, agriculture, and industry appeared earlier than general-interest periodicals. The monthly *Registro Mercantil de Manila* debuted in 1824, while the bilingual (Spanish-English) *Precios Corrientes de Manila* was established in 1839.

The Press in the Early Twentieth Century

In South Asia, the story of the press is intertwined with independence movements. The press in Pakistan is a direct descendant of the Muslim League press of pre-independence India, founded primarily to advocate for a separate Muslim state on the Indian subcontinent. By 1925, the Muslim press had grown in size and circulation and comprised about 220 newspapers in nine languages, including Urdu (the first Urdu journal had been founded in 1836), English, and Bengali.

Muhammad Ali Jinnah, who assisted in founding the first Muslim news agency in the 1930s, greatly helped the Muslim national cause. He was involved in establishing a number of publications, including *Dawn,* the official organ of the Muslim League, still one of the most powerful dailies in Pakistan.

Until 1947, when India achieved independence from Britain, the spirit of nationalism stimulated the growth of the press. Social and political reforms and nationalism were considered the press's three main objectives. Mahatma Gandhi, India's most widely known leader in the struggle for freedom, was a journalist for 60 years. He used the press to propagate his ideas and views as editor of four weekly newspapers—*Indian Opinion, Young India, Navajivan,* and *Harijan.* Through these publications, he spread his ideas of freedom and nonviolence through India and to Indians in South Africa as well.

Jawaharlal Nehru, the first prime minister of India, advocated complete freedom of the press. "I would rather have a completely free press, all the dangers involved in the wrong use of that freedom, than a suppressed or regulated press," he said ("Gandhi" 1989, p. 13).

Another towering political figure who made use of mass media during a period of revolution was Dr. Sun Yat-sen of China. When the *China National Gazette* of Shanghai was suppressed in 1903, it merely changed its name and registered under foreign ownership. Probably the best paper of the period was the *Eastern Times* of Shanghai (1904).

During the early years of the twentieth century, the press of Japan was engaged in circulation battles rather than battles for independence. It adopted some of the worst features of British and American yellow journalism and was well read but often unreliable. During the 1930s, the military forced a restructuring of the press, both to conserve supplies and to make the press easier to control. The 1,200 dailies and 7,700 nondailies were reduced to 55 dailies and weeklies by 1943.

The story of postwar press development and the entire history of broadcasting are covered in the regional discussions in this chapter.

Media Overview

News media in Asia are undergoing historic transformations, caught as they are between sweeping political liberalizations on the continent and a global economic slowdown in the wake of a financial crash in the region. Most countries in Asia do not have a libertarian media tradition except perhaps the Philippines, because of American influence, and Thailand, because of Buddhism. But recent political changes on the content have raised new hopes for media freedom. Indonesia, South Korea, and the Philippines have finally emerged as new democracies after mass demonstrations overthrew military governments. Civilian government returned to Thailand after a military coup in the 1990s, and in Taiwan, martial law was lifted in 1987. In each of these countries, democracy arrived only after decades of suppression at the hands of governments run by generals. Elsewhere on the continent, China, India, and Vietnam have started economic reforms, which resulted in opening up to the outside world, participation in the private economy, and greater information flow.

Taking advantage of the hard-won freedom and the new opportunities, the news media in these countries experienced phenomenal growth, as if releasing pent-up energy. The number of newspapers and magazines doubled or even trebled, and reporters are allowed to explore new territories that used to be taboo. In South Korea, the number of newspapers increased from 28 in 1987 to 115 in 1997, while in Taiwan, the number jumped from 31 in 1988 to 360 in 1998. Even in China, "investigative reporting" has entered the vocabulary of reporters. *Caijing*, a financial magazine started in 1998, is now known for its investigative pieces about publicly listed companies.

The biggest constraints on the media in Asia today are the financial crash in 1997 and the global economic slowdown, which have resulted in a sharp drop in advertising spending, the closure of newspapers, mass layoffs of editorial staff, and tougher competition in the industry.

With the media under extreme pressure for survival, media ethics are being tested. Sensationalism and corruption are serious problems. Some journalists in Thailand, India, South Korea, and China take bribes in exchange for withholding damaging information or writing promotional stories even though it is illegal to do so. Abuse of rights and freedom of the press prompted calls for press responsibility.

Despite the progress toward democracy in various countries in Asia, self-control and government attempts at control are still an important issue facing the news media. Self-censorship among Asian journalists may be deeply rooted in their belief in the nation-building role of the news media. After all, development journalism originated in Asia—in India and the Philippines—and it is still the mainstream in Asian journalism today, even though it is practiced in different ways. In India and the Philippines, it takes the form of diffusion of innovations to the rural areas, while in South Korea and Japan it means cooperation with those in power. Government control of the media can also be exercised in the name of nation-building or national interest. In Singapore and Malaysia, ethnic or religious topics are off-limits for fear of racial conflicts. In China, some labor unrests are kept out of the press for fear of chain reactions.

News media in Pacific island countries are still developing and, to a great extent, depend on foreign aid and expertise for the operation of some of the media and training of the staff. Australia and New Zealand, in particular, have close ties to the news media in the region. The two countries have set up radio stations specifically for listeners in the island countries in the South Pacific. And one paper in Tonga, *Taimi 'o Tonga*, is based in New Zealand. Most of the countries in the Pacific have a democratic political system. However, governments in the region from time to time take actions to silence the media when news coverage of government corruption becomes too critical.

Print Media

Asia has a large number of newspapers with real mass circulation, most of them concentrated in East Asia. At the top of the list is Japan. By 2002, *Yomiuri Shimbun* of Japan was the only paper in the world to boast a circulation of over 10 million, and it is registered in the *Guinness Book of Records*. *Asahi Shimbun,* also of Japan, has a circulation of more than 8 million. Three other top dailies in Japan have circulations ranging from 2 million to 4 million, according to Japan's Audit Bureau of Circulation (Saito 2000, p. 579). And those numbers are only for the morning editions of the Japanese papers. China's *Reference News*, the top-circulation newspaper in the country, has a circulation of 2.74 million, while the *People's Daily*, the central party paper and second in circulation, has a circulation of 1.86 million (*China Journalism Yearbook* 2001). Nine other provincial newspapers in China have circulations of more than 1 million each. South Korea has four papers with circulations of 2 million each.

The wonder with the press industry in the region does not stop at the mass circulations. The readership in Asia is much larger than is suggested by the circulation numbers, which in some cases are only the tip of the iceberg. For example, *Thai Rath* of Thailand has a circulation of 1 million, but its readership is as high as 8.9 million (Ekachai 2000, p. 440). The same is true of *Kompas* of Indonesia, which has a circulation of 525,000 but a readership of 2.04 million (Idris and Gunaratne 2000, p. 291). One reason may be the high population density in these countries. Another reason may be social. In China, it is common for offices to subscribe to newspapers for their staff. And some individuals subscribe to newspapers using their office address, which ensures more reliable delivery. Students in dorms and employees living in company housing for single people customarily share newspapers. Pass-along readership is typically high across the region. China also has newspaper display windows in busy streets, where passers-by can read news of the day.

The reason why Asians are avid newspaper readers may be that the Asian culture values reading and education. Many people in Asia read newspapers not just to be informed and entertained, but also to be educated. Another obvious reason for large circulation is the size of population. In fact, the circulation of newspapers in some Asian countries could be much higher if their literacy rate could be improved, such as India, with the rate standing at 53.5 percent, and Pakistan, at 41 percent.

East Asia

Today any foreign visitors to China expecting to be exposed to monolithic and tightly controlled communist media will have a big surprise in store for them. The media in China are increasingly driven by market pressure since the country began economic reforms and opened up to the outside world. With the national economy substantially decentralized and increasingly market-oriented, the Chinese media today are quite diversified and commercialized. With access to the Internet widely available for a monthly fee, complete control of information is no longer technically feasible.

Print media in China are experiencing an explosive growth as people have realized that newspapers and magazines can be money makers, in addition to having a political role. One journalism scholar, Fang Hanqi, said the industry has become "a pillar of the national economy" ("International News" 2000), whereas formerly it was mostly regarded as a political tool. In 2001 there were 2,007 newspapers and 8,725 magazines published in China (*China Journalism Yearbook* 2001). Newspapers using the languages of ethnic minorities total 84. To prepare for the competition with foreign media, as China is now a member of the World Trade Organization (WTO), 16 newspaper groups have been formed, including the China Daily News Group, the Guangming Daily Group, the Economic Daily Group, and the Wenhui-Xinmin Group.

Besides the *Reference News* and the *People's Daily*, other top-circulation papers include papers targeting the student population, such as *Elementary Students' Journal* (1.75 million), *China Early Teens Journal* (1 million), *Elementary School Students' Math Journal* (2 million) (*China Journalism Yearbook* 1998), and *English Guide*, 2 million; evening papers in Canton, Nanjing, and Shanghai, with a circulation of around 1.5 million each; TV guides in major metropolises; and digest papers such as *Baokan*

Wenchai (1.47 million) and *Weekly Digest* (1.2 million). *Nanfang Weekend* (1.5 million) and *Huanqiu Times* (1 million) are also quite popular. *Soccer News, Legal News Pictorial,* and *China Farm Machinery Safety Journal* enjoy large circulations as well.

Top-circulation newspapers show a clear trend in China: with the exception of the *People's Daily*, which is the central Chinese Communist Party paper, educational and entertainment newspapers are the most popular. In Beijing, Shanghai, and Tianjin, the three largest metropolises, TV guides lead the circulation of all papers in the city, with evening papers, which are less political and carry more human interest stories, a close second. Newspapers in China today cannot afford just to stay politically correct by keeping a stern face and teaching people lessons. They have to be competitive and profitable by appealing to their readers. They need to have a real market now. With the economic reforms, they have to make themselves viable economic entities, especially local papers.

To be competitive in a situation of economic decentralization, some newspapers and magazines in China are pioneering investigative journalism, despite strong resistance from local governments. Corruption is rampant in China and it causes public discontent. It is so bad that the head of the State Administration for Production Safety, Zhang Baoming, called on the media for more active participation in the investigation of major industrial accidents, almost every one of which, he said, was connected with corruption ("Giving" 2002). Gone are the days when the party could dismiss public opinion. Now the government places high hopes on the media to fight corruption, *People's Daily* said. One new magazine, *Caijing,* made a name for itself for muckraking investigation of the financial service sector. However, muckraking is directed only at lower-level officials. The other end of the attention-getting continuum is sensationalism. Tabloids are no longer a rarity in China.

For the vast spectrum of the press in a country as large as China, the government keeps a closer watch over papers run by the central government and the Chinese Communist Party than over local papers. The press law, which is being debated in the Chinese legislature, will in a way define journalists' rights in news gathering and will formalize relations between the government and the media.

Reference News, published by the official Xinhua news agency, is the largest newspaper in China, with a circulation of 2.7 million. It is a Chinese translation of news stories published in the foreign media. The paper is likely to retain its leading position as it will take some time for the percentage of the population with access to the Internet and who know a foreign language to increase. *People's Daily,* with a circulation of 1.86 million, remains the voice of the party. It is the place where people inside and outside China look for signs of political and policy changes. *China Daily,* which is perhaps more widely known outside China than inside, is a product of China's economic reforms. Started in 1981, it is the only national English-language daily newspaper in China. It serves the English-speaking and English-learning population in China and the world community at large. *China Daily's* web site is one of the 10 Chinese sites that have the highest hits. Many of the major Chinese newspapers can be accessed on the Internet today, including *People's Daily.*

The magazine market in China has witnessed even bigger changes and expansion. A Chinese magazine used to educate, not entertain. "Consumer magazine" is a novel concept, and the magazine titles were limited. Today an amazing number of bookshelves parade a dazzling array of consumer magazines in bookstores and libraries. Wherever you go, you see magazines—on the curbside, at subway newsstands, and in the post offices. There is a title for every demographic group, interest, or hobby, and more titles crowd the market of sports, fashion, and women's interests. Who would have imagined finding the Chinese versions of *Elle* and *Vogue* on newsstands in China today? News magazines are on the rise as well.

In Hong Kong, the expected and hyped drastic change in the press after the turnover of sovereignty to China in 1997 did not happen. The Hong Kong press is as vibrant and competitive as ever. Talk of communist China taking away the freedom of the press in Hong Kong has proved to be more fiction than fact five years after the return of Hong Kong to the People's Republic of China. "Hong Kong has continued to enjoy the same political and civic rights and freedoms as before" (So, Chan, and Lee 2000, p. 528). However, self-censorship on the part of the press is becoming a concern (Kubiske 2000).

Hong Kong is a media-saturated society. In the 1970s it was known as "the city of a hundred newspapers" (*China Journalism Yearbook* 1998, p. 717). Today, Hong Kong publishes around 50 newspapers every day and 693 magazines and journals. About 30 of the newspapers are in Chinese, 10 are in English, and the rest are in other languages or are bilingual. About 24 of the papers cover mostly local and world news; three focus on financial news (Hong Kong hosts one of the four major stock markets in the world), and the rest are the popular press or tabloids, which lead circulation in Hong Kong and thrive on sensationalism, gossip, crime, and pornography.

Politically, Hong Kong used to have press on the left, right, and center. But with the folding of the Taiwan-supported *Kung Sheung Daily News* and the *Hong Kong Times* in 1984 and 1991, respectively, the rightist press ceased to exist in Hong Kong. As it became apparent that Hong Kong would soon return to China and it was very unlikely that the Taiwan government would recover the mainland, the rightist press lost its appeal. But *Ta Kung Pao* and *Wen Wei Po* continued their positive coverage of mainland China. In 1997, *China Daily* started its Hong Kong edition in the former British colony, which marked the first time a mainland English paper entered the island.

The elite press in Hong Kong, including the *South China Morning Post, Ming Pao Daily News,* the *Hong Kong Economic Journal,* and the *Hong Kong Economic Times,* is depoliticizing its news coverage (So, Chan, and Lee 2000, p. 533) because of the economic pressure precipitated by *Apple Daily*'s sensationalism and self-censorship after 1997. *Ming Pao Daily News* and the *Hong Kong Economic Journal* are the most read newspapers among intellectuals and the best-quality Chinese newspapers in the territory. The change of ownership of the conservative, influential, and very profitable *South China Morning Post* and *Ming Pao Daily News,* both opinion leaders despite small circulation compared with the popular press, caught media attention when both were bought by Chinese-Malaysian tycoons who have a heavy investment in China (So, Chan, and Lee 2000, p. 535).

Leading the press market in circulation are the *Oriental Daily News* and the *Apple Daily.* Together the two tabloids commanded 75 percent of the newspaper market in 1997–1998. The duo was locked in price wars in 1995 and 1997, which drove several smaller papers out of the market and made serious papers less serious.

Hong Kong's free media environment has attracted international publications like *Asiaweek* and the *Far Eastern Economic Review*. Both the *Asian Wall Street Journal* and the *International Herald Tribune* have offices and printing plants in Hong Kong, from where copies circulate throughout the region.

However, in Taiwan, media were not free until 1987, when martial law was ended, and the freeze on newspaper license applications was lifted, in 1988. The press industry took off. The number of newspapers jumped from 31 to 360 in 1998, including nondailies (Wang and Lo 2000). But only 40 have a wide readership (*Republic of China Publication Yearbook* 1999). The number of newspaper pages has increased too, from 12 to more than 50 over the weekend for big papers like the *United Daily News* and *China Times.* Because press freedom is relatively new in Taiwan, the industry has yet to adjust to the new environment.

Entering the new millennium, the press industry in Taiwan faces new challenges. Impacted by a slowing economy, Taiwan's only sports paper, the *Great Sports Daily,* and the island's first Internet newspaper, the *Tomorrow Times*, shut down ("Slumping" 2001). Two other papers, *Taiwan Shin Wen Daily News* and *Taiwan Shin Sheng Daily News,* are not doing well financially, and *Taiwan Daily News* has incurred debt. The expansion of the cable television industry and the ensuing decline in readership and competition for advertising, which account for about 70 percent of newspapers' revenue, contributed to the industry's woes ("Slumping" 2001). Another major factor for the industry's difficulties is the saturation of media on the island. With a population of 23 million, the market may be too small for 21 national newspapers—more than twice the number in Malaysia, which has a similar population size. Most of the smaller papers can afford the losses because their owners are looking more for political and social influence than profits ("Slumping" 2001).

Today, the *United Daily News Group* and the *China Times Group* share about 60 percent of the island's daily newspaper circulation and more than 75 percent of newspaper advertising. The *Liberty Times* managed to reach the top category with aggressive and often controversial promotional strategies, including offering lottery prizes to new subscribers (Wang and Lo 2000).

Magazines in Taiwan never experienced a freeze on licenses during the martial law years and became the favorite medium for political dissidents. After martial law was lifted, the dissident magazines recorded major growth.

North of Taiwan, Japan is a newspaper giant, with the highest-circulation newspapers in the world, and is known for its press freedom in Asia. Japan has five national daily newspapers, all based in Tokyo. *Yomiuri Shimbun, Asahi Shimbun, Mainichi Shimbun, Nihon Keizai Shimbun,* and *Sankei Shimbun* together give Japan a daily newspaper circulation of 580 copies per 1,000 people, the highest in the world, which means that an average family of four gets more than two dailies everyday. All of the Big Five, except perhaps *Sankei*, have similar viewpoints on major issues. As profitable companies with mass readerships, the papers see no need to rock the boat.

Among the explanations offered for the high circulation figures are Japan's homogeneous population, large middle class, high-density urbanization, heavily used public transportation, and high literacy rate. The answer may lie in the broad-based content of the newspapers, which has something for everyone, from comics to fact-laden news stories. All of these factors are coupled with a phenomenal circulation system whereby each adult contractor (students are too busy studying) distributes an average of 250 copies in 2 hours. About 93 percent of households get a home-delivered paper. Many of the papers sold at newsstands are "sports" (real sports, entertainment, and soft-core pornography) dailies.

The Big Five dailies have numerous media and nonmedia holdings, ranging from English-language dailies to baseball teams. The "sister papers" of the Big Three join the *Japan Times* to provide a choice of four English-language daily publications. The papers from early on have sponsored projects and events from art exhibits to Antarctic explorations, making them an integral part of national life and attracting readers in the process.

Yet not all is rosy in the Japanese print media picture. Readers spend fewer minutes with newspapers as trust in reporting has somewhat declined. Further, whereas newspapers used to stand out as the mass medium, since about 1970 television has emerged as an equal force. Since 1975, television has displaced newspapers as the leading advertising medium.

Newspapers carry comics, but the phenomenal cartoon appetite of the Japanese has created its own industry. About two-thirds of all magazines are *manga*, books or magazines that use a cartoon-panel format. The most popular *manga* publication, *Shonen Jump*, has a weekly circulation of about 3.4 million ("U.S." 2002). The publication is to launch *U.S. Shonen Jump*, targeted to American boys and teens. *Manga* run the gamut from science fiction to how-to manuals, pornography, and economics.

Beyond *manga*, Japanese have thousands of monthly and weekly magazines to read. Unlike newspapers, they are sold in stores, not by subscription. Like newspapers, a handful of Tokyo-based companies dominate the market.

Striking parallels exist between Taiwan and South Korea. Both broke from an authoritarian press system in 1987 after achieving dazzling economic success. In both Taiwan and South Korea, advertising dollars buoy an emerging free publication industry. But today's Korean press faces serious challenges as the economy slows down, and the government arrested owners of major newspapers for tax evasion, prompting outcry over political pressure on a critical press.

The Korean press experienced substantial growth after military dictatorship ended. In 1984, South Korea had 25 daily newspapers, including six with a nationwide circulation of more than 700,000 each. Now the country hosts more than 100 dailies and thousands of new periodicals. The largest and most prestigious papers, *Dong-A Ilbo* and *Chosun Ilbo*, both founded in 1920 and with a circulation of more than 2 million each, maintain many foreign bureaus. The other two major dailies, *Joong-ang Ilbo* and *Hankook Ilbo*, have a circulation of 2 million each. The two English-language dailies are the *Korea Times* and the government-owned *Korea Herald*. When control over the media relaxed, the ban on Japanese magazines and comic books was also lifted, just as in Taiwan. All these major national dailies target the elite and the conservative class and are mostly pro-business and pro-government. Despite legal freedom, the press club system and the custom of *chonji* (gifts to journalists) make for a cozy rather than adversarial relationship between journalists and those in power. Sometimes journalists even demand *chonji.* Going against this trend, the *Hankyoreh Shinmun,* established in 1988, forbids the acceptance of *chonji.* Popular with young readers, this new daily attacks both the Korean establishment and the United States while sympathizing with North Korea.

Compared to South Korea, the press of North Korea lacks variety, veracity, and vitality. Foreign publications are carefully excluded, although elites can get a digest of world press reports. A major task of the media is to enhance the personality cult of the present leader, Kim Jong Il, son of Kim Il Sung, who died in 1994 after almost five decades of rule. One six-page issue of the party paper *Rodong Sinum,* which has a circulation of 1 million, referred to the two men more than 200 times.

South Asia

The press in India is among the oldest and freest in South Asia. It is also one of the most influential in the developing world. Its growth has been phenomenal. At the time of independence from British rule in 1947, only 300 dailies and 2,700 periodicals were being published in the country (Goenda 1996). By 2000, more than 5,000 newspapers and approximately 25,600 periodicals were being published in 92 languages and dialects, with a combined circulation of about 68 million copies. More than 70 newspapers have a circulation in excess of 100,000. The distribution of print media in India is largely an urban phenomenon, with about 80 percent of circulation confined to cities where only 20 percent of the country's population lives. About 30 percent of newspapers are published in the four major cities of Delhi, Bombay, Calcutta, and Madras.

Despite a literacy rate of only 52 percent, the English-language press plays an influential role in the country's political milieu. Mostly owned by large business concerns, English-language publications reach the educated elite throughout the country as well as abroad and are looked on by the government as a barometer of public opinion. Five newspapers rank as elite papers: the *Times of India,* the *Statesman,* the *Hindustan Times,* the *Indian Express,* and the *Hindu.* The English-language dailies are serious in content and tone and are widely known for their comprehensive national and international coverage as well as independent views.

Until the 1970s, English-language publications dominated the print scene. Now Hindi has made a sharp jump, as have other languages. The total circulation of the Hindi press is 19 million; that of the English-language press is 12 million, and the circulation of newspapers in all other languages combined is 37 million. The phenomenal growth of Indian-language newspapers was due to improved literacy rate, economy, and technology, as well as increased political awareness among people.

The regional language press constitutes the bulk of mainstream journalism in India and has a much higher readership than the English-language press. It played an active role in the struggle for Indian independence and still remains the most sought-after vehicle to reach the increasingly literate nonAnglophone provincial population.

Newspapers in India have a huge influence on public opinion as 35 percent of newspaper readers are in the age group of 14 to 24 years. The 1990s saw major growth in investigative journalism in the country. Because terrestrial TV and radio are controlled by the government, newspapers and magazines appeal to readers of every political hue, from die-hard capitalists to die-hard communists.

The news magazines carrying investigative stories have become especially widespread over the last decade. One of the most influential is *India Today* (circulation about 900,000), a political news fortnightly published in New Delhi. In the past few years, however, readership of other periodicals has fallen. But the competition is sharpening in specialized fields. Two areas of new interest are business magazines and technology. *Business Today, Business World*, the *Economic Times,* and *Technocrat,* launched fairly recently, are doing well in terms of circulation.

Discussions about the press in Pakistan must take into account the reality that a majority of the population of Pakistan, about 62 percent, cannot read or write. Today there are 1,330 newspapers in print in Pakistan, although only 1 percent of the population buys a newspaper (Isa 2001, p. 137). A slightly larger number buys a magazine, which totals 1,623. The print media in Pakistan are independent of the government and are mostly privately owned. The influence that the print media have is disproportionate to the number of people who buy newspapers. Major issues of public concern are debated in the newspapers, which help mold and influence public opinion. Given the long absence of democracy and the government's control of TV and radio, newspapers in Pakistan have become the de facto instruments for social change.

Newspapers in Pakistan are mostly in English and Urdu. Among the major national Urdu language dailies are *Jang* (largest circulation daily), *Nawa-i-Waqt, Mashriq* (government-owned), and *Hurriyat.* The major English-language dailies are *Dawn,* the *Muslim,* the *Nation,* and the *Pakistan Times.* The English-language dailies are mostly conservative, whereas the Urdu dailies are more aggressive in expressing viewpoints.

A majority of newspapers are full of political news and essays and hardly carry any cultural and entertainment news. Another characteristic of Pakistani press is its religious orientation.

Weekly news magazines are also widely read in Pakistan. *Akhbar-e-Jehan* (News of the World), a weekly news magazine, has the largest circulation. The Pakistani periodicals dealing with literary and cultural subjects, religion, sports, films, women, science, medicine, health, trade, tourism, and so on are also quite popular.

In the smaller South Asian nations such as Sri Lanka, Bangladesh, Nepal, and Bhutan, prospects for the press have brightened. Sri Lanka has seen a tremendous growth in newspapers and other publications over the past two decades, especially since 1977, when President J.R. Jayawardene considerably relaxed the press controls imposed by previous regimes. In 1979 alone, the circulations of Sri Lanka's newspapers increased by more than 30 percent.

Sri Lanka has a high literacy rate of 89 percent, the highest in South Asia. As a result, Sri Lanka has an extensive reading public. There are many newspapers published in Sri Lanka in English, Sinhala, and Tamil (12 dailies and 84 weeklies).

Some of the well-known general-interest periodicals are *Ferguson's Ceylon Directory, Reader's Relish, Outlook, Public Opinion* (in English), *Ceylon Government Gazette* (in English and Tamil), and *Sinhala* and *Subasetha* (in Sinhalese). Some children's and women's magazines have also become quite popular.

The Bangladesh press also has grown considerably since martial law ended there in 1979. Today, 146 daily newspapers are published in the country. The daily *Ittefaq* (Unity) is the largest-circulation daily published in Bengali language, and *Inquilab* (Revolution) is the second largest. The largest and most influential English-language daily is the *Bangladesh Observer.* Other well-known English-language papers are *Bangladesh Times, New Nation, Daily Stat,* the *Daily Telegraph, Morning Sun, Financial Express,* and *Daily Life.*

Weekly newspapers are quite popular in Bangladesh. Presently, there are approximately 242 weeklies and 132 monthlies, besides several fortnightlies and quarterlies. *Holiday* is the largest-circulation newsweekly in English, and *Bichitra* (Unusual) is the largest-circulation Bengali newsweekly.

In 1998, Nepal had 29 dailies with an estimated circulation of 260,000. Nepali-language newspapers account for more than 82 percent of the circulation. English-language newspapers follow, with more than 16 percent of the circulation (Rao and Koirala 2000, p. 140). The institutionalization of private-sector newspapers began in the mid-1990s, when individuals and companies established newspaper companies to publish dailies. The new constitution of 1991 boosted people's confidence in the industry.

The oldest and the major Nepalese-language newspaper is *Gorkhapatra* (35,000 circulation). Among the major English-language newspapers, *The Rising Nepal,* the oldest English-language daily, established in 1961, is a semiofficial newspaper. The newsweeklies *Jagaran, Spotlight,* and a host of political mouthpieces, bulletins, and literary magazines are also quite popular.

Bhutan, with less than 1 million population, can now boast of publishing its own national newspaper. *Kuensel* (The Enlightener), the country's only newspaper, was sanctioned by the government in 1986 to operate as a weekly. Before 1986 it was a small government newsletter. The newspaper is printed in English, Nepali, and Dzongkha, the official language of Bhutan. Circulation is about 8,500 in English, 2,850 in Dzongkha, and 630 in Nepali. The 12-page tabloid consists of national and international news and features, sports, public notices, and a letters page. It also contains photographs, comics, and a crossword puzzle. Besides the newspaper, there are two general-interest periodicals in Bhutan, *Kuenphen Digest* and *Kuenphen Tribune,* both of which are published in English. In 1997, *Kuensel* received 18 percent of its funding from the government.

In Afghanistan, years of fighting have reduced the media infrastructure in the country to practically nothing. Even before the Taliban came to power, fighting across Kabul in the early 1990s damaged buildings and precious equipment. American bombing in late 2001 destroyed more communication facilities. Journalism also suffered greatly as many skilled journalists left the country. Freedom of expression has been severely restricted in recent times. The new government of Hamid Karzai has promised freedom of the press. The development of the press industry in Afghanistan will to a large extent depend on how successful efforts at rebuilding the country are.

Southeast Asia

Since Vietnam embarked on a market-oriented economic reform and began integrating itself into the world marketplace, more and more people in Vietnam have realized that in today's business world, information is crucial to any enterprise. As a result, there was a boom in the information industry in the country in 1999. Almost every province, ministry, and industry had its own newspapers and magazines, which led Vietnamese lawmakers to complain about a "publication glut" ("Publication" 1999). The lawmakers deemed the glut a waste of Vietnamese press when they discussed a revised press law.

However, in 1997, the press in Vietnam was affected by the Asian financial crisis, just like the industry elsewhere in the region. Circulations of most newspapers were down. Hardest hit were the English-language newspapers, such as *Saigon Times Daily* and *Vietnam News*. About 80 percent of *Saigon Times Daily*'s readers are foreign investors and businesspeople, and many of them were forced to leave the country as a result of the crisis.

There were 8,000 journalists and freelancers working in Vietnam in 2001.

In Laos, the lone newspaper of note, the *Vientiane Times,* which promotes itself as "the gateway to democracy," publishes weekly in English. Generically, the content is little different from what one might find in any U.S. metropolitan daily.

Two newspapers of some substance operate in Cambodia, *The Cambodia Daily* and *The Phnom Penh Post,* both in English. The *Post* promotes itself as representing "Cambodia's independent news and views." The *Asia Observer* also provides Cambodian news and background, and the *Khmer Kampong Speu* offers daily news from the Funcinpec Party. The nonprofit Cambodian Information Center generates what it calls neutral news announcements related to Cambodia.

In Myanmar (Burma), a one-party socialist state, the Information Ministry closed two dailies in 1993 and started three new ones: *Kyehmane* (the Mirror), *Myanmur Lh Lin,* and the latter's English-language version, *New Light of Myanmar,* which continues to publish in a sometimes volatile journalistic climate. In 2002, the World News Network offered an on-line English newspaper, *Burma Daily* (available at Burmadaily.com), which covers Burmese politics, business, economic news, and sports. An underground press flourishes in parts of the country.

In Thailand, a constitutional monarchy and the only country in Southeast Asia with an official Information Act, nothing negative is ever written about the royal family, but almost everyone else is fair game. Politicians and wealthy businessmen use bribes and favors more than restrictive laws to influence stories, which can range from colorful to sensational to downright libelous.

Thailand has scores of daily, weekly, and monthly publications printed in Thai, Chinese, Japanese, German, and English. Two English-language dailies, the *Bangkok*

Post and the *Nation,* have more reliable, less scurrilous content than many of their competitors.

South of Thailand, Malaysia has a tame, development-oriented press, the main constraint on which is a prohibition against publishing anything that might adversely affect national cohesion in this complex society, whose ethnic makeup is Malay (44 percent), Chinese (36 percent), Indian (10 percent), and other groups. Newspapers in various languages reflect this diversity, with some papers away from Kuala Lumpur combining several languages in one publication.

The largest publishing house, the New Straits Times Group, produces the nation's largest English-language daily, the pro-government *New Straits Times.* The group also includes *Berita Harian,* a Malay-language daily. Another English-language daily, *The Star,* used to oppose the government. However, after being banned in 1987, it returned subdued and chastened, having lost many of its reporters to other professions. The lively Chinese press has considerable freedom because authorities do not attend much to outlying periodicals and because the Chinese engage in commerce rather than politics. Other Malaysian newspapers include *Business Times* (English), *Daily Express* (English, Bahasa Malaysia, and Kadazan), *Nanyang Siang Pau* (Chinese), and *The Star* (English).

The Malaysian government has often been critical of the Western media. In May 2002, the Southeast Asia Press Alliance (SEAPA) protested Malaysia's Parliamentary Secretary to the Ministry of Information, Zainuddin Maidin, for remarks made on the eve of World Press Freedom Day. Maidin accused Thai and Filipino journalists of being agents of the Western media imperialists ("Malaysian" 2002).

Singapore, which occupies a 244-square-mile island off the tip of the Malay Peninsula, broke politically with Malaysia in 1965. It has the same ethnic groups as Malaysia but in different proportions: Chinese (67 percent), Malay (15 percent), and Indian (6 percent). By mutual agreement, Malaysia and Singapore newspapers are not distributed in each other's territory.

Thus, the daily newspapers published in Singapore serve a varied readership. Because of a bilingual educational system, many residents read both English and Chinese publications. Indeed, former Prime Minister Lee Kuan Yew encourage the use of English as an integrative force and an aid in international commerce. The number of dailies has fallen since 1980, mainly because of government action to shut them down. The *Eastern Star, Singapore Herald, New Nation,* and *Singapore Monitor* all have ceased publication.

One company, Singapore Press Holdings, dominates the newspaper scene in the city-state. Its flagship publication, the *Straits Times,* has a circulation of about 280,000. Founded in 1845 by Robert Carr Woods, when Singapore had a population of only 40,000, the *Straits Times* served the commercial interests in the seaport. During the Japanese occupation, many staff members were interned.

As if to compensate for frequent closings, new papers spring up frequently in Singapore. In 1988 the *New Paper,* modeled on *USA Today,* began publishing with an appeal to young readers. It promised to avoid politics and offered fun-to-read stories. As if this were not enough for the city-state's 2.7 million people, some 3,700 foreign publications, including the Asian *Wall Street Journal* and *Time* magazine, are imported into the island, but not without certain travails.

In Indonesia, there has been an explosion of press freedom after dictator General Suharto was ousted in 1998. Since then the press industry has experienced ups and downs as a result of the political changes in the country and the financial crisis in the region. The press industry in Indonesia has a hierarchical order—a national press and a regional press (Idris and Gunaratne 2000, p. 275)—very similar to China's press system. Both dailies and nondailies fall into these two categories. But unlike many other countries in the region, Indonesia also has an identifiable and successful rural press.

In Indonesia, newspapers are published in Bali, Jakarta Raya, Java, Jawa Barat, Riau, and Sumatra. One of the most respected and largest dailies is *Kompas*, published in Jakarta, with about 504,000 in circulation in 2000, according to the World Association of Newspapers' *Yearbook*. Because of its serious style and coverage of international events, it appeals to the elitist class of Indonesia. Other Indonesian newspapers include *Indonesian Observer* and *The Jakarta Post*, both published in English. *Jawa Pos, Pikiran Rakyat, Republika, Suara Merdeka, Surabaya Post*, and *Waspada* are all published in Indonesian. *Media Indonesia*, though smaller in circulation, is an outspoken paper.

Magazines published in Indonesia include *Inside Indonesia*, printed quarterly by the Indonesian Bureau of Resources and Information Programs, and *Tempo*, a weekly news magazine published in Indonesian, Japanese, and English. *Tempo* also produces a Philippine edition.

In the Philippines, before the declaration of martial law in 1972, newspapers flourished. In 1972 all media establishments were confiscated or closed, with the exception of the *Daily Express* and Kanlaon Broadcasting's radio and television stations, owned by the family and friends of Ferdinand Marcos. In the final years of Marcos's rule, only four daily newspapers were publishing in Manila. However, within two years of Marcos's fall, 30 daily newspapers were being published in Manila.

The *Manila Bulletin*, with an estimated circulation in excess of a quarter of a million, is the nation's largest and most respected serious paper, supporting the Philippines in its nation-building efforts. *The Philippine Daily Inquirer*, founded in 1985, criticized the Marcos regime and became a very powerful opposition paper. Both the *Bulletin* and the *Inquirer* are published in English. The *Inquirer*, with an estimated daily circulation around 150,000, it is the second largest paper in the Philippines. *The Philippine Star*, founded in 1986 by Maximo V. Solven, is the nation's third largest paper. Among other important Manila dailies are *Business World*, published in English, and *Chinese Commercial News*, which is published in Chinese and offers an on-line version. The *Filipino Express* (English), *Ilocos Times* (English), *Newsline* (English), and *Sunday Punch* (English) are all published weekly.

The Pacific

Most Pacific countries have only one radio station or one newspaper (Gounder 2000). Most papers in the region have small circulations. But since the late 1990s, thanks to desktop publishing, increased literacy, citizen interest in voting rights, and better coverage, circulations of newspapers have registered rapid growth in the Solomon Islands, New Guinea, Vanuatu, Fiji, and the Samoas (Lael 1997). In Pacific countries, government media are giving way to private enterprise, and the viability of private media has been made possible through desktop publishing. A case in point is the *Solomon Star,* which has grown in circulation from 1,000 to 6,000 in its decade of independence with the help of the new technology (Lael 1977).

Papua New Guinea, located north of Australia in the Pacific, claims to have one of the most influential and independent newspapers in the South Pacific, the *Post-Courier.* Papua New Guinea has a larger population than New Zealand but a much less developed press. Like its economic, military, and technical spheres, the press of Papua New Guinea partially depends on Australia. *The Post-Courier* is owned by Rupert Murdoch's News Ltd, other Australian interests, and minority shareholders, such as individual Papua New Guineans (Robie 1999).

The *Post-Courier* is the largest-selling national newspaper in Papua New Guinea, with a daily circulation of 30,000 in 2001 ("Your" 2002) and is published Monday through Friday in English. The *Post-Courier* has a long tradition of vigorous and outspoken reporting. Its circulation reached a peak of 41,000 in 1994. It dropped after a rival daily newspaper, the Malaysian-owned *National,* was launched. After the *Post-Courier* edged back again with steady circulation increases over the next three years, circulation of all of Papua New Guinean newspapers dropped sharply in 1998 in the face of an economic recession. *The National,* also an English daily, had a circulation of 21,036 in 2001, according to the Audit Bureau of Circulations of Australia. In an effort to expand its presence in Papua New Guinea, South Pacific Post Ltd., a subsidiary of News Ltd., planned to launch a chain of community- and provincial-level newspapers in Papua New Guinea.

After a military leader staged a coup in 1987, Fiji's private press was subjected to censorship. Now, with civilian government restored, Suva is regaining its place as the publishing center of the Pacific Islands. The long-established *Fiji Times,* with a circulation of about 27,124 in 2001, competes with the newer *Daily Post,* established in 1987. The *Daily Post* is far from a strong contender, with a circulation of only around 12,000. Another daily, the *Fiji Sun,* had a circulation of 10,000 in 2001, according to the Australian Audit Bureau.

There are two weeklies in Tonga, *Time of Tonga* and *Tonga Chronicle,* with circulations of 8,000 and 5,000, respectively. Other newspapers in the region include *Pacific Daily News,* of Guam, *Cook Island News* and *Samoa News,* of American Samoa. *The Island Tribune,* of Micronesia, *Samoa Observer,* of Samoa, and *Saipan Tribune,* of the Northern Mariana Islands.

Electronic Media

Electronic media in Asia, especially East Asia and parts of Southeast and South Asia, are highly developed. Both radio and television broadcasting began in some parts of Asia soon after they were established in the West. The Philippines, an early adopter, had radio service in the 1920s and television by 1953; Thailand, another pioneer, established radio in 1931 and television in 1954. By the mid-1960s, 18 Asian countries had television. Today, only certain Pacific islands lack TV service. In some areas of electronic media, Asia is the leader. In Singapore, the whole country is wired for cable and Internet access. In fact, Singapore was the first country in the world to set up a national Internet web site, Singapore InfoMap (Kuo and Ang 2000, p. 414). Malaysia is a strong contender with Singapore to be the center of communications in the region. Both China and India have launched communication satellites to beam TV programs to the far corners of their territories, and both conduct commercial launches for other countries.

But the development of electronic media in Asia is rather uneven, with East Asia far ahead of South Asia in general. Within Southeast Asia, development is also unbalanced: there are huge differences between Singapore and Cambodia, for example. The differences in electronic media penetration are surprising, with South Korea's radio and TV receiver penetration rates at 103.9 and 34.8 per 100 people, respectively, in contrast to the radio and TV receiver penetration rates for Myanmar of respectively 9.6 and 0.59 per 100 people.

For the electronic media industry, Asia is an ideal regional market, because Asians have the tradition of immigrating to neighboring countries, especially Chinese, Indians, and the Filipinos. And some cultural influences reach beyond borders, such as Confucianism, Buddhism, and Islam. Diversity and common influence make Asia receptive to regional media, such as Hong Kong-based STAR TV (Satellite Television Asian Region), which sends out programs in Mandarin, Hindi, and English to East Asia, South Asia, and the Arab world, giving it a potential audience of half of the world's population. Being one of the most prominent regional satellite and cable television operations in the world, STAR TV takes programming from a number of sources, principally the United States, Hong Kong, China, Taiwan, India, and Japan. Seeing STAR TV's dizzying profit potential, Rupert Murdoch's News Corporation fully acquired STAR TV by the end of 1995. Revenues come from advertisers in many countries who want to reach STAR TV's audience of about 2 million.

Another regional television news service, Asiavision, has been a major source of news for and about Asia since its launch in 1984.

Developed as they are, electronic media in Asia are mostly tightly controlled by governments for political, social, or cultural reasons.

East Asia

China has more than 10,000 radio stations, covering 90 percent of the population, and more than 3,000 television stations, covering about 88 percent of the population, according to the web site chinatoday.com. By 2001, the number of Internet users in China had reached 30 million, and the number of web sites totaled more than 260,000. A survey on media use published in 2000 found that Beijingers spent seven minutes on average on the Internet every day, much less than the time they spent on traditional media such as newspapers or television. The survey also found that people in Beijing spent an average of two hours 17 minutes on television every day,

58 minutes on newspapers, 57 minutes on books, 41 minutes on radio, and 40 minutes on magazines (*People's Daily*, 19 May 2000). The survey was conducted by a media research institute affiliated with the Renmin University in Beijing, which is known for its journalism program.

Most people in urban China were first exposed to television in 1976 when the funeral of the late Party Chairman Mao Zedong was broadcast on TV. TV sets were provided by the government for public viewing. They were black-and-white TVs about 8 inches in size. That was in the 1970s. Today, TV has become the richest and hottest medium in China because of its impact and power and its entertainment programming. A survey by A.C. Nielsen Media International showed that in 2001, China's television stations reaped $8.1 billion in total advertising revenue, $5.2 billion more than newspapers and $7.9 billion more than magazines.

Television stations in China, like radio stations, are set up along administrative lines: national, provincial, municipal, county, and some communes. They provide news three times a day and entertainment programs, the most popular of which are TV show series, a genre similar to soap opera but with a faster pace, and imported TV programs. Some interactive quiz shows are also becoming very popular. News programs start invariably with official meetings. But other news shows can be nerve-racking for some government officials, such as *Jiaodian Fangtan* on CCTV, which is a kind of talk show that focuses on hot issues, mostly problems. The show has become so popular and has such an impact that it is said Chinese Premier Zhu Rongji has to watch every show.

CCTV is the most powerful and influential television station in China. It can make or break an enterprise. Many enterprises and local governments are ready to pay television stations to do a favorable story about them. Paid news is a serious problem in the industry. There are rules and regulations banning such payment, but often the temptation of money proves too strong to resist.

About access to foreign media, Chinese audiences nowadays can watch programs from ESPN and movies on HBO, but only elite hotels and newsrooms such as the one at *China Daily* have access to CNN. Government regulations ban satellite dish receivers from rooftops or balconies, but many people still install them. China is a large country, and it is difficult to implement the law to the letter.

Radio is still a popular source of news for people in both urban and rural areas because of its convenience. Morning radio news is the most popular. Only in some remote mountainous areas do rural residents still depend solely on radio for news and entertainment. The development of the electronic media in China is rather uneven. Early in 2002, Chinese Vice-Premier Li Lanqing called for improved radio and TV programs in remote western regions ("Vice-Premier" 2002). He said that expanding the radio and TV networks to the inland regions was of great importance in promoting economic development, social stability, and ethnic harmony in the border regions. Media's role in nation-building is always high on the agenda of the government.

Overseas, China Radio International, formerly known as Radio Beijing, represents the voice of the Chinese government. The radio station broadcasts news in 43 languages to the whole world. It has a wide following as well. In 1997, when the station sponsored a knowledge contest on tourism and investment in Sha'anxi, about 260,000 listeners from 155 countries sent in their answers.

The next big challenge for China's TV and radio industry is China's commitments to WTO to open up markets. To prepare for the competition with foreign media, a state radio, film, and television conglomerate was established in 2001 that includes all the major players in the industries.

Internet use is expanding very fast in China as net surfers and domain names keep rising. Foreign capital is trying to get into the fast-developing sector as well. On-line recruitment took off in 2001 as college graduates found it a convenient means to hunt for jobs. The net has also been used for sex education because the topic is an embarrassing one for Chinese parents and children and even at schools. There are many regulations regarding the use and operations of the Internet, especially concerning news, politically sensitive material, and violence and sexual content. Details of regulations are discussed in the government–media relations section.

In Hong Kong, the electronic media are very well developed technologically, and Hong Kong's TV entertainment programs are popular not only in Asia but in Chinese communities overseas as well. Of the limited stock of Chinese movies in American video stores, a sizable portion are kung fu films made in Hong Kong.

Every household in Hong Kong has access to television—about 2 million of them. Hong Kong has more than 38 TV channels for local viewers and hosts several influential regional TV broadcasters as well, such as STAR TV, Chinese Television Network, and Chinese Entertainment Television (So, Chan, and Lee 2000, p. 537). The "Phoenix" channel run by STAR TV was the first to broadcast in Mandarin in Hong Kong in 1996 (*China Journalism Yearbook* 1998). Hong Kong has two commercial radio broadcasters, and each has three channels. Compared with TV popularity in Hong Kong, less than half of the people in Hong Kong listen to radio every day. The Internet is easily accessible in Hong Kong with the island's advanced telecommunications technology.

In Taiwan, although the press is now mostly free, there is still control over the electronic media. The Radio and Television Broadcast Law stipulates that all programs are subject to prior censorship except for news (Wang and Lo 2000, p. 668).

After martial law was lifted, the number of television and radio stations increased. For a long time Taiwan had three television stations, owned by the government, the army, and the KMT (the Nationalist Party). In 1993 the government lifted the ban on new TV stations. In 1997 a new TV station, Formosa Television, came into being with financial support from the opposition party. In 1998, public television went on the air. The expansion of the radio industry followed a similar path. After the government approved additional frequencies for applicants in 1993, private, local radio stations witnessed rapid growth, breaking the domination of national and metropolitan radio stations. Although three of the five television stations and a large number of the radio stations are owned by the government, the army, and the KMT, many of them are commercial in nature (Wang and Lo 2000, p. 671).

Media expansion improves diversity but cuts the profit margin. Broadcasting is even more saturated than the print media in Taiwan, Chen Kuo-hsiang, president of the *China Times Express,* said ("Slumping" 2001). In 2001, Taiwan had seven 24-hour cable TV news channels.

In Japan, the electronic media operate under a dual broadcasting system—the public broadcaster (NHK) and commercial broadcasters (Saito 2000). NHK is Japan's sole public broadcaster. It is independent of both government and corporate sponsorship and relies almost entirely on household reception fees. Commercial broadcasters are affiliates of national networks.

Japan's broadcast law reflects both political needs and cultural values. It stipulates that domestic broadcast programs should not disturb public security, good morals, and manners; should be politically impartial; should broadcast news without distorting facts; and should clarify points of views on controversial issues from different perspectives.

For overseas coverage, Japan's electronic media make frequent use of satellites and have numerous overseas correspondents. Japan has a larger corps of correspondents in the United States than any other country. However, Cooper-Chen (1994) found NHK's news reporting to be the least international of five countries studied.

In entertainment TV programming, Japan's exported animated cartoons for children are universally popular, and it imports major movies. However, it has virtually stopped importing regular series, which means that it must produce all of its own programming—about 150 hours a week for most stations. Considering only one genre, the quiz show, viewers have a choice of 32 domestically produced weekly programs that differ markedly from game or quiz shows anywhere else in the world.

As for the future, TV saturation—one set per 1.8 people—means NHK cannot expect increased revenues from new customers. Nor can TV advertisers expect much more attention to their messages, since the average Japanese already watches 4 hours a day. But the Internet market in Japan is still expanding. While Europe is building expectations of what its mobile Internet will be, the Japanese market has already created 35 million subscribers to the mobile Internet services.

The penetration of television in South Korea stands at nearly 100 percent. There are two public broadcasting networks, KBS and MBC, and one commercial network, SBS, in South Korea. It also has one government-owned educational broadcasting network, EBS, and cable television companies (Heo, Uhm, and Chang 2000). Korean broadcast programming focused on national and political interests until the 1980s, but since then programs have become more commercial.

In 2001, the credibility of public broadcasting was cast into doubt when it supported the government's "newspaper directives," which initiated outside regulation of newspaper sales and advertising (Jim 2001; Kim 2001). In the broadcast sector, the Korea Broadcasting Advertising Corporation, a government agency that sets the advertising rates, has maintained a monopoly over the entire broadcast advertising industry in Korea since its establishment in 1981 (Heo, Uhm, and Chang 2000), which means all Korean and foreign advertisers have to deal with the government agency if they want to buy airtime.

South Korea has more than 200 TV sets per 1,000 people, while North Korea has only 12. In recent years, relations between the two sides have relaxed, but still little South Korean content gets through to the North, since all radios have fixed dials to receive domestic programs only.

South Asia

In 2001, representatives from South Asian countries gathered for a workshop on community radio in the small town of Kothmale in Sri Lanka. Organized by the University of Sri Lanka and UNESCO, the workshop aimed at working out a plan to make community radio a reality in South Asia and encouraging cooperation among community radio advocates in South Asia. Radio remains the principal broadcast medium throughout most of South Asia, and in some places, especially rural areas, where illiteracy is widespread, it is more important than newspapers. It is particularly well suited to the communication needs of nations with a multiplicity of languages and cultures and where mountainous terrain (such as in Afghanistan and Nepal) is a formidable obstacle to television transmission. The development of inexpensive battery-operated transistor sets has greatly increased the size of radio audiences everywhere. Some governments have made radio programs more available to rural masses by establishing community listening centers.

In India, many new players have entered the broadcast industry over the past 10 years, most of them private. Satellite television has established its presence and power over the Indian market. Although multiple players are an indication of democracy and plurality, the vast majority of the Indian population and their interests are underrepresented in the media. It is not surprising that programming is targeted at a small segment of the urban and semiurban middle class, which wields significant buying power.

With the media explosion in the country, the government-controlled media, Doordarshan (Distant Vision) and All India Radio (AIR), have realized that they are no longer the sole providers of media content. However, while admitting private corporate players to the media playing field, the government has remained deaf to calls for community radio and community television.

Milestones in the Indian broadcast industry include the first satellite broadcasting, in 1975, which helped take television signals to remote areas for entertainment, education, and development. The Gulf war of 1991 was another major landmark influencing television scene in the country, when CNN was the first to beam transnational signals on the war. These transmissions by CNN opened up enormous possibilities. A large number of young entrepreneurs saw the potential of this as a viable business activity. They initiated the present mode of distributing satellite signals through a cable network to individual households. Rupert Murdoch's STAR TV network followed CNN into the market in India in 1992, providing programs ranging from soap opera to movies, music, sports, and news.

Today, out of 70 million TV households of the country, about 37 million receive satellite channels. The increase in the number of channels has been exponential, especially in the Indian regional languages (Joshi 2000).

Doordarshan now faces real competition. Gone are the days of monopoly, as this national television authority of the government of India has to reorient itself to compete with its rivals. In 1993, Doordarshan launched five new satellite channels. After more than 30 years in operation, Doordarshan has grown into a giant network.

All India Radio is one of the largest radio systems in Asia, with 170 stations broadcasting for a total of more than 700 hours a day. The programs, which are radiated from 190 transmitters, cover 95.7 percent of the population spread over 85 percent of the country's area. No other medium in the country has a comparable capacity to reach such a gigantic mass of people.

As a development-oriented radio station, AIR regularly broadcasts programs on family planning, health, hygiene, nutrition, vocational training, farming, industries, and various other aspects of rural life. AIR also provides programs for special audiences, which include women and children, students, youth, and senior citizens.

In Pakistan, the government decided to free the electronic media from government monopoly in 2000. The adviser to the chief executive on information, Javed Jabbar, said that a framework was being evolved to allow Pakistan Television (PTV) and Radio Pakistan to compete with private channels ("Government" 2000). But PTV and the Pakistan Broadcasting Corporation will continue functioning in the public sector. The government has no plans to privatize radio and television in Pakistan, but private individuals will be able to set up their own TV and radio stations ("Private" 2000). The government also reduced Internet connection charges for Internet service providers by more than 50 percent in an attempt to boost use of Internet and the information technology industry.

Radio Pakistan has been providing information, education, and entertainment for listeners since it came into existence in 1947. In Pakistan's multilingual, largely rural society, radio is an extremely powerful communication vehicle that transmits programs in 21 languages. In cities, three of every four households have radios, and in villages, two of three households have radio sets.

The Central News Organization of Radio Pakistan offers Home Service, External Services, and World Service to keep the listeners abreast of latest news. The radio is also considered an effective medium for farm broadcasting. Introduced on an experimental basis in 1966, farm programs have become an integral part of Radio Pakistan. Over 60 percent of the farmers depend on Radio Pakistan for agricultural information and guidance. Eighty percent of Pakistan's population lives in villages, and radio plays a tremendous role as an instrument of change, education and information.

Pakistan's television reaches more than 82 percent of the total population. Its five production centers provide more than 7 hours of transmission daily to over 10 million viewers. Like India, Pakistan also uses television to promote adult literacy. PTV has devised seven major educational programs covering adult functional literacy and formal school/college education.

Radio in Bangladesh is still a government operation, supported by license fees, government subsidies, and advertising. The daily combined broadcasts of all nine stations of Radio Bangladesh total 92 hours. In 1990, there were 406,000 licensed radio receivers in use.

The Bangladeshi government believes in the global free flow of information and made an epoch-making decision of allowing the use of dish antenna to receive foreign television programs via satellites, which is banned in quite a few Asian countries.

Radio is extremely popular in Sri Lanka and is financed by license fees and advertising revenues. Radio programs consist of news, music, and cultural programs and are broadcast in six languages: Sinhalese, English, Hindi, Urdu, Tamil, and Arabic.

Experimental TV began in 1979 as a private venture and was sold to the government later that year. There are three other television networks in Sri Lanka: Rupavahini, another government network; MTV, an independent network TV; and Telshan, which provides countrywide transmissions of local and foreign programs on four channels.

Nepal's broadcast environment has changed radically since the country's transition to multiparty democracy in 1990. New broadcast policies, legislation and regulations have allowed for public interest, community, and commercial FM stations as well as satellite TV distribution via cable and some limited local TV broadcasting.

Radio is used extensively for educational purposes, especially for the rural population. Radio offers programs in agriculture, public health, and family planning. Radio news is broadcast in English, Nepali, Newari, Hindi, and Maithili.

Television in Nepal began in 1982, and the age of satellite communications in the Himalayan Kingdom was ushered in in October 1982 with the installation of the Satellite Earth Station. As the Nepalese are sports fans, there is a separate sports channel, Prime Sports.

Bhutan Broadcasting Service started as Radio NYAB (National Youth Association of Bhutan) in 1973. It broadcasts local, national, and international news as well as developmental issues and music every day in four languages: English, Nepali, Dzongkha, and Sharchop (Eastern Bhutanese). Bhutan had no domestic television service until 1999 (Conlon 2000), when the government believed that the country was ready to produce its own programs. Concern exists that the popularity of foreign films may undermine traditional Bhutanese values and culture. In the absence of television, urban Bhutanese watched rented foreign movies.

In Afghanistan, years of fighting and repression have destroyed the infrastructure of the broadcast industry. American bombing in November 2001 destroyed radio and television transmitters. As a result, the broadcast industry in Afghanistan had to start from scratch.

In Afghanistan, the need for public-service broadcasting has never been greater. A public service broadcaster in the country has to be concerned about a broader clientele, even the nonconsuming classes. It needs to determine and meet the needs of the illiterate, poverty-stricken villager watching TV or listening to radio on a community set in some far-away corner of the country. It needs to worry about minorities—ethnic, religious, linguistic, class or caste—and meet their requirements.

The interim administration of Afghanistan issued a press law in February 2002 that observes the International Convention of Human Rights in order to ensure the liberty of speech. The law allows Afghan citizens, political parties, organizations, and the government of Afghanistan to set up audiovisual establishments. The government's monopoly was thereby dissolved.

Southeast Asia

Myanmar (Burma), Cambodia, Laos, and Vietnam all have state-run, strictly controlled systems. Radio Myanmar programs music extensively, with its spoken messages reinforcing the ideological content of the press. Television came to the country in 1980. Currently, MRTV, the government-operated Myanmar television, broadcasts on Channel 6, with a number of repeaters distributed around the country. Radio Myanmar is also government operated. Myawaddy Television is operated by the military.

The Voice of Cambodia, a nonprofit, non-governmental organization (NGO) established in 1995, broadcasts in English on an AM frequency and on several shortwave frequencies received in South America. Remarkably free of the typical governmental controls, it claims to promote democracy, freedom of speech, freedom of the press, and freedom of expression. Voice of Cambodia International provides on-line news and music programs on a radio station web site. In addition, there are seven national television networks, two of which also operate FM radio stations, and a national radio network, National Radio of Cambodia.

Television came to Vietnam in 1966, introduced by the U.S. government in the midst of the war. There are three principal entities: Central Television, the State Committee for Radio and Television, and the Voice of Vietnam (VOV). The last operates two national services and numerous local ones. There are three national television networks, VTV 1, 2, and 3. The first programs news in English and French, the third in music, art, sports, and advertising. There are also five regional television networks.

Laos, in addition to taking advantage of signals from Thailand, has national radio and television networks, both of which are government operated. TVNL offers a separate mix of international programs. Radio Free Asia is also available via shortwave, as is Voice of America. Radio Nationale Lao provides external radio programming in Cambodian, English, French, Thai, and Vietnamese.

Thailand has six television networks, including Royal Thai Army Television. There is also a Royal Thai Army Radio outlet. There are more than a dozen cable and satellite television broadcasters, including Buddhism and Christianity channels. Almost all Thai operators have official status through links with the military, public universities, the royal household, and similar entities, but private entrepreneurs often handle the actual program scheduling, then share profits with the operators. About 90 percent of Bangkok homes have TV sets. Content includes both Thai and foreign syndicated material, much of the latter from the United States. The independent producers previously concentrated on entertainment but now have begun news analyses, news magazines, and on-site, probing reporting.

In Malaysia, the Ministry of Information keeps tight control over broadcasting. Radio-Television Malaysia (RTM), established in 1963, runs two TV channels, receiving revenue from licenses and commercials. It also operates seven radio networks. The government party, UMNO, owns most of the shares in a third TV channel. RTM operates out of a modern $19 million facility in Kuala Lumpur. There are also dozens of local radio stations, virtually all broadcasting on FM frequencies.

On Malaysian TV, advertising for products such as tobacco, alcohol, and blue jeans is forbidden, as are scenes of sex and violence. Entertainment content, including imports, must reflect Malaysian values. News programs portray the government positively. CNN is not available.

Singapore's Ministry of Communications and the Singapore Broadcasting Authority (SBA) control much of what occurs in television and radio in Singapore. The SBA's purpose is to regulate and promote the broadcasting industry in Singapore. The Singapore Broadcasting Corp. (SBC) broadcasts in Malay, English, Chinese (Mandarin and a number of dialects), and Tamil. In addition to Singapore television broadcasting, Radio Corporation of Singapore (RCS), operates 13 domestic and three international stations. Overseas radio service blankets much of Southeast Asia with broadcasts in English, Mandarin, and Malay. Radio East West programs 20 channels of music.

Anticipated eventual media privatization may not end censorship, even on pay TV, however. As in Malaysia, sex, violence, homosexuality, and drug use may remain forbidden topics. Public affairs programs, which in the past stressed racial tolerance and national unity, are also expected to change little. Still, in March 1999, Channel NewsAsia, an arm of profit-driven MediaCorp, launched an English-speaking television operation in Singapore, promising "insights from the inside" in programming "created for Asians by Asians."

Because Indonesia is made up of isolated islands scattered across thousands of miles and has a low literacy rate, radio is the nation's only true "mass" medium. The state-owned Radio Republik Indonesia (RRI) is the largest network in the country, founded in 1945, within days of the country's declaration of independence.

The current policy of RRI is directed at improving the broadcast quality available to formalized groups of rural listeners, who play an important part in the nation's overall information strategy. That strategy is aimed at creating an equal and balanced flow of information.

Televisi Republik Indonesia (TVRI), the state-owned television service, started in 1962 with the cooperation of the Japanese government in preparation for the Fourth Asian Games. Today there are television broadcasting stations in major towns and hundreds of transmitters in various provinces, which enable the population in border areas and remote places to watch national programs. Privately owned television networks or stations include Rajawali Citra Televisi Indonesia, Surra Citra Televisi, and PT Indosiar.

Indonesia has its own domestic communications satellite system, Palapa, which was launched in 1976. As a result, television is received in the most isolated villages and has enabled the cultures of smaller minority groups to be exposed nationally.

Currently in Indonesia there are five national television networks, eight cable or satellite television broadcasters, three national radio networks, 700 local radio stations, over 650 of them privately owned, and three shortwave broadcasters.

In the Philippines, with the "free access" policy of the new governments after Marcos, radio stations and television channels are multiplying. Radio may be the most important medium in the rural reaches of the country. Studies indicate that radio programming, including broadcast music, serials, mysteries, soap operas, and contest shows, is within reach of the bulk of the population. Radio talk shows are increasingly popular and influential. Most radio stations are owned and controlled by powerful, wealthy families. The Catholic Church also exerts tremendous influence over the Philippines' population through its group, Radio Veritas, which runs 45 radio stations throughout the Philippine islands. Radio Veritas's programming is aired in about 35 dialects. There are five privately owned television networks and one public network in the country.

It is clear that television penetration, at least in terms of receivers per capita, is greatest in Singapore, with Thailand and Malaysia not far behind. Elsewhere, however, particularly in Myanmar, Cambodia, and Laos, penetration is minimal. The implications are especially grave in countries where use of print media is restricted because of low literacy rates, such as Myanmar, Cambodia, and Laos. Elsewhere, substantially greater literacy rates may offset to some degree the lack of access to television.

Internet journalism is developing a substantial presence in a number of Southeast Asian countries, among them Thailand, the Philippines, Malaysia, Indonesia, Singapore, and Cambodia.

In Thailand, the *Chiang Mai News* is distributed in English, and *Thainews* in Thai. The Philippines have four Internet news sources, all of which distribute their product in English: *GMAQuest, Philippine Headline News, South Hearld,* and *Tarlac News*. Malaysia has *The Edge* and *Malaysia Kini,* both published in English, and *Malaysia Daily News,* published in German. In Indonesia there are six Internet news sources, and in Singapore two. Indonesian outlets include *Astaga.com* (Indonesian), *BerPolitik* (Indonesian), *Eramuslim* (Indonesian), *Detikcom* (Indonesian), *Indonesian Observer* (English), and *Mandiri* (English). In Singapore, *Electric News Paper* is published in English. So is *NTUC News*. Vietnam's *Mekong Sources.com* offers business information, daily news, weekly editorials, and news clips concerning energy, agriculture, telecommunications and the stock market. *Vietnam New Headlines Online* offers worldwide business, political, and governmental news about Vietnam, and *Vietnam News.net* provides similar fare. Khmer news and other information is offered on the Cambodian News and Information web site.

The Pacific

Many Pacific radio stations are still under the control of the governments, either directly or indirectly, and are heavily influenced by their colonial history—the influence from Europe, Australia, and New Zealand (Craddock 2000). The development of electronic media in the Pacific region faces many problems, including funding, government interference, low salaries, inadequate training, outdated equipment, and multiple languages. Despite those difficulties, radio serves as the only timely link between many islands and the rest of the world. Even those islands that lack a daily newspaper have a radio system.

The Cook Islands Broadcasting Corporation incorporates public broadcasting aims into its radio objectives. In the Marshall Islands, the radio system is a mixture of public service radio, commercial broadcasting, and automated satellite radio feeds for United States military personnel and families. A number of radio stations in the South Pacific and television stations broadcast "stale news," because "to try and be the first with the news is more the exception than the rule" (Craddock 2000). To beef up news coverage, Radio New Zealand International and Radio Australia supply much of the up-to-date news on the Pacific events. The Australian station has several reporters around the Pacific; the New Zealand station relies on a few freelancers and telephone interviews.

As a commercial venture, radio is unlikely to be sustained by market forces in the small Pacific countries. Radio Tonga and the Solomon Islands Broadcasting Corporation run side businesses to bring in money for their station funds, such as selling electric appliances and servicing other electronic equipment (Seward 1999). Other stations supplement their operation funds with payments for broadcasting birthday calls, pending events, and death notices, a unique flavor to Pacific radio through the broadcasting of personal family histories.

In Papua New Guinea, there are eight AM radio stations, 19 FM stations, 28 shortwave radio stations, and three television stations. In Samoa, Radio 2AP has a staff of three serving a population of more than 170,700, while in Tonga, a population of about 97,800 is served by eight staff members involved in radio news production (Seward 1999).

For the television industry, except for funding problems, virtually all Pacific nations and dependencies could link into Intelsat even if lack of facilities and staff limited local productions. Although television has been established in several island states, videocassette systems continue to thrive throughout the region. A cassette circulation network is a creative alternative to television in places that cannot or choose not to go the TV route.

News Services

The existence of myriad news agencies in Asia holds out both hope for better information availability and the specter of managed news flows. The various patterns found in Asia include the presence of a government agency only, government and private agencies operating side by side, private agencies only, private agencies subject to indirect government control, and regional cooperation of various kinds.

There are two regional news services in Asia. The Asia News Network is a network of national daily newspapers published in Asian cities. Depthnews, a development news service established in 1969, caters to clients throughout the Asian region and serves as a voice for Asian development journalism. *Depthnews* stands for development, economics, and population themes.

Most Asian countries have national government news agencies; the exceptions are Bhutan, Fiji, Taiwan, and Japan. The national agencies in Asia range from those that act solely as gatekeepers, such as the Korean Central News Agency of North Korea, which controls domestic consumption of news from regional and international sources, to those that do active local reporting.

East Asia

China has two news agencies. One is Xinhua, the other is the lesser-known China News Service, targeted toward the overseas Chinese population. Both are owned by the government. For domestic news, Xinhua has more than 30 bureaus across the country, employing nearly 3,000 people. Oversease, Xinhua has 101 bureaus in 92 countries, employing more than 500 people. In 35 other countries, Xinhua hires locals as its editorial staff. In overseas bureaus, Xinhua correspondents are classified as diplomats and enjoy diplomatic immunity. With a total staff of more than 5,000, including staff at its headquarters in Beijing, it transmits about 50,000 words daily to the Chinese media and about 60,000 words overseas in six languages. It also monitors all incoming news. To be competitive economically, Xinhua has added several publications of its own: the *Xinhua Daily Telegraph, Economic Reference News, Outlook,* and *Semimonthly Talk.*

China News Service also has bureaus inside and outside China, employing about 500 people. The agency claims to be the first in Asia to put a Chinese-language media outlet on the Internet.

The only news agency in Hong Kong is Hong Kong China News Agency, established in 1956 (*China Journalism Yearbook* 1998). Its target audience is overseas Chinese media and people in Hong Kong, Macao, and Taiwan, which are its areas of news coverage as well.

Kyodo is a nonprofit cooperative organization run on an annual budget, that is primarily made up of membership dues and revenues from nonmember subscribers. It has bureaus in about 40 countries. For its large domestic clientele, it produces more than 200,000 Japanese characters a day, while for overseas subscribers it sends out about 40,000 words a day in English. The English service has recently responded to increased demands for news about Japanese sports.

Jiji Press, a business-oriented private agency, also was born in 1945. Like Kyodo, it produces domestic Japanese and overseas English stories, and it also sends out about 12,000 words a day in Chinese.

South Korea, North Korea, and Mongolia all have government news agencies.

South Asia

Among South Asian countries, India has a diverse national news agency system, including four major agencies and several other specialized agencies. The largest and the most widely known is the privately owned Press Trust of India (PTI), a nonprofit cooperative owned by the country's newspapers like the Associated Press of the United States. Established in 1947, PTI supplies news to 450 newspapers in India and scores abroad. All major TV and radio channels in India and several abroad, including the BBC in London, receive the PTI service. With a staff of over 1,600, including 400 journalists, PTI has more than 100 bureaus across the country and foreign correspondents in major cities of the world.

In Pakistan, there are three major news agencies. News Network International (NNI), established in 1992, is the largest independent international news agency in the country. Besides providing services to more than 100 national and regional newspapers, published in English, Urdu, and Sindhi languages, NNI has subscribers in America, Europe, the Far East, South Asia, Central Asia, the Gulf states, and the Middle East. NNI has a network of 700 correspondents, reporters, and stringers throughout Pakistan. The other two news agencies are Pakistan Press International (PPI) and The Associated Press of Pakistan (APP).

Bangladesh has three news agencies: Bangladesh Sangbad Sangstha, a news service in English, owned by the government; United News of Bangladesh, a computerized news service with latest equipment established in 1988; and Development Features Agency.

Sri Lanka has two news agencies, Lankapuvath (National News Agency of Sri Lanka) and Sandesa News Agency.

Nepal's news agency, the Rashtriya Samachar Samiti, was founded in Kathmandu in 1962. The agency is owned by the government and its chairman is appointed by the government.

Bhutan has no news agency.

Southeast Asia

With UNESCO's encouragement, a number of countries established national news agencies in the 1970s. In late 1980s, Burma, Cambodia, Laos, Indonesia, Malaysia, the Philippines, Singapore, and Vietnam all had government news agencies. Cambodia's pro-Vietnamese news agency, Sapordamean Kampuchea, employs more than 100 reporters, making it that nation's largest single news operation. Thailand's Thai News Agency is an exception in its freedom from direct government control.

Pursuant to a 1967 act of parliament, one of the largest Southeast Asia news agencies, the Malaysian National News Agency, was established in 1968 under the country's Ministry of Information. Known as Bernama, the agency has offices in all Malaysian states, correspondents in Singapore and Jakarta, and stringers in Washington, D.C., London, Manila, New Delhi, Dhaka, and Melbourne. In late 1998, Bernama began dissemination of its news product via an audiovisual element known as Bernama TV. It has since added the Internet as a distribution channel.

Indonesia has three national news services. Antara, meaning "between" in Bahasa Indonesian, is the major agency.

In the Philippines, with the restoration of press freedom in 1987, the government-owned Philippine News Agency was discontinued. However, a local news agency operates in Mindanao, publishing the weekly *Minda News* under the auspices of the Mindanao News and Information Cooperative Center.

The Thai News Agency (TNA), with headquarters in Bangkok, is a subsidiary of the Mass Communication Organization of Thailand (MCOT), which operates under the jurisdiction of Thailand's prime minister. TNA content is distributed via MCOT television and radio networks and the Internet.

The Vietnam News Agency (abbreviated to TTXVN in Vietnamese, VNA in English) is the official news service of Vietnam. Directly attached to the government, VNA is authorized to make official statements reflecting the country's views on important national or international issues.

The Pacific

PACNEWS, the Pacific News Agency Service, may be the only news agency in the region. Its members include almost all the Pacific island countries. The news agency provides comprehensive coverage of regional events and issues for members and commercial clients. News information is gathered from both broadcasting and stringers, and is then provided every weekday through facsimile or by e-mail.

Government–Media Relations

Asia is a very diverse continent in terms of political system. Government–media relations vary from country to country. Of the major theories of the press regarding global press systems, namely authoritarian, libertarian, communist, social responsibility, development, and democratic-participant (Downing 2002, p. 22), examples of each can be found in Asia, from the libertarian press in Japan to state-owned media in Vietnam and China, where media are supposed to promote party policies, and from development journalism in the Philippines and India to an authoritarian press in Singapore and Malaysia, where governments are very sensitive to critical news coverage and their racial and religious diversity, and thus keep a close watch over the media.

If there is one commonality regarding the media in Asia, it is their role in nation building. Many of the Asian countries were colonies of Western powers before the Second World War. They became independent only after the war, which flattened many of these countries. High on the agenda of national governments across Asia was economic development, which is a long-term goal, given the low starting point and large populations. It is no coincidence that development journalism originated in the Philippines and India. Development journalism comes in many shapes and forms. In more democratic societies, government and the media are partners in nation-building, whereas in societies where governments exercise more control, the media are used as a tool for publicizing government policies and plans and can be punished for disrespect for the governments or their top officials.

Control mechanisms on the press include annual licensing of publications, exorbitant security deposits, confiscation, cutting allowable circulation, controlling newsprint and official advertising, and outright closure. Journalists can be punished under sedition, libel, security, or martial law provisions.

East Asia

In China, news media are owned by the state. The media are expected to follow Communist party and government policies. News media are regarded as a tool for national development, education, information, and entertainment. Media are supposed to be a bridge between the party and the people. The government keeps media in line through regulations and through the appointment or removal of editors.

Ding Guangen, head of the Publicity Department of the Central Committee of the Chinese Communist Party, emphasized in one speech that under no circumstances can the news media alter its role as the voice of the party and the people ("Party" 2001). He said that news media should help promote reform, safeguard social stability, and create a sound environment for the socialist cause with Chinese characteristics. Interestingly, he also said journalists should listen to public opinion in order to tell the truth and write news stories that can stand the test of time.

To formalize government–media relations in China, a press law is being debated in the legislature. Journalists and judges are calling for legislators to enact the law to guarantee the rights of journalists in news gathering. Deputies to the National People's Congress, China's parliament, proposed the enactment of a press law in 2000, and a drafting group has been set up to work on the law. The need for the law arose when some government officials refused to be interviewed by the media. In other cases, journalists' video cameras were broken and some reporters were even manhandled by local governments. Anhui Province took the lead in issuing a regulation in 2000 banning its government from refusing interviews with the press ("Press Law" 2000). Other provinces and cities followed suit. The government now needs the media to fight corruption.

To regulate news on the Internet, the Netnews Bureau of the China Internet Information Center declared in 2000 that commercial web sites without traditional news media background enjoyed no right of news coverage. The government also blocks some sites, such as CBS, CNN, BBC, and *L.A. Times*, for politically sensitive material, and blocks other sites for content deemed objectionable, such as sex and violence. But Fox News, MSNBC, *The New York Times*, *The Washington Post*, *The Christian Science Monitor*, *USA Today*, and ABC can be accessed inside China. It is hard to judge the standard for blocking sites as access availability keep changing. In September 2002, the search engine Google was briefly blocked and rerouted to a Chinese web site, resulting in a media uproar over control of information in China. The action against Google was believed to be prompted by the unflattering information retrieved about former President Jiang Zemin and to be part of the media tightening before the upcoming party congress later in the year.

Relations between the government and media in Hong Kong have been in the spotlight of the world media since Hong Kong was returned to China in 1997. In the five years after the turnover, China has kept its promise of "one country, two systems" regarding Hong Kong affairs, giving Hong Kong a high degree of autonomy except in the areas of foreign affairs and defense. Today Hong Kong remains a capitalist society and maintains its free and open economic system. Media in Hong Kong are mostly privately owned enterprise and are treated as such by the Hong Kong government. In the absence of much government intervention, the operation of Hong Kong's media market depends on the state of the advertising industry (So, Chan, and Lee 2000, p. 539).

Ironically, freedom of the press and freedom of expression were clearly enshrined and entrenched in Hong Kong's written constitution for the first time after 1997 (Cheung 2002, p. 191). The colonial government in Hong Kong had "notoriously illiberal ordinances" to control the press, even though it seldom used them

(So, Chan, and Lee 2000, p. 542). Many of these laws were repealed since 1985, after Britain and China signed the treaty to return Hong Kong to China.

Hong Kong law professor Anne S. Y. Cheung called for attention to the threat to press freedom from the judiciary branch (Cheung 2002). She said, "The problem is that most of the Hong Kong SAR judges are trapped in the pre-constitution mindset" (p. 215). She said the judges value deference to authority more than the respect of civil liberties. She concluded that unless there is an awakening in the judicial attitude, the struggle to protect press freedom in Hong Kong would be a constant uphill battle (p. 193).

In Taiwan, governments have embarked on a road of liberalization since 1987, lifting martial law, repealing the ban on new licenses for newspapers, television, and radio stations, and relaxing policies of control over the media in general. The discussions of Taiwan's independence used to be off limits in the press. Now there are papers openly advocating it, which has a lot to do with the changes in the government in Taiwan. KMT, which is against Taiwan independence, used to be the ruling party. Now the opposition, the People's Progressive Party, is in power and supports independence.

In the electronic media sector, the government still faces challenges in regulating the industry. By the late 1990s it had become obvious that the existing legal framework was no longer adequate as new technologies blurred the line between the media, telecommunications carriers, and computer systems.

Japan and South Korea both have democratic political systems and their media legally are free from government intervention or influence. But media in both countries are described as a "lapdog" rather than a watchdog (Freeman 2000). Confucian thought is a dominant influence in Japan and South Korea even though the Chinese philosopher-educator lived more than 2,000 years ago. Confucius believed that a strong state is the ultimate goal and that all individual interest should give way to national interest. He hoped that the government would be strong and kind and would take care of its people. Confucian philosophy clearly prescribed a patriarchal role for the government. Japan and South Korea prospered under state-guided capitalism. For "national interest," media in Japan and South Korea exercise heavy self-censorship and go easy on the government.

In Japan, controversial media bills—laws to protect personal data and human rights—are being introduced. Ignoring protests from newspapers and broadcasters, Prime Minister Junichiro Koizumi's cabinet approved a bill aimed at outlawing "excessive reporting activities" and "violations of privacy" by reporters (*The Statesman*, March 10, 2002). Japanese legislators and critics pointed out that the bills would put unreasonable restraints on the media ("Media Bills" 2002).

Since South Korea returned to civilian government in late 1980s, the media in South Korea are finally free from the tight control of military strongmen. However, mainstream media in South Korea have always been pro-government except the recent flare-up between the government and the media in 2001 over alleged tax evasion by major newspapers. The government ordered tax investigation of the newspapers and levied astronomical back taxes and jailed media owners, major shareholders in *Donga Ilbo* and *Chosun Ilbo*, the two largest papers in the country.

The *Chosun Ilbo* (Nam 2001) contended that the government crackdown occurred because of the paper's criticism of government policy toward North Korea. It said the government was trying to apply psychological pressure. The government' actions prompted protest from the international media. However, the government's actions were supported by many civic groups. The South Korean government also controls the media through advertising.

South Asia

Governments in most South Asian nations try to restrain the press by providing "guidance" for national development. Media should cooperate, according to the "guidance," by stressing positive, development-oriented news and by supporting government policies and plans for national development.

Besides promoting a guidance concept, most governments use direct censorship, suspend offending newspapers, and arrest journalists who do not conform to the official policy. Direct censorship is prevalent in Sri Lanka, Bangladesh, and Nepal.

In Sri Lanka, direct censorship is permitted under the antiterrorism law and parliamentary privileges can be invoked to shield parliamentary discussion. As a result of direct censorship, Sri Lanka's mainstream publications do not contest the government's viewpoint directly or probe its activities thoroughly. Military censorship is tight in the country because of on-going guerrilla warfare in the country.

The path to press freedom in Sri Lanka may still be long and winding as the court cases against a prominent editor in the country prompted a letter to the Sri Lankan President by the International Press Institute (IPI) in 2001, stating that the institute was deeply concerned over the use of the Sri Lankan criminal defamation laws to intimidate Victor Ivan, a local newspaper editor who exposed corruption and abuse. Ivan, a respected journalist in Sri Lanka who has been honored for his work by the University of Colombo, the Colombo Law College, and the Editors Guild of Sri Lanka, was facing four separate criminal defamation charges over stories about the alleged corrupt conduct of a police officer, apparent abuse in a children's home, a series of articles discussing the administration of the Dalada Maligawa, a Buddhist temple, and an article alleging misconduct on the part of the deputy minister of health.

The war on terrorism puts the media in Pakistan in a spotlight. The Pakistan constitution protects the right to information, even though the absence of a specific freedom of information law is acutely felt. Pakistan is a relatively open society where even when the government sends journalists to court in order to restrain the media, the independent courts often strike down on the government. However, attempts by the government to "guide" the media never stop.

Speaking at a reception in 2002, Punjab Information Minister Mahmood Ahmad urged journalists to support the "government efforts for the promotion of responsible and positive journalism in the country and discourage sensational and yellow journalism" ("Newsman" 2002).

Major political changes took place in Nepal in 1990 as a result of a successful people's movement for the restoration of democracy. The new constitution of 1991 guarantees freedom of expression and thought in general. Article 16 states that every person shall have the right to demand and receive information on any matter of public importance (Rao and Koirala 2000). The press in Nepal helped bring about the political changes in the country after three decades of repression by promoting a freer government and protesting against the restrictions.

The relationship between the media in Afghanistan and the future government is still uncertain as the war on terrorism drove the Taliban from power and installed a transitional government, which has given some new hope for the freedom of the press in the country. The new government pledged an independent and pluralistic media at a three-day seminar held in Kabul in September 2002. The Minister of Information and Culture endorsed this declaration: "The declaration recognizes that Afghanistan must have new laws to protect and promote the media and enable it to play in a important role in making the government open, transparent and accountable and giving all members of society a voice" ("International" 2002).

Even as recently as 2001, the media in Afghanistan were beset by harsh restrictions imposed by the Taliban. Today, journalists in Afghanistan still face the threat of violence for military commanders and others.

India has prided itself on its democratic political system and its long-established tradition of a free and fair press. The only exception was the Emergency Rule under Indira Gandhi (*Statesman*, April 18, 2002). She tried to restrain and censor newspapers. With the lifting of Emergency Rule, Indian press reverted to what is generally considered a free press philosophy in the Western tradition.

The press in India plays a significant watchdog role. Newspapers and news magazines are constantly engaged in aggressive reporting exposing corruption, malfeasance, and nepotism on the part of the authorities in power. Investigative journalists have been quite outspoken in revealing the financial scandals of politicians, including prime ministers. Almost all leading papers have been critical of the government in power.

Like many other Asian nations, the Indian government is still trying to control access to information by introducing a new Freedom of Information Bill in early 2001. Cusbrow R. Irani (2001) criticized the bill by charging that the bill was drawn up by bureaucrats for the benefit and protection of bureaucrats. Liberty of the press must constantly be fought for in most South Asian countries, where the governments allocate newsprint, control advertising quotas, stipulate registration rules, and operate the broadcast media.

Southeast Asia

Confucian influence is also strong in Singapore, where control of the media is very similar to that in Malaysia. In both countries, government knows best and makes sure that the people receive only the right information. When charges are made in the news media against the government or its officials, the government is quick to file libel charges in the courts. Race and religion are taboo topics in both countries.

The Singapore press operates within a strict legal framework (Kuo and Ang 2000, p. 406). Singapore's constitution provides the right to freedom of speech and expression, but that right is limited only to citizens in Singapore, which means that foreign media do not have the right to comment on or to criticize Singapore's domestic politics.

The Newspapers and Printing Presses Act of 1974, the dominant law policing the press, requires annual licensing of daily newspapers. A 1986 amendment to the act gives the government the power to restrict the circulation of foreign publications that engage in domestic politics. The Singapore government fiercely guards not only its political system, but also its culture. Soft-porn and alternative lifestyle publications are handled under the Undesirable Publications Act.

Broadcasting is licensed as well, including the Internet. The Singapore Broadcasting Authority exercises censorship directly through a code of practice. As in China, satellite dishes for private viewing are banned except for the international and financial communities.

In 2002, survey results by the Freedom House for the bulk of Southeast Asia show that media in Burma, Cambodia, Laos, Singapore, Malaysia, and Vietnam were classified as not free, with the situation in Laos deteriorating (Sussman and Karlekar 2002). In Indonesia, too, where media were classified as partly free, open access to information and freedom to publish were being eroded by political extremists and renegade law enforcement. Only in the Philippines and Thailand were media classified as free.

In Indonesia, press licensing has ended, and there are new legal prohibitions against press bans and censorship. But despite its partly free press status, most private, commercial television stations continue to be owned by or have management ties to former President Suharto's family. Private radio stations are required to broadcast material daily that is prepared by government sources, though stations are at liberty to offer their own news programs.

In the tenuous democracy of the Philippines, hundreds of radio stations and newspapers proffer disparate perspectives and opinions. The constitution, ratified in 1987, says: "No law shall be passed abridging the freedom of speech, of expression, or of the press, or the right of the people peaceably to assemble and petition the government for redress of grievances." The Philippine media operate under one of the laxest systems of state supervision in Asia (Coronel 2000). Since the country returned to civilian rule, no government body oversees or supervises the press. No license or permit is required to publish a newspaper or magazine.

In Thailand, while media can and do offer diversified perspectives, prison terms can be levied for various journalistic transgressions, including insulting the head of state. The press, broadcast media, and the Internet are prohibited from distributing material regarded as sexually explicit or as promoting ethnic, racial, or religious hatred or intolerance. Moreover, there is no legal framework guaranteeing access to public information. Here as elsewhere, journalists are subjected to threats and physical attacks, as well as government and economic pressure designed to limit criticism of officials and their behavior. Warnings have been issued to a number of publications, and recalcitrant media are punished through punitive use of advertising allocations.

In Malaysia, annual renewal of licenses is required for print and broadcast outlets, and the renewal often depends upon government-friendly coverage. Radio

Television Malaysia, the country's state-operated, chief electronic outlet, is predictably deferential in its treatment of government policies.

In Vietnam, all news media are state-owned, and news content is controlled through antidefamation and national security constraints imposed on journalists and publishers. While government policies may be criticized with relative impunity, the Communist party cannot. Unofficial national policy prohibits dissent, and critics have been arrested.

In Laos, the lesser-known communist country in Asia, all newspapers and broadcast media are owned by the government, which rigorously controls content. Legislation mandates pro-government news coverage and imposes criminal penalties on those found to have published "misleading" news on the Internet. Reports viewed as contrary to prevailing political dogma or conflicting with governmental objectives can be the basis for prison terms of five to 15 years.

All Burmese media are owned and content carefully controlled by the military junta governing the country, now known as Myanmar. Coverage of a number of subjects is proscribed, and pre-publication censorship is not unusual. Foreign journalists are frequently denied admission to the country and are obliged, as a consequence, to report in absentia, usually from Thailand.

In Cambodia, criticism of the government is viewed as treasonous. Among the results is that journalists typically turn to government officials, who are invested in maintaining the status quo, as sole sources of authoritative information. While the private press is sometimes critical of government policies, it is also subject to whimsical application of a 1995 law allowing the government to impose a 30-day moratorium on publication and to impose criminal penalties as well. Almost all TV stations are owned by government officials or their associates.

The Pacific

In the Pacific countries, media suppression does not reach the magnitude seen on the Asian continent. In Papua New Guinea, for example, critical viewpoints are allowed on the government-controlled radio system. But still Pacific news media are waging a "constant battle" against government pressure but remain a vital barometer of the region's well-being, as chiefs and politicians in the Pacific use influence drawn from tradition, custom, and honor of authority as a shield for immunity from criticism and unlawful actions (Seward 1999).

Pacific Weekly Review ("Media Freedom" 2002) reported that the Cook Islands attempted to stifle scrutiny of the "big lies" of politicians over the Pacific solution on asylum seekers, the war on terrorism, and a bitter exchange between media commentators. The new Port Vila–based regional newspaper said: "In the Pacific, there is a general acceptance of the need for a free press, which can help in nation-building and in creating open and accountable governments." But incidents threatening press freedom occur from time to time. The paper listed threats made against *Cook Islands Herald* publisher George Pitt by a government that had suggested "Zimbabwe-style" press restrictions and called on governments not to use the war on terrorism as an excuse to crack down on freedom of expression.

The threat to press freedom in the region is vigorously alive (Seward 1999). The Tongan Crown Prince once said that there is no need for democracy to flourish. Many of the government officials in Pacific island countries regard democracy and freedom as Western concepts that do not suit their society. Even though globalization and world culture do have an impact on media in the region, it remains a fact that when an event is to be covered for the media, it is most likely to be explored by a journalist outside the region. The most typical news from Pacific commentators is silence (Seward 1999).

Concepts of Media Freedom

Media freedom is available to more people in Asia today than 15 years ago, and media responsibility and ethics have become a big concern in new democracies. Credibility of the media is in serious crisis because of sensationalism, factual inaccuracies, self-interest of the press owners, and self-censorship.

When we examine the state of the press freedom in Asia, it would be helpful to use the "four theories" concept (Siebert, Peterson, and Schramm 1956, 1963), which have now expanded into five or six theories (Hachten 1987, 1992; Downing 2002), as a tool. But we have to remind ourselves that we are borrowing a yardstick developed in the West to measure Oriental media systems, and we may run the risk of pigeonholing media systems in theory concepts that do not fit. The same caution should be exercised when we examine Freedom House's rankings of press freedom in the world. How accurately do those indexes reflect the reality of press freedom in those countries?

For example, Japan is rated in the Freedom House survey as having the freest press in Asia in 2002, with an index of 17, where 100 equates with total government control. The other end of the spectrum is North Korea, with an index of 96. But does Japan have the freest press in Asia? The Japanese press operates under a unique "press club" system, which channels information from the government and corporations to the journalists. The press clubs act as gatekeepers and suppliers of information to the media. The system is criticized for discouraging independent and thorough reporting and for the uniformity of content in the Japanese press. Because Japanese journalists hesitate to break corruption stories (because of their close ties to the news sources through the press clubs), Japanese journalism has been described as a "pro-establishment style of journalism" (Saito 2000). When the Asian financial crash first hit in 1997, the media in Japan were criticized for not keeping the people informed about the problems and irregularities of the financial sector. The press in Japan may be free from government control, but it is to a great extent controlled by other social institutions such as the press clubs and social and professional norms regarding what is acceptable professional behavior. Given that much social control, industry pressure not to compete, and self-censorship, can we still say Japan has the highest degree of media freedom in Asia? The standards used in the Freedom House survey to measure media freedom may have to be reconsidered.

However, Western theories of the press can be helpful in classifying media systems in the world in broad terms, even though countries put under the same label may vary greatly regarding media freedom. Of all the theories of the press developed so far, the four most helpful for studying Asian media systems are authoritarian, libertarian, communist, and development journalism.

Anarchist Libertarianism

In Indonesia, Taiwan, and the Philippines, news media are enjoying unprecedented freedom after decades of government suppression and repression. After long periods of rule by a strongman, authoritarian governments in these countries gave way to democratically elected but weak governments, which have yet to establish trust and credibility among the people. When governments are weak and their rule is ineffective, media enjoy complete freedom from government control. Also, when the rules, regulations, and bans were first lifted, the enthusiasm to start up news media organizations was high, and the number of newspapers in these countries no longer requiring license sharply increased.

But the crowded market and the financial crash forced many of the new papers to close down. As competition intensified, freedom of the press was abused and yellow journalism ruled. In Indonesia, now that the media enjoy so much freedom, the main problem is a lack of ethics among journalists. More and more journalists are violating the most sacred principle of the profession: tell the truth ("Press Credentials" 2000). Journalists in Indonesia today are accountable to no one but themselves and their proprietors. The ministry of information was abolished, and gone also is the licensing mechanism. In 1999, a new press law was put in place to guarantee freedom and promise punishment for those who obstruct the profession.

Free as they are, Indonesian journalists still face violence and intimidation in their profession. In 2000, there were 106 cases of oppression against journalists and the media, with almost half of them, 47 cases, perpetrated by the public ("Journalists" 2001). The government also is trying to intervene in the business as well. It reversed almost four years of relaxing media restrictions by banning one of the highest-profile foreign correspondents working in the country (Aglionby 2002). Freedom is still vulnerable and fragile in Indonesia.

In Taiwan, which started to enjoy press freedom after martial law was lifted in 1987, media still have to learn how to use that freedom responsibly. Political discussions are much more open in the press, even though the media spend a lot more energy on crime stories or the private lives of public figures than investigating the government. A magazine, the *Scoop Weekly*, included a VCD of an alleged sexual encounter of a female legislative candidate. The magazine argued that the VCDs were given to the readers as "evidence" supporting the veracity of its investigative reporting ("Freedom" 2001). Reporters in the rush to be the first to get the story out sacrifice accuracy in their reporting rather than find credible sources to check out the facts. And sometimes news gathering and reporting get in the way of solving kidnapping cases. "The freedoms that were so hard to obtain, ironically, now threaten some parts of a society that considers the press the enemy because of its influence and power" (Luwarso 2002) "Freedom of the press" has been condemned as the "freakdom of the press." Some members of the public even called for the press to be brought under control again.

The electronic media in Taiwan still have close ties to the government and political parties. Nine legislators host TV or radio talk shows, and six lawmakers serve as chairmen of newspapers and TV stations (Tsai 2001).

The Philippine press today claims itself to be the freest in Asia, even though broadcasting is subject to greater regulation. Sheila S. Coronel (2000) described the Philippine press as "rowdy," "vibrant," "pluralistic," and "anarchistic." She said Filipino journalists are noisy and powerful. Media exposes have caused the resignation of officials and raised public awareness about important issues. Because of their recent past, Filipino journalists guard their freedom fiercely and are strong believers in the adversarial role of the press as the watchdog of the government.

However, press freedom in the Philippines has been pushed to the extreme and is often abused. Media are being criticized for irresponsible and sloppy report-ing, for "checkbook journalism," and for using their freedom to commercially exploit the public's taste for the sensational (Coronel 2000). The news media have also used their freedom to outdo rivals in the race to peddle newspapers and television programs. Media owners sometimes use their newspapers to defend and advance their business and political interests.

The threat to press freedom in the Philippines today mostly comes in the form of economic pressure rather than government intervention. The press sometimes has to soften critical reporting because of withdrawal of advertisements, bribery, or the linking of business success in other sectors to the editorial line of the owner's newspaper. Media in the Philippines remain vulnerable to pressures on their proprietors and protective of the interests of their owners (Sison 2001).

Reporters sometimes have to defend press freedom with their lives. The Philippines have a high casualty rate of community journalists. There is less toler-ance for critical reporting in the provinces. The New York–based Committee to Protect Journalists puts the number of Filipino journalists killed since 1986 at 33 (Coronel 2000). Many of these killings remain unsolved.

Self-Censoring Libertarianism

Japan and South Korea probably have the most self-censored press in Asia, despite the fact that journalists in both countries may be the best trained in the region. Even though constitutions from both countries guarantee the freedom and independence of the media, newspapers in both countries choose to operate under the press club system.

Both Japan and South Korea have a political system of Western democracy, but their culture is clearly Asian and deeply rooted in Confucianism. Media would rather choose to respect the government and big business than muckraking them, as the media are often conscious of what kind of image the government wants to have.

A typical example is the self-censorship exercised by Japanese journalists in discussions of the imperial family. When Emperor Hirohito died in January 1989 after 62 years of rule, Japanese television showed scenes of Japanese invasion from the 1930s and 1940s. However, the programs neither showed footage of the "rape of Nanking," called in Japan "the Nanking incident," in which 300,000 civilians in the city of Nanjing were massacred by the invading Japanese troops, nor did it discuss in any depth the occupation of Korea. The emperor was portrayed as peace-loving but manipulated, with no alternative explanations offered.

Investigative journalism has never been the strong suit of Japan's mass media. Accuracy and insight mark the material that the media produce, but much of what is going on in the government or the big business does not appear in the media. Willingly sustaining a culture of secrecy, journalists from both countries failed to keep the public informed about the inside story of the financial industry and left them in the dark when the financial crash hit.

Laurie Anne Freeman (2000) has said the media cartels in Japan are composed of the unholy trinity of press clubs, industry associations, and media conglomerates, which makes it possible to muzzle the press, restrain competition, within the media and abuse the public trust. Media in Japan want to keep the status quo, because the industry is doing very well financially.

Hong Kong and Thailand border on anarchist libertarianism and self-censoring libertarianism. Illogical as this may sound, it is the reality of the news media in both countries. Journalists censor themselves when it comes to politically sensitive stories or when it has anything to do with the royal family but resort to yellow journalism when it concerns market competition and nonpolitical stories.

When Hong Kong was officially turned over to China, about 8,000 journalists landed on the island to cover the event, and the Western media focused on the future status of press freedom in Hong Kong. The predictions were very gloomy. Today the media in Hong Kong are still free and open in criticizing the government and its officials. A survey of Hong Kong's news media will produce a spectrum of opinions and interpretations of events. Hong Kong media are as diverse as before. "Contrary to widely held predictions, Hong Kong has continued to enjoy a high degree of press freedom as China seems to have kept its promise of not interfering with the SAR's [Hong Kong's] internal affairs" (So, Chan, and Lee 2000, p. 534). Before 1997, the British government allowed the press to operate freely as long as the press did not pose any real threat to social stability and colonial rule. The colonial government did not exercise censorship or other forms of control outside the general laws. After 1997, the situation has remained largely the same (So, Chan, and Lee 2000).

However, not everyone in Hong Kong agrees that press freedom is as healthy as before 1997. Right before the fifth anniversary of the return of Hong Kong to mainland China, the Hong Kong Journalists Association issued a report stating that the Hong Kong government suppresses public opinion, restricts people's right to assemble, and attacks dissidents. The China News Service (Yu 2002) contradicted such claims. It cited diverse opinions and unreserved criticism of the government in Hong Kong press as evidence of press freedom and said that 95 percent of Hong

Kong's daily rallies and demonstrations are legal. Rallies and demonstrations average six per day.

Self-censorship can be a major threat to an independent and free press in Hong Kong, according to Dan Kubiske (2000). "Some journalists and media are exercising self-censorship for fear of real or imagined pressure from China" (So, Chan, and Lee 2000). However, Arnold Zeitlin, director of the Freedom Forum office in Hong Kong, said that self-censorship is no stronger in Hong Kong today than it was under the British or it is in the United States (Kubiske 2000). The *South China Morning Post* was criticized for less than aggressive reporting about China because the owner of the paper reportedly wants to protect his investment on the mainland.

In Thailand, the royal family is off limits to the media. Like Japan and South Korea, Thailand has a culture of secrecy. Given freedom of the press, journalists are not using that freedom vigorously. Roderick Macdonell, director of the World Bank's investigative journalism program, called on the media in Thailand to step up investigative journalism to help curb corruption and keep the public better informed (Changyawa 2001). However, journalists sometimes abuse that freedom in competition for market share and in inserting bias in covering local controversies ("News That" 2001).

Confucian Authoritarianism

Ever since the appearance of the press, authoritarian media systems have been the most common. Hachten defines this concept as constant direct or implied control from above, with consensus and standardization as a goal and dissent an "annoying nuisance" (1981, p. 17). As long as the press operates within mutually understood boundaries, the government does not intervene.

In Singapore, both the government and the tamed press see the media as a partner with the government in development. One official expressed his distaste for James Bond–style journalists who attack national leaders at will; the pro-government *Straits Times* agreed. It warned Westerners in an editorial not to apply the American ideal of press freedom to a multiethnic society such as Singapore. Similarly, a Malaysian official warned against applying Western-style individual liberties in a non-Western context.

Singapore and Malaysia may be the loudest voices among Asian nations in promoting "Asian values," which emphasize putting the interest of the country, the family, or the group above the interest of the individual, in contrast to Western values of individual rights and freedom. Luwarso (2000) said that Malaysia, Singapore, and Brunei frequently resort to "Asian values," where government controls press freedom and political activity in order to guarantee economic growth. He called Asian values a thinly veiled pretext for authoritarianism and said that Southeast Asia sees its press as a government tool, a "free and responsible" press.

However, governments emphasize responsibility more than freedom. The press is constantly asked to account for itself. Heads of government keep a close eye on the press because they believe that press freedom will lead to anarchy, conflict, and instability. Threats to press freedom mostly come in the form of licensing, lawsuits, and intimidation directed at journalists.

In Singapore, there is more infotainment available than information. All forms of imported material must first pass the censors of the Films and Publications Department. All compact disks and electronic mail are also censored. Singapore's three Internet service providers and one cable television operation all have links to the government. The People's Action Party, Singapore's ruling party, dominates ownership of the mass media through the state enterprise Singapore Press Holdings (Luwarso 2000).

Singapore has the greatest concentration of international media in the region, but the government keeps tight control of the foreign media by limiting their circulation in the country. If foreign media offend the government, their circulation will be cut as a punishment. As a result, foreign media start to censor themselves as well.

In Malaysia, Prime Minister Mahathir Mohamad, a loud critic of Western culture, often emphasizes the social role of the media and sometimes questions the power of the press. News media in Malaysia can be critical of the government and occasionally provoke the wrath of government leaders, especially the prime minister. But the mainstream media are mostly tame and compliant, and thus lack credibility among the public.

Access to information in both Malaysia and Singapore is limited by many existing laws, including colonial-era laws, Official Secrets Acts, Internal Security Acts, and Printing Presses and Publications Acts ("Regional" 2002). But both countries are opening up due to economic factors, leading to various changes relating to disclosure of information.

Not all authoritarian media have a Confucian root. Pakistan is a relatively open society (Isa 2001, p. 146). The press enjoys a lot more freedom than the electronic media. The constitution in Pakistan prohibits the ridicule of Islam, the armed forces, or the judiciary. The country has a strong and independent court system, which sometimes becomes the protector of press freedom and the integrity of public discourse. In one such case Pakistan's Supreme Court struck down an order of the central government prohibiting the publication of a periodical, *The Mirror* (Isa 2001, p. 142). But the government still has strong influence over the media by providing "guidance."

The press in most Pacific island countries belongs more with the authoritarian press model than with the libertarian model, even though it generally enjoys more freedom than the press on the Asian continent. Despite the existence of a critical press and sometimes even radio, governments do take actions against the media, such as the expulsion from Fiji of two German PACNEWS personnel, the relocation of this news service to New Zealand to circumvent editorial control by the Fiji government, and the banning of the Samoa opposition leader from the government-owned Apia radio station—2AP (Seward 1999). There is no live news from this radio station. After the news is written, it is cleared by the prime minister's office.

In 1996, a New Zealand-based Tongan newspaper publisher who had crusaded for democracy in his island kingdom was jailed for contempt of parliament ("Tongan" 2002). Another case in Samoa concerns the publishers of *Samoa Observer,* Sano Mailfa and his wife, who were threatened with physical violence, their plant was burned, and their advertising was cut off for accurately reporting the issuance of illegal passports, rocketing national debt, and details of the crash of a government aircraft in western Samoa (Lael 1997). In Papua New Guinea the government barred three prominent Papua New Guineans from discussing controversial legislation on a talk radio show (Robie 1995). Media controls are also an issue in the Cook Islands when the government bans journalists, attacks the media, and makes it difficult for foreign journalists to visit the country (Robie 1995).

Reforming Communism

Of the remaining communist countries in the world, quite a few are in Asia, including China, Vietnam, North Korea, and Laos. Although North Korea has changed little since the late ruler Kim passed along the power to his son Kim, communism in China, Vietnam, and, to a lesser extent, Laos, however, has taken a new direction as Vietnam and Laos are following China's example in implementing the economic reforms.

According to Hachten (1987), the communist concept holds that a free press, divisive by its very nature, gets in the way of the key job of nation building; by contrast, state-owned media can pursue in unison their tasks of agitating, propagandizing, and organizing. News is any information that serves the state.

That description of communist media is still relevant in today's China. News media in China are still owned by the state, even though state ownership of other industries is on a sharp decline. The government emphasizes a lot more of the "positive role" of the media, that is, what media should report and how media can help national development, rather than what the media should not cover, which often gets killed through self-censorship in the newsroom.

A typical example would be the speech given at the Communist party school in Beijing by party leader Jiang Zemin on May 31, 2002, in which he gave his "three represents" theory for the first time. Jiang's "three represents" theory calls on the party to represent the development trend of China's advanced productive forces, the orientation of China's advanced culture, and the fundamental interests of the overwhelming majority of the Chinese people. His speech is promoted as a new development in Marxist theory and an important political, ideological, and theoretical preparation for the 16th Party Congress to be held later in the year ("Hu" 2002). The "three represents" has become the focus of news coverage in all the mainstream media, be it print, electronic, audio, or visual. Coverage will be for several months until the government is sure that everyone in China gets the point.

What is forbidden from the Chinese news media is diversity of opinion on "sensitive" political topics. When it comes to Fa Lung Gong, for example, there is only one voice, the party's voice. However, Chinese media in the twenty-first century carry a lot more real news than just party voices. In the Chinese press today, there is no lack of negative stories, such as stories about corruption, crime, industrial accidents, or natural disasters, although some labor unrest in the country is hidden from public view for fear of chain reactions. Some journalists in China now say there is plenty of press freedom in China, especially for local papers, so long as the press does not print anything against the party or the political system.

The real free press existed in China in 1989, when the Chinese press covered the mass student-led demonstrations in Beijing before the crackdown by the government. All the official media, including Xinhua News Agency and the *People's Daily*, covered the news events as they were happening in the street without "guidance" from above. But after the troops were sent in to stop the mass demonstrations on June 4, the official version and interpretation of events dominated media coverage.

Because television developed in the post-Mao era, it followed a different pattern from that of the press. According to Rivenburgh (1988), television functions less for political consolidation and more as an entertainment medium.

Internet, the latecomer in the news media, provides a real freedom forum today for the Chinese. Chinese web sites Sina.com, Sohu.com, and China.com all offer free and spirited discussions and sharp criticism about government policy regulating Chinese athletes joining foreign sports clubs. People not only criticize the government policy, they also blame the journalists for siding with the government. Discussion topics are not limited to sports but include political events as well.

News media in Vietnam are in a very similar situation as in China. Its media are owned and controlled by the government. They remain an arm of the government and extol the virtues of the Communist Party. But media in Vietnam are also opening up and the press is freer than it was a decade ago (Lamb 2002). In terms of freedom, the press has been getting better and more aggressive. A clearer press law should help media get more freedom. Hong Phuong, a local journalist, said: "We are now having debates more on 'responsibilities and morals of journalists' than on free press." ("News Often Wounds" 2001).

In the Vietnamese press, readers can find stories on official corruption, slumping exports, the sluggish pace of economic reforms, or the widespread use of drugs. The country's 7,000 journalists routinely report on issues ranging from smuggling to prostitution.

News media in North Korea and Laos are still tightly controlled by the government.

Development Media

Most South Asian governments provide guidance for their news media and use the media as tools for national development. Development media are popular in South Asia may be because all of the countries in the area are underdeveloped. The country in South Asia that is best known for development journalism is India, which is the largest developing country in the region. Ever since its independence from the British Empire, the goal of the national government as well as that of aspiring journalists has been national economic development, even though common goals do not necessarily translate into positive coverage of the government in the press.

People in India expect the newspapers to "don a steering mantle when the need may arise," according to Vivek Goenka, chairman and managing editor of *The Indian Express* (1996). The press in India has largely fulfilled that role. Goenka said that Indian newspapers could not be passive disseminators of news. They have to reflect plurality of opinion and encourage debate, with an objective to serve society and uplift falling societal values.

The Indian Express positioned itself as a responsible corporate citizen only by not stepping up coverage of socially relevant issues, such as the environment, health, and the development of women and children, but also by organizing activities in these areas, such as cancer detection camps and races against pollution. The paper also created campaigns on important social issues such as dowry, old age, and female feticide, and covered these campaigns in its group publications. The paper also had its readers constitute special action groups under the banner "Express Citizens Forum," which directly took up civic and other issues of their city. In this way the paper effectively turned its readers into active information users and agents of change within their communities.

In Sri Lanka, the mass media play a role as a channel and means for environment education. A recent environment awareness study showed that most people in both urban and rural areas cited different organs of the media as their primary source of environmental education, especially the print media. Television was the next major source of information for the urban population, while radio was for the rural population.

Media Economics and Special Problems

Mass media in Asia derive revenue from subscriptions, advertising (both private and government), user fees for public television and cable television, government or institutional subsidies, and allied enterprises. The large circulations of leading papers in Asia produce an income that can only be envied by their Western counterpart. And the mass media generated huge profits when an increasing amount of advertising dollars flowed to the media as a result of the Asian economic miracle before the financial crash in 1997.

The news media in East Asia and Southeast Asia were hit hard by the financial crash in 1997, which swept through Japan, South Korea, Taiwan, Hong Kong, Singapore, Thailand, Indonesia, the Philippines, and Malaysia. Advertising spending plummeted in Thailand and Indonesia (Eng 1998). Budgets for programming and news gathering were drastically reduced. Papers were closed and editorial staffers were laid off. In Thailand, about 3,500 journalists lost their jobs in 1997–1998, and few of those jobs had been replaced, according to a seminar on freelance journalism and the challenge of globalization organized by the International Federation of Journalists. The mass layoffs forced some veteran journalists in Thailand to open coffee stalls instead (Eng 1998).

The media in some Asian countries such as South Korea, are still recovering from the impact of the crash. In South Korea the media are becoming more competitive and the government is relaxing the rules regarding foreign investment in the media. However, the media in Hong Kong, Taiwan, and Vietnam are still dealing with the impact of the economic slowdown. Because Hong Kong's media market is much larger than its geographic area, the media industry is still vibrant. In 1999, the

TV industry took the lead in display advertising revenue (45 percent), followed by newspapers (36 percent), magazines (12 percent), radio (4 percent), and outdoor (3 percent), according to A.C. Nielsen's Adex data for Hong Kong.

One problem for the Hong Kong press is that competition for circulation results in lower editorial standards and yellow journalism when one paper lures talent from its rival with higher pay. Price wars can erupt again if the need is felt or imagined. And when that happens, it impacts the whole industry negatively.

The same problem plagues Taiwan. The slowing Taiwan economy makes the competition for advertising even tougher. Some papers adopted unethical practices in promotion and in the kind of advertising they run, such as ads for gambling, superstition, and even prostitution.

However, the problem is not unique to Hong Kong and Taiwan. News media in Indonesia, Thailand, the Philippines, and Cambodia were also criticized for sensationalism. Being the first and the loudest seemed to be the key to survival. Because advertising dollars are harder to come by in slower times, the pressure for the media to compete for the smaller pie of advertising spending is intense, which, unfortunately, instead of driving up the quality of media product, drives down its quality when some media operators keep a close eye on the lowest common denominator. In the rush to compete for audience, the lowest common denominator keeps getting lower, which has done great harm to the credibility of the industry and in some cases caused the total loss of respect for the media. Journalism ethics is, to a great extent, compromised in the pursuit of market share.

Chinese media face very different issues. China was barely scratched by the financial crash because the Chinese currency is still not convertible on the international money market. In 2001, China topped the Asia-Pacific advertising market with $11.2 billion spent, a 16 percent increase over 2000, an A.C. Nielsen survey showed. But media competition is heating up as well in China and Vietnam. Since Vietnam followed the suit of China in implementing economic reforms that emphasize the role of the market and the private sector, both countries have substantially cut state subsidies for the media, with the exception of the Internet, which is regarded as a new frontier and a new playground for the battle of the minds. Media now have to make themselves competitive for advertising dollars, just like their counterpart in noncommunist countries. They are required to be at least semi-independent financially. Media in China and Vietnam are caught in a bind: they have to be commercially successful and politically correct at the same time. No government official is studying the possibility of such a miracle; media are simply told that that is the order of the day. That is a real challenge to the editors caught in such systems and would tap the potential of any competent editors anywhere in the world.

To attract a larger audience, investigative reporting has appeared in both China and Vietnam, with some official encouragement as corruption worsens. But how far the media can go, and where they should draw the line in muckraking, are far from clear. One thing is certain: the survivors and casualties in the media market can tell a lot about the direction the media in these two countries are going and the market in which they operate.

The Chinese media not only have to compete with other national or local media in the country, soon they will face very strong competition from foreign media and foreign capital now that China has joined the WTO. During the negotiations on China's accession to the WTO, European and American countries persistently demanded that China open up the markets of service trade, including publication, film, and television. Although China has not promised to open its media market so far, in the long run, in keeping with the WTO principles of trade liberalization, the gradual opening of the media market to a certain degree is an inevitable trend. Within three years after China's entry into the WTO, China will gradually open the sales and retail market of publications to the outside. Foreign capital will not be satisfied with selling only the Chinese publications but will pin its hope on bringing the foreign publications into the Chinese market. Foreign capital can now hold as much as 30 percent of the stake of Internet service provider and Internet content provider firms in Beijing, Shanghai, and Guangzhou. The percentage will rise to 49 percent in 14 cities a year after the entry date. Two years after entry, there will be no geographic limits on overseas investors. To get ready for the challenge, Chinese media are speeding up the forming of publishers' groups to pool media resources.

To China, WTO is not only an economic issue. Already media in the country are talking about the possible "corrosive role" of transnational media on local culture.

A concentration of ownership in the form of media conglomerates, monopoly, or oligopoly characterizes much of the Asian press. The Singapore Press Holdings is a major publishing and printing group in Southeast Asia. The group publishes and distributes 11 newspapers and eight magazines. Its business activities also include the publication and distribution of telephone directories in Vietnam; a 35 percent stake in an English business daily, *Business Daily*, in Thailand, delivery over computers (AsiaOne and Newslink) and telephones (Audiotex); a joint venture with the incorporation of CyberWay, the third Internet access provider in Singapore; a 35 percent stake in MobileOne, to spearhead its thrust into the mobile phone and paging businesses; and a 20 percent stake in the consortium of Singapore CableVision, which will invest nearly $500 million in a nationwide cable TV network.

In Hong Kong, Sing Tao Holdings gets the word out, and in more than one language. The company publishes *Sing Tao Daily*, the oldest Chinese-language newspaper in Hong Kong, as well as the English-language newspaper *The Standard* (formerly called *Hong Kong iMail*). The company owns Chinese-language newspapers in Australia, Canada (through a joint venture with *Torstar*), and the United States. In addition to newspapers, Sing Tao also has real estate operations.

In Japan, media conglomerates form an oligopoly that controls news flow and discourages diversity in content. The big three, Asahi, Mainichi and Yomiuri, have many editions that cover the whole country. For newspapers, half of their revenue comes from advertising and the other half comes from sales. Television takes the lion's share of the advertising revenue, about 44 percent.

In South Korea, the trend toward monopoly ownership of the media is speeding up. In India, a few major national newspaper chains dominate the system.

Even in China, where all the news media are state-owned, media conglomerates are being formed as well with encouragement from the government to get ready for the competition with foreign capital and foreign media.

As media conglomerates get bigger, media owners are becoming more powerful. Across Asia, and especially in new democracies such as Indonesia, the Philippines, Taiwan, and South Korea, a historical shift in the control of the media from the government to powerful media owners is occurring. The media owners mostly look out for their own economic interests and bow to government pressure, in the case of Singapore and Malaysia, to protect those interests.

The self-interest of media owners is not the only factor compromising the integrity of the journalism profession. Corruption of journalists is widespread in Asia because the salaries of reporters in the region are mostly low, as in China, Indonesia, Thailand, the Philippines, Vietnam, and Cambodia. Envelopes stuffed with cash are handed out at press conferences by businesses and institutions. Gifts in the form of stocks, free trips, and free meals are also available in some of these countries. In Vietnam, one serious case shocked the public when it was revealed that one journalist received a bribe of up to $200,000 ("News Often Wounds" 2001). Corruption of journalists makes the public cynical about the profession. The larger and more prestigious media organizations in these countries try to clean up their ranks by making rules and regulations banning such freebies.

Asia is a continent with very unbalanced economic development in its urban and rural areas. Serving the rural population, which in some countries includes many illiterates, is still a big challenge for the news media, especially the press. In countries less developed than Japan and Singapore, the profitability and accessibility of an urban base have accentuated a tendency for newspapers to serve city dwellers. The gradual penetration of television into rural areas does not overcome the need for print media and literacy. There is also the fear that imported film and TV fare may smother local cultures and have a negative impact on the younger audience.

For the Pacific island nations, funding has always been tight for media operations and training. In 1996, the Pacific Islands News Association was declared financially insolvent and was revitalized in 1997 (Lael 1997). Financial independence is a hard-to-reach goal for most of the media in the region, which depend heavily on foreign aid. However, the U.S. Information Agency, which had in the past been generous in funding journalism training, pulled out of the South Pacific in 1997 (Lael 1997). Many French, English, Canadian, Australian, New Zealand, and German benefactors withdrew, perceiving a greater need for philanthropy in Eastern Europe and Hong Kong.

Journalism Education and Training

In some parts of Asia and the Pacific, many journalists still get their training on the job. Despite this tradition, Asia has more institutes and academic programs in communications than any other region in the world except North America. About half of these follow the U.S. pattern, offering a degree in communications or journalism that combines academic study with practical experience.

East Asia

There is a boom in journalism education in China as the government supervision of the press loosens, and journalism in China is getting more competitive and professional. The fact that both Beijing University and Tsinghua University, two of the most prestigious universities in China, set up their own journalism schools in 2001 and 2002, respectively, testifies to the popularity of the program and the need for trained journalists in China. Some of the more prominent master's programs in journalism are offered by the Graduate School of the Chinese Academy of Social Sciences, People's University, Beijing Broadcast College, the School of Journalism of China (run by the Xinhua news agency), Fudan University, Nanjing University, Jinan University and Wuhan University.

South Asia

Of all the countries in South Asia, India has the largest number of universities and colleges—over 50 in total—that offer journalism and mass communication programs, and many of the programs are quite comprehensive. Some of these academic programs offer doctoral degrees in communication. India also has quite a few education and research centers in journalism and communication, which are the best equipped in the region, including the Indian Institute of Journalism and New Media (IIJNM), which was founded in Bangalore in 2000 and trains students in a broad range of skills, teaches concepts involving the gathering, editing, and presentation of information, and prepares them for a career in journalism. The Sri Sri Center for Media Studies, also in Bangalore, aims to train entry-level media professionals. One of the best training institutions in South Asia is the Indian Institute of Mass Communication, which was set up in New Delhi in 1965 as a center for advanced study and research in mass communication. With India's resources in journalism education, it not only provides training for journalists in the country, but also training for journalists in neighboring countries.

Southeast Asia

The media in Southeast Asia are undergoing tremendous change and at the same time are in urgent need of improving their professionalism. Medialink, a global corporate media communications services company, reported that two needs were highlighted in the training of journalists. First is the need for experienced trainers, because the senior or experienced journalists chosen to become trainers often do not have experience or training as trainers. The second is the need for in-house and institutional training with the help of communications corporations like Medialink. To meet the need, Medialink organized a training-of-trainer workshop in Bangkok 2000 for trainers from the key journalism training institutions in Cambodia, India,

Indonesia, Laos, Malaysia, Philippines, Thailand, and Vietnam. The two weeks of intensive training was conducted by a professional trainer of trainers from India and a high-level journalism trainer from Australia.

Journalism education in Southeast Asia can be as emerging as short-term courses or workshops in Cambodia and Laos or as comprehensive and advanced as Singapore's. The Asian Media Information and Communication Center (AMIC) in Singapore is a premier communication center for information, research, education, and promotion of mass communication in the Asia-Pacific region. Established in 1971 with the support of the Singaporean government and Friedrich-Ebert-Stiftung, it is actively engaged in communication documentation, research, training, publishing, and media development.

The center has a close working relationship with the School of Communication and Information, Nanyang Technological University (NTU), Singapore. The school, established in 1992, has become one of the premier communication schools in Asia within a short span of 10 years. It has an international faculty, and 20 percent of its students come from other countries as well. It also has state-of-the-art facilities and close ties to the media and information industries.

The Pacific

The two more important journalism programs among the Pacific island countries are offered by the University of Papua New Guinea and the University of the South Pacific based in Suva, capital of Fiji. Australia and New Zealand both help with the training of journalists in the region by providing scholarships for students and hosting regional workshops, conferences, and awards to improve the quality of journalists and journalism.

Prospects for the Future

News media in Asia are at a crossroads. They have the potential to rise above yellow journalism, shake off the shackles of self-censorship, and wean themselves from corruption to reach real greatness, and perhaps they can help redress the unbalanced flow of information between the North and South with their technological capabilities. The World Association of Newspapers predicts ("Newspaper" 2002) that newspaper circulation in Asia will experience double-digit growth in the next four years, while sales decreases in Europe and North America will slow, following two decades of decline. The forecast says that in Asia, circulation will grow about 13 percent between 2002 and 2006. Circulation in the European Union is forecast to decline around 4 percent from 2002 to 2006. In North America, circulation will fall slightly more than 1 percent for the same period.

Or the media in Asia can pass up this historic opportunity to reach true greatness by continuing the downward spiral of sensational journalism and self-censorship to remain a lapdog. Freedom of the press is fragile in Asia. If abuse continues, it can bring on a crackdown on the media by the government supported by the public.

The media in Asia have never had a better opportunity to fully develop, given the sweeping liberalization trend across the continent, the economic strength of many of the countries in the region despite the financial crash, and the vast and solid readership base. The key to the success of Asian media lies in the maturing of the media in exercising press freedom and in pushing for the frontier of press freedom. For the new democratic countries in the region, it will take some time for the media to learn to use that freedom responsibly rather than taking advantage of it to gain a competitive edge. Culturally bound, self-censoring journalists will have to look beyond the interests of their own organization and the image of the government to care about the interests of the public as a whole. It will take some time for the Asian media to take off, as they need time to recover from the impact of the financial crash and current global economic slowdown.

In the case of China, the hope lies in the younger generation of Chinese leaders and a press law that is being debated. Some Chinese leaders are already advising newspaper editors to "liberalize their thinking," which can be a welcome sign for the future development of Chinese media.

Globalization of the media is no longer a vision, it is a reality, even for a country like China, which would be unimaginable in the past. With China being a member of the WTO, Chinese media have no choice but to get prepared for the competition with foreign media. The same is true for many other countries in Asia. There are already strong and successful regional media in Asia, such as STAR TV, and some leading newspapers and magazines, which have a regional circulation. The next step is going global. Asian media are fully equipped, both in their hardware and software, to take the next step. The question is whether the editors and journalists in the region have the vision and the will to take that step. We hope they do.

In Pakistan, journalists are calling for and being trained in "peace journalism" in regard to the coverage of conflicts in Kashmir ("Realistic" 2000). In today's world, peace journalism is more urgently needed than at any other time in human history, and it points to the future role of the ubiquitous global news media.

Bibliography

Aglionby, John. "Indonesia Bans Foreign Journalist." *The Guardian*, 18 March 2002.

Bangladesh Basic Information and Media Guide. Bangladesh: Ministry of Information, 1993.

Bishop, Robert. *Qi Lai! Mobilizing One Billion Chinese: The Chinese Communication System*. Ames: Iowa State University Press, 1989.

Changyawa, Porpot. "Journalists Reminded of Role to Help Curb Corruption." *Bangkok Post*, 13 December 2001.

Cheung, Anne S. Y. "One Step Forward, Two Steps Back: A Study of Press Law in Post-Colonial Hong Kong." *Journalism Communication Monographs* 3, no. 4 (Winter 2002): 189–226.

China Journalism Yearbook. Beijing: China Journalism Yearbook Press, 1998, 2001.

Clark, Judith. "Training Journalists in an Emerging Democracy: The Case of Cambodia." *Asia-Pacific Media Educator* 8 (January–June 2000) 82–98.

Conlon, C. J. "Bhutan." In *Handbook of the Media in Asia,* edited by Shelton A. Gunaratne, 67–83. New Delhi: Sage, 2000.

Cooper-Chen, Anne. *Games in the Global Village: A 50-Nation Study of Entertainment Television.* Bowling Green, Ohio: Popular Press, 1994.

Coronel, Sheila. *The Philippines: After the Euphoria, the Problems of a Free Press.* Paper presented at a conference, "Transparency, Asian Economic Crisis and the Prospects of Media Liberalization." University of Sydney, Australia: Research Institute for Asia and the Pacific, 2000.

Craddock, Pat. "Review: Unique Flavor of Pacific Public Radio." *Pacific Journalism Review* 6, no. 1 (January 2000) 121–132.

Downie, Sue. "Journalism Training in Laos, Cambodia and Vietnam." *Asia-Pacific Media Educator* 8 (January–June 2000). Available: http://www.uow.edu.au/crearts/journalism/APME/contents8/Downie.html.

Downing, John D. H. "Drawing a Bead on Global Communication Theories." In *Global Communication,* edited by Yahya R. Kamalipour, 21–39. Belmont, Calif.: Wadsworth/Thompson Learning, 2002.

Ekachai, Daradirek. "Thailand." In *Handbook of the Media in Asia,* edited by Shelton A. Gunaratne, 429–461. New Delhi: Sage, 2000.

Elmore, Cindy. "Rigors of the Japanese Press." *Editor & Publisher* 129, 15 June 1996, 120.

Eng, Peter. "Economic Woes Pummel Thai, Indonesia media." *Columbia Journalism Review* 37, no. 2 (July/August 1998): 58–59.

"Freedom Comes with Responsibilities" (editorial). *Taipei Times,* 19 December 2001.

Freeman, Laurie Anne. *Closing the Shop: Information Cartels and Japan's Mass Media.* Princeton, N.J.: Princeton University Press, 2000.

"Gandhi to Gandhi: Views on Press." *India Abroad,* 25 August 1989, 13.

"Giving the Media a Greater Voice." *People's Daily,* 31 March 2002. Available: http://english.peopledaily.com.cn/200203/31/eng20020331_93207.shtml.

Goenka, Vivek. "Journalism in India: A Changing Perspective." *Editor & Publisher,* 129, 22 June 1996, 68.

Gounder, Christine. "Insight Report on Pacific Environment." *Wansolwara News* 5, no. 2 (June 2000): 9.

"Government to Free Electronic Media." *Dawn,* 4 April 2000.

Hachten, William. *The World News Prism.* Ames: Iowa State University Press, 1981.

———. *The World News Prism,* 2nd Edition. Ames: Iowa State University Press, 1987.

———. *The World News Prism,* 3rd Edition. Ames: Iowa State University Press, 1992.

Hamzah, Bahreen. "Certificate Presentation for Photo Journalism Workshop." Asia Intelligence Wire, 12 April 2001.

Heo, Chul, Ki-Yul Uhm, and Jeong-Heon Chang. "South Korea." In *Handbook of the Media in Asia,* edited by Shelton A. Gunaratne, 611–637. New Delhi: Sage, 2000.

"Hu Calls for Study of Theories." Ximhua News Agency, 3 September 2002. Available: http://www.16congress.org/cn/english/features/41290.htm.

Idris, Naswil, and Shelton A. Gunaratne. "Indonesia." In *Handbook of the Media in Asia,* edited by Shelton A. Gunaratne, 263–295. New Delhi: Sage, 2000.

International News Media Seminar Starts." *People's Daily,* 21 October 2000. Avalable: http://fpeng.peopledaily.com.cn/200010/21/eng20001021_53221.html.

"International Media Aeminar in Afghanistan." BBC World Service, 24 September 2002.

Irani, Cusbrow R. "Freedom of Information in India: Some Reflections." In *Freedom of Information: An Asian Survey,* edited by V. Iger, 125–134. Singapore: Asian Media Information and Communication Center, 2001.

Isa, Qazi Faez. "Freedom of Information in Pakistan: Pressing Need for Action." *Freedom of Information: An Asian Survey,* 135–148. Singapore: Asian Media Information and Communication Center, 2001.

Jin Seong-ho. "Newspaper Self-Regulatory Committee Resigns en Masse." *Chosum Ilbo,* 24 April 2001. Available: http://srch.chosun.com/cig-bin/english/search?did=35960&OP=5&word=NEWSPAPER%20.

Joshi, Subhash. "25 Years of Satellite Broadcasting in India" (columns in English), October 2000. Available: Orbicom.uqam.ca.

"Journalists Face Violence, Intimidation." *Jakarta Post*, 3 May 2001, 2.

Juan, Chee Soon. *Media in Singapore.* Presented at a cConference, Transparency, Asian Economic Crisis and the Prospects of Media Liberalization. University of Sydney, Australia: Research Institute for Asia and the Pacific, 2000.

Kim, Jee-woon. "Strayed Broadcasting." *Chosum Ilbo*, 26 April 2001. Available: http://srch.cho-sun.com/cgi-bin/english/search?CD=333554431&SH=1&FD=1&OP=3&q=strayed+broadcasting.

Kubiske, Dan. "Press Freedom in Hong Kong: No Easy Answers." *Quill*, 88, no. 3 (April 2000): 38–40.

Kuo, Eddie, and Peng Hwa Ang "Singapore." In *Handbook of the Media in Asia*, edited by Shelton A. Gunaratne, 402–428. New Delhi: Sage, 2000.

Lael, Morgan. "South Pacific Circulation Grows." *Quill* 85 (October 1997): 7.

Lamb, David. "Free Enterprise But Not Freedom of the Press." *Nieman Reports* 56, no. 2 (Summer 2002): 69–71.

Luwarso, Lukas. "'Freakdom' of the Press: Keeping Indonesia Free for All." *Taipei Times*, 5 April 2002, 13.

———. "The Paradox of Freedom in Southeast Asia." *Jakarta Post*, 3 May 2000, 000.

"Media Bills' Require Changes." *Japan Times*, 25 May 2002. Available: http??www.japan-times.co.jp/ cgi-bin/getarticle.pl5?ed20020525al.htm.

"Media Freedom Day 2002 Focuses on Corruption." *Post-Courier*, 2 May 2002, Local Section 5.

"Media in Constant Battle over Press Freedom." *Pacific Weekly Review*, 30 September 2002–6 October 2002.

Momin, Sajeda. "Gagging the Press Modi Intimidates Press to Cover Up Carnage." *The Statesman*, 18 April 2002.

Nam-Shi-wook. "The Truth Behind the Tax Investigation." *Chosun Ilbo*, 25 September 2001.

"News Often Wounds, But More Often It Heals." *Saigon Times*, 5 October 2001.

"News That Didn't Make News." *Bangkok Post*, 30 August 2001.

"Newsman Urged to Follow Code of Ethics." *Dawn*, 8 July 2002.

"Newspaper Circulation Set for Asian Rise." *Irish Examiner*, 31 July 2002.

"Papua New Guinea: Pacific Investigative Award Address." *Journalism Studies*, 14 February 1998.

"Party Publicity Chief on China's Media Work." *People's Daily*, 29 October 2001.

"Press Credentials." *Jakarta Post*, 14 July 2000.

"Press Law Needed to Protect Reporters." *China Daily*, 25 December 2000.

"Private Radio, TV Stations to Go On Air Next Year." *The News*, 26 April 2000.

"Publication Glut a Waste of Vietnam's Press, Say Deputies." *Saigon Times*, 10 May 1999.

Rao, Sandhya, and Bharat Koirala. "Nepal." In *Handbook of the Media in Asia*, edited by Shelton A. Gunaratne, 132–154. New Delhi: Sage, 2000.

"Realistic Approach on Kashmir Stressed." *Dawn*, 10 April 2000.

"Regional Overview." *Bangkok Post*, 1 April 2002.

Republic of China Publication Yearbook. Taipei: Government Information Office, 1999.

Rivenburgh, Nancy. *China: The Television Revolution.* Paper presented at an AFJMC convention, Portland, Ore., July 1988.

Robie, David. "Media: *Post-Courier* Shrugs Off Buy-Out Claims." *Asia-Pacific Network*, 11 January 1999.

———. Editorial. *Pacific Journalism Review*, 2, no. 1 (November 1995).

Saito, Shinichi. "Japan." In *Handbook of the Media in Asia*, edited by Shelton A. Gunaratne. New Delhi: Sage, 2000.

Saksi, a web site of independent journalism in Malaysia, no. 8, June 2000.

Seward, Robert. *Radio Happy Isles: Media and Politics at Play in the Pacific.* Honolulu: University of Hawaii Press, 1999.

Siebert, Fred, Theodore Peterson, and Wilbur Schramm. *Four Theories of the Press.* Urbana: University of Illinois Press, 1956.

———. *Four Theories of the Press,* 2nd Edition. Urbana: University of Illinois Press, 1963.

Singh, Shailendra. "Bad Governance 'Root Cause' of Pacific Woes, Says Chandra." *Wansolwara Online,* 12 June 2002.

Sison, Marites N. "Philippines: Elusive Access to Information." *World Press Review* 48, no. 12 (December 2001). Available: http://www.worldpress.org/specials/press/phil.htm.

"Slumping Economy Hits Taiwan's Crowded Media Market." *People's Daily,* 5 June 2001.

So, Clement, Joseph Man Chan, and Chin-Chuan Lee. "Hong Long SAR (China)." In *Handbook of the Media in Asia,* edited by Shelton A. Gunaratne, 527–551. New Delhi: Sage, 2000.

Statistical Yearbook 2001. Geneva: UNESCO, 2002.

Sussman, L., and K. Karlekar. *The Annual Survey of Press Freedom.* New York: Freedom House, 2002.

"Tongan Press Crusader Kalafi Maola Wins Freedom Award." *Pacific Media Watch,* 28 September 2002.

Tsai, Ting-I. "Scholars Debate Future of Taiwanese Media." *Taipei Times,* 17 December 2001.

"Two Pacific Winners of New PIMA/AUT Scholarships." *Pacific Media Watch,* 5 October 2002.

"U.S. Shonen Jump Anime Magazine Previewed at Comic-Con." *Write News,* 9 April 2002.

"USP Academic Tells of 'Crisis of Conscience.' " *Pacific Journalism Online,* 23 January 2001, 3162.

"Vice-Premier Calls for Wider Radio, TV Coverage in Inland Regions." *People's Daily,* 9 January 2002.

Wang, Georgette, and Wen-Hwei Lo. "Taiwan." In *Handbook of the Media in Asia,* edited by Shelton A. Gunaratne 000–000. New Delhi: Sage, 2000.

Whymant, Robert. "Japan Bill to Cub Press." *Statesman,* 9 March 2002. Available: http://www.thestatesman.net/page.arcview.php?clid=8&id=31896&usrsess=1.

"Your Nambawan Newspaper Wins International Award." PNG *Post-Courier,* 16 August 2002.

Yu, Ruidong. "Hong Kong Media Reported More Freedom of Speech After Turnover" (translated from Chinese). Chinanews.com.cn, 4 July 2002.

Web Sites

http://corporate.mediacorpsingapore.com/news/index.htm
http://corporate.mediacorpsingapore.com/philosophy.htm
http://kidon.com/media-link/indonesia.shtml
http://kidon.com/media-link/malaysia.shtml
http://kidon.com/media-link/singapore.com
http://sonora.indosat.net.id/new/about.html
http://www.abs-cbn.com/international/aboutus.html
http://www.amic.org.sg/amic.html
http://www.antara.co.id/e_profil.asp
http://www.asiaobserver.com/cgi-ocal/anacondaodpp.pl?passurl=/Regional/Asia/Cambod
http://www.asiaobserver.com/cgi-ocal/anacondaodpp.pl?passurl=/Regional/Asia/Vietnam
http://www.asiasource.org/profiles/cfm
http://www.bernama.com.my/history.htm
http://www.burmadaily.com
http://www.camnet.com.kh/cambodia.daily/top.htm
http://www.channelnewsasia.com/can/aboutus-new/index.htm
http://www.comn.usm.my/intro.htm
http://www.communique.no/dvb/programs/statements.html
http://www.dailyexpress.com.my/
http://www.dailyexpress.com.my/about.cfm
http://www.metrotvnews.com/profile.asp
http://www.indosiar.com/welcome/about.htm
http://www.ipl.org/div/news/browse/ID/
http://www.ipl.org/div/news/browse/MY/

http://www.ipl.org/div/news/browse/PH/
http://www.ipl.org/div/news/browse/SG/
http://www.ipl.org/div/news/browse/TH/
http://www.itm.edu.my/acactr/ptar/english/html/index.html
http://www.kidon.com/media-link/cambodia.shtml
http://www.kidon.com/media-link/laos.shtml
http://www.kidon.com/media-link/philippines.shtml
http://www.kidon.com/media-link/thailand.shtml
http://www.kidon.com/media-link/vietnam.shtml
http://www.mcot.org/aboutmcot.asp
http://www.mindanews.com/
http://www.mindanews.com/others/aboutus.html
http://www.myanmar.com/nlm/
http://www.onedr.net/RFB/rfb.html
http://www.philexport.org/philradio/cities.htm
http://www.phnompenhpost.com/TXT/now.htm
http://www.rsi.com.sg/
http://www.thaiaktuell.com/TA/enginf.htm
http://www.tvradioworld.com/region2/ins/
http://www.tvradioworld.com/region2/mla/
http://www.tvradioworld.com/region2/mya/
http://www.tvradioworld.com/region2/phl/
http://www.tvradioworld.com/region2/sng/Radio.asp
http://www.tvradioworld.com/region2/vtn/
http://www.vnagency.com.vn/Public/newse.asp
http://www.vocri.org/about.html

18

Australasia

Stephen Quinn

Australians are some of the hungriest media consumers in the world. Newspaper and magazine readership is one of the highest internationally, on a per-capita basis. Almost all Australian homes possess, on average, two television sets, and most households own four or more radios. More than half the adult population accesses the Internet. Figures are unavailable for Internet consumption by people younger than 18, but a similar pattern is likely. New Zealanders are also major media consumers. This chapter looks first at Australian media and journalism, and then transfers its attention to New Zealand.

Australia

Australia's press has traditionally been regarded as free, but no provision in either the federal constitution or any of the state constitutions explicitly guarantees freedom of speech. Australia inherited the traditional English view that freedom of speech is best protected by common law. Some unsuccessful attempts have been made to incorporate a guarantee of free speech, alone or with other human rights, into the Australian constitution. But the constitution is notoriously difficult to amend because change requires a national referendum with a two-thirds majority.

Media Regulation

The Australian Press Council, a voluntary body established in 1976 by the Australian Journalists' Association and the country's major publishers, promotes press ethics. It investigates and deals with complaints about press conduct. Funding comes from its constituent bodies. The council provides an independent and free service. The Australian Broadcasting Authority (ABA) administers the Broadcasting Services Act. Among other things, the ABA considers issues of ownership and control, licensing, program content, and the handling of complaints. Section 53 of the Act says no person is allowed to control television broadcasting licenses whose combined area exceeds 75 percent of the population, or more than one license within a license area.

Section 57 prohibits foreigners from control of a television license, and total foreign interests must not exceed 20 percent. Section 54 says a person cannot control more than two radio licenses in the same license area. Section 60 prevents anyone from controlling a commercial television license and a commercial radio license in the same area, or a commercial television license and a newspaper associated with that license area, or a commercial radio broadcasting license and a newspaper associated with that license area. As of August 2002 these laws were under review, but current regulations negate the possibility of convergence.

Print Media Ownership

Australia has a high concentration of ownership. Rupert Murdoch's News Ltd. controls almost 68 percent of the capital-city and national newspaper market by circulation, 76 percent of the Sunday newspaper market, 47 percent of the suburban newspaper market, and 23 percent of the regional newspaper market. John Fairfax Publishing controls about 20 percent of the metropolitan and national daily newspaper publishing, runs three regional dailies and a number of ancillary country newspapers, and controls about half the suburban circulation in Sydney and Melbourne. Rural Press, largely owned by a branch of the Fairfax family, which no longer has an interest in John Fairfax, publishes a large number of daily and weekly regional and country newspapers, as well as *The Canberra Times*.

Australian Provincial Newspapers publishes 14 regional daily newspapers in Queensland and northern New South Wales, plus a host of weekly country newspapers and suburban newspapers in Melbourne. West Australian Newspapers publishes the Perth daily, *The West Australian*, a regional daily, a number of country newspapers, and has a large interest in most of the Perth suburban newspapers.

Print Media

Australia has 49 daily newspapers. Analysts distinguish between capital-city (or metropolitan dailies) and dailies in smaller population centers (usually referred to as regional newspapers). Ten metropolitan and two national dailies are published in the capital cities of the five states and two territories. Half of the 12 are published in the two largest population centers, Sydney (4 million) and Melbourne (3.4 million). Australia's population in August 2002 was 19.7 million. All other capitals have one daily paper. Table 18.1 shows Monday–Friday circulations.

Another 37 dailies publish in the regional areas. Their circulations tend to be much lower than the metropolitan dailies. Each day 2.4 million people read the two national and 10 metropolitan dailies, compared with 0.6 million who read the 37 regional dailies. About 100 weekly or twice weekly newspapers, mostly free, circulate in city suburbs. Another 250 country newspapers publish one to three times a week.

Magazines

More than 1,600 magazines appear regularly in Australia. An unknown number of titles are imported on a regular or irregular basis. As of mid-2002, Australians spent U.S.$12 million a month buying magazines. Australians consume magazines at a prodigious rate relative to other English-speaking nations: a quarter of all people read an average issue of a weekly women's magazine, a third of the population read a monthly women's magazine, and almost one in three people read a general-interest magazine.

News Agencies

The main news agency in terms of content for Australia's media is Australian Associated Press (AAP), headquartered in Sydney. All of the major international agencies—Associated Press, Reuters, and Agence France-Presse—cover the country and region from offices in Sydney. AAP bases reporters in all capital cities and London.

In 1998 the joint federal secretary of the Australian Journalists' Association, Chris Warren, estimated that Australia had somewhere between 8,000 and 10,000 working journalists. Most were employed in print. Warren estimated that somewhere between 2,500 and 3,000 worked on metropolitan dailies, with another 800 to 1,000 working on regional dailies. The figures were "ballpark" because no accurate totals were kept. The 1996 Census reported that 14,354 people said they worked "in journalism and related professions," with 52 percent of the total (7,455) working as journalists.

Broadcast Media

Commercial radio started in Australia in 1923 in Sydney, spreading to other cities the next year. In 1932, then Prime Minister Joseph Lyons inaugurated the Australian Broadcasting Company, modeled on the BBC. It became the Australian Broadcasting Corporation (ABC) in 1980. Over time the ABC has grown to become the country's largest broadcaster, entertainment, and marketing organization. The ABC employs about 600 domestic journalists, plus correspondents in 14 foreign bureaus. The ABC's editorial and programming independence is guaranteed by legislation. In 1997, ABC news celebrated 50 years of providing an independent broadcast news service.

Figures from the Australian Broadcasting Authority as of July 1998 show a total of 212 commercial radio stations in the country, equally divided between FM and AM. Of that total, 38 were in metropolitan areas and 174 in regional areas. The ABA reports that the trend since 1996 has been the growth of monopoly markets in regional areas. The Special Broadcasting Service (SBS) began in 1975 with radio stations in Sydney and Melbourne, broadcasting four hours a day in eight languages. SBS was established to define and foster Australia's cultural diversity in accordance with its charter obligation to provide multilingual and multicultural radio and television services that inform, educate, and entertain all Australians and "reflect Australia's multi-cultural society." As of August 2002, it was broadcasting in more languages than any other network in the world: 68 languages were spoken on SBS Radio. As well, it broadcasts audio-on-demand services in more than 50 languages.

Television

Commercial television started in Australia in 1956, though it took about a decade before TV reached all areas of the nation. By the early 1990s most people had access to five free-to-air channels: the national broadcaster, the ABC; a network that reflects Australia's multicultural background, SBS Television; and three national commercial networks: Seven, Nine, and Ten. The Australian Broadcasting Corporation (ABC) was discussed earlier. SBS Television broadcasts in more than 60 languages. The three national commercial networks are described below, along with the major regional broadcasters.

Seven Network. The Seven Network controls five metropolitan and a regional television license, with a potential audience reach of 72.1 percent of the population. It also has a number of pay TV interests, including a 33 percent stake in Sky News. The largest shareholder is chairman Kerry Stokes (34 percent). In July 2001 the company acquired 50 percent of the Australian and New Zealand magazine business of PMP Limited.

Nine Network. Publishing & Broadcasting Ltd. (PBL) owns the Nine Network and the major magazine publisher, Australian Consolidated Press (ACP). PBL controls three metropolitan and one regional television license, giving it a reach of 51.5 percent of the potential audience. ACP publishes 65 magazines and its share of the circulation of the top 30 Australian magazines is 41.5 percent. It has a joint on-line venture (ninemsn) with Microsoft Corporation.

Ten Group Ltd. Ten controls five metropolitan television licenses, with a potential audience reach of 64.9 percent of the population. The largest shareholder is Canada's CanWest Global Communications (chairman, Izzy Asper), which holds a 14.9 percent voting interest and an overall 57.5 economic interest in the company.

Southern Cross Broadcasting Australia Ltd. Southern Cross has one metropolitan and four regional television licenses, with a potential audience of 21.5 percent of the population. It also controls six metropolitan radio licenses and Sky Radio. The largest shareholder is the Ten Group Ltd. (14 percent).

Prime Television Ltd. Prime has eight regional television licenses, with a potential audience of 25.1 percent of the population. The largest shareholder is Paul Ramsay Holdings Pty Ltd. (39 percent); Ramsay is the chairman.

WIN Corporation Pty Ltd. WIN controls one metropolitan and nine regional television licenses, with a potential audience of 26.1 percent of the population. WIN also has a radio station. The major shareholder is chairman Bruce Gordon.

Telecasters Australia Ltd. Telecasters Australia controls five regional television licenses, with a potential audience of 18.8 percent. The major shareholder is a corporation, Permanent Trustee Australia (17 percent).

New Zealand

New Zealand enjoys a high level of freedom of expression. The concept received statutory endorsement in the Bill of Rights Act of 1990. Section 14 states that "everyone has the right to freedom of expression, including the freedom to seek, receive, and impart information and opinions of any kind in any form." Sir John Jeffries, chairman of the New Zealand Press Council, noted that independent international studies on freedom of expression usually rate the country in the top bracket.

Regulation

The New Zealand Press Council, founded in 1972, is a self-regulatory body that operates in a fashion similar to that of its Australian counterpart. The main difference is funding: it all comes from publishers. The council's main role is the resolution of complaints, but it also promotes press freedom. The Broadcasting Act of 1989 established the Broadcasting Standards Authority as an independent statutory body. Its mission is to encourage broadcasters to develop and maintain program standards that "respect human dignity and reflect current social values."

Print Media Ownership

New Zealand's two biggest media groups are Independent Newspapers Ltd. (INL) and Wilson & Horton. INL is the country's largest media company. In 1964 Rupert Murdoch, owner of News Ltd. in Australia, made his first overseas newspaper purchase—a 29.57 percent stake in the Wellington Publishing Company, which publishes *The Dominion*. As of mid-2002 News Ltd.'s holding in INL stood at just under 50 percent. INL owns or controls the major papers in Wellington, Hamilton, and Christchurch. It also owns *TV Guide* and two-thirds of the pay television operator, Sky Network Television Ltd. INL aggregates the content from its newspapers to supply its Internet site, Stuff (http://www.stuff.co.nz), which describes itself as "New Zealand's leading news and information web site."

Wilson & Horton operates in four areas: newspaper publishing (nine daily newspapers and 32 free community papers), new Internet-based media, specialist publishing (including two weekly magazines), and commercial printing via its subsidiary, W&H Print Ltd. The company has a one-third shareholding in the 53 stations of The Radio Network (TRN), the country's largest commercial operator. APN News and Media Ltd.—itself controlled by Independent News and Media PLC, a Dublin-based company with extensive media interests in Ireland, the U.K., Australia, South Africa, Mexico, and Portugal—owns Wilson & Horton. The company publishes New Zealand's biggest circulating daily, the *New Zealand Herald*.

Print Media

A unique feature of the print media environment in New Zealand is the high proportion of afternoon daily newspapers compared with morning dailies, despite an international trend toward morning publication. Of the country's 24 dailies— four in metropolitan cities and 20 in regional areas—16 appear in the afternoon. The four metropolitan publications all appear in the morning. The last traditional metropolitan afternoon daily, *The Evening Post*, published in the capital, Wellington, closed on June 29, 2002.

By way of comparison, in 2001 the United States had 776 morning dailies and 704 evening papers. Fifty years earlier, evening papers dominated, with 1,450 evening dailies and 322 morning dailies (Newspaper Association of America 2002). Several things help explain the New Zealand phenomenon. One major factor is the way the New Zealand Press Association operates. It provides a huge amount of content aimed at an afternoon publication schedule. "Its enormous domestic and international output is both affordable and critical for the survival and relevance of evening newspapers" (Tidey 2002, p. 144). The press association operates as a cooperative, and members pay fees based on circulation. A small paper thus receives a huge amount of content for relatively low cost. The intense parochial focus of local communities represents another factor, along with the fact that nowhere in the country are daily newspapers in serious head-to-head contest. Two main groups own most of the papers, which means that "strategic considerations also offer some protection." Tidey concludes that afternoon papers are likely to survive in New Zealand "for quite some time yet" (Tidey 2002, p. 144).

Magazines

New Zealand's magazine industry is unusual, in world terms, in having two of its four major publishers owned by newspaper publishing groups—Wilson & Horton and INL. The largest magazine publisher is ACP Media. This company also owns Netlink, one of the country's two major magazine distributors. The second largest publisher is the INL Group, which encompasses INL Magazines and News Media Ltd. INL owns the other major magazine distributor, Gordon & Gotch (NZ) Ltd., which accounts for 55 percent of all titles circulated in the country. The third largest magazine publisher is New Zealand Magazines, part of the Wilson & Horton newspaper group. The fourth largest, Pacific Magazines, is a division of PMP Communications in Australia.

These companies publish major consumer magazines such as *Woman's Day* (ACP), *New Zealand Woman's Weekly* (NZ Magazines), and *New Idea* (Pacific). Other consumer magazine publishers include Readers Digest, Time, and the New Zealand Automobile Association. The last publishes *AA Directions*. A significant publication, despite its relatively low circulation, is *The National Business Review*, a weekly tabloid (circulation 14,398 on March 31, 2001). The rest of the magazine market consists of medium to small niche publications. The country has perhaps 140 multititle publishers. About 700 magazines are published in total. Of these, 165 are listed with the New Zealand Audit Bureau of Circulations (ABC).

News Agency

The New Zealand Press Association (NZPA), which started in 1879, is owned by the country's daily newspapers and supplies them with a 24-hour national and international news service. NZPA's main newsroom in the capital, Wellington, distributes about 1,000 pieces of information every 24 hours. These come from its reporters, the daily newspapers, overseas wire services, and other sources, such as the New Zealand Stock Exchange. NZPA is unique in the way its member newspapers contribute copy for redistribution to other papers. Copy flows into and out of the Wellington headquarters, rather than the one-way traffic at other news agencies. This has the added benefit of keeping costs low. NZPA has about 40 journalists. Most are based at the head office in Wellington, with a handful located in Sydney, Auckland, Christchurch, and at the parliament in Wellington.

Broadcast Media

State-funded public broadcasting began in New Zealand in 1925. Public broadcasting has traditionally been seen as a social service, designed to reflect and develop the country's identity and culture. In many ways radio followed the mission statement of the first director-general of the BBC, Lord Reith, who famously maintained that broadcasting should "inform, educate and entertain" its audience. Various forms of restructuring led to the formation of Radio New Zealand (RNZ), a state-owned enterprise established under the Broadcasting Act of 1995. A state-run enterprise is semi-independent in terms of structure but is required to pay an annual dividend to the government. RNZ broadcasts 24 hours a day and operates three networks: a high-quality talk service called National Radio, Concert FM for fine music, and an AM network. This network broadcasts all sittings of parliament. When parliament is not sitting, the transmitters carry programs from the Radio Rhema Broadcast Group.

RNZ News and Current Affairs provide a comprehensive news and information service for all networks. Its bulletins are written and presented in a style that "recognizes the intelligence and interest" of its audience. "Stories are put into context and follow a strict policy of impartiality" (RNZ on-line 2002). A short-wave service, Radio New Zealand International, broadcasts throughout the South Pacific. New Zealand On Air funds National Radio and Concert FM, which are free of advertising. NZ On Air's brief is to promote and foster development of New Zealand's culture on the airwaves by funding locally made television, public radio networks, and access radio.

Television

New Zealand was a latecomer to the television age. The BBC started the world's first public service in 1936, and NBC began broadcasting three years later. New Zealand's first transmission did not start until June 1961, though the government had permitted experimental broadcasts from 1951. The first network newscast did not appear until almost a decade after transmission started. Before then, news was structured on a regional basis. A second network, Network Two, appeared in 1975. Funding for the Broadcasting Corporation of New Zealand (BCNZ), modeled on the BBC, came from a television license and limited advertising. The first privately owned free-to-air network, TV3, debuted in 1989. Eight years later a Canadian company, CanWest, which had owned TV3 since 1991, established a fourth national channel, TV4. In 1988 the BCNZ separated into radio and television arms. The television arm became a state-run enterprise known as Television New Zealand (TVNZ). It operates two national networks known as TVONE and TV2. TVNZ's charter requires it to provide a strong focus on maintaining New Zealand's cultural identity. Pay television in the form of Sky Television entered the market late relative to international trends, in 1990. It went digital in 1998 and as of late 2002 offered just over 40 channels.

Journalism Education

The two countries approach journalism education differently. In Australia, most new reporters start work after graduating from one of the country's 37 universities. Many have degrees in communication or journalism from the 22 programs offering a major in journalism, though a trend is emerging to employ people with specialized degrees such as law or economics. Journalism education in New Zealand has traditionally been more practical. Many graduates emerged from a one-year industry-controlled diploma in journalism taught through polytechnics (similar to American community colleges). In the 1990s polytechnics lobbied to gain university-status to attract more students. This produced a rise in undergraduate numbers. Popular courses such as journalism became part of university degrees. New Zealand's three main journalism programs are now based at universities in Auckland, Wellington, and Christchurch.

Industry influence is strong, and it influences educators' teaching methods. In the mid-1990s, employers threatened to boycott employing graduates of a polytechnic course in the capital, Wellington, unless it was restructured (Thomas 1999).

Assessment focuses on student writing and tutors work one on one, correcting student work. "Work attachment, where students are attached to a newspaper, is an integral part of most of our courses as are internships where students work in a newspaper office or elsewhere in the media industry for several weeks" (Thomas 2000). Skills-based training is standardized via the New Zealand Journalists' Training Organization (NZJTO). About 80 percent of graduates find jobs. The NZJTO reports about 2,500 journalists in the country.

Figures for graduates in Australia are not precise because the country is bigger and less centralized. Some estimates suggest that about 250 to 300 of the 1,000 who graduate each year get a job in journalism or related areas. Universities protect their autonomy, so it is unlikely that an organization such as the NZJTO will emerge in Australia. The two biggest newspaper groups, News Ltd. and Fairfax, run training programs. They employ trainees who are mostly graduates. During their one-year program, trainees attend courses one day a week while working on a newspaper. Their training includes shorthand and lectures from prominent journalists.

Issues for Discussion

Concentration of ownership remains an issue in both countries. Journalists have expressed concern about their ability to write about contentious issues. Academic Bill Rosenberg noted that in 1993, the London-based magazine *Index on Censorship* commented that Australians were "losing some of their liberty to dissent" because of a "potent increase" in the concentration of media control. Rosenberg concluded that the issue was "even more true of New Zealand today" (2002 p. 86). The worldwide trend toward convergence is unlikely to occur in Australia because of Section 60 of the Broadcasting Services Act, which prohibits ownership of a daily and a television license in the same market. The big New Zealand companies with their range of assets are positioned to try convergence and are actively considering their options.

Bibliography

Newspaper Association of America. "Facts About Newspapers 2002." Available: http://www.naa.org/info/facts02.

Newspaper Publishers' Association of New Zealand. "Information About Newspapers 2000–2001. Wellington: NPANZ, 2001.

Rosenberg, Bill. "News Media Ownership." *Pacific Journalism Review* 8 (June 2002): 59–95.

Thomas, Ruth. *Industry Influences on Journalism Training: Thoughts for the Future.* Paper presented at the Journalism Educators' Association of New Zealand conference, December 2000. Available: http://www.wintec.ac.nz/jeanz/conference_thomas.html.

———. "Learning News Writing: A Process Intervention in a Product Setting." Master's thesis, University of Auckland, 1999.

Tidey, John. "Death in the Afternoon." *Australian Journalism Review* 24, no. 1 (July 2002): 141–145.

Related Web Sites

Australian Associated Press: http://aap.com.au
Australian Broadcasting Authority: http://www.aba.gov.au
Australian Broadcasting Corporation: http://www.abc.net.au
Australian Press Council: http://www.presscouncil.org.au
Magazine Publishers Association of New Zealand: http://www.mpa.org.nz
Magazine Publishers of Australia: http://www.magazines.org.au
New Zealand Press Association: http://www.nzpa.co.nz
New Zealand Press Council: http://www.presscouncil.org.nz
Prime Television: http://www.primetv.com.au
Radio New Zealand: http://www.rnz.co.nz
Southern Cross Broadcasting: http://www.southerncrossbroadcasting.com.au
Telecasters: http://www.telecasters.com.au
Television New Zealand: http://www.tvnz.co.nz
WIN Corporation: http://www.wintv.com.au/wincorp

19

Latin America

Donn Tilson and Rick Rockwell

John Gunther (1966) once described Latin America as a region "in the state of active flux, grasping for a future, with fundamental . . . impulses for change apparent almost everywhere" (p. xii). That description holds true today. In some respects, there are hopeful signs in the region, including the rise to power of new political voices in Mexico under the Fox administration and an increasingly politically active citizenry in Ecuador. At the same time, many age-old problems persist, such as widespread poverty and unemployment, corruption, and *caudillo*-style government. It is indeed a region in transition of great promise and of promises unkept. Hopefully, it will not remain as Brazil has been characterized in a *carioca* proverb: "Brazil is the land of the future—and always will be" (Gunther 1966, p. 1).

A Confluence of Forces

A review of the region (Figure 19.1) suggests that privatization, free-market reforms, democratization, telecommunications, and globalization are transforming the economic, political, media, and cultural landscape. Such forces have spurred the development of business, the promotional sector (public relations, advertising, and marketing), and higher education communication curriculum. For example, as economic reforms have created more opportunities for multinational corporations, including global media giants, advertising and public relations consultancies have followed their business clients into the Southern Hemisphere to handle their media relations and other promotional needs. Today, such consultancies—Ogilvy & Mather Worldwide, Burson-Marsteller, and Edelman, among others—operate offices or affiliates in the major capitals of Latin America, often with regional head-

Portions of this chapter appeared in slightly different form in *Toward the Common Good: Perspectives in International Public Relations,* edited by D. Tilson and E. C. Alozie, and are reproduced here by permission of the editors and publisher.

FIGURE 19.1 *Latin America and the Caribbean*

quarters in South Florida. In turn, growth in the promotional sector has facilitated, if not accelerated, the commodification of society (Wernick 1991), ushering in a world of MTV, Wal-Mart, Coca-Cola, and English-language television advertising and programming, even as media outlets have proliferated.

The Media Landscape

The media landscape in the region is interesting and dynamic. Latin America has a long tradition of print media. For example, by the mid-nineteenth century, Argentina already had a well-established newspaper system, as did Brazil and Mexico (Salwen and Garrison 1991). Traditionally, Latin American newspapers have been more literary and more political than their U.S. counterparts (Cole 1996). Today, according to Tilson (*Media* 1999), many newspapers provide excellent, professional coverage (such as *El Clarín* in Argentina and *La Prensa* in Nicaragua), often modeling themselves after the *New York Times* and other high-quality papers like *El País* in Spain (some examples are *Jornal do Brasil* and *Reforma* in Mexico). In addition, a number of newspapers now provide exclusive business coverage—*Gazeta Mercantil* in Brazil, *El Financiero* and *El Economista* in Mexico, and *Economía Hoy* and *Reporte* in Venezuela (Tilson [*Media*] 1999).

Increased business opportunities in the global media market have expanded the horizons of such papers and also opened the door for competing publications. In 1999, Grupo de Diarios America, an association of 11 major Latin American dailies, located its world headquarters in Coral Gables, Florida (a municipality of Miami-Dade County). The association represents more than two million subscribers and a vast network of internewspaper intelligence sharing (Tilson [*Media*] 1999). GDA executives felt that the U.S.-based location positioned the association "to become the most effective and efficient media buy in the region" with multinationals interested in the Latin American market (Grupo de Diarios America 1999). Agencia Estado, Brazil's largest news agency, joined Business Wire Global Latin American Network, a news delivery service, in 1998, and provides text, photos, and audio and video feeds to more than 250 media, both within the region and internationally (Tilson [*Media*] 1999).

Similarly, U.S. print news publications have expanded their reach into Latin America. *Newsweek en Español*, with bureaus in Mexico, Chile, and Argentina, publishes throughout the region. Luer and Tilson (1996) also note that

> *Time, Newsweek,* and *Business Week* have published English-language editions in Latin America for several years. *Fortune* introduced a Latin American edition in 1993. *The Wall Street Journal* added a weekly edition in Central America and Bolivia in early 1996. *The Miami Herald* began delivering its international edition via satellite to Panama and Colombia in early 1996. (p. 26)

Such expansion often is in partnership with Latin American print media. *The Miami Herald,* for example, has eight partner publishers throughout the region, serving 12 major markets; English-language international satellite editions are produced in association with *The Tribune* (the Bahamas), *La Prensa* (Panama), and *Diario Hoy* (Ecuador), among others, with a daily average paid circulation of more than 16,000 readers (R. Beatty 2002).

Television and radio, however, are the most dominant media in Latin America and continue to grow in influence. For example, from 1970 to 1988, the number of television stations in the region multiplied from 205 to 1,459 as countries and media conglomerates set up satellite and cable networks (Martin-Barbero 1995, cited in Tilson ["Against"] 1999). In Brazil, considered by many to be a "television nation," "more households have televisions than refrigerators" (Vanden Heuvel and Dennis

1995, p. 104). Virtually everyone has access to radio; it is the most pervasive and free communication medium in the region (Cole 1996). Throughout Latin America, radio and television, with their greater proportion of entertainment content, like *telenovelas* (soap operas), draw immense audiences, whereas newspapers are read more by the highly educated and those interested in politics (Cole 1996).

Such tremendous growth has given birth to major Latin American media conglomerates and also attracted foreign broadcast media multinationals into the region. According to Tilson and Newsom (2001):

> Cable television now reaches more than 15 million households in Latin America, and some 30 networks have established their operations in South Florida within the past five years. Major media include USA Latin America, Sony TV, Nickelodeon, Gems, HBO Latin America, MTV Latin America, Discovery Communications Latin America, MGM Networks Latin America and the Cisneros Television Group, which is a partner in Galaxy Latin America, the DIRECTV Provider and the world's largest private satellite operator. (pp. 41–42)

The Brazilian communications giant, Organizaçoes Globo, touts a stable of subsidiaries, including *O Globo*, the nation's second largest newspaper, TV Globo (part of Rede Globo, the multinational, multimedia TV component), considered "the world's fourth or fifth largest network" (Stevenson 1994, cited in Montenegro 2004), and Globo Cabo, Brazil's top cable-TV operator, among other entities. Grupo Cisneros has 37,000 employees, investments and syndication concerns in at least 40 countries, and revenues of $3.7 billion (Mayorbe 2002).

Along with Globo, Televisa of Mexico continues its dominance as one of the most important television networks in the world. Although Cisneros may now be a larger operation, Televisa is still considered the broadcaster that reaches the most people in Latin America, producing more than 44,000 hours of programming annually (Tricks 2000). Televisa's production of *telenovelas* for export worldwide, along with its news and other syndication services, makes it a force in the dynamic world of global television. In 2000, Televisa had $1.4 billion in sales and about 14,000 employees (Tricks 2001). During the 1990s, Televisa expanded into direct and partial ownership of various networks outside of Mexico, including partnerships in Peru, Chile, and Guatemala. With Grupo Cisneros, Televisa also reacquired considerable holdings in Univision, the most popular Spanish-language network in the United States (Sinclair 2002). Although the Mexican government encouraged the formation of a new challenger to Televisa in the 1990s in the form of TV Azteca, the older network found a way to revamp its programming to win the ratings challenge, making it the choice of 80 percent of Mexican viewers. Televisa is also one of the major stakeholders in the Sky Latin America satellite service, along with Rupert Murdoch's News Corporation, Globo, and TCI from the United States (Fox and Waisbord 2002).

Like Televisa, TV Azteca has moved beyond domestic concerns to syndicate programming in Latin America and has established partnerships or direct ownership of networks in Guatemala and El Salvador. TV Azteca also formed a strategic partnership with Telemundo, the Spanish-language competitor to Univision in the United States. The U.S. network NBC acquired Telemundo in 2001 (James 2001). Another Mexican broadcasting force of note is Angel González, who runs various network and local television operations from his headquarters in Miami (Rockwell and Janus 2001). Including six local television operations in Mexico, González has television holdings in at least nine countries in Latin America and the Caribbean. In 1998, his operations had revenues of $100 million (Paxman 1999).

Additionally, Ted Turner's 24-hour Spanish-language network, CNN en Español, has been broadcasting CNN-signature-style international news and feature programming since 1997, following the signing of distribution agreements in Argentina, Colombia, and half a dozen other Latin American countries. The programming is fed from bureaus in Mexico City, Buenos Aires, Rio de Janeiro, and Santiago, Chile (Luer and Tilson 1996).

Problems of Reform

Some argue that economic, social, and political changes have ushered in more open and democratic societies with greater economic opportunities. Others contend, however, that the confluence of outside and indigenous special interests has only benefited ruling oligarchies and exacerbated unemployment and poverty in the region while further contributing to a climate of corruption and institutional violence (Tilson ["Against"] 1996, 1999). Indeed, as Shifter (1997) has noted about the unequal progress of antipoverty programs in Latin America compared to the advance of democracy in the region, "Improving the quality of democracy may not necessarily enhance efficiency and help deliver the kinds of benefits that citizens demand" (p. 115). Weak democratic institutions throughout the region that are meant to shore up accountability, representation, and the rule of law have left strong executive power in place for the most part. The media also have often shirked any sense of a public service mission in favor of the pursuit of profits. Consequently, very little reporting of quality is aimed at the immense poverty of the region. Some of this relates to the oligarchic nature of media ownership in the region. As a consequence, journalists in the region have been caught dead center in the vortex of such issues, both as investigative reporters and, often, as targets of harassment and violence.

Poverty

A closer look at the economies in the region shows both sides of the argument. According to the World Bank, the number of poor has grown from 136 million in 1986 to 180 million, but as a percentage of overall population, it has declined since 1992 from 40 percent to 34 percent currently; moreover, projections suggest that poverty levels will fall to 24 percent by 2015 even as the total number of poor increases to 147 million (Oppenheimer ["Gloomy"] 2001). Of further concern, however, is the increasing concentration of wealth in the region. The United Nations'

Human Development Report 2001 details severe disparities in income, with the richest 20 percent of the population earning a disproportionate share as compared with the poorest 20 percent. In general, Latin America, which began privatizing state-run industries and implementing free-market reforms in Chile, Mexico, and Argentina in the mid-1980s, has the widest gap between rich and poor in the world, with the richest 20 percent having 30 times the income of the poorest 20 percent (Oppenheimer ["Latin America Leads"] 2001). Several countries top the list, not only in the hemisphere but also in the world—Bolivia (highest income 38 times that of the poorest), Honduras (38 times), and Nicaragua (28 times). According to the Inter American Development Bank's *Development Beyond Economics 2000* study, the region's average per-capita income has declined from 50 percent to 30 percent of the average in the developed world since 1950 (Bussey 2000). Haiti, Guatemala, and Nicaragua rank the lowest in the hemisphere on the United Nations' Human Development Index (Pierri 2002). The index is based on a number of social indicators, including per-capita income, school attendance, literacy rates, and life expectancy. Argentina attained the highest point on the index in Latin America, finishing in 34th place. By contrast, Haiti ranked 146, Guatemala was listed at 120, and Nicaragua at 118.

The InterAmerican Development Bank's *Development Beyond Economics 2000* study argues, moreover, that privileged classes that rule such societies do little to support public policies necessary to provide vital social services to the poor (Oppenheimer ["Latin America Leads"] 2001). An InterAmerican Development Bank report corroborates the inequities in economic development and places the responsibility squarely on the shoulders of public institutions—government administrations, justice systems, and electoral bodies; as Ricardo Hausmann, IDB chief economist, noted, "Latin American countries have problems with the rule of law, corruption and the ineffectiveness of government" (Bussey 2000, p. 9E). In Argentina and Peru, for example, hundreds of thousands of workers lost their jobs when industries were privatized, but few provisions were made for their retraining, outplacement, or social welfare. Freitag (2004) reports that unemployment and underemployment in Peru now stand at 61 percent of the population, and 90 percent of Peruvians spend 80 percent of their income on food.

Corruption

While no one country or region has a monopoly on corruption, it seems that privatization of state-run industries in developing nations "has been the foremost source of corrupt payments," according to Dean Klitgaard of the Rand Graduate School (Bussey 1998, cited in Tilson ["Against"] 1999, p. 70). As during the Salinas administration in Mexico, "corrupt government officials . . . have given privatization deals and other business contracts to associates," which discourages investors and inhibits the flow of free-market reform benefits to society (Tilson ["Against"] 1999, p. 70). Indeed, the number of Mexican billionaires increased from two in 1991 to 24 in 1994 as many garnered the winning bids in the sale of government industries through their association with the Salinas presidential family and the ruling Institutional Revolutionary Party (PRI, Spanish initials) (Oppenheimer and Ellison 1996, cited in Tilson ["Against"] 1999, p. 70). Since winning office in a historic election in 2000, President Vicente Fox has made fighting corruption a top priority of his administration.

A review of two studies issued almost simultaneously indicates that corruption inhibits the flow of foreign capital into the general economy, with government officials and economic oligarchies often monopolizing such funds for their private interests. A Miliken Institute study of credit availability in 31 emerging nations (Fields 1998) ranked Chile fifth among the top in liquidity and five other Latin American nations in the middle to bottom ranks—Peru (13), Brazil (14), Mexico (21), Ecuador (20), and Venezuela (25). These rankings seem to correlate with those in a 1998 and a 2002 Transparency International corruption index based on residents' and nonresidents' perceptions of the level of corruption in each country. In 1998, Chile (20) ranked among the least corrupt of the 85 nations reviewed, while other Latin American nations ranked in the middle to bottom: Peru (41), Brazil (46), Mexico (55), Ecuador (77), and Venezuela (77) ("Survey" 1998). In a 2002 study of 100 nations, countries in Latin America maintained similar rankings, with Chile and Uruguay scoring above the norm in the region, Brazil (45), Mexico, and Colombia (58) emerging toward the middle, and Venezuela (81) and Ecuador (89) slipping farther toward the bottom; other nations at the lower end included Argentina (70), Guatemala and Nicaragua (81), Haiti (89), and Paraguay (98) (Bussey 2002). Corruption has become so endemic in Paraguay, for example, particularly smuggling operations by customs and port administration officials, that the Industrialists Association "sarcastically asked the government for jobs in corruption-rife sectors, so they can save their own firms and turn around the country's economy" ("Paraguay" 2002). Leading newspapers have regularly featured the alleged corrupt activities of customs and port officials, which prompted a government investigation of their personal assets and a review of anticorruption laws.

Of course, not all journalists in the region have been immune to the corrosive influence of "crony capitalism." Peru during the administration of President Alberto Fujimori (1990–2000) is a case in point. Fujimori, who portrayed himself as "the Lee Iacoca of Latin America" (Freitag 2004), launched an aggressive neoliberal economic plan built on the privatization of industry and a worldwide promotional campaign to recast Peru's image as a "business-friendly," progressive country. Privatized sectors eventually included mining, petroleum distribution, salt, cement, banking, telecommunications, power generation, and the national airline, realizing U.S. $2.8 billion in proceeds in 1994 alone (Freitag 2004). However, "while the economy improved under Fujimori's neoliberal policies—evidenced especially by the drop in inflation from 40 percent per month to 1–2 percent per month—social costs included sharp increases in unemployment and poverty" (Freitag 2004). Popular opposition soon began to grow with oil workers' union protests against the sale of a major refinery in 1996 and a decline in public support in opinion polls by 2001. In November 2001, according to Freitag (2004), "following revelations of corruption, and fearing investigation and charges," Fujimori disappeared into a self-imposed exile in Japan. A major investigation of corruption in the administration ensued in

2002. Freitag (2004) notes that the investigation "was extended to include possible manipulation of public opinion through considerable financial incentives extended to media that supported the government (Chauvin 2001). The Administration, in fact, outspent Procter & Gamble in 1999, becoming the nation's largest advertiser. By early 2000, four of the top-spending advertisers in Peru were government agencies, lavishing tens of millions of dollars on sympathetic media."

Freitag (2004) further observed that "It's ironic that the final blow to the Fujimori Administration was the repeated broadcast on Peruvian television of a hidden-camera video showing . . . Vladimiro Montesinos [Presidential security advisor] handing a wad of cash to an opposition congressman in exchange for his switching parties. Others present on the video included a top advertising agency executive and then-vice president of Peru's largest network. In separate audio recordings, Montesinos tells the network vice president how to slant news coverage in favor of the administration."

Multiple sets of criminal charges have since been filed against Fujimori for corruption, and against many of those in his administration for embezzlement, particularly for the use of privatization proceeds for personal enrichment, and for drug and arms trafficking. According to Johnson ("Corrupt" 2002, p. 19A), "investigations have led to the imprisonment of a former attorney general, two Supreme Court justices, four television station owners, a former president of Congress, four other legislators, and 14 generals." In May 2002, Peru's Special Prosecutor's office "asked the courts to name government-appointee trustees to run two TV networks, Channels 4 and 5," since the former owners were in jail "accused of receiving multimillion dollar bribes from Montesinos" (Chauvin ["Peru-controlled"] 2002). A state trustee also was requested to take control of *Expresso*, in the absence of its former executive editor, who was accused—and who has admitted to the charges—of receiving almost $3 million from Montesinos "to slant news coverage in Fujimori's favor"; the Miami-based Inter-American Press Association argued against the request, contending that it would compromise freedom of expression. Montesinos, who fled to Panama within a week of the televised airing of the tapes (September 14, 2000), was eventually arrested in Venezuela. In July 2002, a Peruvian court found Montesinos guilty of abusing his authority, sentenced him to nine years plus in prison, and imposed a fine of $2.85 million; more than 60 other cases currently were pending against him (Chauvin 2002). That August, Switzerland returned $77.5 million in funds "originated from corruption-related crimes" traced back to Montesinos and a former head of the Joint Chiefs of Staff; the money—commissions on arms trafficking and embezzlement of military budgets—is the tip of some $782 million traceable to more than 200 people that corruption investigators have identified and "represents a staggering amount of money for a relatively poor country like Peru . . . fighting to overcome an economic crisis" (Chauvin 2002, p. 11A). To date, Peruvian officials have recovered $145.8 million from the foreign bank accounts of Montesinos and the former chief of Peru's armed forces, and believe that Montesinos accounts still hide several hundreds of millions of dollars more. Moreover, an assistant prosecutor believes that Fujimori "'has at least as much as Montesinos'" (Johnson ["Plundered] 2002). Japan has repeatedly rebuffed requests from Peruvian officials to extradite Fujimori to stand trial. Meanwhile, the administration of Alejandro Toledo has attempted to press ahead with privatization, even though more than 60 percent of Peruvians oppose it. A decision to sell two state-owned power companies in June 2002 was quickly suspended following a week of violent public protests and the imposition of a state of emergency in southern Peru.

While the corruption of the Peruvian media may be extreme, it is by no means unique in the region. Garvin (1999) reports that government payoffs to journalists "are customary throughout much of Latin America, where salaries for journalists are usually very low. Those who work in the news business often find that they are expected to supplement their income off the job . . . an entry-level newspaper reporter makes as little as $350 a month." In Nicaragua, for example, "many reporters and editors routinely supplement their income with under-the-counter payments from officials looking for favorable stories—or seeking to avoid unfavorable ones" (Garvin 1999). In 1999, aides to then President Arnoldo Alemán, seeking to discredit then Comptroller Agustin Jarquin, a political enemy who was preparing to run for president in 2001, revealed more than $120,000 in payoffs by Jarquin to some 63 journalists, including the news-talk show host of Nicaragua's top-rated TV station, "to ensure favorable publicity that would polish Jarquin's image as a corruption fighter" (Garvin 1999). Such payoffs date to the Somoza government, and other perks, including government-sponsored low-cost housing for journalists in Managua, easy-term home mortgages, and annual duty-free imports of cars, have become institutionalized benefits (Garvin 1999).

Jarquin counterpunched with a campaign in 2000 to expose the corruption of President Alemán. Jarquin's zeal was propelled a bit by party allegiance; he is a Sandinista, and Alemán is the leader of the Liberal Party. Alemán's government is notorious now for the various corruption schemes that have turned up since he left office. However, at the time, Alemán's schemes were still mostly hidden. As he unearthed the beginnings of the Alemán scandal, Jarquin paid Danilo Lacayo, the anchor of Nicaragua's favorite television program, *Buenas Dias Nicaragua*, to regularly carry items from Jarquin's office. Lacayo was also paid to share his own investigative material with Jarquin. But when Jarquin's deal with Lacayo leaked out, the Comptroller General was the one headed to jail, and Lacayo lost his prominent television job (Dye, Spence, and Vickers 2000).

The story continued to develop in 2002, following the election of President Enrique Bolaños, when prosecutors in Nicaragua found $124 million "in questionable government and private transfers," which they believe ended up in the pockets of Alemán, his family, relatives, and associates; they further contended that another $1.8 million "in illegal government expenditures [was used] to cover the former president's American Express card purchases" (Oppenheimer ["Nicaragua's"] 2002). Arrest warrants for four relatives and six associates of Alemán were issued on charges of corruption, fraud, and money laundering.

In Panama, so many scandals, "including bribes to government officials and assembly members," have rocked the administration of President Mireya Moscoso that in September 2002, she asked the United Nations for help in battling corruption. In that regard, she turned to the UN Agency for Development, requesting that the office formulate "a plan of integrity for human development to prevent all elements of corruption in our society and promote ethical, civic and moral values" ("President" 2002).

In Mexico, Long (2004) observes that "at times, the media, as with government and other institutions, have been a part of the entrenched corruption that afflicted Mexico for all of the twentieth century . . . the media received its marching orders—and frequently plain brown enveloped filled with pesos—from the dominant political party and other special interests . . . in many cases, the cash changed hands before stories were written; on occasion, the envelope came in appreciation for a certain story or placement." Long (2004) also notes the once widespread use of the printing of *gacetillas,* or government (a k a PRI)-purchased advertising space designed to look like news stories: "In some cases, entire pages of newspapers were covered with government propaganda . . . newspapers became dependent on the insertions for their revenue flow, and there was a natural desire to make sure nobody harmed the cash cow. Reporters came to depend on them, too, because many papers gave a commission to those whose beats generated the income."

In Central America also, newspapers and radio stations often sell advertising that masquerades as news. In El Salvador and Nicaragua such ads are called *campos pagados.* Some Salvadoran papers, however, have adopted the practice of labeling *campos pagados* as "paid space," much as is done in Costa Rica and the United States. Such hidden advertising can also be found in Guatemala, Honduras, and Panama.

Long (2004) notes that the practice in Mexico began to decline in the late 1980s, during the Salinas administration, when the media were granted limited additional freedom. Similarly, President Fox has curtailed the use of the *embute,* the regular government supplemental payment to journalists. Much of the official corruption flowing from the president's office, in fact, had already been stopped by Fox's predecessor, Ernesto Zedillo, who notably ended the practice of lavish, all-expenses-paid junkets and travel for reporters covering the president (Lloyd 2000).

Outside of presidential circles, however, the largesse in Mexico still flows. Journalists still remain in the employ of various political parties, corporate entities, and even drug traffickers. During the 1990s, a variety of ways were used to bribe reporters besides direct cash payments—free cars, free or discounted gasoline and long distance usage, jewelry, cases of liquor, prostitutes, expensive meals, and airline tickets, among other methods (Rockwell 2002).

Although the climate to combat corruption may be improving in Mexico, other Latin American countries saw corrupt influences gaining stronger footholds in the 1990s. For instance, the 1997 elections in Honduras were tainted by the influence of drug money (Payne 1998). Notably, the winner of that election, Carlos Flores, also owns *La Tribuna,* one of the more successful newspapers in Honduras. During an international conference on journalism, a reporter from the popular Honduran network Radio America noted that reporters on the presidential beat in Tegucigalpa received large government supplements to the paychecks from their media outlets (Fliess 1999).

Such "corruption" of the public channels of communication, encouraged by "a heightened level of business activity [which] invites more official and corporate corruption," also is a consequence of the "unethical and illegal behavior [that] has extended itself to the promotional sector" (Tilson ["Against"] 1999, p. 71). As Sharpe (1992) noted, it has been common practice for corporations "to hire licensed journalists for the preparation of news releases" (p. 104). When such "hired guns" submit stories, the media "generally accept that material without change or question because to offer such a challenge would be an affront to another licensed journalist" (Sharpe and Simöes 1996, p. 288). In some cases, a journalist actually may hold two jobs, one with a media outlet and another with a corporation.

Still, some of the leading public relations consultancies in Latin America now report a sea change in such behavior. Ketchum Senior Partner and CEO David Drobis noted in 1998 that "we're finally seeing the demise of the time-honored practice of so-called 'informal journalism'—or paying the media for placement of your story. Nevertheless, personal relationships are still very important when dealing with the media in Mexico, Argentina or Brazil" (p. 9). In interviews with the leading public relations firms in Mexico, Long (2004) similarly reported a change in attitude on both sides of the news desk. One of the principals in Zimat Golin/Harris noted that—according to Long—"media bribes have been almost eradicated. . . . Today those who take payments are an endangered species. Nobody controls the media in this country anymore . . . for years, the media feared the government would lift its radio-TV concessions or its lucrative print advertising. No longer." Also according to Long (2003), an official at Edelman Public Relations Worldwide claims that "Mexico's news media are becoming more professional. 'We see many new, young and serious-minded professionals pursuing journalism, especially covering business and technology' . . . [while] it is common in a client presentation to be asked, 'How much of the budget goes to the journalists?', today, the answer is 'zero' in the business arena, though . . . the practice of paying bribes to reporters may die more slowly in the political sector" (Long 2004). A Fleishman-Hillard executive observed further that "younger Mexicans are becoming more trusting of the media, and reporters and editors are learning how to use the freedoms they acquired with the end of authoritarian rule. It is a given . . . that the public will gain from a better-informed media" (Long 2004).

Institutionalized Censorship and Violence

The media in Latin America often have the led the fight against corruption, and have paid a high price for such investigative work. Newspapers led the way in the fight against government corruption in the 1990s. In the early part of the decade, Venezuela's *El Nacional* exposed the corruption of President Carlos Andrés Pérez, and he eventually resigned, although while still in office, he ordered the forced closure of the paper (Vanden Heuvel and Dennis 1995). In Brazil, the investigative work of a variety of publications, including *Veja, Jornal do Brasil*, and *Fólha de São Paulo*, opened the debate about political corruption that eventually led to the end of the presidency of Fernando Collor de Mello (Lins da Silva 2000). In Argentina, the corruption investigations started by *Pagina 12* took a decade to gain momentum and eventually snuffed out the political career of former President Carlos Menem (Waisbord 2000). In Guatemala, although it came too late to stop corruption flowing from the president's office, investigative reporting by *Prensa Libre* and *elPeriodico* revealed the various corruption scandals of the Arzú administration. The investigative campaign by the papers during 2000 helped as Arzú's party disassembled itself after he left office, leaving Guatemala's National Advancement Party a shell of its former self (Weissert 2000).

Courageous journalists who do choose to expose corruption (both corporate and governmental), drug dealing, and arms trafficking often find themselves in harm's way. Such journalists daily face harassment, "legal, administrative and economic pressures," and death threats (Kudlak ["Climate"] 2001, p. 66). Many are murdered. In 2001, according to the International Press Institute, "eleven journalists were killed in Colombia, two in Mexico . . . and one each in Bolivia, Brazil, Costa Rica, Guatemala, Haiti and Paraguay" (Kudlak ["Climate"] 2001, p. 66). In 2000, 17 journalists were murdered, including eight in Colombia (Inter-American Press Association 2001). In 2002, the Committee to Protect Journalists (CPJ) ranked Colombia as the second worst country in which to practice journalism in the world (Webster 2002). According to the International Press Institute, the country is considered "the most dangerous . . . in the Americas to work in as a journalist," with "vast areas . . . outside government control," and those "who attempt to expose corruption and other illegal activities, or report on . . . the civil war" are continually in danger; journalists are kidnapped by leftist rebels, "forced to leave the country or go into hiding because of death threats" even as media outlets are bombed (Kudlak ["Climate"] 2001, p. 66). For example, Francisco Santos, the news editor of *El Tiempo* and an activist against kidnapping, fled into exile "after speaking out against the violence and intimidation meted out by Colombia's illegal armies of the left and right" ("Assault" 2000, p. 35). The violence in Colombia, which has escalated in the past decade, is part of a civil war that has stretched on for almost 40 years (Smyth 2002) and is also aimed at clergy, politicians, and ordinary citizens. The lethal mix of paramilitaries, drug gangs, and left-wing guerrillas includes the prominent rebel groups FARC and ELN, both formed in 1965, and the EPL, the smallest, founded in 1967–1968 (Wickham-Crowley 1992).

Violence against journalists has been declining in Mexico. Between 1970 and 1998, more journalists were murdered in Mexico than in Colombia during the same period (Rockwell 1999). Only three journalists were killed in Mexico in the past two years, which is notable because during the 1990s Mexico had climbed near the top of the CPJ watch list. Instead of violence directed by corrupt bureaucrats and politicians, as was common in the 1970s and 1980s, repression of journalists in Mexico is now directed by drug gangs, and sometimes by corrupt elements of the police employed by drug traffickers. All of the journalists killed in recent years have worked in areas close to the U.S.- Mexico border and have filed critical reports about drug trafficking (Smeets ["Mexico"] 2002).

Like Mexico, although violence against journalists has subsided in Guatemala since the end of the country's 36-year guerrilla war, journalists there still face threats. Since peace accords were signed in 1996, Guatemala has averaged about one journalist killed annually. In 2001, Jorge Mynor Alegria Armendariz was murdered after discussing official corruption on his radio program based in Izabal Department (Smeets ["Guatemala"] 2002). The newspaper *elPeriodico* also faced a number of threats for investigating the powerful Guatemalan military and revealing corruption in the administration of President Alfonso Portillo. Portillo's Communication Minister Luis Rabbe was forced to resign his post after *elPeriodico* discovered Rabbe had organized a rock-throwing protest at the newspaper's headquarters (Bounds, Emmott, and Webb-Vidal 2001).

In Peru, according to the International Press Institute, "the departure of president Alberto Fujimori has led to a freer and more independent print and broadcast media" but journalists continue "to report cases of threats [and] attacks . . . particularly at the hands of public officials in the country's interior" (Kudlak ["Climate"] 2001, p. 67). During Fujimori's administration, the government seized the television station Frecuencia Latina–Canal 2 in retaliation for its reports about corruption, murder, torture, wiretapping, and drug trafficking by officials and the military, including a story about the 1992 massacre of nine students and a professor at La Cantuta University, attributed to paramilitary death squads in collusion with government intelligence personnel (Reyes 1998). Canal 2 owners Baruch Ivcher and Jose Arrieta, head of the station's investigative unit, went into exile, and the station was turned over to more loyal supporters of the administration (Simon 1999). Still other journalists were arrested on charges of "terrorism." Ivcher has since returned from exile and reclaimed his station, and the journalists released from prison. Peru's Truth and Reconciliation Committee is investigating allegations of atrocities during Fujimori's administration, including a 1991 massacre of more than a dozen people in a poor Lima neighborhood; Fujimori faces murder charges for allegedly approving the attack as well as for the murders at La Cantuta University ("Fujimori" 2002).

While the media in the Caribbean are generally free of government interference (with the exception of Cuba), harassment of and attacks on journalists in Haiti by police and supporters of President Jean-Bertrand Aristide have been increasing. Journalists are considered "participants in the struggle for political power"; in one instance, a broadcast journalist was macheted to death by a pro-government mob (Kudlak ["Climate"] 2001).

U.S. corporations and public relations consultancies share some of the blame for such violence. U.S. consultancies, for example, have counseled some of the most violent and corrupt regimes in the hemisphere (Tilson ["Against"] 1999), including Duvalier in Haiti (Hill & Knowlton), Somoza in Nicaragua (Norman, Lawrence, Patterson, and Farrell), and Argentine leaders during the nation's "dirty war" against suspected dissidents in the 1970s (Burson-Marsteller). Such representation has done little to endear Latin Americans to the United States or its interests in the region. Further, a report issued following the 2001 Summit of the Americas in Quebec indicated that foreign and domestic corporations in Latin America do little to promote the welfare of employees or the local community. The report urges corporations to work proactively with government to institute private-sector initiatives to improve social conditions and to strengthen codes of conduct with anticorruption measures. Such corporate responsibility should be a priority for public relations professionals who counsel top management, and good citizenship an integral part of every strategic public relations plan. In so doing, the profession can best serve not only its own interests and those of its employers, but also the interests of the societies in which they operate.

Of course, there are many other ways to silence journalists from reporting the truth. As noted earlier, the use of government-purchased advertising space is still very much in practice in the region. In 2001, governments in Argentina, Honduras, Nicaragua, and Uruguay, in particular, "sought to intimidate the media by using official advertising to either reward or punish the media" (Kudlak ["Climate"] 2001, p. 66). According to the International Press Institute, a number of legislatures have passed laws "that require journalists to possess degrees, licenses or membership in special associations in order to exercise their profession" (Kudlak ["Climate"] 2001, p. 66). In an exception, Panama rescinded two laws in 1999 originally adopted during the regime of General Omar Torrijos that required journalists to be licensed and that imposed fines and imprisonment on reporters who "discredited" government institutions (Martinez 1999, p. 3a).

All too often, however, journalists do face charges of criminal defamation, libel, and slander. In Chile, for example, a former presidential candidate brought insult and libel charges last year against three *El Metropolitano* reporters, even though some provisions of the country's State Security Law were repealed to provide more press freedom and the return of exiled journalist Alejandra Matus from the United States (Kudlak ["Climate"] 2001, p. 67). In Venezuela, Montenegro (2004) reports that, in April 2000, "a provincial law passed by the state of Apure allows local police to detain journalists who publish negative information about the regional authorities and politicians."

President Hugo Chávez generally has been at odds with the media since his election in 1998, arguing that "he has been the victim of unfair coverage by the opposition-aligned news media" ("Marchers" 2002). Presidential aides have threatened tax audits against newspaper publishers—forcing out Teodoro Petkoff, a Chávez critic and the editor of *El Mundo* in 1999, for example—which prompted a judge to order the arrest of an *Exceso* reporter and publisher on defamation charges (both fled into hiding), and have filed similar suits against other media, including Pablo Lopez, the publisher of the weekly newspaper *La Razón* (Johnson 2000). A June 2001 Venezuelan Supreme Court decision, codifying the constitutional right to "truthful information," adds further legal muscle to a "judiciary . . . dominated by Chávez supporters, to punish those media that criticize the policies of the president and his government" (Kudlak ["Climate"] 2001, p. 67). In August 2002, Chávez created a new Information Ministry, headed by the former director of two state radio stations, to counterbalance "what he calls the local news media's unfair coverage of his government" ("Chavez" 2002).

Journalists reported that they were harassed and attacked by mobs during the violence and protests that swirled around the unsuccessful coup to bring down Chávez. One photographer was killed in the violence and another was paralyzed. At least 50 other people were killed in the violence surrounding the attempted coup. Reporters also feel they are being squeezed in the political struggle between President Hugo Chávez and media oligarchs (González Rodriguez 2002). International journalism groups have flagged Venezuela as one of the problem areas for the safety of journalists in the hemisphere, and have criticized Chávez for creating an antimedia mood in his country. Also, human rights groups criticized Venezuela in the late 1990s for allowing police and military forces to routinely use torture and violence against detainees (Shifter 1997). Colombia, Peru, Brazil, and Mexico were also on that infamous list.

In Cuba, the independent press has been under siege for decades. Journalists are "routinely harassed, threatened and detained . . . often with the goal of 'persuading' them to leave the country" (Kudlak ["Climate"] 2001, p. 66). President Fidel Castro's communist government does not recognize the island's some 100 independent journalists or the independent news agencies they work for. Generally considered to be "counterrevolutionaries," these journalists, according to the International Press Institute, are

> not allowed to publish or broadcast in Cuba . . . are forced to fax their stories to the United States, or dictate them over the telephone. . . . Their phone calls are monitored, they are prevented from traveling freely, and they are routinely put under house arrest. . . . Typewriters must be registered and owning a fax machine or photocopier without authorization is punishable by imprisonment. The Internet is also severely regulated. (Kudlak ["Cuba"] 2001, p. 79)

Gag laws in Cuba carry sentences of up to 14 years for "dangerousness," "disseminating enemy propaganda," and "insults against officials" (Kudlak ["Cuba"] 2001, p. 79). While three journalists were released from Cuban prisons in 2001, Bernardo Arévalo Padrón, founder of *Línea Sur Press,* an independent news agency, "remained incarcerated, serving a six-year prison term for 'insulting' the president" (Kudlak ["Climate"] 2001, p. 66).

In March and April 2003, the Castro government arrested as many as 100 people in an island-wide sweep of its best known and most vocal dissidents, including independent labor union and political party leaders, supporters of the Varela Project, a grassroots movement calling for free elections and other political reforms, and more than two dozen independent journalists. Economist Martha Beatriz Roque and Raúl Rivero, one of Cuba's most prominent independent journalists, were among those detained. Many of the dissidents were charged "with violating a much-criticized law that makes it a crime to support subversion and acts that would break the internal order and destabilize the country" (San Martin ["Spate"] 2003, p. 2A). The European Union, various nations, human-rights groups, and press organizations condemned the arrests (San Martin ["Cuba"] 2003).

Roque and more than a dozen others facing life sentences subsequently went on trial behind closed doors with at least 43 other defendants as did Rivero, who faced 20 years in prison. On April 7, Cuban courts sentenced the defendants to as much as 27 years in prison; Roque and Rivero each received 20 years, and another independent journalist, Omar Rodriguez Saludes, was sentenced to the longest term—27 years (San Martin ["Cuba"] 2003).

Less than a week later, on April 11, three Cuban men arrested for the attempted hijacking of a ferry to the United States were convicted on terrorism charges and executed by a firing squad. A few days later, the remaining imprisoned dissidents were convicted and sentenced. In total, some 75 dissidents were given prison terms from 6 to 28 years, with an average sentence of 19 years (Johnson 2003).

Democracy

Good governance and a "clean" media are essential to the economic, social, and political well-being of a society. Most important for the future of the hemisphere, however, as noted almost a decade ago by various Latin heads of state attending the Summit of the Americas in Miami in December 1994, "corruption in both the public and private sector weakens democracy and undermines the legitimacy of governments" ("Declaration of Principles" 1994, p. 14). It was just such public fatigue with corruption that prompted a change in Mexico's presidency in 2000 after 71 years of rule by the Institutional Revolutionary Party and that climaxed in massive protests driving several administrations from office in Ecuador and ousting five presidents in less than three weeks in Argentina in 2001, while also leaving 28 dead and a nation in bankruptcy. By the time the de la Rúa Administration collapsed in Argentina, political expenditures were estimated at U.S. $2–4 billion for almost one million federal and provincial employees, with many party loyalists rewarded with lifetime "political spoils" jobs protected by law (Oppenheimer ["Argentines"] 2001). With the average public-sector worker making almost twice that of private-sector employees, and federal legislators earning 200 times that amount, it is not surprising that only 15 percent of the public said they trusted Congress, down from 75 percent in 1983, when the nation returned to democracy (Oppenheimer ["Gloomy"] 2001). Public dissatisfaction with corruption and underperforming economies has prompted impatience with "proto-democracies" throughout the region (Shifter 1997) and has also resulted in major regime change in Peru, Venezuela, and Brazil. Some might even question whether some of the governments in Latin America truly were democracies. Given the corruption and oligarchic media power on display in countries such as Honduras, such combinations had more in common with the new oligarchies of the post-Soviet states. Some experts have dubbed these emerging systems "polyarchies," a system with democratic forms but run by a coterie of power at the top (Robinson 2000).

In general, popular support for democracy has been eroding throughout Latin America. A regional poll conducted in April–May 2002 by Cima-Barometro Iberoamericano (which includes several Gallup affiliates) reports popular support below 30 percent for a majority of presidents; only President Fox of Mexico and President Lagos of Chile recorded positive ratings of 45 percent or higher (Oppenheimer ["Most"] 2002). Some of the lowest tallies of respondents who considered their nation's leader "very good" or "good" included Chávez, 5 percent (Venezuela); Toledo, 10 percent (Peru); Duhalde, 16 percent (Argentina); and Cardoso, 20 percent (Brazil). Moreover, according to the survey, "political parties are equally discredited," with public trust of these institutions generally under 20 percent; confidence levels in Venezuela (11 percent), Peru (10 percent), Argentina (8 percent), Brazil, Bolivia, and Ecuador (6 percent each) are among the lowest (Oppenheimer ["Most"] 2002). The results echo a Latinobarometro 2001 poll that revealed a drop from 60 percent to 48 percent in support for democracy across the region; in some countries, such as El Salvador and Brazil, only 25 percent and 30 percent polled thought that "democracy was preferable to any other kind of government," with the most trusted institutions being the Catholic Church (76 percent) and television (70%) (Oppenheimer ["Dear"], ["Latin America Suffering"] 2001). Not surprisingly, disenchanted citizens often choose not to vote in national elections. Voter turnout in presidential and congressional elections throughout the region within the past few years has been abysmal. Abstention rates have ranged from 61 percent (1999 presidential elections in El Salvador and Guatemala) to 42 percent (2001 congressional elections in Argentina) to 40 percent (2002 presidential elections in Costa Rica) to 34 percent (2001 presidential elections in Honduras), "produc[ing] politically weak presidents that have a hard time governing" (Oppenheimer ["Latin American Elections"] 2002). Understandably, some of the disenchantment reflects "frustration about the region's economic slump" and "dashed high expectations that democracy would automatically bring about better living standards" (Oppenheimer ["Latin American Elections"] 2002). More important, however, according to Oppenheimer, "recent corruption cases in most countries—now getting widespread exposure thanks to an increasingly independent press—have taken a toll on people's trust in politicians."

In Ecuador, for example, "crony capitalism" is a major recurrent theme that has plagued a host of government administrations (Tilson ["Public"] 1999). In a review of *The Miami Herald* from January to September 1998, news stories cited corruption charges against Ecuadorean ex-Presidents Fabian Alarcón and Abdala Bucaram, Interior Minister Cesar Verduga, Foreign Minister Diego Paredes, and presidential advisor Eduardo Sierra; charges were also later filed against Bucaram Vice President Alberto Dahik and Press Secretary Enrique Proaño (Tilson ["Against"] 1999, p. 71). In one week of political chaos that preceded Bucaram's flight to safe haven in Panama in February 1997—with a reported $300 million stolen from government accounts—Ecuador had three presidents before congress and the military finally brokered a deal; half of the ex-president's cabinet joined him in exile or escaped to Miami (Tilson ["Against"] 1999, 2003). In June 2002, the country's Finance Minister and four other high-ranking officials in the ministry were accused of demanding bribes from various city mayors ("Ex-Minister" 2002). As noted, public confidence in political parties in Ecuador is only 6 percent, one of the lowest levels in Latin America (Oppenheimer ["Most"] 2002).

The effects of corruption on public confidence in democracy have not been lost on the United States. The Bush administration has taken an increasingly harder line on corrupt officials using the United States as a haven to escape prosecutors or hide illegal funds. In 2002, the U.S. State Department revoked the visas of public officials from Ecuador, Nicaragua (ex-Alemán functionaries), and more than 20 Guatemalans, and was moving to pull the visas of corrupt business owners and bankers. As Otto Reich, U.S. Assistant Secretary of State for the Western Hemisphere, told a trade and investment conference in Washington, "We have declared war on corruption. . . . Corruption in Latin America undermines the very systems that we are trying to support, the democratic systems, the development of societies" (Johnson ["Corrupt"] 2002).

Toward the Common Good

As multinational corporations, advertising and public relations consultancies, and media conglomerates, together with their partners in the hemisphere, reshape Latin American society, they should pause to consider the long-term consequences of their actions. While a certain degree of "progress" is desirable, if not inevitable, other "reforms" should be carefully weighed not so much against what is to be gained as against what is to be lost. As Tilson ("Against" 1999) notes:

> Are the new commercial enterprises, communications technologies, and free-market reforms serving the common good or are they increasing the social, political and economic inequities in society? If such developments are not addressing basic social needs, what is the future of democracy in the region? We would do well to consider that a basic moral test of society is the welfare of its most vulnerable members and that a community of conscience is required to orient public and private life toward the fundamental dignity of all human beings. (p. 72)

While the media can and should play an important role in exposing injustice and dishonesty, a broader view of community requires government, business, the media, and the public to work together to fashion societies that are free from corruption, institutional censorship and violence, and economic exploitation. In so doing, a society can create an economically and politically healthy, stable environment in which human rights are respected, citizens can participate in government, and the fruits of labor are equitably shared. Such a truly "civil" society will require personal sacrifice from government officials, corporate executives, journalists, and all citizens, and a transformation of personal and professional lives. In the final analysis, though, the courage to pursue the path that includes the common good in all decisions ultimately will be a blessing for all peoples, not only in Latin America but also around the world.

Bibliography

"The Assault on Democratic Society in Colombia." *The Economist* (March 2000): 34–35.

Beatty, Robert. Personal communication, 12 September 2002.

Bounds, A., R. Emmott, and A. Webb-Vidal. "Press Finds It a Struggle to Stay Free in Latin America." *The Financial Times* (London), 4 July 2001, 3.

Bussey, J. "Anti-Corruption Summit Seeks Solutions." *The Miami Herald*, 3 April 1998, 3C.

———. "Despite Reforms, the Americas Continue to Lag Much of the World." *The Miami Herald*, 21 May 2000, 1E.

———. "Latin America Low on Corruption Scale." *The Miami Herald*, 29 August 2002, 2C.

Chauvin, L. "Montesinos Receives 9–Year Sentence." *The Miami Herald,* 2 July 2002, 5A.

———. "Peru Gets Secret Fortune Linked to Former Spy Chief." *The Miami Herald,* 11A.

———. "Peru-Controlled Newspaper Would Hurt Press, Group Says." *The Miami Herald,* 1 May 2002, 14A.

"Chavez Creates Information Ministry." *The Miami Herald,* 21 August 2002, 10A.

Cole, R. *Communication in Latin America: Journalism, Mass Media, and Society.* Wilmington, Del.: Scholarly Resources, 1996.

"Declaration of Principles." Statement of Summit of the Americas, Miami, Fla., 11 December 1994.

Drobis, D. *Still Young at 75.* Speech to University of South Carolina College of Journalism and Communications, Columbia, October 1998. New York: Ketcham.

Dye, D. R., J. Spence, and G. Vickers. *Patchwork Democracy: Nicaraguan Politics Ten Years After the Fall.* Cambridge, Mass.: Hemisphere Initiatives, 2000.

"Ex-Minister Is Targeted in Corruption Scandal." *The Miami Herald,* 26 June 2002, 5A.

Fields, G. "Group: To Stay Afloat, Increase Liquidity." *The Miami Herald Business Monday,* 26 October 1998, 11.

Fliess, M. "Honduran Press Called Tarnished by Corruption." *free!* [Internet journal of the Freedom Forum], 13 September 1999. Available: http://www.freedomforum.org/international/1999/9/13mediaatmill.asp.

Fox, E., and S. Waisbord. *Latin Politics, Global Media.* Austin: University of Texas Press, 2002.

Freitag, A. "Perú's Fujimori: The Campaign to Sell the Administration's Neoliberal Policies." *Toward the Common Good: Perspectives in International Public Relations,* edited by D. Tilson and E. Alozie. Boston: Allyn and Bacon, 2004.

"Fujimori Declines to Talk to Commission." *The Miami Herald,* 11 September 2002, 16A.

Garvin, G. "In Nicaragua, News Handouts May Be Money." *The Miami Herald,* 19 April 1999, 8A.

González Rodríguez, S. "Cannon Fodder." The Committee to Protect Journalists [Internet database], 2 August 2002. Available: http://www.cpj.org/Briefings/2002/ven_aug02/ven_aug02.html.

Grupo de Diarios America. *The Miami Herald,* 25 March 1999, 3C.

Gunther, J. *Inside South America.* New York: Harper and Row, 1966.

Inter-American Press Association. "Impunity: Cases," October 2001. Available: http://www.impunidad.com/statistics/stats11_15_01E.html. Accessed 11 September 2002.

James, M. "Univision Strikes Pact with Televisa." *The Los Angeles Times,* 21 December 2001, 1C.

Johnson, T. "Chavez, Media at Odds." *The Miami Herald,* 12 March 2000, 1A.

———. "Corrupt Latin Leaders Could Lose Assets in U.S., Bush Envoy Says." *The Miami Herald,* 7 September 2002, 18A.

———. "Plundered Peru Struggles to Find Missing Treasure." *The Miami Herald,* 2 September 2002, 1A.

Kudlak, M. "A Climate of Intimidation: The Americas." *IPI Report 2001 World Press Freedom Review* (December 2001): 66–67.

———. "Cuba." *IPI Report 2001 World Press Freedom Review* (December 2001): 79–81.

Lins da Silva, C. E. "Journalism and Corruption in Brazil." *Combating Corruption in Latin America,* edited by J. S. Tulchin and R. H. Espach, 173–192. Washington, D.C.: Woodrow Wilson Center Press, 2000.

Lloyd, M. "Turning to New Page, Workers Oust Embattled Head of Mexico Paper." *Boston Globe,* 4 November 2000, C1.

Long, R. "The Other 'New' Mexico: Public Relations Accelerates the Move to a Legitimate Democracy." *Toward the Common Good: Perspectives in International Public Relations,* edited by D. Tilson and E. Alozie. Boston: Allyn and Bacon, 2004.

Luer, C. and D. Tilson. "Latin American Public Relations in the Age of Telecommunications, JC Penney and CNN." *Public Relations Quarterly* 41 (1996): 25–27.

"Marchers Hail Chávez, Who Faces Recession, Revived Foes." *The Miami Herald,* 25 August 2002, 15A.

Martin-Barbero, J. "Comunicación e Imaginarios de la Integración." *Taller de Comunicación,* 1995.

Martinez, K. "Panama Drops Restrictions to Free Press." *The Miami Herald,* 21 December 1999, 3A.

Mayorbe, J. A. "Venezuela and the Media: The New Paradigm." *Latin Politics, Global Media,* edited by E. Fox and S. Waisbord, 176–186. Austin: University of Texas Press, 2002.

Montenegro, S. "Public Relations in Latin America: A Survey of Professional Practice of Multinational Firms." *Toward the Common Good: Perspectives in International Public Relations,* edited by D. Tilson and E. Alozie. Boston: Allyn and Bacon, 2004.

Oppenheimer, A. "Argentines Want Politicians to Tighten Their Belts, Too." *The Miami Herald,* 22 July 2001, 6A.

———. "Dear Mr. President: Latin America Needs Your Attention." *The Miami Herald,* 5 August 2000, 8A.

———. "Gloomy Times: Latin Americans' View of the Future No Longer Shiny as in Early '90s." *The Miami Herald,* 17 June 2001, 1L.

———. "Latin America Leads World in Inequality, U.N. Study Says." *The Miami Herald,* 12 July 2001, 14A.

———. "Latin America Suffering 'Democratic Fatigue.' " *The Miami Herald,* 18 October 2001, 6A.

———. "Latin American Elections Marred by Decline in Voting." *The Miami Herald,* 30 May 2002, 11A.

———. "Most Latin Presidents Unpopular with Own People." *The Miami Herald,* 14 July 2002, 7A.

———. "Nicaragua's Ex-President May Set a Larceny Record." *The Miami Herald,* 5 September 2002, 9A.

"Paraguay Entrepreneurs Want In on Corruption." *The Miami Herald,* 22 August 2002, 2C.

Paxman, A. "Ghostly Titan Works Below the Radar." *Variety* (31 May 1999): 23.

Payne, D. W. *Storm Watch: Democracy in the Western Hemisphere into the Next Century.* Washington, D.C.: Center for Strategic and International Studies, 1998.

Pierri, R. "Human Development Backsliding Says UNDP." Inter Press News Service, 24 July 2002.

President Asks U.N. Help in Fighting Corruption." *The Miami Herald,* 2 September 2002, 7A.

Reyes, G. "Ex-Agent Tells of Torture, Wiretaps in Peru." *The Miami Herald,* 19 March 1998, 16A.

Robinson, W. I. "Polyarchy: Coercion's New Face in Latin America." *NACLA Report on the Americas* 34, no. 3 (November–December 2000): 42–48.

Rockwell, R. "Killing the Messenger: Methods of Media Repression in Mexico." *Mexico: Facing the Challenges of Human Rights and Crime,* edited by W. Cartwright, 199–216. Ardsley, N.Y.: Transnational Publishers, 1999.

Rockwell, R. "Mexico: The Fox Factor." *Latin Politics, Global Media,* edited by E. Fox and S. Waisbord, 107–122. Austin: University of Texas Press, 2002.

Rockwell, R., and N. Janus. "Stifling Dissent: The Fallout from a Mexican Media Invasion of Central America." *Journalism Studies* 2, no. 4 (2001): 497–512.

Salwen, M., and B. Garrison. *Latin American Journalism.* Hillsdale, N.J.: Lawrence Erlbaum, 1991.

San Martin, N. "Cuba Attacks Dissent with Prison." *The Miami Herald,* 8 April 2001, 1A.

———. "Spate of Hijackings Prompts Rare U.S. Warning to Cubans." *The Miami Herald,* 3 April 2003, 1A.

Sharpe, M. "The impact of social and cultural conditioning on global public relations." *Public Relations Review* 18 (1992): 103–107.

Sharpe, M., and R. Simões. "Public Relations Performance in South and Central America." *International Public Relations: A Comparative Analysis,* edited by H. Culbertson and N. Chen, 273–297. Mahwah, N.J.: Lawrence Erlbaum, 1996.

Shifter, M. "Tensions and Trade-offs in Latin America." *Journal of Democracy* 8, no. 2 (1997): 114–128.

Simon, J. "How Fujimori Uses Spies to Tighten His Grip on Peru." *The Miami Herald,* 4 February 1999, 29A.

Sinclair, J. "Mexico and Brazil: The Aging Dynasties." *Latin Politics, Global Media,* edited by E. Fox and S. Waisbord, 123–136. Austin: University of Texas Press, 2002.

Smeets, M. "Guatemala." *Attacks on the Press in 2001,* edited by R. M. Murphy, 187–189. New York: Committee to Protect Journalists, 2002.

Smeets, M. "Mexico." *Attacks on the Press in 2001,* edited by R. M. Murphy, 193–194. New York: Committee to Protect Journalists, 2002.

Smyth, F. "Colombia: Bad Press." *Attacks on the Press in 2001,* edited by R. M. Murphy, 16–24. New York: Committee to Protect Journalists, 2002.

Stevenson, R. *Global Communication in the Twenty-first Century.* New York: Longman, 1994.

"Survey Says Denmark Least Corrupt; U.S. Tied for 17th." *The Miami Herald,* 23 September 1998, 8A.

Tilson, D. "The Commodification of Latin America: A Confluence of Telecommunications, The Media and Promotion." *World Communication* 25 (1996): 133–141.

———. "Against the Common Good: The Commodification of Latin America." *Media Development* 46 (1999): 69–74.

———. "Privatization and Government Campaigning in Ecuador: Caudillos, Corruption and Chaos." *Toward the Common Good: Perspectives in International Public Relations,* edited by D. Tilson and E. Alozie. Boston: Allyn and Bacon, 2004.

———. *The Media Landscape in Latin America and Crisis Management.* Speech to the International Association of Tanker Owners, INTERTANKO, Houston, Texas, April 1999.

———. "Public Relations in Emerging Democracies: The Government Campaign in Ecuador to Sell Privatisation to Key Publics." *Ecquid Novi* 20, no. 1 (1999): 80–94.

Tilson, D., and D. Newsom. "Marketing the Americas: A Vision for a New World Union." *International Journal of Commerce and Management* 11, no. 1 (2001): 34–53.

Tricks, H. "Monarch of the Mexican Airwaves. *The Financial Times* (London), 15 May 2000, 14.

———. "Televisa Set to Axe 730 Jobs as Income Slides." *The Financial Times* (London), 19 April 2001, 20.

Vanden Heuvel, J., and E. Dennis. *Changing Patterns: Latin America's Vital Media.* New York: The Freedom Forum Media Studies Center, 1995.

Waisbord, S. *Watchdog Journalism in South America: News, Accountability, and Democracy.* New York: Columbia University Press, 2000.

Webster, N. "Pause in Praise of Free Press." *Montreal Gazette,* 4 May 2002, B7.

Weissert, W. "Congressmen Quit in Guatemala; Former Ruling Party in Disarray." *The News* (Mexico City), 7 June 2000, 13.

Wernick, A. *Promotional Culture: Advertising, Ideology and Symbolic Expression.* London: Sage, 1991.

Wickham-Crowley, T. P. *Guerrillas and Revolution in Latin America.* Princeton, N.J.: Princeton University Press, 1992.

20

North America

William Briggs

Canada and the United States share the world's longest borders, more than 5,000 miles, largely unguarded (Figure 20.1). As each other's leading trading partner, more than $1 billion crosses this border daily, along with a huge flow of people. Imagine, therefore, the surprise on September 12, 2001, when armed guards occupied border crossings and challenged cross-border traffic at gunpoint. But that's just one way in which the terrorist attacks on the United States on September 11, 2001, changed the relationship between these two North American democracies overnight, and changed everything else as well, including the media.

According to Orville Schell, dean of the Graduate School of Journalism at the University of California at Berkeley, the terrorist attacks and the ensuing war on terrorism have been a wake-up call for how negligent the West has been covering the news of the rest of the world. "The great paradox is that the word globalization is on everyone's lips while the American media, at least, has been in great default mode in terms of covering it. I think September 11 was a shocking reminder that we literally did not know what was going on between Tel Aviv and Hong Kong. There's very little by way of permanent [media] presence out there" ("Q&A" *Newsweek* 2002).

In the ensuing interval, the United States and Canada have grown closer than ever, participating in military and intelligence activities and with greater economic integration, with increased calls for a customs union or an open border for workers and visitors. Media in both countries recognized the anniversary of the terrorist attacks with days of high-quality news coverage focusing on how the societies had changed, each from its own national perspective.

At the end of the day, however, Canada has withstood the economic, security, and media onslaught from its neighbor and focused on core Canadian values like civil liberties and multiculturalism. Meanwhile, the United States hotly debated in the press the trade-off between personal liberty and collective security as it fought off the psychological effects of the attacks and the ensuing economic recession. More

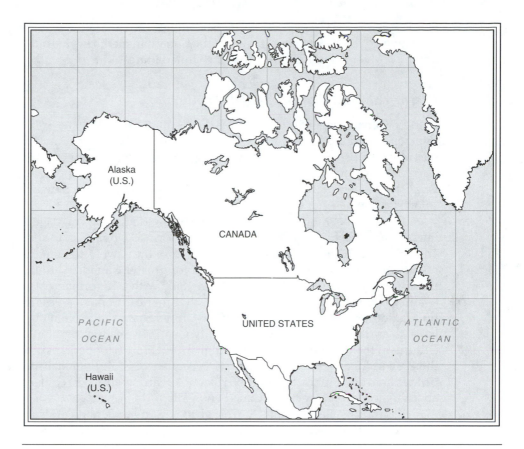

FIGURE 20.1 *North America*

similar than different, the two North American media systems nevertheless are the products of different philosophies and historical backgrounds. This chapter explores the evolution and character of those parallel systems that so greatly influence the media of the entire world.[1]

Canada

Author and global observer Pico Iyer summed it up by saying, "[Canada is] the only country in the world that sits right next to the planet's dominant superpower, which it resembles just enough to be reminded constantly of the differences" (2000, p. 158) The great majority of Canadians live within a hundred miles of the border. They watch American (i.e., U.S.) television, listen to U.S. radio, and often cross the border to shop or attend sporting events. But much energy is spent trying to keep that same American culture at bay. For example, Canadian content laws require broadcasting to air at least 30 percent Canadian-made programming, and U.S. filmmakers making movies in Canada must employ a percentage of Canadians to be eligible for attractive government grants. How did the Canadian media evolve out of a colonial empire and the economic shadow of the United States?

Historical Context of Canadian Media

Modern Canada began its evolution as the result of a pair of wars. British victory in the French and Indian War (1754–1763) determined that North America would be part of the British Empire, and largely English speaking. The other war that shaped Canada's destiny was the American Revolution, when tens of thousands of British loyalists fled north from the Thirteen Colonies, joining the indigenous French colonists, who refused to join the rebellion.

From the beginning, the population was divided along language and cultural lines. As early as 1791, the British government formed Upper Canada (later Ontario) and Lower Canada (modern Quebec). The provinces were reunited in 1840 as a result of the Durham Report, which called for greater Canadian autonomy within the empire. Dominion status followed in 1867, with new provinces added as the country expanded westward across North America. Canada's vast size, distinct population groups, and proximity to the United States have often made it a challenge to create a unified Canadian identity. Centuries of attempts at integrating the cultures of the two founding groups, English and French (or perhaps of assimilating the French into the English), have proved unsuccessful. Regionalism, influences from Britain and France, and the need to fend off an expansionist United States have all influenced the character of Canadian media.

It is impossible to dismiss the role of geography in Canada's development. All major geographic features—mountain ranges, rivers, plains, prairies, and coastlines—run north to south and are shared with the United States. Thus, many Canadians identify more strongly with their regional counterparts in the lower 48 states or Alaska than with their fellow citizens across the country. Canada is also thinly populated, and three-quarters of the population lives within a few hundred miles of the U.S. border, mostly along the corridor from Windsor and Toronto to Montreal and Quebec City. Creating a national identity across this vast continent required superhuman feats of engineering, transportation, and communication. Even today, communication holds the far corners together, overcoming geographic barriers, distance, and weather.

As with the population, the early media were transplanted from the American colonies when Boston editor John Bushnell established the *Halifax Gazette* in 1752. The first paper in Quebec, the bilingual *Quebec Gazette* (1764), survives today as part of the *Quebec Chronicle-Telegraph,* arguably North America's oldest surviving newspaper. The short-lived *Nova Scotia Magazine and Comprehensive Review of Literature, Politics and News* was the first British North American periodical.

Newspaper development in the eastern provinces was temporarily interrupted by war with the United States in 1813. An enlarging business community requiring advertising outlets made the press more self-sufficient and less dependent on the government for subsidies. It also made the press more critical of government.

This tension marked the period between the Constitutional Act of 1791 and the Rebellions Losses Act of 1849. Libertarian press principles were asserted when Joseph Howe was found guilty of seditious libel but nevertheless acquitted. With the arrival of the first iron printing press in 1839, the layout of newspapers changed and became more inviting.

The dominion expanded from the original four provinces of New Brunswick, Nova Scotia, and Upper and Lower Canada with the addition of Manitoba (1870), British Columbia (1871), and Alberta and Saskatchewan (1905). The Yukon Territory was established in 1898 to help administer the gold fields of the Klondike Gold Rush. These decades saw considerable emigration into the western provinces, much of it from the United States. But the press came from eastern Canada. *The Victoria Gazette and Anglo American* and the French-language *Le Couriler de la Nouvelle Caledonie* were both established in British Columbia in 1858. *The Edmonton Bulletin* began in Alberta in 1880. By 1900, 1,266 newspapers served Canada, accompanying settlers and gold seekers into the west. The telegraph facilitated east–west news flow, and coverage was further improved with the founding of the Canadian Press Association in 1859.

Technological innovations, such as the rotary press, helped attract mass audiences. Advertising revenues climbed. Daily publications increased from 23 in 1864 to 121 in 1900. In the twentieth century, population growth, urbanization, immigration, the Great Depression and technological change all contributed to newspaper growth, particularly in the western provinces and Canadian north. The trend toward media consolidation and single-newspaper cities began, so that by the 1960s, seven publishing interests controlled half of the 110 daily papers. The three major groups were Free Press Publications, Southam Company, and Thompson Company. Papers began looking better, but their content was duller, less localized, less personalized.

The advent of Canadian broadcasting came with the granting of the first license for sound broadcasting to the Marconi Wireless Telegraph Company. Canadian Reginald Fessenden had been the first person to transmit voice and music over the air, on Christmas Eve, 1906. Three federal broadcasting acts (1932, 1936, and 1958) created the Board of Broadcast Governors, the broadcast regulatory agency, and the Canadian Broadcasting Corporation (CBC). Private television stations formed their own network in 1961, linking stations in 80 cities. The Broadcasting Act of 1968 replaced the Board of Broadcast Governors with the Canadian Radio-Television and Telecommunications Commission (CRTC), and established a mixed system of public and private broadcasting with a single regulatory agency. Canadian broadcasting enjoys ownership protection with the requirement that 80 percent of voting shares be held by Canadians and that directors and chairpersons be Canadian. The CRTC also established minimum requirements for radio, ensuring a level of Canadian broadcast programming and stimulating the industry. While broadcasting ascended, however, Canadian magazines, never flourishing, continued to struggle against U.S. competition. When the O'Leary Commission (Royal Commission on Publications) was established in 1960, Canadians read U.S. magazines three-to-one over domestic publications, and two U.S. publishing companies, Time Inc. and Reader's Digest, controlled 40 percent of Canadian newsstand sales.

Legal Environment of Canadian Media

Canada is a fully independent nation but retains the British queen as its own. A Governor General is appointed by the queen and acts in her stead as head of state, but not of government. Canada remains a member of the British Commonwealth. If the United States is built upon the fundamental principles of life, liberty, and the pursuit of happiness, then Canada is founded upon the principles of peace, order, and good government. Canada embodies elements of both the British and American governmental systems. Cabinet ministers, responsible to a parliament, serve at both national and provincial levels. Federalism holds the provinces together and assures each a degree of local independence.

Until the passage of the Canada Act in 1982, whereby the British Parliament granted Canada control of its own constitution, Canadian press freedom was not part of its constitution and could be applied only to federal laws. The courts generally asserted press freedom but based their decisions on technicalities. With the Canada Act came a Charter of Rights and Freedoms that includes "freedom of thought, belief, opinion and expression, including freedom of the press and other media of communication." However, this freedom is not absolute. Such freedoms are "subject only to reasonable limits prescribed by law as can be demonstrably justified in a free and democratic society."

Canada has long been skeptical of American-style populism and has long viewed government as benign. As Canada became more Americanized, it adopted more notions of press freedom, but it has never abandoned the legitimate rights of government to prevent the press from going too far. The Canada Act leaves it to the courts to decide the extent to which limits on fundamental freedoms can be justified. A pair of laws enacted in 1983 delineates press behavior. The Privacy Act protects citizens from invasion of privacy. The Access to Information Act provides access to governmental records, with five mandatory and 12 discretionary exemptions. The act is limited to citizens and declared permanent residents of Canada. The various provinces have passed similar statutes.

Part of Canada's inheritance from Britain is a long tradition of secrecy. Receipt and divulgence of classified information is actionable in court, although high-profile cases in 1978 and 1989 were unsuccessful. The Emergencies Act allows government to suspend civil liberties during times of emergency, such as in Quebec in 1970. The Canadian press is also more restricted in it coverage of crime and criminal trials. The media are proscribed from releasing information about a defendant's prior criminal record, or other information that might interfere with his or her right to a fair trial. But Canada's long-standing practice of protecting certain parties in court cases is coming under increasing criticism from the media and may be rendered obsolete by technology. A 1996 Manitoba murder case has the attention of the Canadian Supreme Court. If the court sides with the media, it will alter the balance between police protecting their secrets and the public's right to know. The Internet and satellite TV make it increasingly difficult to use publication bans to protect police techniques. The identity of juveniles in trials is protected. The British Columbian Supreme Court allows journalists to record the proceedings for accuracy, but not for broadcast. Libel and defamation cases are usually tried in civil court. As in the United States, truth, fair comment, and privilege are allowed as media defenses. However, Canada has no statute regarding reporting on public officials. In the area of obscenity law, the Canadian Supreme Court ruled in 1982 that obscenity provisions in the criminal code do not violate the guarantee of freedom of expression in the Charter of Rights and Freedoms. Voluntary press councils exist at provincial or regional level but have no legal authority. The Canadian Broadcast Standards Council oversees broadcasting, maintaining a strong relationship with the CRTC.

Canada faces many of the same difficult and complicated issues related to the rapidly changing media and communications industries as the United States does. But prior to the Canada Act of 1982, the operating constitution was similar in principle to that of the United Kingdom, and courts were primarily concerned with jurisdictional decisions between the provinces and the federal government. In the last two decades, the Canadian Supreme Court has had to tackle myriad issues defining the relationship between government, the media, and society, issues the United States has had two centuries to wrestle with. Much of the Canadian media policy over the past century has been the formulation of laws to protect and develop Canadian media and cultural industries and to foster national unity and cultural identity. Now, Canada must also face new technologies, such as the Internet and satellite delivery systems, that increasingly make national borders—and national media policy—irrelevant.

Print Media in Canada

Canada is a nation of concentrated media ownership. Today, 105 dailies circulate approximately 5.16 million copies. Circulation has slowly declined over the past decade. The major cities of Canada all support more than one daily newspaper. Edmonton, Calgary, and Vancouver have two papers, while Montreal and Ottawa claim three. Toronto, Canada's largest city, has five daily papers: the *Toronto Star* (2001 weekly circulation 3.41 million), *The Globe and Mail* (2.18 million), *The National Post* (2.05 million), the *Toronto Sun* (1.71 million), and *Metro Today*, a free commuter paper that circulates 200,000. Together these papers reach 75 percent of Toronto's households. *The Globe and Mail* is considered Canada's national newspaper, and maintains a number of foreign correspondents as well. It compares with *The New York Times* as a paper of record and is aimed at educated, affluent readers, particularly the business class. *The Star* is considered the more liberal paper, *The Post* the more conservative.

If Canadians read newspapers for their distinctive political stance, they also bemoan a certain sameness in their papers. CanWest Global, for example, owns a third of the English-language market. Bell Globe Media, the telephone concern, now owns Thompson Corporation, of Toronto, once Canada's largest communications company, and is now publisher of *The Globe and Mail*. Bell Globe Media also owns CTV, the largest private TV network. The chains tend to homogenize the news for wide distribution, creating a certain dullness in the press.

The Canadian Press Wire Service, a cooperative, contributes to the sameness of Canadian publications, since the same papers contribute and publish the wire service copy. The CPWS does not maintain a large foreign correspondents network and is dependent upon Associated Press (AP), Reuters, and Agence France-Pesse (AFP) for international news, adding to the notion that Canada sees the world through U.S. reporting.

In 1997, international publisher Conrad Black purchased the 14-newspaper Southam chain and launched *The National Post* to compete with *The Globe and Mail*. *The National Post* was never financially successful, and in 2000 Black divested all of his communication holdings to CanWest Global Communications, creating an unprecedented media conglomeration. The CanWest empire includes media in Australia, Northern Ireland, and New Zealand, as well as 14 English-language metropolitan dailies, television stations, a news portal, and scores of community newspapers in Canada. In 2001, CanWest instituted a policy of corporately written national editorials for all its dailies. Letters to the editor and columns contrary to the corporate viewpoint were discouraged, producing a single (conservative) viewpoint across the nation. Prominent journalists were let go or resigned. Media observers questioned the heavy-handed tactics, censorship, and the aggressiveness of the owners so soon after being awarded cross-media ownership. A national debate has ensued over concentration of ownership and the role of political objectivity. Clearly, CanWest, with 2001–2002 revenues of $1.46 billion, sees itself as a global player and envisions expanding its playing field to the United States and the rest of the world.

The number of Canadian community newspapers continued to grow during the 1990s but plateaued as advertising revenues dried up during the recessionary first years of the 2000s. Nevertheless, more than five million Canadians receive a community newspaper. In addition, Canada has a wide variety of ethnic newspapers, specialized newspapers, supplements and shoppers.

In general, the Canadian magazine industry lacks the critical population mass to support a vibrant magazine industry editorially or with advertising. The Canadian magazine industry has been continually affected by direct U.S. competition, and substantial federal intervention has kept it afloat.

Most of the 1,500-plus Canadian magazines are consumer publications, with the balance divided between business and specialty publications. Canada's largest circulating English-language magazine is the general interest *Macleans*, with a circulation of 512,000.

When the Royal Commission on Publications (O'Leary Commission) determined in 1960 that three-quarters of magazines read in Canada were American, and that *Time* and *Reader's Digest*, in Canadian editions, controlled 40 percent of newsstand sales, legislation followed disallowing income tax deductions for advertising aimed at the Canadian market but placed in non-Canadian publications. However, this 1966 law exempted *Time* and *Reader's Digest* until it was amended in 1975. At that point, *Time* abandoned its Canadian edition and *Reader's Digest* spun off a Canadian affiliate company. Canadian advertising revenues increased by more than a third.

However, by the end of the 1990s, Canadian magazines were still looking to the government for help, and the government was still responding with cultural initiatives. Rather than close its borders to American magazines, which still represent about 80 percent of newsstand sales, Canada has sought to penalize magazines that publish split runs (parallel editions of the same publication with minor editorial differences and different advertising content) and the Canadian companies advertising in them. In 1997, the World Trade Organization ruled that Canada remove an earlier, similar law. The law seems particularly aimed at *Time Canada,* the split run with the largest circulation (320,000). For multinational advertisers, it is even simpler to reach the Canadian market (for free) by simply advertising in border-crossing U.S. magazines. These magazine wars are a skirmish in the larger globalization wars of free trade versus protectionism.

Canadian book publishers are more keenly aware of their need to serve a Canadian market than U.S. publishers. And while healthy, Canadian publishing is nevertheless dominated by the United States. Two-thirds of titles in Canadian bookstores are published in the United States. Thus, some publishers are more determined to seek out Canadian authors and themes.

Electronic Media

Writing in *The Cultural Industries in Canada,* Michel Filion concludes,

> In Canadian radio's first phase, American airwave imperialism posed a serious threat to the Canadian radio industry. Since direct state involvement began in 1932, American influence has become subtler. . . . [The] last phase of evolution has seen the competition from private stations become official, while regulatory mechanisms are put in place to contain American influence and promote a Canadian cultural identity. This remains the ultimate objective of state intervention in broadcasting. (Dorland 1996, p. 138)

Canadian radio is ubiquitous. From the birth of the technology the airwaves have been considered public property, and the state has held regulatory authority over them. The Broadcasting Act of 1932 created the Canadian Radio Broadcasting Commission (CRBC), ushering in the golden age of public radio in Canada. In reality, Canadian broadcasting has always been a compromise between nationalism and commercial interests. By 1958, the private sector was allowed to create its own networks in parallel with public radio. Adapting to the arrival of television, radio moved into automobiles and became transistorized. The evolution of FM radio coincided with radio's transition to a largely music format medium.

Today, Canadian commercial radio provides music, news-talk, and sports programming. Public CBC radio offers a noncommercial music and alternative programming option, called Radio 1, and a higher culture (classical music, opera) station, Radio 2. Public radio is in reality state radio and is not dependent on the larger mass markets of its commercial cousins. Commercial stations tend to serve local markets. Licensing regulations require that music programming contain a percentage of Canadian products, although the amount varies, depending on the musical genre. Rock music stations must play the most Canadian music, 30 percent, under a formula called the MAPL (Music, Artist, Producer, Lyrics) System. Music meeting two of those four criteria, such as a Canadian singer and songwriter, is considered Canadian. In reality, the appeal of American popular culture and the relative paucity of Canadian product undermine attempts at managing cultural programming.

Canadian broadcasting has developed as a hybrid, shifting toward privitization but with a private sector increasingly reliant on public subsidies and government regulation. The Canadian Broadcasting Corporation remains the centerpiece of Canadian broadcasting. The CBC produces radio and television programming in both English and French, and produces the internationally distributed 24-hour *Newsworld*. Both noncommercial radio and commercial TV strive to be distinctive rather than competitive. The distinction between CBC and independent broadcasting is, however, increasingly blurred.

A small market, dual language requirements, and easy cross-border reception of U.S. programming have always made it more economic for Canadian broadcasters to import U.S. programs and sell them to Canadian audiences rather than to produce comparable programming at home.

Despite the increased spending on Canadian programming by the country's largest private broadcasters, CTV and Global, viewership of those shows is in decline. In 1999, barely 12 percent of what was watched during prime time on CTV was Canadian produced, down from 17 percent in 1997. On Global, the decrease was from 7 percent to 5 percent. Both TV networks had made large commitments to spending on Canadian production as conditions of recent acquisitions. Indeed, television watching across Canada has declined to 21.6 hours per week in 1999 from a peak of 23.5 hours in 1988. But less television viewing doesn't necessarily mean less time in front of the screen, as increases in watching DVDs, videos, and logging onto the Internet confirm.

There are more than 1,800 cable systems operating in Canada, offering customers dozens of channels. Cable operators and broadcasters alike have engaged in a decade-long period of consolidation and expansion through takeovers, new channels, and new technologies. While Canadians are intrigued with the new digital channel offerings coming on-line, only about a tenth of them are willing to pay for the new bundled programming. The uncertain future direction of the CBC keeps everyone else perpetually jockeying for position in a changing broadcast environment. One of the players looking to expand globally is the previously mentioned CanWest Global Communications Corp. Another global television network combining commercial and public approaches is WETV, a publically funded attempt to counterbalance the developed world's stranglehold on television by providing production and distribution for underrepresented countries and indigenous cultures worldwide. Canadian, foreign, and United Nations development funds financed its 1996 start-up. Small audiences in partnership countries view WETV worldwide.

Minority broadcasting is a significant issue in a country where multiculturalism is official policy. The Aboriginal People's Television network (APTN) began in

1999 to better serve Inuit and various other aboriginal peoples. Not only does it broadcast specialized programming, native peoples largely staff it, and much of the programming is in native languages.

Clearly, the overriding cross-cultural challenge for Canadian media is its dual-language responsibility. Quebec declined to sign Canada's new constitution in 1982 for lack of special consideration for Quebec's linguistic and cultural differences, and two other provinces declined to ratify a subsequent agreement giving Quebec unique status. Quebec nearly approved a referendum to secede. Thus, Canada walks the tightrope of national disintegration. The existence of the North American Free Trade Agreement (NAFTA) makes Quebec separation even more possible if not probable. French-language broadcasting has reinforced Francophone identity, in addition to providing programming and commercial messages. Ironically, the CBC produces more English-language programming than any of the U.S. networks and more French programming than the national system of France. Francophone programming is available in all metropolitan areas, although its reach is not as strong as in English. All Anglophone Canadian schoolchildren study French in school, but the crossover market is not large. Research shows a slightly different CBC news agenda for French and English audiences. Francophone audiences tend to be more parochial, more provincial, and more interested in other Francophone countries. Three French networks serve the Francophone audience: Société Radio-Canada, TVA, and Television Quartre Saisons. While much of Quebec can easily access U.S. media, especially in Montreal, the preference is to import French, rather than U.S., programming.

Convergence and New Media

Canada is recognized as a world leader in Internet penetration, with more than half of all Canadians having Internet access. This contrasts with almost universal television penetration and cable or satellite subscription rates above 80 percent. So, while not an immediate threat to traditional media, the Internet is nevertheless siphoning off some of viewers' time. Half of Canadians surveyed say they are spending less time watching television, listening to radio, or reading newspapers, books, and magazines. Young Canadians spend 2.5 hours more per week on-line than their U.S. counterparts and are 95 percent more likely to use a high-speed Internet service. The most popular use of the Internet by Canadians is for electronic mail. But the desire for news and other information is also strong. And at this point, traditional and new media can converge.

Internet use by French-speaking Canadians, however, is substantially less, 44 percent compared to 58 percent of Anglophone Canadians, suggesting that the digital divide between the nation's two language groups is likely to widen.

The idea of convergence underlies many of the decisions being made by Canadian corporations and regulatory agencies, as Canada moves into the fast lane on the information superhighway. Convergence in its technical, functional, and corporate manifestations is the most important policy issue Canadian communication faces. "This is because convergence relates closely to such basic geopolitical trends and issues as the erosion of national sovereignty and the concomitant growth in transnational corporate power; the controversy over whether government should be a major policy planner as opposed to merely a market facilitator; the debate over whether information/communication are to be treated as instruments of social/political/cultural policy, or merely as commodities; questions of continued universal access to telecommunications and information in the context of widening gaps between the information rich and the information poor" (Babe, cited in Dorland 1996, 284–285).

Historically, information has been afforded public good status, but this is in opposition to the deregulated, market-driven forces of globalization. Canada has always treated its media as a public resource, not as a commodity (in contrast to the U.S. decision to withdraw from UNESCO over the commodity issue). Squaring convergence with traditional Canadian values will be a delicate maneuver.

Movies and Film

From the early days of motion pictures, Canada has spun in the orbit of Hollywood. From Canadian stars such as Mary Pickford to Hollywood-made movies about survival in the Yukon, Canada has seen itself in the movies through the filter of California sunglasses. In 1939, the federal government established the National Film Board of Canada, to produce and distribute Canadian films that would positively interpret Canada to the world. Telefilm Canada was established in the 1960s to support the television and feature film industry. The majority of these government-subsidized projects are made for television, many of them documentaries or otherwise of significant social content. The rise of private-sector companies, most small but several eventually offering public-sector shares, signals a shift in the Canadian film industry. These companies, such as Cineplex, Alliance, and Alias, have benefited from a government-stimulated environment and Hollywood's (as well as other nations') desire for cost-effective partnerships. The relatively weak Canadian dollar, good locations, lots of "American" actors and extras, and an insatiable hunger for product sent U.S. production companies into Canada in droves. Today, more than nine out of ten movies in Canadian theaters are foreign. As with much of its media, Canadian film has witnessed the collision of an industry in the marketplace with Canadian cultural public policy initiatives.

Media Education and the Future

Journalism and mass communication education in Canada has developed in its own unique way. While early models included Columbia University and other U.S. institutions, today media students receive specialized journalism training at a dozen major institutions across English and French Canada. Leading institutions include Carleton University, Ottawa, and Ryerson University, Toronto, which offer baccalaureate programs; the University of Western Ontario, London, and the University of British Columbia, Vancouver, which offer graduate-level programs; and the Université du Quebec, in Montreal, and the Université Laval, Quebec City, which offer French-language programs.

Canadian education tends not to stream its communication programs. The market is too small, and students tend to be more broadly trained across different media platforms. Public relations and advertising are frequently taught at the community college level, which is considered terminal. In a tightening, competitive marketplace, many baccalaureate degree holders are returning to the community colleges for hands-on training. Many of the degree-granting institutions also provide continuing education and professional development seminars and courses.

Yet the traditional emphasis on careers in journalism, such as the one at Carleton University, with its Centre for Investigative Journalism, face many of the same challenges as the industry, according to Peter Johansen, past chairman of the department at Carleton. "We have to respond to the convergence talking place in the industry. While we still believe in graduating students who excel in a given area, say reporting, rather than trying to be all things to all people, we also acknowledge the need for some cross training and the willingness to acquire new skills as they come on-line. This refers to the faculty as well as the student" (Johansen 2002).

A core democracy with a sophisticated media system, Canada enters the twenty-first century full of hope and promise, but with British and French baggage and one eye on the United States. Driven by the psychological need for a unique national identity and culture, and tempered by the need to pay for it in a globalizing world, Canada juggles the public and the private to maintain a media culture all its own.

The United States

When, centuries from now, archaeologists (or interplanetary visitors) examine the remains of the U.S. civilization, it well may be that they declare the American media empire to be the dominant feature of our times. Media from the United States offer the most far-reaching news and entertainment options available in the world. U.S. media are particularly global, as domestic programming and copy are exported to, viewed or read, imitated, and smuggled into every corner of the globe. Domestic U.S. stories often dominate international headlines. American popular culture is admired or despised worldwide. Proponents of globalization point to American media as messengers of liberal democracy. Opponents assail the surge of cultural imperialism. Characteristically, American media is big. More than half of the largest global media conglomerates are American owned. Those archaeologists may be right.

At home, Americans are truly a mediated society: they spend an average of nine hours daily with media, watching one of their multiple television sets or listening to their car radio while negotiating clogged highways, or increasingly interacting with their computers by playing games, downloading music, exchanging e-mail messages, or surfing the World Wide Web. Fueling all this media activity is an enormous advertising industry representing hundreds of billions of dollars as it relentlessly dominates a consumer society.

It is also a free society—arguably the freest in the world. This is in large measure due to the watchdog function of the American press, warily guarding the democracy against abuse and corruption in government, business, and society, and protected by the guarantees of the First Amendment of the Constitution, ensuring freedom of speech and of the press. Balancing the needs for corporate profits with fairness, accuracy, and responsibility in an atmosphere of permissive commercialism is the challenge for U.S. media in the twenty-first century.

In many ways the press of the United States mirrors the republic it serves. From its colonial beginnings it has been assertive, rebellious, and independent-minded. No less an observer of American society than Alexis de Tocqueville marveled at the widespread nature of the frontier press and saw it as the cement between an exuberant population and their youthful democracy. The trend toward global media hegemony today is in many ways a natural continuance of the themes of manifest destiny that tamed a continent and became an industrial and commercial force long before world wars pulled the United States into global involvement. Press systems reflect the societies that house them. A look at the historical context of the American press helps explain its current state.

Historical Context of the U.S. Media

The press in America developed right along with the country. From colonial beginnings, through revolution, westward expansion, civil war, industrialization, world wars, cold war, and superpower status, the press has reflected, critiqued, and cheered on the United States.

Like its British antecedents, the press in colonial America was licensed by the government and subject to prior restraint and penalties for printing seditious libel. Evolving from pamphlets and handbills, the first newspaper was Benjamin Harris's *Publick Occurrences Both Foreign and Domestick,* in 1690. It lasted but a single issue. The first continuously published newspaper was John Campbell's *Boston Newsletter,* begun in 1704. A competitor, The *Boston Gazette,* began in 1719, and in turn, its printer, James Franklin, launched his own paper, *The New England Courant.* While Franklin was in jail for seditious libel, his younger brother, Benjamin, ran the paper, beginning his own illustrious career as a journalist and publisher. The 1735 acquittal of publisher John Peter Zenger in a seditious libel case did not establish legal precedent, but it did allow truth as a defense and became a symbolic victory for emerging press freedom.

Increasingly emboldened, the press became highly partisan as the rift with England widened. Tory (pro-British) publishers were often persecuted. Colonial revolutionaries such as Thomas Paine and Samuel Adams used the press to mold public opinion toward independence, often using woodcut illustrations by Paul Revere and other artisans. The Stamp Act (1765), a tax on legal documents and newspapers, infuriated editors. The press was in large measure responsible for forging an "American identity" among colonists. During the Revolutionary War, the colonial press traded news throughout the colonies and helped hold the colonies together.

Following independence, the new nation operated under the Articles of Confederation. A constitution was developed in 1787 and its supporters, called Federalists and led by Alexander Hamilton and James Madison, wrote and published an extensive series of essays, known as the Federalist Papers, explaining the new Constitution and urging ratification. Anti-Federalists, championed by Thomas Jefferson, also published highly partisan essays and political attacks. With the inclusion of a Bill of Rights, whose First Amendment guarantees freedom of speech and press, the Constitution was ratified by the states. A highly partisan political press marked the early years of the new nation.

Though closely aligned with political patronage through the early decades of the nineteenth century, the press gradually became a more commercial enterprise, relying on advertising and subscriptions instead of political parties. The arrival of the "penny press" with Benjamin Day's *New York Sun* (1833) shifted the audience to the emerging middle class and immigrants in large cities. James Gordon Bennett's *New York Herald* (1835) signaled the arrival of reporter-generated stories and news beats, such as police news. Emphasis was placed on human interest and local stories. Along the frontier, small papers borrowed stories freely from one another for a news-hungry population. By 1844, the development of the telegraph separated communication from its dependence on transportation. Reporters covering the Mexican War (1846–1848) made use of the new telegraph. By 1861, the telegraph linked the Atlantic and Pacific coasts.

With the election of Abraham Lincoln as president in 1860, southern states sensed a shift in political power to the North and a threat to their slavery-based economy, and began to secede from the union. Civil War followed. Abolitionists had long used the press for antislavery essays. William Lloyd Garrison's *Liberator* was absolute in its demand for the end of slavery. Elijah Lovejoy, a white editor murdered by a pro-slavery mob, became a martyr. Harriet Beecher Stowe's *Uncle Tom's Cabin* became the most widely read book in the world after the Bible and brought the issue of slavery to the forefront of national debate. The ensuing war (1861–1865) saw brigades of correspondents compete to cover the battles and profile the generals, with varying degrees of accuracy and objectivity. Military censorship was rampant. The new technology of photography allowed artists to make woodcuts for publication from photographs, and the public flocked to see the actual photographs of battlefield carnage taken by Mathew Brady and other photographers, bringing the horror of war home to thousands.

Post–Civil War industrialization brought with it advances in printing production and expansion of newspapers, magazines, books, and other printed material. The press reflected the growing urbanization of the country, and crusading—if sensationalist—publishers such as Joseph Pulitzer and cartoonist Thomas Nast targeted big city corruption. Pulitzer's excesses peaked during a circulation war with William Randolph Hearst and their coverage of the Spanish American War (1898). A cartoon character of the day gave rise to the expression "yellow journalism." The century ended with a wave of reform journalism, including "muckraking" that attacked social ills and influenced government legislation.

Government persuasion techniques during World War I were transferred to the private sector as a way to burnish the image of big business. Ivy Lee and Edward Bernays helped pioneer a new media industry of public relations. Meanwhile, Lee De Forest and his audio tube had advanced the early efforts of Marconi in radiotelephony. The war stimulated research, and civilian applications became possible with the cooperation of government and industry in creating the Radio Corporation of America in 1919, headed by David Sarnoff. Radio networks soon followed as advertisers discovered a way to reach mass audiences relatively cheaply. Radio and moving pictures became the entertainment mainstay during the 1920s and 1930s, when government also used its tremendous reach to soften the effects of the Depression and prepare the nation for eventual entry into World War II. The Federal Communications Commission was established in 1934 to help ensure that broadcasting operated in the public interest. Photojournalism came of age with the advent of large-format, glossy magazines such as *Life* in 1936.

Allied victory in World War II ushered in a period of prosperity, and the acquisition of choice was a television set. Television technology had been adapted to military use during the war, but its civilian popularity was unprecedented. Veteran war correspondents, led by Edward R. Murrow, set a high standard for television news, and many of America's favorite entertainers made the transition to television. Radio, the movies, and print publications all had to adjust to the arrival of television, as TV would later have to adjust to the arrival of cable and the Internet. Some of the more recent developments are detailed in the sections that follow.

Government–Press Relations and the Law

The United States is a nation of law, and all law is tested against the Constitution, which reigns supreme. When the original states ratified the Constitution, there was much debate and concern about specific protection against government infringement on individual liberties. The first ten amendments, known as the Bill of Rights, placed restrictions on the power of the federal government and remanded much authority back to individual states.

The First Amendment to the Constitution is the bulwark of press freedom. It states:

> Congress shall make no law respecting an establishment of religion, or prohibiting the free exercise thereof, or abridging the freedom of speech, or of the press, or the right of the people peaceably to assemble, and to petition the government for a redress of grievances.

For over 200 years, journalists have thrived under the protection of the First Amendment and rallied to its defense at every challenge. Nevertheless, there has endured a tension between the government and its unofficial "fourth estate," the press. Prior restraint was precluded by the First Amendment, and after a brief reintroduction of laws against seditious libel, primarily in the form of the Alien and

Sedition Act (1798–1801), the federal government yielded to scrutiny by an aggressive press playing its role in the democracy by informing the people about the workings of their government.

In recent years, landmark court decisions have reinforced the notions of press freedom in the United States, notably in *New York Times v. Sullivan* (1964) and *New York Times v. U.S.* (1971), commonly known as the Pentagon Papers case.

In *Times v. Sullivan*, the U.S. Supreme Court turned back efforts by a state government official to bring a civil libel suit against the press. The decision has made it difficult for civil officials to bring defamation lawsuits against their critics as a means of silencing them. Writing in the Sullivan decision, Justice William Brennan wrote, "[There should be] a profound national commitment to the principles that debate on public issues should be uninhibited, robust and wide open." And, the court argued, citizens not only have the right but also the duty to criticize government. However, a steady stream of libel cases over the years demonstrates that many courts are sensitive to the special First Amendment issues involved in the constantly evolving area of libel law.

In 1971, the *New York Times* published stories based on leaked classified material about U.S. involvement in Vietnam. The U.S. Attorney General brought an injunction against the *Times* on the grounds of national security. It was a case of prior restraint that went quickly to the Supreme Court. The Court ruled that "Any system of prior restraints of expression comes to this Court bearing a heavy presumption against its constitutional validity."

In 1972, another collision occurred between the press and the administration of President Richard Nixon. Burglars had been caught breaking into the Democratic Party headquarters at the Watergate apartment complex in Washington, D.C. Reporters for the *Washington Post* connected them to the Republican Party's presidential reelection committee. Over the ensuing months, a trail of lies and cover-ups was disclosed that eventually ended its way back to the office of the President himself. When altered tapes of Nixon's conversations in the White House were disclosed during Senate hearings before a national television audience, the Nixon presidency unraveled and ultimately led to his resignation in 1974. It was a high-water mark for the press, although its role in bringing down a sitting president has been exaggerated. A generation of young journalists modeled themselves after investigative *Post* reporters Carl Bernstein and Bob Woodward. The reputation of the government, however, was at low ebb. The cynicism of the American public, already heightened by the Vietnam War, became complete. Public mistrust and antipathy toward government—and by some toward the press—endures to the present.

More recently the Supreme Court has generally been reluctant to hear major press freedom cases. U.S. libel laws remain more protective of the press than anywhere in the world, although those protections are not likely to be expanded greatly in the near future. There is an area, however, that bears watching as the press and government continue to almost literally cross swords—war coverage.

Wars make big stories. Audiences are captivated and crave information, especially when U.S. service personnel are involved. The Vietnam War was fully covered by its own battalions of journalists, who ignored the military press hand-outs and covered the war at will. Vietnam was the first television war, and the sight of body bags and other carnage did not sit well with the American public. When respected television newsman Walter Cronkite expressed misgivings about U.S. involvement in Vietnam during a newscast, there was a perceptible shift in American public opinion, and President Lyndon Johnson is said to have remarked that was when he lost the backing of the American people.

Some military and government officials believe the press "lost Vietnam." In subsequent American military operations, such as Grenada (1983), Panama (1989), and the Persian Gulf war (1990–1991), the government has increasingly made it difficult for the press to have access to the war zones and otherwise has placed obstacles in reporters' way. In the current Bush administration, Vice President Dick Cheney and Secretary of State Colin Powell had been part of the command structure during the Gulf war. They seem even more inclined to keep the press under control now during this new era of war against terrorism. Following the Gulf war, the American press subjected itself to close scrutiny and found it lacking. Since then, the press has called for greater access during times of hostilities, pointing out that there have been very few instances where the press has acted irresponsibly with sensitive stories.

Michael Getler, ombudsman for the *Washington Post*, said:

> The press will always find ways to cover the story. If the military seriously restricts coverage, reporters will find other sources and other ways to cover the war, as they should. The public's best interests are served by an enlightened relationship between the military and the media, when both sides make an honest stab at solving some of the problems that naturally arise in a way that does not interfere with military operations and security, but allows an independent account of America at war to be recorded. (Getler 2001, p. 26).

During the Iraq war, in a dramatic change of policy, the Pentagon authorized U.S. and foreign journalists to be "embedded" with military units throughout the theater of war. Viewers and readers got first-hand battlefield accounts, often in real-time, unparalleled in the history of reporting. However, critics pointed out that such coverage was often disjointed and lacked context and worried that the journalists traded objectivity for such unprecedented acccess. Had the military cleverly co-opted the press to its advantage, or had the public been better served than ever? Additionally, more than a thousand journalists covered the Iraq conflict in the more traditional "independent" mode.

Although the print media in America operates free from government regulation, the same cannot be said for broadcasting. Broadcasting operates in the public interest, under licensure from the Federal Communication Commission. The FCC, established in 1934, regulates ownership and allocates frequencies to broadcast operations, since the broadcast spectrum is a finite resource. An FCC license for a radio or television station is a lucrative property. Challenges to ownership, from underrepresented community groups, for example, have been largely unsuccessful. FCC forays into influencing programming have been met with resistance. Broadcasting enjoys the same First Amendment protection as its print relatives.

In the 1980s, a wave of deregulatory thinking accompanied the arrival of the Ronald Reagan Administration in the United States (and the Thatcher government in the United Kingdom). Broadcasting was among the industries opened up to market forces (although broadcasting had always been a commercial venture in the United States). Deregulation brought about a reduction in record keeping, streamlined license renewal, and increased the number of media holdings an individual could own. These free-market policies have continued into the present, generating a rash of media mergers and consolidation, as well as the Telecommunications Act of 1996. One victim of deregulation was the Fairness Doctrine.

Debate over the Fairness Doctrine illustrates a sea change in media thinking. For almost 40 years, the Fairness Doctrine had mandated that broadcasting air opposing sides of controversial issues. In the spirit of government deregulation, and mindful of developing new technologies such as cable, the FCC moved to rescind the Fairness Doctrine. By the turn of the century, the Fairness Doctrine had withered away, including the equal-time provision for political candidates. Stations are now free to present controversial issues unilaterally, and the government is further removed from programming decisions.

The Telecommunications Act of 1996 replaced an older court order that had broken up the telephone monopoly, AT&T. It forced local telephone companies to open their networks to competition, while letting them compete in the long distance market and compete in areas they were formerly denied by law or regulation. Thus broadcasting, cable, and telephone companies began jockeying for position in an ever-changing marketplace and a yet-to-be-determined technological environment. Ownership opportunities were further expanded. A V-chip to block objectionable programming was mandated, and provisions against pornography and other indecent material on the Internet were instituted. A portion of the broadcast spectrum was reserved for digital television services. In signing the legislation, President Bill Clinton said:

> For the past three years, my administration has promoted the enactment of a telecommunications reform bill to stimulate investment, promote competition, provide open access for all citizens to the Information Superhighway, strengthen and improve universal service and provide families with technologies to help them control what kinds of programs come into their homes over television. As a result of this "act", consumers will receive the benefits of lower prices, better quality and greater choice in the television and cable services, and they will continue to benefit from a diversity of voices and viewpoints in radio, television and the print media. (Scherr 1996, p. 2)

Currently, federal regulators are considering loosening rules limiting ownership of radio and television stations and newspapers even further in a natural extension of deregulation. Expected revisions would make cross-ownership of media in a given market much easier, and would facilitate mergers of large media firms. Critics charge this will limit diversity of media ownership and opinion even more.

Contemporary Media Industries

Print Media—Newspapers. Contrary to conventional wisdom, paper has not disappeared with the Internet, and print media are still flourishing. People still do read. After all, the enormous baby-boom generation grew up with print and has formed a strong attachment. What has happened, however, is that fewer Americans are reading newspapers. Newspaper readership is down, particularly among young adults and the younger segment of the baby boomers.

In the year 2000, 47 percent of those surveyed indicated that they were newspaper readers, down from 58 percent in 1994. This trend seems to break down squarely along generational lines. For readers over age 50, newspapers are the most read medium. Newspaper readers seem to be more interested in national and international news than young people, who read other things. The challenge for newspapers is to find other subjects that attract young readers. But young readers are not news averse. On the contrary, they express interest in religion, entertainment, business, sports, and health news and follow the news in other media. The future viability of newspapers depends to no small extent on attracting these younger readers. While circulations may remain stable for the short term, due to legions of loyal baby boomers, the aging population of readers will eventually have to be replaced.

During the period of deregulation many media companies merged and went public. Corporate earnings began to vie with the public interest as the rationale for media efforts. With companies publicly traded on the stock exchanges, editors were faced with stockholder ownership as demanding as any nineteenth century pub-lisher. And as news became more of a corporate enterprise, the nature of the product changed in an ongoing effort to attract readers. Newspapers created more special-interest sections; news became "softer," with more emphasis on lifestyle issues, celebrities, and features. Today, three out of four American newspapers are chain-owned. Few American cities are served by more than a single daily newspaper, usually a morning paper. Many chains have diversified into other communication activities such as magazines, broadcasting, or cable. In a triumph of market research, the Gannett Company launched *USA Today* as a national newspaper in 1982. Although criticized for lack of serious content, *USA Today*'s use of graphics, positive stories, and a carefully formulated editorial mix has defied the critics and attracted a wide readership over the past two decades.

Newspapers are increasingly relying on new technologies. New offset printing techniques have led to greater use of color. Many newspapers distribute their product on-line to customers, and offer computerized retrieval capability. *USA Today, The Wall Street Journal, The New York Times,* and *The Washington Post,* among others, transmit daily or weekly editions via satellite for global distribution. *The International Herald Tribune,* a joint venture between *The New York Times* and *The Washington Post,* is printed via satellite in 11 cities around the world and distributed in most of the world's countries.

The leading daily circulation newspapers are:

1. *USA Today* (Gannett)   2.21 million
2. *The Wall Street Journal* (Dow Jones)   1.82 million
3. *The New York Times* (New York Times Co.)   1.19 million
4. *Los Angeles Times* (Tribune Co.)   985,798
5. *New York Daily News* (Zuckerman)   733,099
6. *New York Post* (NewsCorp)   562, 639

Although the New York newspapers experienced a circulation increase follow-ing the terrorist attacks of September 11, 2001, *USA Today* and *The Los Angeles Times* experienced a decline in circulation.

According to the Newspaper Association of America:

- Nearly six in ten adults in the top 50 U.S. markets read a daily newspaper, and nearly seven in ten read a Sunday paper.
- Nationally, more than 56 million newspapers are sold daily, with a pass-along readership of two readers per copy. On Sunday the number increases to more than 60 million.
- More than 1,000 newspapers in the United States have sites on the World Wide Web.
- Among adults who read an on-line newspaper, more than two-thirds read a printed daily; more than three-quarters still read a printed Sunday edition. Most on-line readers report no change in their print reading habits.
- More than half of newspaper readers read the classified advertising section, more than twice their usage of on-line classified services.
- Newspaper advertising expenditures in 1999 totaled $46.3 billion, one-fifth of all advertising expenditures and 3 percent more than television.

Print Media—Magazines. Magazines have been a companion print medium to newspapers since before the American Revolution. Magazines have provided space for many of the greatest writers and thinkers of their time, and the most pressing issues of their day. Far from dying out, the magazine medium has proved extremely adaptable to economic trends and societal shifts, as well as to changes in media technology. From the political tracts of the eighteenth century through the literary journals, abolitionist essays, women's publications, and muckrakers' exposés, magazines endured. With photography, magazines like *Life* brought pictures into the home long before television. After television, magazines evolved from general interest to special interest to niche. Many advances in graphic design and printing take form in magazines. Today, there are more than 12,000 consumer magazines and even more trade, technical, and professional journals. Of the hundreds of magazines begun annually, almost all fail within a couple of years for lack of capitalization or lack of audience appeal. Although many magazines struggle to survive, the ones successful at capturing advertising dollars prosper, such as the 600-page *Vogue*.

Areas of current interest among consumer magazines include health and fitness, gardening, family leisure, computing, travel, fashion, and cooking. *Modern Maturity*, aimed at an aging, growing demographic, circulates well over 20 million. Pocket-sized publications such as *Readers' Digest* and Rupert Murdoch's *TV Guide* circulate upward of 15 million. Half of the top ten magazines are women's publications such as *Better Homes and Gardens* and *Family Circle*. Many magazines make use of technology to publish international editions in several languages. Trade, technical, and professional journals offer industry-specific news and features of use to occupational markets. Many are widely circulated, although little known outside their specific industry. Magazines enjoy anywhere between $10 and $15 billion in advertising revenues, depending on the overall economy. In the most recent recession, many magazines, particularly those targeting high technology, succumbed because of lack of advertising. In recent years, many magazines have added web pages to their offerings, and there have been a number of high-visibility webzines published exclusively on the Internet. Despite the advantage of being on-line, webzines are still in their infancy, searching out an audience and advertiser base. Countless thousands of "zines," small-scale, often home-produced hybrids between newsletters and magazines, are published for very specific, targeted markets.

Electronic Media. Broadcast media dominate American life. Radio, the senior medium, reaches 80 percent of the population daily, either at home, over one of an average of five receivers, increasingly in the car, or at some other venue. Radio revenues exceed $10 billion from the roughly 5,000 commercial AM stations, the nearly 5,000 commercial FM stations, and the approximately 1,600 public or non-commercial stations.

By 1920, what had been a hobbyist's experiment with radio technology had been transformed into an entertainment medium eagerly seized upon by a mass market. Differing opinions and criteria place the first radio station in San Jose, California, or Pittsburgh, Pennsylvania. But commercial broadcasters immediately took control, and the medium has been commercially driven almost since its inception. Within a decade almost half the households in America owned radio sets, over which they listened to popular entertainment and the calming messages of President Franklin D. Roosevelt during the Great Depression and the dark days of World War II. In postwar years, the new medium of television lured away both radio's audience and many of its biggest stars and most popular programs. Radio, in turn, adapted by seeking narrower audiences for music or news programming. The expansion of FM radio with its superior sound quality captured most of the music audience by the 1970s and 1980s, while AM radio increasingly relied on news and listener call-in talk formats. Despite television's popularity, radio remains the most versatile, portable medium, particularly in times of emergency.

Television, the most popular medium in the country, has penetrated virtually every home in America. Consider these facts:

- Each week the average child spends 20 times more minutes warching television than talking with his or her parents.
- Teenagers spend 900 hours in school each year, but 1,500 hours watching television.
- The average American watches an equivalent of 52 days of TV per year.
- By age 65, the average American adult will have spent nine years of his or her life in front of the TV.
- Two-thirds of Americans watch TV while eating dinner.

Television technology, delayed during World War II, changed the lifestyles of millions of Americans, who clustered around small black-and-white screens to watch their favorite programs. Television was dominated until the 1980s by three major networks: ABC, CBS, and NBC, headed by radio and television pioneer David Sarnoff. However, the advent of Community Access Television (CATV), now popularly called cable television, broke the networks' dominance. By the 1990s two-thirds of American homes were wired for cable television and a third of TV programming was non-network. Other challenges came from new networks, including Rupert Murdoch's Fox Broadcasting Company; the WB Television Network, owned by Warner Bros.; and UPN, owned by Viacom. Though still attracting large audiences, the original three networks realized enough slippage that by the end of the 1990s, all three had been acquired by new owners: NBC by General Electric, CBS by Viacom, and ABC by Capital Cities (Disney). In addition, the Corporation for Public Broadcasting, created by Congress in 1967, provides about 20 percent of the budgets for more than 600 public, noncommercial radio and television stations. The balance of their funding comes from foundations, corporate underwriting, and viewer pledges. Much of public television's daytime programming, such as *Sesame Street*, is aimed at children.

Cable television has expanded from providing reception in mountainous or remote locations to providing a hundred or more channels over coaxial or fiber-optic cables. Once considered merely a common-carrier public utility, cable now represents many of the innovations in broadcasting, such as Home Box Office (HBO) and Ted Turner's Superstation, which distribute their programming via satellite. Turner also founded the Cable News Network (CNN), the first 24-hour, all-news station, which came into its own with nonstop live coverage of the events of the Gulf war in 1991. Today, many people unable to access cable television or who want even more programming choices can install their own satellite receiving dish from companies, such as DirecTV, using direct broadcast satellites (DBS). The notion of broadcasting has been recast as narrow casting, where smaller, special-interest audiences can have their own channels, while allowing the cable operators and content providers to still make a profit through advertising and subscriptions. Concern over rising monthly cable rates in a deregulated marketplace caused

Congress to partially deregulate the cable industry, again treating it as a public utility.

In terms of news programming, networks and local stations differ significantly. According to the Project for Excellence in Journalism, network news is more abstract, with defense, foreign affairs, and the economy accounting for a large portion of the newscast. A lone anchorperson fields reports from a cadre of correspondents. Local news is presided over by a family-like grouping of male and female anchors, a weatherman, and a sports anchor, who engage in small talk and present short news stories. The study suggests more community coverage, more enterprise reporting, better sourcing of stories, longer stories, and more reporters with longer lead times as a way of regaining viewers siphoned off by the Internet and other activities. The terrorist attacks of September 11, 2001, temporarily brought viewers back to their local stations. But will they stay (Project for Excellence in Journalism 2001)?

Existing technologies are converging and new technologies are emerging, but America remains a television culture. It is the primary source of news for most Americans, a habit, an escape, perhaps even a necessity. It has been critiqued and criticized unlike any other industry. Its effect on children has been hotly debated. It has been called too violent, too bland, too lowbrow, and too much of everything else. A former chairman of the FCC called it "a vast wasteland." But amid the clutter of advertising, the reruns, the banality, and the boosterism, there are nuggets of entertaining, enlightening, and uplifting programming that make TV the most popular medium in history.

News Services

The Associated Press (AP) is the dominant news service in the United States. Founded in 1848 as a way to share the cost of international reporting, AP is uniquely owned as a not-for-profit member cooperative. Today, AP's World Services provides news and features in six languages to some 8,500 international print, photography, and broadcasting customers in more than 110 countries. This membership cooperative is a counterpoint in a highly competitive industry. Members pay for the content they receive and, in turn, agree to share the news with other members. This concept hastened the development of objective reporting.

A second news service, United Press International (UPI), has experienced a long downward spiral in its business fortunes in recent years. Once an aggressive competitor with AP, today UPI has sold off its broadcasting arm (to AP), has been acquired by the Unification Church, and is struggling to find an Internet presence.

Several U.S. newspapers or newspaper chains and broadcast companies maintain a somewhat lesser degree of intermedia cooperation and often syndicate their own product to subscribers. Notable is the availability of the various CNN broadcast services on a 24-hour basis. The federal government is also a major player in the distribution of news and information. In 1998, the United States Information Agency was restructured, and the newly created International Broadcasting Bureau (IBB) is responsible for disseminating news and public affairs programming through the Voice Of America, WORLDNET Television and Film Service, and Radio and TV Marti, aimed at Cuba. The cold war rhetoric of these propaganda arms has been tempered by an increased emphasis on trade and commerce issues. However, public diplomacy efforts in both print and broadcast media aimed primarily at the Middle East were enhanced by the U.S. Department of State in response to the terrorist attacks of 2001.

Internet and Interactive New Technologies

Each successive technological innovation has expanded the reach of the media while forcing existing media to adapt and perhaps change. The telegraph, radio, movies, television, cable, satellite, and now digital communication have all shaped the direction of mass communication. Today, well over half of U.S. homes have computers, and most enjoy access to the Internet. Many others use computers on the job. However, research suggests that unlike the democratizing effect of radio or television, the wired revolution remains largely the tool of the more educated and more affluent. President Bill Clinton called it the "digital divide." Taking the society as a whole, the heavily computerized United States (along with other industrialized nations) represents the "haves" in a world increasingly characterized by the disparity between the haves and the have-nots.

The Internet, relying on widely separated but interconnected computer systems, was originally designed as a military solution to the threat of communication disruption due to nuclear attack. By the end of the twentieth century, the Internet was being used for everything from news to shopping, entertainment, and distance learning. The Internet was siphoning customers from traditional media. At the same time, traditional media were embracing Internet technology to complement their original print or broadcast product. While some people were bypassing traditional media reporting by using the World Wide Web, others consumers were simply using the web to access traditional media services in a new technological format. Major media companies, such as AOL TimeWarner, competed with technology giants, such as Microsoft, to maximize audience share and retain competitive advantage in a constantly changing technological marketplace, as well as occasionally in the courts. Competition looms fierce between computer, coaxial cable, and fiber-optic service providers for access to the consumer's household hookup and subscription revenues.

Global Mass Culture and Media Imperialism

American media is big business and getting bigger. Propelled by deregulation at home and the worldwide trend of merger-mania, U.S. media firms have engorged themselves on smaller competitors and now dominate the globe. The largest media conglomerates, along with nationality and 2001–2002 revenues are:

General Electric	U.S.	$127.0 billion
Sony	Japan	57.1
Vivendi	France	51.1
AT&T	U.S.	49.8
AOL TimeWarner	U.S.	40.2
Disney	U.S.	24.5
Viacom	U.S.	23.2
Bertelsmann	Germany	17.0
News Corp.	Australia	12.6

The four top-grossing conglomerates—G.E., Sony, Vivendi, and AT&T—have diversified into other ventures beside media. AOL TimeWarner is the largest media corporation, owning America Online, Netscape, TimeWarner publications, CNN, HBO, Turner Entertainment, cable, film, music, and TV production, as well as major league sports franchises. By any measure, the United States dominates the news and entertainment production and flow for the world.

Domestically, mainstream media reflect the interests and mores of the large majority of citizens, and this is the group advertisers most desire to reach. So too, globally, Western media, led by the United States, reflect the capitalistic, democratic values of the more-developed nations of the Northern Hemisphere. The effect of this media dominance is as complex as the debates over globalization. Do U.S. values subvert and swamp the cultural traditions of less-developed nations that are unable to compete against media empires? Or does exported U.S. media offer a lifestyle of consumer choice and political freedom that will advance the lives of millions? Why does Western news largely ignore the developing world, except in times of crisis? From marketing to programming to satellite technology, the rest of the world has little choice but to avail itself of U.S. media. When cries of media imperialism reached a crescendo in the 1980s, the United States withdrew from UNESCO, and only recently has it announced plans to rejoin that world body. But the debate continues in a new century of change.

Advertising and Public Relations

The decade of the 1990s represented a period of considerable growth and profitability for the advertising industry and its quieter but equally effective partner in persuasion, public relations. Riding the crest of the runaway bull market economic expansion, advertising and public relations helped drive share prices to dizzying heights, launching entrepreneurial start-up companies and then taking them public. It was a period that saw revenues rise and ad rates climb to more than $1 million for a 30-second television commercial during the National Football League Super Bowl. Agencies grew, merged, and provided plenty of employment.

But as all good things seem to end, the Internet-company bubble burst by the year 2000. Share prices tumbled. Companies folded. And with the steep decline in advertising revenue, media constricted. Small publications went out of business. Layoffs beset advertising and public relations agencies and media firms alike. Many blamed advertising and public relations for artificially hyping the value of start-up companies that still lacked any products to take to market. Even large global communication conglomerates felt the impact. Cash rich, many had acquired big public relations agencies as a way to offer broader services to their clients and as a hedge against an advertising downturn. Some had proved profitable investments. Other public relations agencies, however, had been overvalued, and the parent companies found themselves servicing high levels of acquisition debt in a soft business climate. Currently, three-quarters of the top grossing public relations agencies, including such U.S. firms as Weber Shandwick, Fleishman-Hillard, Hill & Knowlton, and Burson Marstellar, are owned by global diversified holding companies, such as Omnicom, Interpublic Group (IPG), or WPP, which also own such major advertising agencies as BBDO Worldwide, DDB Worldwide, FCB Worldwide, McCann-Erickson, J. Walter Thomson, Ogilvy& Mather, and Y&R Advertising.

A significant trend in recent years has been the consolidation of advertising and public relations functions under the umbrella term of integrated marketing communication (IMC). In IMC, all activities designed to move goods and services in the marketplace, such as advertising, publicity, sales promotion, direct mail, trade shows, and special events, are coordinated under a single management function. This trend has been implemented in corporations and agencies alike.

Advertising is no longer just about media placement of advertising messages aimed at a mass audience. Today's advertising practitioner must know niche marketing, interactive media, relationship marketing, and brand development. Advertising is a worldwide business, but the United States is the largest advertising market and New York is the capital. Domestic advertising expenditures for all media are in the neighborhood of a quarter of a trillion dollars per year, with daily newspapers, broadcast television, and direct mail responsible for nearly two-thirds of that total. In recent years, however, cable television and newer technologies such as the Internet have been claiming larger shares of the media pie. This new technological revolution has changed advertising significantly, moving it away from reliance on mass media toward more specialized media aimed at smaller audiences with select interests. Of course, technology has also provided the tools for the audience to skip over the commercials altogether.

Half of all U.S. advertising billings are generated by the largest 500 agencies. Many of these in turn are owned by the giant global holding companies mentioned previously. The largest U.S. agency brands, ranked by 1999 fee income, are Grey Advertising ($536 million), J. Walter Thompson Co. ($496 million), McCann Erickson Worldwide $467 million), FCB Worldwide ($453 million), and Leo Burnett USA ($397 million). By providing full client services with global reach, these giant agencies obtain an economy of scale and greater efficiency. However, critics argue they restrict competition and monopolize the media, while overwhelming nascent advertising industries in developing markets.

Advertising adds desirability to the products it promotes. It adds value to brands, stimulates competition, and gives the consumer higher quality and more choice. But advertising also continues to face social criticism for campaigns aimed at children; advertising in schools, such as the Channel One project; and for health-related issues such as tobacco and alcohol advertising. By the end of the 1990s, settlements in a series of lawsuits against the tobacco industry resulted in severely curtailing tobacco advertising efforts. When Seagram, the Canadian liquor conglomerate, defied a 60-year-old voluntary ban by reintroducing liquor advertising into American broadcasting, state and federal governments as well as consumer groups moved to restrict alcohol advertising. However, the Federal Trade Commission, the government's watchdog on advertising, was substantially downsized during the Reagan administration's era of deregulation, making advertising monitoring more problematic. Generally, the First Amendment of the U.S. Constitution protects commercial speech. A case involving Nike Corporation currently before the U.S. Supreme Court may possibly further define the limits of commercial speech protection and affect the practices of advertising and public relations communicators in the future.

Public relations in its many forms and functions is an estimated $10 billion per year industry in the United States and enjoys a growth rate roughly equal to the country's gross domestic product (GDP). As many as a quarter of a million people work in public relations in the United States. Public relations practitioners handle media research and media relations, counseling, public affairs, fund raising, publications, and creating positive relationships with a variety of publics, such as the government, the community, employees, or shareholders. Practitioners work for corporations, public sector organizations, and not-for-profit firms. The federal government is the single largest employer of public relations personnel.

Media Diversity in a Changing Environment

Demographically, California signals the future of America. The majority in the state is now Spanish speaking. The most common surnames are Rodriguez and Gonzales. In San Jose, the 11th largest city in the United States, the most common surname is Vietnamese, Nguyen. Nationally, companies are retooling their branding, marketing, and advertising campaigns to tap the estimated $1.3 trillion—20 percent of the national total—in minority spending power. Mainstream media is diversifying into these markets with, bi- or trilingual pages, supplements, and separate publications. Local broadcasting is also targeting the ethnic communities, although not as quickly as cable, where entire channels are devoted to ethnic news and entertainment programming. Non-English Internet content is growing.

At the same time, a small, tenacious group of ethnic publishers and broadcast owners struggle to meet the diverse needs of their communities and compete for advertising revenue. Media directories list ethnic publications of various groups in the hundreds. Broadcast outlets are far fewer. The black press, for example, has functioned since the end of the Civil War. The ethnic press has accompanied each successive wave of immigration into the United States.

Media employment for minority journalists, broadcasters, and other communicators is a priority in industries anxious to effectively serve and sell to the growing minority communities. Qualified applicants are highly sought after and recruited. But the applicant pool is small. Women fare better than ethnic minorities in finding media jobs, filling one-third to two-thirds of positions, depending on media segment. Women still encounter the so-called glass ceiling in their attempts to infiltrate upper management. Launching their own publication or agency is a common tactic to advance careers. Ethnic practitioners make up about 20 percent of the workforce, but very few are represented in the executive suite.

Preparing Tomorrow's Journalists and Communicators

Communication education in the United States remains healthy, despite a recessionary economy and chronically low starting salaries in the industry. More than 400 colleges and universities offer degrees in mass communications. There has even been a slight upturn in journalism enrollment since the terrorist attacks of September 11, 2001. Communication students are roughly equally distributed between print and broadcast journalism, public relations, and advertising. More than 10 percent of communication students are pursuing advanced degrees. Virtually all communication industries require a college degree for entry-level positions. About a quarter of college and journalism programs are accredited by the Association for Education in Journalism and Mass Communications (AEJMC), meeting standards in curriculum, faculty scholarship, diversity, budget, facilities, and public service.

Communications graduates find jobs in advertising and public relations, broadcasting, and print. About a quarter of graduates continue their education or work outside of communications.

As in the industries they are preparing students for, the primary issue of the twenty-first century for U.S. schools of mass communication is convergence. Nationwide, journalism schools are increasingly teaching students how to present news in more than one medium. Thus students are being prepared for multimedia careers. Since the audience already seeks out news in a multiplatform environment, schools are adapting to the new reality. While some media and some educational programs simply transfer their print content to the web, others have embraced convergence seriously, using and teaching streaming video, web production, and cross-platform publishing, after teaching research, writing, and critical thinking. Similarly, public relations and advertising programs are cross-training their students to meet the needs of contemporary agencies and integrated communications departments. Not only does convergence challenge the students to learn multiple platforms, it also challenges the curriculum to make hard choices of what to teach and what to expect students to learn elsewhere. Faculty members are also challenged to upgrade their own skills, and increasingly skills courses are being taught by working professionals.

A complementary challenge facing journalism education is the proper role of the discipline within the academy. Columbia University, long the paragon of job skills education for the profession, as well as home to the prestigious Pulitzer prizes, has been rocked by an administrative decision to reevaluate the role of journalism in higher education. How to balance the skills and scholarship has been a longstanding debate in academe. Proponents line up on both sides of the theory versus practicum divide. Orville Schell, dean at University of California's graduate program in journalism, disagrees that journalists can learn their skills on the job. "Media outlets have abdicated bringing young journalists up the food chain, from copy boy to reporter, so there's a need for journalism schools," he says. But he calls for more courses in history, economics, and literature, not mass communications theory. Other schools advocate in-depth study and research in the areas of mass communications. The debate in the United States is a century old; vocational education and scholarly pursuits have been uncomfortable bedfellows since Aristotle. The debate goes on. But the extensive U.S. system of higher education should be able to provide a home for both schools of thought, to the ultimate benefit of the democracy (Walsh and Fogg 2002).

Conclusion

A core democracy with a sophisticated media system, Canada enters the twenty-first century full of hope and promise, but with British and French baggage and one eye on the United States. Driven by the psychological need for a unique national identity and culture, and tempered by the need to pay for it in a globalizing world, Canada juggles the public and the private to maintain a media culture all its own.

Unfettered by regulation and fueled by huge quantities of advertising revenues, U.S. media act out the global role one would expect of a superpower. Often the media play a lead in formulating the public agenda and participating in public diplomacy. Media are the major form of "white propaganda" on behalf of liberal capitalist democracies in a world characterized by globalization. Driven by technological innovation, U.S. media constantly merge and evolve into new organizations, seeking media convergence and market dominance. While its critics are many, both foreign and domestic, U.S. media will continue to exert an enormous influence over the entire world for a long time to come.

Note

1. The author thanks the authors of this chapter in the third edition, Herbert Strentz and Vernon Keel, for their scholarship and conceptual framework, which made the task of updating the chapter much more rewarding. In some cases, where updating was not called for, their work is retained, along with references from the third edition.

Bibliography

"A Chronicle of Freedom of Expression in Canada (part 1, 1914-1994)." Available: http://www.hackcanada.com/canadian/freedom/freedomchron/chronicle.htm. Accessed 24 August 2002.

"A Chronicle of Freedom of Expression in Canada (Part 2, 1995–present)." Available: http://www.hackcanaca.com/canadian/freedom/freedomchron/recent.html. Accessed 24 August 2002.

Akin, David. "Canadian Youth Online More Than Americans: Survey by Forrester." *Financial Post,* 31 January 2001. LexisNexis: http://www.libaccess.sjsu.edu:2072?universe/document?_m2e639bld737014c8dc8249f335ad628f&_docnum=88&wchp=dGLbVlz-1S1A1&_md5=5b502279efb614c58a0bd5a3aaa40cb8. Accessed 24 September 2002.

American Society of Newspaper Editors (ASNE). "Newsroom Minorities Top 10 Percent, ASNE 1993 Survey Shows." News release. Reston, Va.: ASNE, 30 March 1993.

Annenberg Public Policy Center. "Media Usage by Families and Children for 2000," 26 June 2000. Available: http://www.media-awareness.ca/eng/issues/stats/usetv.htm#meduse. Accessed 24 August 2002.

Bass, Warren. "Silence of the Press: Canada's Horrific Unreported Trial." *Columbia Journalism Review* (September/October 1993). Available: http://www.cjr.org/year/93/5/canada.asp. Accessed 16 August 2002.

Barnouw, Erik. *A History of Broadcasting in the United States.* Vol. 1, *A Tower of Babel (to 1933).* New York: Oxford University Press, 1966.

———. *A History of Broadcasting in the United States.* Vol. 2, *The Golden Web (1933–53).* New York: Oxford University Press, 1968.

———. *A History of Broadcasting in the United States.* Vol. 3, *The Image Empire (From 1953).* New York: Oxford University Press, 1970.

Beattie, Earl. "In Canada's Centennial Year, U.S. Mass Media Influence Probed." *Journalism Quarterly* 44, no. 4 (Winter 1967): 667–672.

Beauchesne, Eric. "Internet Clicking With Youth: Nine of 10 Teenagers Have Been Online, Overall Use Soars: Survey." *The Standard* (27 March 2001). LexisNexis: http://www.libaccess.sjsu.edu:2072/universe/document?_m=b7e9775b88291e9051C833444846e8f&_docnum=8&wchp=dGLbVlZ-1S1A1&_md5=84c7a8affd514b654c078a758426b5b4. Accessed 24 September 2002.

Blanshay, Marlene. "Canadian TV Sucks: Six-Year-Old Repeats of Drivel, Lumberjack Contests—No Wonder So Many People Want U.S. Satellite TV, Which Is Now Illegal Here." *Montreal Gazette,* 27 May 2002, LexisNexis: http://libaccess.sjsu.edu:2073?universe/document?_m64861911946bb84682f9b302baa66317&docnum=15&wchp=dGLbV1z-1S1A1&_md5=ffc04d8afcc793496f87d25c1b1385. Accessed 24 August 2002.

Brown, Barry. "Canada, Land of Newspaper Barons." *Media Life,* 16 August 2002. Available: http://www.medialifemagazine.com/news2002/aug02/aug12/5_fri/news5friday.html. Accessed 16 August 2002.

"Cable TV Subscribers Dip While DHT Demand Rises." *The Vancouver Province,* 21 June 2001, A32. LexisNexis: http://libaccess.sjsu.edu:2073/universe/document?_m=99d4d9d488511971-cfd554e73b905&ducnum=51&wchp=dGLbVtb-1S1A1&_md5=eaa0dc43fb8b05b6179211d6e53d6e53d0d27>. Accessed 24 September 2002.

Campbell, Richard. *Media and Culture,* 2nd Edition. Boston: Bedford/St. Martin's, 2000.

Canada: A Portrait. Ottawa, Ontario: Minister of Supply and Services, 1992.

Canada, Communications Division. *Canada Year Book 1994.* Ottawa, Ontario: Statistics Canada, 1993.

Canadian Association of Internet Providers. "Copyright & Other Policy Issues." Available: http://www.caip.ca/issues/copyright/aug1501-2.htm. Accessed 21 August 2002.

Canadian Newspaper Association. "2001 Circulation Data, Based on 6 Months March 2001." Available: http://www.can-ajc.ca/newspapers/facts/circulation.asp?search=all&language=English. Accessed 19 August 2002.

"Canada Will Put Different Spin on 9/11." *The Kitchener-Waterloo Record,* 20 August 2002, B5. LexisNexis: http:libaccess.sjsu.edu:2073?universe/document?_md2a5710ef3f14f6347-c1254d691f01bf&_docnum=1&wchp=dGLbV1z-1S1A1&_md5=8816842d502cdc6c1ffd55642389ffd7. Accessed 24 August 2002.

Canam–Supreme Court of B.C., 12 October 1999. Available: http://www.scacanada.com/bcsupremecourt.html. Accessed 23 August 2002.

Christians, Clifford G., John P. Ferre, and P. Mark Fackler. *Good News, Social Ethics and the Press.* New York: Oxford University Press, 1993.

Cobb, Chris. "Divas Lead Cultural Export Surge: Pop Superstars Help Put Canada's Balance of Cultural Trade in the Black." *The Ottawa Citizen*, 21 June 2001, A1. LexisNexis: http://libaccess.sjsu.edu:2072?universe/document?_m=6b2caa971e2ce299fc588c17d821d06a&_docnum=52&wchp=dGLbV1z-1S1A1&_md5=75751cd4c51d082c19725cal1787693. Accessed 24 September 2002.

Commission on Freedom of the Press. *A Free and Responsible Press.* Chicago: University of Chicago Press, 1947.

Cornacchia, Charyl. "Gimme Shelter: Publications Devoted to Home Comforts—the Shelter Magazines—Are Doing Surprisingly Well in a Troubled Economy." *The Vancouver Sun*, 1 February 2002, E6. LexisNexis: http://libaccess.sjsu.edu:2072/universe/document?_m=dc9d80fca2439cb7a0780186f3f4df86&docnum=18&wchp=dGLbV1z-1S1A1&_md5=497a44dcfb37a02165d533119ea991d5. Accessed 24 September 2002.

"Coverage a Balancing Act for Media." *The Regina Leader-Post*, 2 November 2001, A3. LexisNexis: http://libaccess.sjsu.edu:2073/universe/document?_m=2b31d034c84d5333157e4f8f44e9daa5a&docnum=64&wchp=dGLbV1z-1S1A1&_md5=897fd43498130c593456d8f61ed4bb09. Accessed 24 August 2002.

Desbarats, Peter. *Guide to Canadian News Media.* Toronto: HarcourtBraceJovanovich, Canada, 1990.

Diekmeyer, Peter. "Little long-term effect on ad sales: But terrorist attacks have distracted public, making it hard for advertisers to make impact." *Montreal Gazette*, 9 October, 2002, C2. LexisNexis: http://libaccess.sjsu.edu:2073/universe/document?_m2b31d034c84d533157-e4f8f44e9daa5a&_docnum=66&wchp=dGLbV1z-1S1A1&_md5=b6803303c34da7059a613b52c8e3e700. Accessed 24 August 2002.

Dordick, Herbert S., and Georgette Wang. *The Information Society: A Retrospective View.* Newbury Park, Calif.: Sage, 1993.

Dorland, Michael. *The Cultural Industries in Canada.* Toronto: James Lorimer, 1996.

Ellis, David. *Split Screen.* Toronto: Friends of Canadian Broadcasting, 1993.

Emery, Michael, Edwin Emery, and Nancy L. Roberts. *The Press and America: An Interpretive History of the Mass Media*, 9th Edition. Boston: Allyn and Bacon, 2000.

Emmert, Fredric A. "U.S. Media in the 1990s: Part I. Overview and the Print Media." Available: http://usinfo.state.gov/usa/infousa/media/media1cd.htm. Accessed 32 August 2002.

Emmert, Fredric A. "U.S. Media in the 1990s: Part II. The Broadcast Media." Available: http://usinfo.state.gov/usa/infousa/media/media2cd.htm. Accessed 32 August 2002.

Emmert, Fredric A. "U.S. Media in the 1990s: Part III. The Media and Society." Available: http://usinfo.state.gov/usa/infousa/media/media3cd.htm. Accessed 32 August 2002.

Eng, Dinah. "Targeting New Markets." *Presstime*, June 2002. LexisNexis: http://libaccess.sjsu.edu:2073/universe/document?_m=c06af606c5d00eecb8f24d1b105020d&docnum=5&wchp=dGLbV1z-1S1A1&_md5=300f9db200a8be0e6eaa684e4103a14d. Accessed 24 August 2002.

"Federal Government Reminded That Advertisers Are the Engine Driving Canadian Broadcasting System; Advertising Associations Present Case to Standing Committee on Canadian Heritage." *Canada NewsWire*, 18 April 2002. LexisNexis: http://libaccess.sjsu.edu:2072/universe/document?_m65c62d27eaa7f708baa3828c17d91645&_docnum=40&wchp=dGLbV1z-1S1A1&_md5=49e94eb970f21487ac9d526013bb9ba. Accessed 24 September 2002.

Ferguson, Marjorie. "Invisible Divides: Communication and Identity in Canada and the U.S." *Journal of Communication* 43, no. 2 (1993): 42–57.

Folkerts, Jean, and Dwight L. Teeter, Jr. *Voices of a Nation: A History of Mass Media in the United States*, 4th Edition. Boston: Allyn and Bacon, 2002.

Getler, Michael. "Challenges: The Press and the Pentagon." *Columbia Journalism Review* 40, no. 4 (November/December, 2001): 26.

"Global National Wins Awards for Sept. 11 Coverage." *Calgary Herald*, 28 May 2002, B11. LexisNexis: http://libaccess.sjsu.edu:2073/universe/document?_m=e7ce46635e7b1bd9be-92bda3f0a747ed&docnum=156&wchp-dGLbV1z-1S1A1&_md5=7341911e53e2172d6871dedd6a77a9c. Accessed 24 August 2002.

Greenaway, Norma. "52% of Us Saying No to the Net." *Montreal Gazette,* 12 June 2002, A1. LexisNexis: http://libaccess.sjsu.edu:2072/universe/document?_mdadfb0ac4beaa756-a0509b668b1bc8c7&_docnum=4&wchp=dGLbVtb-1S1A1&_md5=bc640c29c3495af7ec3bc a54d005d61b. Accessed 24 September 2002.

Gwyn, Richard. "No Need to Fear Closer Ties to the U.S." *Toronto Star,* 23 June 2002. http:// friendscb.ca/articles/torontoStar/torontostar020623-2.htm. Accessed 19 August 2002.

Hackett, Robert. "Covering Up the 'War on Terrorism': The Master Frame and the Media Chill (Top Ten Questions Undercovered by the Dominant U.S. Media)." *Canadian Business and Current Affairs* 8, no. 3 (Fall 2001): 8–11. Available: http://libaccess.sjsu.edu:2073/universe/cocu-ment?_m1cfb8b88925f78fc38cd4f1bb8b82dlb82d1b&docnum=106&wchp=dGLbV1z-1S1 A1&_md5=7f86473383768f6c9a405c186da9e0fc. Accessed 24 August 2002.

Halberstam, David. *The Powers That Be.* New York: Knopf, 1979.

Haggett, Scott. "Newspapers Turn the Page after Slump." *Calgary Herald,* 24 April 2002, C1. LexisNexis: http://libaccess.sjsu.edu:2072/universe/document?_m=b7e9775-b88291e9a051-c833444846e8f&_docnum=19&wchp=dGLbV1z-1S1A1&_md5=013d1a57d 085cc85ac5ccc7d8310b1c4. Accessed 24 September 2002.

Head, Sydney W., and Christopher Sterling. *Broadcasting in America,* 5th Edition. Boston: Houghton Mifflin, 1987.

Holmes, Helen, and David Taras. *Seeing Ourselves: Media Power and Policy in Canada.* Toronto: HarcourtBraceJovanovich, Canada, 1992.

Innis, Harold A. *The Bias of Communication.* Toronto: University of Toronto Press, 1951.

Iyer, Pico. *The Global Soul.* New York: Vintage Departures, 2000.

Jobb, Dean. "Fighting Publication Bans." *Canadian Business and Current Affairs* 8, no. 4 (Winter 2002): 12–14. LexisNexis: http://libaccess.sjsu.edu:2073/universe/document?_m=fcae826027c05-b17d25c729c31d932c9&_docnum=40&wchp=dGLbV1z-1S1A1&_md5=7ac68e14204364dd 38e29443e6238903. Accessed 24 August 2002.

Johansen, Peter. Personal interview by William Briggs, 25 September 2002.

Joyce, Grag. "B.C. Supreme Court Allows Recorders Inside Courtroom, But Not for Broadcast." *Yahoo Headlines,* 5 June 2002. Available: http://ca.news.yahoo.com/020605/6/mv7v.html. Accessed 24 August 2002.

Kamalipour, Yahya R. *Global Communication.* Belmont, Calif.: Wadsworth, 2002.

Kesterton, W. H. *A History of Journalism in Canada.* Toronto: McClelland and Stewart, 1967.

Kohut, Andrew. "Young People Are Reading, Everything But Newspapers." *Columbia Journalism Review* (July/August 2002). LexisNexis: http://libaccess.sjsu.edu:2073?universe/docu-ment?_m=c06af606c5d00eecb8f24d1b1050202d?_docnum=2&wchp=dGLbV1z-1s1A1&_ md5=dc5ed160b9883cfcI753aabe62c1b645. Accessed 24 August 2002.

Leonard, Thomas C. *The Power of the Press: The Birth of American Political Reporting.* New York: Oxford University Press, 1986.

Levy, Leonard W. *Emergence of a Free Press.* New York: Oxford University Press, 1985.

MacAffee, Michelle. "Six Out of 10 Canadians Say Culture Is Threatened by Americans: Poll." *Canadian Business and Current Affairs,* 30 June 2002. LexisNexis: http:libaccess. sjsu.edu:2072/universe/document?_m=99d4d9d488511971cfd554e73b0fb905&_docnum= 59&wchp+dGMbVtb-1S1A1&_md5=9b3edd00354e36e978e764fl8cd51c6a. Accessed 24 September 2002.

McMurray, Sandy. "Less TV Is Net Gain." Available: http://www.pollara.ca/new/LIBRARY/sur-veys/net_gain.htm. Accessed 19 August 2002.

McPhail, Thomas L. *Global Communication: Theories, Stakeholders, and Trends.* Boston: Allyn and Bacon, 2002.

Martin, Robert, and G. Stuart Adam. *A Sourcebook of Canadian Media Law,* revised edition. Ottawa, Ontario: Carleton University Press, 1991.

Marzolf, Marion. *Up from the Footnote: A History of Women Journalists.* New York: Hastings House, 1977.

Merrill, John C. *The Dialectic in Journalism: Toward a Responsible Use of Press Freedom.* Baton Rouge: Louisiana State University Press, 1989.

Miller, Sally M., Editor. *The Ethnic Press in the United States: A Historical Analysis and Handbook.* Westport, Conn.: Greenwood Press, 1987.

Moore, Aaron J. "A Chill in Canada." *Columbia Journalism Review* (July/August 2002). Available: http://www.cjr.org/year/02/2/moore.asp. Accessed 16 August 2002.

Mott, Frank Luther. *American Journalism: A History, 1690–1960.* New York: Macmillan, 1962.

Newspaper Association of America. "Canadian Daily Newspapers." Available: http://www.naa.org/info/facts00/28.html. Accessed 3 August, 2002.

——. "Employment of Women and Minorities." Available: http://www.naa.org/info/facts00/32.html. Accessed 25 Aug 2002.

——. "Journalism Graduates." Available: http://www.naa.org/info/facts00/25.htm. Accessed 25 August 2002.

——. "Highlights: The Year in Review." 2000. Available: http://www.naa.org/info/facts00/33.html. Accessed 25 August 2002.

——. "Newspaper, Voice and Online Services." Available: http://www.naa.org/info/facts00/18.html. Accessed 25 August 2002.

——. "Number of U.S. Daily Newspapers." Available: http://www.naa.org/info/facts00/11.html. Accessed 22 August 2002.

——. "U.S. Daily Newspaper Circulation." Available: http://www.naa.org/info/facts00/12.html. Accessed 22 August 2002.

——. "Top 20 U.S. Newspaper Companies by Circulation." Available: http://www.naa.org/info/facts00/15.html. Accessed 25 August 2002.

——. "Total U.S. Non-Daily Newspapers." Available: http://www.naa.org/info/facts00/27.html. Accessed 25 August 2002.

——. "U.S. Daily Newspaper Advertising Expenditures." Available: http://www.naa.org/info/facts00/08.html. Accessed 25 August 2002.

——. "U.S. Daily and Sunday Newspaper Readership Demographics." Available: http://www.naa.org/info/facts00/03.html. Accessed 25 August 2002.

——. "U.S. Daily and Sunday/Weekend Newspaper Reading Audience." Available: http://www.naa.org/info/facts00/02.html. Accessed 25 August 2002.

——. "U.S. Newspaper Online Readership." Available: http://www/naa/org/iinfo/facts00/19.html. Accessed 25 August 2002.

"Newspaper Industry Rebounding, Says CAN." *Windsor Star,* 24 April 2002, A15. LexisNexis: http://libaccess.sjsu.edu:2072/universe/document?_m=dc9d80fca2439cb7a0780186f4df86&_docnum=15wchp=dGLbV1z-1S1A1&_md5=1deda95cee55d3c7ecb4cac57d502f8f. Accessed 24 September 2002.

New York Times Co. v. Sullivan, 376 U.S. 254 (1964).

New York Times Co. v. United States, 713 U.S. 403 (1971).

O'Neill, Juliet. "Net users no recluses, study finds." *Montreal Gazette,* 12 December 2001, A1. LexisNexis: http://libaccess.sjsu.edu:2072/universe/document?_mdabfb0ac4-beaa756a0509b668b1bc8c7&_docnum= 2&wchp=dGLbVtb-ISIAI&_md5=3d9761c5b8b6-eb72170c8c54810e254e. Accessed 24 September 2002.

Peterson, Theodore. *Magazines in the Twentieth Century.* Urbana: University of Illinois Press, 1964.

Pollard, James E. *The Presidents and the Press.* New York: Macmillan, 1947.

Project for Excellence in Journalism. "Gambling With the Future." *Columbia Journalism Review* 40, no. 4 (November/December 2001, supplement).

"Q & A: How 9-11 Changed Media Coverage." *Newsweek* Web Exclusive, 12 May 2002. Available: http://www.msnbc.com/news/695680. Accessed 12 May 2002.

Raboy, Marc. Les *Média Québécois: Presse, Radio, Télévision.* Câblodistribution. Boucherville, Québec: Gaetan Morin Editeur, 1992.

Regan, Tom. "Courtroom Secrecy Is Under Fire in Canada." *The Christian Science Monitor,* 3 July 2001. Available: http://www.csmonitot.com/durable/2001/07/03/p7s1.htm. Accessed 24 August 2002.

Romanow, Walter I., and Walter C. Soderlund. *Media Canada.* Mississauga, Ontario: Copp Clark Pitman, 1992.

Scanlon, Joe. "Putting Terrorism and Its Aftermath into Context: The Quality of News Reports After the September 11 Attacks." *Canadian Business and Current Affairs* 8, no. 3 (Fall 2001): 16–17. LexisNexis: http://libaccess.sjsu.edu:2073/universe/document?_m1cfb8b88925f78fc38-cd4f1bb8b82d1b&_docnum=113&wchp=dGLbV1z=1S1A1&_md5=b4ccd89c4e649783370 2340e4488edcd. Accessed 24 August 2002.

Schecter, Barbara. "Homegrown Viewing Falls, CRTC Data Show: CTV, Global Spend More." *National Post*, 22 February, 2002, C4. LexisNexis: http://libaccess.sjsu.edu:2073/universe/ document?_m6bc0119f9f848d8fl4b125c64e96583c&_docnum=30&wchp=dGLbVtb-1S1A 1&_md5=e3753582a690488aff096f7b7cda980d. Accessed 24 September 2002.

———. "You Expect Us to Pay More for That: TV Viewers 'Aren't Clamouring' for More." *National Post*, 21 June, 2001, C1. LexisNexis: <http://libaccess.sjsu.edu:2073/universe/document?_ m=6bc0119f9f848d8f14b125c64e9658c&_docnum=46&wchp=dGLbVtb-1S1A1&_md5=87 69a040f339d98fde22065b4348857f9>. Accessed 24 September 2002.

Scherr, Edmund F. "Fact Sheet: Telecommunications Act of 1996." Available: http://usinfo.state. gov/usa/infousa/media/telecomc.htm. Accessed 23 August 2002.

Schudson, Michael. *Advertising: The Uneasy Persuasion.* New York: Basic Books, 1984.

Scotton, Geoffrey. "Media Integration a Work in Progress: Publishers Agree Convergence Way of Future." *Calgary Herald*, 25 April 2002. LexisNexis: http://libaccess.sjsu.edu:2073/uni-verse/document?_mdc9d80fca2439cb7a0780186f3f4df86&docnum=23&wchp=dGLbV1z-1S1a1&_md5=fe57elb45d9ec612fl602eab21b622d7. Accessed 24 September 2002.

Shaw, David. "Foreign News Shrinks in Era of Globalization." *Los Angeles Times*, 27 September, 2001. Available: http://www.commondreams.org/headlines01/0927-03.htm. Accessed 19 April 2002.

Shaw, Mary-Liz. "Holding the Line: Two Neighboring Nations Try to Raise Their Defenses While Staying Friends." *Milwaukee Journal Sentinel*, 10 March 2002, 1A. LexisNexis: http:libac-cess.sjsu.edu:2073/universe/document?_m1cfb8b88925f78fc38cd4f1bb8b82d1b&_docnum =119&wchp=dGLbV1z-1S1A1&_md5=eb4ef04c1560007285267c8956a23728. Accessed 24 August 2002.

Singer, Benjamin D. *Communications in Canadian Society.* Scarborough, Ontario: Nelson Canada, 1991.

Smith, Anthony. *Goodbye Gutenberg: The Newspaper Revolution of the 1980s.* New York: Oxford University Press, 1980.

Smith, Jeffery A. *Printers and Press Freedom: The Ideology of Early American Journalism.* New York: Oxford University Press, 1988.

Soderlund, Walter C., Paul Gedelovsky, and Martha F. Lee. "Trends in Canadian Newspaper Coverage of International News, 1988–2000: Editors' Assessments." *Canadian Journal of Communication* 27, (January 2002): 73–87. LexisNexis: http://libaccess.sjsu.edu:2073/uni-verse/document?_m=d25710ef14f6347c1254d691f01bf&_docnum=9&wchp=dGLbVIz-1S 1A1&_md5=dcd25e450a4f512881cb6c10ccf3325f. Accessed 24 August 2002.

Steffens, Lincoln. *The Autobiography of Lincoln Steffens.* New York: HarcourtBraceJovanovich, 1931.

Stein, Nicholas. "Magazine Trade Wars." *Columbia Journalism Review* (January/February 1999). Available: http://www.cjr.org/year/99/1/canada.asp. Accessed 16 August 2002.

Steinhart, David. "Canadians Top Net Bankers, U.S. Leads Shopping Stakes: Ipsos-Reid Poll." *National Post*, 22 August 2001, C7. LexisNexis: http://libacces.sjsu.edu:2072?universe/ document?_m6bc0119f9f848d8fl4b125c64e96583c&_docnum=38&wchp=dGLbVtb-1S1A 1&_md5=add477b0fe343cc8d31aa33cc39a61c4. Accessed 24 September 2002.

Stephens, Mitchell. *History of News from the Drum to the Satellite.* New York: Viking, 1988.

Stevenson, Robert L. *Global Communication in the Twenty-First Century.* New York: Longman, 1994.

Steward, Gillian. "Is There Any Room for Stories Unrelated to the September 11 Attacks? Conver-gence Has Made That Difficult to Answer." *Canadian Business and Current Affairs* 8, no. 3 (Fall 2002): 20–21. LexisNexis: http://libaccess.ejsu.edu:2073/universe/document?_ m=285696b8cd31b46dc1f6dd16534bb166&_docnum+329&wchp=dGLbV1z-1S1A1&_md 5=c07d1f92ef26d105b0042e65749592fe. Accessed 24 August 2002.

Stothart, Paul. "A Culture Strong and Free: The Doomsayers Predicted That a Trade Deal with the U.S. Would Spell the End of the Cultural Sovereignty. They Were Wrong." *The Ottawa Citizen* A13. LexisNexis: http://libaccess.sjsu.edu:2072/universe/document?_m=99d4d9d-488511971cfd554e73b0fb905&_docnum=75&wchp=dGLbVtb-1S1A1&_md5=da26087a7b d00b3fae94fcb65487148ee. Accessed 24 September 2002.

Taras, David. *The Newsmakers: The Media's Influence on Canadian Politics.* Scarborough, Ontario: Nelson Canada, 1990.

Tibbetts, Janice. "French Isolated in 'Digital Divide,' Report Finds." *National Post,* 26 March 2002, A9. LexisNexis: http://www.libacess.sjsu.edu:2072/universe/document?_m= 1414e22c064aefc05ed3b7a7980a29b3&_dounum=85&wchp=dGLBtb-1S1A1&_md5=8cc46 ba10385c4d3711d74e555d70552. Accessed 24 September 2002.

Tolusso, Susan. "Broadcast Policy Report: Good News for Producers." *Playback,* 27 November 2002, 6. LexisNexis: http://libaccess.sjsu.edu:2072/universe/document?_m= 99d4d9d-488511971cfd554e73b0fb905&_docnum=66&wchp=dGLbVtb-1S1A1&_md5=36efa1b9511 a11e6f9a907fbc441768bc. Accessed 24 September 2002.

"TV Facts." Available: http://www.girltech.com/Sports/SP_hfacts.html. Accessed 23 August 2002.

Vanderburg, Geoffrey. "Couch-Potato Time Falling—Maybe: Albertans Watch Television the Least, StatsCan Study Says." *Edmonton Journal,* 26 January 2001, A3. LexisNexis: http://www. libacess.sjsu.edu:2072/universe/document?_m6bc0119f848d8fl4b125c64e96583c&_docn um=33&wchp=dGLbVtb-1S1A1&_md5=b56731fb897baaced54d75e628d11065. Accessed 24 September 2002.

Von Jenna, Yvonne. "Navigating Turbulent Waters." *Interactive Multimedia Arts and Technologies Association.* Available: http://www.imat.ca. Accessed 23 August 2002.

Wall, Barbara. "Review of Key Legal Decision in 2000," 15 December 2000. Available: http://www. gannett.com/go/newswatch/2000/december/nm1215-5.htm. Accessed 24 August 2002.

Walsh, Sharon, and Piper Fogg. "Editing the Mission." *Chronicle of Higher Education* 48, no. 40 (9 August 2002).

Weaver, David A., and G. Cleveland Wilhoit. *The American Journalist: A Portrait of U.S. News People and Their Work.* Bloomington: Indiana University Press, 1986.

Wilcox, Dennis L., Glen T. Cameron, Philip H. Ault, and Warren K. Agee. *Public Relations: Strategies and Tactics.* Boston: Allyn and Bacon, 2003.

Wolseley, Ronald E. *The Black Press, U.S.A.* Ames: Iowa State University Press, 1990.

Contributors

Oliver Boyd-Barrett (*Chapter 3, Global and National News Agencies: The Unstable Nexus*) is professor in the Department of Communication, California State Polytechnic University, Pomona. He has several publications in the field of international communications, including *The International News Agencies, Le Trafic des nouvelles* (with Michael Palmer), *Contra-Flow in Global News* (with D. K. Thussu), and *The Globalization of News* (with Terhi Rantanen). Currently he is researching media coverage of the war on terrorism. Boyd-Barrett pioneered the adaptation of international communications courses to distance learning, both at the Open University (United Kingdom) and at the Centre for Mass Communications Research, University of Leicester (United Kingdom). He has also researched and published on issues related to educational and management communications. E-mail: OBoydBarrett@csupomona.edu

William Briggs (*Chapter 20, North America*) is a professor in the School of Journalism and Mass Communications at San Jose State University, San Jose, California. An internationally known educator in the field of strategic communication, Briggs was the founding director of both the Global Studies Institute and the Pacific Rim Institute at San Jose State University. He has lectured and conducted faculty development programs in a number of countries, including China, Singapore, Hong Kong, Taiwan, the Philippines, Thailand, Vietnam, Australia, New Zealand, South Africa, Belgium, the United Kingdom, Canada, and Mexico. At San Jose State University Briggs teaches widely across the graduate and undergraduate curriculum. The degree program in public relations is consistently ranked among the top such programs nationally. He was twice faculty advisor to national championship entries in the Public Relations Society of America Case Studies competition. He served as an Academic Senator and is active in university governance. He has twice served on the executive board of the International Association of Business Communicators and has studied cross-cultural communication at the East West Center, Honolulu. Professionally, Briggs has been an active communications consultant, broadcast and print journalist, editor, and public relations manager. He has received or shared several national and regional awards. His publication record lists more than 80 articles, most notably on globalization and on crisis management. E-mail: wbriggs@pacbell.net

Catherine Cassara (*Chapter 14, The Newly Independent States of Eurasia*) is an associate professor of journalism at Bowling Green University in Bowling Green, Ohio, where she teaches undergraduate courses in international press and media history, as well as courses in news writing, reporting, and editing. At the graduate level, she teaches courses in media history, news framing, and research methods. She is the author of articles and book chapters on human rights and American newspapers and on international news flow patterns in American newspapers. Her current research focuses on human rights and the U.S. media, the framing of international news, and the role of journalism in transitional societies. She has been active for years through the International Communication Division of the Association for Education in Journalism and Mass Communication, serving as head of the division in 1996–1997. A former newspaper journalist, she holds a doctorate in mass media from Michigan State University (1992) and a master's degree in journalism from Michigan State University (1987). In 1989 she received an IREX fellowship to study Russian. She earned a bachelor's degree in Russian studies from the University of Virginia in 1976. E-mail: ccassar@bgnet.bgsu.edu

Arnold S. de Beer (*Chapter 12, News—The Fleeting, Elusive but Essential Feature of Global Journalism*) is professor emeritus in the Department of Journalism, University of Stellenbosch, South Africa, where he teaches international journalism, mass communication theory, and qualitative research methods. He is former professor and head of the Department of Communication at Potchefstroom University and the Department of Communication at Free State University, South Africa, and director of the Institute for Communication Research, Potchefstroom. He is the research director of Media Tenor SA—Institute for Media Analysis, and the founder and editor of *Ecquid Novi—The South African Journal for Journalism.* Other positions he holds include board member of *Journalism Studies, Communication,* and *Communicare;* council member of the International Association for Media and Communication Research and acting chair of the International Communication Division; chair of the African Council on Communication Education—Media and Society Division; member of the Appeals Board of the South African Press Ombudsman; first recipient of the Communication Educator of

the Year award, from the South African Public Relations Institute; first university professor to become a South African APR; former president of the South African Communications Association; member of the South African Broadcasting Corporation board and Executive Committee; and member of the South African Press Council. His published research includes works on media and democracy in South Africa; conflict and peace; violence against women and children in the media; journalism education and training; international news flows and international communication; and news theory and history. E-mail: asdebeer@sun.ac.za

Mark Deuze (*Chapter 9, Global Journalism Education*) is assistant professor in the Department of Communication, University of Amsterdam, the Netherlands, and researcher at the Amsterdam School of Communication Research. He received his bachelor's degree in journalism at the Tilburg School for Journalism, the Netherlands, a master's degree in history and communication studies from the Rand Afrikaans University in Johannesburg, South Africa, and a doctorate in social sciences from the University of Amsterdam, the Netherlands. In 2002–2003 Deuze was a Fulbright scholar at the University of Southern California's Annenberg School for Journalism. His research focuses on the characteristics of journalists and (thus) news cultures, and particularly aims to explore the evolution of skills, standards, and values in journalism in the context of changing society, technology, and economy. From 2002 to 2005 he will be visiting a number of countries to study the ways in which journalism educators and students of the media give meaning to the changes and challenges confronting journalists in contemporary global society. His recent publications include papers in journals such as *Journalism Quarterly, Asia Pacific Media Educator, Journalism Educator, Journal of Mass Me-*

dia Ethics, Ecquid Novi, and the *European Journal of Communication.* Several papers have been published exclusively on-line in *First Monday, Ejournalist,* and the *Online Journalism Review.* E-mail: deuze@pscw.uva.nl

Lyombe S. Eko (*Chapter 16, Sub-Saharan Africa*) is an assistant professor of journalism and mass communication, Department of Communication and Journalism, University of Maine, Orono. His doctorate is from Southern Illinois University at Carbondale (1997). Eko teaches courses in mass media law and regulation, mass communication, and techniques of video production. Areas of research and academic specialization are comparative mass media law and policy, visual communication, African communication studies, and international communication. Eko is an active member of the Broadcast Education Association, and won first place in the association's 2000 scholarly research paper competition. He has published in *Communication Law and Policy* (journal of the Law and Policy Division of the Association for Education in Journalism and Mass Communication); *Communications and the Law,* the *Journal of Black Studies,* and *Ecquid Novi,* the South African journal for journalism research. Eko has also published several book chapters on communication theory and on African communication. Before joining the University of Maine, Eko was an editor and translator at the African Broadcasting Union (URTNA) in Nairobi, Kenya. Before joining URTNA, he was a journalist with Cameroon Radio and Television Corporation. He has produced several video documentaries on African topics. Three of them won honorable mention at festivals in Germany and Canada. They have been broadcast throughout Africa and on WNYC, New York. They are now part of the holdings of several American and Canadian universities. Eko is currently the faculty member of a digital video lab and The Maine Channel, the University of Maine's closed-circuit student cable television system. E-mail: Lyombe_Eko@umit.maine.edu

Lianne Fridriksson (*Chapter 13, Western Europe*) is an associate professor at Baylor University, where she teaches graduate-level courses in research methods, mass communication theory, international communication, and political communication. A former newspaper reporter and editor, she has twice been named a Fulbright scholar, once to Victoria University in Wellington, New Zealand, to research media coverage of antinuclear issues, and once to the University of Iceland and National Library of Iceland, to research government–media relations. She holds a doctorate and a master's degree from the University of Texas and has taught journalism at the University of Texas, Southwest Texas State University, and the University of Kansas. Fridriksson's research focuses on international political communication, human rights, and international security issues. She has presented or published research in the United States, Australia, Israel, Iceland, Denmark, New Zealand, Canada, Mexico, South Korea, and Sweden. E-mail: Lianne_Fridriksson@baylor.edu

Peter Gross (*Chapter 14, Eastern Europe*) is a professor at California State University–Chico (CSUC), Department of Journalism. Multilingual, he has worked and traveled extensively in Western and East/Central Europe, the former Soviet Republics, Taiwan, India, and Cuba. He is the author of *Entangled Evolutions: Media and Democratization in Eastern Europe* (Johns Hopkins University Press/Woodrow Wilson Center Press, 2002) and *Mass Media in Revolution and National Development: The Romanian Laboratory* (Iowa State University Press, 1996), for which he received the 1996 American-Romanian Academy of Arts and Sciences book award. He is co-author of *Eastern European*

Journalism: Before, During, and After Communism (Hampton Press, 1999), which was nominated for the 1999 Kappa Tau Alpha book award. He also authored or co-authored four books published in Europe. He serves on the editorial boards of the AEJMC's international communication bulletin, *The Global Network,* a quarterly mass communication journal of the East/Central European Network of Journalism Educators; *Dilemma,* a national intellectual weekly published in Bucharest, Romania; and *Mediakutato,* a Hungarian media studies journal published in Budapest, Hungary. Gross serves as the AEJMC International Division's chair for teaching standards and formerly served as chair of the Markham International Student Paper Competition and chair of Professional Freedom and Responsibility. He is a member of the International Communication Association, the European Network for Trans-Integration Research, the South East European Studies Association, the Society for Romanian Studies, and the Association for the Advancement of Slavic Studies. E-mail: peergross77@hotmail.com

Paul Grosswiler (*Chapter 8, Continuing Media Controversies*) was a senior Fulbright scholar in journalism in 2000 at China's Wuhan University, where he taught media ethics and critical media studies and began conducting research on Chinese journalism ethics. He is the author of a book on the media and social theories of Canada scholar Marshall McLuhan, *The Method is the Message: Rethinking McLuhan Through Critical Theory,* published by Black Rose Books in Montreal in 1998. He has published articles and book chapters focusing on Tanzanian media worker attitudes, the U.S. press and foreign policy, cultural studies and postmodernism, media ecology, critical media theory, and political communication and new technology. His articles have appeared in *Ecquid*

Novi, the *Journal of International Communication,* the *Canadian Journal of Communication,* the *Journal of Communication Inquiry,* and the *Harvard International Journal of Press/Politics.* He has presented his research at conferences of the Canadian Communication Association, the Media Ecology Association, the International Communication Association, and the Association for Education in Journalism and Mass Communication. He earned a Ph.D. in journalism at the University of Missouri in 1990 and is an associate professor of journalism at the University of Maine, where he teaches international mass communication, history of mass communication, media ethics, opinion writing, and editing. E-mail: PaulG@maine.edu

Minabere Ibelema (*Chapter 16, Sub-Saharan Africa*) holds a Ph.D. in mass communication from Ohio State University and is associate professor of communication studies at the University of Alabama at Birmingham (UAB). Before joining the UAB faculty, he was associate professor of journalism at Eastern Illinois University. Before then, he was associate professor at Central State University (Ohio). Ibelema is the co-editor of *Afro-Optimism: Perspectives on Africa's Advances* (in press) and author of numerous journal articles and book chapters on press freedom and professionalism, mass media, culture and development, and foreign press coverage of Africa. One of his book chapters appeared in *Africa's Media Image,* winner of the Society of Professional Journalists Signa Delta Chi Research Award in 1993. His other articles have appeared in *Free Speech Yearbook, Journal of Development Communication, Newspaper Research Journal, Journal of Radio,* and *Journalism & Mass Communication Educator,* among others. Ibelema has had journalistic stints at *The Birmingham News, The Capital-Journal* (Topeka), and the *Dayton Daily News* (Ohio). He has also had articles published in various other newspapers and magazines, including *Essence* magazine, the *Cleveland Plain Dealer,* the *St. Louis Post-Dispatch, The Christian Science Monitor,* the *Sunday Times* (Nigeria), and the *National Concord* (Nigeria). He has served as faculty adviser for student newspapers at Central State and Eastern Illinois universities. E-mail: mibelema@uab.edu

Dean Kruckeberg (*Chapter 6, International Journalism Ethics; Chapter 14, Russia*) is professor and coordinator of the mass communication division in the Department of Communication Studies at the University of Northern Iowa. His consulting work has included review of the mass communication programs at the United Arab Emirates University in 1993. He was part of the team that developed the public relations degree program at that university in 1994. Kruckeberg was a speaker at workshops in Russia and Latvia in 1998. Also in 1998, Kruckeberg presented programs about journalism and public relations in Bulgaria. In 2002 he was invited to lecture in Sweden to the Swedish Public Relations Association; at Orebro University; and at the Communicare Seminar at Mid Sweden University. He is co-author of *Public Relations and Community: A Reconstructed Theory,* which won the first annual PRIDE Award from the National Communication Association Public Relations Division and is author of book chapters, articles, and papers dealing with international public relations and its ethics. Kruckeberg is co-author of *This Is PR: The Realities of Public Relations.* He was 1995 national Outstanding Educator of the Public Relations Society of America and was 1997 recipient of the Pathfinder Award from the Institute for Public Relations. He is co-chair of the Commission on Public Relations Education. E-mail: kruckeberg@uni.edu

Mitchell Land (*Chapter 16, Sub-Saharan Africa*) is director of the Mayborn Graduate Institute of Journalism at the University of North Texas in Denton. Land worked in media development for the francophone countries of Africa for 15 years before joining professorial ranks in 1989. His research has focused on the political role of television in Cote d'Ivoire and on the status of independent newspapers in Cameroon. For the last two years, he has led the Mayborn Institute in helping Eduardo Mondlane University, Mozambique, launch an undergraduate journalism program. Land is currently co-editing a practical media ethics book that demonstrates how to analyze cases by applying the philosophical principles of utilitarianism and communitarianism. Land has published in the *Howard Journal of Communication, Journal of Communication, Critical Studies in Mass Communication, African Urban and Rural Studies, Judicature,* the *Business Research Yearbook Journalism & Mass Communication Quarterly,* and *African Technology Forum.* Land's work includes scholarship, pedagogical innovations, and outstanding service to the university and community. He studied French language and culture for two years at the Universite de Haute Bretagne and the Institut de la Touraine in France. His Ph.D. is from the University of Texas, Austin, in international/development communication and cultural anthropology. E-mail: mland@unt.edu

P. Eric Louw (*Chapter 11, Journalists Reporting from Foreign Places*) is senior lecturer and director of communication programs at the School of Journalism and Communication, University of Queensland in Brisbane, Australia. He has a Ph.D. from the Center for Cultural and Media Studies, University of Natal (Durban), and an M.A. in political science from the University of South Africa. He previously taught at the University of Natal (Durban), University of South Africa (Pretoria), and Rand Afrikaans University (Johannesburg), and has been a journalist for the

Pretoria News. Louw's primary area of research is political communication. His books are *The Media and Cultural Production* (Sage) and *South African Media Policy* (Anthropos), and he co-authored *The South African Alternative Press* (Anthropos). He is currently writing another book, *The Media and Political Process* (Sage). During the 1980s, Louw was involved in the process of establishing South Africa's (anti-apartheid) alternative press and was a founder and chair- person of non-government organization engaged in development communication work in South Africa. E-mail: e.louw@uq.edu.au

John C. Merrill (*Chapter 1, Global Press Philosophies; Chapter 2, International Media Systems: An Overview*), a teacher of journalism, English, and philosophy for half a century, is currently professor emeritus at the School of Journalism, University of Missouri–Columbia. He was a pioneer in international communication studies, writing the first textbook in comparative journalism (*A Handbook of the Foreign Press*) in the late 1950s. He has taught at the University of Missouri for 25 years and at various other American and foreign universities for 25 years. Merrill is a World War II veteran (Navy), serving in the amphibious forces in both the Atlantic and Pacific theaters. He holds a bachelor's degree in English/history, a master's degree in journalism (LSU), a doctorate in mass communication (Iowa), and a second master's degree in philosophy (Missouri). He has lectured in some 80 countries and is the author or editor of more than 30 books. He was the editor of the first three editions of *Global Journalism*. E-mail: MerrillJ@missouri. edu

Orayb A. Najjar (*Chapter 15, The Middle East and North Africa*) is associate professor of communication, Northern Illinois University, DeKalb. She has a doctorate in journalism from Indiana University, Bloomington.

Najjar trained at the BBC and worked for seven years as a TV director in Jordan. Her publications include entries in Volume 4 of *Encyclopedia of International Media and Communications*, "Jordan, Status of Media in," "West Bank and Gaza, Status of Media in"; six entries in *Censorship: A World Encyclopedia* (Fitzborn Dearborn Publishers, 2001); "Freedom of the Press in Jordan 1927–1998," in *Mass Media and Society in the Middle East* (Hampton Press, 2001); Can This Image Be Saved? in *Islam and the West in Mass Media: Fragmented Images in a Globalizing World* (Hampton Press, 2000); *Palestine, Mass Media in the Middle East* (Greenwood Press, 1994); "Dear Israeli Chief-Censor . . . Sincerely Yours, The Palestinian Editor-in-Chief: Censorship, Negotiation, and Procedural Justice," in *Studies in Cultures, Organizations, and Societies* (vol. 5, 1999); "The Ebb and Flow of Press Freedom in Jordan, 1985–1997," in *Journalism and Mass Communication Quarterly* (vol. 75, no. 1, Spring 1998); and "The 1995 Palestinian Press Law: A Comparative Study," in *Communication Law and Policy* (vol. 2, pp. 41–103, 1997). Najjar is working on a book tentatively entitled *Popular Mobilization and the Palestinian Press: Five Case Studies*, based on her Fulbright research in the West Bank. E-mail: onajjar@niu.edu

Douglas Ann Newsom (*Chapter 7, Global Advertising and Public Relations*) is the senior co-author of three textbooks: *Media Writing* (with the late James Wollert), *This Is PR* (with Judy VanSlyke Turk and Dean Kruckeberg), and *Public Relations Writing: Form and Style* (with the late Bob Carrell). She is co-editor of a book of women's colloquium papers, *Silent Voices* (also with Bob Carrell). Newsom's degrees from the University of Texas at Austin include a bachelor's degree in journalism, a B.F.A. in broadcasting (1955), a master's degree in journalism (1956), and a doctorate (1978). A Fulbright lecturer in India in 1988 and Singapore in 1998–1999, she also has done public relations workshops in Singapore, South Africa, Bulgaria, Hungary, Romania, Poland, Vanuatu, and Latvia. In addition to teaching at Texas Christian University, she is a public relations practitioner and serves on the board of directors of a publicly held company. E-mail: d.newsom@tcu.edu

Allen W. Palmer (*Chapter 14, Eastern Europe*) is the coordinator of international media studies at Brigham Young University in Provo, Utah, where he has taught since 1988. His work has focused on international communication problems, particularly on problems of media globalization. His writing has appeared in *International Journal of Communication, Media and Society, Gazette, Science Communication, Public Understanding of Science,* as well as chapters in several anthologies, including *Global Communication,* edited by Yahya Kamalipour (2001). He has taught as a visiting professor in Mauritius, Benin, Kosovo, and the Philippines. E mail: allen_palmer@byu. edu

Paul Parsons (*Chapter 4, Barriers to Media Development*) is a professor and dean of the School of Communications at Elon University in North Carolina. Previously he served 16 years at Kansas State University, where he was Seaton professor, associate director of the School of Journalism and Mass Communications, and the recipient of three university teaching awards. Parsons was a Fulbright professor at the China School of Journalism in Beijing in 1992–1993 and a visiting professor of communications at Nanyang Technological University in Singapore in 1999–2000. After graduating from Baylor University, he spent 10 years as a newspaper reporter, state Capitol correspondent for United Press International, and state broadcast editor for the Associated Press in Arkansas before pursuing an academic career. He was selected as a recipient of a Rockefeller

Foundation Fellowship in Religious Studies for Journalists at the University of North Carolina at Chapel Hill, completed a master's degree from the University of Arkansas at Little Rock, and earned a Ph.D. in communications at the University of Tennessee. He is the author of two university press books and numerous book chapters and articles on international communications, the most recent an article on news framing in the *Asian Journal of Communication.* E-mail: parsons@elon.edu

Gregg Payne (*Chapter 17, Asia and the Pacific*) holds a bachelor's degree in journalism from the University of Arizona, a master's degree in mass communication from San Diego State University, and a Ph.D. in communication from the University of Utah. His research includes comparative studies of newspaper and Internet credibility; media uses and gratifications investigations involving magazines, newspapers, and the Internet; and the function of media in construction, maintenance, and repair of communities defined by common interests, rather than spatial boundaries. His interest in international journalism is linked to intercultural issues associated with the media-community nexus. Payne's research has been published in the United States and abroad. He teaches research methodology at the University of California, Irvine, and is an adjunct faculty member in the department of communication at Chapman University in Orange, California, where he teaches a variety of courses in mass and interpersonal communication. He is president of Quantum Communication, a consulting firm that specializes in the development of research-based communication programs, and is a former magazine editor and publisher. E-mail: quantmcom@aol.com

Stephen Quinn (*Chapter 18, Australasia*) is director of the Center for Media Training and

Research College of Communication and Media Sciences, Zayed University, Dubai, in the United Arab Emirates (www.zu.ac.ae/cmtr). He also taught journalism in the United Kingdom, Australia, and New Zealand. He is a co-author of *Bridging the Gulf: Communications Law in the United Arab Emirates* and author of *Knowledge Management in the Digital Newsroom* (Focal Press, 2002), *Digital Sub-Editing and Design* (Focal Press, 2001), *Newsgathering on the Net*, 2nd edition (Macmillan, 2001), and *The Art of Learning* (UNSW Press, 1999). He is the only academic on the international advisory counsel for Newsplex (www. newsplex.org/counsels.shtml). Between 1975 and 1990 he worked as a reporter, editor, and columnist in Australia, Thailand, the United Kingdom, and New Zealand, including the *Bangkok Post,* the Press Association in London, BBC-TV, the Australian Broadcasting Corporation, Independent Television News in London, Television New Zealand, and *The Guardian* in London. Since becoming an academic in 1991, he has maintained industry links by contributing to newspapers and magazines, working as a freelance editor, and delivering training courses. To date he has run courses in Australia, the United Kingdom, New Zealand, the United States, Hong Kong, South Africa, Lebanon, and the United Arab Emirates. E-mail: Stephen. Quinn@ zu.ac.ae

Terhi Rantanen (*Chapter 3, Global and National News Agencies: The Unstable Nexus*) is director of the master's program in Global Media and Communications at the London School of Economics. Most of her research has been done on news agencies, which provide excellent case studies for the study of globalization and the introduction of new communications technologies. One of the outcomes of her work is *The Globalization of News* (Sage, 1998). Rantanen's most recent research concerns the impact of globaliza-

tion on media and communications in contemporary Russia. It contributes to theoretical debate by relativizing the concepts of globalization and new communications technologies, as well as analyzing and describing their impact on a little-known case, what was formerly called "a sixth of the world." Her latest book, *The Global and the National: Media and Communications in Post-Communist Russia,* was published by Rowman and Littlefield in 2002. E-mail: T.Rantanen@lse.ac.uk

Rick Rockwell (*Chapter 19, Latin America*) is an assistant professor of journalism at American University in Washington, D.C. He teaches courses on broadcasting, the Internet, and ethics. He has more than two decades of experience in the media as a reporter, producer, and news manager. He has worked for ABC News as a TV and radio producer, The Discovery Channel as a senior producer, and PBS' *NewsHour* as a freelance reporter. As a television reporter and producer, Rockwell reported from Nicaragua during the Contra War and covered Pope John Paul II's visit to Central America in the 1980s. He has covered the last two Mexican presidential elections and the 2001 Nicaraguan elections for various news organizations, including the Associated Press. He is a contributor to the recent book, *Latin Politics, Global Media* (University of Texas Press) and to such publications as *The Baltimore Sun* and *In These Times.* He is the co-author of the forthcoming book, *Media Power in Central America* (University of Illinois Press). E-mail: rockwell@american.edu

Robert L. Stevenson (*Chapter 5, Freedom of the Press Around the World*) is Kenan Professor of Journalism and Mass Communication at the University of North Carolina at Chapel Hill. He has taught in Mainz, Munich, and Dresden (Germany) and in Budapest, and for shorter periods in Romania, Australia, and Great Britain. He is the author of *Global Communication in the 21st Century* (Longman, 1994), *Communication, Development, and the Third World* (Longman, 1988), and *Foreign News and the New World Information Order* (with Donald L. Shaw, Iowa State University Press, 1984). E-mail: robert_Stevenson@unc. edu

Elanie Steyn (*Chapter 16, Sub-Saharan Africa*) teaches news media and corporate communication at the School of Communication Studies, Potchefstroom University, South Africa, where she is a doctoral candidate. She is also a director of Scribe Communications North West, and former manager of research and information, Small Business Advisory Bureau, as well as a former researcher at the Institute for Communication Research, Potchefstroom University. She is the deputy editor of *Ecquid Novi*. As director of Scribe Communications North West, Steyn is involved with a number of media, communications, and research projects for clients such as local and provincial SMMEs, government departments, universities, and investment corporations. Her involvement in research projects includes qualitative and quantitative surveys for among others, provincial government departments and other organizations. As researcher at the Institute for Communication Research, Steyn contributed to a number of national and international research projects on the media (e.g., international news coverage of the 1992 Olympic Games in Barcelona), papers for national and international media conferences (e.g., on the relationship between media and society, media policy), chapters for national and international textbooks (*Mass Media Towards the Millennium, Global Journalism, Press Freedom and Communication in Africa, South African Media Policy*), and has published research articles in accredited South African media and journalism journals (e.g., *Ecquid Novi, Communicatio*). E-mail: komefs@puknet.puk.ac.za

Donn J. Tilson (*Chapter 19, Latin America*) is an associate professor of public relations at the University of Miami's School of Communication. The first in Europe to graduate with a doctorate in public relations (from the University of Stirling), he has published and lectured internationally on corporate public relations, including as a European University Public Relations Confederation Visiting Scholar at Complutense University in Madrid and Autónoma University in Barcelona. He is co-editor of the forthcoming book *Toward the Common Good: Perspectives in International Public Relations* (Boston: Allyn & Bacon). He is a member of the Public Relations Society of America's College of Fellows; he serves on the editorial board of *Ecquid Novi*, the research journal for journalism in South Africa; and he is a former book review co-editor of *Journalism Studies*, an international journal published in cooperation with the European Journalism Training Association. He is a participating faculty member of UM's Institute for Cuban and Cuban-American Studies and Center for Latin American Studies. Prior to joining UM, he served as a public relations manager for BellSouth for 16 years, directing the company's charitable contributions and educational relations programs in Florida. In 1999 he was inducted as a Knight of the Equestrian Order of the Holy Sepulchre of Jerusalem, one of the oldest Orders of Chivalry in the world. E-mail: dtilson@miami.edu

Katerina Tsetsura (*Chapter 6, International Journalism Ethics; Chapter 14, Russia*) is a doctoral candidate in the department of communication at Purdue University. She received her Diploma (eqivalent to MA) in Journalism from Voronezh State University in Russia and an MS in Communication from Fort Hays State University in Kansas. Tsetsura has worked as a free-lance journalist in Russian media for five years and was a director of the first Black-Soil region teenagers' news agency "Teenpress," as well as editor-in-chief of the popular Voronezh teenagers' newspaper *Pyatnitsa*. She also worked as a public relations director and consultant for a nonprofit organization in the Black-Soil region of Russia. Her current research interests include media elations in Russia and CIS countries, ethics in international public relations, and issues of freedom of speech in countries with emerging democracies. E-mail: tsetsura@purdue.edu

David H. Weaver (*Chapter 10, Journalists: International Profiles*) is the Roy W. Howard Professor in Journalism and Mass Communication Research in the School of Journalism at Indiana University, Bloomington. He is author of *Videotex Journalism* (Erlbaum, 1983) and senior author of *Media Agenda-Setting in a Presidential Election* (Praeger, 1981), *The American Journalist* (Indiana University Press, 1986, 1991), and *The American Journalist in the 1990s* (Erlbaum, 1996). He is co-author of *Newsroom Guide to Polls and Surveys* (Indiana University Press, 1990), *The Formation of Campaign Agendas* (Erlbaum, 1991), and *Contemporary Public Opinion* (Erlbaum, 1991). He is co-editor of *Communication and Democracy* (Erlbaum, 1997), editor of *The Global Journalist* (Hampton Press, 1998), and co-editor of *Mass Communication Research and Theory* (Allyn and Bacon, 2003). He has published numerous book chapters and articles on U.S. journalists, the role of the media in political campaigns, newspaper readership, foreign news coverage, and journalism education. Several of his books have been translated into Greek, Japanese, and Korean. Although not specializing in international communication, he has had a long interest in comparative, cross-national research on journalism education, media agenda-setting in politics, global news coverage, and studies of journalists. His bache-

lor's and master's degrees in journalism are from Indiana University, and his Ph.D. in mass communication research is from the University of North Carolina at Chapel Hill. E-mail: weaver@indiana.edu

Jiafei Yin (*Chapter 17, Asia and the Pacific*) is an associate professor of journalism, Central Michigan University. She received her master's and doctoral degrees from the School of Journalism, University of Missouri. Her bachelor's degree is in English and American literature, from Nanjing University in China. She worked for *China Daily*, the country's only national English-language daily newspaper, from 1982–1993 as a wire editor, reporter, copy editor and chief copy editor. Her responsibilities included the international news page, and national and financial news pages. Yin has been teaching at Central Michigan University since 1996. She has taught courses in media writing, information gathering for the media, newspaper editing, media in contemporary society, American media history, and international and cross-cultural communication. She has started an exchange program between her department and the *China Daily*. Her teaching and research interests are mainly in the areas of print media, international communication, and international studies. She has done research comparing public journalism and development journalism, on international advertising, and international news coverage. She has presented papers at AEJMC conventions, the international conference sponsored by the Center for Global Media Studies, co-authored papers for the World Congress of Sociology, and published in the *Journal of Advertising Research* and the *Asian Journal of Communication*, and co-authored for *Operant*. E-mail: jiafei.yin@cmich.edu